MANAGEMENT SCIENCE FOR DECISION MAKERS

MANAGEMENT SCIENCE FOR DECISION MAKERS

LARRY M. AUSTIN
Texas Tech University

PARVIZ GHANDFOROUSH
Virginia Polytechnic Institute and State University

WEST PUBLISHING COMPANY

MINNEAPOLIS/ST. PAUL

NEW YORK

LOS ANGELES

SAN FRANCISCO

WEST'S COMMITMENT TO THE ENVIRONMENT

In 1906, West Publishing Company began recycling materials left over from the production of books. This began a tradition of efficient and responsible use of resources. Today, up to 95 percent of our legal books and 70 percent of our college and school texts are printed on recycled, acid-free stock. West also recycles nearly 22 million pounds of scrap paper annually—the equivalent of 181,717 trees. Since the 1960s, West has devised ways to capture and recycle waste inks, solvents, oils, and vapors created in the printing process. We also recycle plastics of all kinds, wood, glass, corrugated cardboard, and batteries, and have eliminated the use of styrofoam book packaging. We at West are proud of the longevity and the scope of our commitment to our environment.

Composition: Carlisle Communications
Artwork: Brian Betsill
Text design: Melinda Grosser for *silk*

Production, Prepress, Printing and Binding by West Publishing Company.

COPYRIGHT © 1993 By WEST PUBLISHING COMPANY
610 Opperman Drive
P.O. Box 64526
St. Paul, MN 55164-0526

All rights reserved

Printed in the United States of America

00 99 98 97 96 95 94 93   8 7 6 5 4 3 2 1 0

Library of Congress Cataloging-in-Publication Data

Austin, Larry M.
    Management science for decision makers / Larry M. Austin, Parviz Ghandforoush.
      p.   cm.
    Includes bibliographical references and index.
    ISBN 0-314-01243-5
    1. Management science. I. Ghandforoush, Parviz. II. Title.
T56.A88   1993
658.4'03—dc20

92-21119
CIP

Dedicated to **Jill** and **Terri,** who make it all worthwhile. L.M.A. and P.G.

PREFACE

In most present texts on quantitative methods of management science/operations research (MS/OR), there is a strong emphasis on understanding the mathematical details of algorithms used to solve models introduced by the text. The traditional approach to teaching algorithms is "hand solution." Before the proliferation of computers and the availability of sophisticated software, such an emphasis was necessary so that we could solve the models.

This emphasis compromised other equally appropriate emphases, such as:

- Developing problem solving and model formulation skills
- Understanding real-world problems (instead of textbook problems whose models we can solve by hand calculation methods)
- Appreciating the assumptions that underlie the models (and their methods).

With computers and software for solving MS/OR models accessible to virtually everyone, we need to reassess the emphasis on hand solution of models.

We intend this textbook for use in graduate-level management science courses for prospective or practicing executive decision makers. Such courses typically are required in the second year of master's degree programs, such as Master of Business Administration (MBA); Master of Science (MS) in Business Administration, Economics, or Industrial Engineering; and Master of Industrial Management (MIM); etc. *For convenience, we refer to such programs in this preface and throughout the book by the generic term "MBA."*

An MBA student needs to learn how to formulate and analyze models to enhance his or her problem solving and decision-making abilities, and is much less concerned with the technical details of algorithms used to solve these models. Therefore, we geared the organization and substance of this book, toward problem formulation, model conceptualization, and problem analysis—not hand solution of small textbook models.

For all practical purposes, knowledge of management science required by the practicing manager should be identical to that required by the MBA student. Decision makers need to have substantive understanding of what models are available, how to build them, and how to use the resulting solutions as an aid to problem solving. Consequently, this text would serve equally well as an MBA textbook or as a reference book on MS/OR models for the practicing manager.

In view of the specific pedagogical needs of the MBA student and the practicing manager, we adopted the following goals and criteria for the design of this text.

- To emphasize the development of problem solving and model formulation skills, including:
  a) Recognizing how and when a particular type of model can be of value; and
  b) The ability to construct a model of the problem.
- To carefully consider the assumptions that underlie each model and its associated algorithm(s).

- To introduce the student to a variety of real-world or realistic problems and their models through the use of complex minicases.
- To articulate the art and science of decision analysis under conditions of certainty, risk, and uncertainty.
- To employ a managerial perspective that focuses on decision making rather than mathematical solution techniques.

In addition, this book places a strong emphasis on "what if" in addition to the usual "what's best." We demonstrate to MBA students how to use management science models to gain insight into problems.

In this text we do not "force" a quantitative approach to decision making and management. Rather, we include decision factors that are *intuitive, subjective, judgmental, and unquantifiable* as an inherent component of each real-world minicase. We illustrate how only a proper mix of quantifiable and nonquantifiable considerations can lead to a satisfactory solution strategy.

We treat decision making at all levels of the organizational hierarchy. At each level, modeling begins with an assessment of which factors or variables are within the decision maker's capacity to influence and which factors the decision maker can only observe. All model formulations, therefore, begin and end with a specified decision maker's perspective of the problem. Nor do we avoid the complexity that usually accompanies real-world decision making.

MBAs AND COMPUTER SOFTWARE

It is clear that successful use of this textbook for graduate courses depends heavily upon the availability of microcomputer software that implements the various MS/OR algorithms. There are more than a dozen such packages for IBM-compatible microcomputers, to include D&D [1], Management Scientist [2], STORM [3], QSB+ [4], MSS [5], and ORS [6]. Rather than arbitrarily selecting one of these packages as our vehicle in this book, we invoke the fictitious package that we call **SAMS** (**S**imulated **A**lgorithms for **M**anagement **S**cience). **SAMS** is a generic approach to modeling with microcomputer software that will permit adopters of this text to select their preferred packages in the market. It has a spreadsheetlike input mechanism and report format similar to those of most available packages.

ORGANIZATION OF THE TEXT

The text begins with a discussion of modeling as both art and science. We discuss the importance of modeling, and introduce the notation used in the text. We characterize the model building process in some generality. In detail, we discuss the criteria by which the manager classifies the problem and chooses an appropriate model to represent it. Chapter 1 presents all of these ideas. The remainder of the text consists of four parts:

DECISION MAKING UNDER CERTAINTY

Chapters 2 through 6 are about decision making under certainty. The first four chapters address deterministic mathematical programming models—linear programming, integer programming, network programming, and nonlinear programming. Chapter 6 deals with deterministic dynamic programming.

DECISION MAKING UNDER RISK

Chapters 7 through 12 describe models related to decision making under risk. Chapter 7 discusses matrix decision models, decision trees, expected value and opportunity loss, Bayesian analysis, and the concept of economic utility. Chapter 8 deals with queueing (waiting-line) models, while Chapter 9 describes the use of simulation in the decision environment. Chapter 10 discusses Markov chains. Chapter 11 describes the extension of probabilistic concepts to project management (PERT). Chapter 12 introduces basic principles of scientific inventory management.

DECISION MAKING UNDER UNCERTAINTY

Chapters 13 through 15 discuss models for decision making under uncertainty. Chapter 13 covers the classical matrix decision model. Chapter 14 introduces modeling with multiple objectives and goal programming. Chapter 15 presents some useful graphical tools and multiattribute choice models that don't "fit" elsewhere in this part of the text.

MANAGEMENT SCIENCE AND THE FUTURE

The Epilogue presents our view of the "high tech" future of 2000 A.D.

ORGANIZATION OF EACH CHAPTER

Most chapters follow a uniform format to give continuity and coherence to the book. A typical chapter consists of the following sections:

a. **Underlying Assumptions.** Here we give managerial meaning to such concepts as linearity and multistage decision making. We also describe problem classes appropriate for this type of model.
b. **Modeling.** Here we describe the models verbally and present an intuitive description of the corresponding mathematical representations. We omit terms that have to do with the algorithm(s) used to solve the model (e.g., in linear programming—artificial variable, pivot, entering and exiting variable, revised SIMPLEX). This section devotes particular attention to how we formulate models of this type, and what the data requirements are.
c. **Solution Approaches.** Section c is an intuitive description of the algorithm(s) used to solve models of this type. In this section, we describe the algorithms by analogy or by use of graphical and tabular illustrations.
d. **Developing Alternative Solutions.** Here we deal with sensitivity studies and parametric analyses of model solutions that we can perform to assist in developing alternative solutions to the problem.
e. **State of the Art Topics.** Section e briefly describes state-of-the-art topics, such as computational considerations related to problem size and potential difficulties encountered during computer implementation. Our purpose in including these brief discussions of advanced models is to make potential and practicing managers aware that the models exist. To discuss these topics in detail would take us well beyond the scope of this book; to omit them would convey an incomplete—and therefore erroneous—impression of the dynamic nature of management science.
f. **Minicases.** In this section, we present from two to five minicases—hypothetical and actual short cases that illustrate applications of the model(s) to real or realistic problems. Several cases are adaptations of term project reports submitted by our MBA students over the years at Virginia Tech and Texas Tech. Not all minicases report successful applications—some describe *unsuccessful* applications and why the applications were unsuccessful. These minicases reflect the complexity of the real-world decision environment.
g. **Summary.** Section g summarizes the material presented in the chapter and provides an overview of the chapter contents.
h. **Problems for Analysis and Practice Models.** In this section, we first present end-of-chapter problems that will stimulate and challenge MBA students. We include "unworked" minicases that expose students to some of the complexities of problems they will encounter after graduation. Then we provide some small, unadorned practice models that MBA students can use to become familiar with available software.
i. **References and Additional Reading.** Section i contains chapter references and suggestions for additional reading.

THE PHILOSOPHY OF THE BOOK

This book emphasizes the problem-definitional aspects of MS/OR usage, and recognizes a need for coping with the complexity of the real-world decision environment. It treats such complexity with candor, and it presents tools for characterizing and analyzing the complexity of the real world. It takes a managerial perspective of decision analysis.

Although the writing style is informal, *this is a deadly serious book*. It is not about algorithms. It is about the difficult, complex, and frustrating process of managerial decision making. If the book has a "theme," we can best describe it by the following phrase, which we repeat several times herein:

*MODELS DON'T MAKE DECISIONS—
MANAGERS DO.*

ACKNOWLEDGEMENTS

For their incisive comments on the drafts of the book and for the raw materials for several minicases, we are grateful to our MBA students—present and past—at Texas Tech and Virginia Tech. We wish also to thank our respective universities for their logistical support and our faculty colleagues for their help and encouragement.

In preparing this book for publication, we were extremely fortunate to have the advice and assistance of some excellent reviewers. Special thanks go to Steve Bechtold at Florida State University, Warren Boe at the University of Iowa, Mike Hanna at the University of Houston—Clear Lake, Don Harnett at Indiana University, Lori Kaplan at the University of Tennessee—Knoxville, Bill Pinney at the University of Texas—Arlington, Alan Raedels at Portland State University, Steve Replogle at Arkansas State University, and Rick Wilson at Oklahoma State University.

Special thanks are in order to the professionals at West—particularly Rick Leyh, Jayne Lindesmith, and Jessica Evans.

L.M.A., P.G.

References

1. Anderson, D., D. Sweeney, and T. Williams. *Management Scientist*. St. Paul: West, 1991.
2. Chang, Y., and R. Sullivan. *QSB+: Quantitative Systems for Business Plus*. Englewood Cliffs, NJ: Prentice-Hall, 1989.
3. Dash, G. and N. Kajiji. *Operations Research Software*. Homewood, Ill.: Richard D. Irwin, 1988.
4. Dennis, T., and L. Dennis. *Microcomputer Models for Management Decision-Making* 2d ed.). St. Paul: West, 1988.
5. Emmons, H., and D. Flowers. *STORM Personal Version 3.0*. Englewood Cliffs, N.J.: Prentice-Hall, 1991.
6. Nelson, T. *The Management Science System*. Homewood, Ill.: Richard D. Irwin, 1988.

CONTENTS

PREFACE vii

1.
PROBLEMS, MODELS, DECISIONS, & SYSTEMS 1

Problems and Decisions 2
Model Classification 2
Model Building—An Art and a Science 5
    Step 1: Statement of the Purpose 6
    Step 2: Clarification of the Values 7
    Step 3: Determination of the System 7
    Step 4: Identification of the Problem 8
    Step 5: Formulation of the Model Structure 9
    Step 6: Collection of the Data 9
    Step 7: Validation of the Model 9
    Step 8: Selection of the Algorithm 10
    Step 9: Derivation of Feasible Policies 11
    Step 10: Determination of the Most Appropriate Policy 11
    Step 11: Implementation of the Policy 12
Notation 13
Some Classical Problems in Management Science 14
    Resource Allocation Problems 14
    Capital Investment Decisions in Risky Environments 15
Caveats and Comments on Building and Using Models 16

Summary 18
Problems 19
References and Additional Reading 21

PART ONE
DECISION MAKING UNDER CERTAINTY (DMUC) 23

2.
LINEAR PROGRAMMING MODELS 26

Underlying Assumptions 26
    Additivity 27
    Divisibility 27
Building LP Models 27
    An Orderly Approach to Model Building 28
Model Formulation: Two Examples 31
    LO-CAL Candy Company 32
    Teletronix Industries, Inc. 34
The SIMPLEX Algorithm: An Intuitive Description 36
    The SIMPLEX Algorithm 37
    A Graphical Example 38

Developing Alternative Solutions 40
    Standard Computer Output 41
    Decision Variables 43
    Slack Variables 43
    Ranging Analysis on Resource Availability 45
    Ranging Analysis on Objective Coefficients 45
    "What If" Analysis 46
    A Caveat for Decision Makers 46
    Teletronix Industries Revisited 47
Extensions of the SIMPLEX Method 49
    Some Bits and Pieces 49
    Unbounded and Infeasible Solutions 50
    Duality Theory 51
Some Advanced Topics 52
    Lower-Bounded Variables 52
    Upper-Bounded Variables 53
    Dantzig-Wolfe Decomposition 53
MINICASE: Wiseacre 55
MINICASE: William Hill Distillery 60
MINICASE: Incremental Profit Program 64
MINICASE: Racquet 67
MINICASE: Security 71
Summary 74
Problems for Analysis 75
Practice Models 88
References and Additional Reading 90

3.
INTEGER (LINEAR) PROGRAMMING MODELS 92

Underlying Assumptions 92
Integer Modeling 93
    Natural Integer-Valued Variables 93
    Modeling with Surrogate Integer Variables 94
    Modeling with Zero-One Decision Variables 103
Solution Approaches: An Intuitive Description 106
    Branch and Bound 107
    Cutting Planes 110
    Zero-One Models 112
Developing Alternative Solutions 112
    Alternatives with Branch and Bound 112
    Alternatives with Cutting Planes 112
    Sensitivity Analysis in ILP 112
Extensions of ILP Modeling 114
    Reduction to Zero-One Models 114
    Traveling Salesman Model 115
MINICASE: Disk-o-Tech 117
MINICASE: BLL, Inc. 121
MINICASE: Backpacking 123
Summary 128
Problems for Analysis 128
Practice Models 141
References and Additional Reading 144

4.
MODELING WITH NETWORKS 145

Underlying Assumptions 147
Network Modeling and Algorithms 147
    Shortest Route Through a Network 147
    Longest Route Through a Network (CPM) 150
    Minimal Spanning Tree Model 154
    Optimal Network Flow Model 157
        Transportation Models 158
        Assignment Models 163
        Transshipment Models 164
    Comments on Network Modeling 165
Developing Alternative Solutions 166
    Descriptive Network Models 166
    Optimizing Network Models 168
State of the Art in Network Modeling 168
    The Chinese Postman Model 168
    Multicommodity Network Flows 169
    Imbedded Networks 169
    The Min-Cut/Max-Flow Theorem 169
MINICASE: Meter Readers 170
MINICASE: Center for Professional Development (CPD) 172
MINICASE: POLKA 175
Summary 177

Problems for Analysis 177
Practice Models 187
References and Additional Reading 189

5.
NONLINEAR PROGRAMMING MODELS 191

Underlying Assumptions 192
Nonlinear Modeling 193
    A Pricing Model 193
    An Inventory Control Model 195
    A Scrap Minimization Model 197
    A Container Cost Minimization Model 197
    Genesis of NLP Models 198
NLP Solution Approaches: An Intuitive Description 199
    Indirect Methods 199
    Direct Methods 200
    Linearization 200
    Miscellaneous Methods 204
Developing Alternative Solutions 204
State of the Art in NLP 205
MINICASE: Colossus of Roads 206
MINICASE: Beau-Kay, Inc. 210
Summary 214
Problems for Analysis 215
Practice Models 222
References and Additional Reading 223

6.
DISCRETE DYNAMIC PROGRAMMING MODELS 224

Underlying Assumptions 224
Multistage Modeling 226
    Time-Sequenced Decisions 226
    Separability 227
    Order-Independent Allocation 228

Dynamic Programming: An Intuitive Description 228
    The Elusiveness of Recursive Optimization 230
    The "Curse of Dimensionality" 231
Developing Alternative Solutions 232
State of the Art in Dynamic Programming 232
    Continuous Dynamic Programming 233
    Nonsequential Multistage Optimization 235
MINICASE: Air Traffic Control 235
MINICASE: Cabana Bananas 238
MINICASE: Touring Europe 241
Summary 243
Problems for Analysis 244
Practice Models 248
References and Additional Reading 249

PART TWO
DECISION MAKING UNDER RISK (DMUR) 251

7.
A STRUCTURE FOR DECISION MAKING UNDER RISK 254

Structuring the Decision Environment 254
A DMUR Model 255
    Assessing State Probabilities 255
    Sequential Decision Processes 257
Decision Criteria for DMUR Models 257
    The Expected Monetary Value Criterion 258
    The Expected Opportunity Loss Criterion 259
The Value of Information 260
    The Value of Perfect Information 260
    The Value of Imperfect Information 261
An Optimizing Algorithm for Decision Tree Models 264

Sensitivity Analysis of DMUR Models 266
    Analysis of Prior Probabilities 267
    Dominated Alternatives 267
    The Posterior Distribution 267
The Concept of Economic Utility 268
    An Underlying Assumption 268
    Utility Functions 269
    Building Utility Functions 270
State of the Art in DMUR 271
    Continuous Prior Distributions 272
    The Newsboy Model 273
    On the Frontier 274
MINICASE: Jack Legg Associates 275
MINICASE: High Tor 280
MINICASE: King Cotton 282
MINICASE: D-Day 284
Summary 287
Problems for Analysis 287
Practice Models 297
References and Additional Reading 298

8.
WAITING LINE (QUEUEING) MODELS 300

Underlying Assumptions 300
    The Calling Population Subsystem 301
    The Queueing Subsystem 301
    The Service Facility Subsystem 302
    The Integrated Queueing System 303
Building Queueing Models 303
    Some Useful Notation 307
    Some Caveats in Using Queueing Models 307
Solution Approaches: An Intuitive Description 308
    Notation 308
    Some Known Results for Queueing Models 308
Developing Alternative Solutions 312
    Arrival and Service Time Distributions 312
    Arrival and Service Rates 313
    An Example of Sensitivity Analysis 313

State of the Art in Queueing Models 314
    Some General Parameter Relationships 314
    Advanced Models 315
MINICASE: ICQ 315
MINICASE: Gourmet 318
Summary 320
Problems for Analysis 321
Practice Models 326
References and Additional Reading 326
Appendix: Closed-Form Analytical Results for Two Models 327

9.
DISCRETE SIMULATION MODELS 328

Underlying Assumptions and Definitions 332
    Activities and Events 332
    Entities and Attributes 333
    Approaches to Discrete Simulation 334
Mechanics of Discrete Simulation Model Formulation 334
    A Neighborhood Grocery Store Example 334
    Random Number Generation 338
    Probability Distributions 339
    Sampling in Simulation 342
    Discrete Simulation Results 344
Solution Approaches: An Intuitive Description 344
    General Purpose Simulation System (GPSS) 344
    SIMSCRIPT II.5 346
    SLAM—A Simulation Language for Alternative Modeling 347
State of the Art in Simulation 348
    Visual Interactive Simulation 348
    Knowledge Engineering 348
    Continuous Simulation 348
MINICASE: Savin E. Lavin, Inc. (Continued) 349
MINICASE: Cabana Bananas (Revisited) 350
Summary 356
Problems for Analysis 357
References and Additional Reading 363

Appendix: Continuous Simulation Models 365

10.
MODELING WITH MARKOV CHAINS 370

Underlying Assumptions 371
Modeling with Transition Matrices 372
Solution Approaches: An Intuitive Description 373
    Recurring Markov Processes 373
    Transient Markov Processes 375
Developing Alternative Solutions 377
State of the Art in Markov Chain Analysis 377
    Time of First Passage 377
    Dynamic Programming in Markov Chains 378
MINICASE: An Officer and a Gentleman 379
MINICASE: Lemmon Rent-a-Car 383
Summary 385
Problems for Analysis 386
Practice Models 391
References and Additional Reading 392

11.
PROJECT SCHEDULING 393

Underlying Assumptions 393
    The Beta Distribution 395
    Approximation to the Beta Distribution 395
Modeling with PERT 396
Solution Technique: An Intuitive Description 398
Sensitivity Analysis 400
PERT/COST 401
    Project Management with PERT 401
Advanced Concepts in Project Scheduling and Management 402
    GERT and Q-GERT 402

    PERT-Simulation 402
    Some Caveats 403
MINICASE: Audit Trail 404
MINICASE: GYRO 410
Summary 412
Problems for Analysis 413
Practice Models 415
References and Additional Reading 416

12.
INVENTORY MANAGEMENT 418

Types of Inventories 418
Types of Inventory Models 419
Underlying Assumptions 419
    Demand 419
    Order Quantity 419
    Lead Time 419
    Procurement Costs 420
    Operating Costs 420
Modeling an Inventory System 421
    Procurement Cost 422
    Holding Cost 422
    Ordering Cost 422
    Total Cost 423
    Constraints 423
Solution by Discrete Simulation 423
    Closed-Form Solutions 424
The Simulation Model 427
Advanced Concepts in Inventory Management 427
    Multiechelon Inventory Models 427
    Periodic Review Inventory Models 428
    Material Requirements Planning 429
    Just-In-Time Production System 430
MINICASE: EOQ at AFLC 430
MINICASE: Keep on Truckin' 433
Summary 437
Problems for Analysis 438
Practice Models 439
References and Additional Reading 440
Appendix: Incremental Price Breaks, No Constraints 441

PART THREE
DECISION MAKING UNDER UNCERTAINTY (DMUU) 443

13.
CLASSICAL DECISION MODELS UNDER UNCERTAINTY 445

Underlying Assumptions 445
Modeling Under Uncertainty 446
    The MAXIMIN Criterion 446
    The MAXIMAX Criterion 448
    The MINIMAX Regret Criterion 448
    The Insufficient Reason Criterion 451
Deriving Useful Solutions 452
Risk and Utility 452
State of the Art in Modeling Under Uncertainty 452
MINICASE: Apteryx Aircraft Company 453
MINICASE: D-Day Revisited 456
Summary 460
Problems for Analysis 460
Practice Models 462
References and Additional Reading 464

14.
MODELING WITH MULTIPLE OBJECTIVES 465

Underlying Assumptions 465
    Matrix-Vector Notation 466
    Commensurable Functions 467
    Incommensurable Functions 467
MOLP Modeling 468
    MOLP Models Requiring Commensurability 468
    MOLP Models Not Requiring Commensurability 472

Solution Approaches: An Intuitive Description 477
    The MAXIMIN Model 478
    The Linear Combinations Model 480
    The Preemptive Goal Prioritization Model 480
    The Preemptive Goal Programming Model 481
Developing Alternative Solutions 481
State of the Art in MOLP 482
    Utility Transformations for Incommensurable Objectives 482
    Modeling with Fuzzy Sets 483
    Non-MOLP Multiple Objective Models 483
MINICASE: SofSneez 483
MINICASE: Spacetrek 490
MINICASE: Budgeting in Blacksburg 494
Summary 499
Problems for Analysis 499
Practice Models 505
References and Additional Reading 507

15.
VISUAL AND MULTIATTRIBUTE CHOICE MODELS 508

Underlying Assumptions 509
Graphical Techniques: An Intuitive Description 509
    Charts for Project Planning and Scheduling 511
    Morphological Methods and Models 514
    Matrix Modeling 520
Multiattribute Choice Models 522
A Multicriterion Decision Model 526
    Critical Factors 526
    Quantitative Factors 527
    Qualitative Factors 527
    The Evaluation Measure 528
    A Project Selection Model 528
    The Strategy Control Component 529
MINICASE: MIPS 529
MINICASE: T. N. Crumpets 533

Summary 537
Problems for Analysis 538
Practice Models 541
References and Additional Reading 542

 EPILOGUE
MANAGEMENT SCIENCE & THE FUTURE 543
The Art of Constructing a Crystal Ball 543
Assumptions: The World of 2000 543
Deductions: The World of 2000 544
Implications: The World of 2000 545
References and Additional Reading 547

APPENDIXES
A. Standardized Normal Distribution 549
B. Unit Normal Linear Loss Integral 550

GLOSSARY 551

INDEX 557

MANAGEMENT SCIENCE FOR DECISION MAKERS

CHAPTER 1

Problems, Models, Decisions, and Systems

This book is concerned with making decisions that solve problems. The main thesis of this book is as follows:

> The use of management science (MS) models can make us better decision makers and problem solvers.

Models help us to better understand problems and enable us to evaluate courses of action in making decisions. They reflect the structure of the system we use them to represent. A model is a **paradigm**—a description and explanation of the relationship of the parts of the problem to one another or of the problem to its environment.

Everyone uses models as a basis for making decisions. An oil firm executive gathers information in the form of printed data, listens to the opinions of others, and concludes that the firm must raise retail gasoline prices in accordance with increases in the price of crude. An economist reads the consumer price statistics and decides that more stringent controls on the money supply must be applied. An MBA student keeps close track of his or her course performance to determine how much effort he or she will require to achieve the desired grades. In each case, we formulate a **mental model** as a basis for making decisions. Even our interpersonal responses stem from models. Psychologists say that our mental model of ourselves—our self-image—strongly colors our personality.

Our mental concepts of a particular situation represent the model—either explicit or implicit—that we use to make decisions in both private and professional life. At times, that mental model is biased, fuzzy, incomplete, inaccurate, or just plain wrong. Obviously, the response or decision stemming from that mental model will probably be wrong also, and we must face the consequences of the misguided decision. The point is, *we make all conscious decisions on the basis of models*. The question, then, is not whether to use models but rather what kinds of models to use.

Consider a stockbroker poring over market projections on the screen of a personal computer. The broker's mental model of the stock market suggests that the market will continue to go up in the short run before dropping drastically. In light of this mental model, the stockbroker is advising clients to sell their holdings. If the stockbroker has many colleagues who share the same view of the market, the simultaneous advice those colleagues give to investors could actually cause the predicted downturn to occur. Thus, in this case, the mental model becomes self-fulfilling. Such are the hazards of forecasting models in the managerial sciences. Gloom-and-doom predictions may create the very factors responsible for drastic downward readjustments.

Clearly, models influence managerial behavior that weighs heavily upon the outcomes of the system itself. Self-image models, furthermore, tend to be consistently self-fulfilling.

This book focuses on management science (MS) models, and its premise is that such models are better decision aids than mental models alone. Actually, we use such models to influence, formalize, and concretize the mental models we use to make all decisions. An **MS model** is a model that encompasses quantitative, mathematical, or graphic forms. We distinguish it from the verbal models that make up much of the literature in business, economics, sociology, political science, and psychology.

We assert that MS models will enable us to make better decisions. We must address such questions as, What form do these models take? What data do we need? How do we formulate these models? How do we solve these models? The answers to these questions constitute most of the content of this book.

PROBLEMS AND DECISIONS

Problems arise whenever there is a *perceived* difference between what is desired and what is. In the language of the economist, wherever expectations differ substantially from realizations, a problem occurs. Problems serve as motivators for doing something. Since what we do must begin with a decision about what to do, problems ultimately lead to decisions (see Figure 1.1). *The goal of* **decision making** *is mitigating or alleviating perceived problems.*

In Figure 1.1a, a problem leads to a **decision** about that problem without the input from an MS model. The decision could be to do nothing for now. The decision will thereafter have an impact that will either diminish or exacerbate the problem. We will observe the effect on the problem, and this will lead to further decisions about the problem in question.

The plan and purpose of this book is to insert into the decision process the use of MS models (Figure 1.1b). We study the problem in the framework of its own system to enable contextual understanding of the problem. Thereafter we can develop an MS model of the "problem system." This is the essence of the so-called systems approach popularized in recent years by Churchman [2] and others. A good problem solver should try to develop the largest possible perspective of that problem. This is tantamount to understanding the problem within the context of its own system.

MODEL CLASSIFICATION

We can classify models in a variety of ways. For example, *purpose, perspective, degree of abstraction,* and *content* represent four classification criteria.

FIGURE 1.1 Relationships among models, problems, and decisions

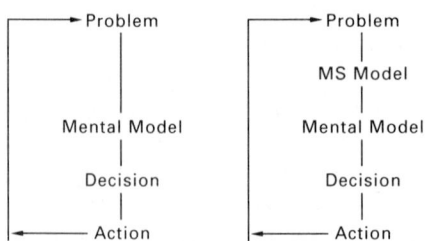

Models classified according to **purpose** would require our considering the uses to which we can put models. We can use models for planning, forecasting, training, behavioral research, or some combination. Both planning and forecasting models improve the decision-making acumen of managers and represent the two most widely used purposes to which managers can put models. A training model might enable pilots to increase their skills in flight simulations, whereas a behavioral research model could explain why the behavior of people, organizations, or animals is likely to manifest itself in a certain way.

Models classified according to **perspective** fall into two basic categories: *descriptive* and *prescriptive*. Descriptive models try to describe an existing situation as it actually is. Prescriptive models, on the other hand, attempt to describe an existing situation as it ideally should be. A company's accounting and bookkeeping records, for example, represent a descriptive model of the company's actual earnings structure—for example, net earnings around 5% of gross investment. However, resident within the minds of top-level management is an "ideal" model with earnings of 8 percent. Managers evolve a plan for taking the firm's earnings, as indicated by the descriptive model, a step in the direction of the prescriptive model.

Models classified according to **degree of abstraction** are either isomorphic or homomorphic. An **isomorphic model** is one in which every component in the real-world system has a corresponding component in the model. Such models have components that are in one-to-one correspondence with components in the real world. On the other hand a **homomorphic model** is one in which each component in the model may represent many components in the real-world system. In this case, the correspondence is one-to-many. Most of the models we describe in this book are one-to-many in the sense that one component may represent more than one component in the real system.

We most often classify models according to **content.** We recognize four categories: mental models, physical models, verbal models, and MS models.

Mental models are the basis for all human behavior. Since our mental faculties are limited, there is a limit to the number of factors we can consider simultaneously. Psychologists tell us this limit *is seven plus or minus two*. MS models serve as information input to mental models. Clearly, to be of any value, MS models must produce results that we can easily understand.

Science, engineering, and architecture make wide use of physical models. Aeronautical engineers build miniature models of aircraft and place them in wind tunnels to study stability, aircraft dynamics, and air flow characteristics. Architects use models of planned new construction to enable planners to get a three-dimensional perspective of the structure and to thus assess the overall aesthetic appearance. Flight simulators are physical models used to train pilots. Dress designers fabricate physical models of dresses that they thereafter test for marketability.

Verbal models make up much of the literature in business, economics, sociology, psychology, political science, and history. A classic example of a verbal model is the energy-economy-environment enigma about which people have written so much over the past 20 years. A typical verbal model follows.

> Americans have witnessed how an emphasis upon the environment has contributed to a growing demand for liquid fuels in the transportation sector that at times were in short supply. To provide sufficient fuel, the United States had to increase oil imports. To offset the balance-of-payments drain, the United States tried to encourage a commensurate increase in the export of agricultural produce.

Pollution controls applied to new automobiles caused increases in auto prices. Rises in the price of imported crude oil also produced price increases that reverberated throughout the economic system. These price increases served only to further fan the fires of inflation already burning because of excessive demand and insufficient supply of goods and services.

The succession of concurrent fuel price increases forced the federal government to lower pollution and safety standards to allow for the use of cheaper low-grade fuels. The use of cheaper fuels then resulted in greater amounts of sulfur and nitrous pollutants being dumped into the air and water.

We can trace the behavior of the energy-economy-environment system to the decisions that industry and government implemented and the consequences derived from those decisions.

Oswald Spengler and Arnold Toynbee have separately espoused models of history. In *The Decline of the West*, [9], Spengler suggested in 1945 that Western civilization was in the winter of its life cycle and would die by the 23rd century. In 1954, Toynbee [11] proposed a linear evolutionary model of history. Civilization evolves from primitive to more sophisticated forms; civilization survives by deploying increasingly sophisticated solutions to increasingly difficult problems. Other models of history claim that history is shaped by the moving forces of courageous people. Such models are obviously verbal in form and content.

The last model category is the MS model. We may further classify the MS model into ever more specific model forms. We choose, in this book, to classify models according to the decision environments for which the models are most appropriate (see Table 1.1). Decision making can occur under the conditions of **certainty, risk,** and **uncertainty.** We can classify MS models as to whether they are appropriate for decision making under each of these conditions, as we show in Table 1.1.

In Figure 1.1, we tried to depict the relationship between a problem and the decision that addresses the problem. **Decision making under certainty** simply suggests that we can characterize as *certain* the system (and inputs received from the environment) in which the problem is embedded; that is, we have perfect knowledge about the system (including its inputs). Obviously, we can know and understand very few systems perfectly. Even so, for many systems this may be an appropriate assumption. Under such conditions we refer to the problem as **deterministic.** Of particular interest are the possible future states of the environment, since these states influence the inputs from the environment. If we assume that we know the future perfectly, then we face decision making under certainty.

TABLE 1.1 Decision environments and MS models discussed in this text

Decision Making Under Certainty	Decision Making Under Risk	Decision Making Under Uncertainty
Linear Programming Models	Bayesian Analysis and Expected Utility Models	Classical Decision Models
Integer Programming Models	Waiting-Line Models	Models Involving Multiple Objectives
Modeling With Networks	Discrete Simulation Models	Visual and Multiattribute Choice Models
Nonlinear Programming Models	Markov Chain Models	
Discrete Dynamic Programming Models	Project Scheduling Models	
	Inventory Management Models	

Decision making under risk involves a problem embedded in a system that we do not know perfectly. We use probability theory to characterize our imperfect knowledge about the system and about any inputs received from the environment. We assign probabilities to the possible futures in accordance with the likelihood of their occurrence. In this case, we have some knowledge of the system and its environment, but we do not have perfect knowledge.

Decision making under uncertainty involves a problem embedded in a system and an associated environment with a large number of components and a substantial amount of interaction between and among the components. Sometimes the problem under consideration involves a system that is so complex that managers do not well understand its structure. Under such circumstances it is important that managers have access to model-building tools that will enable them to structure models of their systems so that they can identify gaps in understanding. At other times we may be unable to estimate appropriate probability structures for our problem, or perhaps we must incorporate multiple goals or objectives in the solution of our problem.

A moment's comparison of Table 1.1 with the chapter titles of this book discloses a striking similarity. This book will introduce you to each of the model types listed in Table 1.1 so that you can thoroughly understand when (and how) to use them. Of course, whether to use a linear programming model or a **discrete simulation** model will depend on the type of problem being considered. We address this subject under "Step 4: Identification of the Problem" in the following section.

MODEL BUILDING—AN ART AND A SCIENCE

The following definition of an MS model is more general than most: *An MS model is a quantitative representation of a process that includes those components relevant to the problem at hand.* The reference to *relevance* here is significant. All models contain information about the system; however, they contain less information than the system contains within itself, and that information is at times organized differently. The components and the data that are to be included in (as well as excluded from) the model are based exclusively upon the purposes of the model-building exercise. For instance, Coyle [3] suggests that the level of detail in structure is dependent on the manager's input if the purpose is to model the system from the vantage point of the manager who controls or influences the system.

The fact that the model contains less information than the real system is an advantage in a way, because it simplifies the situation by eliminating superfluous detail. For example, Thesen [10] states that "all aspects of the real situation not relevant to the purpose of the model can be ignored." For complex systems, however, Thesen points out that all elements directly or indirectly seem relevant to the stated purpose. The model builder consequently faces the difficult problem of defining the "relative relevancy of different elements of the real situation." This is one reason why model building will remain a mixture of both art and science.

Following Thesen [10], we define the art or **process** of model building as "the act of (1) identifying information relevant to a problem area; and (2) creating a real or imaginary entity containing this information suitable for the purposes of this effort." It follows that thorough knowledge and understanding of the system are indeed essential.

We represent the process of model building and its subsequent use by 11 steps (see Table 1.2). Since the 11 formal steps to model building are too many for us to remember easily (recall the seven plus or minus two rule), we choose to group them

TABLE 1.2 Eleven steps to better modeling and happier managing

Phases	Steps to Better Modeling
Scenario	1. Statement of the purpose 2. Clarification of the values 3. Determination of the system
Problem	4. Identification of the problem
Model	5. Formulation of the model structure 6. Collection of the data 7. Validation of the model
Solution	8. Selection of the algorithm 9. Derivation of feasible policies 10. Determination of the most appropriate policy 11. Implementation of the policy

into four basic categories: *scenario*, *problem*, *model*, and *solution* (SPMS). Subsequent discussions will use these four categories, and the examples, minicases, and most end-of-chapter problems will incorporate the SPMS method of description.

The *scenario* portion of the minicases describes the purpose of the model, the values that impinge upon the modeling process, and the system. The *problem* portion of the minicases further explains the system and the actual problem that motivates the study. The *model* portion deals with the construction and validation of the model. The *solution* portion describes the algorithm used, the results (in terms of a recommended strategy that the algorithm produced), and the effect of implementing the strategy upon the actual problem and system. The following discusses in some detail each of the 11 steps to successful modeling.

STEP 1: STATEMENT OF THE PURPOSE

Of all the approaches that one can take, the MS modeling approach is the only one that deals explicitly with characterizing reality in such a way that one can use symbolic processing to arrive at logical and rational decisions. This systematic way of dealing with a very necessary element in human thinking usually involves determining and justifying a set of objectives and purposes or goals for the model-building initiative. A well-defined statement of the purpose of the model-building exercise will guide the manager in determining what he or she should include in or omit from the model.

Consider a classroom. Class is in session, and students fill the room, each busily taking notes. The instructor is using a chalkboard and a transparency projector and screen to convey important concepts. The classroom also contains textbooks, chairs, writing materials, and the instructor's notes and transparencies.

If someone were to ask you to model this situation, which of the components would you include in your model? Would you include the students? Probably. You might also include the textbooks and writing materials. You might leave out such items as the lights, the walls, and the chairs. Why? No one has told you what the purpose of the modeling exercise is. Hence, you have no criteria for deciding what you should include and what you should omit.

Suppose that the purpose is to study the process of learning within the framework of the classroom alone. You would then necessarily include the students, the instructor, and the instruction taking place between these components. Of lesser importance would be such components as lecture notes and textbooks. You would omit altogether such objects as chairs and the chalkboard. The purpose, then, is the yardstick by which we measure relevance—the basis of inclusion and exclusion of any element in the environment (system) of the problem of interest.

STEP 2: CLARIFICATION OF THE VALUES

Our values are the primary standards we use for weighing various alternatives and deciding among them. Values, therefore, play a very important role in decision making. A **value** is a criterion, goal, state, or standard by which we perceive or express normative or ideal circumstances. Managers continually use values to assess, measure, or compare existing real-world conditions and performance.

In terms of modeling, the manager should ask, How do my values influence my perception of the problem? Specifically, how do my values influence my perceptions of (a) what is, (b) what is desired, and (c) what needs to be done to move from what is to what is desired?

We sometimes refer to values relating to "what is desired" as *ends values* and values relating to "how to achieve what is desired" as *means values*. In general, we find substantial agreement over ends values but substantial disagreement over means values. It is easy to get management to agree that earnings should exceed 8% of gross investment. However, considerable controversy arises when managers begin discussing the means by which they can achieve such a goal. The advertising manager believes they can achieve the goal through more extensive and aggressive advertising. The production manager believes that they can achieve it through modernization of production facilities. And so it goes.

STEP 3: DETERMINATION OF THE SYSTEM

Before we can develop an MS model, we must determine a clear definition of the system. In general, this amounts to drawing a boundary around all components that we believe to be a part of the system. Figure 1.2 is a block diagram of an abstract system. The small triangles represent elements or components. Only those contained within the block or rectangle are part of the system.

FIGURE 1.2 A block diagram representation of a general system

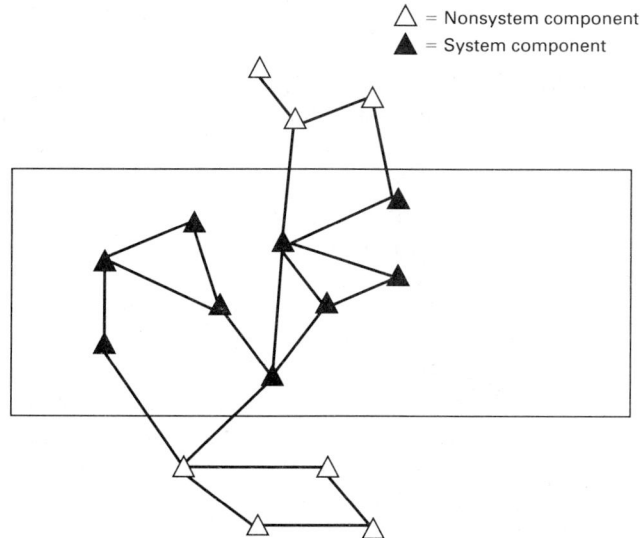

Systems are sets of elements or components and a set of relationships among the interacting elements. The word *universe* refers to all elements and entities in existence. Since, in general, a given system does not make up the entire universe, we must treat the concept of a boundary in connection with the definition of a system. The **boundary** specifies which components are a part of the environment. The **environment** of the system, then, comprises all components that are not within the system itself. The manager should address the following questions as part of the effort to define the system:

1. From whose perspective will we study the system? Normally, we should study the system from the perspective of the manager of the system.
2. What criteria should we use to select components or variables to characterize the system? Ordinarily, the analyst should choose only sufficient variables to fulfill the purpose and perspective (the internal, or endogenous, variables).
3. What criteria should we use to delineate the system boundary? What is the degree of separability of the system from its environment? Will the system boundary change with time?
4. What criteria should we use to select the variables that influence the system but that the system does not influence? These are the input, or exogenous, variables, or parameters.
5. What criteria should we use to select those variables representing the outputs of the system (those quantities that we are measuring)? The outputs may or may not be the same as the internal variables.

The definition of the system might therefore consist of the following steps:

1. Determine the inputs or points of influence accessible to the manager.
2. Determine the outputs or observables measured by the manager.
3. Determine the components that make up the system.

In deciding whether we should include a component within the boundary of the "system," we should ask at least two questions:

1. Can one of the manager's inputs influence that component?
2. Can one of the manager's outputs observe that component?

If the answer to both of these questions is no, the component does not belong within the boundary of the system. Systematically considering every conceivable component in this way will enable the manager to properly determine the system and its boundary.

STEP 4: IDENTIFICATION OF THE PROBLEM

Before we can model problems, we must first identify and define them. Identification begins with considering the process or system that surrounds and encompasses the problem. Which of the following terms best characterizes the process: certainty, risk, or uncertainty? Is there an essential dependence upon time that we must take into consideration? Are there special characteristics that require deliberate attention, such as linearity, integer-valued decision variables, a network, or stages of decisions?

The manager's responses to these questions will determine the type of model that is most appropriate. For example, a problem, which we know to be deterministic, may involve a certain level of complexity, and there may be a certain time dependence that we must take into consideration. Based upon these attributes, the manager may choose a continuous simulation model to study the problem. A manager may feel that a decision involves a certain amount of risk. The manager first lists the decision alternatives at his or her disposal. Which alternative to use is largely contingent upon which "future" will occur. In a risky environment, the manager does not know with certainty which possible future will occur.

STEP 5: FORMULATION OF THE MODEL STRUCTURE

At this point, we have stated the model's purpose, determined the system, and identified the problem. We now know what type of model to use and can begin actually fabricating the model **structure**—the relationships that will eventually characterize the model. These relationships could be constraints, equations, or expressions, as we shall see in forthcoming chapters.

We must identify and include relevant variables and relationships. Once formulated, the relationships will dictate what data we need. The data collection step meets these data requirements. In some cases, we may structure relationships to take advantage of existing or available data.

The actual strategy for model construction will depend strongly upon the problem identification step. For example, if the problem complexion is one of certainty and there isn't an essential time dependence, we will usually construct a static optimization model. On the other hand, if the problem is embedded in a time-dependent system, we might use simulation. The details of construction of the model will depend strongly upon the type of model we choose. We will describe such details as we discuss each of the model types in their respective chapters.

The model construction step will involve two activities: actual formulation of the model, followed by the model's computer implementation. We will say more about these activities later in the text.

STEP 6: COLLECTION OF THE DATA

This book emphasizes understanding the data requirements for each model that the book presents. We discuss how we can obtain such data (if not already available) together with how to guesstimate unknown and unobtainable data items. One of the benefits we get from a model-building exercise is enhanced comprehension of what data are important to the model—and thus to the decision itself.

Figure 1.3 illustrates the relationships between the MS model, the algorithm, and the data. We should perform data collection in parallel with the actual formulation of model structure so that we can construct the model around data that are readily available—and so that we can better understand the data requirements for the model-building exercise.

STEP 7: VALIDATION OF THE MODEL

Validation is the exercise of comparing the model against reality to ascertain the model's authenticity and appropriateness. The term **verification** denotes the task of making certain the computer implementation of the model contains no errors and is essentially free of bugs. In general, a model is verified if its computer implementation

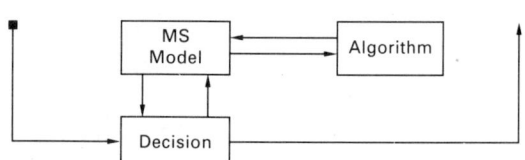

FIGURE 1.3 Relationships among the MS model, the associated algorithm, and data

does exactly what we require and conforms to the specifications for the model. If a manager hires specialists to perform the computer implementation, it is the specialists' primary responsibility to ensure verification of the computer code that embodies the model. Clearly, verification represents a subtask that we must complete to validate the model.

In validation, the manager is usually interested in four areas: data validation, structure validation, behavior validation, and overall validation. In data validation, the manager double checks the data to determine where soft data (data that possess a high degree of uncertainty) exist. The manager should instruct his or her management science specialist to perform sensitivity studies on these values so that he or she can assess the effect of large variations in their magnitudes upon the results produced by the model. If the results are sensitive to a coefficient or parameter whose data value is soft, the manager must try to measure this parameter value more accurately. Such measurement can be expensive—too expensive, perhaps, to be compatible with the manager's budget. In such instances, the manager must live with the uncertainty.

The second concern in validation is the structure of the model. Here two types of errors can arise: errors of omission and errors of commission. An omission error occurs whenever we omit an important relationship (be it a constraint, an equation, or whatever) or variable. Commission errors occur when we include superfluous or improperly formulated relationships. We can eliminate these errors by submitting the structure to examination by others familiar with the system and its problem and by comparing the structure with other model structures developed for similar problems.

We next perform behavioral tests of validity. The term **behavior** denotes the results or outputs produced by the model. Such tests usually involve inspection of the results or outputs and their evaluation for plausibility and practicality. Implausible results may suggest that the model has serious structural or data defects. In any modeling exercise, the manager starts with an incomplete understanding of both structure and behavior. By playing one against the other, the manager can increase his or her understanding of both. The end result is a better understanding of the process or problem the manager is trying to manipulate and control.

The intent of the last battery of validation tests is to examine the overall validity of the model. Once again the manager, assisted by an analyst, examines the model's data, structure, and outputs. The difference this time is that we have detected and corrected all bugs and deficiencies in the data, structure, and behavior. The examination this time is a final check on the overall compatibility and consistency of the model's data, structure, and behavior.

STEP 8: SELECTION OF THE ALGORITHM

Solving the models espoused in this book will require that we use algorithms. An **algorithm** is a logically ordered sequence of steps required to provide a satisfactory solution for the model. We do not necessarily have to encode the algorithm into a computer program, but this is usually the case. While it is true that all computer programs are algorithms, not all algorithms are computer programs. In particular, you can sometimes use a manual method to find the solution required by the model. This is also an algorithm. For models of any size, we generally use computerized algorithms because of the greatly diminished computational effort required. We could not solve most real-world models without a computer.

In general, we actually select the solution algorithm during the Formulation of Model Structure phase, because codifying the model will require a prior determination of the algorithm we will use. The model we encode must be compatible with the solution algorithm we choose for it.

This book emphasizes knowing how to use the computer algorithms and available packages. The manager needs to know how to prepare the inputs and how to interpret the outputs from these packages. This is especially true when the manager does not hire a specialist to perform his or her computer implementations. The manager does not need to be an expert in the mechanics of the algorithms in the same sense that one does not need to know details about the electrical circuitry of a radio, television set, electric razor, or telephone to use these devices. However, an intuitive understanding of how each algorithm works is certainly of significant value.

For some types of models there are several algorithms that we could employ in the solution. We can solve a linear programming model, for example, using ordinary SIMPLEX, dual SIMPLEX, or revised SIMPLEX. We can solve nonlinear programming models by numerous algorithms. In some cases, the issue of which algorithm to choose is one merely of **efficiency**—computer time required for solution. In other cases, a bad choice of algorithm may lead to suboptimal results. It is important in some cases to be able to recognize from the characteristics of the model what algorithm is likely to be "best" in terms of a successful result and computer time requirements.

This book employs two basic types of algorithms in the solutions of the models: heuristic and optimizing. **Heuristic algorithms** are able to produce satisfactory (but not necessarily optimal) solutions to models, whereas **optimizing algorithms** produce optimal solutions to models. Some researchers have likened the search for an optimal solution to the search for a needle in a haystack. In view of the very considerable computation often required to find optimal solutions, we sometimes defer to heuristic algorithms and satisfactory solutions that require far less computation.

STEP 9: DERIVATION OF FEASIBLE POLICIES

We can perform this step and the one that follows it automatically by the algorithm or manually by the manager or his or her modeler. Optimization algorithms, for example, can automatically generate feasible policies. An optimization algorithm is one that searches for an optimal policy through iteration. By optimal we mean a policy that maximizes or minimizes a criterion representative of the manager's values. We use the word **policy** rather than *decision* here because the result is really a coordinated collection of decisions. Policies are **feasible** if they satisfy a manager-specified set of restrictions or constraints on acceptable policies.

While optimization algorithms have the capability to automatically generate feasible policies, such is generally not the case for simulation algorithms. This is one of the major differences between simulation and optimization. We must therefore specify manually the policies we want tested when using **simulation models.**

STEP 10: DETERMINATION OF THE MOST APPROPRIATE POLICY

The "most appropriate" policy is a value-laden managerial consideration based in part upon the information provided by MS models. The manager must examine the policies provided in the printed or displayed output produced by the computer run. **Optimization models** automatically report the resultant optimal policy, which is optimal only insofar as the model is concerned, since it rarely represents the optimal policy in reality. The optimal policy serves its purpose by providing us with greater insight, intuition, and understanding about the problem.

For simulation models, we determine the most appropriate policy generally through a manual process of "cut and try." We generate a set of policies that in some sense covers the "policy space." We perform a separate simulation run for each policy, examine output of these runs, and "pick a favorite." Then we generate a second battery of policies in close proximity to the favorite one and conduct a second battery of simulation experiments. We may do this iteration as many times as we wish. Finally, we arrive at a policy that appears most appropriate of those examined, and this step is complete.

There are a few instances in which an optimization algorithm is connected to a simulation model. In such cases, the optimization algorithm performs automatic generation and evaluation of policies just as it did for static optimization models.

STEP 11: IMPLEMENTATION OF THE POLICY

Once the chosen policy is decided upon, the manager must implement it. No further objections or reservations should remain with regard to the policy in question, as the manager should have resolved them in earlier steps. Once the policy is activated, the manager must follow up the implementation to ensure the following:

1. A smooth transition.
2. A faithful activation that adheres to the intent of the chosen policy.
3. An improved behavior or performance consistent with the behavior predicted by the model for this policy.

We need to take seriously these eleven steps to "better modeling and happier managing." Managers need to be involved in all of these steps, even though they may delegate details of accomplishing any particular step to a management science specialist. Studies show that the greater the manager's involvement and participation in the model-building process, the more likely the manager will be to put to use any insights or recommendations derived from the modeling exercise. If the manager is separated by a considerable distance from an applicable MS model, any conclusions, insights, or recommendations accruing from the model will be unlikely to have much of an impact. This is because the manager is unacquainted with the structural assumptions built into the model in the form of constraints and equations and therefore is unlikely to place much confidence in the model. We say that the model suffers from problems of **credibility** in such cases.

In classic studies [4, 12] of major models formulated to study and solve problems in the public sector, researchers found that as many as two-thirds of these models failed to achieve their avowed purpose in the form of actual policy intent. This represents literally millions of wasted public dollars. The reason for these failures are many:

1. Failure to identify a specific client, manager, or policymaker whose perspective we should use in the model formulation exercise.
2. Failure to include the appropriate set of managerial inputs and outputs that would enable the manager to use the model as a policy-testing instrument.
3. Failure to make the structural assumptions inherent within the model comprehensible to the manager.

All of the alluded-to shortcomings contribute to the distance that separates the manager from the model. This book, therefore, encourages as much managerial involvement and participation in the modeling process as possible. Such involvement creates confidence, acceptance, and comprehension in the manager's mind. Consequently, the MS model begins to frame, shape, and influence the manager's mental model until decisions begin to reflect the insight, intuition, and understanding received from the MS modeling exercise. This is the goal of all MS models and MS modeling.

Managerial involvement in the modeling process is important for other reasons. One of the primary benefits of the model comes from an exposure to the modeling process itself. The development of an MS model forces the manager and his or her modeler to address important questions about the problem that the manager may have never considered before. A model never contains as much information about the real system as we must acquire in order to formulate it. Modelers are rarely diligent enough to record every conceivable consideration that arose in the construction of the model. And if they were, few managers would take the time to read and understand the voluminous material that results. All such learning is by nature vicarious, whereas the understanding that accrues from participation in the model-building exercise itself is active learning. Thus, the primary benefit that we may derive from any model-building exercise may just be the understanding that went into development of the model itself. To deny any manager such benefits would be counterproductive.

NOTATION

This section introduces the reader to sufficient notation (and some additional definitions) to enable a comprehension of the material to follow. Mathematical notation is the language of management science. To avoid misunderstanding, managers must develop at least a superficial familiarity with the mathematical jargon of management scientists.

The most important symbolic entity we discuss in this book is the decision variable, which we shall consistently denote by x_j. The subscript j tags x as the jth decision variable in a collection of n such variables (most problems involve many decision variables, and we must distinguish among them). As used here, the word **variable** connotes something whose value we don't know but need to determine by means of the model (and its associated algorithm and data). The term **coefficient** denotes an entity that remains constant, whose value we know from data, and that we use in the solution of the model.

Many of the models we discuss in this book involve linear functions and expressions. Two very prominent formulations arise in linear optimization models:

$$x_0 = c_1 x_1 + c_2 x_2 + \ldots + c_n x_n \tag{1.1}$$

and

$$a_{i1} x_1 + a_{i2} x_2 + \ldots + a_{in} x_n \leq b_i \tag{1.2}$$

Here there are n decision variables x_j; the terms c_j, a_{ij}, and b_i are coefficients (constants). It is customary to also write Equations (1.1) and (1.2) as follows:

$$x_0 = \sum_{j=1}^{n} c_j x_j \tag{1.3}$$

and

$$\sum_{j=1}^{n} a_{ij} x_j \leq b_i \tag{1.4}$$

where the symbol Σ denotes summation.

In addition to these conventions, we will sometimes use function notation. For example,

$$y = f(x)$$

denotes that y is a function of a single variable x. For the case of n variables, $n > 1$, this becomes

$$y = f(x_1, x_2, \ldots, x_n)$$

We employ function notation when we do not know whether the assumptions of linearity hold. In the absence of such knowledge, Equations (1.3) and (1.4) become

$$x_0 = f(x_1, x_2, \ldots, x_n) \tag{1.5}$$

and

$$g_i(x_1, x_2, \ldots, x_n) \leq b_i \tag{1.6}$$

We should understand that the "$\leq$" operator in Equations (1.2), (1.4), and (1.6) may be replaced by an "$=$" or a "$\geq$" operator in these relations. Thus, a particular model may involve several relations of the form Equation (1.4) or Equation (1.6), some of which have $\leq$ operators, some of which have $=$ operators, and some of which have $\geq$ operators.

Finally, we shall have occasion to use a transformed variable in a model rather than the variable itself. If x_j is the variable, then x'_j is the transformed or replaced variable we use in the solution. The algorithm will return a value for x'_j; it is up to the user to translate this numeric value into a value for x_j.

SOME CLASSICAL PROBLEMS IN MANAGEMENT SCIENCE

Before delving deeply into the substance of management science, we will introduce some general problems that we can address by management science methods. These problem descriptions should serve to impart a flavor for the power, diversity, and generality of management science methods.

RESOURCE ALLOCATION PROBLEMS

Every business manager is confronted from time to time with a rather general problem—how to get the most out of the resources available. The manager is responsible for allocating limited resources to the products and services he or she provides to the consumer or customer. Specifically, the manager wants to know how much of each product or service to provide to maximize profits. Since resources are limited, constraints are placed on the amount of product or service the manager can offer. The decision maker seeks that product mix that will realize the greatest net return. Depending upon the nature of the problem, the resources might be money, materials, labor, machine capacities, warehouse space, or some other factor whose availability affects the decision at hand. The problem is a recurring one in such areas as financial planning, production scheduling, purchasing, and marketing strategy.

The following is a typical mathematical form for such a problem that is linear:

$$\text{MAX } x_0 = \sum_{j=1}^{n} c_j x_j, \tag{1.7}$$

$$\text{ST: } \sum_{j=1}^{n} a_{ij} x_j \leq b_i, \quad i = 1, 2, \ldots, m \tag{1.8}$$

All $x_j \geq 0$

For a multiproduct, multiresource industry, the variable x_j would represent the amount of product j to produce, c_j would represent the profit contribution of each unit of product j, a_{ij} would represent the amount of resource i needed by j, and b_i would represent the amount of resource i that is available. Since our objective is to determine how much of each product to produce to maximize profit, Equation (1.7) represents a mathematical formulation of the objective or goal or purpose, while Equation (1.8) represents the constraints imposed by limited resources upon the achievement of that objective. The symbolism "$i = 1, 2, \ldots, m$" in Equation (1.8) denotes that there are m such constraints of the form

$$\sum_{j=1}^{n} a_{ij} \leq b_i$$

As an example of a resource allocation problem consider the following situation.

The Scenario: Ten years from now you are managing a commercial airframe manufacturing operation in which you mass-produce three different types of airplanes. These aircraft, which we designate in a model as x_1, x_2, and x_3, respectively, share many of the same resources, including the same engines, avionics package, seats, and manufacturing facility. The objective is to determine how many of each type of aircraft to produce—to determine product mix. The market will buy as many of these airplanes as your facility can produce. However, there are certain constraints on the number of aircraft that your resources and your facility impose upon the product mix. Your purpose is to maximize your return.

The Problem: The system in this case is your manufacturing facility. The environment would include the suppliers of parts for your manufacturing facility and market demand for your product. You are fortunate in that the market is bullish and will buy all that you can produce. You can count on your suppliers to produce and ship (on time) the requested number of parts that you procure. These considerations make your decision one involving certainty—to find that number of aircraft of each type that will maximize profit. Moreover, you obviously don't wish in any given production period to produce (and procure parts for) a fraction of an airplane. Your decision variables must thus be integers (whole numbers)—a special characteristic that you must accommodate.

The Model: This is an example of an integer (otherwise linear) programming model (discussed in Chapter 3).

CAPITAL INVESTMENT DECISIONS IN RISKY ENVIRONMENTS

Occasionally, a manager must decide whether additional capital investment will contribute to the firm's profit-making potential. Such an investment would expand production (or service) capacity. However, the manager is unable to determine with certainty whether market demand will be strong enough to fully utilize the additional capacity once it is in place. For example, a plastics manufacturing manager must decide whether he or she needs additional plastic presses. An apartment landlord must decide whether to build additional apartments. An oil drilling manager must decide whether to purchase another drilling rig.

As managers, we must consider several important factors. First, how much additional capital outlay do we require? Second, what probable return on investment can we realize? This latter question will depend upon the future strength of the marketplace, which we do not know with certainty. Thus, risk characterizes such problems.

The manager's job is to weigh the risks against the profit potential of the investment to make an appropriate decision.

As an example of a capital investment decision, let's consider the commonplace problem of buying a car.

The Scenario: You are an MBA student with a spouse, three children, and a live-in mother-in-law. The price of gasoline is near an all-time high, and your aging auto is a ten-year-old medium-sized gas-guzzling sedan. You are to decide whether to replace the car.

The Problem: To bring matters to the point of crisis, your car has finally broken down—the automatic transmission will not shift out of Park. After doing some data collection and research, you find that in the next five years fuel prices will

1. Increase by 50% with probability 0.5.
2. Increase by 100% with probability 0.3.
3. Increase by 10% with probability 0.2.

On the basis of this information you define your problem as one involving risk.

The Model: You begin by listing the alternatives:

1. fix old car
2. buy new car
3. buy used car
4. buy bicycle

Next you list the values that will impinge on your selection of an alternative:

1. comfort
2. safety
3. operating costs
4. status
5. cost of initial investment

You consider the total system and environment in which your problem is embedded. An important factor in the environment of this problem is the cost of fuel for the automobile. However, you do not know this cost with certainty.

The Solution: The solution to this problem will vary considerably from person to person. Depending upon the temperament and perspective of the decision maker, models will recommend different solutions. (We will analyze problems of this type in Chapter 7.)

CAVEATS AND COMMENTS ON BUILDING AND USING MODELS

Management science methods do not always succeed. We can usually attribute failures to one or more of the following:

1. Insufficient managerial involvement.
2. Overly optimistic expectations.
3. Cost overruns.
4. Fitting the problem to the technique rather than selecting the model that best fits the problem.
5. Failure to use known information.
6. Failure to consider the total system.

7. Failure to use an unbiased, unparochial value structure with which to evaluate the results.
8. Failure to use accurate data.
9. Failure to recognize the difference between a solution to a model and a solution to the problem.

Some managers believe that once they have defined the problem, they can safely turn it over to a technical analyst. Unfortunately, this usually results in a model that is incomprehensible to—and therefore unusable by—the manager.

At the same time, managers are too often taken in by modelers who are overly optimistic about the capabilities and strengths of a particular technique. The effect of such exaggerated optimism is to build expectations in the mind of the unseasoned user that are too high and that the user can never achieve. Such a tendency to oversell MS models and their attendant algorithms has in some instances given management science a bad name, and some oversold clients and users have become sadly disillusioned as a result.

In addition, some technical analysts tend to grossly underestimate the costs associated with a given modeling study. We should view as unrealistic the time requirements to complete each phase (as suggested by the modeler).

Perhaps one way to mitigate these difficulties somewhat is to make use of **decision support systems**—software packages that enable a manager to quickly and inexpensively build models without assistance from a modeler. Using such systems gives managers better control of all assumptions, structure, and data that go into the model. A decision support system consists of a model base, a data base, and a user interface. Ease of use is one of the primary design considerations for these packages, which are usually interactive.

The manager should be eclectic in terms of his or her consideration of the total spectrum of possible methods and models that he or she should apply. In addition, the manager should give ample consideration to the total system and the ultimate causes of any problem. Does the proposed solution suboptimize for a small department, or does it contribute to the goals of the entire organization? Is there any omitted relevant information? Is the perspective on the problem unbiased and nonparochial? These questions represent still other potential pitfalls that can make a difference between success and failure of the model.

Still another caveat relates to computers, algorithms, and software for solving models. As your *most* obedient servants, these tools do precisely what you tell them to do—nothing less and nothing more. They cannot recognize faulty or erroneous input data. They cannot spot the logical flaws that resulted in a linear model for a highly nonlinear underlying problem. Computer scientists have an expression—garbage in, garbage out—that sums it up neatly. The orderly, impressive-looking computer printout tends for some managers to become authoritative, and managers forget that the output is only as good as the input.

The last caveat has to do with the difference between decision making and analysis. If an analyst tears off the computer printout from a model and scurries to you with "the solution to the problem," you must know better. If a computer program can make decisions, who needs you? The point, of course, is that mathematical models are important aids to you, the decision maker. What most analysts ignore is that, for example, typical industrial applications of linear programming computer packages deliver an optimum solution to the model and there will usually be thousands of other solutions with objective values within a fraction of a percent of the optimum one. We should exploit this wealth of alternatives when we as decision makers consider factors exogenous to the model.

SUMMARY

Models are ubiquitous. We find we cannot even discuss models without using models. The question of whether to use models, therefore, is meaningless. The choice is really only one of alternative models.

We have, in this chapter, tried to describe management science, operations research, and the systems approach as sister disciplines with much overlap and having, as it were, the same parent—namely, World War II and the associated logistical and managerial problems that it brought on. Each of these disciplines is concerned with models. Today the terms *management science* and *operations research* are largely synonymous—both involve the use of models that have mathematical, quantitative, or graphical forms. We call these models MS (management science) models and distinguish them from mental models, physical models, and verbal models.

We suggested that MS models are devices for creating insight, intuition, and understanding about a problem. We should therefore regard MS models as media for guiding and enlightening the mental models of managers. Thus, we should be able to reduce the final results produced by MS models to seven plus or minus two components or concepts so that we can assimilate them into a mental model.

We found that we can classify MS models according to the type of decision environment for which they are most appropriate and according to any special characteristics they might have. In this book, for example, we consider three such decision environments: certainty, risk, and uncertainty. We discussed types of models appropriate under each category of decision environment as well as model building. We proposed a systems approach to modeling by using an eleven-step method organized into four phases: scenario, problem, model, and solution.

We suggested that managers would want to participate substantially in all four phases of the model building process. Such involvement would enable decision makers to acquire the full benefit of the modeling process and would ensure that the model ultimately reflects more closely their views and perspectives of the object system.

We then presented notation to be used in forthcoming chapters and introduced several classic situations to give you a feel for the kinds of problems that we can model. We considered some classical problems, including a resource allocation problem and a decision problem in a risky environment. Finally, we presented some caveats for model usage.

In this chapter we promoted the MS modeling approach to problem solving and decision making. You may be inclined to ask, "Does the MS modeling approach have shortcomings that I as an aspiring manager should know about?" The basic problem with the MS modeling approach is that we are always deceived to some extent about the character of reality and that every model is wrong—sometimes even dangerously so.

Why, then, do we have the audacity to espouse MS models? Business organizations started with simple things and mechanisms, which grew or evolved into more complex things, which further evolved into the extremely complex mechanisms of today. To cope with the increased complexity, we needed more sophisticated models. MS models met this challenge by enabling managers to augment their cognitive capacities with constructs that enhanced understanding and comprehension of complex systems and problems. The limitation on continued growth and competence in solving complex problems rests in part upon the MS modeling literacy of managers and prospective managers. Toward this end, let us proceed.

KEY TERMS

algorithm
behavior
boundary

certainty
coefficient
content

credibility
decision
decision making
decision making under certainty
decision making under risk
decision making under uncertainty
decision support systems
degree of abstraction
deterministic
discrete simulation
efficiency
environment
feasible
heuristic algorithms
homomorphic model
isomorphic model
MS model
mental model
models

optimization models
optimizing algorithms
paradigm
perspective
policy
problems
process
purpose
risk
simulation models
structure
systems
uncertainty
validation
value
variable
verbal models
verification

PROBLEMS FOR ANALYSIS

1. Provide at least three definitions for *model*.
2. Characterize the process of model building.
3. Discuss each of the following:
   decision making under certainty
   decision making under risk
   decision making under uncertainty
4. Discuss the differences and similarities between MS models and other types of models.
5. Discuss why a precise statement of the purpose of the model-building activity is critical to the success of the initiative.
6. Take a problem of interest to you through the SPMS method of description (as far as you can).
7. Indicate what model type you would use for each of the following situations and why:
   a. A leather wallet company is considering hiring additional leather workers to expand into the belt business. The manager has access to plenty of raw leather at reasonable prices and knows where he can obtain quality buckles. The largest financial commitment is the requirement for additional leather workers. The company has established an esteemed reputation for its top-of-the-line wallets, which sell at well above average prices. However, the belt market is very competitive, and there are already many quality belt manufacturers in the business.
   b. A manufacturer makes five different types of television sets. The company has established a reputation for quality and reliability that is unequaled in the marketplace. The market for television sets remains strong. The company is currently experiencing some difficulty getting the necessary raw materials. The various TV sets made by this manufacturer share many of the same components that are in limited supply. The ultimate consideration is how many of each type of TV set to manufacture.
   c. A large suburban bank is considering adding more teller stations to its drive-in bank facility. It knows the arrival frequency of its automobile banking customers and wants to know how many tellers to add so that no customer will have to

wait longer than five minutes. Currently, the average waiting time is eight minutes during peak periods of customer demand.
   d. A large federal bureaucracy wishes to study the future of the social security system in its country. The work force provides revenues for the social security system, while the elderly population receives these revenues in the form of payments. As time progresses, the elderly population increases, while the work force remains stable or declines slightly during periods of recession.
8. We often conduct managerial problem solving and decision making in groups, which involves consensual agreement among the members of the management team. While we might easily agree on objectives, the means to achieve those objectives are far more controversial. What approaches would you suggest as strategies for resolving conflicts relating to the means by which we can reach an agreed-to set of objectives?
9. For each situation in Problem 7, determine the following:
   purpose
   values
   system
   endogenous variables
   inputs or exogenous variables
10. How would you settle a dispute involving a pair of managers over a particular department that each is claiming belongs to his or her management "system"? Is it possible that the same department could report to and receive management directives from more than one manager (as in matrix management)?
11. Explain what advantages accrue from a systems approach to model building.
12. Validation involves four basic stages. What are they?
13. The decision situation faced by a manager is organized in the form of a decision tree. After considering her decision alternatives, the manager decided upon three: A, B, and C, as shown. A consideration of alternative A led to the realization that only outcome 1 or 2 could accrue from its implementation. We know the probabilities of these outcomes. If we implement alternative B, only one outcome—outcome 3—is possible. If we implement alternative C, outcomes 4 and 5 are possible. We know the probabilities of these outcomes. What type of decision making model is this?

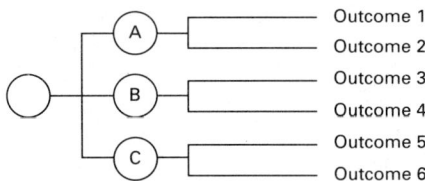

14. A simple technique for analysis of decisions is the use of a list of alternatives to characterize a decision space. When you complete your MBA program, you will face a decision involving your career. Characterize your career decision space. Analyze each alternative you list in terms of probable outcomes. As an example, consider the following:

Decision Space	Outcome
1. Go to work for accounting firm.	Modest income but high job satisfaction.
2. Go to work for manufacturing firm.	Modest income; bad location.
3. Go to work for consulting firm.	Somewhat better income; less job security.
4. Start own company.	Bankruptcy or tremendous wealth.

15. You have a handful of job offers on which you must make an ultimate decision. Describe what procedure you will use in evaluating the offers and deciding among them.
16. We recommend a term project in this course. Design a procedure for selecting a topic for the term project. If the professor tells you that the goal is "demonstration of a functional comprehension of the models presented in this book," does that help? Why or why not?
17. Discuss some basic differences between optimization models and simulation models.

REFERENCES AND ADDITIONAL READING

1. Ackoff, R., and P. Rivett. A *Manager's Guide to Operations Research*. New York: Wiley, 1963.
2. Churchman, C. *The Systems Approach*. New York: Dell, 1968.
3. Coyle, R. "On the Scope and Purpose of Industrial Dynamics." *International Journal of Systems Science* 4 (1973): 397–406.
4. Fromm, G., W. Hamilton and D. Hamilton. *Federally Supported Mathematical Models: Survey and Analysis*. National Science Foundation—RANN publication number NSF-RA-S-74-029 (available from U.S. Government Printing Office, Washington, DC 20402, #038-000-00221-0), 1974.
5. Gupta, J. "Management Science Implementation: Experiences of a Practising OR Manager." *Interfaces* 5 (1975): 84–90.
6. McCormack, M. *What They Don't Teach You at Harvard Business School*. New York: Bantam, 1988.
7. Pascale, R., and A. Athos. *The Art of Japanese Management*. New York: Simon & Schuster, 1981.
8. Peters, T., and R. Waterman. *In Search of Excellence*. New York: Warner Books, 1982.
9. Spengler, O. *The Decline of the West*. New York: Knopf, 1945.
10. Thesen, A. "Some Notes on Systems Models and Modelling." *International Journal of Systems Science* 5 (1974): 145–152.
11. Toynbee, A. A *Study of History*. New York: Oxford University Press, 1954.
12. Ways to Improve Management of Federally Funded Computerized Models. National Bureau of Standards, Number LCD-75-111, 1975.
13. Woolsey, R. "The Measure of MS/OR Applications, or Let's Hear It for the Bean Counters." *Interfaces* 5 (1975): 74–78.

PART ONE

Decision Making Under Certainty (DMUC)

Part 1 considers decision-making environments for profitably modeling problems by ignoring or assuming away such basic realities as the riskiness, uncertainty, and complexity inherent in real-world situations. In the jargon of decision theory, Part 1 addresses decision making under certainty (DMUC). Specifically, the five chapters of this part operate under the following assumptions:

1. We assume that probability distributions for all parameters and decision variables needed for modeling problems have zero variance—that is, they are represented by their means, and we refer to them as deterministic.
2. The managerial problem we are modeling can be focused (for the purposes of this model) on a single objective that we wish to optimize.

There are, of course, few if any real-world problems that *strictly* meet these assumptions. Why, then, should we include such models in a text that addresses potential and practicing managers? The answer is simple and compelling. Models are not problems, and the optimal solution to a model of a problem provides nothing more than insight into the solution of the problem. Managers have used the models we discuss in Part 1 with great success in business, industry, and the public sector to provide such insight to hundreds of thousands of managerial decision makers. The key point here is that the assumptions apply to the *model*, not to the problem. We must recognize the outputs from models exactly for what they are—information based on a simplified representation of reality. Thus, the decision maker must take into account conflicting objectives and probabilistic considerations in finding a viable solution to the problem. Seldom or never can we include *all* constraints affecting a managerial problem in a mathematical programming model of the problem. We must deal with issues such as social, legal, or political considerations external to the model. As we shall repeatedly stress, solutions generated by models constitute only one input to the decision-making process.

The following is a brief discussion of the major deterministic, single-objective MS models.

DETERMINISTIC OPTIMIZATION MODELS

Managerial problems that we can profitably model by the techniques in this section tend to be operational or tactical, and the models are usually optimizing in nature.

That is, they seek sets of values for decision variables that maximize profit, minimize cost, and so on. (The models we discuss in Part 2 are also single-objective models. We treat multiple-objective models in Part 3.)

MATHEMATICAL PROGRAMMING MODELS

Four of the models we will discuss in Part 1—linear programming, integer programming, network programming, and nonlinear programming—are subsets of a modeling approach with the generic name of **mathematical programming.** The term *programming* here carries the connotation of "planning" and not "computer programming," although, as we shall see, these highly sophisticated models would be of little or no practical value without the existence of high-speed electronic computers.

All mathematical programming models fit a very general format. First, we define a mathematical function to represent the goal or objective of the problem. We call this function the **objective function.** Next, we identify the restrictions, limitations, or **constraints** on the problem. We use a separate mathematical function to represent each such constraint. All functions are made up of **decision variables** and **coefficients** (constants).

LINEAR PROGRAMMING (LP) MODELS

The LP model is by far the most common form of mathematical programming model in use. Resource allocation problems, blending problems, dietary problems, and problems involving vehicle scheduling represent a few of the myriad problem classes to which LP is applicable. Nearly every industrial sector of the economy makes some use of LP, including the petrochemical industry, the automobile industry, the small appliance industry, and the advertising industry. At the same time, we find extensive use of LP within the various sectors of government, where managers use such models to make allocation decisions. Nearly every major component of a large firm could make use of LP for such disparate applications as personnel planning, production planning, marketing planning, and product planning. Such models consist of a linear representation of the goal or objective of the system and linear representations of the restrictions or limitations imposed on the system. We discuss LP models in Chapter 2.

INTEGER PROGRAMMING (IP) MODELS

Integer programming models arise, for example, in capital budgeting situations. We can also use them to help solve managerial problems involving go/no-go decisions or situations where the end result is either a yes or a no for each of a collection of decision variables. For example, suppose that we have proposed several new products but cannot start all of them at once. We define a separate decision variable for each product. After we solve the model, each decision variable will have a value of one or zero—a one meaning that the associated product will be included in the product line and a zero meaning the opposite.

As a further example of a classic IP problem, consider the task of assigning n instructors to as many courses. We must assign each instructor one and only one course. This problem recurs in assignment situations, such as the assignment of jobs to machines, movies to theaters, and personnel to positions. The typical decision variable is a zero-one decision variable, which is one if we should assign a particular instructor to a specific course and zero otherwise. The gamut of possible problems to which we can apply IP includes such classics as the problem of loading a knapsack, of finding a minimum distance (or cost) tour for a traveling salesperson, and of distributing fixed costs over an arbitrary number of items to produce. We discuss these and other problems in Chapter 3.

NETWORK PROGRAMMING MODELS

Many problems that we can model as IP problems result in immense constraint sets and/or a very large number of decision variables. In some cases, solution of these models by IP optimization techniques is either impossible or prohibitively expensive in terms of computer time. However, we can model some important classes of these problems as networks (sets of nodes connected by arcs) and find optimal solutions to the models with special techniques developed for this purpose. For example, the Defense Fuel Supply Center procures five billion gallons of aviation fuel for the armed services. This procurement requires five bidding cycles per year to supply 300 Department of Defense installations and involves complicated bids from more than 100 suppliers.

An LP model of the problem, with the objective of minimizing total procurement and transportation costs, did not incorporate several bidding features—and required eight hours of computer time on an IBM 370/145 to produce a suboptimal solution. Researchers subsequently modeled the problem as a network (we discuss this problem in detail as a minicase in Chapter 4). Other applications have reported successful network modeling of mathematical programming formulations with more than a million decision variables.

NONLINEAR PROGRAMMING (NLP) MODELS

Many different types of NLP models are discussed in Chapter 5. While the majority of mathematical programming applications employ linear approximations, there are some problems for which we cannot ignore the degree of nonlinearity. Such nonlinearities occur, for example, in product pricing, ordering with quantity discounts, and inventory control. In production systems, we observe nonlinear relationships empirically in per-unit production costs, process yields, and quality characteristics. In financial circles, a classic model for portfolio design requires that we minimize the level of risk, where we measure risk as a quadratic function of the decision variables. NLP becomes increasingly important as models take on greater sophistication and endeavor to characterize the nonlinearities of the real world.

RECURSIVE OPTIMIZATION MODELS

Discrete dynamic programming (DP) is an optimization modeling technique that employs the principle of recursion. Problems in this class usually require a sequence of managerial decisions (or we can model them so that they appear to be of this form), so that the current decision depends only on the previous one. Dynamic programming is the subject of Chapter 6.

The model types we will discuss in Part 1 are all basically static optimization models.

KEY TERMS

coefficients
constraints
decision variables

objective function
mathematical programming

CHAPTER 2

Linear Programming Models

Linear programming (LP) models of economic, industrial, and social problems are all-pervasive. Such models are used

- by commercial airlines to schedule aircraft/flight crews
- to optimize the mix of ingredients in pet food
- to optimize product mix in hard goods manufacturing
- by large commercial banks to manage their balance sheets
- for long-range capacity planning in production facilities
- to minimize trim waste in the paper industry
- by investment firms to optimize portfolio selections

The list of applications is seemingly endless, and trade and academic journals report new applications weekly. It is not an overstatement that if all currently operational LP models were simultaneously destroyed, American business and industry would grind to a halt overnight.

And yet, operational LP has been around only since 1947. George Dantzig invented a solution technique called the **SIMPLEX algorithm,** which was nothing more than a mathematical curiosity until the advent of the high-speed electronic computer. Applications burgeoned in the 1960s and 1970s, and today LP is a widely accepted and routinely used modeling technique.

What is the nature of this mathematical tool that has found its way into the boardrooms and management information systems of business, industry, and public sector organizations? LP has many definitions, ranging all the way from the mathematically precise to the simplistic (and therefore misleading). For the potential or practicing manager, none of these definitions is particularly helpful, since none succeeds in capturing the broad diversity of problems that we can profitably model by LP.

Instead of trying to describe the *model*, why not describe the aspects of *problems* that lend themselves to modeling by LP? The following section does precisely that.

UNDERLYING ASSUMPTIONS

Most managerial problems involve one or more **objectives** we wish to attain and **constraints** under which we—the decision makers—must operate. As noted previously, no model will ever capture all of the elements of an actual problem. However, if the model can represent certain aspects of the problem, the output from the solution of the model may provide useful insights.

What kinds of problems are candidates for modeling with LP? Recalling that our modeling environment is **deterministic** and **single objective**, it must also possess two basic characteristics: **additivity** and **divisibility**.

ADDITIVITY

To model a problem with LP, we must be able to safely assume that we can add the individual costs or profit contributions of the various products or processes to obtain an accurate total of costs or profit. Stated another way, there are no interdependencies among the decision entities. For example, if a laptop computer and a leather carrying case sell separately, but the case sells at a discount when purchased along with the calculator, we obviously cannot assume that the two items are independent. A morbid example might be the separate effects of taking sleeping pills and drinking martinis as opposed to the effect of taking them together. Most people would agree that the latter is apt to be infinitely worse than the former rather than merely additive.

DIVISIBILITY

The key aspect of a problem as regards its appropriateness for modeling by LP is divisibility. There are two considerations. First, the process we are modeling must be operating above a level at which economies of scale are a factor and below a level at which diminishing returns affect the outcome. In determining an efficient product mix in production planning, for example, there may be products that, if selected for production, would involve a one-time setup cost for the production line. We cannot model such a problem as a linear program, since cost per unit of production is different for every level of production (i.e., as production level rises, more and more units share in the initial setup cost). Note, however, that when the number produced grows large, we may approximate the problem *at that time* fairly closely by LP.

Second, nonintegral values of the decision variables must make managerial sense. If a small airline, for example, were trying to optimize its fleet mix of six aircraft and the LP model indicated an optimal purchase of 2.78 MD-9s and 3.22 Boeing 767s, our decision maker would hardly be pleased with such a result. As another example, suppose a portfolio manager wishes the decision variable x_1 to be one if he or she should include the common stock ROK (Rockwell International) in the portfolio and zero if not. We can only imagine the manager's exasperation at having the LP model return the output "$x_1 = 0.57$."

The net effect of the additivity and divisibility assumptions is that we should be able to express mathematically as linear functions both the objective of the manager and the constraints under which he or she must operate. The next section discusses the art and science of building such models.

BUILDING LP MODELS

Chapter 1 has already addressed some of the principles of modeling discussed in this section. However, these principles are so critical to successful modeling that we can justify the redundancy. **The following section (An Orderly Approach to Model Building) is one of the most important parts in the book. Please read it carefully, and then read it again.**

AN ORDERLY APPROACH TO MODEL BUILDING

In Chapter 1, the model phase of our SPMS methodology included three subphases: formulating the model, collecting the data, and validating the model. Since mathematical programming models (of which LP is a special case) exhibit the same mathematical pattern—an objective function that is some function of the decision variables, and a set of equations or inequalities in the decision variables that constrain the objective function—we can generalize much of the following to nonlinear models as well.

Our orderly approach to model building in linear programming focuses on the three subphases noted in the previous paragraph: formulating the model, collecting the data, and validating the model.

FORMULATING THE MODEL

Model formulation implies model selection and careful definition of decision variables before formalizing the mathematical statement of the problem. In deciding to use a linear programming model, make certain that your problem meets the requirements of additivity and divisibility closely enough so that no potentially misleading results emerge from the computer. Take into consideration the large amount of data required for LP modeling and make sure that those data are available in a timely and cost-effective manner.

Above all, remember that model selection is the *decision maker's* responsibility, not a technical analyst's.

Why is this so? Model selection is a macro (managerial) decision because only the decision maker knows what part the analytical results from the model will play in the decision process, and the relative sophistication required of those results will thus depend on factors exogenous to the model and of which a technical analyst will probably be unaware. For example, if factors such as labor problems, environmental pollution considerations, and financial exigencies constrain a product mix problem so heavily that all is needed is a feasible mix, it is unlikely that an LP model will provide a useful solution. Thus, managerial involvement in model selection is crucial to the success of the effort.

If we deem an LP model appropriate, the next step is to carefully define the decision variables. Recall from Chapter 1 that a decision variable represents a specific entity over which a decision maker has control. For example, the "number of steel-gray, four-door, fully equipped Taurus LX cars to produce in the Detroit factory in August 1994" is a decision variable that the Ford-Detroit plant manager can control; "how many cars are sold" is not. The important point is that we must define all decision variables precisely and unambiguously.

We are now ready to formulate the model of our problem. We have already defined our objective in previous SPMS steps. Our next step is to state the constraints under which we must operate. A useful and often insightful approach is first to state the objectives and constraints verbally. Let us illustrate this point with an example problem.

The Scenario: You are the chief executive officer (CEO) of a commercial aircraft manufacturing company that produces three aircraft models: a two-engine, a three-engine, and a four-engine model. Your objective is to maximize total profit contribution generated by manufacturing the three types of aircraft.

The Problem: The purchasing manager indicates that she can obtain limited numbers of engines, avionics packages, and seats each month. Furthermore, the limited supply of peripheral equipment (e.g., landing gear assemblies, cockpits) places restrictions on the numbers of each type of aircraft that you can produce. Finally, there is an overall limitation on the number of aircraft that you can produce each month due to plant capacity.

The Model: It appears that we have a deterministic, single-objective problem and that additivity is present. However, a result that includes "fractions of airplanes" makes no sense, so that one aspect of the divisibility assumption does not hold. Even so, let us continue the modeling process even though the resulting model might be flawed.

The monthly decision variables are apparent: (1) how many two-engine aircraft to produce, (2) how many three-engine aircraft to produce, and (3) how many four-engine aircraft to produce. Let us now construct a verbal model of the problem.

Objective: Maximize total profit contribution.
Constraints

1. Engine availability is limited.
2. Avionics package availability is limited.
3. Seat availability is limited.
4. There is an upper limit on production of two-engine aircraft.
5. There is an upper limit on production of three-engine aircraft.
6. There is an upper limit on production of four-engine aircraft.
7. There is an upper limit on total aircraft production.

If we are satisfied with our verbal model, the next step is to construct the mathematical version. The formal statement of an LP model is

$$\text{OPTIMIZE } x_0 = \sum_{j=1}^{n} c_j x_j \tag{2.1}$$

$$\text{S T: } \sum_{j=1}^{n} a_{ij} x_j \begin{Bmatrix} \leq \\ = \\ \geq \end{Bmatrix} b_i, \ i = 1, \ldots, m \tag{2.2}$$

In Equation (2.1), OPTIMIZE may be either MINIMIZE or MAXIMIZE, and the objective function is a linear function of the decision variables x_j, $j = 1, \ldots, n$.

Equation (2.2) indicates that there are m linear constraints that may be equations ("=") or inequalities ("$\leq$" or "$\geq$"). Since our aircraft manufacturing example has three decision variables ($n = 3$) and seven constraints ($m = 7$), the general mathematical LP model is

$$\text{MAX } x_0 = \sum_{j=1}^{3} c_j x_j$$

$$\text{S T: } \sum_{j=1}^{3} a_{ij} x_j \begin{Bmatrix} \leq \\ = \\ \geq \end{Bmatrix} b_i, \ i = 1, \ldots, 7$$

COLLECTING THE DATA

In our general LP model stated in Equations (2.1) and (2.2), there are

n cost or profit margin coefficients (c_j)
m constants on the right-hand side of the constraints (b_i)
mn "technological coefficients" on the left-hand side of the constraints (a_{ij})

Thus, for a problem with 25 decision variables and 20 constraints (a modest problem in the real world), the decision to develop an LP model of the problem involves collecting $25 + 20 + 25 \times 20 = 545$ numbers. Unlike in some textbooks, we cannot conveniently pluck these $n + m + mn$ numbers from thin air, to appear neatly assembled in a table. Depending on the nature of the problem and the decision environment, we must sometimes forcibly extract them from the accounting department or painstakingly sift them out of production records or estimate them from incomplete financial transaction records. If our organization happens to have a sophisticated, highly integrated management information system, so much the better. But even a good MIS is no cureall. In our manufacturing illustration, for example:

$$n + m + mn = 3 + 7 + 7 \times 3 = 31$$

Once we have assembled the numbers, it's time for a healthy exercise in managerial skepticism. Remembering garbage in, garbage out, we should consider the data to be "garbage" until proven otherwise. For example, decimal points are notoriously nomadic, wandering to places they don't belong. Moreover, the level of confidence in data accuracy may vary for the various inputs to the same model. As an illustration, personnel and labor costs taken from time cards may be highly reliable, while numbers estimating stockout or back-order costs in the inventory system may be only guesstimates—or at best scientific guesstimates. In any case, the manager must recall and take into account any known weaknesses in the data when he or she uses the analytical results from the model in the decision process.

Data for the aircraft manufacturing illustration are as supplied by the production and procurement departments (Table 2.1):

Since there are three decision variables ($n = 3$) and seven constraints ($m = 7$), the mathematical version of our verbal model would be as follows:

MAX	$x_0 =$	$500{,}000x_1 +$	$650{,}000x_2 +$	$900{,}000x_3$		profit
S T:	1.	$2x_1 +$	$3x_2 +$	$4x_3 \leq$	60	engines
	2.	$x_1 +$	$x_2 +$	$2x_3 \leq$	35	avionics
	3.	$135x_1 +$	$175x_2 +$	$245x_3 \leq$	3500	seats
	4.	x_1		$\leq$	8	2-engine
	5.		x_2	$\leq$	15	3-engine
	6.			$x_3 \leq$	10	4-engine
	7.	$x_1 +$	$x_2 +$	$x_3 \leq$	30	plant capacity

VALIDATING THE MODEL

After formulating the model and collecting the data, we must take one final precautionary measure before preparing the data for computer analysis—a check for dimensional consistency. That is, we must assure that we have stated the objective function and constraints in consistent units of measurement. For example, in our aircraft production illustration, our objective is to MAXIMIZE x_0, where x_0 is "dollars of profit contribution." To check for dimensional consistency, we note that "profit contribution

TABLE 2.1

	Aircraft Type			Limits/ Available
	2-engine x_1	3-engine x_2	4-engine x_3	
Profit contribution/unit	$500K	$650K	$900K	
Engines/unit	2	3	4	60
Avionics/unit	1	1	2	35
Seats/unit	135	175	245	3500
# 2-engine	1	0	0	8
# 3-engine	0	1	0	15
# 4-engine	0	0	1	10
Total aircraft	1	1	1	30

in dollars per unit of two-engine aircraft produced" is $500,000 and that the dimension of decision variable x_1 is "number of two-engine aircraft produced." When we multiply $500,000 by x_1, the resulting dimension is

$$\frac{\$ \text{ of profit contribution}}{\text{No. 2-engine AC produced}} \text{ (No. 2-engine AC produced)} = \$ \text{ profit}$$

We get the same result for x_2 and x_3, so that the objective function is dimensionally consistent. We use the same procedure with the constraints. For example, the first constraint indicates that there is a limited supply of engines, so that the right-hand side of this constraint (60) has the dimension "no. engines." The left-hand side of the constraint has terms such as $2x_1$, whose dimensions are

$$\frac{\text{No. engines}}{\text{No. 2-engine AC produced}} \text{ (No. 2-engine AC produced)} = \text{No. engines}$$

so that we have a consistently valid statement in terms of dimensions.

After assuring that our objective function and constraints are dimensionally consistent, we should have our technical analyst prepare the data in the form in which we will feed them to the computer for eventual analysis. As decision makers, we must personally make sure that all the numbers are in their proper places and accurate. Commas in a computer-ready data set—much like decimal points—seem to have a mind of their own. One misplaced comma, or one erroneous data item, or one omitted variable or constraint, is sufficient to turn the entire data set into "garbage." Once satisfied that the data are complete and accurate, the manager should have the analyst run the LP package using the data as input and bring him or her the preliminary solution to the model. If the LP solution looks reasonable from a managerial perspective, the model validation phase is complete. If it does not, you need to start over.

MODEL FORMULATION: TWO EXAMPLES

The minicases and problems at the end of this chapter provide a wide variety of scenarios intended to develop model formulation skills. Because of the criticality of this phase of LP modeling and analysis, however, let us introduce our fictitious computer user interface LPS (Linear Programming Synthesizer), who will lead us step by step through the formulation of a small (but realistic) LP model.

LPS: LPS on line. I am ready to assist you in formulating a linear model of your problem. What is your name?

PERCY: My name is Percy. Our family owns and operates the LO-CAL Candy Company. I have an MBA from a local university, but none of the cases we studied seems to be similar to the problem we have at hand.

LPS: Tell me about your problem, Percy.

PERCY: Our company manufactures five lines of candy, and it takes five different ingredients to make them. I have the production data right here—and I also have the profit contribution per package of each product [Table 2.2]. Would you like to see the data?

LPS: Enter them, please.

LPS: Got it. What's the problem?

PERCY: We are closing the plant (at the beginning of next week) for a month to modernize our facilities. The problem is that we have an inventory of perfectly good ingredients in stock and we want to make one more production run before closing the line. The raw materials will spoil if we don't use them. The foreman says we have enough ingredients to make about 200 packages of each brand, for a total profit contribution of $1,080. He's right, of course, and that would use up most of the light chocolate, but I think we could do better. So the CEO (my father) offered to give me any profits I can generate in excess of $1,080. You'd probably like to see the current inventory, so examine Table 2.3.

LPS: Got it. (Short pause) Percy, it appears you have a classic example of a linear product mix problem. Before we find a solution, though, let me ask some questions. Are you sure those ingredient amounts are right for each product? Two pounds of chocolate per package of Diet-Buster seems very high, and the 0.05 pound of sugar per package of Goo-Chew is an order of magnitude different from the other four products.

PERCY: No, LPS, those figures are accurate—it's the nature of the products. Anything else bother you?

TABLE 2.2

Product	Profit per Package	Ingredients (pounds per package)				
		Dark Choc	Light Choc	Sugar	Caramel	Asstd. Nuts
Nuts 2-U	$1.00	0.80	0.20	0.30	0.20	0.70
Bite O'Heaven	0.70	0.50	0.10	0.40	0.30	0.10
Chocochunk	1.10	1.00	0.10	0.60	0.30	0.90
Diet-Buster	2.00	2.00	0.10	1.30	0.70	1.50
Goo-Chew	0.60	1.10	0.20	0.05	0.50	0.00

TABLE 2.3 Inventory (in pounds)

Ingredient	Amount on Hand
Dark chocolate	1,411.0
Light chocolate	149.0
Sugar	815.5
Caramel	466.0
Nuts	1,080.0

LPS: Well, per-unit profit contributions are always tough to estimate. Do you use a different setup for different products? Is one (or more) of the products new? Also, who took the inventory of ingredients? Are you sure it's accurate?

PERCY: We've been making all five products for 15 years, and the profit contributions are accurate. As for the inventory, I took it myself—and I'm certain each of the amounts is within 3% of the actual availability.

LPS: One more thing, Percy. Technically, an LP model might give answers in fractions of packages. Could you handle that?

PERCY: Sure. I always take the scraps home to my German shepherd. He loves candy.

LPS: O.K. We're going to let the five decision variables x_1, x_2, x_3, x_4, and x_5 represent the number of packages respectively of Nuts 2-U, Bite O'Heaven, Chocochunk, Diet-Buster, and Goo-Chew to produce. Your objective appears to be maximization of total profit contribution, which is just the sum of the five individual profit contributions. Your constraints are the amounts of the five ingredients available. I'm also going to constrain your decision variables so that they can't take on negative values. Remember, now, when we solve this model we may not get whole packages. Here is the model:

$$\text{MAX } x_0 = x_1 + 0.7x_2 + 1.1x_3 + 2x_4 + 0.6x_5 \qquad (2.3)$$

$$\text{S T: } \quad 0.8x_1 + 0.5x_2 + x_3 + 2x_4 + 1.1x_5 \leq 1411 \qquad (2.4)$$

$$0.2x_1 + 0.1x_2 + 0.1x_3 + 0.1x_4 + 0.2x_5 \leq 149 \qquad (2.5)$$

$$0.3x_1 + 0.4x_2 + 0.6x_3 + 1.3x_4 + 0.05x_5 \leq 815.5 \qquad (2.6)$$

$$0.2x_1 + 0.3x_2 + 0.3x_3 + 0.7x_4 + 0.5x_5 \leq 466 \qquad (2.7)$$

$$0.7x_1 + 0.1x_2 + 0.9x_3 + 1.5x_4 \leq 1080 \qquad (2.8)$$

$$x_1, x_2, x_3, x_4, x_5 \geq 0 \qquad (2.9)$$

PERCY: That looks vaguely familiar—you said it's a linear programming model? I guess Equation (2.3) is the objective and the inequalities of Equations (2.4) to (2.8) stand for the constraints on dark chocolate, light chocolate, sugar, caramel, and nuts, respectively. What's the solution?

LPS: Percy. I've already solved the model, and I'll show you the optimal values of the decision variables in a minute to make sure my solution appears to make sense. But I'll warn you—you're not quite ready until

TABLE 2.4

Variable	Description	Value	
x_0	Profit	$1,509.09	
x_1	Nuts 2-U	454.50	packages
x_2	Bite O'Heaven	58.78	packages
x_3	Chocochunk	-0-	packages
x_4	Diet-Buster	503.99	packages
x_5	Goo-Chew	9.13	packages

you absorb the rest of this chapter. Here's my solution [Table 2.4]: Does it make sense?

PERCY: I guess so, and I make $429.09 for myself! I'm sort of disappointed that your solution doesn't produce any Chocochunk at all—it's one of our favorites. And we might have a problem selling more than 500 packages of Diet-Buster. Could you give me some other solutions that change these two products around without cutting into my profits too badly?

LPS: You asked an interesting question, Percy. I'll see you again later in this chapter, when you'll be able to understand my answer. This is LPS, over and out.

TELETRONIX INDUSTRIES, INC. [17]

In this model formulation session, our decision maker is Cynthia Sizer, head of the mechanical engineering department of Teletronix Industries (TI). Since Cynthia is an experienced LP modeler, LPS conducts her session in the BRIEF mode. That is, LPS dispenses with the chitchat it indulged in with Percy and gets down to business.

LPS: Ready. Name, please.
CYNTHIA: Cynthia Sizer—CS.
LPS: Scenario please, CS.
CYNTHIA: My company, TI, wants to prototype a voice-driven computer communications device. The EE team has the electronic technology just about whipped. My ME people will make the plastic case.
LPS: Check, CS. Problem, please.
CYNTHIA: We've always used the polymer ABS for plastic cases, since its heat-deflection properties are superior—and since it also meets minimum standards for ultraviolet stability, strength, and shrinkage rate. ABS is expensive, however, and management is becoming more and more cost conscious because of the increasingly competitive market. So I'm looking into the possibility of a blend of several compatible materials to try to reduce costs.
LPS: Objective is cost minimization. Decision variables are fractions of each compatible material to include in the blend. Additivity and divisibility OK?
CYNTHIA: Yes, LPS. Total cost is the sum of individual material costs. No setup or integer variable problems, either.

TABLE 2.5

Material	Variable Name	Cost ($ per pound)
Polystyrene	PS	$0.70
Talc	TA	0.15
Glass beads	GL	1.85
Regrind	RE	0.10
Polypropylene	PP	0.50
ABS plastic	AB	1.00

LPS: Good. We'll work this on a per-pound basis. Give me the names of the materials, their costs per pound, and a two-letter variable name for each material. We'll be using the SAMS format for output. OK?

CYNTHIA: OK. Here goes.

LPS: Got it. Any constraints on mix? If not, you should obviously use 100% of RE.

CYNTHIA: Yes, unfortunately. TA can't be more than 20% because of strength losses. PP is very unstable, so the mixture can't include more PP than 50% of the total of the other base plastics AB and PS. RE has strength implications as well but not as severely as TA—the mixture can include up to 50% RE. OK so far?

LPS: No problem. Continue, please.

CYNTHIA: This one is tricky. The base plastics are AB, PS, and PP, as noted. Too much PS and/or PP causes problems in the extrusion mold, so that at least 60% of the total fraction of base plastics must be AB. Also, the three base plastics must account for at least 70% of the mix.

There are two more constraints. We must limit the total of GL and TA to a maximum of 25%, for cosmetic purposes. Finally, to assure sufficient mold life, we must restrict the amount of GL to be no more than 15% of the mix.

LPS: You missed one constraint, CS—the fractions of materials must sum to 1. Here are the objective function and constraints exactly as you described them. Check them over carefully.

MIN x_0 = 0.7 PS + 0.15 TA + 1.85 GL + 0.1 RE + 0.5 PP + 1 AB

S T:
$$TA \leq 0.2$$
$$PP \leq 0.5\ (AB + PS)$$
$$RE \leq 0.5$$
$$AB \geq 0.6\ (PS + PP + AB)$$
$$PS + PP + AB \geq 0.7$$
$$GL + TA \leq 0.25$$
$$GL \leq 0.15$$
$$PS + TA + GL + RE + PP + AB = 1$$

ALL VARIABLES NONNEGATIVE

```
       ┌──→ SAMS INPUT SCREEN - Linear Programming  ←──┐
       │ NAME?  TELETRONIX INDUSTRIES, INC.            │
       │ MAximize or MInimize?  MI                     │
       │ PROBLEM DESCRIPTION - Optimize per-pound cost of material
       │                       for a plastic case.
       │
       │ Variables      PS     TA     GL     RE     PP     AB    Dir  RHS
       │ Objective      .7    .15   1.85    .1     .5    1.      <
       │
       │ Upper Bound   INF    .2    .15    .5    INF    INF      =
       │ Lower Bound   0.    0.    0.     0.     0.     0.       >
       │
       │ Constraints
       │ BASE MIX      -.5    0.    0.    0.     1.    -.5      <   0.
       │ LB ON AB      -.6    0.    0.    0.    -.6    .4       >   0.
       │ LB ON PLAS    1.     0.    0.    0.     1.    1.       >   .7
       │ UB ON GL,TA   0.     1.    1.    0.     0.    0.       <   .25
       │ SUM TO 1      1.     1.    1.    1.     1.    1.       =   1.
```

FIGURE 2.1 SAMS input screen for Teletronix

CYNTHIA: (Short pause) Looks good, LPS. But you can't give the model to SAMS in that form, can you? Don't all variables have to be on the left side of the equations or inequalities and constants on the right?

LPS: Correct, CS. I have a subroutine that does exactly that, but experience tells me that decision makers like to see the mathematical model exactly as they fed it in. However, if you'd like to see what SAMS will get, here's my call to SAMS on your screen as Figure 2.1. Note that SAMS handles the upper-bound constraints on *TA*, *RE*, and *GL* implicitly—that is, we tell SAMS that these limitations exist by entering the bounds in the row labeled "Upper Bound." This means that we have to enter only five constraints rather than eight. I have **boldfaced** the entries that I input to this module.

CYNTHIA: You're right, LPS. It's harder to check for errors in formulation in this format. What's the optimal solution to my model?

LPS: Already run. Table 2.6 shows you the SAMS LP summary briefing.

CYNTHIA: Interesting result, LPS. The blend costs about 60 cents a pound as opposed to a dollar using the ABS plastic alone. A cost savings of 40% will please my boss. How about sensitivity analysis?

LPS: This is a textbook, CS, so you'll have to wait until later in the chapter, when I'll show you SAMS' full briefing.

CYNTHIA: Fine. Bye.

LPS: LPS out.

THE SIMPLEX ALGORITHM: AN INTUITIVE DESCRIPTION

On a practical level, what goes on inside the black box that generates solutions to LP models is of little interest to a practicing manager. Philosophically, however, it is dangerous to know only what your servant does—and not how. Does this mean that a

TABLE 2.6

TELETRONIX INDUSTRIES, INC.	
QUICK BRIEFING ON OPTIMAL SOLUTION	
Variable	Value
PS	0.05
RE	0.30
PP	0.23
AB	0.42
Objective Function Value = 0.599	

practicing manager should be able to solve small LP models with pencil and paper? It does not—but every manager needs to understand the process and the logic behind it for several reasons.

First, as you will see later in the book, many problems exist that we can model in several ways—with perhaps one model being very much more efficiently implemented than another. Moreover, one model may produce the same solution as another but not have the capability of delivering data on the sensitivity of that solution (more on this later).

Second, many optimizing algorithms work in perfectly logical fashion mathematically but produce optimal solutions with features that sometimes defy managerial common sense. For example, the optimal solution to an LP model has the following curious property: if there are m constraints, no more than m decision variables can have values greater than zero (in the absence of alternative optimum solutions). But we are supposed to avoid constraints, since they represent limitations on managerial freedom of action. Does the above mean that the fewer constraints (unless $m > n$), the fewer decision variables that can be operationally positive and still give an optimal solution to the model? Yes.

For example, in a crude oil cracking problem, if a manager decided (foolishly) to implement the optimal solution to an LP model as the solution to the problem, without intervention, the number of different products would be a function of the number of constraints on production. Taken to its logical conclusion, such a manager—seeing the need (for exogenous reasons) to broaden the range of petroleum-based products produced from a given batch of crude oil—would need to look about for additional constraints! Such an absurdity mandates that managers understand what is occurring in the mysterious bowels of the black box.

THE SIMPLEX ALGORITHM

George Dantzig invented the SIMPLEX algorithm for linear programming in 1947. The algorithm takes its name from the mathematical term *simplex*—a region in n-dimensional space bounded by linear functions (hyperplanes). In algebraic terms, a simplex is the set of all solutions to a system of linear inequalities.

The idea behind the SIMPLEX algorithm is elegantly simple. Suppose we have n decision variables and m inequality constraints, so that we are dealing with an n-dimensional simplex. For example, a triangular pyramid would be a three-dimensional simplex described by $m = 4$ constraints: the three planes that intersect to form the sides, and the plane that intersects with the sides to form the bottom. Since we are interested in locating a point in or on this pyramid (the feasible region) that makes the value of another plane (the objective function) as large (maximization) or as small (minimization) as possible, it is logical that such a point must lie on the surface (boundary) of the pyramid, so that we can ignore the interior in our search for an optimal solution to our model.

Moreover—and this is the key to understanding how the SIMPLEX algorithm works—we can show that an optimal solution to an LP model (if there is such a solution) must occur at a **vertex** of the simplex represented by the set of constraints of the model. In our pyramid example, there are exactly four feasible vertices—the points where each combination of three planes intersect. Instead of having to concern ourselves with the infinite number of points on the boundary of the feasible region, we therefore need only to examine the finite number of feasible vertices.

Admittedly, the number of candidate solutions may be rather large. For example, in a moderate-sized LP problem with 50 decision variables and $20 \geq$ constraints, the number of vertices is approximately 50,980,740,270,000,000,000, which is roughly 50 quintillion! Surprisingly, computerized versions of the SIMPLEX algorithm routinely solve LP models hundreds of times this size in seconds (or at most minutes) on high-speed computers.

We can best explain the power of the SIMPLEX method by analogy. Let us represent the feasible vertices (most, in practice, are not feasible solutions to the LP model) as footholds on a mountain and suppose that an intrepid climber wishes to reach the top (*solve a maximization problem*). She or he will, of course, never try to gain footing on a foothold in space (*an infeasible vertex*), and the climber wishes to move from one foothold to the next and thereby ascend nearer the top (*increase the value of the objective function*). Occasionally, the climber may be forced to move sideways to an adjacent foothold at the same distance from the top (*encounter a degenerate iteration*), but eventually will find a foothold that leads upwards (*the algorithm is guaranteed to converge to the optimum*). Thus, because of the "upward-seeking" nature of the climber (*the SIMPLEX algorithm*), the fact that we do not consider "sudden-death" footholds in space (*we avoid infeasible solutions*) and that it is impossible to move horizontally around the mountain to return to a previously occupied foothold (*infinite cycling cannot occur*), we have a very efficient climbing strategy that uses only a very small percentage of possible footholds (*iterates through a minimal number of vertices*).

Mathematically speaking, the SIMPLEX algorithm does nothing more than solve sets of m equations in m unknowns—changing out one variable at a time until it finds the optimal set, or *basis*.

A GRAPHICAL EXAMPLE

Although dealing with "toy problems" is usually not particularly insightful, in this instance a graphical illustration using a two-dimensional problem is useful in understanding how the SIMPLEX algorithm works. (See Figure 2.2.)

$$\text{MAX } x_0 = 16 x_1 + 17 x_2 \tag{2.10}$$

$$\text{S T:} \quad 3 x_1 + 5 x_2 \leq 15 \tag{2.11}$$

$$8 x_1 + 9 x_2 \leq 36 \tag{2.12}$$

Toy $\qquad 5 x_1 + 4 x_2 \leq 20 \tag{2.13}$

Problem $\qquad 2 x_2 \leq 5 \tag{2.14}$

$$2x_1 \leq 7 \tag{2.15}$$

$$x_1, x_2 \geq 0 \tag{2.16}$$

The feasible region is the shaded area in Figure 2.2. We can demonstrate that there are theoretically 21 possible vertices for this toy problem, some of which appear as black dots in Figure 2.2. Note, however, that only the six vertices labeled A, B, C, D, E, and F are feasible—that is, they satisfy all five formal constraints and the nonnegativity restrictions on x_1 and x_2.

FIGURE 2.2 (a) Feasible region for toy model (b) Graphical solution of toy model

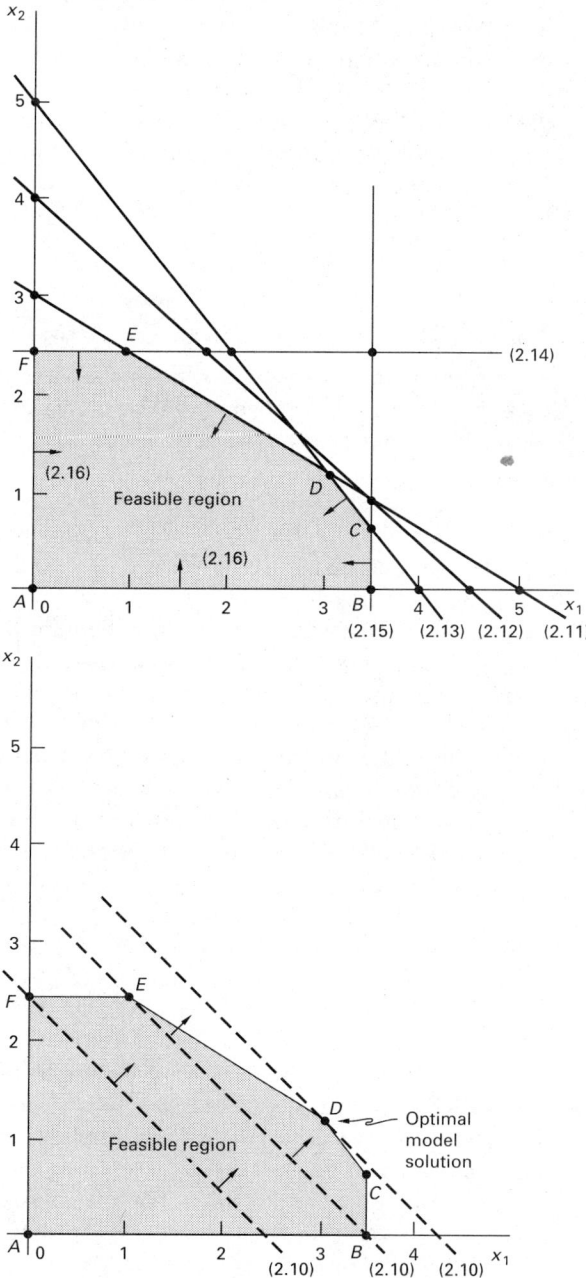

The dashed lines in Figure 2.2b represent the objective function at three positions. The SIMPLEX algorithm begins at point A (the origin), and moves first to point F ($x_1 = 0$, $x_2 = 2.5$), with an objective value of 42.5. The second iteration moves to point E ($x_1 = 0.83$, $x_2 = 2.5$), with an objective value of 55.8; the third and final iteration locates the optimum point D ($x_1 = 3.08$, $x_2 = 1.15$), with x_0 (the maximum feasible value of the objective function) = 68.8.

Recalling the mountain-climbing analogy, note that each successive "foothold" was indeed feasible and that the "climber" did make progress at each step until he or she reached the "top." In geometric terms, observe that the objective hyperplane (a dashed line in this case) moved parallel to itself, in the direction of increasing value, until it reached the optimal vertex point. From the graph, it is intuitively obvious that an optimal solution to an LP model must include a vertex.

So much for our toy problem. Operational LP models may have thousands of decision variables and hundreds or even thousands of constraints, so that the graphical example we presented is good only to provide insight into the operation of the SIMPLEX algorithm. Efficient computerized packages that implement the algorithm are widely available.

DEVELOPING ALTERNATIVE SOLUTIONS

At this point, let us step back and scan the terrain over which we have traveled. In preparing to use linear programming as an aid to problem solving, we took a careful look at the major characteristics of the problem to be certain that the LP model was appropriate. We discussed model building—and we heavily stressed data collection and analysis. A broad discussion of the SIMPLEX algorithm for solving LP models ensued.

Before discussing the details of developing useful information from the computer output of an optimizing LP model, we need to dwell for a moment on the nature of solutions to LP models. For example, our toy problem illustrated in Figure 2.2 has—as we saw—only six feasible vertex points. Thus, as theory points out, it depends only on the slope of the objective function—and whether we are minimizing or maximizing—as to which of these six points is an optimal point. Two observations are in order. First, if the objective hyperplane x_0 happens to be parallel to one of the constraints in the direction of optimization, there will be **alternate optimal solutions**. Although having sets of optimal solutions to work with is highly desirable, the truth is that for most real LP models, this happenstance rarely occurs, so that in most cases, the alternate optimal solution is a mathematical oddity.

Second, please note that if we do not insist on *the optimal solution to the model*, we have made a giant step in a managerial sense. Why? Because there is literally an infinite number of such solutions! For example, in our toy problem, suppose we would be willing to back off about five percent from the optimum value of x_0 (68.8) to a value of 65. Graphically, we have moved the objective hyperplane a bit southwest, so that $x_1 = 3$, $x_2 = 1$ is now on the new objective hyperplane (i.e., $3 \times 16 + 1 \times 17 = 65$). Thus, every point in the thin polyhedron bounded by constraints # 1, 3, 5 and by the new objective function is a feasible solution to the model and with objective values in the range [65, 68.8]. Figure 2.3 is a simplified version of Figure 2.2, illustrating this phenomenon.

Note in Figure 2.3 that within the shaded area, x_1 can now range from 2.4 to 3.5 and x_2 can range from about 0.5 to 1.6 (not simultaneously, of course). One way to view this result, in a general sense, is that we have traded off some possible profit

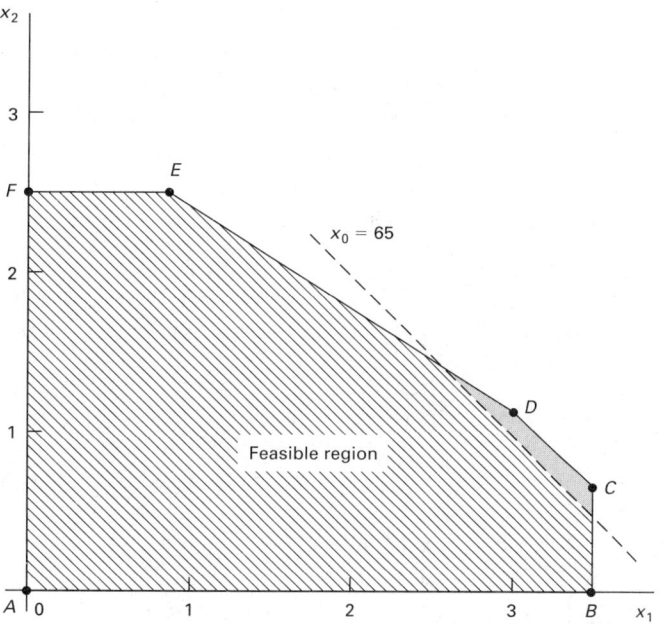

FIGURE 2.3
Good suboptimal solutions to toy model

FIGURE 2.4
SAMS input screen for LO-CAL

```
┌─► SAMS INPUT SCREEN - Linear Programming      ◄─┐
│  NAME?   LO-CAL CANDY COMPANY                    │
│  MAximize or MInimize?  MA                       │
│  PROBLEM DESCRIPTION - Optimize mix of candies for largest
│                       profit contribution.
├──────────────────────────────────────────────────┤
│  Variables    N2-U   BO'H   CHOC   DIET   GOOC   Dir  RHS
│                                                  
│  Objective    1.     .7     1.1    2.     .6     ┌─┐
│                                                  │<│
│  Upper Bound  INF    INF    INF    INF    INF    │=│
│  Lower Bound  0.     0.     0.     0.     0.     │>│
│                                                  └─┘
│  Constraints
│  DARK CHOC    .8     .5     1.     2.     1.1    < 1411.
│  LITE CHOC    .2     .1     .1     .1     .2     <  149.
│  SUGAR        .3     .4     .6     1.3    .05    <  815.5
│  CARAMEL      .2     .3     .3     .7     .5     <  466.
│  NUTS         .7     .1     .9     1.5    0.     < 1080.
└──────────────────────────────────────────────────┘
```

contribution for managerial flexibility in decision making. This is one of our goals—throughout this chapter and the rest of the text. And, incidentally, it should be your goal as a potential or practicing manager.

STANDARD COMPUTER OUTPUT

Figure 2.4 is the input screen and Table 2.7 is the resulting SAMS output to the LO-CAL Candy Company problem. Let us examine the product from this package.

The first item in the output is our LO-CAL Candy Company input screen exactly as we gave it to SAMS. The full solution briefing follows. We gave SAMS 35 numbers

TABLE 2.7

LO-CAL CANDY COMPANY
FULL BRIEFING ON OPTIMAL MODEL SOLUTION

Maximum Objective Value = 1509.09

Decision Variable	Optimal Value	Reduced Cost
N2-U	454.48	0.00
BO'H	58.78	0.00
CHOC	0.00	0.01
DIET	503.99	0.00
GOOC	9.13	0.00

Constraint	Type	Slack	Shadow Price
DARK CHOC	<	0.00	0.05
LITE CHOC	<	0.00	2.50
SUGAR	<	0.00	1.01
CARAMEL	<	0.11	0.00
NUTS	<	0.00	0.23

POST-OPTIMALITY ANALYSIS OF RIGHT-HAND SIDE VALUES

Constraint	Type	Lower Bound	Current Coefficient	Upper Bound
DARK CHOC	<	1403.05	1411.00	1411.26
LITE CHOC	<	137.13	149.00	150.04
SUGAR	<	795.41	815.50	815.89
CARAMEL	<	465.89	466.00	INF
NUTS	<	1079.68	1080.00	1096.04

POST-OPTIMALITY ANALYSIS OF OBJECTIVE COEFFICIENTS

Decision Variable	Lower Bound	Current Coefficient	Upper Bound
N2-U	0.98	1.00	1.05
BO'H	0.35	0.70	0.74
CHOC	0.00	1.10	1.11
DIET	1.98	2.00	2.96
GOOC	0.56	0.60	0.70

as input to our model; we got back 61 numbers in the solution briefing! The briefing consists of four sections: decision variables; constraints; post-optimality analysis of right-hand side values of the constraints; and post-optimality analysis of the objective function coefficients. Let's explore the meaning of these numbers in some detail.

DECISION VARIABLES

This section of the briefing indicates the optimal values of the objective function and the decision variables (in the column labeled "Optimal Values") for this model, and we can verify that the solution is the same as the one LPS shared with Percy.

The column labeled "Reduced Costs" contains vital information for the decision maker, although the label hardly suggests that this is the case. Reduced costs are associated with the decision variables x_j, $j = 1, \ldots, n$. All x_j that have positive values in the optimal model solution have reduced costs of zero. If there are no alternate optimal solutions to the model, all other x_j have positive reduced costs. The size of the reduced cost for a particular variable gives an indication of how close that variable is to becoming a "contender."

In our LO-CAL model, CHOC has a value of zero and a reduced cost of about one cent. What this means is that if the profit contribution for Chocochunk had been only one cent greater, it would have been included in the model's optimal mix. In general, for total profit maximization models, the values of the reduced costs indicate how tight the pricing structure is for a product line. In this particular model, it means that if he wished, Percy could include some packages of Chocochunk at very little degradation in total profit, since total profit would decrease at the rate of one cent per package (within certain limits).

In most LP models of real-world problems, large reduced costs (relative to their objective coefficients) should raise a managerial red flag. They could be signaling errors in estimation or perhaps in data input. But they could also be signaling an underlying problem, such as inappropriate pricing policies.

SLACK VARIABLES

The SIMPLEX algorithm cannot deal with systems of inequalities—it must have systems of equations on which to operate. By the simple device of adding nonnegative variables that take up the slack between the left-hand and right-hand sides of $\leq$ constraints, we meet this condition. In our LO-CAL problem, therefore, the actual model that SAMS saw was as follows:

MAX

$\quad$ 1 N2-U + 0.7 BO'H + 1.1 CHOC + 2 DIET + 0.6 GOOC $\qquad$ (2.17)

S T:

DARK CHOC $\qquad$ (2.18)

0.8 N2-U + 0.5 BO'H + 1 CHOC + 2 DIET + 1.1 GOOC + S1 = 1411

LITE CHOC $\qquad$ (2.19)

0.2 N2-U + 0.1 BO'H + 0.1 CHOC + 0.1 DIET + 0.2 GOOC + S2 = 149

SUGAR $\qquad$ (2.20)

0.3 N2-U + 0.4 BO'H + 0.6 CHOC + 1.3 DIET + 0.05 GOOC + S3 = 815.5

CARAMEL (2.21)

0.2 N2-U + 0.3 BO'H + 0.3 CHOC + 0.7 DIET + 0.5 GOOC + S4 = 466

NUTS (2.22)

0.7 N2-U + 0.1 BO'H + 0.9 CHOC + 1.5 DIET   + S5 = 1080

0 <= N2-U, BO'H, CHOC, DIET, GOOC, S1, . . . , S5 (2.23)

Handily, the SAMS LP module itself puts in the slack variables $S_1, \ldots, S_5$.

The values of the slack variables constitute important information for the decision maker. If a particular slack variable has a positive value, at optimality for the model, we say that constraint is **nonbinding**. That is, if the solution to the model *happens* to be a viable solution to the problem, that constraint is really not a managerial constraint at all. On the other hand, if the slack variable has a value of zero, the limitation represented by the constraint is **binding** and represents a very real limitation to managerial alternatives. For example, if the constraint represents a required raw material, the limited supply available directly affects the level of profit contribution we can attain. Note in the LO-CAL model that the optimal model solution uses all of the ingredients except a fraction of a pound of caramel.

We call the shadow prices associated with the constraints in an LP solution, variously; dual prices, Lagrange multipliers, or marginal utilities. The middle term in the foregoing derives from a mathematical formalism attributed to a famous French mathematician; the term *shadow price* has an intriguing cast, so we choose it in favor of the mundane-sounding but accurate "marginal utilities."

IMPORTANCE OF SHADOW PRICES

There is a shadow price associated with each slack variable—and therefore with each constraint. The shadow prices are the values exhibited under the heading "Shadow Price" in the SAMS printout of the solution to our LO-CAL model (Table 2.7). The shadow price indicates the change in total profit contribution that would occur, *given a unit change in the availability of resources represented by that constraint.* For example, the shadow price for the first constraint is 0.05. This means that if the right-hand side of the first (dark chocolate) constraint had been 1,412 rather than 1,411, the total profit contribution would have been about five cents higher. Within certain bounds that we shall discuss later, we can consider shadow prices to be **rates of change**, so that if the right-hand side of the second constraint (light chocolate) had been 151 instead of 149, the total profit contribution would have been higher by 2($2.50) = $5, etc. (assuming that the current set of nonzero variables, or **basis**, remains the same).

Note in the printout that the shadow price of the fourth constraint is zero—which means that increased availability of the associated resource (caramel) would have no effect whatsoever on total profit contribution. This comes as no surprise, since the value of the slack variable associated with this constraint (S_4) is positive. Obviously, if our optimal model solution didn't use up all of this resource, an additional increment wouldn't be of any value to us.

One might observe at this point: "What good is there in knowing shadow prices? We had only 149 pounds of light chocolate, after all—that's why it's a constraint!"

Good question. And the answer is in two parts. First, the value "149" may be anything from a guesstimate to a precisely computed quantity. It is here that the decision maker should heed the previous imprecation to recall any weaknesses in or uncertainties about the input data. If "149" was a "soft" number, the entire analysis is no better than it is. A quick calculation for the LO-CAL model reveals that a 5% error in this number would mean approximately a 1.2% error in total profit contribution. The supply of sugar (third constraint) is also critical. With a shadow price of about $1, a 5% change in the value "815.5" (the right-hand side of the constraint) would result in a 2.7% error in total profit contribution. Logic and managerial common sense tell us that one reaction might be to go back and try to obtain more reliable estimates of these critical data items—if at all possible. On the other hand, looking at the value of the slack variable for the nonbinding constraint (S_4), we see that we have almost no cushion in the caramel supply, even though its constraint is technically nonbinding. Thus, for practical purposes, caramel supply is actually a binding constraint.

Second—and most important—the LP solution has focused managerial attention on the bottlenecks in our problem. If such analysis in general does nothing more than this, it will have made a most significant contribution to the decision maker. After all, the inventory of raw materials in a blending problem like LO-CAL is not chiseled on stone tablets and handed down from on high. Such resource limitations are the result of managerial decisions. Can we somehow trade off the surplus resources represented by some nonbinding constraints for additional units of the scarce (binding) resources? Does the increased profit contribution exceed the cost of acquiring additional units? In other words, the model has done its job; it is now time for the decision maker to do hers or his.

RANGING ANALYSIS ON RESOURCE AVAILABILITY

The b_i, $i = 1, \ldots ,m$ on the right-hand sides of the constraints usually represent limitations on resource availability and thus are critical inputs to the model and the decision process. One simple type of ranging analysis is to compute—one at a time, and holding the other values fixed—the ranges over which the true values of these parameters may vary without changing the current set of variables (both decision variables and slacks) that are nonzero in the optimal model solution. SAMS exhibits this information in the third section entitled "Post-Optimality Analysis of Right-hand Side Values." These results help give the manager additional insight into the possible effect of data inaccuracies, as well as focus managerial attention on critical resources. For example, as long as the right-hand side of the nuts constraint (b_5) remains between 1079.68 and 1096.04, all else being equal, the current optimal model solution set remains unchanged. As we observed earlier, b_4 (caramel supply) can increase indefinitely without affecting the current solution set. Note also the very narrow range associated with the supply of dark chocolate, so that a small error in either direction would result in a different basic optimal solution to the model. In models of real problems, this is critical information for decision makers.

RANGING ANALYSIS ON OBJECTIVE COEFFICIENTS

In many LP models of problems, the most difficult numbers to estimate are the coefficients in the objective function (c_j, $j = 1, \ldots ,n$). If the objective happens to be cost minimization, the task is somewhat easier than the converse—maximization of total profit contribution. The reason for this is simple. "Profit contribution" includes both net profit (the bottom line) and contribution to overhead expenses not directly related to the decision variable. For this reason, we must estimate the overhead contribution using some assumed range of activity level for the variables. As we have previously noted, we cannot accurately model with linear programming a production line situation in which there is a possibility of incurring a one-time setup cost for one or more items. For these reasons, post-optimality analysis on the objective coefficients is very important.

The SAMS Linear Programming module will perform ranging analysis on the objective function of the model, and the fourth section of the output displays this information under the heading "Post-Optimality Analysis of Objective Coefficients." As long as the values of our objective coefficients are indeed within these bounds, the current basis (set of nonzero decision variables) remains unchanged. Note that the objective function values for our five decision variables in LO-CAL appear to lie quite close to either their lower or upper bounds—with Nuts 2-U *(N2-U)* in a narrow range of both bounds. In the majority of models of real-world problems, ranges on the objective coefficients tend to be very narrow—which means that the accuracy of our estimates of these coefficients is critical.

We can also perform post-optimality analysis on the constraint coefficients, and some sophisticated mainframe packages have this capability. Since the analysis is similar to the two cases previously discussed, we will not address this subject further. For an excellent discussion of this subject, see Wagner [22] or Hillier and Lieberman [15].

WHAT IF ANALYSIS

Reduced costs, shadow prices, and objective function and right-hand side ranging provide invaluable insights into our problem and, in many cases, to the underlying managerial and economic systems in our organization. But they don't actually generate the alternative solutions that we need to find an acceptable solution to the problem. We pursue such an extended analysis in Problem 1 at the end of this chapter, where LPS returns to provide Percy with additional help.

A CAVEAT FOR DECISION MAKERS

At this point, you might be saying to yourself, "There's nothing to this LP stuff—it'll be a snap to use." If so, beware! You are on the verge of being afflicted with the deadly "toy model syndrome." Think ahead for a moment, and imagine that your analyst has just run your 200-variable, 100-constraint problem. Recall that you had directed the analyst to run the program for optimality and then to run it again at 1%, 2% and 5% below optimality. Naturally, you also ordered a complete (simple) post-optimality analysis on each run. Your input consisted of 20,300 neatly arrayed numbers. Your output consists of 243,600 numbers and weighs roughly five pounds! Devoting one second of your attention to each number would require 67.5 hours! The point is that that pile of paper is not **information** (which is what you need for decision making); it is **secondary data.**

The solution to the dilemma is simple. Almost all operational LP models have an auxiliary program that scans the results produced by the optimization model. Using parameters, which you supply (e.g., all input elements within 5% of their upper or lower post-optimality ranges, binding constraints with shadow prices larger than the unit cost of the resources represented), the auxiliary program separates the wheat from the chaff and presents you with potentially valuable information. Is there a cookbook of such parameters? No. Every decision maker faces unique problems, and the elements of those problems may differ widely. The key is to thoroughly understand what the LP model is doing, what indicators it can provide, and what those indicators mean in the context of your decision environment. If you know what you need and if you know what it means after you've gotten it, your technical analyst will see that you get it.

TELETRONIX INDUSTRIES REVISITED

We now return to the session between LPS and Cynthia Sizer to complete the analysis of the Teletronix Industries plastic blending problem.

LPS: Ready to continue, CS?
CYNTHIA: Right. Full SAMS briefing display, please [Table 2.8].
CYNTHIA: The reduced cost of GL is $1.75 per pound. I guess I should have eliminated that variable from the analysis based on common sense. The other material not used in the mix is TA, with a reduced cost of

TABLE 2.8 SAMS output for Teletronix model

TELETRONIX INDUSTRIES MATHEMATICAL MODEL

MIN $0.7\,PS + 0.15\,TA + 1.85\,GL + 0.1\,RE + 0.5\,PP + \quad AB$
S T: BASE MIX
  $-\ 0.5\,PS \qquad\qquad\qquad\qquad + \ 1\,PP\ -\ 0.5\,AB\ <=\ 0.0$
  LB ON $ABSP$
  $-\ 0.6\,PS \qquad\qquad\qquad\qquad -\ 0.6\,PP\ +\ 0.4\,AB\ >=\ 0.0$
  LB ON $PLAS$
  $\quad\ PS \qquad\qquad\qquad\qquad\quad +\ \ PP\ +\quad AB\ >=\ 0.7$
  UB ON GL, TA
  $\qquad\qquad TA\ +\quad GL \qquad\qquad\qquad\qquad\ <=\ 0.25$
  SUM TO 1
  $\quad\ PS\ +\ TA\ +\quad GL\ +\ RE\ +\ PP\ +\quad AB\ =\ 1$
  Upper bounds: $TA <= 0.2\quad GL <= 0.15\quad RE <= 0.5$

FULL BRIEFING ON OPTIMAL MODEL SOLUTION

Maximum Objective Value = .599

Decision Variable	Optimal Value	Reduced Cost
PS	0.05	0.00
TA	0.00	0.05
GL	0.00	1.75
RE	0.30	0.00
PP	0.23	0.00
AB	0.42	0.00

Constraint	Type	Slack	Shadow Price
BASE MIX	<	0.00	−0.13
LB ON ABSP	>	0.00	0.30
LB ON PLAS	>	0.00	0.71
UB ON GL,TA	<	0.25	0.00
SUM TO 1	=	0.00	0.10

TABLE 2.8 SAMS output for Teletronix model—*Continued*

POST-OPTIMALITY ANALYSIS OF RIGHT-HAND SIDE VALUES

Constraint	Type	Lower Bound	Current Coefficient	Upper Bound
BASE MIX	<	−0.35	0.00	0.07
LB ON ABSP	>	−0.42	0.00	0.05
LB ON PLAS	>	0.50	0.70	1.00
UB ON GL,TA	<	0.00	0.25	INF
SUM TO 1	=	0.70	1.00	1.20

POST-OPTIMALITY ANALYSIS OF OBJECTIVE COEFFICIENTS

Decision Variable	Lower Bound	Current Coefficient	Upper Bound
PS	0.50	0.70	1.00
TA	0.10	0.15	INF
GL	0.10	1.85	INF
RE	−INF	0.10	0.15
PP	−1.64	0.50	0.70
AB	0.70	1.00	INF

$.05, but the per pound cost is only $.15. Does that mean that if the cost of *TA* was less than $.10 per pound, the mix would include some *TA*?

LPS: Correct, CS.

CYNTHIA: OK, the binding constraints were the first three and the last one, and none of the upper bounds are binding. That's interesting—the first three are constraints on the base plastics, and the last just assures that the mix totals 100 percent. It appears to me that the base plastics *PS*, *PP*, and *AB* are "driving" my problem.

LPS: I agree, CS. Note in the "Shadow Price" column that the shadow prices for constraints (1), (2), and (3) are −0.13, +0.30, and +0.71, respectively. Recall that for a minimization model, SAMS presents shadow prices for ≤ constraints as negative numbers and for ≥ and = constraints as positive numbers—for the convenience of the user.

CYNTHIA: Got it, LPS. But what do the shadow prices mean in a model like this one? There aren't any scarce resources as there are in a product mix problem.

LPS: Good question. Look at the right-hand side ranging analysis on the third constraint. Since b_3 had a value of 0.70, then—all else remaining the same—you would get the same materials in the optimal model mix for $0.50 \leq b_3 \leq 1$. Recalling that the shadow price for this constraint is

+0.71 and noting that a decrease in b_3 *loosens* this $\geq$ constraint and therefore reduces the cost of the mix, for $b_3 = 0.5$, $x_0^* = 0.599 - .20 \times .71 = 0.457$.

CYNTHIA: I see. If I could get by with only 50 percent base plastics in the mix, I could lower the per-pound price from about $.60 to about $.46. I think I'll have our chemist recheck her lab analysis on that requirement.

Another thing, LPS. In the mechanical engineering business, there's an old saying—simple is better. What kind of price per pound would result if we stuck to just the base plastics *PS*, *PP*, and *AB*? If you have to solve another model, just give me the cost and the mix—I don't need to see the full SAMS output.

LPS: I do have to solve another model, CS. I can't answer your question easily from the printout. (Short pause) . . . Here's your solution.

Cost per Pound		$	.800000
Percent	PS	=	0
	PP	=	40.000000
	AB	=	60.000000
	Check total	=	100.000000

CYNTHIA: That's it, LPS! We'll convert immediately to the 40/60 mix of PP/AB at a savings of 20%—there's no retooling needed to make that change. Then when our chemist rechecks her analysis, we'll reconsider the original optimal model mix and perhaps pick up additional savings. Thanks—you've been a big help.

LPS: LPS out.

EXTENSIONS OF THE SIMPLEX METHOD

This section picks up the bits and pieces that we purposely avoided earlier in the interest of clarity. It also discusses some of the more sophisticated extensions that are quite useful in practice.

SOME BITS AND PIECES

All is not quite as simple as it appeared in our toy problem, and we must address certain other possibilities.

"$\geq$" OR "$=$" CONSTRAINTS

In the case of a "$\geq$" constraint, we must subtract a "surplus variable" from the left-hand side to turn it into an equality. The shadow price for a surplus variable has precisely the reverse connotation as the shadow price for a slack variable. Think of it this way. Increasing the b_i for a $\leq$ constraint in effect loosens the constraints on the model and permits the possibility of improving the value of our objective function. Exactly the reverse is true for a $\geq$ constraint, since increasing b_i tightens the constraining force on the problem. Therefore, we interpret the shadow price conversely in the two cases.

How about a natural = constraint? We need no slack or surplus variable to transform it into an equality, so how do we find a shadow price if our computerized LP package does not do it automatically for us? The simplest way to handle this situation is to write the = constraint as two constraints, as follows:

$$\sum_{j=1}^{n} a_{ij}x_j = b_i \tag{2.24}$$

is equivalent to:

$$\sum_{j=1}^{n} a_{ij}x_j \leq b_i \tag{2.25}$$

and

$$\sum_{j=1}^{n} a_{ij}x_j \geq b_i$$

One then interprets either shadow price in the usual way.

VARIABLES WITH UNRESTRICTED SIGNS

In some situations, it makes sense for certain decision variables to take on negative values in an optimal solution, and some available computerized packages handle this feature explicitly. However, one of the computational requirements of the SIMPLEX algorithm is that all variables be nonnegative. We solve this problem easily by the addition of a single dummy variable z as follows. Suppose the first k decision variables in an LP model of stock portfolio selection carry the option of buying the stock (x_j positive) or selling the stock short (x_j negative). We replace these k variables with the following transformation:

$$x_j = z - x'_j, \quad j = 1, \ldots, k \tag{2.26}$$
$$z, x'_j \geq 0 \tag{2.27}$$

Note in Equations (2.26) and (2.27) that if it is preferable to buy stock j, the algorithm will emerge with a value of $z > x'_j$. If a short sale is optimal, the model generates the $x'_j > z$. The remarkable thing about this transformation is that it only takes one variable z to unconstrain many decision variables x_j, $j = 1, \ldots, k$.

UNBOUNDED AND INFEASIBLE SOLUTIONS

Instead of returning pages of numbers, the black box will sometimes return a single page with the cryptic comment "unbounded solution" or "no feasible solution." The former case means that some variable or variables can increase (decrease) without limit, so that we can make the objective function as large (small) as we wish. This, of course, is a mathematical possibility but an operational silliness. It means only that you have made an error in modeling the problem or assembling the data. Consider yourself extremely lucky if you get back an indication of "unbounded solution"—the SIMPLEX algorithm has discovered your error for you.

The "no feasible solution" result is an entirely different matter. This may, of course, have come about because of modeling or data error, in which case you are again lucky. More likely, however, is the possibility that the LP model of your problem is actually overconstrained. What you have uncovered, if this is the case, is an incipient managerial disaster. For example, you may have overcommitted the production line with an operationally impossible mix of advance orders. You may have adopted an investment strategy that cannot meet SEC requirements. Or you may have targeted for a percentage of market share that your present advertising budget cannot achieve. To be absolutely candid, if we could explicitly include all possible constraints in optimization models, most such models would return the output as "no feasible solution." Models that allow for the attempt to attain multiple objectives are one answer to this problem, and we discuss them in Chapter 14.

DUALITY THEORY To the MS/OR specialist, something called "duality theory" is one of the most important theoretical constructs in all of mathematical programming. For example, it forms the basis for the theoretical underpinnings that explain the meaning of shadow prices. Duality theory and its implications have led to major algorithmic developments in nonlinear programming (Chapter 5) and network modeling (Chapter 4) as well. We would insist that our technical analysts be well versed in this topic.

There is also a potentially useful computational device based on duality theory with which the practicing manager should be familiar. Consider the LP problem P that follows:

$$\text{MAX } x_0 = \sum_{j=1}^{n} c_j x_j \tag{2.28}$$

(P)

$$\text{S T:} \quad \sum_{j=1}^{n} a_{ij} x_j \leq b_i, \, i = 1, \ldots, m \tag{2.29}$$

$$x_j \geq 0, \, j = 1, \ldots, n \tag{2.30}$$

Duality theory demonstrates that we can solve the following problem DP, which is closely associated with P, merely by inspecting the optimal solution to P:

$$\text{MIN } y_0 = \sum_{i=1}^{m} b_i y_i \tag{2.31}$$

(DP)

$$\text{S T:} \quad \sum_{i=1}^{m} a_{ji} y_i \geq c_j, \, j = 1, \ldots, n \tag{2.32}$$

$$y_i \geq 0, \, i = 1, \ldots, m \tag{2.33}$$

Note that DP is just P with the objective functions and constraint right-hand sides changing places and with the constraint coefficients transposed. We can show that $x_0 = y_0$ at optimality and that the y_i are the shadow prices for P.

Admittedly, the managerial utility of the preceding is not immediately obvious. However, computational difficulty with the SIMPLEX method is largely a function of the number of constraints—and much less so as regards the number of variables. Suppose your (primal) problem looks like the semi-toy problem DP with 10 decision variables and 20 constraints. There will be 20 surplus variables and 20 artificial variables (needed to obtain a feasible starting solution), for a total of 50 model variables. For this small problem, there are about *47 trillion* vertices.

Now consider the corresponding problem P, which has 20 decision variables and 10 constraints. We must, of course, add 10 slack variables (but not artificials), for a total of 30 model variables. In this case, our problem has about *30 million* vertices, which is less than one ten-thousandths of one percent of the number of vertices in DP! Since we can obtain the solution for DP by inspecting the optimal solutions for P, the computational advantage of solving P instead of DP is obvious. Moreover, some real-world LP models are so large that they won't even fit in the computer available to solve them. If the dual problem will fit, we have breached a computational chasm with this handy device. Finally, some sophisticated computer LP codes incorporate something called DUAL SIMPLEX, which solves the dual problem directly. Please consult an OR/MS technical specialist for details.

This small peek under the immense tent of duality theory is similar to viewing one frame of *Gone With the Wind*. If any of you readers stray from the world of managerial decision making into the technical briar patch of OR/MS, you will unquestionably see the entire movie—several times.

SOME ADVANCED TOPICS

Most texts of this nature avoid some or all of the following topics because of their mathematical complexity. Since we are not concerned with mastering algorithmic details—and since these topics are important modeling tools—we discuss them briefly in the following sections.

LOWER-BOUNDED VARIABLES

Many LP models contain constraints that express lower bounds on some or all of the decision variables. For example, if the variables x_j, $j = 1, \ldots, n$, represented production levels for n products and the marketing department had already accepted advance orders for the products in the amounts L_j, there would be n constraints of the form

$$x_j \geq L_j, j = 1, \ldots, n$$

As previously noted, since the number of constraints drives computational complexity in the SIMPLEX method, it is always advantageous to delete constraints whenever possible (without changing the nature of the model).

We can do away with lower-bound constraints by a simple transformation. For every decision variable with a lower bound, we make the substitution:

$$x_j = x_j' + L_j, j = 1, \ldots, n \tag{2.34}$$

$$x_j' \geq 0 \tag{2.35}$$

After we have optimized the model, we merely reverse the transformation to recover the optimal values of the original decision variables.

Like several available packages, SAMS handles lower bounds implicitly without having to either make the transformations or include the constraints themselves. In the

CHAPTER 2 LINEAR PROGRAMMING MODELS 53

row labeled "Lower Bound" in the input screen, we need only enter the lower bounds for affected variables (the SAMS default value is, of course, zero).

UPPER-BOUNDED VARIABLES

Consider the problem of scheduling part-time nurses in a large hospital. Among the many constraints that we must consider, suppose that state laws require payment of retirement and other benefits to nurses who work more than 20 hours in any week. We wish, therefore to impose constraints to assure that our part-timers work no more than 20 hours in any week. Let x_{ij} be the decision variables representing the number of hours that part-timer i works in week j, and assume that there are n part-timers. If our planning horizon is 13 weeks, these upper-bound constraints would appear in the model as follows:

$$x_{ij} \leq 20; \: i = 1, \ldots, n; \: j = 1, \ldots, 13 \quad (2.36)$$

You may be thinking: "I'll bet there's a transformation like Equation (2.34) that lets us do away with the upper-bound constraints (2.36). Let's see: that would be—$x_{ij} = 20 - x'_{ij}$." Sorry, but it won't work. Such a transformation certainly limits x_{ij} to an upper bound of 20, but what if the computer decided to make some $x'_{ij} = 30$? Nurse i would have to come in on week j and *unwork* ten hours—a result so absurd that it deserves no further comment.

However, like SAMS, many sophisticated LP packages do have a feature called "implicit upper bounding." This feature is usually not automatic, however, and the analyst must explicitly summon it. In SAMS' input screen, we place upper bounds in the row labeled "Upper Bound" for each affected variable (the default is $+\infty$). Implicit upper bounding greatly expedites the solution process and allows solution of some large problems with many upper-bounded variables that otherwise would not even fit in the computer.

DANTZIG-WOLFE DECOMPOSITION

There is a class of very large LP models that technical specialists call **block diagonal (BD) models**. Other authors refer to the underlying problem as multidivisional or multiple time period in nature. For example, an LP model with three such blocks, divisions, or periods, would have the appearance of the schematic in Figure 2.5.

For the sake of clarity, let us discuss this BD problem in terms of a realistic example. Suppose BD is the aggregate LP model for a product mix problem for a

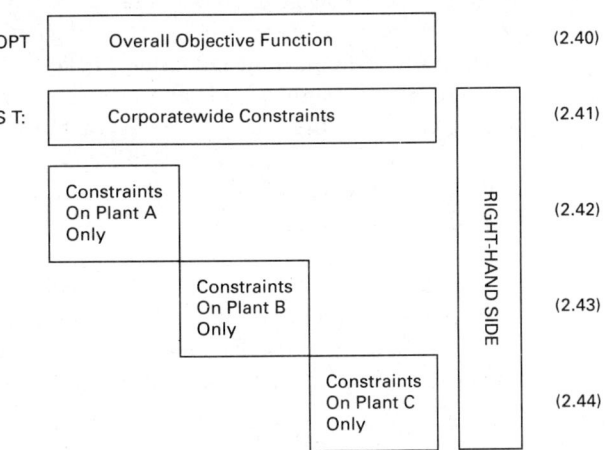

FIGURE 2.5
Block diagonal LP model

modest-sized manufacturing firm with three semiautonomous plants that produce different products. The plant managers are vice presidents of the firm and have historically had profit center responsibility.

The objective function (2.37) represents the total profit contribution of the three plants, and—naturally—the CEO of the company wishes to maximize it. The constraints (2.38) represent scarce resources, which the corporate managers will allocate to the plants, and might involve restrictions on capital investment, corporate MIS availability, trained quality control inspectors, etc.

Constraints (2.39), (2.40), and (2.41) pertain specifically to the internal constraints within each of the three plants, and we note that these constraint sets do not overlap each other (thus the term *block diagonal*). Therefore, if it were not for the existence of corporatewide constraints (2.38), the three plant managers could separately optimize their own individual models and report the results separately to the CEO. However, the corporatewide constraints (2.38) do exist, and they may represent overriding considerations that the CEO must account for. The task of the CEO, then, is to divide these resources among the three plants in such a way that the CEO optimizes the overall corporate profit contribution.

You might observe—from an analytical point of view and assuming that the corporate computer is large enough—that there's not much of a problem here. All the CEO needs to do is to request the data in constraints (2.39), (2.40), and (2.41) from the three plant managers, run the overall model BD and analyze the results, and return the optimal values of each set of decision variables to the appropriate plant manager. What's the big deal? *Models don't make decisions: Managers do.*

Although corporate headquarters could certainly obtain the required data from the plants, decision makers at that level are most likely unfamiliar with the day-to-day operation of the plants. The decision environment no doubt differs widely from plant to plant, and the plant managers are paid to know those environments and make good decisions based on their knowledge.

A product mix handed down to a plant manager from headquarters might not even be feasible because of considerations exogenous to the model. Besides, if corporate headquarters is going to make such detailed decisions, who needs a plant manager with the rank of vice president? The answer to this rhetorical question is obvious to anyone familiar with business and industry.

We now turn to the Dantzig-Wolfe decomposition approach to the multidivisional LP model, but we avoid the mathematical details. The approach is an iterative one—and one of the most clever optimization devices in all of OR/MS.

Basically, corporate headquarters makes an allocation of resources represented by the b_i in constraints (2.38) and asks the plants to return their results. Based on these results and the shadow prices that accompany them, corporate revises its resource allocation in such a way that overall profit contribution will increase. We iterate this process until the shadow prices eventually stabilize at their optimal values. This is a highly oversimplified description of what is happening, but adequate for our purposes.

In addition to the multidivisional application, note the purely computational aspects of this technique. If we have a monster LP model that won't fit on our computer but has a block-diagonal structure, we can solve it iteratively using Dantzig-Wolfe decomposition by breaking it down into smaller, more manageable pieces. As we must realize, it is a great deal more difficult to solve one 1000×1000 model than it is to solve ten 100×100 models—even considering the multiple solutions required in the iterations of the Dantzig-Wolfe technique.

MINICASES

Wiseacre [5]

THE SCENARIO

Jackson Browne Mize is a retired physician who has taken up large-scale gardening as a form of relaxation and owns a rectangular plot of land 150 by 200 feet. Since he is already in the highest income tax bracket, he gives away some of the produce to his friends. Even so, the 30,000-square-foot plot yields so much that over half of the vegetables go to waste. Because gardening is excellent exercise as well as enjoyable, Dr. Mize still wishes to plant the entire plot.

THE PROBLEM

Dr. Mize's son, an MBA student at a nearby university, suggested that his father donate the excess produce to churches and synagogues in the less affluent part of town. They could sell the vegetables through a co-op at reduced prices and give Dr. Mize a receipt for their value. Dr. Mize could then claim his donation as a deduction on his income tax return. The good doctor liked the idea and has decided to plant beans, corn, cucumbers, onions, squash, and tomatoes. Within certain constraints, he wants to determine the optimal mix of crops that would maximize his tax deduction. The following are some considerations that he has to take into account:

1. The 200 foot side of the plot runs north-south. Dr. Mize will plant crops with the rows running east-west so that the prevailing wind will pass down the rows instead of broadside.
2. Corn is wind pollinated, so the doctor must plant at least four rows to get maximum yields.
3. Dr. Mize wants to plant at least 10% but not more than 30% of his plot in each of the five vegetables other than cucumbers. Because cucumbers tend to be high yielding, he wants to restrict their planting to no more than 15% of the plot.
4. From a gardening guide, Dr. Mize's son found the space requirements for the six vegetables and obtained yield estimates (per plant) from a local farmer, who gave separate estimates for good, average, and bad years. A vegetable co-op supplied estimates of wholesale prices. Table 2.9 exhibits these parameters.

THE MODEL

Dr Mize's son recognized his father's problem as one that he could model and analyze by linear programming and chose the decision variables x_j, $j = 1, \ldots, 6$, as the number of rows of vegetable j to plant (in alphabetical order). In actuality, there were three LP models—one each for yields in good, average, and bad years.

The objective function coefficients c_j are the revenues per row for each vegetable. For example, we compute the per-row revenue for beans (c_1) as follows:

Good year: $c_1 = \dfrac{150 \text{ ft/row}}{3 \text{ ft/plant}}$ (2 lb/plant $\times$ \$0.39 revenue/lb.)

$\quad\quad\quad\quad\quad\; = \$39$ revenue/row

Average year: $c_1 = 50[(1.5)(\$0.39)] = \$29.25$ revenue/row

Bad year: $\quad c_1 = 50[(1.0)(\$0.39)] = \$19.50$ revenue/row; etc.

Table 2.10 summarizes the objective coefficients.

The model for a good year is as follows:

MAX

$x_0 = 39x_1 + 45x_2 + 405x_3 + 40.91x_4 + 229.5x_5 + 141.38x_6$ \hfill (2.42)

S T: $3.5x_1 \leq 60$ \hfill (2.43)

$\quad\quad 2.5x_2 \geq 60$ \hfill (2.44)

$\quad\quad\quad\quad 5x_3 \leq 30$ \hfill (2.45)

$\quad\quad\quad\quad\quad\quad x_4 \leq 60$ \hfill (2.46)

$\quad\quad\quad\quad\quad\quad\quad\quad 3x_5 \leq 60$ \hfill (2.47)

$\quad\quad\quad\quad\quad\quad\quad\quad\quad\quad 3x_6 \leq 60$ \hfill (2.48)

$\quad\quad x_2 \geq 4$ \hfill (2.49)

$3.5x_1 \geq 20$ \hfill (2.50)

$\quad\quad 2.5x_2 \geq 20$ \hfill (2.51)

$\quad\quad\quad\quad 5x_3 \geq 20$ \hfill (2.52)

$\quad\quad\quad\quad\quad\quad x_4 \geq 20$ \hfill (2.53)

$\quad\quad\quad\quad\quad\quad\quad\quad 3x_5 \geq 20$ \hfill (2.54)

$\quad\quad\quad\quad\quad\quad\quad\quad\quad\quad 3x_6 \geq 20$ \hfill (2.55)

$3.5x_1 + 2.5x_2 + 5x_3 + x_4 + 3x_5 + 3x_6 \leq 200$ \hfill (2.56)

$\quad\quad\quad\quad\quad\quad x_j \geq 0, j = 1, \ldots, 6$ \hfill (2.57)

TABLE 2.9 Parameters for Wiseacre Case

	Vegetables					
	Beans	Corn	Cucumbers	Onions	Squash	Tomatoes
Spacing						
Feet Between Plant	3.00	1.00	1.0	0.33	2.00	2.00
Feet Between Row	3.50	2.50	5.0	1.00	3.00	3.00
Yield/Plant						
Good year	2.00 lb	6 ears	30	0.60 lb	18	6.50 lb
Average year	1.50 lb	5 ears	25	0.50 lb	16	5.50 lb
Bad year	1.00 lb	4 ears	22	0.45 lb	14	4.00 lb
Wholesale Price	\$0.39	\$0.05	\$ 0.09	\$0.15	\$ 0.17	\$0.29

TABLE 2.10 Objective coefficients for Wiseacre Case

	Beans	Corn	Cucumbers	Onions	Squash	Tomatoes
Good year	$39.00	$45.00	$405.00	$40.91	$229.50	$141.38
Average year	$29.25	$37.50	$337.50	$34.09	$204.00	$119.63
Bad year	$19.50	$30.00	$297.00	$30.68	$178.50	$ 87.00

Constraints (2.43) to (2.48) are the upper bounds (15% for cucumbers, 30% for others) on space for each vegetable, constraint (2.49) imposes the requirement that at least four rows of corn be planted, and constraint (2.56) limits the size of the total crop to be 200 feet north/south.

We can easily solve the model with a computer LP module in its present form. However, we note that constraint (2.51) is nonbinding, since constraint (2.49) will assure that we plant at least four rows of corn. Furthermore, constraints (2.50) to (2.55) are merely lower bounds on the variables.

If we let

$$x_j = \frac{x'_j + 20}{\text{No. ft. between rows}}, j = 1, \ldots, n, \qquad (2.58)$$

and make this transformation in the model, we have the much smaller (but equivalent) LP model:

MAX
$$x_0 = 11.1x'_1 + 18x'_2 + 81x'_3 + 41x'_4 + 99.8x'_5 + 47.1x'_6 + 54.85 \qquad (2.59)$$

S T:
$$\begin{aligned}
x'_1 &\leq 40 & (2.60) \\
x'_2 &\leq 40 & (2.61) \\
x'_3 &\leq 10 & (2.62) \\
x'_4 &\leq 40 & (2.63) \\
x'_5 &\leq 40 & (2.64) \\
x'_6 &\leq 40 & (2.65) \\
x'_1 + x'_2 + x'_3 + x'_4 + x'_5 + x'_6 &\leq 80 & (2.66) \\
x'_j \geq 0, j = 1, \ldots, 6 & & (2.67)
\end{aligned}$$

SOLUTION TO THE MODEL

When using SAMS, explicitly making the lower-bound transformation is unnecessary. In fact, 12 of the 13 nonredundant constraints are lower or upper bounds, leaving a single explicit constraint (2.56) to reflect the size of the plot available. Figure 2.6 is the SAMS input screen, and Table 2.11 is the detailed SAMS report for a good year.

The optimal solution to the original model is identical for all three objectives (good, average, bad) (see Table 2.12).

FIGURE 2.6 SAMS input screen for Wiseacre

```
┌──► SAMS INPUT SCREEN - Linear Programming  ◄──┐
│  NAME?  WISEACRE: GOOD YEAR                    │
│  MAximize or MInimize?  MA                     │
│  PROBLEM DESCRIPTION - Maximize profit for charity by
│                        optimally planting a garden plot.
├────────────────────────────────────────────────┤
│  Variables     X1     X2     X3     X4     X5     X6    Dir  RHS
│  Objective    39.    45.   405.   40.5  229.5  141.38    <
│  Upper Bound  17.14  24.    6.    60.    20.    20.      =
│  Lower Bound   5.71   8.    4.    20.     6.67   6.67    >
│  Constraints
│  PLOT SIZE     3.5    2.5   5.     1.     3.     3.      <   200.
└────────────────────────────────────────────────┘
```

TABLE 2.11

WISEACRE
FULL BRIEFING ON OPTIMAL MODEL SOLUTION

Maximum Objective Value = 10769.18

Decision Variable	Optimal Value	Reduced Cost
X1	5.71	−125.94
X2	8.00	−72.82
X3	6.00	169.37
X4	20.00	−6.63
X5	20.00	88.12
X6	16.67	0.00

Constraint	Type	Slack	Shadow Price
PLOT SIZE	<	0.00	47.13

POST-OPTIMALITY ANALYSIS OF RIGHT-HAND SIDE VALUES

Constraint	Type	Lower Bound	Current Coefficient	Upper Bound
PLOT SIZE	<	170.00	200.00	210.00

POST-OPTIMALITY ANALYSIS OF OBJECTIVE COEFFICIENTS

Decision Variable	Lower Bound	Current Coefficient	Upper Bound
X1	−INF	39.00	164.94
X2	−INF	45.00	117.82
X3	235.63	405.00	INF
X4	−INF	40.50	47.13
X5	141.38	229.50	INF
X6	121.50	141.38	229.50

TABLE 2.12 Variable values

Variable	Vegetable	No. of Rows	Revenue Good	Revenue Average	Revenue Bad
x_1	Beans	5.71	$ 222.85	$ 167.14	$ 111.43
x_2	Corn	8.00	360.00	300.00	240.00
x_3	Cucumbers	6.00	2,430.00	2,025.00	1,782.00
x_4	Onions	20.00	810.00	675.00	607.60
x_5	Squash	20.00	4,590.00	4,080.00	3,570.00
x_6	Tomatoes	16.67	2,356.33	1,983.83	1,450.00
	Total Profit		$10,769.18	$9,230.97	$7,761.03

Constraint	Type	Shadow Price
Beans	Lower bound	$29.77
Corn	Lower bound	23.12
Cucumbers	Upper bound	2.38
Onions	Lower bound	3.95
Squash	Upper bound	29.02
Tomatoes	Both	—
Land	Upper bound	47.13

SOLUTION TO THE PROBLEM

To simplify planting, Dr. Mize decided on 6 rows of beans and 16 full rows of tomatoes. This reduced the total revenue by about $83 (for a good year) but made working the plot much easier for Doctor Mize and still resulted in a feasible solution.

The doctor was surprised at the high shadow price associated with an additional 150-foot row (e.g., $47.13 per row for a good year). However, his son pointed out that the insistence upon at least 10 percent of the crop being planted in beans and 10 percent in corn and that no more than 30 percent be planted in squash would significantly reduce the total tax deduction that he could generate on the present plot.

Finally, Dr. Mize—impressed with his son's cleverness—asked him: "Son, what if we hadn't known about linear programming and I had decided to plant one-sixth of the plot with each kind of vegetable. What sort of tax deduction would I have gotten, say, in a good year?"

"Good question, Dad," replied the son, "and I knew you were going to ask it. First of all, that would violate your constraint of not planting more than 15% in cucumbers.

If we ignore that constraint and plant 25 row-feet in each vegetable, the total writeoff would be about $6,857 in a good year, so that linear programming would have made you about $3,912 in additional deductions."

"Son," chuckled Dr. Mize, "I'm impressed."

William Hill Distillery

THE SCENARIO

J. William Hill III is the CEO, chairman of the board, and production manager for William Hill Distillery, Inc. (WHD). The firm produces and distributes a line of beverages popular in the region. WHD manufactures three basic product lines—Dew, Moon, and Lightning—but each line comes in either light or dark (depending on the type of corn used) and low or high potency (depending on cooking time). Therefore, WHD essentially manufactures 12 distinct products.

The market for all three products is excellent, with demand always exceeding supply. WHD's distribution channel is currently at capacity, which is the reason WHD cannot increase production.

THE PROBLEM

One cloudy Sunday afternoon, the firm's industrial intelligence network learned that several people representing the IRS were planning what they hoped to be a surprise visit to the WHD distillery and intended to arrive in 72 hours. Mr. Hill concluded that good business practice dictated the temporary dismantling of the distilling equipment, but the 72-hour warning would allow him to produce another batch from his on-hand inventory of corn (150 bushels of light and 225 bushels of dark). Table 2.13 gives cooking time, corn requirements, and profit contribution per 10-gallon batch of each brand.

In addition to the limited supply of corn and brewing time, there are other factors that complicate Mr. Hill's problem.

1. WHD's marketing department has already accepted orders for 50 gallons (5 batches) of Dew light, but the customer will take either low- or high-potency product.
2. To keep the still from clogging on long production runs, WHD must make at least one-third of the batches with dark corn.
3. Sales records indicate that about 40% of previous sales have been high-potency products, so Mr. Hill wishes to produce at least this amount.

THE MODEL

Mr. Hill's older sister Roberta, the company's management science analyst, observes that the problem could be modeled by LP—except that the number of batches cannot be fractional. She decides to model the problem as a linear program anyway to see what happens.

TABLE 2.13 Parameters for William Hill Distillery

Brand		Bushels Corn/ 10-gal Batch		Cooking Time Minute/10-Gallon Batch	Profit Contribution/ 10-Gallon Batch
		White	Dark		
Dew	LL	3		60	17
	LH	5		85	25
	DL		2	45	16
	DH		3	95	28
Moon	LL	4		80	28
	LH	6		120	40
	DL		3	85	24
	DH		5	130	36
Lightning	LL	5		115	43
	LH	8		125	48
	DL		6	145	44
	DH		7	180	52

LL = light corn, low potency   **LH** = light corn, high potency
DL = dark corn, low potency   **DH** = dark corn, high potency

The object is obviously to maximize total profit contribution, and the decisions involve the number of batches of each of the 12 products to run. She lets x_{ij} = number of batches of the ith brand and the jth type to produce, $i = 1,\ldots,3; j = 1,\ldots,4$. (For example, x_{23} would represent Moon, dark low-potency). The LP model is as follows:

$$\text{MAX } x_0 = 17x_{11} + 25x_{12} + 16x_{13} + 28x_{14} + 28x_{21} + 40x_{22}$$
$$+ 24x_{23} + 36x_{24} + 43x_{31} + 48x_{32} + 44x_{33} + 52x_{34} \quad (2.68)$$

S T:
$$3x_{11} + 5x_{12} + 4x_{21} + 6x_{22}$$
$$+ 5x_{31} + 8x_{32} \leq 150 \quad (2.69)$$
$$2x_{13} + 3x_{14}$$
$$+ 3x_{23} + 5x_{24} + 6x_{33} + 7x_{34} \leq 225 \quad (2.70)$$
$$60x_{11} + 85x_{12} + 45x_{13} + 95x_{14} + 80x_{21} + 120x_{22}$$
$$+ 85x_{23} + 130x_{24} + 115x_{31} + 125x_{32} + 145x_{33} + 180x_{34} \leq 4320 \quad (2.71)$$
$$x_{11} + x_{12} \geq 5 \quad (2.72)$$
$$x_{11} - x_{12} + 2x_{13} + 2x_{14} - x_{21} - x_{22}$$
$$+ 2x_{23} + 2x_{24} - x_{31} - x_{32} + 2x_{33} + 2x_{34} \geq 0 \quad (2.73)$$
$$- x_{11} + 1.5x_{12} - x_{13} + 1.5x_{14} - x_{21} + 1.5x_{22}$$
$$- x_{23} + 1.5x_{24} - x_{31} + 1.5x_{32} - x_{33} + 1.5x_{34} \geq 0 \quad (2.74)$$
$$x_{ij} \geq 0, i = 1,\ldots,3; j = 1,\ldots,4 \quad (2.75)$$

Constraints (2.69) and (2.70) are the limits on available light and dark corn, respectively, and constraint (2.71) represents the 72 hours (4,320 minutes) remaining until the IRS agents arrive. Constraint (2.72) guarantees that WHD will fill the advance order, and constraints (2.73) and (2.74) impose the desired restrictions on runs with dark corn and runs of high-potency product, respectively.

SOLUTION TO THE MODEL

The optimal solution to the model emerged from SAMS as in Table 2.14.

SOLUTION TO THE PROBLEM

Since the model solution was obviously not implementable because it involved fractional batches, and since WHD had no ILP computer code, Roberta experimented a bit with rounding to produce a feasible solution to the problem (see Table 2.15).

TABLE 2.14 SAMS output for William Hill Distillery

WILLIAM HILL DISTILLERY
FULL BRIEFING ON OPTIMAL MODEL SOLUTION
Maximum Objective Value = 1545.90

Decision Variable	Optimal Value	Reduced Cost
X11	0.00	−1.40
X12	5.00	0.00
X13	36.01	0.00
X14	3.38	0.00
X21	0.00	−4.40
X22	0.00	−3.80
X23	0.00	−4.80
X24	0.00	−3.20
X31	0.00	−1.90
X32	15.63	0.00
X33	0.00	−4.00
X34	0.00	−3.20

Constraint	Type	Slack	Shadow Price
LITE CORN	<	0.00	1.30
DARK CORN	<	142.83	0.00
TIME	<	0.00	0.32
ADV ORDER	>	0.00	−6.30
LB DARK C	>	58.16	0.00
LB ON HIGH	>	0.00	−1.60

TABLE 2.14 SAMS output for William Hill Distillery—*Continued*

POST-OPTIMALITY ANALYSIS OF RIGHT-HAND SIDE VALUES

Constraint	Type	Lower Bound	Current Coefficient	Upper Bound
LITE CORN	<	25.00	150.00	172.84
DARK CORN	<	82.17	225.00	INF
TIME	<	3770.31	4320.00	8188.28
ADV ORDER	>	0.00	5.00	22.08
LB DARK C	>	−INF	0.00	58.16
LB ON HIGH	>	−12.22	0.00	61.60

POST-OPTIMALITY ANALYSIS OF OBJECTIVE COEFFICIENTS

Decision Variable	Lower Bound	Current Coefficient	Upper Bound
X11	−INF	17.00	18.40
X12	23.60	25.00	31.30
X13	14.92	16.00	39.74
X14	25.90	28.00	30.55
X21	−INF	28.00	32.40
X22	−INF	40.00	43.80
X23	−INF	24.00	28.80
X24	−INF	36.00	39.20
X31	−INF	43.00	44.90
X32	44.96	48.00	53.60
X33	−INF	44.00	48.00
X34	−INF	52.00	55.20

TABLE 2.15

Variable	Value	Variable	Value
X12	5 batches	S1	5 bushels
X13	36 batches	S2	141 bushels
X14	4 batches	S3	16 minutes
X32	15 batches	S4	0 excess
		S5	60 excess
		S6	0 excess

Profit Contribution: $ 1,533

In addition, Roberta recommended to Mr. Hill that he schedule the Dew-dark, low-potency (x_{13}) run last, since it produced the lowest profit batches and could be cut short if more than the 16 minutes of getaway time seemed desirable.

When Roberta presented Mr. Hill with the results of her analysis, he was pleased and decided to implement her recommended product mix. He was also intrigued by the shadow prices in the original LP solution. It was obvious that WHD's accepting advance orders of Dew-light cost additional profits, since the associated shadow price was $6.30 per batch. Moreover, the light corn supply shortage cost WHD $1.30 per bushel in profits, even though there was an astonishing overage of more than 140 bushels of dark corn. There was obviously an inventory management problem that he needed to attend to when operations resumed.

Finally, there was a problem with the pricing strategy for Moon products, since none ended up in an optimal solution. Mr. Hill made a mental note to look into the advisability of repricing (or perhaps discontinuing) this product line after the dust had settled from the IRS visit.

Incremental Profit Program [14]

THE SCENARIO

Mike Rowe, CEO and founder of Arizona Silicon Products, Inc. (ASP), pored thoughtfully over the sales forecasts by ASP's three sales regions for next fiscal year. Projected profit for the company's five computer component products was $5.139 million based on sales estimates, an increase of 28% over the current year. This was typical of the explosive growth that ASP experienced in the three years since Mike started the company.

THE PROBLEM

When Mike compared sales forecasts with the output from ASP's LP program that optimized product mix, the same aggravating situation cropped up again: ASP had the capacity to produce more of certain products than its three regional sales divisions were able (or willing?) to sell. Table 2.16 illustrates Mike's problem.

TABLE 2.16 Profit/production capacity analysis

Product	Optimal Production (units)	Forecast Sales (units)	Profit Potential	Profit/Forecast Sales	Difference
RAM	1,000,000	1,000,000	$1,435,000	$1,435,000	—
ROM	3,612,000	2,000,000	1,191,960	660,000	$531,960
LIN	1,000,000	1,000,000	630,000	630,000	—
IC	3,000,000	3,000,000	264,000	264,000	—
MP	1,215,000	1,000,000	2,612,250	2,150,000	462,250
TOTAL	9,827,000	8,000,000	$6,133,210	$5,139,000	$994,210

If ASP's sales organizations could sell everything the company could produce in the ROM and MP lines, Mike could add almost a million additional dollars to the bottom line. Mike called in his vice president for marketing and laid out the numbers. But the VP insisted, as he always did, that ASP's salespeople were overworked and underpaid and would have to strain just to make the forecast sales figures—much less sell additional units of ROM and MP.

After Mike dismissed the marketing chief, he turned his attention back to the numbers. He suddenly realized that he had considerably *understated* the additional profit potential. The profit contribution figures for the eight million units of forecast sales included all overhead and fixed costs; a higher level of sales would in effect reduce per-unit costs and result in even higher overall profits. Something had to be done.

Mike called in ASP's vice president for human resources, who listened carefully to his narrative, paused thoughtfully before replying, and spoke as follows:

> "Mr. Rowe," she said, "your mistake was allowing the vice president for marketing to set sales quotas before you knew what production potential would be. People are so very predictable—once they lock onto a particular quantitative goal or objective, it immediately becomes an upper bound on their capabilities—regardless of their actual performance potential. However, if you try to unilaterally raise sales quotas at this point, you'll only make matters worse. Would you like an alternative?"
>
> "Yes," responded Mike. "I need help on this one."
>
> She continued. "I'm not an economist, but I do know that per-unit profit contribution increases as sales volume increases—as long as that volume doesn't approach the level of diminishing returns. Why don't you consider something like an **incremental profit program** (IPP) that allows the sales regions to compete for higher sales quotas in return for bonus commissions on incremental sales? If you work it right, ASP could receive the current level of profit contribution for the additional sales, and the sales people could earn the *incremental* difference."

THE MODEL

Mike decided to concentrate first on the MP line, since the high profit contribution ($2.15) meant that he would need fewer incremental sales for good results than would be the case for ROM ($.33 profit contribution). He called up the marketing budget on his terminal (see Table 2.17).

TABLE 2.17 Fiscal year marketing budget: MP

Expense Item	Per-Unit Marketing Expense			Budget
	Region I	Region II	Region III	
Personnel	$.095	$.100	$.100	$100,000
Travel	.018	.020	.025	25,000
Promotion	.010	.010	.010	15,000
Totals	$.123	$.130	$.135	$140,000
FY sales quotas (units)	200,000	400,000	400,000	Expense $130,600

Mike's first thought upon seeing the cost data on MP was to model his problem as an LP model. He let x_1, x_2, and x_3 represent the sales quotas for regions I, II, and III, respectively, with the idea of maximizing total sales. There were six constraints: remain within the total personnel, travel, and promotion budgets and assign at least the current sales quotas to each region. He entered the following model into his LP SIMPLEX package:

$$\begin{aligned}
\text{MAX } x_0 = \quad & x_1 + x_2 + x_3 \\
\text{S T:} \quad & 0.095x_1 + 0.100x_2 + 0.100x_3 \leq 100{,}000 \\
& 0.018x_1 + 0.020x_2 + 0.025x_3 \leq 25{,}000 \\
& 0.010x_1 + 0.010x_2 + 0.010x_3 \leq 15{,}000 \\
& x_1 \geq 200{,}000 \\
& x_2 \geq 400{,}000 \\
& x_3 \geq 400{,}000 \\
& x_1,\ x_2,\ x_3 \geq 0
\end{aligned}$$

After checking his input data, Mike stared at his LP model uneasily. Something was wrong—but he couldn't put his finger on it.

SOLUTION TO THE MODEL

Mike invoked his SIMPLEX algorithm, and the instant he saw the solution (Table 2.18), he realized his modeling error.

Mike had considered the subconstraint on the personnel budget for MP binding, which meant that there was about $3,210 excess budget available for travel and about $4,895 excess for promotion. He grinned sheepishly—glad that he was alone in his office.

TABLE 2.18

Optimal $x_0 = 1{,}010{,}526.316$

Variable	Value	Reduced Cost
x_1	210,526.316	0
x_2	400,000.000	0
x_3	400,000.000	0

Constraint	Slack or Surplus	Dual Price
1	0.000	0.105300
2	3,210.527	0.000000
3	4,894.737	0.000000
4	10,526.316	0.000000
5	0.000	0.000053
6	0.000	0.000053

SOLUTION TO THE PROBLEM

Turning off the computer console, Mike picked up a scratch pad and a pencil.

> "Let's see, now. There is a total unbudgeted expense for MP of $140,000 − $130,600 = $9,400. Since region I has the most efficient marketing cost of $0.123 per unit, there is enough budget money for them to sell $9,400/$0.123 = 76,423 units, for an additional profit at the current margin of $2.15 × 76,423 = $164,309. As a rule of thumb, that increment would generate actual profit contribution of about $2.35, or about 8.5% above current margin."

Getting the VP for marketing back into his office, Mike Rowe announced the IPP and instructed him to offer region I an additional quota of 76,000 units of MP at an 8% bonus. If they took it, the other (less efficient) regions would have the opportunity to bid on some or all units, but at lower bonuses that reflected their higher marketing costs.

The moral for this minicase is: *Don't let MS models get in the way of solving problems.*

Racquet [18]

THE SCENARIO

Armadillo Racquet Club was founded in 1981 by Ace Freely, its owner-manager. With 400 members in 1992, it is the most successful venture of its kind in the western part of the state. Facilities include four indoor tennis courts, eight outdoor courts, tennis shop, weight room, aerobics facility, whirlpool, saunas, and locker rooms. Monthly dues cover nontennis activities, so that the hourly charge for tennis courts represents profits.

The four cold-weather months (November–February) see heavy usage of the four indoor courts.

THE PROBLEM

Ian Ball, the head tennis pro, has always been responsible for scheduling indoor courts during months of cold weather. However, complaints from influential members mounted rapidly last year. Ian, it seemed, dislikes giving lessons in the morning, so his practice has been to reserve premium afternoon hours for his lessons. Since Ace is a good enough manager to know that suboptimizing by catering to one person's preferences is unacceptable, he has taken over the winter scheduling responsibility himself for the coming season.

There are six revenue-producing activities associated with the four indoor courts, as outlined in Table 2.19.

Several constraints complicate Ace's problem:

1. The club is open 92 hours per week, so only 4 × 92 = 368 hours of court time is available.
2. Of the 344 court hours available for nonleague play, Ace feels strongly that at least half (172 hours) should be available for individual court reservations by members.

3. League play, a very popular activity, uses 24 hours of court time each week.
4. The head pro, who gives individual and both types of group lessons, is willing to work no more than 40 hours per week. Both the head pro and assistant pro must be present for lessons.
5. The assistant pro also gives individual and group lessons and wishes to work up to 50 hours per week.
6. Ace's instincts tell him that at least ten court hours should be reserved for adult group sessions.
7. Since younger players represent the future of the club, Ace has specified that at least 20 hours of court time be reserved for junior group sessions.

THE MODEL

Ace frowned as he looked over the numbers. This certainly had the appearance of an LP model, with six decision variables and seven constraints. Maximizing revenue was certainly an appropriate criterion, since the head pro and assistant pro were paid commissions rather than salaries. Additivity looked O.K. as well, and Ace felt good about ignoring probabilistic considerations.

The divisibility thing, however, bothered him. He couldn't really schedule fractions of an activity, but perhaps he could round a model solution to get usable results. He constructed the LP model as follows:

$$\text{MAX } x_0 = 20x_1 + 16x_2 + 30x_3 + 25x_4 + 8x_5 + 28x_6$$

S T:
$$x_1 + x_2 + 1.5x_3 + 1.5x_4 + 1.25x_5 + 4x_6 \leq 368$$
$$1.25x_5 \geq 172$$
$$4x_6 = 24$$
$$x_1 + 1.5x_3 + 1.5x_4 \leq 40$$
$$x_2 + 1.5x_3 + 1.5x_4 \leq 50$$
$$1.5x_3 \geq 10$$
$$1.5x_4 \geq 20$$

all $x_j \geq 0$

TABLE 2.19 Revenue-Producing activities

Decision Variable	Activity	Court Hours	Revenue for Activity
x_1	Individual lessons/head pro	1.00	$20
x_2	Individual lessons/assistant pro	1.00	$16
x_3	Adult group lessons	1.50	$30
x_4	Junior group lessons	1.50	$25
x_5	Individual court reservations	1.25	$ 8
x_6	League play	4.00	$28

SOLUTION TO THE MODEL

Table 2.20 shows the SAMS output for this LP model. Ace fiddled with the LP output to produce the rounded solution in Table 2.21.

This solution violated the seventh constraint slightly, but this was entirely satisfactory to Ace, who then turned his attention to the LP printout.

SOLUTION TO THE PROBLEM

The shadow price for the head pro's time was quite high—$13.60 per hour. It was useless to pursue that line, however; Ian was adamant about working no more than 40 hours per week. However, the assistant pro's time carried a shadow price of $9.60, and the young man was eager for extra work. Four extra hours represented almost 1% increase in revenue per week. Perhaps the assistant pro could be persuaded to work a bit more during the winter season.

By including lower bounds explicitly as constraints, we find that forcing group sessions was expensive—$9.60 per session for adults and $12.93 for juniors. But individual court reservations amounted to $1,816 of the $3,039 weekly revenue, and limiting training might mean fewer future players. Ace felt it prudent to invest scarce court time in this way.

The really interesting number was the $6.40 shadow price for total court time availability. Staying open one extra hour per week meant an additional four court hours, or $25.60 in additional revenue per week. That was worth investigating!

TABLE 2.20 SAMS output for Racquet

RACQUET
FULL BRIEFING ON OPTIMAL MODEL SOLUTION

Maximum Objective Value = 3038.93

Decision Variable	Optimal Value	Reduced Cost
X1	10.00	0.00
X2	20.00	0.00
X3	6.67	0.00
X4	13.33	0.00
X5	227.20	0.00
X6	6.00	0.00

Constraint	Type	Slack	Shadow Price
TOT HOURS	<	0.00	6.40
IND LESS	>	112.00	0.00
LEAGUE<	<	0.00	0.60
LEAGUE>	>	0.00	0.00
HEAD PRO	<	0.00	13.60
ASST PRO	<	0.00	9.60
ADULT GRP	>	0.00	−9.60
JUNR GRP	>	0.00	−12.93

TABLE 2.20 SAMS output for Racquet—*Continued*

POST-OPTIMALITY ANALYSIS OF RIGHT-HAND SIDE VALUES

Constraint	Type	Lower Bound	Current Coefficient	Upper Bound
TOT HOURS	<	256.00	368.00	INF
IND LESS	>	−INF	172.00	284.00
LEAGUE<	<	24.00	24.00	24.00
LEAGUE>	>	24.00	24.00	24.00
HEAD PRO	<	30.00	40.00	152.00
ASST PRO	<	30.00	50.00	162.00
ADULT GRP	>	0.00	10.00	20.00
JUNR GRP	>	0.00	20.00	30.00

POST-OPTIMALITY ANALYSIS OF OBJECTIVE COEFFICIENTS

Decision Variable	Lower Bound	Current Coefficient	Upper Bound
X1	10.40	20.00	INF
X2	6.40	16.00	INF
X3	−INF	30.00	44.40
X4	25.00	25.00	44.40
X5	0.00	8.00	8.75
X6	25.00	28.00	INF

TABLE 2.21 Rounded model solution

x_0:	Total revenue per week	$3,039
x_1:	Individual lessons/head pro	10
x_2:	Individual lessons/assistant pro	20
x_3:	Adult group lessons	7
x_4:	Junior group lessons	13
x_5:	Individual court reservations	227
x_6:	League play	6

A glance at the ranging analysis on right-hand sides confirmed that the current mix was optimal for the model over a wide range of RHS values for all constraints. However, the ranging analysis on revenue coefficients was revealing. Ace could apparently raise prices on individual court reservations from $8 to $8.75 without changing the current model solution, generating an additional $170 per week. Perhaps he could propose the price increase to the board as a surcharge to go into a fund to building heated covers for some of the outside courts. Ace found a solution to his problem.

Security [20]

THE SCENARIO

Security and Fail-safe Engineering, Inc. (SAFE) is a high-tech, service-oriented firm involved in the design and construction of large federal computer systems. The company employs a wide range of technical specialists, but the success of most contracts depends on the quality and availability of the computer security engineering staff.

The federal government has a growing need for computers that can be trusted not to compromise national security. The company had foreseen this need and had begun training highly specialized security engineers several years ago. Even so, the demand had grown faster than new security engineers could be trained. To exacerbate the problem, rival computer engineering companies were attempting to lure SAFE's security engineers with absurdly high salary offers. It was a vexing problem.

THE PROBLEM

The immediate problem, however, was allocating the time of SAFE's security engineers to ongoing projects. On federal contracts, hours budgeted for security engineering must be used for that purpose; funds budgeted for unused hours must be returned to the procuring agency.

Chip Hertz, the manager of the Security Engineering Section, pored over the work schedule for the coming week. He currently had six security engineers on his staff, and there were seven hot projects under way. Chip fully expected the backlog to grow in the weeks and months ahead and desperately needed a flexible, reliable system for assigning security engineers to projects. Engineering requirements are stated in person-weeks, so that a requirement for eight person-weeks of effort can be met by two engineers working for four weeks, four engineers working two weeks, etc. The problem was complicated by the wide divergence in experience among his six security engineers; that is, Chip could not treat the six engineers as homogeneous resources for assignment to projects. Chip had a challenging task!

Chip's planning horizon was the next eight weeks. Security engineering requirements for the seven current projects in person-weeks are as follows:

Project #	1	2	3	4	5	6	7	Total
Agency	ASP	BUG	CAT	DOG	EMU	FOX	GNU	
Person-weeks	8	20	8	8	2.4	8	4	58.4

Although there were six engineers on the staff, three had one-week vacations planned in the next eight weeks, so that availability of engineers was as follows:

Engineer #	1	2	3	4	5	6	Total
Name	Hal	Ike	Joe	Kay	Len	Moe	
Person-weeks	7	7	8	8	7	8	45

The factor that complicated Chip's problem was the special nature of assignments of engineers to projects. There were four distinct categories, as follows:

1. The engineer must work on this project.
2. The engineer should work on this project unless demand exists elsewhere.
3. The engineer should not work on this project unless no acceptable substitute is available.
4. The engineer must not work on this project under any circumstances.

Chip then assembled the engineer/project table (see Table 2.22).

The only other consideration Chip had to deal with was that the DOG project (#4) absolutely had to be completed.

THE MODEL

Chip noted that were it not for the special restriction on the DOG project, he could model his scheduling problem nicely as an ordinary transportation problem (see Chapter 4). At any rate, Chip had a fairly simple linear programming situation. But what could he use as an objective function? All he really needed was a feasible solution. Then it occurred to him that he could consider the project/engineer assignment categories to set up a maximizing objective function that represented the *best* feasible assignment; he used weights of 100, 10, 5, and 0 for categories #1, #2, #3, and #4, respectively. He briefly considered omitting the variables with a zero coefficient altogether but then realized that he wanted a general model that he could use over and over in the future.

TABLE 2.22

Project # Agency	1 ASP	2 BUG	3 CAT	4 DOG	5 EMU	6 FOX	7 GNU
Hal	3	3	2	1	4	2	3
Ike	3	3	1	4	4	1	3
Joe	3	2	2	4	1	4	3
Kay	1	2	2	4	4	4	3
Len	3	2	2	4	4	2	3
Moe	3	2	2	4	4	4	3

Letting x_{ij} represent the assignment to project i of person-weeks of engineer j, the assignment LP model is as follows:

$$
\begin{aligned}
\text{MAX } x_0 = \quad & 5x_{11} + 5x_{12} + 5x_{13} + 100x_{14} + 5x_{15} + 5x_{16} \quad (2.76)\\
+ \quad & 5x_{21} + 5x_{22} + 10x_{23} + 10x_{24} + 10x_{25} + 10x_{26}\\
+ \quad & 10x_{31} + 100x_{32} + 10x_{33} + 10x_{34} + 10x_{35} + 10x_{36}\\
+ \quad & 100x_{41} + 0x_{42} + 0x_{43} + 0x_{44} + 0x_{45} + 0x_{46}\\
+ \quad & 0x_{51} + 0x_{52} + 100x_{53} + 0x_{54} + 0x_{55} + 0x_{56}\\
+ \quad & 10x_{61} + 100x_{62} + 0x_{63} + 0x_{64} + 10x_{65} + 0x_{66}\\
+ \quad & 5x_{71} + 5x_{72} + 5x_{73} + 5x_{74} + 5x_{75} + 5x_{76}
\end{aligned}
$$

$$\text{S T:} \quad \sum_{i=1}^{7} x_{ij} = 7, \; j = 1,2,5 \tag{2.77}$$

$$\sum_{i=1}^{7} x_{ij} = 8, \; j = 3,4,6 \tag{2.78}$$

$$\sum_{j=1}^{6} x_{ij} \leq 8, \; i = 1,3,6 \tag{2.79}$$

$$\sum_{j=1}^{6} x_{2j} \leq 20 \tag{2.80}$$

$$\sum_{j=1}^{6} x_{5j} \leq 2.4 \tag{2.81}$$

$$\sum_{j=1}^{6} x_{7j} \leq 4 \tag{2.82}$$

$$\sum_{j=1}^{6} x_{4j} = 8 \tag{2.83}$$

Note that constraints (2.77) and (2.78) are the constraints on person-weeks of engineer time available, while constraints (2.79) to (2.82) express engineering requirements on projects other than DOG (#4). The absolute requirement that we complete DOG is imposed in constraint (2.83).

SOLUTION TO THE MODEL

A summary of the model solution is in Table 2.23. Note that ASP, DOG, and EMU are covered; BUG, CAT, and FOX are partially covered; and GNU has no coverage at all.

SOLUTION TO THE PROBLEM

If you solve this model with a computerized LP package, note in the printout that the reduced costs associated with variables x_{25}, x_{33}, x_{35}, x_{36}, x_{62}, x_{45}, and x_{46} are zero and

TABLE 2.23

Project # Agency	1 ASP	2 BUG	3 CAT	4 DOG	5 EMU	6 FOX	7 GNU
Hal				7			
Ike			7				
Joe		4.6		1	2.4		
Kay	8						
Len						7	
Moe		8					
Covered	8	12.6	7	8	2.4	7	0
Not covered	0	7.4	1	0	0	1	4

that none of these variables are positive in the solution. What this means is that there is a wealth of alternate optimal solutions to this model. A management analyst investigating this problem would undoubtedly generate several (or all) of these solutions for consideration by the decision maker.

SUMMARY

This chapter has introduced you to the widely used optimization modeling technique called linear programming (LP). You should now be able to recognize problems that you can model by LP and build those models. You should realize that you know just enough about the technical details of the SIMPLEX algorithm to appreciate its dependability but not nearly as much as a technically trained analyst.

This chapter also introduced you to the assumptions of linear programming: additivity and divisibility. It has addressed the very important issues of LP model construction involving model selection, data collection and analysis, and model validation. We presented examples of LP model formulation using interactive dialogue with LPS. Then we presented an intuitive description of the SIMPLEX algorithm and described a graphical example. We described a typical LP solution printout (SAMS) in terms of the information content it contained beyond mere presentation of the optimal model solution. We gave meaning to such terms as *shadow price*, *reduced cost*, and *slack* and explained their managerial significance.

We also described in detail the information that followed Post-Optimality Analysis. While other programs may use somewhat different formats and terms, you will find that you retain comprehension across formats and programs once you understand a specific data format (such as SAMS). Ranging analysis, for example, always applies to ranges over which right-hand sides and objective function coefficients can vary without causing the current optimal set of decision variables to change.

The chapter then discussed extensions of LP modeling and analysis that are useful in practice. We treated such issues as interpreting shadow prices for $\geq$ and $=$ constraints, handling variables that can legitimately take on negative as well as positive values, and what has gone wrong when the computer reports that the solution is unbounded or that the solution is infeasible. The chapter then treated with equal care such topics as duality theory, lower-bounded variables, upper-bounded variables, and Dantzig-Wolfe decomposition.

In Chapter 3, we will relax the requirement of divisibility and consider integer (otherwise linear) programming models. As we shall see, this seemingly innocuous change leads to an order of magnitude increase in solution difficulty. Nevertheless, integer (otherwise linear) modeling is extremely important in practice.

KEY TERMS

alternate optimal solutions
basis
binding constraint
block diagram models
incremental profit program
information

nonbinding constraint
rates of change
secondary data
SIMPLEX algorithm
vertex

PROBLEMS FOR ANALYSIS

Note: Analysis of many of these problems requires a computer software implementation of the SIMPLEX algorithm.

1. **The Scenario:** We return to the LO-CAL Candy Company discussions in the chapter.

   The Problem: Recall that Percy, our highly educated but poorly equipped young MBA graduate, wished to solve an optimal product mix problem that arose in his family's firm, the LO-CAL Candy Company.

   The Model: With the assistance of LPS, Percy had built and checked out an LP model of his problem.

   Solution to the Model: LPS had already displayed the solution of the LP model to Percy but had shown him only the optimal model values of the objective function and the five decision variables. Later in the chapter, we returned to the LO-CAL model as a vehicle for our discussion of post-optimality analysis. Let's return once more and do an in-depth what-if analysis model.

   Solution to the Problem:
   a. Recalling Percy's disappointment that no production of Chocochunk (CHOC) was in the model solution and noting that the reduced cost for CHOC was $0.01 at optimality (compared to a per-unit profit contribution of $1.10), change the profit contribution by one cent from $1.10 to $1.11 and rerun the model using a computer-based SIMPLEX algorithm. Are you surprised at the very large value at which CHOC entered the solution?
   b. Note the very high shadow price of $2.50 per pound for light chocolate. Suppose that Percy could purchase additional light chocolate for $1.50 per pound with his own money. Alter the original model in the following ways:

      1. Let y be a variable representing "additional pounds of light chocolate" and change the RHS of the second constraint to "$149 + y$." When you bring y to the left side of the inequality, the constraint becomes:

         0.2 NUTS + 0.1 BITO + 0.1 CHOC + 0.1 DIET + 0.2 GOOC − 1 Y <= 149

      2. Subtract $1.5y$ from the objective function to represent the cost of additional light chocolate.

      Solve this model and verify that Percy could purchase about 112 additional pounds of light chocolate and improve his profit by about $43.

c. Recall that Percy was uncertain about LO-CAL's ability to sell more than 500 packages of Diet-Buster (DIET). What would happen if we added a constraint: DIET $\leq u_4$, where u_4 represents the maximum sales of Diet-Buster that Percy believes he can attain? Use $u_4 = 200$, 300, and 400 and note the results.

d. Recall that Percy was certain that the inventory figures for the five ingredients were within 3% of his estimates. By examining the right-hand side (b_i) ranging analysis, could this small error result in a different optimal product mix from the current one?

e. Perform the following analysis. Enter the original model, but add the following constraint:

1 NUTS + 0.7 BITO + 1.1 CHOC + 2 DIET + 0.6 GOOC $\leq$ 1509

This constraint is referred to as an "objective cut" and has the effect of reducing the total profit contribution from $1,509.09 to $1,509 — less than one one-hundredth of 1 percent. Note the solution to this new model and check to see whether CHOC (Chocochunk) has a positive value. What will happen is that CHOC will take on a nonzero value, and the resulting model solution will have an objective value of $1,509. This exercise parallels our earlier discussion illustrated in Figure 2.3.

Note in your model solution that all five candies are included in the mix and that all raw materials are used up. Is this, in some sense, a perfectly priced line of goods?

2. **The Scenario:** The Daley Paper Company manufactures heavy-duty wrapping paper in large rolls, which are a standard 200 feet long and 150 inches wide. It cuts these large rolls to custom widths, on order, using huge slitting machines that have many cutters that the operator can space differently for every run.

The Problem: The profit margins in this highly competitive industry tend to be narrow, and the problem of trim waste is a serious one. For example, suppose the production supervisor received the following orders from the sales department for today's production run:

Width (Inches)	Number of Rolls
16	300
24	400
48	200
60	100

We see that one run of 100 rolls might involve setting one cutter at 60 inches, one at 108 inches (one 48-inch roll), one at 132 inches (one 24-inch roll), and one at 148 inches (one 16-inch roll), satisfying 400 of the orders with two inch-rolls of trim waste. But is this the best strategy?

The Model:
a. Can we profitably model this problem as a linear program? If so, what are the decision variables? What is the objective function? What are the constraints? (*Hint:* There are 24 feasible ways to set the cutters to produce the above widths without having end-trim waste as large as 16" per roll).

b. In attempting to minimize end-trim waste, your LP model might ignore possible over-production above the orders for today's run. Since Daley is a custom shop, there may never again be an order for an odd size produced on a given day, and over-production is really additional waste. How can we model this problem to minimize *total* waste—not just end-trim waste?

3. **The Scenario:** The College of Business Administration at Chex State University wished to build a faculty with overall excellence in teaching, scholarly research, and service to the profession and its various publics. One obvious though unrealistic way to do this is to demand and expect excellence in all three areas from every faculty member. Another way is to expect basic levels of competence in all three areas but allow each faculty member to excel in the area in which he or she is most competent.

The Problem: One incentive to faculty members is the annual pay raise based on performance during the past year (sometimes referred to as a merit raise). In an attempt to quantify the relative importance of each category (and two subcategories of teaching and service)—and to stimulate a basic level of competence in each—the faculty voted the percentage weights in each category and subcategory as in Table 2.24.

Annually, an elected five-member Dean's Merit Advisory Committee meets many long hours to analyze faculty annual reports. Using a complicated rating scheme that uses ratings ranging from 4 for outstanding to 0 for poor, the committee eventually arrives at five lists of faculty members in rank order—from most productive to least—in each of the four subcategories and in Research. The problem, then, is to use those rankings to generate an overall order of merit that reflects the twofold policy of the college: (1) that each faculty member should achieve a minimum level of performance in all three broad categories and (2) that the college should reward each faculty member for achieving excellence in her or his strongest suit.

The Model:
a. Recognizing that we are dealing with subjective assessments that the committee transforms into ordinal rankings, can we model this problem as a linear program? Why or why not?
b. Numbering each faculty member randomly and letting s_{ij} be the ranking (in reverse order of competence) by faculty member i on subcategory j, write an LP model that maximizes each faculty member's overall merit score in relation to all other faculty members. Note that you will need to construct three separate models—one for each academic rank.

TABLE 2.24

Category	Variable	Academic Rank		
		Full Professor	Associate Professor	Assistant Professor
Teaching				
Student evaluation	x_1	5%–25%	5%–25%	5%–25%
Other	x_2	15%–35%	15%–35%	15%–35%
Overall		30%–60%	30%–60%	30%–60%
Research	x_3	10%–60%	15%–60%	20%–60%
Service				
Institutional	x_4	5%–20%	5%–20%	5%–20%
Other	x_5	0–40%	0–35%	0–30%
Overall		5%–50%	5%–45%	5%–40%

c. Use your models to generate overall merit ratings for the following fictitious B-school faculty members (Table 2.25). Rank them in order of overall merit.
d. Comment on the efficacy of using an approach similar to this in determining pay raises for your present or potential employees in business or industry. What are the advantages? What are the potential pitfalls?

TABLE 2.25

Faculty Member	Average Merit Committee Scores				
	Teacher Evaluation	Other Teach.	Research	Inst. Serv.	Other Serv.
Kirk Krypton (Associate Prof.)	3.0	3.1	3.4	3.2	3.5
Sam Socrates (Full Prof.)	3.7	3.4	0.7	2.9	1.1
Mike Michener (Assistant Prof.)	0.4	1.3	3.8	0.2	2.2
Susan Sununu (Full Prof.)	1.9	1.2	1.7	3.9	3.7
Ann Averidge (Assistant Prof.)	2.8	2.7	2.7	2.9	3.2
Wanda Wood (Associate Prof.)	1.6	0.6	0.3	1.1	0.4

4. **The Scenario** [10]: Arthur Pedick, M.D., F.A.C.S., is the founder and CEO of Arthur Pedick Associates (APA), a small firm that specializes in providing proprietary software products to the health care industry. More specifically, the APA software monitors costs and other benefits associated with work-related injuries and disease in the workers' compensation program. Costs to American industry currently exceed $60 billion per year, so that significant savings can be realized by prevention and monitoring of on-the-job injuries.

The company has two basic products—BoneScan, which involves onsite gathering of injury information by medical specialists, and PhoneScan, which uses sophisticated telephone interviews to collect the data. By carefully tracking injury cases to assure that proper medical attention is being received, these software packages have demonstrated cost savings to employers in the neighborhood of 20% to 40%.

The Problem: Pat Sternum, APA's management science specialist, sat on the edge of the huge chair across from Arthur Pedick's desk.

"Dr. Pedick," she began, "as you know, we now charge $200 per case for BoneScan and $100 per case for PhoneScan. But costs have risen, and my analysis shows that we won't cover our costs next year at those prices. Our profit contributions will be only $25 and $32.50 per case for Bone and Phone, respectively. I can make a strong case for raising our prices by $25 for each product, to $225 and $125, so that our new per-case profit contribution would be $50 and $57.50."

Pedick frowned. "Patty, I don't like to raise prices, but I'm open to suggestions. If we raise prices, won't we lose business to our competitors?"

"I don't think so," answered Sternum. "Medical costs are rising at a higher rate than the price increase I'm proposing. Besides, we run the highest quality operation in the business. People will pay more for first-class service."

"O.K., run it through the computer and give me some data. Here are the options."

1. We can't raise prices on 1,000 existing BoneScan and 2,000 existing PhoneScan cases—they are on multiyear contracts, and we charge current prices.
2. There is a new program next year to wholesale BoneScan software with a sales price of $125 and an expected profit contribution of $52.50 per case.
3. A special version of PhoneScan for small businesses (LoneScan) is planned for next year. LoneScan is priced at $100 per case and carries a profit contribution of $37.50 per case.
4. With our current computing setup, we can handle a maximum of 10,000 total cases per year.
5. Our four salespeople can generate a maximum of about $250,000 each in *new* gross sales in direct (not wholesale) sales, so we can't plan for more than $1 million in business from these three products.
6. We must attract at least $50,000 in sales for the LoneScan small business product to make it viable.
7. To keep the salespeople on their toes, I don't want the number of new PhoneScan cases sold to be more than 80% of all new business.

The Model:
a. Should Pat attempt to model this product mix problem using linear programming? Why or why not?
b. The LP model for this problem has six variables and six constraints (not including the nonnegativity constraints). Write the LP model of the doctor's problem.

Solution to the Model: Use a computer SIMPLEX algorithm to find the optimal solution to your model.

Solution to the Problem: If your LP algorithm provides reduced costs, shadow prices, and ranging analysis, answer the following questions:

a. Comment on the new pricing policy for Bonescan and the new wholesale product as compared to the other two new products. (*Hint:* Analyze reduced costs.)
b. How serious is the limitation on APA's computer facilities that leads to a limitation on total cases sold of 10,000? (*Hint:* Look at the shadow price for the total cases constraint.)
c. How sensitive is the optimal model solution to errors in estimating the profit contribution for the new LoneScan product?
d. Experiment with the constraint that limits the number of the new PhoneScan product from exceeding 80% of new sales. Try 60%, 70%, 90%; then do away with the constraint altogether.
e. Refer to the shadow prices associated with forcing the model to honor existing multiyear contracts at current prices. Comment on the advisability of signing multiyear contracts at a fixed price in an environment of rising costs.

5. **The Scenario:** Ice Train, Inc. (ITI) is a discount store that specializes in television sets. The firm stocks four models: a small portable, an economy model (12-inch screen), a standard model (19-inch screen), and a deluxe model (25-inch screen). The holidays are just around the corner, and the store manager is preparing to place her annual order.

    The Problem: ITI's warehouse will accommodate only 120,000 cubic feet of boxed television sets, but the manager believes that the demand for the portable, economy, and standard models will be very strong this year. Sales for the deluxe model, however, have never exceeded 5,000 units, and the manager would not wish to stock more than this number. She has already received layaway orders as follows: portable—1,000; economy—1,500; standard—1,200, and deluxe—500. She will, of course, have the order include at least these amounts.

The profit contributions for each model and their per-unit volume in cubic feet are as follows:

	Model			
	Portable	Economy	Standard	Deluxe
Profit contribution($)	40	55	125	200
Volume(ft³)	2	3	6	9

This year, ITI is offering a special. Customers who purchase a deluxe model can get a special deal on a portable television if they wish. The profit contribution for this package deal is $220.

The Model:
a. Can we model and analyze this problem using linear programming? Why or why not? (*Hint:* Consider the assumption of additivity.)
b. Ignore the effect of the special offer and model the remaining problem as an LP model. Note that if your computerized MS package has SAMS' implicit bounding capability, you don't have to explicitly include the lower-bound constraints. If not, you can remove them by employing the transformations "$x_j = x'_j + L_j, j = 1, \ldots, 4$," where the L_j are the layaway orders for each of the four models. Thus, there are only two operational constraints: the limitation on warehouse space and the upper bound on the deluxe model.

Solution to the Model: Letting x_j = number of each model to order, $j = 1, \ldots, 4$, in increasing order of size, verify that the optimal model solution is as in Table 2.26.

Solution to the Problem:
a. Note that variables x_1 (portable) and x_2 (economy) are at their lower bounds and that x_4 (deluxe) is at its upper bound at optimality. What does this fact suggest

TABLE 2.26

Variable	Description	Value
x_0	Profit	$2,549,583.33
x_1	Portable	1,000.00
x_2	Economy	1,500.00
x_3	Standard	11,416.67
x_4	Deluxe	5,000.00

Shadow Prices		
Warehouse space		$20.83 per ft³
Upper bound on deluxe		12.50 per unit

about the effect of taking advance layaway orders for the cheaper models and about the effect of limited demand for the deluxe models, on total profit contribution? Relax these lower bounds one at a time and observe the effect on profit and mix.

b. The reduced cost at optimality for x_2 (economy) is $7.50, which means that the profit contribution would have to increase by at least that much for it to be profitable to order more than the lower bound of 1,500 units. What managerial implications does this have for the firm's pricing and product line strategy?

c. The solution above ignores the special offer that combines certain joint sales of portable and deluxe models. Consider the following possible ways of incorporating this feature into the LP model and determine whether either is satisfactory.

1. Introduce a fifth product consisting of one portable and one deluxe, with a profit contribution of $220 and a volume of $9 + 2 = 11$ cubic feet.
2. Assume that every customer who buys a deluxe (other than the 500 already in layaway) will purchase a portable at the special price and set the transformed variable x'_1 equal to the transformed variable x_4.

d. Note that the shadow price for storage space is $20.83, which is merely 125/6 (per-unit contribution for x_3/per-unit volume for x_3). Explain why this is the case.

e. Suppose we can place orders for the four models only in lots of 144 (one gross) because of shipping policies adopted by the supplier. Do we still have a problem that we can model and analyze profitably by linear programming? Why or why not? (*Hint:* Consider the assumption of divisibility.)

6. **The Scenario [2]:** Blitzen Development International (BDI), a company headquartered in Germany, has acquired undeveloped commercial property in such typical American cities as Berlin, Texas; Pottsdam, New York; and Wittenberg, Ohio. BDI's current project is developing a complex in Stuttgart, Arkansas, that will consist of stores, offices, and apartments.

The Problem: BDI's vice president of planning has learned through market surveys that one must tailor development patterns for different U.S. cities to the peculiar tastes and preferences of the local populace. In Stuttgart, Arkansas, for example, stores and shops must be located on the ground floor, offices on the lower two floors, and apartments on the first three floors.

Further, Stuttgarters express strong preferences for a complex that includes some of all three types of units (apartments, stores, and offices), with some of the merchants and office workers preferring to live and shop where they work to avoid the long drive in heavy traffic to the downtown business district.

BDI's management scientist has analyzed survey responses from Stuttgarters and recommends to the vice president that BDI maintain upper-bound constraints on type of unit as in Table 2.27.

Another consideration is that units of different quality are possible (e.g., soundproofing, interior finishing), with three categories for apartments, two for offices, and one for stores. Table 2.28 gives rental charges in deutschemarks (DM) per square foot per year, and Table 2.29 gives initial construction costs in DM/ft^2 (exclusive of land costs).

The commercial lot on which BDI will build the complex was formerly owned by Joni Mitchell Enterprises and is a very large, beautiful, heavily wooded bird sanctuary—a veritable paradise. Since there is abundant land, there is no constraint on space—BDI will pave over the land not occupied by the building itself for a parking lot. However, BDI has allocated only four million deutschemarks to the project. The vice president of planning wishes to maximize total rental income.

TABLE 2.27

Type of Unit	Level	Maximum Percentage
Apartment	First floor	10%
	Second floor	50%
	Third floor	100%
Office	First floor	60%
	Second floor	75%
Store	First floor	50%

TABLE 2.28 Annual rentals (in DM/ft^2/year)

Type of Unit	Level	Quality Categories		
		1 (Highest)	2 (Medium)	3 (Lowest)
Apartment	First floor	3.00	2.50	N/A
	Second floor	3.00	2.50	N/A
	Third floor	2.50	2.00	N/A
Office	First floor	4.50	4.00	3.50
	Second floor	4.00	3.50	3.00
Store	First floor	3.25	N/A	N/A

N/A = not applicable

TABLE 2.29 Construction costs (in DM/ft^2)

Type of Unit	Level	Quality Categories		
		1 (Highest)	2 (Medium)	3 (Lowest)
Apartment	First floor	18.00	16.00	N/A
	Second floor	17.00	15.00	N/A
	Third floor	16.00	14.00	N/A
Office	First floor	19.00	17.00	13.00
	Second floor	18.00	15.00	14.00
Store	First floor	11.00	N/A	N/A

N/A = not applicable

The Model:

a. Let x_{ijk} be the decision variables that are the number of ft² of unit type i (apartment, office, store) to build on level j (first, second, or third floor) of quality class k (highest, medium, lowest). Can we model this problem as an LP?

b. If the answer to (a) is yes, write the LP model. Be sure to include constraints that force the square footage of the three floors to be the same.

Solution to the Model: Use an LP computer package to solve your model.

Solution to the Problem:

a. By forcing the square footage of all three floors to be the same, we in effect force construction of a three-story complex. Could we model this problem in such a way that we build only two stories if it is more profitable to do so?

b. Impose the lower-bound constraints that force us to allocate at least 25% of the floor space to each type of unit (apartment, store, office). How does this affect total rental income?

c. In its present form, this model allocates space to categories of units without regard for the individual sizes of the units. What if the units are in standard sizes? Might we have unused space left over on one or more floors? Can we address this potential problem with LP? (*Hint:* Consider the second part of the divisibility assumption.)

7. In the Wiseacre minicase, ignore Dr. Mize's restriction of planting no more than 15% of the crop in cucumbers and solve the new model with a computerized SIMPLEX package. Analyze the resulting optimal model solution and explain why it is so markedly different from the original solution.

8. In the William Hill Distillery minicase, renege on WHD's advance order by discarding Equation (2.72) and rerun the model using a computerized SIMPLEX package. Analyze the results carefully.

9. **The Scenario** [19]: Numismatics is the study or collection of coins or medals and is a popular avocation in North America. Coins represent a link with the past, and the 40,000 members of the American Numismatic Association (ANA) enjoy reading about and collecting rare coins. Collectors experience a deep sense of achievement when they assemble a complete set of a certain series of rare coins. Table 2.30 lists certain U.S. coins by denomination, type, and years in which they were minted.

But pleasure of ownership is only one facet of numismatics. Since the number of collectors is increasing rapidly and since the supply of rare coins remains stationary, most numismatists consider themselves to be serious investors. Prices of rare coins have increased sharply in recent decades, experiencing a 19% compound annual growth rate in the period from 1969 to 1991.

Table 2.31 exhibits the various grades of coins recognized by the ANA, listed in decreasing order of desirability. Prices of coins vary dramatically depending on their grade. Grading takes into consideration such factors as weight, striking, toning, and surface of the planchet. Far from being completely scientific, grading is still an art rather than a science. Prices of rare coins are heavily dependent on both grade and rarity.

The Problem: Phillipa Cohen has decided to become a serious coin collector. From the latest issue of *Coin World*, she has selected three coin dealers that appear to be reputable. From the *Coin Dealer Newsletter*, she recorded wholesale prices of several coins of interest and has assembled a table by dealer and type of coin (see Table 2.32).

The following are Phillipa's personal preferences and constraints:

1. Phillipa has $1,000 to invest.
2. She wishes to invest no more than $100 in one-cent coins.
3. Hedzer Tales is a new dealer, and Phillipa's friends have cautioned Phillipa to spend no more than $250 there.

TABLE 2.30 Coins of the United States

Denomination	Type	Years Minted	Denomination	Type	Years Minted
$\frac{1}{2}$¢	Liberty Cap	1793–1797	10¢	Draped Bust	1796–1807
	Draped Bust	1800–1809		Capped Bust	1809–1837
	Classic Head	1809–1836		Liberty Seated	1837–1891
1¢	Flowing Hair	1793		Barber	1892–1916
	Liberty Cap	1793–1796		Mercury	1916–1945
	Draped Bust	1796–1807		Roosevelt	1946–
	Classic Head	1808–1815	20¢	Seated	1875–1878
	Coronet	1816–1857	25¢	Draped Bust	1796–1807
	Flying Eagle	1856–1858		Capped Bust	1815–1838
	Indian Head	1859–1909		Liberty Seated	1838–1891
	Lincoln	1909–		Barber	1892–1916
2¢	Copper	1864–1873		Stand Liberty	1916–1930
3¢	Nickel	1865–1889		Washington	1932–
5¢	Flowing Hair	1794–1795	50¢	Flowing Hair	1794–1795
	Draped Bust	1796–1805		Draped Bust	1796–1807
	Capped Bust	1829–1837		Capped Bust	1807–1839
	Liberty Seat	1837–1873		Liberty Seated	1839–1891
	Shield	1865–1883		Barber	1892–1915
	Liberty Head	1883–1913		Walking Liberty	1916–1947
	Buffalo	1913–1938		Franklin	1948–1963
	Jefferson	1938–		Kennedy	1964–

TABLE 2.31 ANA coin grades

Grade	Abbreviation
Proof	Pr.–60/70
Uncirculated	MS–60/70
About uncirculated	AU
Extremely fine	XF
Very fine	VF
Fine	F
Very good	VG
Good	G
About good	AG

TABLE 2.32 Wholesale values of coins

Denomination	Grade Range	Var.	Coinucopia	Var.	Hedzer Tales	Var.	Lou's Change
1-cent	AU–VF	x_1	0.889		n/a	x_9	0.840
5-cent	AU–XF	x_2	0.713	x_5	0.910	x_{10}	0.804
10-cent	G–MS65	x_3	0.888	x_6	0.823	x_{11}	0.878
25-cent	F–XF	x_4	0.883	x_7	0.845		n/a
50-cent	G–XF		n/a	x_8	0.945	x_{12}	0.812

4. Phillipa is particularly interested in 50-cent coins and wishes to invest at least $400 in them.
5. Coinucopia is an old, reputable firm, and for safety, Phillipa wants to invest at least half of her money there.
   (Note: The numbers in Table 2.32 are wholesale prices divided by retail prices. The x_j are decision variables representing the amount of money to invest in a particular coin to be bought from one of the dealers.)
6. Phillipa would like to maximize the total wholesale value of the coins purchased.

The Model:

a. The LP model for this problem has 12 variables and 5 constraints (not including the nonnegativity constraints). Write the LP model of Phillipa Cohen's problem.
b. Note that all constraint coefficients are either one or zero. Does this suggest that the optimal model solution will be all-integer?

Solution to the Model: Use a computer SIMPLEX algorithm to find the optimal solution to your model.

Solution to the Problem: If your SIMPLEX algorithm provides reduced costs, shadow prices, and ranging analysis, answer the following questions:

a. Note the reduced cost associated with x_4 (25-cent coins from Coinucopia). If the coefficient of x_4 in the objective function were increased by 0.005 (from 0.883 to 0.888), how would the current model solution change?
b. In limiting her total purchase from Hedzer Tales to no more than $250, Phillipa obviously limited the total wholesale value of her collection. Examine the shadow price associated with this constraint to determine how serious this limitation is.
c. Study the ranging analysis on objective function coefficients, with particular attention to x_3. What might this very narrow range of values suggest about the importance of accurately estimating this coefficient?
d. Change Phillipa's total budget from $1,000 to $850 and rerun the model. What happened? Could you have predicted this by examining the ranging analysis on right-hand sides of the constraints?

10. **The Scenario:** The Barrister, Ohio, law firm of Carp, Cavil, and Chafe specializes in contested divorce cases and cases involving damage suits for personal injury resulting from automobile accidents. The attorneys are equal partners in the firm, and since they do not trust one another, there is no managing partner. Thus, when critical decisions have to be made, they always hire a management consultant to resolve their differences.

And their differences are troublesome at times. For example, Ms. Carp's highest priority goal is to diversify the firm into the lucrative medical malpractice business. Mr. Cavil, on the other hand, detests being outdoors and would just as soon get out of the automobile accident racket and concentrate strictly on divorces. Mr. Chafe is an amateur racer and loves the thrill of high-speed ambulance chases.

The Problem: The latest crisis at CC&C involves a three-way disagreement over the current caseload. There are 18 divorce cases and 21 auto injury cases to be assigned; Mr. Cavil, naturally, wants 13 divorce cases and as few automobile accident cases as he can get by with. Ms. Carp and Mr. Chafe also have their preferences, and—if everyone has his or her way—there will be double coverage on eight auto injury cases and no coverage on eight divorce cases. Stalemated once again, our attorneys hire Tab Lowe (a management consultant) to break the logjam.

"Counselors," Tab begins, "linear programming will solve your problem—as it has so many times for others. Just give me the details of your problem and I'll get it into my computer."

Tab listened intently as the problem was described in turn by the three attorneys. He then pored over the case logs for several hours and accumulated the following data:

Average preparation time per case

	Carp (hours)	Cavil (hours)	Chafe (hours)
Divorce	15	18	100
Automobile	25	20	28

He then assigned the six decision variables as follows, where each x denotes the number of cases of each type to be assigned to each attorney.

	Carp	Cavil	Chafe
Divorce	x_1	x_2	x_3
Automobile	x_4	x_5	x_6

Tab decided that the appropriate objective was to minimize the total hours of preparation time for the firm. He also concluded that all 39 cases must be assigned and that Ms. Carp should spend at least as many hours prepping as Mr. Cavil but no more hours prepping than Mr. Chafe.

The Model:
a. In this textbook, we would refer to the consultant Tab Lowe as "a solution looking for a problem." That is, regardless of the nature of a problem, Tab will always conclude that LP is the model to use. Critique Tab's role in setting up this model in light of our conclusions in Chapter 1 and considering the assumptions of LP modeling.
b. Model and solve this six-variable, four-constraint problem as an LP model.

Solution to the Model:
a. The solution to your model involves noninteger values for legal cases and is hardly useful to a decision maker in its present form. Try rounding this solution

to get a good, all-integer feasible solution. (Good luck—the optimal integer solution is $x_1 = 18$; $x_2 = 1$; $x_5 = 12$; $x_6 = 10$; $x_3 = 0$; $x_4 = 0$, for total prep time of 808 hours.)

b. Examine the reduced cost for x_3 in your optimal LP solution. The very large size of this number would immediately signal a problem in a real-world formulation. Now note the relative size of c_3 (the objective coefficient for x_3) as compared to the other c_j. Assume that this number represents a magnitude-of-order error and re-solve the model with $c_3 = 10$. Note that this solution is easy to round to an all-integer solution, yielding a total case preparation time of 655 hours.

c. Note in this solution the relatively high shadow price on the constraint that requires at least 21 automobile cases. What might this suggest about the relative desirability (from a workload standpoint) of automobile versus divorce cases?

Solution to the Problem:

a. Compare the model's solution with the description of the three attorneys' individual preferences as stated in the second paragraph of "The Scenario." What likelihood is there that this model's solution will actually be implemented?

b. Try to imagine a worse misuse of management science modeling and analysis than this situation. If you can, you are indeed most imaginative!

11. a. Consider these two toy models:

    P1

    MAX
    $$x_0 = 3x_1 + 4x_2 + 6x_3$$
    S T:
    $$4x_1 + 3x_2 + 5x_3 \leq 40$$
    $$3x_1 + 2x_2 + 6x_3 \geq 89$$
    $$x_1, x_2, x_3 \geq 0$$

    P2

    MIN
    $$x_0 = 2x_1 - x_2 + x_3$$
    S T:
    $$x_1 - x_2 + 3x_3 \leq 18$$
    $$2x_1 + 2x_2 + 4x_3 \geq 12$$
    $$x_1, x_2, x_3 \geq 0$$

    Solve (P1) and (P2) using a SIMPLEX computer package.

    b. Oops! The right-hand side of the second constraint in (P1) should have been 39 rather than 89 (we misread the advance order quantity), and the objective coefficient of x_2 in (P2) should have been $+1$ rather than -1 (typographical error). Make these changes and try it again.

    c. Write the dual models (D1) and (D2) of the original (P1) and (P2) and solve them with a computerized SIMPLEX package. (*Note:* First change the $\geq$ constraints by multiplying both sides by -1.)

12. **The Scenario:** A regional food company has retained an advertising agency to handle the introduction of its new candy bar, which is made from glandless cottonseed. (There actually is such a thing!) The agency has selected a medium-sized town as a trial market and has identified three viable advertising media: television, radio, and

local newspaper. Obviously, advertising rates for radio and television vary widely depending on length of the spot, time of day, day of week, etc., and rates for newspaper ads vary according to size and placement. The agency in this case is operating with a fixed advertising budget.

The Problem: Since there is a fixed budget, the account executive must decide on a media mix that will get the "biggest bang for the buck." She has available a complete set of rate books for all three media as well as market research data on exposure levels of the various subcategories (size and placement of newspaper ads, ratings for specific radio and TV shows, etc.).

The Model: Can we model this problem effectively as a linear program? Why or why not? (*Hint:* How about the additivity assumption? That is, do people *only* watch television or *only* listen to radio or *only* read newspapers?)

PRACTICE MODELS

1. Use a computerized LP algorithm to solve the following LP problems.

   a.
   MAX
   $$4 \text{ VAR1} + 5 \text{ VAR2} + 6 \text{ VAR3} + 5 \text{ VAR4}$$
   S T:
   $$2 \text{ VAR1} + 4 \text{ VAR2} + 4 \text{ VAR3} - 2 \text{ VAR4} < 184$$
   $$2 \text{ VAR1} + 5 \text{ VAR2} + 4 \text{ VAR3} + 3 \text{ VAR4} < 224$$
   $$5 \text{ VAR1} + 4 \text{ VAR2} - 5 \text{ VAR3} + 10 \text{ VAR4} < 280$$
   all VAR > 0

   b.
   MIN
   $$\text{VAR1} - 2 \text{ VAR2} - 4 \text{ VAR3} + 2 \text{ VAR4}$$
   S T:
   $$-2 \text{ VAR1} + \text{ VAR2} + 8 \text{ VAR3} + \text{ VAR4} > 12$$
   $$\text{VAR1} \quad - 2 \text{ VAR3} \quad > 4$$
   $$\text{VAR2} \quad - \text{ VAR4} > 8$$
   all VAR > 0

2. Add the following constraints to Problem 1 (a) and solve using a computerized package:
   $$-1 \text{ VAR1} + 3 \text{ VAR2} + 3 \text{ VAR3} - 4 \text{ VAR4} > 130$$
   $$3 \text{ VAR1} + 6 \text{ VAR2} - 3 \text{ VAR3} + 1 \text{ VAR4} > 148$$

3. In Problem 2 study the detailed solution report generated by your LP package for each iteration.

4. Use the graphical method of LP to determine the optimal solution for the model:

MIN
$\quad$ 2 VAR1 + 3 VAR2

S T:
$\quad$ VAR1 + 2 VAR2 < 8
$\quad$ 4 VAR1 + 3 VAR2 > 12
$\quad\quad\quad\quad$ 1 VAR2 > 2

all VAR > 0

5. Solve the following LP problem. Are there alternate optimal solutions to this problem? If so, identify such solutions and compare the results.

MIN
$\quad$ 9 VAR1 + 4 VAR2 + 21 VAR3 + 5 VAR4 + 15 VAR5 +
$\quad$ 14 VAR6 + 31 VAR7 + 16 VAR8 + 5 VAR9 + 6 VAR10 +
$\quad$ 22 VAR11 + 11 VAR12

S T:
$\quad$ VAR9 + VAR10 + VAR11 + VAR12 = 105
$\quad$ VAR5 + VAR 6 + VAR 7 + VAR 8 = 90
$\quad$ VAR1 + VAR 2 + VAR 3 + VAR 4 = 70
$\quad$ VAR4 + VAR 8 + VAR12 = 60
$\quad$ VAR3 + VAR 7 + VAR11 = 85
$\quad$ VAR2 + VAR 6 + VAR10 = 75
$\quad$ VAR1 + VAR 5 + VAR 9 = 45

all VAR > 0

6. Perform a sensitivity analysis of cost coefficients and right-hand-side values for the following model:

MIN
$\quad$ 600 VAR1 + 480 VAR2 + 20 VAR3 + 20 VAR4 + 50 VAR5

S T:
$\quad$ 10 VAR1 + 5 VAR2 $\quad\quad\quad\quad$ + VAR5 > 15
$\quad$ 10 VAR1 + 5 VAR2 $\quad\quad\quad\quad\quad\quad\quad$ > 12.5
$\quad$ 20 VAR1 + 8 VAR2 + VAR3 $\quad\quad$ + VAR5 > 25
$\quad$ 15 VAR1 + 12 VAR2 $\quad\quad\quad$ + VAR4 $\quad\quad$ > 20

all VAR > 0

a. Change the objective function coefficient of VAR1 to 700 and rerun the model. What effect does this have on the optimal solution?
b. Change the objective function coefficient of VAR1 to 800 and rerun the model. What effect does this have on the optimal solution?

7. Use an LP package to perform a parametric analysis of the model in Problem 6. Note that if the analysis is performed within the allowable minimum and maximum range, the basis will remain the same.

8. Solve the following model using an LP package:

MAX
$$+ 43\, VAR1 + 27\, VAR2 + 25\, VAR3 + 22\, VAR4 + 45\, VAR5$$
S T:
$$VAR1 + VAR2 + VAR3 + VAR4 + VAR5 \le 10$$
$$VAR2 + VAR3 + VAR4 \ge 4$$
$$6\, VAR1 + 6\, VAR2 - 4\, VAR3 - 4\, VAR4 + 36\, VAR5 \le 0$$
$$4\, VAR1 + 10\, VAR2 - 1\, VAR3 - 2\, VAR4 - 3\, VAR5 \le 0$$
$$\text{all } VAR > 0$$

a. SAMS' detailed report indicates that VAR2 has a reduced cost of -30.18. What does this mean?
b. Constraint (1) has a shadow price of 29.83. What does this mean?
c. Decrease the RHS value of constraint (1) from 10 to 5. Does the solution to the problem change? Explain.

9. Solve the following LP problem using a SIMPLEX package and observe the results. Note that the decision variables of this model are unrestricted in sign.

MIN
$$2\, VAR1 + VAR2 + VAR3 + 5\, VAR4$$
S T:
$$VAR1 - 2\, VAR2 \le 12$$
$$2\, VAR1 + 3\, VAR3 - 1\, VAR4 \ge 8$$
$$VAR2 + VAR3 + 2\, VAR4 \ge 18$$

VAR 2 unrestricted in sign

REFERENCES AND ADDITIONAL READING

1. Austin, L., and J. Burns. *Management Science: An Aid for Managerial Decision Making.* New York: Macmillan, 1985.
2. Barrett, M. Adapted from an unpublished MBA term project report, College of Business Administration, Texas Tech University (1983).
3. Bazarra, M., and J. Jarvis. *Linear Programming and Network Flows* (2d ed.). New York: Wiley, 1990.
4. Bierman, H., C. Bonini, and W. Hausman. *Quantitative Analysis for Business Decisions* (7th ed.). Homewood, Ill.: Richard D. Irwin, 1986.
5. Buddingh, D. Adapted from an unpublished MBA term project report, College of Business Administration, Texas Tech University (1987).

6. Calkins, C. *Reader's Digest Illustrated Guide to Gardening.* Pleasantville, N.Y.: Reader's Digest, 1978.
7. Dannenbring, David G., & Martin K. Starr. *Management Science: An Introduction.* New York: McGraw-Hill, 1981.
8. Dantzig, G. *Linear Programming and Extensions.* Princeton, N.J.: Princeton University Press, 1963.
9. Davis, P. Adapted from an unpublished MBA term project report, College of Business Administration, Texas Tech University (1983).
10. Driskill, Blair. Adapted from an unpublished MBA term project report, Virginia Polytechnic Institute and State University (1987).
11. Eppen, G., F. Gould, and C. Schmidt. *Quantitative Concepts for Management* (3rd ed.). Englewood Cliffs, N.J.: Prentice-Hall, 1988.
12. Forgionne, G. *Quantitative Management.* Hinsdale, Ill.: Dryden Press, 1989.
13. Gass, S. *Linear Programming Methods and Extensions* (3rd ed.). New York: McGraw-Hill, 1969.
14. Goodell, P. Adapted from an unpublished MBA term project report, College of Business Administration, Texas Tech University (1983).
15. Hillier, F., and G. Lieberman. *Operations Research* (4th ed.). Oakland, Calif.: Holden-Day, 1986.
16. Knowles, T. *Management Science: Building and Using Models.* Homewood, Ill: Richard D. Irwin, 1989.
17. Marker, R. Adapted from an unpublished MBA term project report, College of Business Administration, Texas Tech University (1987).
18. Offord, Bill. Adapted from an unpublished MBA term project report, Texas Tech University (1986).
19. Stallings, Mark. Adapted from an unpublished MBA term project report, Texas Tech University (1986).
20. Sturms, Edward D. Adapted from an unpublished MBA term project report, Virginia Polytechnic Institute and State University (1986).
21. Taha, H. *Operations Research: An Introduction* (3rd ed.). New York: Macmillan, 1982
22. Wagner, H. *Principles of Operations Research* (2d ed.). Englewood Cliffs, N.J.: Prentice-Hall, 1975.
23. Williams, A. Mark. Adapted from an unpublished MBA term project report, Virginia Polytechnic Institute and State University (1987).
24. Winston, W. *Operations Research: Applications and Algorithms* (2d ed.). Boston: PWS-Kent, 1991.

CHAPTER 3

Integer (Linear) Programming Models

If we insist that some or all of our decision variables in a linear programming model be integer valued, we refer to the resulting model as an integer (linear) programming (ILP) model. Business, industry, and public sector organizations make wide use of such models, which serve as important aids to decision makers in a variety of applications.

ILP models are useful in two different scenarios. First, and most obvious, fractional values for the decision variables may make no sense. For example, consider the managerial consequences of assigning 2.7 salespeople to a given territory or 3.2 robots to a production line. As another illustration, we buy or sell many items in round lots. Your LP model may indicate the purchase of 15.6 eggs, but the supermarket will undoubtedly refuse to take four eggs out of a dozen-egg carton—much less break one of the eggs and sell you 60% of it. On the other hand, if the values of the decision variables are moderately large, no one would object to rounding nonintegral values to the next largest or next smallest integer to obtain a useful solution. No rational manager would lose much sleep over deciding to order 950 rather than 950.6253 batteries.

The second—and much more important—role for ILP models is in using the ILP algorithm for solving certain models of nonlinear problems. We will discuss this approach in detail in the second section of this chapter.

UNDERLYING ASSUMPTIONS

The underlying assumption of linearity applies to ILP models as it does to LP models—except that some or all of the decision variables are required to take on integer variables in the solution to the model. That is, we relax the second part of the divisibility assumption. If all decision variables must meet the integrality requirement, we refer to the model as a **pure ILP model**; otherwise, we use the term **mixed ILP model**. We will see examples of both.

A word of caution is in order. If you can get usable results without having to insist on integral values of your variables—do so. If we can compare solution techniques to flora, the SIMPLEX algorithm is the White House lawn and ILP algorithms are the South American jungle.

INTEGER MODELING

As noted, ILP models are useful in two quite different contexts—when there are natural integer-valued variables and when we use integers to incorporate other nonlinear features.

NATURAL INTEGER-VALUED VARIABLES

Consider the strategic capacity planning problems faced by managers in manufacturing firms. Large, special-purpose equipment like five-axis milling machines are incredibly expensive, and the decision to purchase two or three of these complex items (to replace less sophisticated equipment, perhaps) represents a capital outlay of several million dollars. Thus, an LP solution to a capital equipment acquisition problem that returned fractional solutions for numbers of multimillion-dollar five-axis milling machines would hardly be useful to the decision maker.

The point is obvious. *If it makes a difference* in the solution of a managerial problem, we should use an ILP model instead of an LP model. On the other hand, if we can round the model solution to integer values to produce useful information, we should avoid the time and expense required for solution of an ILP model.

MODELING WITH SURROGATE INTEGER VARIABLES

As noted previously, the most important function of ILP is in incorporating features of problems that lead to nonlinearities in models of those problems. We will discuss four such approaches in what follows, and we forewarn you that some of the approaches come and go in terms of our being able to grasp how they work. All have one thing in common, however, and that is the tradeoff between increased problem size (both in numbers of variables as well as constraints) and the reduction of nonlinear considerations to manageable modeling and solution approaches.

FIXED-CHARGE PROBLEMS

So-called fixed-charge problems are commonplace in managerial decision making, and examples abound. The decision whether to include a new product in our line most probably involves a setup cost for the production facility as well as a per-unit cost to manufacture the item. For instance, if the variable cost per unit is $50 and the setup cost is $100,000, the decision to produce exactly one item (silly thought) would mean a per-unit cost of $100,050. The average cost of producing two items would be $50,050, and so on. The point, of course, is that the decision not to manufacture the new product generates no cost whatsoever, so that the objective function is nonlinear.

To illustrate how this device works, let us return to our electronic analyst LPS and Percy from Chapter 2.

The Scenario: LO-CAL Candy Company is suspending operations for a month, and Percy is allowed to use the current inventory of ingredients to produce one final batch of candy.

The Problem: Table 3.1 gives the production requirements, inventory of ingredients, and the LP solution to this model.

> **PERCY:** Well, LPS, I need more help. When I proudly showed the production foreman my solution to the product mix problem, he took one look and practically fell down laughing.

TABLE 3.1 LO-CAL production requirements

		Ingredients (pounds per package)				
Product	Profit per Package	Dark Choc	Light Choc	Sugar	Caramel	Asstd. Nuts
Nuts-2-U	$1.00	0.80	0.20	0.30	0.20	0.70
Bite O'Heaven	0.70	0.50	0.10	0.40	0.30	0.10
Chocochunk	1.10	1.00	0.10	0.60	0.30	0.90
Diet-Buster	2.00	2.00	0.10	1.30	0.70	1.50
Goo-Chew	0.60	1.10	0.20	0.05	0.50	0.00

LO-CAL production requirements inventory (in pounds)

Ingredient	Amount on Hand
Dark chocolate	1,411
Light chocolate	149
Sugar	815.5
Caramel	466
Nuts	1,080

Optimal LP solution to LO-CAL model

Variable	Description	Value
x_1	Nuts-2-U	454.50 packages
x_2	Bite O'Heaven	58.78 packages
x_3	Chocochunk	-0- packages
x_4	Diet-Buster	503.99 packages
x_5	Goo-Chew	9.13 packages

LPS: I'm sorry to hear that, Percy. What's the problem?

PERCY: Well, it seems that producing Diet-Buster requires shutting down the production line first and thoroughly cleaning the molds and feeder lines. The foreman says it costs $300 to do a setup for Diet-Buster, which is why LO-CAL seldom produced any in the past. My marginal profit was only $429, and this eats up most of it.

The Model:

LPS: Cheer up, Percy. We can model your setup cost with the integer programming capability of SAMS [Table 3.2]. And we may as well go ahead and get a solution with no fractional packages while we are at it, since this is a relatively small model. Just a second . . . here is my input to SAMS' integer programming module on the screen [Figure 3.1].

LPS: As you can see, Percy, I altered the objective function so that if the zero-one variable y (sometimes called a surrogate variable) takes a value of 1, the model accepts the fixed charge of $300 for setup for Diet-

CHAPTER 3 INTEGER (LINEAR) PROGRAMMING MODELS

TABLE 3.2 SAMS model for LO-CAL with fixed charge

LO-CAL CANDY COMPANY MATHEMATICAL MODEL

MAX
$$NUTS + 0.7\ BITO + 1.1\ CHOC + 2\ DIET + 0.6\ GOOC - 300\ Y$$
S T:
DARK CHOC
$$0.8\ NUTS + 0.5\ BITO + CHOC + 2\ DIET + 1.1\ GOOC <= 1411$$
LITE CHOC
$$0.2\ NUTS + 0.1\ BITO + 0.1\ CHOC + 0.1\ DIET + 0.2\ GOOC <= 149$$
SUGAR
$$0.3\ NUTS + 0.4\ BITO + 0.6\ CHOC + 1.3\ DIET + 0.05\ GOOC <= 815.5$$
CARAMEL
$$0.2\ NUTS + 0.3\ BITO + 0.3\ CHOC + 0.7\ DIET + 0.5\ GOOC <= 466$$
ASSTD NUTS
$$0.7\ NUTS + 0.1\ BITO + 0.9\ CHOC + 1.5\ DIET <= 1080$$
FIX CHG
$$DIET - 1000\ Y <= 0$$

$Y = 0$ or 1; All other variables integer

FIGURE 3.1 SAMS input screen for LO-CAL with fixed charge

```
────► SAMS INPUT SCREEN - Integer Programming ◄────

NAME?  LO-CAL CANDY COMPANY WITH FIXED CHARGE ON DIET
MAximize or MInimize?  MA
PROBLEM DESCRIPTION - Optimize mix of candies for largest
                     profit contribution.
```

Variables	N2-U	BO'H	CHOC	DIET	GOOC	Y	Dir	RHS
Type	I	I	I	I	I	I		
Objective	1.	.7	1.1	2.	.6	-300.	<	
Upper Bound	INF	INF	INF	INF	INF	1	=	
Lower Bound	0.	0.	0.	0.	0.	0.	>	
Constraints								
DARK CHOC	.8	.5	1.	2.	1.1	0.	<	1411.
LITE CHOC	.2	.1	.1	.1	.2	0.	<	149.
SUGAR	.3	.4	.6	1.3	.05	0.	<	815.5
CARAMEL	.2	.3	.3	.7	.5	0.	<	466.
NUTS	.7	.1	.9	1.5	0.	0.	<	1080.
FIX CHG	0.	0.	0.	1.	0.	-1000.	<	0.

TABLE 3.3 SAMS full briefing for LO-CAL with fixed charge

LO-CAL CANDY COMPANY
FULL BRIEFING ON OPTIMAL MODEL SOLUTION
Maximum Objective Value = 1495

Decision Variable	Optimal Value	Reduced Cost
N2-U	0.00	1.00
BO'H	284.00	0.00
CHOC	1168.00	0.00
DIET	0.00	2.00
GOOC	19.00	0.00
Y	0.00	−300.00

Constraint	Type	Slack
DARK CHOC	<	80.10
LITE CHOC	<	0.00
SUGAR	<	0.15
CARAMEL	<	20.90
NUTS	<	0.40
Y	<	0.00

Buster. The sixth constraint I've called "FIX CHG" merely ties the variable $DIET$ to y. If $y = 0$, the constraint forces $DIET$ to be zero also. Otherwise, the "constraint" becomes "DIET $\leq$ 1000," which really isn't a constraint at all (we say that it is redundant).

PERCY: How clever, LPS—and yet how simple! What's the solution? I can't wait to see whether the ILP model saved me some of that $300.

LPS: I think you will be pleased, Percy, and probably surprised as well. Here is the SAMS report [Table 3.3].

Solution to the Model:

PERCY: My word, LPS, the ILP solution has only $14 less profit than the LP solution! Of course, it doesn't recommend making any Nuts-2-U or Diet-Buster, but it says to make a *lot* of Chocochunk—and the LP solution recommended none! And I even have some materials left over, even though the LP solution used up just about everything. Are you sure this solution is correct, LPS?

LPS: (Computer chuckle) Yes, Percy, it is correct. I knew you would be surprised.

PERCY: Wait a minute—there's no shadow price column. Did you forget to compute them?

LPS: Unfortunately, shadow prices are meaningless in ILP, as you will discover later in the chapter. So long for now, Percy.

TABLE 3.4

Decision Variable	ROT	LIT	
Profit contribution	$ 2/gal	$ 5/gal	
Resource			Inventory
Cook time	1 gal/hr	3 gal/hr	48 hours
Corn or	2 bu/gal	3 bu/gal	66 bushels
potatoes	3 bu/gal	6 bu/gal	120 bushels
Jugs	1 jug/gal	1 jug/gal	30 jugs

Mathematically, and in general, the fixed-charge term in the objective function would be as follows:

$$c_j = \begin{cases} F_j + V_j x_j, & \text{if } x_j > 0 \\ 0, & \text{otherwise} \end{cases} \quad (3.1)$$

where F_j is the fixed charge or setup cost, V_j is the variable per-unit cost to produce the new item, and x_j is the number of units produced.

To model this problem as a mathematical program, we introduce a surrogate variable y_j, which we allow to take on only integer values. We then model the problem as follows.

MIN: $x_0 = V_j x_j + F_j y_j +$ everything else $\quad (3.2)$

S T: $\quad 0 \leq x_j \leq M y_j \quad (3.3)$

$\quad 0 \leq y_j \leq 1$ and integer $\quad (3.4)$

where M is a very large number.

If our ILP optimizing algorithm finds that we should produce the new product symbolized by x_j, it will set $y_j = 1$ and pick up the fixed charge F_j in the objective function. The constraint (3.3) becomes "$x_j \leq M$," and since we selected M to be a very large number, the constraint has no effect. On the other hand, if the algorithm determines that we should not produce the new item, it will set $y_j = 0$ and not incur the cost F_j. We have modeled the nonlinear fixed charge.

EITHER-OR SITUATIONS

Consider a much smaller version of the William Hill Distillery minicase from Chapter 2, in which there are only two products in the line—Dew (the standard brand) and Light (the top of the line product). Data for this small problem are in Table 3.4.

Note that there are 48 hours of production time before the IRS agents arrive, 66 bushels of corn and 120 bushels of potatoes in inventory, and 30 jugs for the products. However, observe that we can produce the products *either* with corn *or* with potatoes—they don't require both. You can see that if we gave the IP algorithm *both* constraints, it would produce the *poorest* of the two possible solutions.

What we wish to do is to persuade the algorithm to accept the raw material constraint that gives us the greatest profit and to reject the other (e.g., make it nonbinding). To achieve this result, we write the two constraints as follows, using the surrogate variable y:

(Corn) $\quad$ 2DEW + 3LIT $\leq$ 66 + My $\quad$ (3.5)

(Potatoes) $\quad$ 3DEW + 6LIT $\leq$ 120 + M(1 − y) $\quad$ (3.6)

where y takes on only the values 0 or 1 and M is a large number. Note the effect of this device. If our algorithm sets $y = 0$, Equation (3.5) reduces to the constraint on corn and Equation (3.6) becomes "3DEW + 6LIT $\leq$ 120 + M," which is not a binding constraint, since M is a very large number. On the other hand, if $y = 1$, Equation (3.6) becomes a binding constraint on potatoes and Equation (3.5) becomes redundant.

If we arbitrarily select $M = 1,000$, and after we do the algebra to get all variables to the left side of the inequalities, our model is as in the SAMS model in Table 3.5. The SAMS full briefing of the optimal solution is in Table 3.6.

Note that the algorithm chose $y = 1$, so that potatoes are the preferred raw material, and total profit contribution is \$87. You may wish to verify that the best one can do with corn is a profit of \$86.

In general, we can use the either-or device to allow the model to select between *sets* of constraints. For example, we might be trying to decide where to locate a manufacturing plant and wish to evaluate the profit potential of the two sites. If tax rates, utility costs, labor costs, etc., varied widely between the two sites, we would have two sets of constraints—one for each site. If there were m_1 constraints for the first site and m_2 for the second ($m = m_1 + m_2$), the mathematical form of the either-or modeling would be as follows:

$$\text{Site 1} \quad \sum_{j=1}^{n} a_{ij}x_j \leq b_i + My, \; i = 1, \ldots, m_1 \quad (3.7)$$

$$\text{Site 2} \quad \sum_{j=1}^{n} a_{ij}x_j \leq b_i + M(1 - y), \; i = m_1 + 1, \ldots, m \quad (3.8)$$

where $y = 0$ or 1, and M is our large number.

TABLE 3.5 SAMS model for small William Hill Distillery problem

```
SMALL WILLIAM HILL DISTILLERY MATHEMATICAL MODEL
MAX
            2DEW + 5LIT
S T:
TIME
            DEW + 3LIT            <   48
CORN
            2DEW + 3LIT − 1000 Y  <   66
POTATOES
            3DEW + 6LIT + 1000 Y  < 1120
JUGS
            DEW + LIT             <   30
            Y = 0 or 1; DEW, LIT > 0
```

TABLE 3.6 SAMS solution report for small William Hill Distillery problem

SMALL WILLIAM HILL DISTILLERY PROBLEM
FULL BRIEFING ON OPTIMAL MODEL SOLUTION
Maximum Objective Value = 87

Decision Variable	Optimal Value	Reduced Cost
DEW	21.0	0.0
LIT	9.0	0.0
Y	1.0	0.0

Constraint	Type	Slack
TIME	<	0.0
CORN	<	997.0
POTATOES	<	3.0
JUGS	<	0.0

If our ILP computer algorithm emerges with $y = 1$, the constraints (3.8) are binding and those in (3.7) are not (since the right-hand sides are very large). Conversely, if $y = 0$, the constraints (3.7) are binding and (3.8) are not.

SPECIFIED INTEGER VALUES

In many operational problems, the value of a decision variable may be limited to a small set of feasible integer values. For example, we know that many commercial products are sold by the dozen or even the gross (12 dozen). A solution to an IP model that was not evenly divisible by the lot size would be infeasible. To illustrate this situation, let us return to our "Small William Hill Distillery" scenario from the previous section and assume that the company vends Dew in six-packs and Light in four-packs. Recall that the optimal model solution (using potatoes) was $DEW = 21$; $LIT = 9$; Profit = \$87. This solution is wasteful in the present case, since it discards three jugs of DEW and one jug of LIT.

To incorporate the specified integer value feature, we begin by noting that DEW cannot be larger than 30 (because of the JUGS constraint) and LIT cannot be larger than 16 (because of the TIME constraint). Since DEW sells in six-packs, the maximum number possible is five packs, and likewise the largest number of four-packs of LIT is four. We need to add four constraints to our original LP model, as follows:

$$DEW = 6y_1 + 12y_2 + 18y_3 + 24y_4 + 30y_5$$

$$y_1 + y_2 + y_3 + y_4 + y_5 \leq 1$$

$$LIT = 4y_6 + 8y_7 + 12y_8 + 16y_9$$

$$y_6 + y_7 + y_8 + y_9 \leq 1$$

and $y_1, y_2, \ldots, y_9 = 0$ or 1

TABLE 3.7 SAMS model for small William Hill Distillery problem

---

SMALL WILLIAM HILL DISTILLERY PROBLEM MATHEMATICAL MODEL

MAX
$$2DEW + 5LIT$$

S T:

TIME
$$DEW + 3LIT <= 48$$

POTATOES
$$3DEW + 6LIT <= 120$$

JUGS
$$DEW + LIT <= 30$$

TRANS DEW
$$DEW - 6Y1 - 12Y2 - 18Y3 - 24Y4 - 30Y5 = 0$$

SUM DEW
$$Y1 + Y2 + Y3 + Y4 + Y5 <= 1$$

TRANS LIT
$$LIT - 4Y6 - 8Y7 - 12Y8 - 16Y9 = 0$$

SUM LIT
$$Y6 + Y7 + Y8 + Y9 <= 1$$

All Y = 0 or 1; DEW, LIT > 0

After we do the algebra to get all variables to the left side of the inequalities, our model is as in Table 3.7.

The SAMS quick briefing of the optimal solution is in Table 3.8.

Note that the SAMS L&IP module set $y_2 = 1$ and $y_8 = 1$, so that the optimal solution is two six-packs of Dew and three four-packs of Light, for a total profit contribution of $84. Thus, we have met what appeared to be a rather stringent packaging requirement with a profit degradation of only $3!

Generalization of the specified integer values device is straightforward. If some variable x_j can only take on values 0, $V_1, V_2, \ldots, V_k$, we let $y_1, y_2, \ldots, y_k$ be zero-one variables and substitute the following expression for x_j wherever it appears in the model (or add it to the model as a constraint):

$$x_j = \sum_{i=1}^{k} V_i y_i \tag{3.9}$$

We then add the constraint

$$\sum_{i=1}^{k} y_i \leq 1 \tag{3.10}$$

$$0 \leq y_i \leq 1 \text{ and integer}, \ i = 1, \ldots, k \tag{3.11}$$

CHAPTER 3 INTEGER (LINEAR) PROGRAMMING MODELS

TABLE 3.8 SAMS solution report for small William Hill Distillery problem

SMALL WILLIAM HILL DISTILLERY PROBLEM
QUICK BRIEFING ON OPTIMAL MODEL SOLUTION
Maximum Objective Value = 84

Decision Variable	Optimal Value	Reduced Cost
DEW	12.0	0.0
LIT	12.0	0.0
Y2	1.0	0.0
Y8	1.0	0.0

Constraint	Type	Slack
POTATOES	<	12.0
JUGS	<	6.0

Since each y_i can only be zero or one and since the sum of the y_i values must be less than or equal to one, at most one of the y_i values can be nonzero. We have limited the values of x_j to be one of the allowable values.

VALUES IN SPECIFIED INTERVALS

An extension of the concept of specified integer values for a decision variable is that a variable must either have the value zero or take on a value in one or more specified intervals. As an illustration, let us return to the revised LO-CAL Candy Company problem from an earlier section and tamper with it a bit. The solution is reproduced in the SAMS output in Table 3.9.

Because of marketing and distribution requirements, let us impose the requirements that we do not wish to produce both GOOC and CHOC and that (1) if we produce any GOOC at all, we must produce in the range 300–600 packages, and (2) if we produce CHOC, it must be in the range 600–900 packages. To model this requirement, we need two zero-one surrogate variables y_1 and y_2, and the necessary constraints are as follows:

$300 y_1 \leq GOOC \leq 600 y_1$

$600 y_2 \leq CHOC \leq 900 y_2$

$y_1 + y_2 \leq 1$

There are actually five additional constraints, and the form in which they would be added to our earlier SAMS model is

LB GOOC
$\qquad$ − GOOC $\qquad$ + 300 Y1 $\qquad$ < 0

UB GOOC
$\qquad$ + GOOC $\qquad$ − 600 Y1 $\qquad$ < 0

TABLE 3.9 SAMS full briefing for LO-CAL with values in specified intervals

```
LO-CAL CANDY COMPANY
FULL BRIEFING ON OPTIMAL MODEL SOLUTION
              Maximum Objective Value = 1495
```

Decision Variable	Optimal Value	Reduced Cost
N2-U	0.0	1.0
BO'H	284.0	0.0
CHOC	1168.0	0.0
DIET	0.0	2.0
GOOC	19.0	0.0
Y	0.0	−300.0

Constraint	Type	Slack
DARK CHOC	<	80.10
LITE CHOC	<	0.00
SUGAR	<	0.15
CARAMEL	<	20.90
NUTS	<	0.40
Y	<	0.00

LB CHOC
$$-CHOC + 600\,Y2 < 0$$

UB CHOC
$$+CHOC - 900\,Y2 < 0$$

NUM PROD
$$Y1 + Y2 < 1$$

$Y1, Y2 = 0$ or 1

The SAMS quick briefing of the solution for this model is as in Table 3.10.

Note that SAMS chose to produce CHOC rather than GOOC and that CHOC is at its upper bound in this mix. Also observe that imposing this very stringent requirement on the model reduced our total profit contribution by about 6% (from $1,495 to $1,403) and resulted in additional unused ingredients.

The extension of this modeling device to the general case is fairly obvious, and we suppress it for the sake of simplicity.

OTHER USES OF SURROGATE VARIABLE MODELING

The preceding examples of modeling with surrogate variables are meant only to illustrate the myriad possibilities of this device. We are limited only by our imagination and experience in using this approach in analyzing problems.

TABLE 3.10 SAMS solution report for LO-CAL (revised) problem

```
LO-CAL (REVISED) PROBLEM
QUICK BRIEFING ON OPTIMAL MODEL SOLUTION
           Maximum Objective Value = 1403
```

Decision Variable	Optimal Value	Reduced Cost
BITO	590.0	0.0
CHOC	900.0	0.0
Y2	1.0	0.0

Constraint	Type	Slack
DARK CHOC	<	216.0
SUGAR	<	39.5
CARAMEL	<	19.0
ASSO NUTS	<	211.0
LB CHOC	<	300.0

MODELING WITH ZERO-ONE DECISION VARIABLES

We can model many real-world problems profitably with decision variables that *themselves* take on only the values zero or one. The following paragraphs discuss some of the more useful ones.

GO/NO GO MODELS

Several modeling devices come under the "go/no-go" heading. For example, suppose the decision variables x_j, $j = 1, \ldots, n$, represent possible investments in a portfolio, so that the result "$x_3 = 1$" would mean that we would include the investment represented by x_3, while the result "$x_4 = 0$" would not include the associated stock or bond. To limit the number of different investments to, say, k out of n, we merely include the constraint

$$\sum_{j=1}^{n} x_j \leq k \qquad (3.12)$$

As another example, suppose we wish to include an investment represented by x_2 only if we purchase the investment represented by x_1. As an illustration, suppose x_2 represents Serendipity Semiconductor Trust shares and x_1 represents Serendipity's common stock; we might wish to link the two investments without eliminating the option of buying the common stock and not the trust shares. The following constraint accomplishes the result:

$$-x_1 + x_2 \leq 0 \qquad (3.13)$$

Note that x_2 can be 1 only if $x_1 = 1$ but that x_1 can take on values of 0 or 1 regardless of the values of x_2.

A third situation is that we may want the selection of a particular stock, say x_3, only if we select either x_1 or x_2 and x_1 and x_2 are mutually exclusive (we don't want to select both). Perhaps x_3 is a low-risk investment that we could select to counterbalance high-risk stocks x_1 and x_2, and x_1 and x_2 are so risky that we wish to exclude the possibility of purchasing them both. This takes two constraints, as follows:

$$x_1 + x_2 \leq 1 \tag{3.14}$$

$$-x_1 - x_2 + x_3 \leq 0 \tag{3.15}$$

In constraint (3.14), we limit the selection to either x_1 or x_2 (or neither), and in constraint (3.15) we assure that if $x_1 = x_2 = 0$, then x_3 must be 0 as well.

KNAPSACK MODEL

Another ILP model with a colorful name is the knapsack model. Imagine that our hardy backpacker is preparing to fill a knapsack for a long trek and has several dozen items strewn about on the floor. It soon becomes obvious that not everything will fit into the knapsack, and—even if it could—it would weigh far too much for the backpacker to carry. The backpacker's problem, then, is to fill the knapsack with items of a manageable total weight and at the same time give priority to the items in terms of their importance during the trek.

As a much more significant example, consider the problem of provisioning a Polaris submarine armed with nuclear missiles for a six-month (totally submerged) tour of alert duty. Obviously, there must be enough food and supplies to sustain the crew, but what kind and how many spare parts should the submarine carry? A failure of a part that the crew cannot repair on board and for which there is no spare available could abort the mission. Like the knapsack in our first example, there is limited volume and weight capacity in the submarine.

An interesting business application of the knapsack model is in establishing portfolios of financial instruments, real estate holdings, or other tangible assets. As an illustration, consider the problem faced by MUNI, a specialty brokerage firm that buys entire issues of municipal bonds and makes them available for repurchase by its clients. The managing partner has $10 million to invest and has narrowed his choices (see Table 3.11):

The quality index is a number with a value from 0 (very poor) to 10 (highest safety) computed by the firm's analysts. MUNI wishes to maximize the quality of its holdings while investing no more than $10 million and achieving an annual income of at least 7% (tax-exempt).

The SAMS quick briefing of the optimal solution is in Table 3.12.

Note that the model selected *ATL*, *BOS*, *DEN*, *GAI*, and *IND* for the portfolio, exactly investing the $10 million available and having an average quality rating of $42/5 = 8.4$ (actually, if we weight the quality ratings by price, the average is nearer 8.3). The portfolio produces income of $700,100. As an aside, knapsack models are known to be quite finicky. For example, if we change the price of *ATL* from 1.6 to 1.7 so that the optimal portfolio above is no longer feasible, we get the following result:

Portfolio: BOS, CHI, ELP, GAI, HOU
Average Risk: 8.22 Average Weighted Risk: 8.11
Income: $713,400
Investment: $10 million (exactly)

TABLE 3.11 MUNI list of municipal bond issues

Symbol	Price ($ M)	Quality Index	Annual Income ($000)
ATL	1.6	8.2	113.6
BOS	2.1	7.9	155.4
CHI	1.9	8.5	123.5
DEN	2.5	7.7	192.4
ELP	1.3	7.2	104.0
FRA	3.5	9.1	213.5
GAI	0.9	9.5	53.1
HOU	3.8	8.0	277.4
IND	2.9	8.7	185.6
JAC	2.4	7.0	189.6

TABLE 3.12 SAMS quick briefing for MUNI

MUNI PROBLEM MATHEMATICAL MODEL

MAX
$8.2\, ATL + 7.9\, BOS + 8.5\, CHI + 7.7\, DEN + 7.2\, ELP + 9.1\, FRA + 9.5\, GAI + 8\, HOU + 8.7\, IND + 7\, JAC$

S T:

CAPITAL
$1.6\, ATL + 2.1\, BOS + 1.9\, CHI + 2.5\, DEN + 1.3\, ELP + 3.5\, FRA + 0.9\, GAI + 3.8\, HOU + 2.9\, IND + 2.4\, JAC < 10$

INCOME
$113.6\, ATL + 155.4\, BOS + 123.5\, CHI + 192.4\, DEN + 104\, ELP + 213.5\, FRA + 53.1\, GAI + 277.4\, HOU + 185.6\, IND + 189.6\, JAC > 700$

All variables 0 or 1

MUNI
QUICK BRIEFING ON OPTIMAL MODEL SOLUTION

Maximum Objective Value = 42

Decision Variable	Optimal Value	Reduced Cost
ATL	1.0	0.0
BOS	1.0	0.0
DEN	1.0	0.0
GAI	1.0	0.0
IND	1.0	0.0

Constraint	Type	Slack
Income	>	0.1

The general mathematical formulation of the classical knapsack problem is as follows:

$$\text{MAX } x_0 = \sum_{j=1}^{n} c_j x_j \tag{3.16}$$

$$\text{S T:} \quad \sum_{j=1}^{n} v_j x_j \leq V \tag{3.17}$$

$$\sum_{j=1}^{n} w_j x_j \leq W \tag{3.18}$$

$$x_j = 0 \text{ or } 1$$

In Equation (3.16) the c_j are coefficients representing the level of priority or importance of the items x_j, which are zero-one integer variables (i.e., if $x_j = 1$, we include item j). In Equation (3.17), the v_j are the individual volumes of the items and V is the maximum allowable volume. Likewise, in Equation (3.18) the w_j are item weights and W is the maximum allowable weight. Obviously, there could be other constraints, such as height or width restrictions or shape. The quaint but complex minicase entitled "Backpacking" later in the chapter deals with a knapsack model complicated by several side conditions.

There are other models such as those described above, and only our cleverness and imagination limit the applications of zero-one modeling. The next section discusses computational considerations.

SOLUTION APPROACHES: AN INTUITIVE DESCRIPTION

Harvey Wagner [13] uses such expressions as "quest for a philosopher's stone" and "the search of a lifetime" to describe research into efficient ways to find optimal solutions to ILP models. That is, researchers have for years sought a well-behaved, dependable, and efficient method like the SIMPLEX algorithm, which would "civilize" ILP models. Wagner's terms first appeared in print in 1971. We are not much nearer to the solution now than we were then. Why is this so?

The following is "first cousin" of the toy model in Chapter 2:

$$\text{MAX } x_0 = x_1 + x_2 \tag{3.19}$$
$$\text{S T:} \quad -29x_1 + 42x_2 \leq 147 \tag{3.20}$$
$$5x_1 - 2x_2 \leq 7 \tag{3.21}$$
$$-5x_1 + 7x_2 \geq 21 \tag{3.22}$$
$$x_1, x_2 \geq 0 \text{ and integer} \tag{3.23}$$

As we can see in Figure 3.2, the solution to the "relaxed" LP problem [without integer restrictions in Equation (3.23)] is

$$x_0^* = 10.04; \ x_1^* = 3.87; \ x_2^* = 6.17$$

Why not round off the LP solution to get the ILP solution? You might wish to try this on the above problem some rainy afternoon. After all, since $x_0^* = 10.04$, neither x_1 nor x_2 can be larger than 10, so that there are only $11 \times 11 = 121$ (remember zero) possible combinations of (x_1, x_2) pairs. If you do the enumeration, you will find that

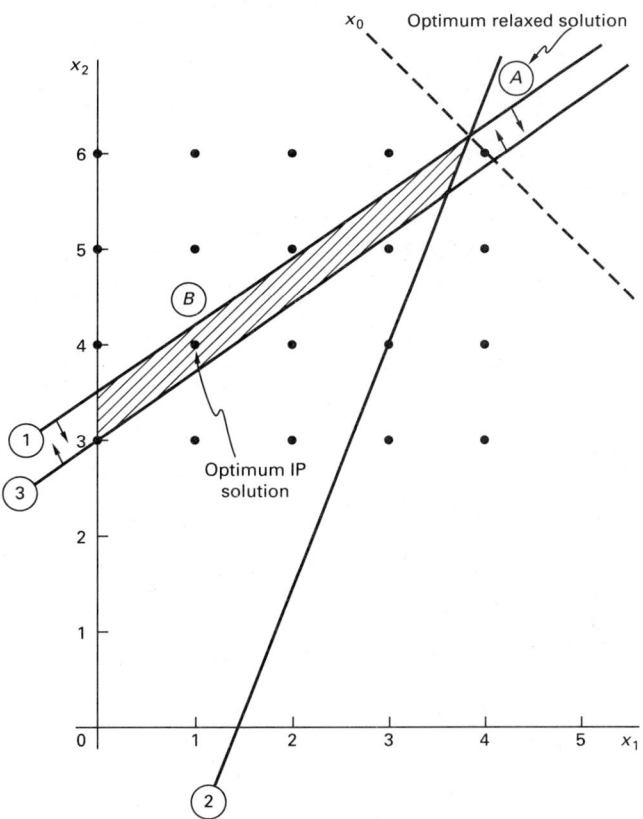

FIGURE 3.2
"First cousin" of the toy model

the solution is $x_0^* = 5$; $x_1^* = 1$; $x_2^* = 4$. So much for rounding when we must have an integral solution to an ILP model.

Let's now briefly discuss three general solution approaches.

BRANCH AND BOUND

In the early 1960s, Land and Doig [10] introduced branch and bound (B&B) as a technique for solving ILP models. B&B was later improved upon by Dakin [5]. Also referred to as a "tree search," B&B is a method for partially enumerating solutions to combinatorial problems in an efficient way. Although we will avoid the mathematical details, the approach is simple and logical; the following allegory illustrates B&B:

> Ernie, a scoutmaster, decides to lead his young charges in Troop 66 on an overnight camping expedition in Fathombranch State Park. The heavily forested park has 30 campsites with trails connecting them in the curiously orderly way depicted in Figure 3.3. One must enter the park at the circle labeled "zero" and may then proceed into the park, always remaining on the trails. The numbered circles represent campsites.
>
> Being a highly conscientious and devoted leader, Ernie decided that nothing but the best will do for his charges, and he is determined to locate the very best campsite in the park for their expedition. He is concerned about the amount of time it would take to investigate all 30 sites but is optimistic that something will turn up to help them avoid that eventuality. Therefore, kerchiefs in place and packs bulging, the troop stands at the entrance. For lack of a better way to start, Ernie flips a coin, and the entourage proceeds down the path to campsite #1.

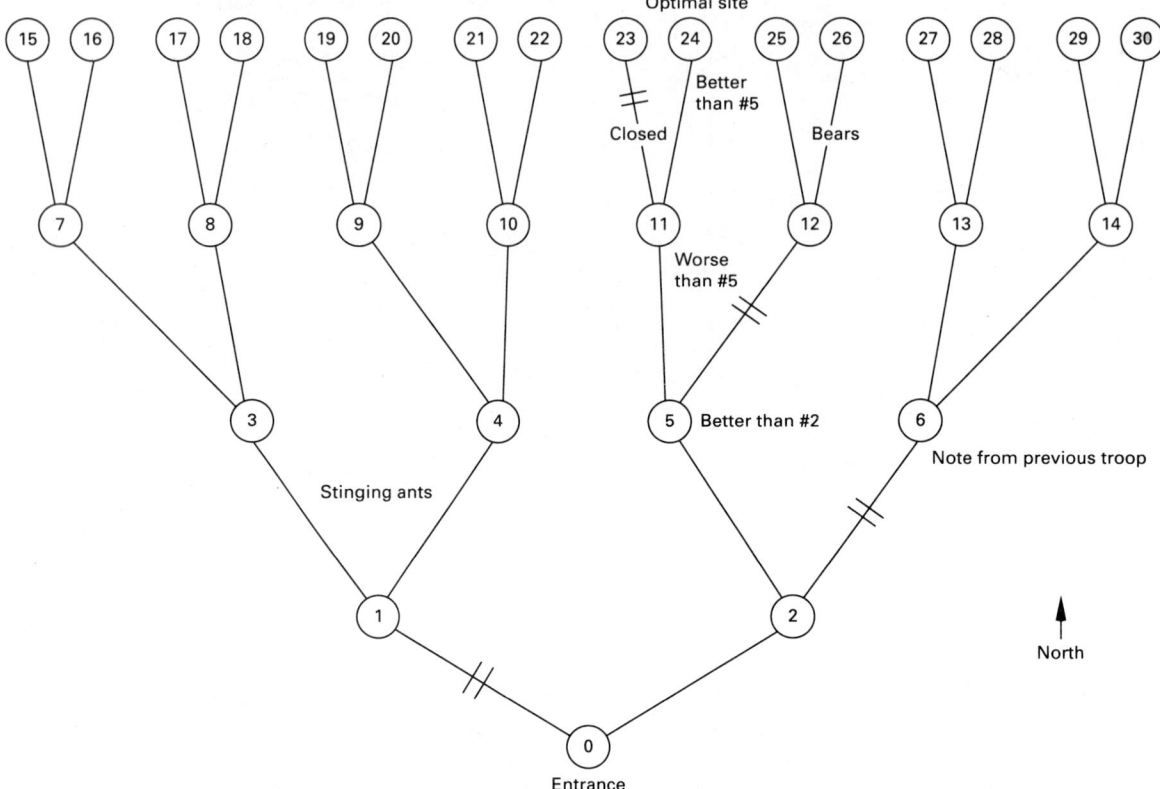

FIGURE 3.3 Fathombranch State Park

Ernie's luck is with him when the troop happens upon a forest ranger at campsite #1. It seems that stinging ants have invaded the entire west side of the park, so that camping on any of those 15 sites would be unacceptable at best. Ernie notes that his problem has been cut in half at one fell swoop and leads the troop back to the entrance and thence down the path to campsite #2.

Campsite #2 is acceptable, but Ernie wants the best. From afar, campsite #6 looks more promising than campsite #5, so the troop makes its way there. Again, they are in luck. A note written by a previous visiting troop and pinned to a tree states: "This is a better campsite than any of those to the north." But Ernie has judged campsite #2 to be better than campsite #6, so it must also be better than the other six to the north. Again, Ernie is most pleased. The troop has eliminated seven additional sites, leaving only eight to go.

At campsite #5, the troop agrees that it is better than campsite #2, so only seven candidates remain. Site #11 looks more promising than site #12 from afar but turns out to be worse than site #5. However, a "temporarily closed" sign on the trail to campsite #23 eliminates it, and a trip to campsite #24 reveals that it is better than site #5. Thus, they have eliminated all sites except #12, #24, #25, and #26.

When the troop arrives at site #12, they spot a family of bears just to the north. Deciding that caution is the better part of valor, they return to campsite #24 for the night. Thus, the troop has found the best available campsite of the 30 by actually visiting only six.

Rather than particularizing B&B to ILP problems at this point, let us discuss its jargon in more general terms. The information from the forest ranger allowed Ernie to **fathom** the entire branch emanating from campsite #1. Since campsite #2 was acceptable, Ernie now had a **lower bound** for the quality of the best campsite. The troop then **branched** to the set of campsites emanating from campsite #6 but found that campsite #6 **dominated** the campsites beyond it and that it was worse than the previous **incumbent** campsite #2. The troop then **backtracked** to campsite #5, since they had fathomed the branch emanating from campsite #6.

The troop then branched at campsite #5, branched again at campsite #11, and found the new incumbent to be campsite #24. One last backtrack to campsite #12 did not replace the present incumbent and allowed only an infeasible branching. So we see that the troop had found the optimal campsite at #24, but it took a backtrack and one more branching attempt to verify that fact.

B&B AND ILP

To solve an ILP problem with B&B, we first solve the associated LP problem with the SIMPLEX algorithm. If all variables are integer-valued, we are done—it must be the solution to the associated ILP problem.

If one or more variables are fractional, the algorithm selects one (which one is not important for our purposes) and solves two more LP problems—one with an additional constraint that limits the variable to be less than or equal to its rounded-down value and the other with a constraint that limits the variable to be greater than or equal to its rounded-up value (it must, of course, be one or the other). If we get no feasible solution to one of the problems, we have fathomed an entire branch. Otherwise we proceed to branch and backtrack, recording integer solutions as they occur, but retaining only the incumbent as a lower bound. Thus we can "cut off" (or fathom) branches in one of two ways—by finding them infeasible or by finding that our current incumbent is better than any solution on that branch.

What a simple and elegant device! However, you may be concerned about all those LP problems that we must solve along the way. We use a device called DUAL SIMPLEX (briefly mentioned in Chapter 2) to incorporate the new constraints into the previous optimal tableau in very few additional iterations. If you are still vaguely troubled about this simple, logical approach (in light of things like "philosophers' stones" and "searches of a lifetime"), read on.

COMPUTATIONAL DIFFICULTIES WITH B&B

As Charlie Brown might observe: "Things are never as simple as they seem." And as usual, Charlie is right. For example, we know what an integer is—it is recognizable instantly and without question by a first grader. But how about the electronic mainframe computer that cost three million dollars? If through almost unavoidable round-off error in the LP solution, the computer determines that $x_1 = 3.99999999$, it will possibly cut off the solution $x_1 = 4$, leaving 3 as the integral result in x_1. We can use something called double precision in the computer to alleviate this difficulty, but nothing will completely eliminate it.

Another serious difficulty with B&B algorithms is that they are entirely unpredictable. That is, on one problem they might locate the optimum solution very quickly because of the nature of the problem and the type of rules used for branching. On other problems, the rules may choose the wrong path many times and end up having to enumerate a high percentage of possibilities. For example, if all our n variables are zero-one variables, there are 2^n possible combinations. If there are 332 such variables, for example, there are about $8.75(10^{99})$ combinations. Researchers have constructed problems with special structures that would lead a B&B algorithm with specific features to enumerate every possible combination of variables. And 332 variables is not very many when we are modeling real-world problems.

However, things are not as bleak as we have portrayed them. Most consider B&B algorithms to be the computational "champs" at the present time, compared to the all-integer cutting plane approach, discussed next. Many operational models are indeed solved successfully by available commercial codes, and you should not abandon integer modeling because solution techniques are less than perfectly dependable.

CUTTING PLANES   The logic behind B&B is simple and obvious—we merely enumerate some of the possible solutions while implicitly discarding most. The all-integer cutting plane approach, on the other hand, is not so simple to understand, in the sense of a nontechnically trained decision maker. We discuss it here, however, because of recent advances in research that make cutting plane algorithms better computational contenders.

Let's try to get a feeling for the mathematically elegant and intuitively appealing cutting plane. A cutting plane is nothing more than an additional constraint derived from the regular model constraints. We incorporate it into the associated LP model by adding it to the constraint set and performing iterations with the SIMPLEX algorithm. In effect, it "cuts off" parts of the LP feasible region without eliminating an optimal integer point.

As an illustration, let's retrieve our toy model from Chapter 2 and take a look at Figure 3.4. Note that there are ten feasible integer (sometimes called lattice) points, represented by the black dots. The dark lines connecting eight of these points describe what is called the **integer hull** of the feasible region. By the same intuition we evoked to understand why an optimal LP solution must include a vertex, it is obvious (we hope) that any solution to the associated ILP problem must be a lattice point on the integer hull of the feasible region.

You're probably thinking, "If we had the three constraints (plus the nonnegativity constraints, of course) that describe the convex hull, we could solve the ILP problem using ordinary SIMPLEX, since the vertices would all be integers." That's precisely what cutting plane algorithms attempt to do—to derive additional constraints called **cuts** from the original model constraints. These cuts remove pieces of the original constraint set in an effort to define as much of the integer hull as needed to form a vertex at the optimal lattice point. Since we are using the ordinary SIMPLEX technique, it will recognize the optimal solution when it finds this vertex. In our toy model, we see that moving the objective function parallel to itself toward the origin encounters the first lattice point at $x_1 = 3$ and $x_2 = 1$. This, then, is the optimal solution to the ILP model.

TYPES OF CUTTING PLANE ALGORITHMS

An in-depth discussion of the mechanics of cutting plane algorithms is inappropriate in this text. Briefly, cutting planes may be fractional or all-integer. The fractional technique of Gomory [8] begins at the optimal solution to the relaxed LP model and cuts off slivers of the feasible region until it locates the optimal lattice point. This technique never locates a feasible lattice point until it locates the optimal one, so no usable solution is available until it does so. This method suffers from computer round-off error just as B&B techniques do.

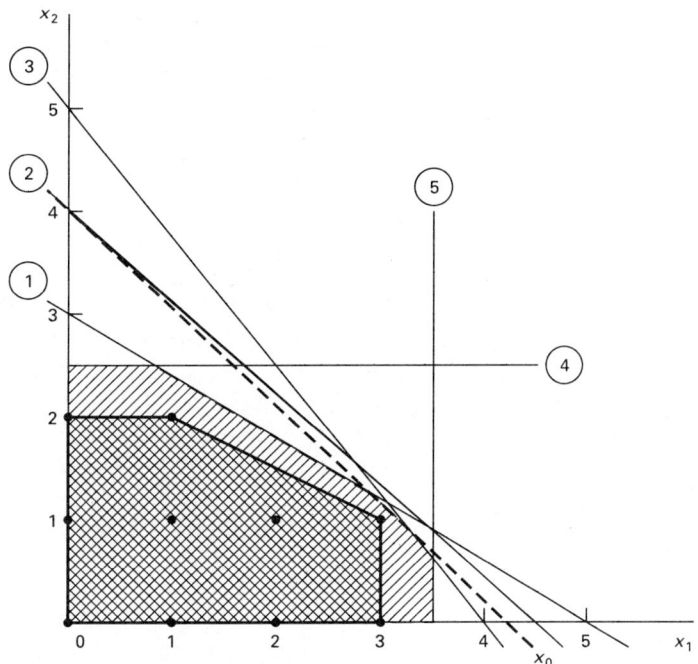

FIGURE 3.4
Example problem revisited

All-integer cutting plane algorithms require that all model parameters be integer valued from the start. This is not particularly a problem, since most input data are rational numbers and we can convert them into integers quite easily. These algorithms generate "cuts" in such a way that each SIMPLEX iteration produces yet another all-integer solution.

Researchers have taken three basic approaches to constructing all-integer cutting plane algorithms: primal, dual, and hybrid (combination of primal and dual). All that managers need to know about this very technical subject is that primal approaches such as Young's **Simplified Primal Algorithm** [15] do not work well in practice. Dual algorithms such as Austin and Hanna's **Bounded Descent Algorithm** [2] and Hanna's **Advanced Start Algorithm** [9] have shown promising results, but the jury is still out at this writing. The **Constructive Primal-Dual Algorithm** of Ghandforoush and Austin [7] is a hybrid technique and appears to work well on highly degenerate models (i.e., there are many zeros in the objective function and the right-hand side of the constraints). The fixed-charge problem discussed earlier is an example of such models.

COMPUTATIONAL EFFICIENCY

All-integer cutting plane algorithms have one very important advantage—they do not suffer from the round-off error inherent in B&B and fractional cutting plane techniques. We merely tell our computer that everything it sees is an integer, and it proceeds to solve the model for us.

However, regardless of their advantages, the truth (at least, at this writing) is that cutting plane algorithms have not performed as efficiently as B&B algorithms on real-world problems. In fact, until a recent flurry of research activity into all-integer cutting planes, researchers had given them up for dead. This recent research has revived hope that researchers can construct efficient algorithms using this elegant approach, but only time will tell.

ZERO-ONE MODELS

As is true throughout this text, investigators have developed special techniques to analyze models with special structures. For ILP models whose variables are all zero-one, Balas [3] invented a technique called the **additive algorithm.** Referred to in the literature as a *partial enumeration* scheme, the additive algorithm works in a way very similar to B&B—taking advantage of the special nature of the integer variables. The technique is very efficient and does not suffer from computer round-off error.

DEVELOPING ALTERNATIVE SOLUTIONS

Everything that we said in the section on developing alternatives in Chapter 2 is also true for ILP except that it is not as tidy for ILP as it was for LP. Unfortunately, there are no such things as shadow prices for ILP models. The reason is that the divisibility assumption in LP resulted in linear—and therefore continuous—constraints and objective function. Since we are dealing in ILP with a set of discrete lattice points, all bets are off in trying to determine rates of change or shadow prices. Does this mean that a decision maker must accept the initial solution to the ILP model as her or his only input? Of course not.

ALTERNATIVES WITH BRANCH AND BOUND

If you are doing your analysis with a B&B code, have your analyst modify the algorithm to print out every feasible integer solution obtained along the way. Alternatively, some computer B&B codes have a "kth best solution" feature, which will find the k (whatever k you wish) solutions having the best objective values.

ALTERNATIVES WITH CUTTING PLANES

As with branch and bound, if we are using a primal code like Young's **SPA,** we can have our programmer save every feasible solution found along the way to attaining optimality. For dual algorithms, unfortunately, the code finds no feasible solutions prior to reaching optimality, so this device is of no value in this regard.

However, cutting plane algorithms do lend themselves to the development of suboptimal (but very good) solutions to maximization problems by the use of an interesting device called the *objective cut*. Suppose we have obtained the optimal solution to the model, x_0^*. By the simple device of adding a constraint,

$$\sum_{j=1}^{n} c_j x_j \leq x_0^* - 1, \qquad (3.24)$$

and continuing the iteration with a dual algorithm like the **SAMS** module, we will eventually derive a feasible solution with a value of "$x_0^* - 1$" or less. Although we are not interested here in the technical details regarding how to derive the cut, it is intuitively appealing that such a cut works in practice. Obviously, we could add such a constraint to the original LP relaxation in a branch and bound algorithm, but—unlike the case when using a cutting plane technique—we must restart the B&B code from scratch.

SENSITIVITY ANALYSIS IN ILP

Since we do not have shadow prices in ILP to guide our sensitivity analysis of the solution to our models, we must resort to ad hoc procedures to check the effects of data inaccuracies on our solution to the model. For example, we give here the "stepsister" of our toy model from Chapter 2 and graph it in Figure 3.5.

CHAPTER 3 INTEGER (LINEAR) PROGRAMMING MODELS 113

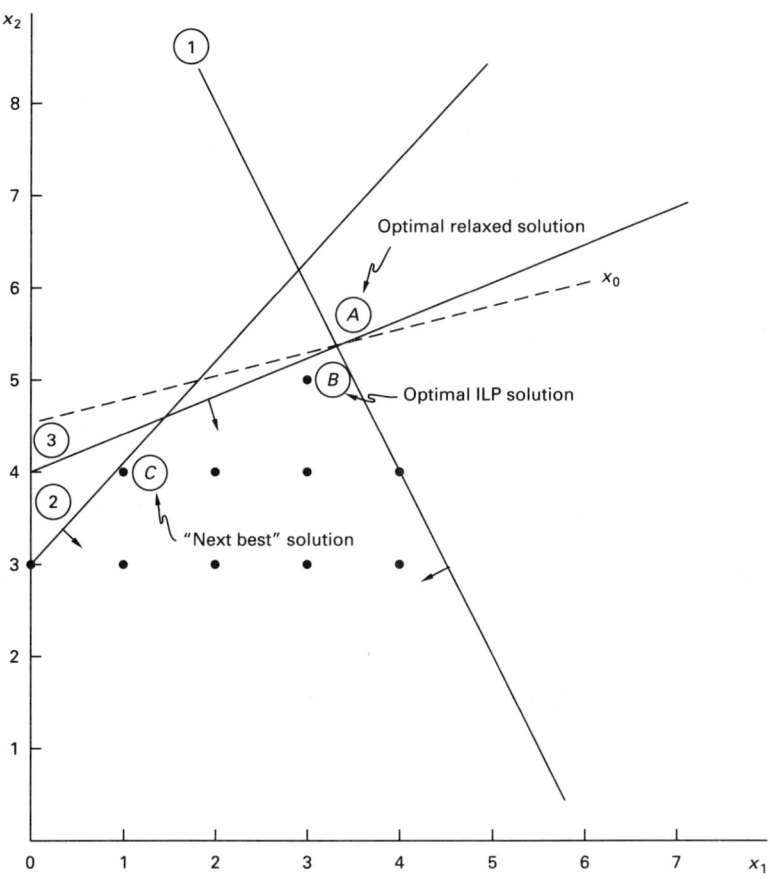

FIGURE 3.5
"Stepsister" of toy model

$$\text{MAX } x_0 = -2x_1 + 7x_2 \tag{3.25}$$
$$\text{S T:} \quad 2x_1 + x_2 \leq 12 \tag{3.26}$$
$$-7x_1 + 6x_2 \leq 18 \tag{3.27}$$
$$-3x_1 + 7x_2 \leq 28 \tag{3.28}$$
$$x_1, x_2 \geq 0 \text{ and integer} \tag{3.29}$$

The optimal values of the relaxed LP solution, the optimal values of the ILP solution, and the values of the "next best" ILP solution are in Table 3.13.

Note from the relaxed solution and from the optimal ILP solution, we might conclude that the resource represented by constraint (3.27) is not particularly a problem, since in both cases the slack is rather large. Since the reverse is true for the first and third constraints, we would be tempted to ignore possible inaccuracies related to constraint (3.27) and concentrate our attention on constraints (3.26) and (3.28). However, if we proceed to find the next best ILP solution in order to develop alternatives, we find that although this solution has a value only about 10% away from the optimal solution, the resource represented by the second constraint is uncomfortably close to depletion, while the first and third are less so. This erratic behavior of ILP models illustrates the difficulty of performing an orderly, dependable sensitivity analysis and is especially troublesome when our model contains many zero-one variables.

TABLE 3.13

	Relaxed Solution	Optimal ILP Solution	"Next Best" ILP Solution
x_0	31.29	29	26
x_1	3.29	3	1
x_2	5.41	5	4
s_1	0.00	1	6
s_2	8.59	9	1
s_3	0.00	2	3

The bottom line to this discussion is that the manager who uses ILP models as an aid to decision making must be acutely aware of the limitations to analysis of the output and must account for those limitations when using that output.

EXTENSIONS OF ILP MODELING

Earlier in the chapter, we looked at some modeling devices commonly used in ILP modeling. Most were straightforward and fairly easy to grasp. This section discusses some more sophisticated—but still useful—ILP modeling devices.

REDUCTION TO ZERO-ONE MODELS

As noted previously, Balas's additive algorithm is a highly efficient technique for solving ILP models with only zero-one variables. What if we could reduce any all-integer ILP model to one that has only zero-one variables? If so, we could take advantage of the power of Balas's technique and avoid having to resort to the B&B or the cutting plane technique.

Suppose in an all-integer ILP model we have available upper bounds u_j for each variable x_j (either explicitly stated or derivable implicitly from the problem constraints). For each variable x_j, we can derive an equivalent expression in terms of the weighted sum of zero-one variables y_{ij} as follows:

$$x_j = \sum_{i=0}^{K} 2^i y_{ij}, \qquad (3.30)$$

where

$$2^K \leq u_j < 2^{K+1} \qquad (3.31)$$

We call the relationships in Equations (3.30) and (3.31) a *binary representation* of x_j, explained in the following example.

Suppose the upper bound is $u_j = 9$ for x_j, so that x_j can take on only the integral values $x_j = 0, 1, 2, \ldots, 9$. Then Equation (3.31) becomes

$$x_j = y_{1j} + 2y_{2j} + 4y_{3j} + 8y_{4j}, \qquad (3.32)$$

since in Equation (3.31), $2^3(= 8) \leq u_j(= 9) \leq 2^4(= 16)$, so that $K = 3$.

TABLE 3.14

x_j	y_{1j}	y_{2j}	y_{3j}	y_{4j}
0	0	0	0	0
1	1	0	0	0
2	0	1	0	0
3	1	1	0	0
4	0	0	1	0
5	1	0	1	0
6	0	1	1	0
7	1	1	1	0
8	0	0	0	1
9	1	0	0	1

To obtain the ten allowable values of x_j, the algorithm would set the y_{ij} values in Table 3.14.

If the upper bound "$x_j \leq 9$" is implicit from the other constraints, we need go no further. On the other hand, if it is an explicit upper bound, we merely replace the constraint "$x_j \leq 9$" with "$y_{ij} + 2y_{2j} + 4y_{3j} + 8y_{4j} \leq 9$."

"But," you may be thinking, "what if I have a small ILP model with only 50 integer variables and the upper bounds are in the neighborhood of 100. For $u_j = 100$, K would be 6—which means that I'd end up with about 350 zero-one variables rather than 50 ordinary integer variables." If you are skeptical about this, recall that as the variable values get larger and larger, we as decision makers become more and more comfortable with rounding the values of the associated relaxed LP model to get "reasonable" solutions to the ILP model. Thus, the binary transformation is useful in those cases in which small upper bounds are involved (e.g., when we are dealing with numbers of airplanes or five-axis milling machines or other costly, low-volume entities).

TRAVELING SALESMAN MODEL

The so-called traveling salesman problem is a prototype model applicable to a great many practical problems. The traveling salesman allegory is as follows. A salesman must visit each of his 11 clients in the southeast. Since he works on straight commission, he must pay his own travel expenses, and gasoline prices are "eating his lunch." If he can find the shortest route that visits each of the 11 towns and gets him home, he can save a lot of money.

Figure 3.6 depicts the salesman's problem, and the triangular matrix in Table 3.15 gives distances between the towns.

"Let's see," he thinks. "Why don't I just lay out all possible routes, figure the distance of each one, and use the cheapest." Good thinking, except that there are 11! (11 factorial) possibilities—that's **39,916,800**. Back to the drawing board.

If we let $x_{ij} = 1$ if the tour should include the leg from town i to town j (and zero if not) and let c_{ij} be the associated distance, we can model the problem as follows:

$$\text{MIN } x_0 = \sum_{i=1}^{12} \sum_{j=1}^{12} c_{ij} x_{ij} \tag{3.33}$$

$$\text{S T:} \quad \sum_{j=1}^{12} x_{ij} = 1, \, i = 1, \ldots, 12 \tag{3.34}$$

$$\sum_{i=1}^{12} x_{ij} = 1, \, j = 1, \ldots, 12 \tag{3.35}$$

$$u_i - u_j + 12 x_{ij} \leq 11, \, i, j = 2, \ldots, 12 \text{ and } i \neq j \tag{3.36}$$

$$x_{ij} = 0 \text{ or } 1 \text{ for all } i, j$$

FIGURE 3.6
Traveling salesman's territory

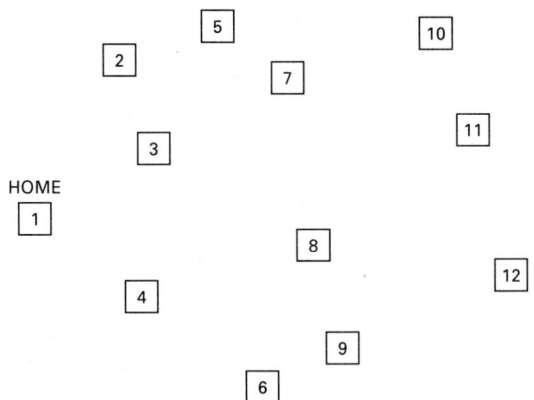

TABLE 3.15 Traveling Salesman distance matrix

NODES		1	2	3	4	5	6	7	8	9	10	11	12
Dist	1	.	50	43	40	78	90	92	94	111	131	134	144
Dist	2		.	32	64	31	103	54	80	110	92	104	127
Dist	3			.	36	44	71	50	56	81	92	93	109
Dist	4				.	79	51	80	66	73	117	112	113
Dist	5					.	103	26	64	101	61	71	106
Dist	6						.	91	53	30	115	98	79
Dist	7							.	44	82	40	50	81
Dist	8								.	38	64	49	50
Dist	9									.	96	77	51
Dist	10										.	28	71
Dist	11											.	44
Dist	12												.

CHAPTER 3 INTEGER (LINEAR) PROGRAMMING MODELS 117

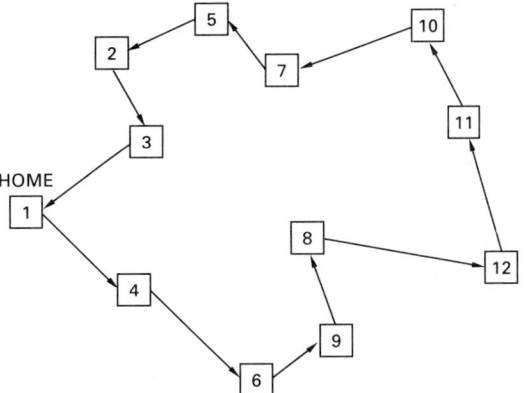

FIGURE 3.7 Solution to traveling salesman's problem

This no doubt requires explanation. Equation (3.33) is the objective function that sums up distances for the n legs of the tour (in our example, $n = 12$). Constraints (3.34) and (3.35) merely assure that each site is a departure point and an arrival point exactly once. This makes sense. But what are constraints (3.36), and where did the u-variables come from? As we have seen before, computers and their associated optimizing algorithms are most obedient—but unbelievably dumb. If we do not include constraints (3.36), we may get a "solution" that contains subtours.

So, in our example, the salesman would not have to enumerate all possible tours. He would merely need to set up and solve an ILP model with 1,440 variables and several hundred constraints.

You should be suspicious at this point. As we shall shortly learn, an ILP model of this size is very difficult to solve with existing techniques. But people solve traveling salesman models involving a hundred or more "stops"—sometimes daily—to assist managers in making decisions. This is yet another example of a model looking for a problem. We can solve traveling salesman models for their optimal solutions by the dynamic programming techniques discussed in Chapter 6. The truth is, however, that we can obtain good (but perhaps not optimal) solutions easily by heuristic (nonoptimizing) algorithms invented expressly for that purpose. The SAMS package contains such a module, and its (not necessarily optimal) solution to our salesman's problem is Figure 3.7.

MINICASES

Disk-O-Tech

THE SCENARIO

Disk-o-Tech, Inc., is a manufacturer of drum-disk memory units that are compatible with several popular minicomputers. The drums are modularized, each having 100 megabytes of memory, and can be wired together to make units of three, four, or six memory packs. Disk-o-Tech plants must perform the hook-up before shipping them to order.

The company has three plants in Ramville, Remburg, and Romtown, with production capacities of 21, 13, and 22 modules per week, respectively. The current week's orders are as follows:

1. Four three-module packs to Tuscaloosa, Alabama.
2. Four four-module packs to Tempe, Arizona.
3. Three six-module packs to Toledo, Ohio.

THE PROBLEM

The memory packs are very fragile and require expensive packaging prior to shipment. They also require special handling during shipment, which adds additional cost. Table 3.16 gives the shipping and handling cost per module. (*Note:* The cost per pack of n modules is merely n times the cost per module.)

The computer memory supply business is highly competitive, and Disk-o-Tech's profit margins have become razor thin. The firm's CEO has turned his attention to cost control as a possible way to retain Disk-o-Tech's market share, and the high transportation outlay caught his eye.

Entering the office of the company's director of distribution, the CEO queries:

"Can't you do any better on the shipping costs? I just got your figures for next week, and the charges come to almost $40,000. That'll put us in the red."

"Boss," replies the director, "here's the schedule I worked out [Table 3.17]."

TABLE 3.16 Disk-o-Tech Shipping Costs

		To		
		Tuscaloosa	Tempe	Toledo
From	Ramville	$600	$ 900	$600
	Remburg	800	800	700
	Romtown	500	1200	600

Note: Costs are per module.

TABLE 3.17 Shipping Schedule

		To			
		Tuscaloosa	Tempe	Toledo	Capacity
From	Ramville			18 (3)	21
	Remburg	12 (4)			13
	Romtown		16 (4)		22
	Requirements	12 (4)	16 (4)	18 (3)	

Note: Shipments are in modules (packs).
Shipping Cost: $39,600

"I know the costs seem high, but you've got to understand what I'm up against. When I put the problem in the computer, the LP package keeps giving me nonsense answers. For example, the last run said to ship 13 modules from the Ramville plant to Toledo, but Toledo wants four-module packs, and I can get only three packs out of 13 modules. What do I do with the extra module? I even tried putting in some extra LP constraints to get it to come out right, but then the computer started giving me answers in fractions of modules. If you want my honest opinion, this LP stuff isn't all it's cracked up to be."

THE MODEL

With the help of a management science consultant, Disk-o-Tech modeled the problem by IP. The key was in recognizing that the decision variables, representing shipments from the three plants to the three customers, must take on specified integer values.

Let x_{ij} = the number of modules shipped from plant i to customer j (i = 1, 2, 3 and j = 1, 2, 3, in the order listed in Table 3.16). Then, for example, x_{11}, x_{21}, and x_{31} represent shipments to Tuscaloosa and must take on values that are multiples of three. Likewise, the variables representing shipments to Tempe and Toledo must take on values that are multiples of four and six, respectively. Mathematically, we formulate the model as follows.

Let y_{ijk} be zero-one variables and let m_j be the module multiples (i.e., $m_1 = 3$, $m_2 = 4$, $m_3 = 6$). Let T_{ij} be the integer part of MIN(S_i, R_j)/m_j, where S_i is the capacity of the ith plant and R_j is the requirement for the jth customer.

For example, T_{22} = integer part of MIN(13, 16)/4 = 3. We then make the following substitutions for the x_{ij}.

$$x_{ij} = \sum_{k=1}^{T_{ij}} k m_j y_{ijk}, \quad i, j = 1, 2, 3 \tag{3.42}$$

For example,

$$x_{22} = \sum_{k=1}^{3} k(4) y_{ijk} = 4 y_{221} + 8 y_{222} + 12 y_{223} \tag{3.43}$$

Then, by adding constraints such as

$$\sum_{k=1}^{3} y_{22k} \leq 1, \tag{3.44}$$

we force x_{22} to take on only the values 0, 4, 8, or 12 (since the y-variables are zero-one). Before making the substitutions for the x_{ij}, the model appears as follows:

MIN $x_0 = 600 x_{11} + 900 x_{12} + 600 x_{13} + 800 x_{21} + 800 x_{22}$
$\qquad + 700 x_{23} + 500 x_{31} + 1200 x_{32} + 600 x_{33}$ (3.45)

S T: $\qquad x_{11} + x_{12} + x_{13} \leq 21$ (3.46)

$\qquad\qquad x_{21} + x_{22} + x_{23} \leq 13$ (3.47)

$\qquad\qquad x_{31} + x_{32} + x_{33} \leq 22$ (3.48)

$\qquad\qquad x_{11} + x_{21} + x_{31} = 12$ (3.49)

$$x_{12} + x_{22} + x_{32} = 16 \tag{3.50}$$

$$x_{13} + x_{23} + x_{33} = 18 \tag{3.51}$$

$$x_{ij} \geq 0, \, i, j = 1, 2, 3 \tag{3.52}$$

In the model, we are attempting to minimize total transportation cost in Equation (3.45). Constraints (3.46) to (3.48) ensure that the plants do not ship more than they are capable of producing, and constraints (3.49) to (3.51) ensure that we fill the customers' orders.

After transforming the above model using the substitution in Equation (3.42), we have a model with

1. 33 zero-one variables
2. 6 original constraints of the form (3.46) to (3.51)
3. 9 constraints of the form (3.44)

SOLUTION TO THE MODEL

A computerized IP package solved this model in five minutes on an AT-compatible microcomputer, requiring 100 branchings. Rather than actually replacing the nine x_{ij} variables with their y-transformations, we merely added the nine transforming equations as constraints. This resulted in a model with 31 zero-one variables, 9 general integer variables, and 15 constraints.

The SAMS solution is in Table 3.18.

SOLUTION TO THE PROBLEM

After inspecting the model solution carefully, the CEO decided to implement the plan without alteration—with savings this week of $9,600 over the original schedule. As it turned out, each plant had at least one excess module, so that if final inspection before shipment discovered a faulty module in a pack, at least one spare would be available. Furthermore, the smallest plant (Remburg) would ship its total output to Tempe and would be concerned only with assembling four-module packs.

Disk-o-Tech used the IP computer package recommended by the consultant routinely thereafter in analyzing its shipping schedule, and the CEO considered the consultant's fee to be money well spent.

TABLE 3.18 Optimal Disk-o-Tech Model Solution

		To			
		Tuscaloosa	Tempe	Toledo	Not Shipped
From	Ramville		4 (1)	12 (2)	5
	Remburg		12 (3)		1
	Romtown	12 (4)		6 (1)	4

Note: Shipments are in modules (packs).
Shipping Cost: $30,000

BLL, Inc.

THE SCENARIO

Business Learning Laboratories, Inc. (BLL), conducts noncredit professional courses for administrators, secretaries, executives, financial and marketing analysts, and others wishing to update and sharpen their technical and administrative skills. The courses vary in length from a day to two weeks and run the gamut from "Interpersonal Skills for File Clerks" to "International Macromarketing for CEOs." Leaders for the majority of the seminars are professors from colleges and universities in the vicinity of the course locations in more than 40 cities across the country. BLL does employ some full-time seminar leaders, however.

The professional development seminar business is lucrative but highly cash-flow intensive. That is, during the busy season, there must be a large amount of cash available to pay for up-front expenses, such as preparation of program materials and room reservations. Except for advance deposits required for certain high-cost programs, revenues tend to lag expenses by two to six weeks.

THE PROBLEM

During the off-season, BLL had followed the practice of letting cash build up in its operational accounts as activity slowed and revenue came in from busy-season programs. Professor Max Float, who taught a program on cash management for the company, found out about this practice. He suggested that BLL look into short-term (30-day) commercial paper as a means of putting idle cash to work during the slow season. Connie Mann, the founder and CEO of BLL, liked the idea and instructed her brokers, CH&S, to propose appropriate investments. CH&S recommended 30-day instruments (see Table 3.19).

In the current period, Connie estimated that BLL had $5,370,000 in excess cash to invest. CH&S recommended buying 10 units of venture capital loans for maximum return (and maximum brokerage fees, of course), and filling out the portfolio with two industrial notes. The high-risk classification of the venture loans bothered Connie, however, and she placed the following managerial restrictions on the composition of the portfolio:

1. We should devote at least 10% of the total investment to each of the three types of instruments other than venture capital loans.

TABLE 3.19 30-Day instruments

Instrument	Denomination	Annual Interest Rate	Risk Class
U.S. treasury bills	$100,000	12%	Negligible
Industrial notes	150,000	14	Low
Second mortgages	250,000	15	Moderate
Venture capital loans	500,000	18	High

2. We should place no more than 50% of the total investment in industrial notes and venture capital loans.
3. We should make no more than 20% of the total investment in second mortgages.

One other consideration is that we must pay a surety fee of $10,000 for the privilege of investing in venture capital loans. Naturally, if BLL does not choose to invest in this instrument, it would not pay the fee. The fee is the same regardless of how large the investment is (other than zero).

THE MODEL

Connie modeled this portfolio problem as an all-integer programming model that included a fixed charge feature to account for the surety fee. Note that we can purchase the four instruments only in integer multiples of their respective denominations, so that fractional purchases are not possible. The model is as follows:

Let x_j = number of the jth instrument to purchase in the given denomination; $j = 1, \ldots, 4$ (in the order given)

$$Y = \begin{cases} 1, & \text{if } x_4 \geq 0 \\ 0, & \text{otherwise} \end{cases}$$

$$\text{MAX } x_0 = 1000x_1 + 1750x_2 + 3125x_3 + 7500x_4 - 10000y \quad (3.53)$$

$$\text{S T:} \quad 100000x_1 + 150000x_2 + 250000x_3 + 500000x_4 \leq 5370000 \quad (3.54)$$

$$100000x_1 \geq 537000 \quad (3.55)$$

$$150000x_2 \geq 537000 \quad (3.56)$$

$$250000x_3 \geq 537000 \quad (3.57)$$

$$150000x_2 + 500000x_4 \leq 2685000 \quad (3.58)$$

$$250000x_3 \leq 1074000 \quad (3.59)$$

$$x_4 - 100y \leq 0 \quad (3.60)$$

$$y \leq 1 \quad (3.61)$$

$$x_1, x_2, x_3, x_4, y \geq 0 \quad (3.62)$$

The objective function coefficients in Equation (3.53) are the one-month proceeds at the stated interest rates. For example, on treasury bills, $c_1 = (0.12)(100,000)/12 = 1,000$. The y-term incorporates the surety fee as a fixed charge. Note in Equation (3.60) that if optimal $x_4 = 0$, then $y = 0$ as well, so that no investment in venture capital loans occurs, and we pay no surety fee. On the other hand, if it is optimal to purchase some of this instrument, x_4 will be greater than zero, forcing $y = 1$ and picking up the $10,000 fee in Equation (3.53).

Constraints (3.54) to (3.59) incorporate the restrictions that Connie Mann placed on the portfolio. We could decrease the size of the model, if necessary, by using a transformation to delete the three lower-bound constraints (3.55) to (3.57).

SOLUTION TO THE MODEL

The output of the optimal solution to the model, as stated, is given in Table 3.20.

TABLE 3.20 30-Day instruments

Instrument	Number to Purchase	Amount Invested	Return
U.S. treasury bills	18	$1,800,000	$18,000
Industrial notes	17	2,550,000	29,750
Second mortgages	4	1,000,000	12,500
Venture capital loans	—	—	—
	39	$5,350,000	$60,250

TABLE 3.21 30-Day instruments

Instrument	Number to Purchase	Amount Invested	Return
U.S. treasury bills	7	$ 700,000	$ 7,000
Industrial notes	1	150,000	1,750
Second mortgages	4	1,000,000	12,500
Venture capital loans	7	3,500,000	42,500
	19	$5,350,000	$63,750

SOLUTION TO THE PROBLEM

Although we can't compute shadow prices for the constraints in IP models, Connie noted several interesting features of the model portfolio. Venture capital loans—the riskiest and highest yielding instrument—were not in the mix, even though none of the lower-bound constraints on the other three were even remotely close to being binding. As an experiment, Connie had her analyst rerun the model, changing from 50 percent to 70 percent the restriction on total investment in industrial notes and venture capital loans. The solution to the new model intrigued her. Table 3.21 is a summary of this solution.

It was apparent that loosening the restrictions allowed the high-risk venture loans to enter at a high enough level to make the $10,000 surety fee worth paying, but the net effect was to substantially increase the level of risk in the portfolio at only a 5.8% increase in return. The message to Connie as a manager was clear: high-risk investments are for high rollers. The 13.5% (annualized) rate of return seemed reasonable for the original portfolio and its low to moderate overall riskiness, and Connie decided to go with the original optimal model solution.

Backpacking

THE SCENARIO

Nelda and Newton, a young DINK (double-income, no kids) married couple, are employees in the EDP facility at Chex State University, and are avid backpackers. They enjoy nothing more than spending a weekend camping in West Texas. Since Nelda is slight of build, she always carries the sleeping bags and the binoculars. Newton carries the bulky pack.

THE PROBLEM

Newton and Nelda are frustrated. It seems that every time they set out on an expedition, they forget to bring one or more critical items. One time they brought four cans of Spam® and no can opener. Another time it was Newton's handheld computer and no batteries. The *next* time, however, they vowed that things would be different. Nelda had audited a management science course in Chex State's B-school and had learned all about integer programming.

THE MODEL

"Newton," commented Nelda, "let's model our backpacking problem as a knapsack problem."

Nelda took a complete inventory of all the things they liked to take along on their excursions. Table 3.22 lists the items by category, each item's per-unit volume and weight, and an importance index for each unit of each item on a scale of 1 (not important) to 20 (extremely important).

Although Newton is only 5′ 2″ tall, he is sturdily built and can carry 80 pounds comfortably. His new backpack can hold about 3,500 cubic inches.

Nelda modeled the problem as a **generalized knapsack problem,** with constraints for weight and volume, as follows. (*Note:* In a generalized knapsack model, we can include *more than one* of each item.)

$$\text{MAX } x_0 = \sum_{j=1}^{28} c_j x_j \quad \text{(importance index)}$$

$$\text{S T: } \sum_{j=1}^{28} w_j x_j \leq 80 \quad \text{(weight constraint)}$$

$$\sum_{j=1}^{28} v_j x_j \leq 3500 \quad \text{(volume constraint)}$$

$$x_j \geq 0 \quad \text{and integer, } j = 1, \ldots, 28$$

SOLUTION TO THE MODEL

Nelda meticulously fed in the parameters for this 28-variable, two-constraint problem to an integer programming module. In less than five seconds, the model produced the summary solution in Table 3.23.

When Nelda saw the solution to her model, she was dismayed.

"Nelda, dear," observed Newton, "we can't go backpacking with only 100 packages of Twinkies and 500 bottles of Sinex spray. You must have made a mistake."

"Never mind," answered Nelda. "These stupid computers only do exactly what you tell them to do—nothing more and nothing less. Let's see,

TABLE 3.22 Items for Backpacking

Type of Item	Item		x_j Variable	w_j Weight (Pounds)	v_j **Volume (Cu. In)**	c_j Importance Weight
Beverages	Prune juice	Pints	x_1	0.30	35	13
	Grape soda	Quarts	x_2	0.60	70	16
	Buttermilk	Quarts	x_3	0.75	70	15
Foods	Spam	Cans	x_4	0.25	27	7
	Powdered eggs	Packs	x_5	0.10	4	11
	Twinkies	2-pack	x_6	0.05	15	16
	Cabbage soup	Jars	x_7	1.20	90	13
	Oatmeal	Boxes	x_8	0.35	200	9
	Wheat germ	Cans	x_9	0.60	90	6
Utensils & cooking supplies	Can opener	Each	x_{10}	0.15	3	7
	Sterno	Cans	x_{11}	0.20	8	1
	Kitchen matches	Boxes	x_{12}	0.10	24	2
	Cooking pot	Each	x_{13}	1.50	300	5
	Plastic forks	Sets	x_{14}	0.25	6	1
Personal care items	Stridex pads	Boxes	x_{15}	0.10	6	12
	Dental floss	Packs	x_{16}	0.05	8	3
	Men's kneesocks	Pairs	x_{17}	0.15	10	11
	Support hose	Pairs	x_{18}	0.18	12	17
	Generic soap	Bars	x_{19}	0.20	8	2
	Sinex spray	Packs	x_{20}	0.15	4	18
Entertainment items	Back issues of *Reader's Digest*	Each	x_{21}	0.12	20	17
	Handheld computer	Each	x_{22}	6.00	240	20
	Batteries	Set	x_{23}	2.00	20	20
	Ukuleles	Each	x_{24}	3.00	800	18
	Camera with zoom lens	Each	x_{25}	5.00	150	16
	B&W film	Rolls	x_{26}	0.10	3	12
	Pet rocks	Each	x_{27}	2.00	25	15
	Pet rock food	Packs	x_{28}	1.00	10	15

TABLE 3.23 SAMS summary solution for Backpacking

BACKPACKING PROBLEM
QUICK BRIEFING ON OPTIMAL MODEL SOLUTION

Maximum Objective Value = 10600

Decision Variable	Optimal Value	Reduced Cost
TWINK	100.0	0.0
SINEX	500.0	0.0

now, we'll have to come up with better instructions in the form of additional constraints."

THE NEW MODEL

1. Let's include at least five units of items in each of the five item types (beverages, food, supplies, personal, and entertainment):

   $x_1 + x_2 + x_3 \geq 5$ (beverages)

   $x_4 + x_5 + x_6 + x_7 + x_8 + x_9 \geq 5$ (foods)

   $x_{10} + x_{11} + x_{12} + x_{13} + x_{14} \geq 5$ (supplies)

   $x_{15} + x_{16} + x_{17} + x_{18} + x_{19} + x_{20} \geq 5$ (personal)

   $x_{21} + x_{22} + x_{23} + x_{24} + x_{25} + x_{26} + x_{27} + x_{28} \geq 5$ (entertainment)

2. Don't take the cooking pot unless powdered eggs or cabbage soup (or both) is included:

   $x_{13} - x_5 - x_7 \leq 0$

3. If Spam is included, be sure to include a can opener:

   $x_4 - x_{10} \leq 0$

4. Take no more than *one each:* can opener, box of kitchen matches, cooking pot, set of plastic forks, computer, and camera.

   Designate $x_{10}, x_{12}, x_{13}, x_{14}, x_{22}, x_{25}$ in SAMS as zero-one variables.

5. Newton is a Sinex junkie, so he should be penalized 500 importance units if any is included:

   Add the term $- 500y_1$ to the objective function, and the constraint

   $x_{20} - 1000y_1 \leq 0,$

   where y_1 is zero-one.

6. If we take any back issues of *Reader's Digest*, we should take at least 6 but no more than 12:

   $x_{22} - 6y_2 \geq 0$

   and

   $x_{22} - 12y_2 \leq 0$

   where y_2 is zero-one.

7. Prune juice comes in four-packs, but we shouldn't take more than 15 pints:

   $x_1 = 4y_3 + 8y_4 + 12y_5$

   and

   $y_3 + y_4 + y_5 \leq 1$

   where y_3, y_4, y_5 are zero-one.

8. For a varied diet, we should take *either* a total of at least 10 units of Spam, Twinkies, and oatmeal cereal *or* a total of at least 12 units of powdered eggs, cabbage soup, and wheat germ, *but not both*.

$$x_4 + x_6 + x_8 \geq 10 y_6$$

and

$$x_5 + x_7 + x_9 \geq 12(1 - y_6)$$

where y_6 is zero-one.

This new model has 16 constraints, 12 zero-one variables, and 22 general integer variables.

SOLUTION TO THE NEW MODEL

The IP module Nelda used required 13 minutes of CPU time on an AT-compatible computer to solve this little problem, branching at 348 nodes in the process. Unfortunately for the backpackers, the optimal solution emerged as in Table 3.24.

When Newton saw the new solution, he was extremely frustrated. The model wanted them to subsist by washing down 68 packs of Twinkies with grape and prune juice, carry a can opener with no cans to open, take four cans of Sterno but nothing to cook, and carry 734 rolls of B&W film but no camera!

> "Nelda," Newton said, "I'd say you completely wasted your time in that management science course!"

TABLE 3.24 SAMS summary solution for new Backpacking

BACKPACKING PROBLEM
QUICK BRIEFING ON OPTIMAL MODEL SOLUTION
Maximum Objective Value = 10026

Decision Variables	Optimal Values	Reduced Costs
PRUNE	4.	0.
GRAPE	1.	0.
TWINK	68.	0.
CAN OP	1.	0.
STERNO	4.	0.
STRIDEX	4.	0.
D FLOSS	1.	0.
BW FILM	734.	0.
Y3	1.	0.
Y6	1.	0.

EPILOGUE

As we noted (forcefully, we hope) in Chapter 1, MS models are not panaceas. This is a classic example of trying to use a sledgehammer (a sophisticated ILP algorithm) to bash a gnat (Nelda and Newton's problem). However, for readers who are more intrigued than amused by this minicase, we return to it as the last end-of-chapter problem and suggest ways to model it more carefully.

SUMMARY

In this chapter, we relaxed the LP assumption of divisibility (at least partially) and discussed the highly utilitarian integer linear programming (ILP) model that resulted.

We noted that ILP models are useful in two distinct contexts: (1) when some or all of the decision variables must take on integer values for a model to be appropriate as an aid to decision making and (2) as devices to effectively model such nonlinear features as fixed charges, either-or constraints, and alternate constraint sets. We also ventured into modeling with zero-one variables and discovered a rich variety of applications of such devices.

Next, we briefly touched on some approaches that we can use to solve ILP models and concentrated our attention on branch and bound (B&B) and cutting planes. We got a feeling for the difficulty we encounter in solving ILP models in general as well as an appreciation of the unpredictability of current solution approaches.

Our discussion of developing alternative solutions for and performing sensitivity analysis on ILP models revealed a greatly decreased capability in this regard as compared to LP models. The fact that shadow prices in ILP have no precise meaning (as they do in LP) was the key shortcoming here. We then briefly discussed some advanced modeling techniques and mixed integer programming.

The next chapter delves into a subset of ILP models that we can model as networks, taking advantage of their special structure to introduce specialized, highly efficient solution techniques.

KEY TERMS

Additive Algorithm	fractional programming models
Advanced Start Algorithm	generalized knapsack problem
backtracked	incumbent
Bounded Descent Algorithm	integer hull
branched	lower bound
Constructive Primal Dual Algorithm	mixed ILP model
cuts	pure ILP model
dominated	Simplified Primal Algorithm
fathom	

PROBLEMS FOR ANALYSIS

1. **The Scenario:** The Rio de Oro Medical Clinic in Aspen, Colorado, is doing a booming business in setting broken limbs, performing physical exams, and tending to various other out-patient services for regular and walk-in customers. Business is so

good that the head nurse, Angela Mersey, has suggested to Dr. Benjamin Dover, the managing physician, that the clinic begin opening on Wednesday afternoons and Saturdays during golf season—a suggestion that Dr. Dover promptly squelches.

The Problem: Because of the demand for its services, the clinic is currently operating at capacity, and waiting lines form almost daily. Bill Dunn, the business manager, expresses his concern to Dr. Dover and Nurse Mersey, noting that the exclusive nature of the clinic's clientele makes it unwise to subject such people to the indignities of lolling about in the waiting room—regardless of how plush it may be.

Dunn suggests that they could convert the physicians' lounge into another examination room, hire another physician and nurse to staff it, and thereby expand the clinic's level of service to meet the demand. An alternative would be to hire a rookie M.D. and a nurse to staff the regular facility on an overtime basis after the regular 10 A.M.–3 P.M. clinic hours (10 A.M. to noon on Wednesday). They might persuade an ambitious young physician to see patients on Wednesday afternoons and Saturdays during golf season—but the premium in pay would be considerable.

"Opening another examination room would cost a bundle," observes Nurse Mersey, "but so would operating the clinic after normal operating hours. Bill, which would be best?"

The Model:
a. Assuming that the objective of the clinic is to maximize total profit contribution and that we can express the constraints on the model with linear relationships, can we model this problem as an ILP model? What integer modeling device could we use to differentiate between the cost of opening another examination room and the marginal cost of overtime operation?
b. Note from a managerial viewpoint that opening another examination room represents a one-time capital outlay that—once made—we cannot recover. On the other hand, the use of overtime gives Ben and Angela a great deal of flexibility in case the forecast patient demand does not materialize. Is there any way to include this feature in a formal ILP model of the problem? If so, how; if not, how can we account for this possibility?

The Solution: Bill Dunn did indeed model the problem as a fixed charge ILP model, and the optimal solution to the model indicated that hiring a rookie M.D. and a nurse to staff the clinic on Wednesday afternoons and Saturdays was the desired solution. However, the forecast demand on Wednesdays and Saturdays did not materialize. The clinic was saddled with the additional expense of an overtime physician and nurse, while the demand on the clinic during regular clinic hours continued to grow.

a. What could have caused this phenomenon?
b. Why did the ILP model fail so miserably in this instance?

2. **The Scenario:** Marijane Moss is majoring in horticulture at Humus State University. A last-semester senior, she has completed all required courses and must enroll in at least 15 elective hours (but no more than 21) to graduate. The electives are not totally free; she must select from a list of courses totaling 36 hours.

The Problem: Marijane's problem is twofold: first, she must have a cumulative grade point average (GPA) of 2.0 (C) to graduate, and she has precisely that at the moment. Second—and more important—she is heavily involved in interviewing for a managerial position in the agribusiness industry, and finding the right position will take time and effort during the coming semester.

Luckily, some of her sorority sisters have compiled a list of senior elective courses and rated the courses on two dimensions: difficulty (from 1 to 10 in increasing order of difficulty) and time commitment required (in hours per week). This list, along with the semester credit hours for each course, is in Table 3.25.

TABLE 3.25

Number	Title	Credit Hours	Difficulty	Time Required
1. SHO 4108	Creative Fertilizing	1	4	8
2. SHO 4309	Houseplant Watering	3	2	12
3. GEO 4312	Plains of New Mexico	3	6	6
4. GEO 4215	Agricultural History of Alaska	2	5	4
5. HEC 4421	Hibiscus in the Home	4	1	7
6. ENG 4335	Farmer's Almanac Review	3	8	5
7. BIO 4241	Pests of North America	2	9	3
8. SOC 4154	House Plants and Rock 'n' Roll Music	1	3	9
9. PSY 4363	Dealing With Vegetables	3	7	6
10. ENV 4578	Air Pollution and Your Turnips	5	10	15
11. AGR 4285	Control of Noxious Grasses	2	6	8
12. LAW 4293	Plants and Their Rights	5	9	13
13. REC 4226	Touring Mesquite Country	2	3	6
	Total credit hours available	36		
	Total time required			102

The Model:

a. Can we model Marijane's problem as an ILP model? If so, what is the objective function? What are the constraints? Do the variables have any special structure?

b. Does the ILP model in (a) (if appropriate) have any special structure that, if recognized, might allow for an efficient solution technique? If so, what special solution technique might be appropriate?

Solution to the Model: We might conclude that we can model this problem as a knapsack model. That is, Marijane wishes to fill her class schedule (knapsack) with items (courses) in such a way that she does not exceed capacity (21 semester credit hours) and that she attains minimum capacity (15 semester credit hours). However, what is an appropriate objective function?

Note that all 13 courses total to a time requirement of only 102 hours per week, so if it weren't for the 21 semester credit hour limit, a student could conceivably take all of them and still get about nine hours of sleep per night. However, in Marijane's case, free time is critical. Marijane needs every hour she can free up to interview with company recruiters. On the other hand, if she selects a set of courses that is too difficult overall, she may not graduate.

One approach to this problem is to model it in two ways: first, *minimize the total difficulty* of the courses, ignoring the time requirement; then, *minimize total time requirement*, ignoring difficulty:

$$\text{LET } x_j = \begin{cases} 1, & \text{if class } j \text{ is included} \\ 0, & \text{otherwise,} \end{cases}$$

s_j = semester credit hours for course j

d_j = level of difficulty for course j

t_j = time required for course j

Then Model 1 (M1)—minimizing total difficulty—becomes

$$\text{MIN } x_0 = \sum_{j=1}^{13} d_j x_j \quad \text{(M1)}$$

$$\text{S T: } 15 \leq \sum_{j=1}^{13} s_j x_j \leq 21$$

$$x_j = 0, 1; j = 1, \ldots, 13$$

Likewise Model 2 (M2)—minimizing total time requirement—becomes

$$\text{MIN } x_0 = \sum_{j=1}^{13} t_j x_j \quad \text{(M2)}$$

$$\text{S T: } 15 \leq \sum_{j=1}^{13} s_j x_j \leq 21$$

$$x_j = 0, 1; j = 1, \ldots, 13$$

The solutions to these two models are in Table 3.26.

Solution to the Problem:
a. We note that course #3 (GEO 4312) and course #5 (HEC 4421) are the only courses that appear in the solutions to both (M1) and (M2). What might we conclude from this "coincidence"?
b. What exogenous factors might she take into consideration when making her final decision? How does Marijane proceed from here?
c. If there were some way to numerically determine the priority of the two objectives "minimize total difficulty" and "minimize total time requirements" and assign a numerical weight to each (e.g., the latter is twice as important as the

TABLE 3.26

For M1

	Course Number				Total
	2	3	5	12	
Credit hours	3	3	4	5	15
Difficulty	2	6	1	9	18 (min.)
Time required	12	6	7	13	38

For M2

	Course Number					Total
	3	5	6	7	9	
Credit hours	3	4	3	2	3	15
Difficulty	6	1	8	9	7	31
Time required	6	7	5	3	6	27 (min.)

former), how might Marijane incorporate this feature into the model? (*Note:* More about this in Chapter 14.)

3. **The Scenario:** Judy Cates and Susan Wynn are partners in a small law firm that specializes in defending their clients against misdemeanor charges (e.g., jaywalking, littering, speeding). Early each Monday morning, they meet to schedule their caseload for the week. Two parameters characterize each case: the time required by either Judy or Susan to prepare each case for court and the due date (docket schedule) set by the court for each case. Since the individual cases are independent of one another, there is no case-dependent sequence to bother with.

   The Problem: The two attorneys must make two basic decisions each Monday morning: which attorney will take which of the cases and in what order they will address the cases. There is no particular advantage in having a case prepared before the time of the docket schedule; however, if they fail to meet the docket schedule for a particular case, the court levies charges on a per-hour tardy basis. Therefore, Judy and Susan decide to set up a schedule that minimizes total tardiness of cases for the week.

   The Model:
   a. Can we model this problem as an ILP model? If you think so, let

   n = number of cases for the week

   p_j = preparation time for case j, $j = 1, 2, \ldots, n$

   d_j = due date (in hours from 7 A.M. Monday) for case j, $j = 1, 2, \ldots, n$

   $$x_{ijk} = \begin{cases} 1, & \text{if attorney } i \text{ processes case } j \text{ in the } k\text{th order} \\ 0, & \text{otherwise,} \end{cases}$$

   $i = 1, 2; j, k = 1, 2, \ldots, n.$

   Write the zero-one ILP model for this problem.

   b. In your model, suppose there are 50 cases in the hopper for a given week. How many decision variables x_{ijk} are there?
   c. Suppose there are 20 attorneys in a large firm and the caseload averages 500 cases per week. How many decision variables are there in this model?

   Solution to the Problem: We refer to this problem in the literature as the "*n*-job, two-machine tardiness model." The terminology comes from a job-shop environment in which two machines (attorneys in this scenario) are available to process (prepare cases on) *n* jobs (cases) with known processing times (preparation times) and due dates (docket schedules). A widely used objective in such situations is minimization of total tardiness.

   The answer to the question: Is this a viable modeling technique for the tardiness problem? is a decided no. Researchers have worked at finding an efficient optimizing solution technique for this model for years —without success. There are, however, heuristic methods that yield "good" solutions in a reasonable amount of computer time, and these techniques are widespread in use.

   If this problem piques your curiosity, think about the following analogy. Consider a pair of traveling salesmen who must jointly visit *n* customers with whom they have set appointments. The time required by each of the two salesmen to travel and conduct business with each customer varies because of personalities, sales techniques, etc. Is the "*n*-job, two-machine tardiness model" nothing more than an extension of the traveling salesman problem?

4. **The Scenario:** TreeTops Airlines (TTA), a small regional air carrier that operates in the Southeast, has received approval to service 12 small cities in Tennessee, Mississippi, and Alabama and to purchase at least 10 passenger aircraft for this purpose.

TABLE 3.27

	Aircraft Models			
	Zoomer	Climber	Air Queen	Chief
Unit cost	$150,000	$215,000	$260,000	$400,000
Passenger capacity	12	16	20	30
Maximum range (miles)	300	400	500	1000
Operating cost ($ per mile)	$1.50	$2.50	$3.00	$4.00

The Problem: Al Aaron, the CEO of TTA, has narrowed his choices to four aircraft models, and some data on these aircraft are in Table 3.27.

Al would like to minimize the average operating cost per mile of the aircraft purchased. TTA has a capital budget of $2.5 million for this procurement. Two additional considerations are that at least six of the aircraft must have a range of 400 miles or more to cover approved routes and that Al would like a total passenger capacity of at least 200 seats for the fleet.

The Model: Note at the outset that the TTA problem is nonlinear, since the objective function (minimize the average operating cost per mile) is written:

$$\text{MIN } x_0 = \frac{1.5x_1 + 2.5x_2 + 3x_3 + 4x_4}{x_1 + x_2 + x_3 + x_4}$$

We call this a **fractional programming model,** and we will discover how to transform such models into linear programming models in Chapter 5.

However, a more basic difficulty with modeling this problem as an integer (otherwise linear) programming model is that it has no feasible solution. (You might try solving the associated LP model, using any objective function you choose, and verify this fact.)

Solution to the Model:
a. Investigate the constraints in an attempt to understand why this problem (as stated) has no feasible solution.
b. If we increase the availability of capital to $2.6 million (from $2.5 million), the model has feasible solutions. Use weighted operating cost as the criterion to minimize (i.e., $x_0 = 1.5x_1 + 2.5x_2 + 3x_3 + 4x_4$) and solve the model as a linear program (initially ignore integer requirements). You should get the following model solution (we also solved the LP version of the fractional programming model, and we also give this solution):

	Variables				
Criterion	x_0	x_1	x_2	x_3	x_4
Weighted operating cost	$27.33	4.44	—	3.33	2.67
Average operating cost	$ 1.91	8.73	6	—	—

Note that we get very different model solutions with the two different criteria.

TABLE 3.28 SAMS summary solution for Treetops Airlines

TREETOPS AIRLINES
QUICK BRIEFING ON OPTIMAL MODEL SOLUTION
Maximum Objective Value = 27.5

Decision Variable	Optimal Value	Reduced Cost
ZOOM	5.0	0.0
CLIMB	0.0	0.0
AIRQ	4.0	0.0
CHIEF	2.0	0.0

Solution to the Problem:

a. The preceding LP solutions are obviously useless to Al Aaron in their present form, since purchasing .44 or .73 of an aircraft is absurd. Experiment with rounding to see if you can find a feasible integer solution to the model and compute the objective value generated by your solution using both criteria.

b. The SAMS summary report of the optimal integer solution to the weighted operating cost model is in Table 3.28. (Note the difference between the integer solution and the LP solution—although the weighted operating costs vary by only $0.17 per mile. Was your "rounded" solution close?)

c. Comment on possible solution approaches to this problem for an international airline that wishes to order 400 large passenger jets and that has a budget of $3.5 billion. Assuming that there were only three or four aircraft models under consideration, would solving the LP model give a usable solution without having to resort to IP algorithms? Why or why not?

d. One way of modeling and solving problems of this type is by transforming them into equivalent zero-one IP models that we can solve with Balas's very efficient additive algorithm. Note that since TTA has only $2.6 million available, the upper bounds on the four decision variables are as follows:

$$u_1 = \$2{,}600{,}000/150{,}000 = 17 \text{ (rounded)}$$

$$u_2 = \$2{,}600{,}000/215{,}000 = 12 \text{ (rounded)}$$

$$u_3 = \$2{,}600{,}000/260{,}000 = 10$$

$$u_4 = \$2{,}600{,}000/400{,}000 = 6 \text{ (rounded)}$$

Thus, we would need five variables for x_1, four variables for x_2, four variables for x_3; and three variables for x_4. Write the equivalent zero-one IP model using the weighted operating cost criterion.

5. Consider the following toy model in integer programming:

$$\text{MAX } x_0 = x_1 + 4x_2$$

$$\text{S T: } 5x_1 + 12x_2 \leq 840$$

$$x_1 + x_2 \leq 90$$

$$-11x_1 + 7x_2 \leq 65$$

$$x_1, x_2 \geq 0 \text{ and integer}$$

a. Ignore the integer restrictions and solve the model with a microcomputer LP package. Your solution should be as follows (approximately):

Decision Variable	Value	Slack Variable	Value
x_0	259.64	s_1	0
x_1	30.54	s_2	2.19
x_2	57.28	s_3	0

b. Add the following constraints to the model in (a), and solve the model.

$$2x_1 + 5x_2 \leq 347$$
$$-x_1 + x_2 \leq 26$$

Your solution should be as in Table 3.29 (exactly).

c. As you may have guessed, the solution in (b) is the optimal solution to the original IP model. The two additional constraints are "cuts" that slice off noninteger portions of the feasible region and create a vertex at the optimal lattice point. Thus, given these cuts, we could solve IP problems using the ordinary SIMPLEX algorithm. How might we go about generating such constraints?

TABLE 3.29

Decision Variable	Value	Slack Variable	Value
x_0	259	s_1	0
x_1	31	s_2	2
x_2	57	s_3	7
		s_4(new)	0
		s_5(new)	0

6. **The Scenario [4]:** Let's return to the Blitzen Development, Inc., problem (Problem 7 in Chapter 2). Recall that this West German commercial real estate developer was planning a three-story building in Stuttgart, Arkansas, containing a variety of stores, offices, and apartments.

The Problem: Table 3.30 gives the restrictions on construction, annual rentals, and construction costs by types.

To make the original problem more realistic, assume that each unit (whether it be an office, a store, or an apartment) contains a fixed amount of floor space, as prescribed by the standard units in Table 3.31.

The Problem: Clearly, this is an integer programming situation. Are decision variables of the zero-one variety or simply nonnegative integers?

The Model: Define decision variables as follows. Let x_j be the number of units of a particular type to construct on a particular floor. Write an objective function based upon total annual rents received from each type of unit. For example, according to the problem statement in Problem 7, Chapter 2, each square feet of floor space on

TABLE 3.30 Restrictions on construction by type

Type of Unit	Level	Maximum Percentage
Apartment	First floor	10%
	Second floor	50%
	Third floor	100%
Office	First floor	60%
	Second floor	75%
Store	First floor	50%

Annual rentals (in DM/ft²/year)

		Quality Categories		
Type of Unit	Level	1 (Highest)	2 (Medium)	3 (Lowest)
Apartment	First floor	3.00	2.50	N/A
	Second floor	3.00	2.50	N/A
	Third floor	2.50	2.00	N/A
Office	First floor	4.50	4.00	3.50
	Second floor	4.00	3.50	3.00
Store	First floor	3.25	N/A*	N/A

Construction costs (in DM/ft²)

		Quality Categories		
Type of Unit	Level	1 (Highest)	2 (Medium)	3 (Lowest)
Apartment	First floor	18.00	16.00	N/A
	Second floor	17.00	15.00	N/A
	Third floor	16.00	14.00	N/A
Office	First floor	19.00	17.00	13.00
	Second floor	18.00	15.00	14.00
Store	First floor	11.00	N/A	N/A

*N/A—not applicable.

the first floor of office quality 1 yields $4.50 rent. Therefore, each unit would yield 800 × 4.5, or $3,600. You can perform similar computations to find objective functions coefficients for the remaining 12 units. You formulate the constraints in a way analogous to the LP model. Consider the final constraint—the market survey constraint that requires that no more than 10% of the total building floor area can be of the office quality 1 type.

TABLE 3.31 Blitzen unit construction standards

Unit Type	Floor Space (in square feet)
First Floor	
Offices, quality 1	800
Offices, quality 2	700
Offices, quality 3	600
Stores, quality 1	1000
Apartments, quality 1	750
Apartments, quality 2	650
Second Floor	
Offices, quality 1	800
Offices, quality 2	700
Offices, quality 3	600
Apartments, quality 1	750
Apartments, quality 2	650
Third Floor	
Apartments, quality 1	750
Apartments, quality 2	650

Let T, total building floor area, be given by

$$T = 800x_1 + 700x_2 + 600x_3 + 1000x_4 + 750x_5$$
$$+ 650x_6 + 800x_7 + 700x_8 + 600x_9 + 750x_{10}$$
$$+ 650x_{11} + 750x_{12} + 650x_{13}$$

Assume x_1 and x_7 represent the number of units of office quality type 1 on the first and second floors, respectively. Then the fraction of the total floor area for office quality 1 is $(800x_1 + 800x_7)/T$ so that

$$\frac{800x_1 + 800x_7}{800x_1 + 700x_2 + 600x_3 + 1000x_4 + \ldots + 750x_{12} + 650x_{13}} \le .10$$

By multiplying both sides of the inequality by the denominator and combining common terms, this expression reduces to the following linear inequality:

$$720x_1 - 70x_2 - 60x_3 - 100x_4 - 75x_5 - 65x_6 + 720x_7 - 70x_8$$
$$- 60x_9 - 75x_{10} - 65x_{11} - 75x_{12} - 65x_{13} \le 0$$

Formulate the remaining constraints.

Solution to the Model: If you have access to an integer programming algorithm that will solve general IP models, use it to solve this model.

Solution to the Problem: How would actual solution of the problem differ from the ILP solution? What extraneous factors would likely change the ILP solution?
To what extent is the final solution influenced by the ILP solution?

7. **The Scenario**: As promised, let's return to our friends Nelda and Newton from the "Backpacking" minicase.

   The Problem: When the couple attempted to model their backpacking problem as a two-constraint generalized knapsack model, they got an absurd solution that included only two items: Sinex and Twinkies. Nelda then made a valiant effort to further constrain the problem but again got a foolish solution to her model.

The Model: Because generalized knapsack models are so very useful in practice as so-called choice models—and *not* because of Nelda and Newton's dilemma—let's investigate some ways that we might get usable solutions from their model. Consider the following ideas:

a. Collapse the variables x_{25} (camera) and x_{26} (film) into a single decision variable, so that the algorithm cannot choose one without the other. Do the same with the pairs x_{22} (computer) and x_{23} (batteries) and x_{27} (pet rocks) and x_{28} (pet rock food).
b. Place common-sense upper bounds on those items for which such bounds are obvious; e.g., x_{11} (Sterno), x_{24} (ukuleles).

TABLE 3.32 Items for Backpacking in indexed order

Item		x_j Variable	w_j Weight (Pounds)	v_j Volume (CU. IN.)	c_j Importance Weight	I_i Index
Sinex spray	Packs	x_{20}	0.15	4	18	30.000
Powdered eggs	Packs	x_5	0.10	4	11	27.500
Twinkies	2-Pack	x_6	0.05	15	16	21.333
Stridex pads	Boxes	x_{15}	0.10	6	12	20.000
Can opener	Each	x_{10}	0.15	3	7	15.556
Support hose	Pairs	x_{18}	0.18	12	17	7.870
Dental floss	Packs	x_{16}	0.05	8	3	7.500
Men's kneesocks	Pairs	x_{17}	0.15	10	11	7.333
Back issues of *Reader's Digest*	Each	x_{21}	0.12	20	17	7.083
Generic soap	Bars	x_{19}	0.20	8	2	1.250
Prune juice	Pints	x_1	0.30	35	13	1.238
Spam	Cans	x_4	0.25	27	7	1.037
Kitchen matches	Boxes	x_{12}	0.10	24	2	0.833
Plastic forks	Sets	x_{14}	0.25	6	1	0.667
Sterno	Cans	x_{11}	0.20	8	1	0.625
Grape soda	Quarts	x_2	0.60	70	16	0.381
Buttermilk	Quarts	x_3	0.75	70	15	0.286
Pet rocks/food	Each	x_{25}	3.00	35	30	0.286
Oatmeal	Boxes	x_8	0.35	200	9	0.129
Cabbage Soup	Jars	x_7	1.20	90	13	0.120
Wheat germ	Cans	x_9	0.60	90	6	0.111
Camera with film & lens	Each	x_{24}	5.10	153	28	0.036
Computer & batteries	Set	x_{22}	8.00	260	40	0.019
Cooking pot	Each	x_{13}	1.50	300	5	0.011
Ukuleles	Each	x_{23}	3.00	800	18	0.008

c. Do a simple ranking analysis on the items for the purpose of possibly eliminating some items from consideration or deciding in advance to include others. That is, since weight and volume are both undesirable, and importance weight is desirable, items that have low importance and relatively high weight and volume might be candidates for elimination. Others with relatively low weight and volume and high importance might be determined in advance. For example, the index

$$I_i = \frac{(\text{importance})_i}{(\text{pounds})_i (\text{cu in})_i}$$

would rank the 25 items [after collapsing variables as in (a)] in this problem as in Table 3.32.

On the basis of this simple analysis, for example, we might decide in advance to include as much Sinex spray, powdered eggs, Twinkies, Stridex pads, support hose, and dental floss as we could possibly use, plus a can opener. Similarly, we might decide that ukuleles, cooking pots, computers, and cameras are too heavy and bulky to take backpacking.

Solution to the Model: Make arbitrary decisions based on the preceding discussion and return to the "Backpacking" minicase to redo the analysis. You will be pleasantly surprised when you do so—and Newton and Nelda will be most appreciative!

Epilogue: Unlike the orderly but complex situation in the Blitzen Development Company problem, real-world problems are often "messy," as in this knapsack scenario. It is not unusual at all for managers to have to do some "preprocessing" on a problem before an MS model can offer assistance.

8. **The Scenario:** Wanda Moore Mooney, chairman of the board of Macon Moore Associates, a private investment firm in Bucks County, thoughtfully reviewed the company's portfolio. Since the death last year of Macon Moore, Wanda's father and founder of the firm, Wanda's current husband Louis N. Mooney has served as president and CEO of the company. And Louis, it appears, is no Macon Moore! The firm had been in the stock market with 90% of its investment assets on Black Monday; its assets had dropped from $100 million to $70 million in one terrifying day. Then, true to form, Louis had liquidated all equity assets the next day and bought gold, which promptly nose-dived as the stock market rebounded in the following weeks. "I suppose it's time for another divestiture," sighed Wanda, thinking of her fourth husband Louis. "But next, I've got to get my hands around the company's portfolio."

The Problem: Wanda was a socialite, a member of the "horsey set," and a philanthropist—not a financial analyst. She realized that she would have to find someone knowledgeable, trustworthy, and attractive to whom she could entrust portfolio management responsibilities for the company. As her mind wandered over her set of acquaintances, the light bulb suddenly illuminated. "Of course!" she vocalized. "I'll hire Macho Dinero!"

Macho Dinero was a handsome young man of uncertain origins but with a brilliant tennis backhand. He had been telling Wanda only last evening at dinner about his MBA from the Cambridge Case Study Institute, with a specialization in investments. She recalled vaguely that he had even mentioned needing a job, since he was ". . . low on bread" or something like that. "Charming young fellow," she mused. "I'll try to talk him into the job of chief financial officer first thing tomorrow."

Wanda was persuasive over lunch, and by the time the chocolate mousse arrived, Macho was the CFO for Macon Moore Associates. However, Wanda was more cautious this time than she had been the last time. Before arranging a meeting with Macho and Dinar Moolah, the company's conservative comptroller, she searched through her desk until she found the handwritten notes her father had left as part of

TABLE 3.33 Macon Moore's rules for investing

1. Invest a minimum of 20% of capital in industrial bonds, certificates of deposit (CDs), and equity securities (stocks).
2. Invest no more than 10% of capital in bonds and 15% in CDs.
3. Invest no more than 25% of capital in stocks.
4. Invest a minimum of 25% in commercial real estate.
5. Invest at least a total of 25% in partnership ventures but don't invest more than 60% in real estate and partnerships combined.
6. Invest in such a way as to maximize after-tax returns.
7. Always stay fully invested.

TABLE 3.34 Investment opportunities

Code	Investment	Cost per unit	After-tax Return per Unit
x_1	Bonds	$ 1,000	$ 75.00
x_2	CDs	10,000	850.00
x_3	Hal stock	150	12.50
x_4	Dec stock	120	10.00
x_5	Land in Maryland	750,000	90,000.00
x_6	Land in Virginia	900,000	100,000.00
x_7	Bo Ski ventures	500,000	55,000.00
x_8	Eye Con ventures	300,000	40,000.00
x_9	C Kord ventures	600,000	80,000.00

his legacy to his daughter. Moore's "rules for investing" were set out in bold strokes on a single sheet of paper, as in Table 3.33.

Wanda briefed Dinar Moolah in advance, and—as usual—Dinar was well prepared when the three met in Wanda's office.

"Ms. Mooney and Mr. Dinero," began Dinar, "I have studied Mr. Moore's rules, and I have assembled some investment opportunities for your consideration. This table [Table 3.34] lists the possibilities. Note that I have coded the investments x_1, x_2, etc., for convenience in discussing them.

"Also," noted Dinar, "Macon Moore Associates appears to have $50 million remaining to invest. I don't have an MBA like Mr. Dinero does, so I don't know how to proceed."

Macho Dinero chuckled confidently. "This is obviously a job for linear programming. It's an elementary task."

The Model:
a. If we let x_j, $j = 1, \ldots, 9$ be decision variables that represent the *number of units of the various investments to purchase*, can this problem be modeled properly as a linear programming model, as Macho Dinero suggests? In particular, consider the assumption of divisibility.
b. The ILP model for this problem has nine variables and eight constraints (not including the nonnegativity constraints). Write the ILP model of Wanda Moore Mooney's problem.

Solution to the Model: Use a computer ILP algorithm to find the optimal solution to your model.

Solution to the Problem: What do you think of the solution that the model obtains? Do you think this portfolio mix is appropriate for Wanda's purposes?

PRACTICE MODELS

Use a computerized ILP algorithm to solve the following integer programming models:

1. For the following model:
   a. Relax the integrality requirement and solve as an LP.
   b. Round off the LP solution to obtain an IP solution.
   c. Solve the model as an ILP.
   d. Compare the results for (b) and (c).

   MAX
   $$560 X1 + 540 X2$$
   S T:
   CONSTR 1
   $$6 X1 + 5 X2 < 15$$
   CONSTR 2
   $$10 X1 + 12 X2 < 30$$
   $$X1, X2 > 0 \text{ and integer}$$

2. Solve the following mixed-integer model:

   MAX
   $$12 \$MKT + 4 MUTUAL + 25 TBILL + TBOND$$
   S T:
   NUMBER
   $$\$MKT + 2 MUTUAL + TBILL + TBOND < 12$$
   RISK
   $$3.5 \$MKT + 3 MUTUAL + TBILL + TBOND < 10$$
   FUNDS
   $$\$MKT + MUTUAL < 5$$
   INSTRUMENTS
   $$TBILL + TBOND < 4$$

   All var > 0

3. Solve the following ILP model:

   MIN
   $$6 X1 + 14 X2 + 6 X3 + 6 X4 + 10 X5 + 14 X6 + 14 X7$$
   $$+ 2 X8 + 6 X9 + 6 X10 + 6 X11 + 10 X12 + 10 X13 + 14 X14$$
   $$+ 14 X15 + 14 X16 + 14 X17 + 2 X18 + 2 X19 + 6 X20 + 6 X21$$
   $$+ 6 X22 + 6 X23 + 6 X24$$

S T:
16" ROLLS

$$9 X1 + 7 X2 + 6 X3 + 6 X4 + 5 X5 + 4 X6 + 4 X7 + 4 X8$$
$$+ 3 X9 + 3 X10 + 3 X11 + 2 X12 + 2 X13 + X14 + X15$$
$$+ X16 + X17 + X18 + X19 > 300$$

24" ROLLS

$$1 X2 + 2 X3 + 3 X6 + X7 + X8 + 4 X9 + 2 X10 + 2 X12$$
$$+ 5 X14 + 3 X15 + X16 + X18 + 3 X19 + 6 X20 + 4 X21$$
$$+ 2 X22 + X24 > 400$$

48" ROLLS

$$X4 + X7 + X10 + 2 X11 + X13 + X15 + 2 X16 + X18$$
$$+ X21 + 2 X22 + 3 X23 > 200$$

60" ROLLS

$$X5 + X8 + X12 + X13 + 2 X17 + X18 + X19 + 2 X24 > 100$$

$$0 < X_j < 1 \text{ and integer}, j = 1, \ldots, 24$$

4. Solve the following fixed-charge model:

MIN

$$2 \text{ FORD} + 3 \text{ CHEVY} + 7 \text{ FIXFORD} + 10 \text{ FIXCHEVY}$$

S T:

LUGSPACE
$$\text{FORD} + 2 \text{ CHEVY} > 10$$

PEOPLE
$$4 \text{ FORD} + 3 \text{ CHEVY} > 22$$

DISTANCE
$$2 \text{ FORD} + 2 \text{ CHEVY} > 15$$

FIXFORD
$$\text{FORD} - 10000 \text{ FIXFORD} < 0$$

FIXCHEV
$$\text{CHEVY} - 10000 \text{ FIXCHEVY} < 0$$

FORD, CHEVY > 0; $0 <$ FIXFORD, FIXCHEVY < 1 and integer

5. Solve the following either-or model:

MAX

$$3 \text{ BUD} + 4 \text{ COO} + 8 \text{ MIL}$$

S T:
PARTY1

$$2 \text{ BUD} + \text{ COO} + \text{ MIL} - 1000 Y > 43$$

PARTY2

$$\text{BUD} + \text{ COO} + 4 \text{ MIL} + 1000 Y > 1024$$

BUD, COO, MIL > 0 $0 < Y < 1$ and integer

6. Find the integer solution to the following go/no go model:

MAX

$0.4\ A + 0.3\ B + 0.4\ C + 0.2\ Y$

S T:
CONSTR 1

$600\ A + 200\ B + 100\ C + 300\ Y < 800$

CONSTR 2

$400\ A + 500\ B + 600\ C + 500\ Y < 1500$

CONSTR 3

$0.5\ A + 0.9\ B + 1.2\ C + 1.6\ Y < 3.5$

$0 < A, B, C, Y < 1$ and integer

7. Find the solution to the following knapsack model formulation:

MAX

$0.5\ PC + 0.3\ GUITAR + 0.2\ 6\_PAK$

S T:
WEIGHT

$100\ PC + 70\ GUITAR + 30\ 6\_PAK < 150$

VOLUME

$PC + 0.7\ GUITAR + 1.4\ 6\_PAK < 3$

$0 < PC, GUITAR, 6\_PAK < 1$ and integer

8. Solve the following capital budgeting model:

MAX

$10000\ PROJ\_1 + 21000\ PROJ\_2 + 38000\ PROJ\_3 + 12000\ PROJ\_4$

S T:
BUDGET

$7000\ PROJ\_1 + 9000\ PROJ\_2 + 12000\ PROJ\_3 + 4000\ PROJ\_4 < 22000$

LABOR

$9000\ PROJ\_1 + 4000\ PROJ\_2 + 8000\ PROJ\_3 + 10000\ PROJ\_4 < 26000$

MIS-SUPP

$5000\ PROJ\_1 + 6000\ PROJ\_2 + 6000\ PROJ\_3 + 5000\ PROJ\_4 < 18000$

ADM-SUPP

$7000\ PROJ\_1 + 7000\ PROJ\_2 + 4000\ PROJ\_3 + 7000\ PROJ\_4 < 21000$

$0 < PROJ\_1, PROJ\_2, PROJ\_3, PROJ\_4 < 1$ and integer

9. Find the solution to the following set covering model formulation:

MIN

$1000\ AXL + 1300\ JON + 800\ BONO + 900\ TOM$

S T:
LOUD

$AXL + JON > 1$

WRITE

$JON + BONO > 1$

SOUL

$BONO + TOM > 1$

BAND

$AXL + BONO + TOM > 1$

$0 < AXL, JON, BONO, TOM < 1$ and integer

10. For the following distance matrix use the traveling salesman method to find the shortest travel route:

City	1	2	3	4	5
1	.	200	60	230	140
2		.	96	138	410
3			.	230	161
4				.	205
5					.

REFERENCES AND ADDITIONAL READING

1. Austin, L., and P. Ghandforoush. "An Advanced Dual Algorithm with Constraint Relaxation for All-Integer Programming." *Naval Research Logistics Quarterly* 30 (1983): 133–143.
2. Austin, L., and M. Hanna. "The Bounded Descent Algorithm for All-Integer Programming." *Naval Research Logistics Quarterly* 30 (1983): 271–281.
3. Balas, E. "An Additive Algorithm for Solving Linear Programs with Zero-One Variables." *Operations Research* 13 (1965): 517–546.
4. Barrett, M. Adapted from an unpublished MBA term project report, Texas Tech University (1983).
5. Dakin, R. "A Tree-Search Algorithm for Mixed Integer Programming Problems." *Computational Journal* 8 (1965): 250–255.
6. Garfinkel, R., and G. Nemhauser. *Integer Programming*. Toronto: Wiley, 1972.
7. Ghandforoush, P. and L. Austin. "A Primal-Dual Cutting Plane Algorithm for All-Integer Programming." *Naval Research Logistics Quarterly* 28 (1981): 559–567.
8. Gomory, R. "An Algorithm for Integer Solutions to Linear Problems." In, R.L. Graves and P. Wolfe (Eds.), *Recent Advances in Mathematical Programming* New York: McGraw-Hill, 1963. (pp. 269–302).
9. Hanna, M. "An All-Integer Cutting Plane Algorithm with an Advanced Start." Unpublished Ph.D. dissertation, College of Business Administration, Texas Tech University (1981).
10. Land, A., and A. Doig. "An Automatic Method for Solving Discrete Programming Problems." *Econometrica* 28 (1960): 497–520.
11. Parker, R., and R. Rardin. *Discrete Optimization*. San Diego: Academic Press, 1988.
12. Taha, H. *Integer Programming: Theory, Applications and Computations*. New York: Academic Press, 1975.
13. Wagner, H. *Principles of Operations Research* (2d. ed.). Englewood Cliffs, N.J.: Prentice-Hall, 1975.
14. Winston, W. *Operations Research: Applications and Algorithms* (2d ed.). Boston: PWS-KENT, 1991.
15. Young, R. "A Simplified Primal (All-Integer) Integer Programming Algorithm," *Operations Research* 16, (1968): 750–782.
16. Zionts, S. *Linear and Integer Programming*. Englewood Cliffs, N.J.: Prentice-Hall, 1974.

CHAPTER 4

Modeling with Networks

All of us encounter **networks** every day. We drive to work, to school, or to appointments on networks of highways, roads, or streets. We switch on the television set and activate a stream of electrons through the circuits of the set, magically plucking "M*A*S*H" reruns from the air. The office or university rumor mill is a network, as is the complex system of routes that commercial airlines fly. Since networks are ubiquitous in daily life, it seems reasonable to suppose that we can model and analyze many business, industrial, and social problems using such a framework.

What is a network in the technical sense we are interested in exploring? We will begin with a cryptic definition. *A network is a set of nodes connected by arcs.*

When we know what **nodes** and **arcs** are, and precisely what **connected** means, we will understand the above definition of **network**. As usual, we will create a working definition by analogy and example.

Figure 4.1 is a network that Harry Driver, a CPA with a "Big Six" accounting firm, faces each weekday morning. Harry and his family live in the peaceful suburb of Sourceburg, and Harry must commute each morning by automobile to his office in the busy metropolis of Sink City. The circles in Figure 4.1 represent major road intersections, (nodes) and the lines connecting them represent major thoroughfares (arcs). Arrows at the end of arcs represent allowable directions of travel, so that arcs G→F and L→J, for instance, represent one-way streets or roads, and the darkened arcs with arrows at both ends (e.g., A↔M, or Kamikaze Freeway) represent two-way streets or roads.

There obviously are many routes that Harry can take to or from work. For example,

Home to Work: Sourceburg → D → H → G → F → I → O → Sink City
    or   Sourceburg → A → M → Q → R → O → Sink City

Work to Home:
            Sink City → P → O → L → J → G → C → D → Sourceburg
    or   Sink City → R → Q → M → A → Sourceburg

Note in Figure 4.1 that Harry *cannot* go directly from C to F or from L to Sink City, since arcs do not connect these nodes. Note also the wide differences among nodes in terms of access and egress. For example, there is only one way to access node H (from D), and only two nodes that are directly accessible from H (nodes G and K). On the other hand, node O (Bedlam Circle) must be very busy during rush hour, with access available from four nodes, and egress available to six nodes. In our example, Harry

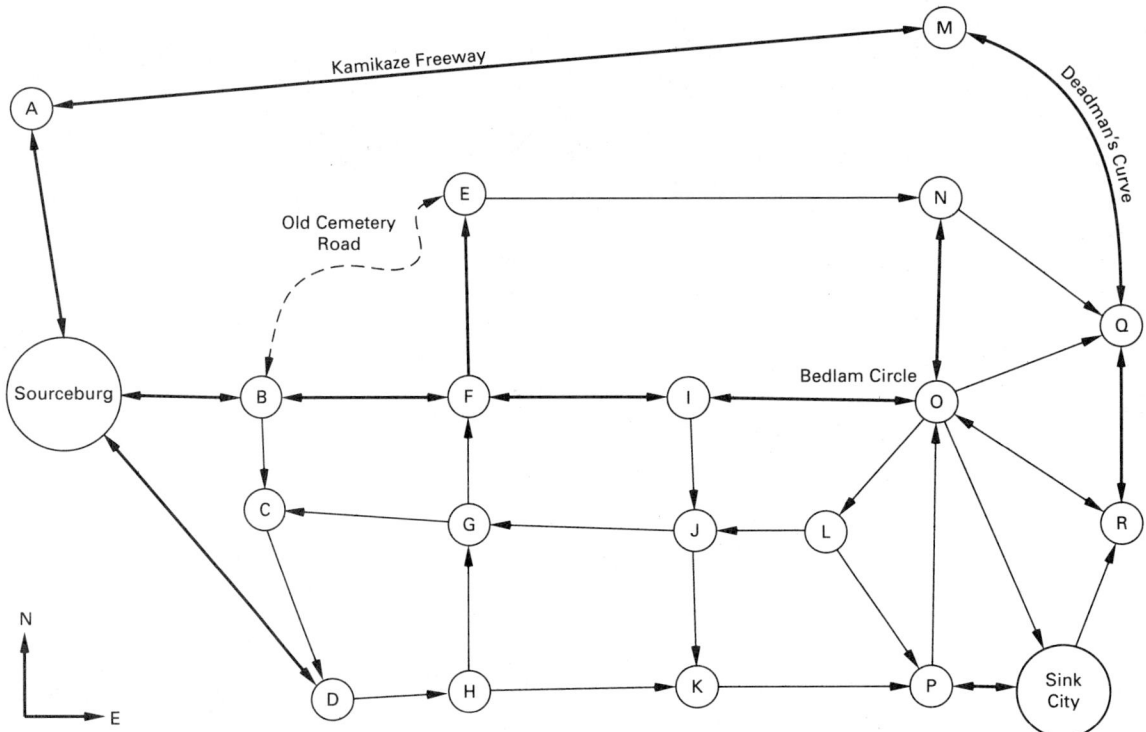

FIGURE 4.1 A commuter network

Driver may wish to select one route to work and perhaps a different route by which to return home, based on one of several criteria. One criterion might be to minimize total distance traveled, in which case Harry has the problem of finding the shortest route through a network. Another reasonable criterion might be minimization of total travel time to and from work, which we call a minimum cost (i.e., minimum time in Harry's case) route through a network. There are other possible criteria, such as "minimize danger to life and limb," which would probably involve a route that avoids high-speed, heavily traveled streets or roads (Sourceburg → B → C → D → H → G → F → I → J → K → P → Sink City might qualify).

As we shall shortly see, the preceding scenarios do not begin to exhaust the possibilities of modeling problems as networks. But what advantage do we gain by using this approach? If we recall ILP models from Chapter 3, we used zero-one variables to model situations in which a particular attribute or object is active in an optimal solution ($x_{ij} = 1$) or inactive ($x_{ij} = 0$). We can easily verify that Figure 4.1 contains 47 distinct arcs (note that we must consider two-way arcs to be two separate arcs), so that we may use 47 zero-one variables to represent the inclusion or exclusion of each arc from the desired route. If we add constraints that assure that the resulting solution is a **path** (an unbroken chain of arcs from source to sink), minimizing some weighted sum of these variables (e.g., total distance, total travel time) results in a zero-one ILP model.

But we already know the answer to the question at the beginning of the preceding paragraph: network models take advantage of special problem structures to develop special, highly efficient algorithms—some of which we will discuss later in the chapter. But in the case of network models, there is another important advantage in a managerial sense in that we can represent networks graphically in such a way that we considerably enhance our understanding of the underlying problem. As an illustration, modeling Harry's drive-to-work problem in Figure 4.1 as a zero-one ILP model would involve 47 variables and 600 constraints. We would gain very little managerial insight by poring over the resulting mathematical symbols. On the other hand, we immediately grasp the nature of the problem when we see the graphical representation in Figure 4.1.

UNDERLYING ASSUMPTIONS

Since network models are all special cases of zero-one ILP models, we see that at a minimum they must conform to the basic assumptions discussed in Chapter 3. But while we can model all network problems as zero-one ILP models, the converse is *not* true. As an illustration, let's return to Figure 4.1 and suppose that Harry Driver is attempting to minimize his driving time from Sink City to Sourceburg. Let us impose one, seemingly innocuous, additional condition that Harry is not allowed to turn left at F while traveling northbound from G. Note that this does *not* remove arc F-B as a viable route for cars coming from I—only for those coming from G. We call this restriction a **side condition,** and it effectively prevents us from modeling this problem as a network. Note that an ILP model easily accommodates this side condition by use of an if-then constraint (refer to Chapter 3); that is, we impose the restriction "if $x_{GF} = 1$, then $x_{FB} = 0$." Unfortunately, there is no way to represent such a restriction in the network itself.

The basic underlying assumption that permits modeling a problem as a network is that the problem has what is sometimes called the "semi-Markov property." This impressive-sounding label means only *that there are no relationships between arcs other than those defined by associated nodes* and that nodes must define the *same* relationships for each incoming and outgoing arc. This concept will become clearer as we explore various network models.

NETWORK MODELING AND ALGORITHMS

This section discusses four basic and very useful network models: (1) shortest route, (2) longest route, (3) minimal spanning tree, and (4) optimal flow.

SHORTEST ROUTE THROUGH A NETWORK

We have already seen an example of a shortest route model—the network in Figure 4.1 representing Harry Driver's commuting problem. It is worth noting at this point that shortest does not necessarily refer to physical distance. Perhaps a more descriptive title might be "Least Cost Route Through a Network," where the total "cost" to be minimized might be distance, time, expense, traffic density, exposure to speedtraps, etc. At any rate, the shortest route model involves identifying a cost c_{ij} for each arc (noting that c_{ij} may not be equal to c_{ji}), and the solution entails finding a path from source (origin) to sink (destination) that minimizes the sum of costs on the traversed arcs.

Before discussing an example, we must first address a subtle but important point regarding network configurations. If all costs for each arc are nonnegative, we may proceed to find the shortest route (least-cost path) through the network without further complication. However, if some or all of the costs are negative, we must determine whether we are dealing with an *acyclic* or a *cyclic* network. Stated simply, an acyclic network is one in which it is impossible to leave a node and traverse a path that returns to the same node. For example, the network in Figure 4.1 is not acyclic, since we can proceed from I to J to G to F and back to I. Note that if the sum of costs on this closed loop happened to be negative, our minimizing algorithm would cycle merrily through the loop over and over—decreasing the value of the objective function with each tour. Obviously, if the sum of costs was positive, the algorithm wouldn't behave in this unusual way. For now, we will assume that all costs on arcs are nonnegative, and thus avoid the problem of cycling. When we address longest-route problems in the next section, however, we will deal with this problem directly.

SHORTEST ROUTE MODEL—AN EXAMPLE

Consider the overhaul-or-replace problem for expensive equipment, such as an injection molding machine. Suppose we have just purchased one of these behemoths for $5 million, and we must plan to either overhaul the current machine or purchase a new one, each year for eight years into the future. Let

P_i = replacement cost at beginning of year i, $i = 0, \ldots, 7$

O_j = maintenance cost after j consecutive years, $j = 0, \ldots, 7$

There is obviously a "best" strategy to follow, since we will assume that replacement costs rise with inflation and that maintenance costs escalate both because of inflation and because of rising costs associated with maintaining aging equipment (i.e., it costs more to maintain a three-year-old injection molding machine than it does a one-year-old one). Obviously, we could model this problem as an ILP model, since it is a go/no-go problem. However, we can also model it as a network, as in Figure 4.2.

FIGURE 4.2
Repair or replace model

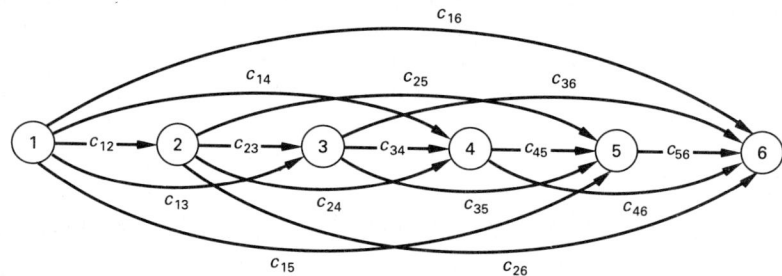

TABLE 4.1

Year	Operating Expense For the Year ($ 000)	Replacement Cost at End of Year
1	150	700
2	180	1,200
3	216	1,868
4	259	2,508
5	311	3,126
6	373	3,724
7	448	4,310
8	538	4,645

To illustrate how this model works, consider the repair or replace problem in Table 4.1 for the Qwerty Company, which uses an extrusion molding machine to manufacture the plastic keys for computer terminals and PCs.

We interpret these data as follows. If, for example, we decide to keep the new machine for three years before buying a new one, the cost of a new replacement (with trade-in) is $1,868,000. The cost of operating a new machine for three years is

$$\$150{,}000 + \$180{,}000 + \$216{,}000 = \$546{,}000$$

Thus, our total costs for the three-year period would be

$$\$1{,}868{,}000 + \$546{,}000 = \$2{,}414{,}000$$

Our problem is to operate the extrusion molding machine over an eight-year "window" and to minimize the total operating and acquisition cost. We assume in eight years that technological advances will have made the equipment obsolete, so that the equipment's terminal value is zero.

We number the initial node "0" to represent the point of purchase of the machine, and we need eight additional nodes to represent the end of years 1–8. Note that we need eight arcs from node 0 to the other nodes, seven arcs from node 1, six arcs from node 2, etc., so that our network has $(8 + 7 + 6 + 5 + 4 + 3 + 2 + 1) = 36$ arcs. The input screen to SAMS' distance networks module is shown in Figure 4.3 (costs are in $ million). The SAMS solution is

---

QWERTY CORPORATION
QUICK BRIEFING ON SHORTEST PATH TO YR8

Origin	Route	Distance
YR0	YR2→YR4→YR6→YR8	6.12

FIGURE 4.3 SAMS Input Screen for Qwerty

```
───▶  SAMS INPUT SCREEN - Network Modeling      ◀───

NAME?    QWERTY CORPORATION        TYPE?  Shortest Route
MAximize or MInimize?  MI
PROBLEM DESCRIPTION - Find optimal repair or replace
                     policy for molding machine
```

	YR0	YR1	YR2	YR3	YR4	YR5	YR6	YR7	YR8
YR0	.	.85	1.53	2.414	3.313	4.242	5.213	6.247	7.120
YR1	.	.	.85	1.53	2.414	3.313	4.242	5.213	6.247
YR2	.	.	.	.85	1.53	2.414	3.313	4.242	5.213
YR3	.	.	.	.	.85	1.53	2.414	3.313	4.242
YR4	.	.	.	.	.	.85	1.53	2.414	3.313
YR5	.	.	.	.	.	.	.85	1.53	2.414
YR6	.	.	.	.	.	.	.	.85	1.53
YR7	.	.	.	.	.	.	.	.	.85
YR8	.	.	.	.	.	.	.	.	.

In this example, operating costs are so high and depreciation on the machine is so rapid that it is preferable to replace the machine with a new one every two years. Note that this strategy saves a total of $1 million when compared with the strategy of keeping the machine for eight years.

As another example, consider the problem faced by Rollin Stone, the big-time rock promoter, who manages 20 rock groups who tour the United States and average 40 concerts each year. Some of the fastest rising and most sought after groups are in Rollin's stable, and Rollin's organization is responsible for contracting play dates, scheduling trips, and handling all of the other complex logistics involved.

In an idle moment in his office, Rollin does some quick calculations on the back of an envelope. "Let's see," he muses to himself, "there are about six performers on the average in each group, and each group travels about 40 times a year. If airline tickets average out at about $200 a copy, that's almost a million bucks a year! If I could cut that down a few hundred thousand, it would be pure gravy."

Glancing at his wall map of the United States, Rollin notes that his bookings usually include over 150 cities in a given year, so that there are $150 \times 149 = 22,350$ combinations in which a group can play in one city and travel to the next. The matter is further complicated by the fact that the great majority of these combinations are not connected by direct flights; that is, it requires two or more legs to go from one city to another. Finally, by taking advantage of various airline specials, Rollin could make flight reservations for the groups in such a way as to minimize total airfares.

The preceding scenario describes a problem that we can model profitably as a network. The nodes are, of course, the locations in which the 20 rock groups have play dates and other cities that provide airline links between these locations. We can state Rollin's objective rigorously as follows: find the path between each pair of cities in which Rollin schedules play dates, which minimizes the per-person airline fare. If there are n such cities, there are $n(n-1)$ models for shortest routes through a network. (*Note:* Because of airline specials and other factors, the fare from city A to city B is not necessarily the same as from city B to city A. If the fares are identical in every case, there are only $n(n-1)/2$ shortest route models to contend with.)

Although the preceding problem appears to be difficult to solve for large n, we shall see later that there are highly efficient computerized algorithms that can solve problems of the magnitude of Rollin's in a few seconds on a personal computer.

SHORTEST ROUTE ALGORITHMS

Highly efficient algorithms for finding the shortest route through networks have been around for many years. Basically, these algorithms implicitly perform SIMPLEX-like operations directly on the arc distances (or other criteria) and use shadow prices—and duality theory—to construct minimal paths. The most useful techniques automatically discover the shortest route from every node to every other node in the network, so that our rock promoter Rollin Stone would be able to solve his travel cost minimization problem quickly and efficiently. In fact, researchers have solved massive problems with hundreds of thousands of arcs in seconds (or at worst minutes) on modern, high-speed computers.

LONGEST ROUTE THROUGH A NETWORK

Other than the special case of a New York cabbie who takes tourists from Kennedy Airport to their downtown Manhattan hotels, why would anyone be interested in finding the longest path through a network? If we use our imagination, many such situations come to mind. For example, if arcs in a network represent graduate courses,

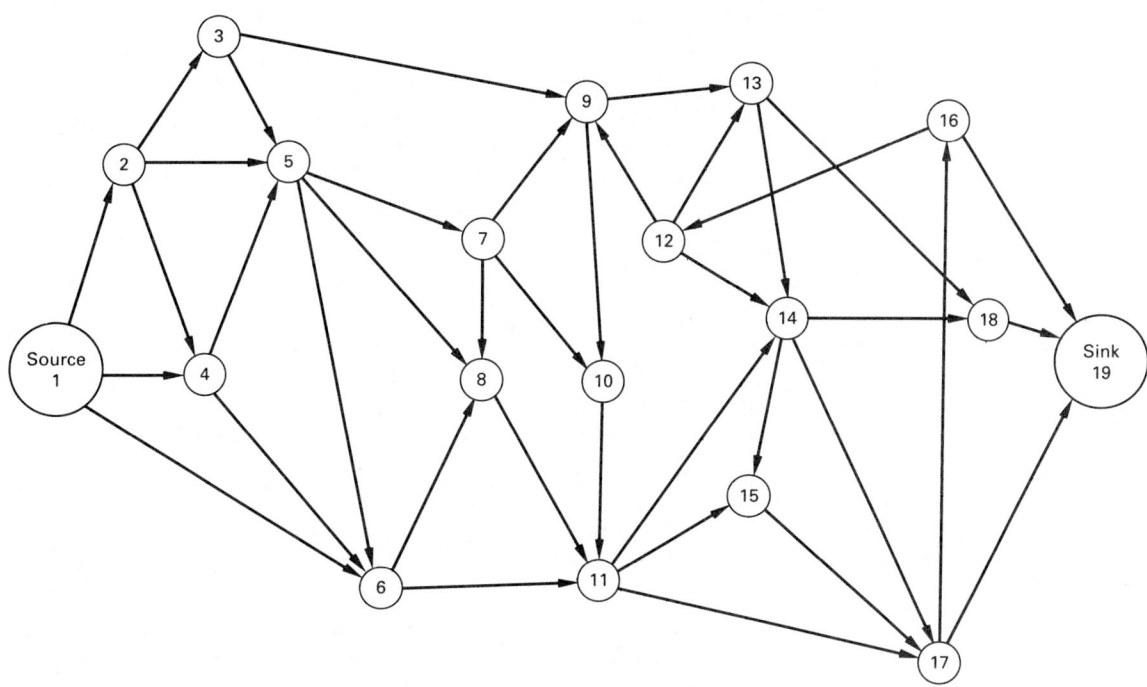

FIGURE 4.4
Cyclic network

the arrangement of nodes and arcs represents the prerequisite structure of our set of MBA courses; and if we can attach a weight to each course to indicate its relative importance, the longest route through the network would represent in some sense the best feasible curriculum attainable. A more recreational example might be to model the network of ski trails at Vail, Colorado, and to ski the mountain in such a way that we traverse the maximum total distance on the way to the bottom. The best known and most widely used application of the longest route model, however, is finding what is known as the critical path through a network representing the activities that constitute a major project. More about this shortly. First, however, we must settle the cyclic vs. acyclic network question.

NODE LABELING IN NETWORKS

In Figure 4.1, which has a total of 20 nodes and 47 connecting arcs, it is a simple matter to visually inspect the network diagram and discover the cycles that exist. However, in large network models of real problems, the network diagram (if we actually hired a draftsperson to draw it) might cover the playing field in a football stadium! Our "eyeball algorithm" would obviously be useless in such a situation.

As a small illustration, consider the 19-node, 39-arc network in Figure 4.4. Can you find a cycle in this small network by visual inspection? Perhaps you can—there are several (e.g., $16 \rightarrow 12 \rightarrow 14 \rightarrow 17 \rightarrow 16$). With 500 nodes and several thousand arcs, however, the task becomes too difficult to do by visual inspection, and we must have an organized method for doing two things:

1. Discovering whether a given network is cyclic.
2. If the network is acyclic, numbering the nodes in such a way that no node can be reached with a path beginning at a higher numbered node.

THE CRITICAL PATH MODEL (CPM)

Consider the contract just signed by Ray Wray, CEO of Ray's Raze and Raise, Inc., (RR&R) to demolish a 200-year-old building in downtown Philadelphia and to subsequently build a 20-story parking garage in its place. We can imagine the thousands of individual activities that such a massive project comprises—as well as the complex set of precedences that exist between and among these activities. As an obvious example, RR&R would certainly want to evacuate the immediate environs before setting off the dynamite to demolish the old building!

From experience, RR&R can estimate the time required to perform each of the many individual activities, but the critical item of managerial information needed is the time to complete the entire project. If we model the activities as arcs in a network and view the associated nodes as events in time (completion of one or more activities, beginning of other activities), we can model the problem in such a way that we maintain precedence relationships in the resulting acyclic network. The longest route through this project network will give the manager an indication of the total time required to complete this project.

In applications, we usually construct project networks by first setting up a macro-network consisting of large-scale activities. In the RR&R illustration, suppose this network consists of 13 macro-activities (see Table 4.2).

Note in Table 4.2 that we can pursue certain activities simultaneously (e.g., activities A, B, and C), while we cannot begin others until we have completed their predecessors (e.g., we must complete A and B before we begin D). Figure 4.5 is the macro-project network for the RR&R example.

Some explanation is in order regarding Figure 4.5. Note, for instance, that the activity arc for E emanates from node 4 and that the activity arcs for C and D terminate

TABLE 4.2 RR&R project macro-activities

Activity	Description	Predecessor Activities	Expected # Days Required
A	Set TNT charges	—	5
B	Evacuate environs	—	4
C	Assemble dump-truck fleet	—	3
D	Detonate TNT	A,B	1
E	Clean up rubble	C,D	7
F	Excavate basement	E	12
G	Erect steel superstructure	E	15
H	Pour concrete foundation	F	10
I	Install electric/plumbing	F,G	8
J	Install flooring	I	15
K	Hang walls	I	20
L	Install elevators	I	7
M	Do finishing work	H,J,K,L	14

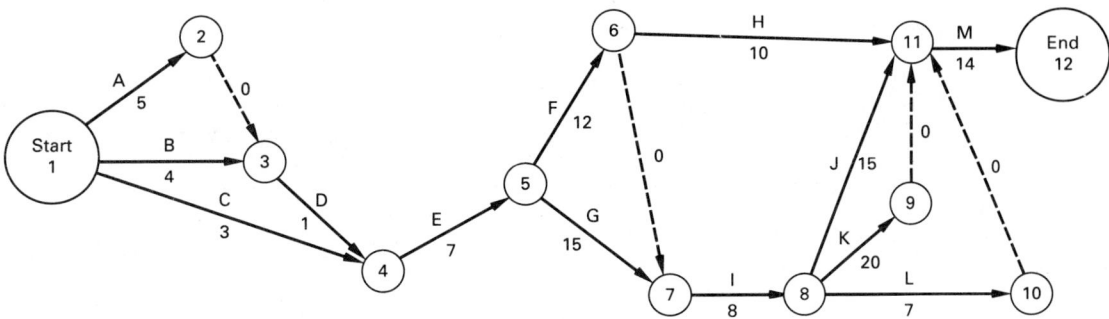

FIGURE 4.5
RR&R macro-project network

in node 4. This means that the earliest time activity E can start is the later of the times that we can complete C or D. This makes sense when we note from the activity descriptions that activities C and D are predecessors of activity E.

But what about the unlabeled dashed line connecting nodes 2 and 3? Couldn't we have connected nodes 1 and 3 with two activity arcs A and B to assure that we complete these activities before we begin D? The answer is yes, we could have; however, in deference to the limited capabilities of our electronic computer, we must use an extra node and a dummy activity to avoid confusion. Here's why. When we assemble the input data for computer analysis of our project network, we must describe each activity with three unique descriptors:

1. Node number at the tail of the arc.
2. Node number at the head of the arc.
3. Activity time of the arc.

If more than one arc had the same nodes as heads and tails, the computer would become hopelessly confused. Thus, we must use additional nodes and dummy arcs (with activity times of zero) to uniquely define the project network for purposes of computer analysis. We see in Figure 4.5 that we also used this device to indicate that both F and G are predecessors of I and that J, K, and L are predecessors of M.

The input screen for SAMS' distance networks module for this model is Figure 4.6. Note that this input screen is laid out as an nxn matrix with a "." originally in each cell. The "." tells SAMS that there is no arc between the two pairs of nodes, so that all we need to do is to insert the 17 distances to enter the RR&R network (in Figure 4.6). Note, however, that we need the actual network diagram to enter this model, since we have four dummy activities we used to indicate precedence relationships.

The SAMS report for the RR&R project network is as follows:

SAMS report for RR&R

RR&R PROJECT
QUICK REPORT ON LONGEST PATH TO N12

Origin	Route	Distance
N1	N2→N3→N4→N5→N7→N8→N9→ N11→N12	70.0

```
┌─────► SAMS INPUT SCREEN - Network Modeling ◄─────┐
│ NAME?  RAYS RAZE & RAISE        TYPE?  Longest Route │
│ MAximize or MInimize?  MA                            │
│ PROBLEM DESCRIPTION - Find completion time of razing and │
│                       construction project           │
├──────────────────────────────────────────────────────┤
```

	N2	N3	N4	N5	N6	N7	N8	N9	N10	N11	N12
N1	5.	4.	3.	.	.	.	.	.	.	.	.
N2	.	0.	.	.	.	.	.	.	.	.	.
N3	.	.	1.	.	.	.	.	.	.	.	.
N4	.	.	.	7.	.	.	.	.	.	.	.
N5	.	.	.	.	12.	15.	.	.	.	.	.
N6	.	.	0.	.	.	.	.	.	.	10.	.
N7	.	.	.	.	.	.	8.	.	.	.	.
N8	.	.	.	.	.	.	.	20.	7.	15.	.
N9	.	.	.	.	.	.	.	.	.	0.	.
N10	.	.	.	.	.	.	.	.	.	0.	.
N11	.	.	.	.	.	.	.	.	.	.	14.

FIGURE 4.6 SAMS input screen for RR&R

The longest path through the network in Figure 4.5 requires a total of 70 days. Usually called the **critical path** for obvious reasons, in our example this path traverses nodes $1 \to 2 \to 3 \to 4 \to 5 \to 7 \to 8 \to 9 \to 11 \to 12$, so that the **critical activities** are A, D, E, G, I, K, and M. Thus, if any one of these critical activities is delayed, the entire project will be delayed.

If you are concerned at this point that constructing a network for a large project might be an extremely complicated and time-consuming chore, please don't be. The SAMS PERT module has an option that accepts details of the project network directly from the activity table so that we do not need to construct the actual network (as in Figure 4.5). However, a visual representation of the project is often a valuable managerial tool as well as a helpful device in assisting us to understand project relationships.

LONGEST ROUTE ALGORITHMS

For the general longest route network model, we can generate an optimal solution by the simple device of reversing the algebraic signs of the distances and employing a shortest route algorithm. In the special case of a project scheduling network, we are interested in knowing the earliest and latest starting times for each activity—as well as the critical path (longest route) through the network. Researchers have developed special algorithms called "two-pass procedures" for such models, but the basic approach remains the same. SAMS' PERT module has this capability as well as the capability of analyzing the probabilistic version of CPM called PERT (Chapter 11).

MINIMAL SPANNING TREE MODEL

The basic purpose of spanning trees is to connect the nodes in such a way that we can reach every node from every other node by traversing designated arcs. A minimal spanning tree consists of a set of $n - 1$ arcs (there are n nodes) such that all nodes are spanned (connected) and the total cost or distance is as small as possible. To illustrate the minimal spanning tree model, consider the following problem of installing a computer local area network (LAN) spine of optical fiber in a small university.

Figure 4.7 shows the locations of the 14 campus sites that need to be connected on the LAN, and the 36 arcs represent utility tunnels already in place. Minimizing the total footage of optical fiber used in the LAN is important for two reasons: fiber is very expensive, and transmission quality is inversely related to total length. SAMS' network distance module has an option for minimal spanning trees that uses the same input format as the longest/shortest route options. For the network in Figure 4.7, only the 36 distances for the actual arcs need to be specified. The SAMS full briefing is in Table 4.3. Thus, the minimal span has a total length of 106 units.

Another familiar problem is one faced by Anita Parr, a former women's golf pro who is now the operations manager for the R. G. Bunker Country Club in Scottsdale, Arizona. Anita's report that the putting greens are in bad shape has elicited action from the board of directors, and Anita has the funds available to install a much-needed sprinkler system. However, Anita is well aware that the cost of installing the system of water pipes depends on the total length of pipe in the system, and she wishes to plan the system in such a way that each of the 18 greens has a sprinkler, water is pumped from a single source near the clubhouse, and total pipe length is minimized. As a side benefit, Anita realizes that water pressure is inversely related to total system pipe footage.

We can model Anita's problem—and a multitude of related problems—as a network in which nodes represent sites that need service (e.g., putting greens) and arcs

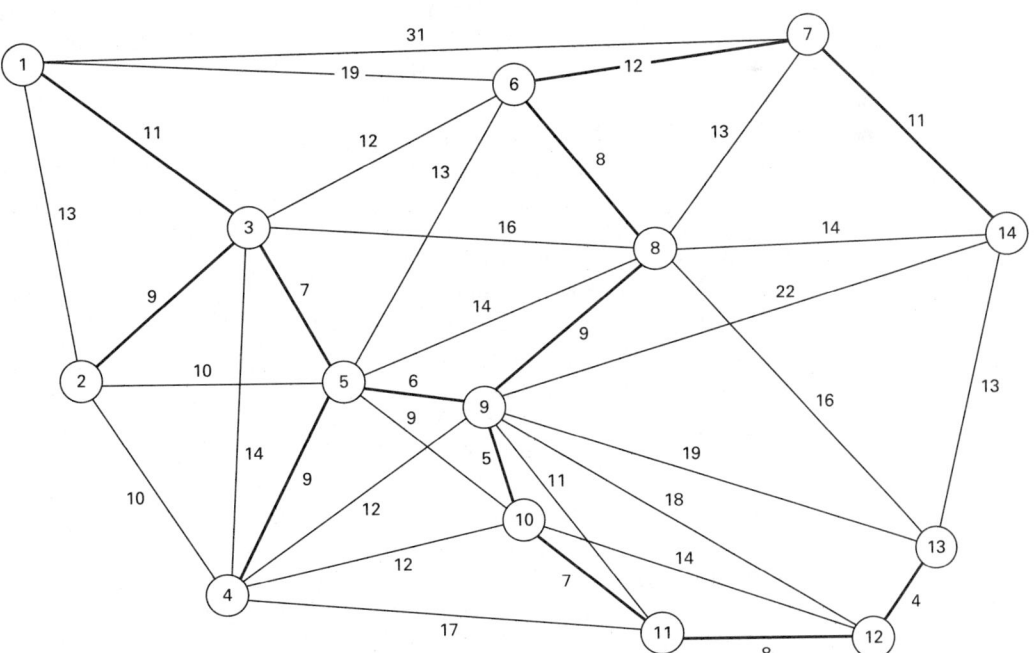

FIGURE 4.7
Minimal spanning tree for computer network

TABLE 4.3 SAMS report for Figure 4.7: Spanning trees

MINIMAL SPANNING TREE
FULL BRIEFING ON COMPUTER NETWORK

Minimal Spanning Tree Length = 106

Connection	Length	Connection	Length	Connection	Length
N1→N3	11.0	N3→N5	7.0	N5→N9	6.0
N9→N10	5.0	N10→N11	7.0	N11→N12	8.0
N12→N13	4.0	N3→N2	9.0	N5→N4	9.0
N9→N8	9.0	N8→N6	8.0	N6→N7	12.0
N7→N14	11.0				

represent access mechanisms (e.g., water pipes). Other illustrations include providing telephone or cable television service to a set of rural communities, scheduling regional airline service, and providing road service among scenic areas in a large national park. We can profitably model such problems using minimal spanning trees.

THE MINIMAL SPANNING TREE ALGORITHM

The minimal spanning tree algorithm is one of the simplest and most elegant optimizing techniques in all of MS. It is one of the very few algorithms that reward "greedy" behavior with an optimal result. For example, in the general linear programming model, we might consider using a greedy approach. That is, we could find the variable with the smallest cost (minimization model) and make its value as large as possible. After reducing the RHSs of the constraints to account for the effect of this variable, we could repeat this process with the next lowest cost, etc., until we have used up all the resources. Unfortunately, this greedy behavior usually leads to a suboptimal—and often very poor—solution.

Although we promised earlier in the text not to belabor MBA students with algorithmic details, the minimum spanning tree technique is so easy to understand and use that we can't resist sharing it in its glorious simplicity (see Table 4.4).

That's all there is to it! If there are n nodes, there will be exactly $(n-1)$ arcs in the minimal spanning tree, so that computational effort depends only on the number of nodes—and not on the number of arcs. If you wish to try out this algorithm, construct the minimal spanning tree manually for the computer LAN in Figure 4.7. You will verify that the darkened arcs denote the minimal spanning tree. If you are still skeptical, you might choose different starting nodes in STEP 1 and confirm that you always get the same answer, with a total spanning distance of 106 units.

In practice, of course, minimal spanning tree models are sometimes immense, so that it may be unlikely that we can actually explicitly draw the network model. Thus, it is important that we have access to a computerized algorithm such as SAMS' network distance module to perform an algebraic analysis.

TABLE 4.4 Minimal spanning tree algorithm

STEP 1:	Choose any node and include the arc for the node closest to it in the spanning tree. Go to STEP 2.
STEP 2:	Scan all nodes currently connected by an arc in the spanning tree and locate the unconnected node that is closest to a connected node. Include this arc in the spanning tree and go to STEP 3.
STEP 3:	If all nodes are connected, stop; we have found the minimal spanning tree. Otherwise, return to to STEP 2.

OPTIMAL NETWORK FLOW MODEL

Perhaps the most widely used network representation is the optimal network flow model. As an illustration, let's view the commuter network in Figure 4.1 in a different way.

Carl Poole is Commissioner of Roads and Streets in Noah County, in which both Sourceburg and Sink City are located. As suburban Sourceburg grows, Carl is concerned that the traffic system leading to Sink City will become saturated, and he wishes to pinpoint bottleneck streets and roads for possible widening. Using standard criteria such as number of traffic lanes, speed limit, and street or road conditions, Carl estimates the maximum traffic flow in vehicles per hour for each street segment (arc) between each major intersection (node). Figure 4.8 graphically depicts Carl's results, with flow capacities annotated on the arcs. (*Note:* On two-way streets, we separate differential flows in each direction by a slash mark, and capacities are in the direction of the arrow.) If Carl can compute the **maximum flow** through this network, streets or roads that are at capacity would be candidates for managerial attention.

We can use SAMS' network flow module to find the maximum possible flow through this network. We have 20 nodes (source, 18 intersections, and sink) and 47 arcs, so this is a nontrivial problem. In building the SAMS data file, note that we input the arcs emanating from the source and entering the sink as follows:

Arc	From	To	Cost	Lower Bound	Upper Bound
SOURCE→A etc.	.	1	1	0	8000
O→SINK etc.	16	.	1	0	19000

The "." tells SAMS that the nodes are origins and destinations. By using a "cost" of 1 for all arcs, the optimal value of the objective function becomes the maximum flow possible in the network.

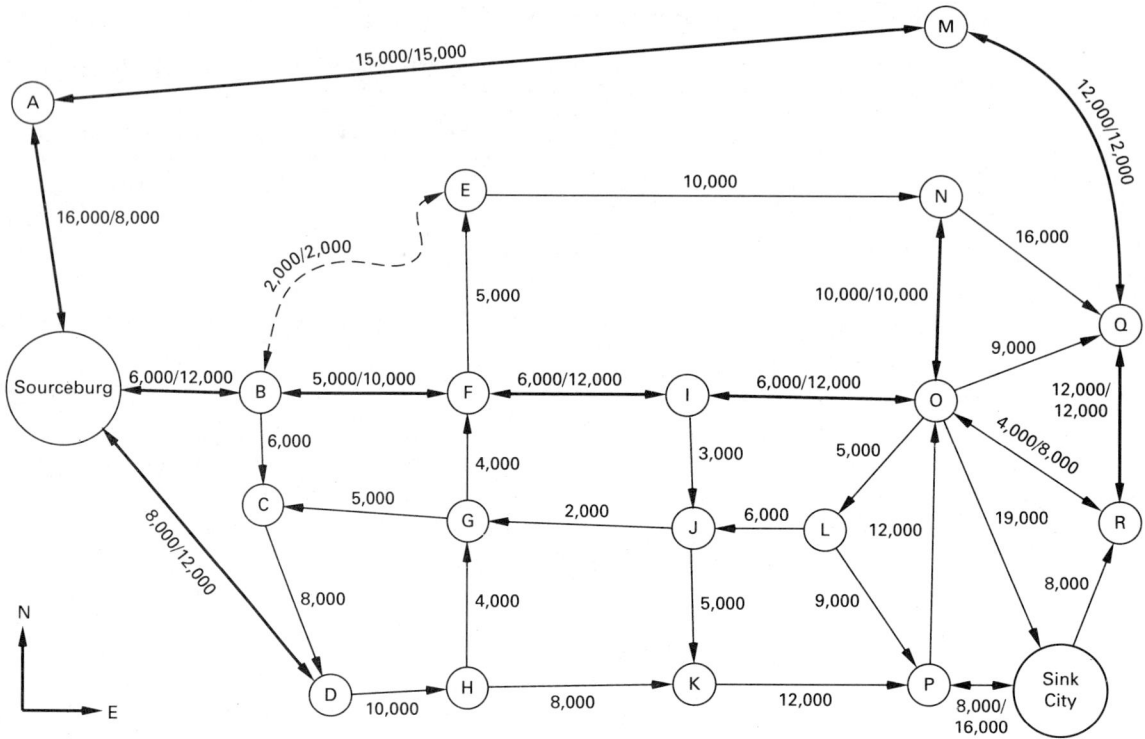

FIGURE 4.8
Noah County road and street system

Taking this illustration one step further, consider the possibility of developing engineering estimates of the maximum possible traffic flows on each road segment resulting from widening the segment, changing the speed limit, etc. If we can estimate the cost of road improvements in dollars per unit of increased flow, we have a classical minimum cost flow model.

There are several special cases of the network flow model, and people use these special situations so widely in practice that they have their own descriptive titles—the transportation model, the assignment model, and the transshipment model. The following sections discuss each of these special cases.

THE TRANSPORTATION MODEL

The **transportation model** is one of the most useful and versatile network flow models. Let's enlist the assistance of an interactive knowledge-based computer program called ONO (optimal network operator), who specializes in network flow modeling and analysis and is unusually empathetic.

THE SCENARIO

  ONO: I feel my brother is in need of help.
  ROLLIN: Help, ONO. My name is Rollin Stone, and I'm a rock promoter.
  ONO: What is the nature of your problem, my brother?
  ROLLIN: I'm trying to help some of my clients schedule charity appearances.

THE PROBLEM

ROLLIN: Four of my more famous clients—Pepper, Jude, Walrus, and Daytripper—are willing to donate a certain amount of their time to worthy charitable causes, and I'm trying to help them control expenses. Let me type in the number of hours of performing time each can donate.

Performer	Hours
Pepper	40
Jude	35
Walrus	25
Daytripper	50
Total hours available	150

ONO: Ah, sweet charity.

ROLLIN: Uh . . . right. Now, three wealthy women representing worthy causes have requested free performances, as follows:

Sponsor	Hours Requested
Lucy	72
Eleanor	34
Yoko	60
Total hours requested	166

TABLE 4.5 Per-hour performing costs

Sponsor	Performer				Needed
	Pepper	Jude	Walrus	Daytripper	
Lucy	$1,300	$1,600	$2,200	$2,500	72
Eleanor	1,500	2,000	1,300	2,100	34
Yoko	1,700	1,400	1,800	1,900	60
Available	40	35	25	50	150/166

ONO: Oh, we are 16 hours short. Perhaps I can help with a tune or two.

ROLLIN: No thanks, ONO. After all, the performances are free, and the worthy causes always pad their requests. At any rate, the costs *per hour* that the four performers will incur for the three causes are in the data currently being entered [Table 4.5]. There it is. How can I minimize my performers' total costs, ONO? Are you sure you can help? You sound a little strange to me.

ONO: I have no personal wisdom in this regard, but I get by with a little help from SAMS [Figure 4.9 and Table 4.6].

ROLLIN: I think I understand, ONO. Pepper does all of his 40 hours for Lucy's cause, and Jude splits time with Lucy and Yoko. That's appropriate. And Walrus donates his 25 hours to Eleanor, while Daytripper splits 50 hours between Yoko (41) and Eleanor (9). There might be some personality or other conflicts here—I'll check out the proposed solution with the performers and sponsors. If this solution is feasible, it will save the rock stars a lot of money—I had estimated about $320,000 using rules of thumb, and this plan would cost $233,500.

ONO: One moment, my brother. Did you not notice that Yoko and Eleanor get all of their requested hours, while Lucy suffers the entire shortfall of 16 hours? Will you not consider alternate paths?

ROLLIN: Oh, I suppose so. I don't want to discriminate against anyone.

FIGURE 4.9 SAMS input screen for Rollin Stone

```
SAMS INPUT SCREEN - Network Modeling

NAME?  ROLLIN STONE CHARITY     TYPE?  Transportation
MAximize or MInimize?  MI
PROBLEM DESCRIPTION - Find optimal assignments of rock
                     groups to charity functions
```

ARC	FROM	TO	COST	LB	UB
1	.	PEPP	0	40	40
2	.	JUDE	0	35	35
3	.	WALR	0	25	25
4	.	DAYT	0	50	50
5	PEPP	LUCY	1300	0	72
6	PEPP	ELEA	1500	0	34
7	PEPP	YOKO	1700	0	60
8	JUDE	LUCY	1600	0	72
9	JUDE	ELEA	2000	0	34
10	JUDE	YOKO	1400	0	60
11	WALR	LUCY	2200	0	72
12	WALR	ELEA	1300	0	34
13	WALR	YOKO	1800	0	60
14	DAYT	LUCY	2500	0	72
15	DAYT	ELEA	2100	0	34
16	DAYT	YOKO	1900	0	60
17	LUCY	.	0	0	72
18	ELEA	.	0	0	34
19	YOKO	.	0	0	60

TABLE 4.6 SAMS summary report for Rollin Stone's problem

```
ROLLIN STONE & ONO
QUICK REPORT ON OPTIMAL ALLOCATION
```

Arc	From	To	Flow	Arc Cost
1	.	PEPP	40	0
2	.	JUDE	35	0
3	.	WALR	25	0
4	.	DAYT	50	0
5	PEPP	LUCY	40	52000
10	JUDE	YOKO	19	26600
12	WALR	ELEA	25	32500
13	JUDE	LUCY	16	25600
14	DAYT	YOKO	41	77900
15	DAYT	ELEA	9	18900
17	LUCY	.	56	0
18	ELEA	.	34	0
19	YOKO	.	60	0
		Total Cost:		233500

ONO: Good-bye. We will meet again. [Problem 3 in the end-of-chapter problems, to be specific.]

Lest this small example mask the importance of the transportation model, let us investigate a somewhat more realistic scenario.

Scarbury Condiments, Inc. (SCI) is a national distributor of spices, supplying 25 supermarket chains with house brands that they package and label themselves. SCI's VP for Production introduced the concept of a basic production unit—a 100-pound bale of assorted spices—and the company's 12 plants process and ship these units to advance orders from 200 supermarket supply points. Production costs vary at each of the 12 plants, as do shipping costs from the plants to the supermarket supply points. SCI's assistant VP is responsible for assigning monthly production quotas to the plants as well as determining shipping patterns.

A bit of reflection reveals that we can model SCI's problem as a linear program. Let

x_{ij} = number of bales shipped from plant i to destination j

c_{ij} = production cost at plant i, plus shipping cost from plant i to destination j

S_i = production capacity of plant i

D_j = demand at destination j

Then we may write the cost-minimization LP model for the SCI problem as

$$\text{MIN } x_0 = \sum_{i=1}^{12} \sum_{j=1}^{200} c_{ij} x_{ij} \tag{4.1}$$

$$\text{S T:} \quad \sum_{i=1}^{12} x_{ij} = D_j, \ j = 1, \ldots, 200 \tag{4.2}$$

$$\sum_{j=1}^{200} x_{ij} \leq S_i, \ i = 1, \ldots, 12 \tag{4.3}$$

$$x_{ij} \geq 0; \ i = 1, \ldots, 12; \ j = 1, \ldots, 200 \tag{4.4}$$

As we have seen, modeling a problem in a certain way and solving the resulting model are two quite different matters. For instance, the LP model above has only 212 constraints: 200 in Equation (4.2) that assure that we satisfy the demands and 12 in Equation (4.3) that limit shipments from each plant to no more than its capacity. However, there are 2,400 variables! If SCI has access only to a microcomputer, it is unlikely that the LP model will even fit in the computer's memory.

Fortunately, we can model problems such as SCI's as transportation models. Figure 4.10 portrays a small transportation model with three *origins* (supply points) A, B, and C, and four *destinations* (demand points) #1, 2, 3, and 4. We added the nodes labeled "Source" and "Sink" in order to represent the system as a network flow model. The numbers in parentheses represent minimum flow and maximum flow, respectively, through the associated arc.

Note how cleverly the network represents the associated LP model. Flow restrictions on the arcs from the "source" node to the "supply" nodes allow no more than the production capacity for each plant to "flow into the plant," so that by something called **conservation of flow,** each plant can ship no more than its capacity. The arcs from origins to destinations are essentially uncapacitated, except that we do not allow negative flow. The arcs from the destination nodes to the "sink" node must allow flows representing the actual demands (since we set both upper and lower bounds at the same

FIGURE 4.10
Transportation network

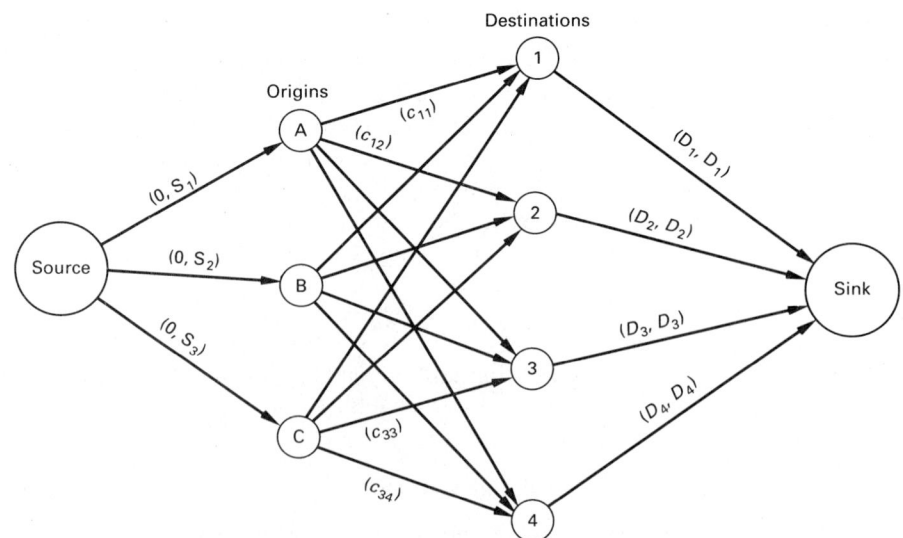

level), so that—again, because of conservation of flow—we meet the demands exactly on the arcs between origin and destination nodes. The optimizing algorithm (discussed later) generates a flow pattern that minimizes the sum of total costs.

We need to address some additional modeling features. If the total supply is greater than the total demand, there is no problem—total flow in the network can never exceed total demand. However, if total demand exceeds total supply, we do indeed have a problem. Some texts advise the modeler to merely add a dummy plant with production capacity sufficient to meet the unfilled demand—with a production and shipping cost of zero for these make-believe units. To a mathematician, this is a logical and elegant procedure; to a managerial decision maker, it is foolishness. We would *never* allow an algorithm to make critical business decisions such as which customer to short on an order when our supply is limited.

The point, of course, is that a network model—or any analytical device for that matter—ignores such niceties as customer goodwill and other exogenous considerations. It is the manager's job to use logic, experience, and common sense to resolve difficulties such as the preceding.

We can deal with other constraints directly in the transportation network. For example, if there are limited shipping facilities between some origins and destinations, we can place upper bounds on the appropriate arcs to reflect this situation. Moreover, suppose we are concerned with economies of scale at the production facilities represented by origins. We merely place appropriate lower bounds on the arcs from the "source" node to the origin nodes. Finally, if we wish to maximize profit contribution (or some other criterion) in a transportation network, we minimize the total "cost" by using the negatives of the c_{ij}s.

THE ASSIGNMENT MODEL

The **assignment model** is a special case of the transportation model, in which all supplies $S_i = 1$ and all demands $D_j = 1$. As an example, consider the problem faced by CompuMax Systems, a small company that sells and provides service for networked computer systems to educational institutions such as school districts and small colleges and junior colleges. Sales teams include a marketing specialist who understands client needs and a technical specialist who tailors computer systems to meet those needs. Since team members work very closely together, it is important that the two members be compatible with each other.

CompuMax has hired 10 marketing specialists and 10 technical specialists. Using a Myers-Briggs personality inventory questionnaire, the company's personnel director has determined an incompatibility index for each marketer and technician. The index ranges from 20, indicating instant hostility, to 1, indicating extremely high compatibility. These indexes are in Table 4.7.

We see that if we designate one group as "origins" and the other as "destinations," we have a simplified transportation problem. What the personnel director wishes to do, of course, is to assign one marketer to each technician in such a way that the total incompatibility score is as small as possible.

We used SAMS' network flow module for both minimization and maximization, and the SAMS quick briefings are listed in Table 4.8. In the minimizing model, six pairings received the lowest possible incompatibility ratings, but the assignment is apparently flawed by the highly incompatible pairing of MAX and CAS. However, MAX and CAS—as one can see by inspecting the incompatibility matrix—are oddballs, so the algorithm assigned them to each other to avoid having *two* highly incom-

TABLE 4.7 Marketing specialists

	\multicolumn{10}{c}{Technical Specialists}
	ANN	BEV	CAS	DOT	EMY	FAN	GIG	HET	INA	JEN
KEN	11	8	15	3	9	17	14	6	12	2
LOU	7	4	13	11	19	2	10	5	18	9
MAX	13	20	19	12	14	11	16	9	15	14
NED	5	8	12	6	1	3	4	7	10	12
ORV	16	7	18	9	13	1	2	17	12	3
PAT	12	3	11	17	5	6	18	2	1	4
QUE	9	1	20	4	7	20	19	1	19	16
ROG	8	6	17	8	11	4	3	4	13	6
SAM	17	2	19	13	14	19	11	3	17	1
TED	12	1	20	1	2	5	6	4	1	13

patible couples! In this case, CompuMax would probably decide to use these two employees in a different capacity and operate with only nine sales teams.

The reason we ran the maximization model was to contrast the best and worst possible pairings. The very large difference highlights the importance of modeling this problem as an assignment model.

The small example just discussed should not mask the importance of assignment models. Managers use them thousands of times each day for dozens of purposes, such as scheduling personnel, assigning aircraft to routes, and routing jobs onto machines.

THE TRANSSHIPMENT MODEL

In its original form, the **transshipment model** was a transportation network with a set of intermediate nodes between origins and destinations. For example, in our SCI problem, suppose the plants shipped their output to a set of six warehouses, which supplied spice bales to supermarket supply points from the warehouses. Although it may not be immediately obvious, we cannot solve this model optimally by first optimizing the shipment between plants and warehouses and then solving a separate transportation problem for warehouses and destinations. This procedure will almost always result in a suboptimal solution to the overall model.

Happily, we can insert the intermediate nodes into the network and construct and bound appropriate arcs, and a network flow model results. As a modeling device, however, transshipment networks are not limited to a single set of intermediate nodes (e.g., warehouses). That is to say, we can easily include several stages of transshipment. An interesting real-world application of this technique was its use in the U.S. Air Force's undergraduate flying training program [3].

TABLE 4.8

```
COMPUMAX—MINIMIZATION
QUICK BRIEFING ON OPTIMAL ASSIGNMENT
```

Row	Column	Arc Cost
KEN	DOT	3
LOU	ANN	7
MAX	CAS	19
NED	EMY	1
ORV	FAN	1
PAT	INA	1
QUE	HET	1
ROG	GIG	3
SAM	JEN	1
TED	BEV	1
Total Cost:		38

```
COMPUMAX—MAXIMIZATION
QUICK BRIEFING ON OPTIMAL ASSIGNMENT
```

Row	Column	Arc Cost
KEN	FAN	17
LOU	EMY	19
MAX	BEV	20
NED	JEN	12
ORV	HET	17
PAT	DOT	17
QUE	GIG	19
ROG	INA	13
SAM	ANN	17
TED	CAS	20
Total Cost:		171

COMMENTS ON NETWORK MODELING

As noted at the beginning of this chapter, network models are special cases of ILP models. We also noted that the visual nature of networks is important in two respects: it gives insight to the underlying problem that mathematical notation cannot give, and it makes network modeling much easier to explain to unsophisticated colleagues. We shall see shortly that researchers have constructed specialized network algorithms and that these techniques are significantly more efficient (in computer implementation) than ILP or even LP algorithms in solving network models.

But how do we recognize problems that can be modeled as networks? In many cases—such as critical path or spanning tree or transportation problems—it will be obvious. In other cases, a network formulation may be far from obvious.

NETWORK FLOW ALGORITHMS

Since problems that we can represent as network flow models are so important in real-world applications, researchers have done a great deal of work in developing efficient optimizing algorithms for such models. Until very recently, researchers thought the colorfully titled "out-of-kilter" algorithm of Ford and Fulkerson [6] to be the most efficient computational technique possible. This approach, as is true for so many others, relies on results from LP duality theory for its power and effectiveness. It uses parameters called "kilter numbers" to characterize network arcs. The nature of these kilter numbers indicates whether the flow restrictions are violated or whether we should increase or decrease current flow in an arc to improve the value of the objective function. This approach is still in wide use in practice.

In recent years, however, researchers have developed and tested highly efficient algorithms that outperform out-of-kilter codes. The basic approach of these new techniques is to take advantage of the specialized structure of so-called generalized networks to greatly increase computational efficiency. The technical details of these techniques are too complex for our purposes, but we note that we can now in a reasonable amount of computer time solve many very large network models that were essentially intractable before.

DEVELOPING ALTERNATIVE SOLUTIONS

As usual, we stress that using the output from quantitative models to develop alternative solutions to underlying problems is a critical managerial activity. You will recall from the previous chapters on LP and ILP that we were dealing solely with optimizing models—i.e., models that sought the best solutions available. Our task, then, was to generate good alternative model solutions that afforded managerial flexibility in finding a solution to the problem we were addressing. Some network models—assignment, transportation, minimal spanning tree, shortest route, minimum cost flow—are also optimizing. Others—finding the critical path in a project network, finding the maximum flow in a capacitated network—are essentially *descriptive* in nature. The following sections deal with these two types of models separately.

DESCRIPTIVE NETWORK MODELS

Consider first the project scheduling problem and the critical path through the project network. How can a decision maker use the output from a package like SAMS to develop managerial strategies? (*Note:* There are no "alternative solutions" in the usual sense for a descriptive model.) Let's examine the output from SAMS' PERT module for the RR&R problem depicted in Figure 4.5 (see Table 4.9).

First and most obvious, we would want to take a close look at our estimates of completion times for activities on the critical path, which are listed first in Table 4.9. Every day that we underestimate these times represents a day added to project completion time, and we want our estimates for the critical activities to be as good as possible.

Next we turn to noncritical activities listed. The column labeled "Free Slack" refers to the number of days these activities can slip or stretch out—all immediate

TABLE 4.9 SAMS PERT module output for RR&R

**RR&R PROJECT NETWORK
FULL BRIEFING ON PROJECT**

Earliest project completion time is 70.

CRITICAL ACTIVITIES

Activity	Start Time		Finish Time		Free Slack
	Earliest	Latest	Earliest	Latest	
SET TNT	0.0	0.0	5.0	5.0	0.0
DETONATE	1.0	1.0	6.0	6.0	0.0
DUMMY1	5.0	5.0	5.0	5.0	0.0
CLEANUP	6.0	6.0	13.0	13.0	0.0
ERESTEEL	13.0	13.0	28.0	28.0	0.0
ELECTRIC	28.0	28.0	36.0	36.0	0.0
HANGWALL	36.0	36.0	56.0	56.0	0.0
DUMMY3	56.0	56.0	56.0	56.0	0.0
FINISH	56.0	56.0	70.0	70.0	0.0

NONCRITICAL ACTIVITIES

Activity	Earliest	Latest	Earliest	Latest	Free Slack
EVACUATE	0.0	1.0	4.0	5.0	1.0
ASSMDUMP	0.0	3.0	3.0	6.0	3.0
EXCAVATE	13.0	16.0	25.0	28.0	3.0
DUMMY2	28.0	28.0	28.0	28.0	0.0
FLOOR	36.0	41.0	51.0	56.0	5.0
ELEVATR	36.0	49.0	43.0	56.0	13.0
DUMMY4	56.0	56.0	56.0	56.0	0.0
CONCRETE	25.0	46.0	35.0	56.0	21.0

successor activities starting as late as possible—without affecting project completion time. In the example, our only serious prospective problem might be with activity B—evacuating people from the vicinity of the old building. We have estimated that this activity will require four days—but we have only one day of slack to play with. We delve into this subject more carefully in Chapter 11.

Finally, managers can use the output from a CPM model to assist in making resource allocation decisions. For example, in the absence of highly restrictive trade union agreements, we could assign fewer workers to activity H (pouring the concrete foundation), effectively lengthening the completion time for this noncritical activity. We could use the resources thus saved to apply to critical activities such as G, I, or J to shorten their activity times—and thus shorten project completion time.

Another purely descriptive network model involves finding the maximum flow pattern through a capacitated network. In our earlier example, Carl Poole of Noah

County used such a model to identify potential bottlenecks in the road and street system. We can use an analysis very similar to the earlier CPM discussion to develop alternative strategies in this type of decision-making situation.

OPTIMIZING NETWORK MODELS

In modeling a problem as a shortest route network model, we are seeking a path from each node in a set of nodes to each node in another (possibly nonexclusive) set. Two different managerial approaches are possible in performing sensitivity analysis on such models. First, analogous to the critical path discussion, the optimizing algorithm has (in a different sense) identified a set of critical arcs that constitute the shortest path through the network. We might wish to carefully recheck our estimates for the "distances" on these arcs to assure that they are accurate enough for our purposes. Second, as discussed in LP and ILP models, there are efficient algorithms that generate the k best solutions to the model and thereby generate good, suboptimal solutions that serve as viable alternatives for the decision maker. In this way, if environmental considerations for some reason make the shortest route nonviable, the manager has good substitutes at hand.

When using minimum-cost flow networks as modeling devices, we are in luck as regards the availability of sensitivity analysis tools. We recall from our previous discussion that the special structure of network models (and especially network flow models) means that we can solve their ILP formulation directly with the SIMPLEX algorithm—assuming that the right-hand sides of the constraints are integers. Since modern, efficient algorithms for solving these problems are based on LP theory, shadow prices are also available to aid us in our sensitivity analysis. Thus, our discussion on developing alternative solutions in Chapter 2 carries over directly for minimum-cost flow network models.

STATE OF THE ART IN NETWORK MODELING

The literature dealing with modeling and solution approaches in networks is rich and varied. This section briefly discusses a few advanced topics and specialized models to get a flavor of this variety, but please understand that our coverage is far from exhaustive. To accomplish this, we would need an entire text of the same size as this book.

THE CHINESE POSTMAN MODEL

Recall from Chapter 3 that the traveling salesman model involves a network with n nodes and with arcs connecting every node to every other node. The object is to visit every node exactly once and return to the starting node in such a way that total distance traveled (or cost incurred, etc.) is a minimum. The well-known Chinese postman problem (named after its formulator M. Kwan, a Chinese mathematician) is a variant of the traveling salesman problem in that some of the nodes are not connected to others by arcs. The object is to travel each arc at least once and return to the original starting point in such a way that the total distance traveled is minimum. This is precisely the problem faced by a postman, hence the name. We can model other real-world problems in this way—e.g., routing of street cleaners, snow removal crews, sanitary engineering teams, political canvassers, and forest fire control teams. At the present writing, however, there is not an efficient optimizing algorithm for

MULTICOMMODITY NETWORK FLOWS

In transportation, transshipment, and assignment models, we dealt with minimizing the total production and transportation cost of supplying a single product to several destinations from several sources—perhaps with one or more intermediate stages, as in the transshipment model. What if we wish to model and solve such a problem involving several different products? This expanded model is called the **multicommodity network flow model**, and finding efficient solution techniques for such models is on the frontier of current research efforts. The underlying problem is that we must keep track of each of the different products or commodities separately. To date, researchers have shown that it is impossible to transform the general multicommodity problem into a single-commodity problem and that—even though all supplies and demands are integer valued—the optimal flow may not be integer.

IMBEDDED NETWORKS

Many large-scale models of complex problems are not themselves networks, but there may be one or more network subproblems imbedded within the larger model (e.g., linear programming). For example, recall that we discussed block diagonal LP models and the use of Dantzig-Wolfe decomposition to break them apart for computational or operational reasons. If the submodels happen to be networks, such as transportation models, we can use highly efficient network optimizing algorithms rather than resorting to the SIMPLEX algorithm. We can model a surprisingly large number of such real-world problems in this way, and a sharp-eyed decision maker should always be on the lookout for such situations.

THE MIN-CUT/ MAX-FLOW THEOREM

We include the result we are about to discuss because it is interesting and intuitively appealing. Ford and Fulkerson discovered and proved the **min cut/max-flow theorem**, which follows:

The maximum flow through a capacitated network is equal to the sum of flows through the minimum cut-set, where a cut-set is defined as any set of arcs that, if severed or "cut," halts all flow from source to sink.

In plain English, the value of the maximum flow through a capacitated network is equal to the sum of flow capacities of the cut-set with the lowest such sum. For example, in the Noah County network in Figure 4.8, arcs O → Sink City and P → Sink City form a cut-set with a total inbound flow capacity of 19,000 + 16,000 = 35,000 vehicles per hour. However, the cut-set Source → A, Source → B, and Source → D has a total outbound flow capacity of 8,000 + 12,000 + 12,000 = 32,000 vehicles per hour, so that the first cut-set is not a minimum cut-set. You might wish to verify from our analysis earlier in the chapter that the cut-set Source → B, D → H, and R → O is indeed the minimum one, so that maximum flow through the network is 26,000 vehicles per hour.

Unfortunately, applying the elegant min-cut/max-flow theorem directly has not been successful in practice. To pique your curiosity, however—and to reinforce a point from Chapter 2—this theorem amounts to a dual formulation of the associated LP problem.

MINICASES

Meter Readers [2]

THE SCENARIO

Eclectic Electric Energy, Inc. (EEE) provides electric power to a region that includes a large portion of West Texas and eastern New Mexico. In its local office in Amarillo, a city of approximately 160,000 people, Meg Watts heads the department responsible for reading electric meters. Meg is a recent graduate of the MBA program at a large state university and concentrated her elective courses in personnel management/organizational behavior. Meg's office staff consists of a secretary, a file clerk, and eight meter readers. Her predecessor had divided the city into 20 zones, with each zone containing 8 subzones, so that the team of meter readers completed one zone every workday. Each month, therefore, the team reads every electric meter in the city. In an attempt to alleviate boredom, the previous supervisor had a policy of rotating the eight readers among the eight subzones in each zone.

THE PROBLEM

Although there had been no turnover among the meter readers for a year, Meg shortly discovered that all was not well in her department. First, upon inspecting the time cards of her readers for the past year, she discovered that the workload among the 20 zones was severely unbalanced. For zones with lower workloads, readers used the extra time to recheck meters that are difficult to read, to reread meters as a result of customer complaints, etc. For high-workload zones, readers routinely used overtime. Meg found that some of the readers didn't mind overtime and liked the extra pay; others resented taking the time away from their families. At any rate, Meg recognized that a restructuring of the zones would involve modeling and solving a very large Chinese postman problem and would take a great deal of time and effort on her part.

A more immediate problem was the structure of the subzones within each zone. One particularly troublesome zone seemed to be zone #7. Since the readers were routinely rotated among the subzones, Meg collected time-card data for the past six months for zone #7 and arranged them in a matrix (see Table 4.10).

The average times for the readers across all subzones varied from 307 minutes for Rajesh (who was known to jog between meters) to 397 minutes for Olga (who was meticulous and hadn't misread a single meter all year). Meg was not concerned about this variance, which was well within the acceptable range of performance standards. What did concern her was the wide variance in average times for subzones across readers—with a low of 274 minutes in #7-4, to a high of 424 in #7-8. Obviously, reallocating zone #7 to new subzones (a smaller Chinese postman problem) at this point would be wasted motion, since Meg intended to reconfigure the 20 major zones in the future.

Still, morale was deteriorating, and overall performance of her unit was unsatisfactory by Meg's standards. Meg felt that she must do something in the short term. Since the crew was scheduled to work zone #7 on Monday of the following week, Meg found her predecessor's scheduling book and noted that next week's schedule would be as follows:

Next Week's Current Schedule

	\multicolumn{8}{c	}{Reader}
	Ramon	Sean	Meiko	Olga	Chen	Rajesh	Babbette	JoeDon
Subzone	4	6	2	1	3	5	7	8
Time	285	330	420	510	315	270	465	450

Total time: 3,045 minutes, or 50.75 worker-hours

TABLE 4.10 Meter reading times for zone 7

Reader	\multicolumn{8}{c}{Subzones}	
	1	2	3	4	5	6	7	8	Average
Ramon	375	360	255	285	270	360	345	405	332
Sean	345	285	225	255	240	330	290	420	311
Meiko	405	420	255	270	285	375	315	390	339
Olga	510	405	330	315	345	390	435	450	397
Chen	480	420	315	270	300	360	450	465	383
Rajesh	270	375	255	240	270	315	360	375	307
Babbette	450	390	330	285	270	405	465	435	379
JoeDon	330	315	255	270	240	345	300	450	313
Average	396	371	278	274	277	360	383	424	345

THE MODEL

Meg Watts recognized that she could model her short-term problem as an assignment model. The nodes were merely the meter readers and the subzones, and the arcs represented the assignment of readers to subzones. Since Meg could assign any reader to any zone, her model would have 16 nodes and 64 arcs. Meg carefully checked her input data and gave it to the company's systems analyst to run.

SOLUTION TO THE MODEL

The analyst used the SAMS network flow module that Meg had installed on EEE's microcomputer to generate a solution to her model. The quick briefing on the optimalmodel solution appears in Table 4.11.

SOLUTION TO THE PROBLEM

Even Meg, who had earned her MBA, was surprised at the difference of over ten worker-hours (615 worker-minutes) between the original schedule and the model-generated assignment—a decrease of over 20 percent. Meg rechecked her input data

TABLE 4.11

METER READERS
QUICK BRIEFING ON OPTIMAL ASSIGNMENT

ROW	COLUMN	ARC COST
RAMON	Z7–3	255
SEAN	Z7–2	285
MEIKO	Z7–8	390
OLGA	Z7–6	390
CHEN	Z7–4	270
RAJESH	Z7–1	270
BABBETTE	Z7–5	270
JOE DON	Z7–7	300
Total Cost:		2430

but found no errors. Out of curiosity, she then had the analyst rerun the model using the MAX criterion in the SAMS network flow module to find the worst possible schedule. The model solution turned out to be the previous schedule! Meg therefore reasoned that using the assignment model would result in an average personnel saving of about 10 percent compared to randomly generated schedules.

Meg had not yet, of course, solved the problem. By demonstrating to her meter readers that the assignment for zone #7 would more evenly distribute the workload and allow each reader to work the same subzone each month, Meg convinced the team of the advantages of applying her approach to all 20 zones. Her announcement that she was reworking the 20 large zones to even out the daily variation in workload was also received positively (if a bit skeptically). ■

Center for Professional Development [10]

THE SCENARIO

The Center for Professional Development (CPD) at a southwestern university is an integral part of the university's business school. The CPD's mission is to design, market, develop, staff, and administer seminars, conferences, and workshops of a nonacademic credit nature. The offerings of the CPD range from one-day short courses to formal, week-long schools; and thousands of people in 64 cities in 28 sunbelt states attend them each year. The objective of the CPD is to deliver the highest quality and to be self-supporting financially.

THE PROBLEM

Early in 1991, the CPD decided to offer a management series of 14 programs for middle and upper middle managers in each of 14 southwestern cities. The CPD would offer each of the one-day seminars (e.g., "Women in the Work Force: A Manager's Role" and "Effective Time Management") in each city at least once in the fiscal year and two or three times in certain cities. It thus needed to schedule and conduct a total of 284 individual seminars. Since this new series was in addition to the CPD's normal complement of programs, the center's staff faced a significant management challenge.

THE MODEL

The associate director of the CPD was also a part-time MBA student at the university. She recognized her problem as being amenable to analysis by the critical path network model, which her class had discussed. (*Note:* She actually used the probabilistic version of the critical path network called Project Evaluation and Review Technique, but here we discuss the deterministic version.)

The associate director first identified 17 mutually exclusive and collectively exhaustive activities involved in scheduling the series of programs and used her judgment and staff input to estimate completion times for each. Table 4.12 summarizes this information, and Figure 4.11 displays the associated network.

TABLE 4.12 CPD scheduling problem activities

Activity	Description	Predecessor Activities	Number of Weeks Required
A	Select seminars	—	2
B	Determine locations and dates	A	7
C	Confirm speakers	A	7
D	Select and order mailing lists	A	5
E	Confirm locations	B	5
F	Design brochures	C,E	3
G	Typeset brochure copy	F	3
H	Print brochures	G	4
I	Send labels to printer/mailer	D	1
J	Mail brochures	H,I	3
K	Conduct registration process	J	5
L	Reconfirm sites/facilities/setups	J	1
M	Order/ship course materials	K	3.5
N	Prepare onsite materials	K	2
O	Ship onsite materials	L,N	1
P	Conduct seminars	M,O	0.2
Q	Final reconciliation of accounts	P	5

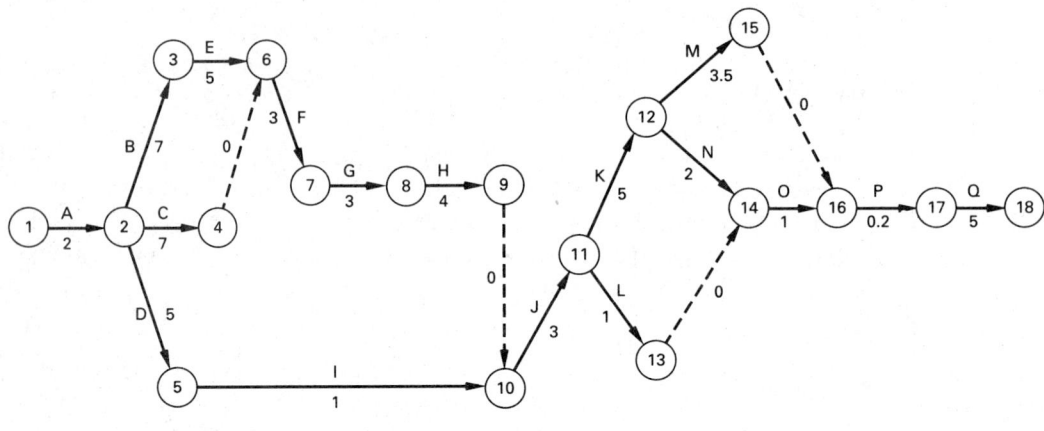

Critical path
Nodes: 1-2-3-6-7-8-9-10-11-12-15-16-17-18
Arcs: A-B-E-F-G-H-dummy-J-K-M-dummy-P-Q

FIGURE 4.11
CPD critical path network

TABLE 4.13 SAMS PERT module output for CPD

CPD PROJECT NETWORK
FULL BRIEFING ON PROJECT

Earliest project completion time is 40.7

CRITICAL ACTIVITIES

	Start Time		Finish Time		
Activity	Earliest	Latest	Earliest	Latest	Free Slack
SELECTSM	0.0	0.0	2.0	2.0	0.0
LOCGATES	2.0	9.0	2.0	9.0	0.0
CONFIRM	9.0	14.0	9.0	14.0	0.0
DESIGNP	14.0	14.0	17.0	17.0	0.0
TYPESETL	17.0	17.0	20.0	20.0	0.0
PRINT	20.0	20.0	24.0	24.0	0.0
MAIL	24.0	24.0	27.0	27.0	0.0
REGISTER	27.0	27.0	32.0	32.0	0.0
ORD/SHIP	32.0	32.0	35.5	35.5	0.0
CONDUCT	35.5	35.5	35.7	35.7	0.0
RECONCIL	35.7	35.7	40.7	40.7	0.0

NONCRITICAL ACTIVITIES

CONFIRM	2.0	7.0	9.0	14.0	5.0
MAILLIST	2.0	18.0	7.0	23.0	16.0
LABELS	7.0	23.0	8.0	24.0	16.0
RECONFRM	27.0	33.5	28.0	34.5	6.5
PRONSITE	32.0	32.5	34.0	34.5	0.5
SHONSITE	34.0	34.5	35.0	35.5	0.5

SOLUTION TO THE MODEL

As indicated in Figure 4.11, the associate director used a minicomputer CPM program to determine the longest route through the network; the critical path is highlighted. Table 4.13 gives the SAMS project management module full briefing. Eleven of the 17 activities appear on the critical path, and the model indicates that the seminar scheduling project will take about 40.7 weeks to complete.

SOLUTION TO THE PROBLEM

As usual, modeling this problem as a critical path network gave the associate director insight into her complex scheduling problem but did not provide a canned solution. Because activities D and I have combined slack of 16 weeks, the associate director can safely delay these tasks to concentrate staff effort on critical activities A, B, E, F, G, and H. On the other hand, activities N and O—while not on the critical path—are very nearly so, with combined slack of only half a week. Finally, the associate director could postpone activity L up to six weeks without affecting total completion time, and activity C has free slack of five weeks.

The CPD used the results of this analysis for planning purposes and monitored its progress against the estimated mileposts generated by the critical path network. This application proved to be so useful that the associate director subsequently planned to incorporate all CPD program scheduling and operation into a larger, more complex network.

Polka [1]

THE SCENARIO

The Department of Defense, through its Defense Fuel Supply Center (DFSC), annually procures about five billion gallons of aviation fuel for the armed services. Three types of fuel are involved, but one particular type—JP-4—dominates the procurement process, with requirements of four billion gallons per year.

DFSC purchases JP-4 through a competitive bidding process that occurs twice each year. Invitations for Bid (IFBs) for a cycle normally involve supplying over 300 military installations, and more than 100 suppliers submit bids. Federal regulations require that DFSC award bids to the lowest bidders (in an aggregate sense), based on "laid down" cost (fuel plus transportation cost). When the authors performed the analysis described below, the total annual cost involved was about $2 billion. In 1992, the same level of requirements would entail a total cost in excess of $5 billion.

THE PROBLEM

On the surface, it appeared that we could model the bid award process as a simple transshipment model, or as a transshipment network. However, there were a wide variety of bidding options available to the suppliers, which greatly complicated the problem. Some of the more vexing of these options (from a modeling point of view) were as follows:

1. There were five modes of transportation (truck, barge, railroad tank car, pipeline, and tanker) available, but some shippers and receivers were limited in their access to one or more modes.
2. There were 53 government transshipment points available for routing and storage purposes.
3. Many of the 100+ bidders had several shipping points, each with limited shipping facilities and fuel supplies. Thus, a particular company could submit bids totaling less than the sum of fuel available at its shipping points.
4. Bidders could submit either destination bids, which included shipping costs, or origin bids, in which the government had to determine the optimal shipping pattern and bear the resulting shipping cost.
5. Price breaks on different quantities were common.
6. Tie-in bids, in which one supplier made its maximum offer contingent upon the award of another (associated) supplier, were common.
7. Suppliers had the option of specifying a minimum acceptable quantity (MAQ) for one or more shipping points, preferring no bid award at all to an award of less than the stated MAQ.

THE MODEL

Since the mid-1960s, DFSC had been using an LP model to generate tentative solutions to the basic bid award problem. It did not use a network model, because it could not model several of the bidding options by such a procedure (e.g., price discounts or tie-in bids). Moreover, the LP model did not incorporate the MAQ bids, since such bids lead to nonlinear constraints. Consequently, DFSC ran the LP algorithm initially, with MAQ bids ignored. If the resulting model solution did not violate the MAQ bids, DFSC managers used the computer output as a basis for developing the bid awards; if the solution did violate some MAQ bids, DFSC disqualified them and reran the LP model without these bids. DFSC repeated this process until it obtained a feasible solution.

As MAQ bids became more and more common, DFSC managers became increasingly concerned that their suboptimal model was producing poorer and poorer solutions. In addition, each run on the agency's IBM mainframe required eight hours, so that repeated runs were becoming a real problem—as regards to both cost and machine access.

SOLUTION TO THE MODEL

At the request of DFSC, the USAF Procurement Research Office, located at the Air Force Academy in Colorado, agreed to act as a consultant to investigate more sophisticated modeling approaches in the bid award problem. The model that finally emerged was dubbed POLKA (Petroleum Oil & Lubricants Out-of-Kilter Algorithm) and consisted of a large minimum cost flow model imbedded within a larger model that accounted for the problem features that the network model could not accommodate. POLKA ran in about *20 minutes* on the DFSC computer and produced an optimal solution. For comparison purposes, we ran POLKA for two previous JP-4 bidding cycles, and it produced solutions that would have resulted in modest savings as a percentage of total cost. (In absolute terms, this means that DFSC would have realized savings of $1 million to $2 million per cycle.) We completely debugged the computer program and wrote a special program to build the data base for the model, and POLKA was operational early in 1973.

SOLUTION TO THE PROBLEM

For those with a wry sense of humor, recall that the Arab oil embargo occurred in 1973—a few months after we installed POLKA. The first JP-4 bidding cycle thereafter produced bids for only 60% of the total requirement. As sophisticated as POLKA was, even *it* couldn't produce 800 million gallons of aviation fuel! The Department of Defense invoked the National Security Act, however, and the armed services got their fuel. Happily, as supplies subsequently increased and bidding again caused supply to exceed demand, POLKA was used—and (as of May 1989) DFSC is still using POLKA in the aviation fuel procurement process.

SUMMARY

This chapter surveyed a special class of ILP models that we can pose and analyze efficiently as networks. In it we noted that these special cases have natural integer solutions whenever the input parameters are all integers.

We first discussed four widely used network models: shortest route, longest route, minimal spanning tree, and optimal flow. As a special case of a longest route model, we introduced the very useful application of project scheduling with the critical path method. We covered transportation, assignment, and transshipment models as special cases of the optimal network flow case.

We addressed post-optimality analysis for two classes of network models: descriptive and optimizing. Our trek through the topic of network modeling ended with some advanced topics such as the Chinese postman model and multicommodity flow models.

In the next chapter on nonlinear programming, we relax the additivity restriction in Chapter 2, and we shall see that the road gets considerably rockier as a result.

KEY TERMS

analog model
arcs
assignment model
connected
conservation of flow
critical activities
critical path
maximum flow

min-cut/max flow theorem
multicommodity network flow model
network
nodes
path
side condition
transshipment model
transportation model

PROBLEMS FOR ANALYSIS

1. **The Scenario:** The head coach of the Dallas Dudes professional football team is preparing to select his starting players for the upcoming season. The team's training camp is located in Dragon's Breath, Arizona, and the combination of three-a-day workouts and the 110-degree heat has already discouraged most of the aspiring rookies (and a few of the veterans as well). The offensive team is set, as are the defensive line and linebackers. Only the four defensive secondary positions are still up for grabs.

The Problem: Eight players remain in contention for starting positions at strong safety (SS), weak safety (WS), right corner (RC), and left corner (LC). The Dudes need two additional players as substitutes, so that two of the eight candidates will get a pink slip and a one-way airline ticket home. The coach wishes, of course, to select the four starters in such a way that the strongest possible secondary results and to choose the two substitutes so that defensive capability is not seriously degraded if one of the starters is injured.

The Model: The head coach instructs his defensive coaches to schedule scrimmages so that each of the eight candidates plays each of the four positions and to rate each candidate in each position on a scale of 1 (terminally inept) to 10 (exceptionally talented). The ratings that resulted are in Table 4.14.

a. How many different ways can the head coach assign players to the four positions, neglecting for a moment the necessity of selecting two remaining players as substitutes?
b. Can we model this assignment problem as a network? If so, how many nodes and arcs are there?
c. What is the nature of an appropriate objective function for this model?
d. What do you think of the additivity assumption inherent in network modeling as it applies to this problem? That is, do you think a player's performance at a position is independent of the other players in the defensive strategy?

Solution to the Model: The head coach instructed the Dallas Dudes' OR analyst to solve the model, which the analyst proceeded to do using the network flow module from the SAMS-like package on the club's microcomputer. Not knowing quite how to handle the selection of substitutes, the analyst first solved the assignment problem by maximizing the sum of scores, with the results as in Table 4.15.

Noting that the total score for this assignment is the highest possible (since it is impossible to include all four of the "10s"), the analyst smugly turned to the problem of choosing the two substitutes. Since the individual scores for both Chauncey and Egbert sum to 27 across the four positions, compared to 26 each for Aloysius and Gherkin, the analyst decided to recommend that the Dudes retain the former as substitutes and—to demonstrate his efficiency—ordered one-way airline tickets for Aloysius and Gherkin.

a. Using an appropriate computer package such as SAMS' network flow module, solve this model to verify the analyst's results.
b. Do you really think he has solved the coach's problem?

TABLE 4.14

| | Position | | | | |
Player	SS	WS	RC	LC	Sum of Scores
Aloysius	6	5	7	8	26
Bertram	3	10	1	10	24
Chauncey	8	8	2	9	27
Dunsinane	10	9	1	2	22
Egbert	9	8	3	7	27
Fauntleroy	3	2	10	9	24
Gherkin	7	6	8	5	26
Helmer	10	5	3	4	23

TABLE 4.15 Defensive secondary

Position	Player	Score
Strong safety	Helmer	10
Weak safety	Dunsinane	9
Right corner	Fauntleroy	10
Left corner	Bertram	10
		39

TABLE 4.16 Defensive secondary

Position	Player	Score
Strong safety	Helmer	10
Weak safety	Bertram	10
Right corner	Gherkin	8
Left corner	Chauncey	9
		37

Solution to the Problem: Upon receiving the "solution" from the analyst, the coach glanced briefly over the results. Several items came to his attention. First, if total scores across the four positions are any indication of overall athletic ability, the four players recommended as starting players were the poorest of the eight. Second, if the coach implemented the analyst's plan and Fauntleroy was subsequently injured in a game, since Chauncey and Egbert both performed very poorly at right corner during the scrimmages, they and would probably be poor substitutes. Third, Fauntleroy performed well at both corner positions, as did Dunsinane at both safety positions. On this basis, the coach decided on Dunsinane and Fauntleroy as substitutes. The coach then had the analyst run the algorithm once again with the other six players, with the result as in Table 4.16. Finding no additional exogenous factors that affected this problem, the coach decided to implement the new solution and sent Aloysius and Egbert home.

2. **The Scenario:** The accounting firm of Upp and Cummings, CPAs, is in the process of planning its auditing schedule for next month. The main office is located in Gaapville, and the firm's three other offices are in Tenkay, Tickenfoot, and Sasburg. For each of the ten clients whose audits are due, the managing partner Juan Upp has estimated how many auditors he will need. These requirements, as well as the numbers of auditors available at each of the four offices, are shown in Table 4.17.

The Problem: Since the firm's audit staff among the four offices varies widely in experience and since the difficulty of audits differs from one client to the next, assigning an auditor from a particular office to a given firm involves a considerable setup cost in terms of preparation time. A poor assignment pattern could cost the firm dearly in terms of inefficient use of its personnel resources. Furthermore, there are additional complications. First, since none of the auditors stationed in Sasburg have experience in oil and gas accounting, they must assign auditors from the other offices to clients #2 and #9. Second, because of company policy, the firm never conducts

TABLE 4.17

	Customer No.										
	1	2	3	4	5	6	7	8	9	10	Total
Auditors needed	4	9	2	12	7	6	9	3	18	5	75

	Office				
	Gaapville	Tenkay	Tickenfoot	Sasburg	Total
Auditors available	35	20	25	10	90

TABLE 4.18 Auditor training costs (worker-hours per auditor)

	Client											
	1	2	3	4	5	6	7	8	9	10	Training	Supply
Gaapville	8	21	15	13	9	17	8	7	26	9	0	35
Tenkay	14	18	17	19	12	6	0	15	24	13	0	20
Tickenfoot	9	15	18	16	16	15	11	13	21	19	0	25
Sasburg	11	M*	14	7	23	9	6	18	M*	7	0	10
Requirements	4	9	2	12	7	6	9	3	18	5	15	90

* M is a very large number.

an audit for a given client with all auditors from the same office. And finally, the 15 available auditors not assigned to audits will go to the same office for required professional training in Bayesian discriminant analysis.

The Model: Juan has his staff estimate the costs in hours c_{ij} for training each auditor from the ith office to audit the jth firm. For $i = 4$ (Sasburg), Juan is careful to make c_{42} and c_{49} artificially large numbers, in effect taking care of the first complication. Although he recognizes his problem as being similar to a transportation problem, he isn't quite sure how to incorporate the second complication—no single-office audits of a client—so he ignores it for the moment. The third complication, he realizes, isn't really a problem, since his supply of auditors exceeds the client requirement. Table 4.18 is a matrix showing the c_{ij}, requirements, and supplies.

The Solution: As Juan had suspected, the solution that emerged from the computer violated the single-office audit policy for eight of the ten clients. See Table 4.19 for this solution. By fiddling with the model solution in Table 4.19, Juan is able to generate a feasible assignment (see Table 4.20).

CHAPTER 4 MODELING WITH NETWORKS 181

TABLE 4.19 Upp and Cummings model solution: auditor assignment

	Client										
Office	1	2	3	4	5	6	7	8	9	10	Training
Gaapville	4	0	2	2	7	0	0	3	0	5	12
Tenkay	0	0	0	0	0	6	9	0	2	0	3
Tickenfoot	0	9	0	0	0	0	0	0	16	0	0
Sasburg	0	0	0	10	0	0	0	0	0	0	0

Total cost: 842 worker-hours

TABLE 4.20 Upp and Cummings feasible solution: auditor assignment

	Client										
Office	1	2	3	4	5	6	7	8	9	10	Training
Gaapville	3	0	1	3	6	1	7	2	2	4	6
Tenkay	0	1	1	0	1	5	2	1	0	0	9
Tickenfoot	1	8	0	0	0	0	0	0	16	0	0
Sasburg	0	0	0	9	0	0	0	0	0	1	0

Total cost: 954 worker-hours

TABLE 4.21 Upp and Cummings worst model solution: auditor assignment

	Client										
Office	1	2	3	4	5	6	7	8	9	10	Training
Gaapville	0	9	0	0	0	6	0	0	18	0	2
Tenkay	4	0	0	12	0	0	0	0	0	0	4
Tickenfoot	0	0	2	0	0	0	9	0	0	5	9
Sasburg	0	0	0	0	7	0	0	3	0	0	0

Total cost: 1,488 worker-hours

a. Noting that Juan's "fiddled solution" is about 4.4 percent more expensive than the optimal (but infeasible) solution, should Juan—in your opinion—go to the additional expense of modeling the problem as an ILP model? Why or why not?
b. To support your answer to (a), derive the ILP model of this problem that explicitly incorporates the single-office policy.
c. Table 4.21 represents the worst possible solution to the network transportation model. Given your estimate of the cost of trained auditor worker-hours, do you think that the time and expense of modeling this problem and solving the model was justified? Why or why not?

TABLE 4.22 SAMS summary report for Rollin Stone's problem

```
ROLLIN STONE & ONO
QUICK REPORT ON OPTIMAL ALLOCATION
```

Arc	From	To	Flow	Arc Cost
1	.	PEPP	40	0
2	.	JUDE	35	0
3	.	WALR	25	0
4	.	DAYT	50	0
5	PEPP	LUCY	40	52000
10	JUDE	YOKO	19	26600
12	WALR	ELEA	25	32500
13	JUDE	LUCY	16	25600
14	DAYT	YOKO	41	77900
15	DAYT	ELEA	9	18900
17	LUCY	.	56	0
18	ELEA	.	34	0
19	YOKO	.	60	0
		Total Cost:		233500

3. **The Scenario:** As promised, we now return to the dialogue between our knowledge-based program Optimal Network Operator (ONO) and the rock promoter Rollin Stone.

   The Problem: ONO has helped Rollin by modeling his transportation problem using the SAMS network flow module.

   Solution to the Model: ONO noticed from the model solution (repeated in Table 4.22) that the entire 16-hour shortage of performing hours was borne by one of the three sponsors—Lucy to be specific—and suggested that perhaps Rollin might wish to consider alternatives.

   Solution to the Problem:
   a. One way to address ONO's concern would be to *decrease the upper bounds* on the arcs Yoko to "." from 60 to 55 and Eleanor to "." from 34 to 29. This will free up an additional 10 hours for allotment to Lucy. Use a network flow package to make this change and note the result.
   b. Another way would be to *increase the lower bound* on the arc Lucy to "." from 0 to 66. Try this and note the result. Also note that there is no way to incorporate this change in a classical transportation tableau, but it is quite easily done in the network flow module.
   c. Are you surprised by your results in (a) and (b)? Did you think perhaps that you would get the same result in each case? Are you just a bit startled that such a radical change in the model resulted in such a small change (%) in the original minimum cost solution?

4. **The Scenario:** The Consolidated Information Agency (CIA) maintains a system of worldwide operatives in 400 foreign cities. Because of the highly sensitive nature of

the agency's responsibilities, all electronic communication with these operatives must be made via special secure voice networks that scramble the message at one end and unscramble it at the other. Volume of message traffic is high, and certain "all-ears" messages that CIA must transmit to each operative arise several times daily. Harry Matta, current director of operations, is inordinately proud of the existing communications system (which he was responsible for installing). The system involves transmitting messages from CIA headquarters in Foggy Bottom, Virginia, directly and individually to each operative, and CIA has compromised only two all-ears transmissions in the past five years.

The Problem: In a cost-cutting mood, Congress passes next fiscal year's budget, which includes a 20% decrease in CIA's operating funds. Harry and his staff go to work immediately to identify areas for cost savings. Harry briefly considers—but ultimately abandons—the idea of withdrawing operatives from Tierra del Fuego and Nova Scotia. However, Harry is stunned to learn that the CIA's long-distance telephone charges are running $23 million per year and are escalating rapidly. Perhaps there is some way to reduce telephone expenditures without sacrificing operational effectiveness.

The Model: The current practice is to transmit all-ears messages directly from headquarters. Since each operative has the capability of contacting other operatives, why couldn't headquarters contact a few directly and have them pass on the message to nearby operatives, continuing the relay until they had contacted all parties? There would still be 400 telephone calls, but many would obviously cost much less than a direct call from headquarters. Harry asks his OR analyst to calculate long-distance charges per minute between all 400 cities and headquarters and recommend a call relay system that minimizes costs.

The Solution:
- a. Does this appear to be a problem that we can model as a network? If so, what are the nodes and arcs?
- b. Assuming that a call from city A to city B may not cost the same as from B to A, how many arcs does this network have?
- c. Can we express a solution to the network model in terms of a minimal spanning tree? If so, how does the CIA problem differ from "normal" problems that we can model as networks of this type?

5. A curious property is associated with transportation networks, called the "more for less" phenomenon. Consider the toy model (Table 4.23) displayed in a classical transportation tableau (still used in many MS/OR texts).
In the transportation tableau, the small numbers in the upper-right corner of each cell are the c_{ij}s—the unit transportation cost from demand point i to supply point j. The other numbers in the illustration represent an optimal solution to the model, and you can easily verify that the minimum total cost is $152.

Suppose, after you have solved the model, demand point #2 increased its order by 5 units (from 10 to 15) and supply point A indicated that it could meet this additional demand by using overtime (producing 16 units rather than 11). Thus, our total shipment has increased by 5 units (from 55 to 60), or about 9 percent. The optimal solution to this new model is in Table 4.24.

You may wish to verify that the total cost of this new shipping pattern is $147 — which is $5 (about 3%) *less* than the original.

- a. Is the preceding result counterintuitive from your perspective? That is, does the fact that we *decreased* costs 3% by increasing shipping volume 9% seem paradoxical? If so, compare the two tableaus and their respective solutions. Can you see that the additional five units of demand and supply allowed us to ship more cheaply from C-2 and A-1, while decreasing the shipment from the higher cost route C-1?

TABLE 4.23 Transportation tableau

		Supply Points				
		A	B	C	D	Demand
Demand Points	1	11 [1]	[6]	9 [3]	[5]	20
	2	[7]	2 [3]	8 [1]	[6]	10
	3	9 [ ]	11 [4]	[5]	14 [4]	25
	Supply	11	13	17	14	55

TABLE 4.24 Transportation tableau

		Supply Points				
		A	B	C	D	Demand
Demand Points	1	16 [1]	[6]	4 [3]	[5]	20
	2	[7]	2 [3]	13 [1]	[6]	15
	3	9 [ ]	11 [4]	[5]	14 [4]	25
	Supply	16	13	17	14	60

b. By how many more units could we increase demand at #2 and supply at A before cost savings ceased?

c. In the *original* model, would *decreasing* demand by #2 actually increase costs? Why or why not? (*Hint:* Increasing managerial options can never result in poorer performance in a technical sense.)

6. Consider the following LP formulation of the maximum network flow model. Let

x_F = total flow through the network

x_{ij} = flow on arc (i, j) from node i to node j

u_{ij} = flow capacity on arc (i, j)

MAX

$$x_0 = x_F \tag{4.5}$$

S T:

$$\sum x_{1j} = x_F \tag{4.6}$$

(1, j in network)

$$\sum x_{kj} = \sum x_{ik} \tag{4.7}$$

(k, j in network)   (i, k in network)

$$\sum x_{in} = x_F \tag{4.8}$$

(i, in network)

$$x_{ij} \leq u_{ij} \text{ for all } i, j \text{ in network} \tag{4.9}$$

Node #1 is the starting node (source), and node #n is the ending node (sink). Constraints (4.6) and (4.8) assure that the flow from the source and to the sink are the same. Constraints (4.7) are called conservation-of-flow equations and guarantee equal flow in and out of each node. The constraints in Equation (4.9) limit the flow on each arc to be less than or equal to its capacity. As an illustration, consider the following simple network flow diagram, and its LP formulation. The numbers on the arcs are flow capacities.

MAX

$$x_0 \qquad\qquad = x_F \tag{4.10}$$

S T:

$$x_{12} + x_{13} \qquad\qquad -x_F = 0 \tag{4.11}$$

$$x_{12} \quad - x_{23} - x_{24} \qquad\qquad = 0 \tag{4.12}$$

$$x_{13} + x_{23} \quad - x_{34} - x_{35} \qquad\qquad = 0 \tag{4.13}$$

$$x_{24} + x_{34} \quad - x_{45} \qquad = 0 \tag{4.14}$$

$$x_{35} + x_{45} - x_F = 0 \tag{4.15}$$

$$x_{12} \leq 10 \tag{4.16}$$

$$x_{13} \leq 18 \tag{4.17}$$

$$x_{23} \leq 8 \tag{4.18}$$

$$x_{24} \leq 6 \tag{4.19}$$

$$x_{34} \leq 9 \tag{4.20}$$

$$x_{35} \leq 12 \tag{4.21}$$

$$x_{45} \leq 16 \tag{4.22}$$

In optimizing algorithms, we use a special modeling device to take care of the upper-bound constraints so that the resulting constraint matrix has the semi-Markov property mentioned earlier.

a. You may wish to verify that the maximum flow through this network is 27 units, as follows:

$$x_{12} = 10 \quad x_{23} = 4 \quad x_{34} = 9 \quad x_{45} = 15$$
$$x_{13} = 17 \quad x_{24} = 6 \quad x_{35} = 12 \quad x_F = 27$$

Check the solution to see whether it meets the conservation-of-flow conditions. Do you see that the minimum cut-set consists of arcs (2,4), (3,4), and (3,5)?

b. What would be the effect if the upper-bound constraint on arc (3,4) were increased by one unit (from 9 to 10)?

c. If the preceding network represented part of the proposed circuit design for a handheld computer and the flow capacities represented current limitations, what could you conclude about the design parameter (capacity) of arc (2,3)?

d. The illustration has 5 nodes and 7 arcs, and its LP formulation involves 8 variables and 12 constraints. Certain real-world network flow models may have thousands of nodes and tens of thousands of arcs. In addition to this complication of sheer size, the LP formulation results in a so-called highly degenerate model—one with many zeros in both the objective function and the right-hand sides of the constraints—and are difficult to solve efficiently. Does this illustration help you to understand the importance of specialized, highly efficient algorithms that take advantage of the network structure?

7. One interesting way of finding the shortest route through a network (given that all arc distances are nonnegative) is to build an **analog model** of the network. We use pieces of string to represent the arcs, and their lengths are proportional to the distances they represent. We then tie the strings together, and the knots represent the network nodes. To "solve the model," one merely grasps the starting node with one hand and the destination node with the other and pulls the string network taut. The length of the resulting line is the shortest distance between the two selected nodes, and the arcs that are taut represent the arcs that make up the shortest route.

a. From a managerial standpoint, would this analog model conceivably have any practical value? Answer as though you were a consultant for a metropolitan emergency ambulance company with units stationed throughout the city and you were dealing with the owner, who came up through the ranks as an ambulance driver.

b. Could we somehow adapt our string model to find the critical path (longest "distance") through an activity scheduling network? If so, what would be the relationship between an activity's duration and the length of the corresponding piece of string? How would you handle dummy activities? How would you determine slack time for noncritical activities?

8. Think about the following entities in terms of modeling and analysis with networks:

a. The electric power system of a city.
b. The United States' decennial census.
c. The curriculum structure of a multipurpose business school.
d. The flow of raw materials and finished goods through an assembly line.
e. Word-of-mouth advertising.
f. A vertically integrated company that sells fast-food franchises.
g. Assigning graduate assistants to professors.
h. Planning the intricate process of a kidney transplant operation.

PRACTICE MODELS

1. Use a network distance module to determine the shortest path through the following network:

		From Node						
		1	2	3	4	5	6	7
To Node	1	0	5	8	11	—	—	—
	2	—	0	3	—	10	—	—
	3	—	—	0	—	6	9	—
	4	—	—	2	—	—	4	—
	5	—	—	—	—	—	—	6
	6	—	—	—	—	—	—	9

2. Use a network distance module to find the minimal spanning tree for the following network:

	1	2	3	4	5	6	7	8	9
1	0	25	60	50	—	—	—	—	—
2	—	0	—	45	20	—	—	—	—
3	—	—	0	40	—	105	—	—	—
4	—	—	—	0	40	125	170	150	—
5	—	—	—	—	0	—	—	100	—
6	—	—	—	—	—	0	75	—	70
7	—	—	—	—	—	—	0	25	95
8	—	—	—	—	—	—	—	0	60
9	—	—	—	—	—	—	—	—	0

3. Find the maximum flow through the following pipeline:

	From	To	Cost	Lower Bound	Upper Bound
Arc 1		PIP1	0	0	5000
Arc 2	PIP1	TAN1	0	0	1000
Arc 3	PIP1	TAN2	0	0	3000
Arc 4	TAN1	TAN2	0	0	500
Arc 5	TAN1	TAN3	0	0	1000
Arc 6	TAN2	TAN3	0	0	1500
Arc 7	TAN2	TAN4	0	0	1000
Arc 8	TAN3	REF	0	0	2000
Arc 9	TAN4	TAN3	0	0	1500
Arc 10	TAN4	REF	0	0	500
Arc 11	REF		0	0	6000

4. Use a network distance or PERT module to analyze the following CPM network:

	Activity Time	Start Node	End Node
Activity 1	6	1	2
Activity 2	6	1	3
Activity 3	12	2	4
Activity 4	14	2	5
Activity 5	12	2	3
Activity 6	6	3	6
Activity 7	5	4	7
Activity 8	4	5	8
Activity 9	3	6	8
Activity 10	2	8	7
Activity 11	7	7	9
Activity 12	4	8	9
Activity 13	6	9	10

5. Use a network flow module to determine the optimal allocation for the following transportation network:

	Norfolk	Rocky Mont	Pulaski	Supply
Roanoke	3	1	1.5	75
Richmond	2	3	2	60
Leesburg	3	5	4	40
Demand	30	65	55	

6. Use a network flow module to solve the following production planning problem:

	Jan.	Feb.	Mar.	End. Inv.	Supply
Beg. Inv.	0	10	20	30	150
Jan. Prod.	100	110	120	130	1200
Feb. Prod.	•	100	110	120	1050
Mar. Prod.	•	•	100	110	600
Demand	1000	1200	900	100	

7. Solve the following plant-warehouse-retail store transshipment problem:

	From	To	Unit Cost	Lower Bound	Upper Bound
Arc 1	.	PL1	0	0	15000
Arc 2	.	PL2	0	0	8000
Arc 3	PL1	WH1	225	0	2000
Arc 4	PL1	WH2	275	0	3000
Arc 5	PL2	WH1	315	0	2500
Arc 6	PL2	WH2	240	0	5000
Arc 7	PL2	STR4	310	0	4000
Arc 8	WH1	STR1	400	0	4500
Arc 9	WH1	STR2	350	0	3000
Arc 10	WH2	STR3	260	0	1500
Arc 11	WH2	STR4	510	0	6500
Arc 12	STR1	.	0	1000	.
Arc 13	STR2	.	0	2000	.
Arc 14	STR3	.	0	1500	.
Arc 15	STR4	.	0	3500	.

8. Find the optimal assignment of part-time nurses to weekdays. Do both maximization and minimization and compare your results.

	Mon.	Tues.	Wed.	Thurs.	Fri.
Nurse 1	3	1	5	2	4
Nurse 2	1	2	3	4	3
Nurse 3	4	5	3	1	2
Nurse 4	4	4	2	1	3
Nurse 5	2	3	4	2	5

REFERENCES AND ADDITIONAL READING

1. Austin, L., and W. Hogan. "Optimizing the Procurement of Aviation Fuels." *Management Science* 22 (1976): 515–527.
2. Baird, B. Adapted from an unpublished MBA term project report, Texas Tech University (1981).
3. Barr, R., F. Glover, and D. Klingman. "A New Alternating Basis Algorithm for Semi-Assignment Networks." Report No. 77-3, Management Science Report Series. Boulder: University of Colorado, 1977.
4. Bazarra, M., and J. Jarvis. *Linear Programming and Network Flows* (2d ed.). New York: Wiley, 1990.
5. Bradley, G., G. Brown, and G. Graves. "GNET, A Primal Capacitated Network Program." Monterey, Calif.: Naval Postgraduate School, Copyright 1975, 1977.
6. Ford, L., Jr., and D. Fulkerson. *Flows in Networks*. Princeton, N.J.: Princeton University Press, 1962.

7. Glover, F., J. Hultz, D. Klingman, and J. Stutz. "Generalized Networks: A Fundamental Computer-Based Planning Tool." *Management Science* 24, (1978): 1209–1220.
8. Hitchcock, F. "The Distribution of a Product from Several Sources to Numerous Localities." *Journal of Mathematics and Physics* 20 (1941): 224–230.
9. Kwan, M. "Graphic Programming Using Odd or Even Points." *Chinese Mathematics* 1 (1962): 273–277.
10. Lutz, J. Adapted from an unpublished MBA term project report, Texas Tech University (1982).
11. Minieka, E. *Optimization Algorithms for Networks and Graphs*. New York: Marcel Dekker, 1978.
12. Parker, R., and R. Rardin. *Discrete Optimization*. San Diego: Academic Press, 1988.
13. Shier, D. "Iterative Methods for Determining the k Shortest Paths in a Network." *Networks* 6 (1976): 205–230.
14. Spira, P. "A New Algorithm for Finding All Shortest Paths in a Graph of Positive Arcs in Average Time $O(n^2 \log 2n)$." *SIAM Journal of Computing* 21 (1973): 28–32.
15. Wagner, H. *Principles of Operations Research* (2d. ed.). Englewood Cliffs, N.J.: Prentice-Hall, 1975.
16. Winston, W. *Operations Research: Applications and Algorithms* (2d ed.). Boston: PWS-KENT, 1991.

CHAPTER 5

Nonlinear Programming Models

Society—including business, commerce, industry, and the public sector—is becoming increasingly complex. Declining productivity, scarce resources, stiffer international competition, and gyrating rates of interest and inflation all dictate that we employ more sophisticated models to understand and perhaps alleviate such problems. One form these sophisticated models can take belongs to the class we call **nonlinear programming** (NLP) models.

Most introductory management science texts do not include a chapter on NLP models. This text does for several reasons:

- To enable you to recognize nonlinear situations that you may encounter in your managerial environment.
- To impart an appreciation of how nonlinearities arise in deterministic optimization models and what NLP applications are commonplace.
- Because this text does not deal with the mathematical details of algorithms, there is no reason to avoid discussing NLP modeling and analysis.

As methods of conducting business become increasingly complicated, more and more firms must relax overly stringent assumptions of linearity in their optimization models to better accommodate the nonlinearities of the real world. A typical example of the increased complexity of business is the pricing of products and services. Products that merchants previously sold separately are now priced together at a discount. At the same time, volume discounts represent a popular form of pricing that introduces nonlinearities into the pricing problem. A retailer must now consider complicated price schedules when replenishing depleted inventories. Such pricing strategies have a significant effect upon sales, so that gross revenue winds up being a nonlinear function of price.

Another frequent situation where nonlinearities arise is the blending of ingredients to produce a product. Blends of metallic alloys, pet food, and gasoline all represent situations where the whole may not be equal to the sum of its parts. Nonlinearities arise chiefly because some product properties, such as octane number and vapor pressure in gasoline, are nonlinear functions of the amounts and properties of each component in the blend.

NLP models have been around a long time, and classical methods for solving some of these models date back to the eighteenth century. As a modeling and optimization technique, NLP is much older than LP, which got its start during World War II.

Until recently, most NLP models belonged to the realms of physics and engineering. Today the use of NLP in business is growing rapidly, or so the literature on business models would suggest. This chapter looks at some typical nonlinear business models and investigates the use of NLP algorithms to solve such models.

UNDERLYING ASSUMPTIONS

In the introduction to this part of the text, recall that we defined something called a mathematical program or—in terminology more germane for our purpose—a mathematical programming model. We repeat this model below for convenience:

$$\text{OPTIMIZE } x_0 = f(x_1, x_2, \ldots, x_n) \tag{5.1}$$

$$\text{S T:} \quad g_i(x_1, x_2, \ldots, x_n) \begin{Bmatrix} < \\ = \\ > \end{Bmatrix} b_i, \, i = 1, \ldots, m \tag{5.2}$$

In Chapter 2, the objective function f and the m constraints g_i were linear functions (because of additivity and divisibility assumptions in the underlying problem), and we explored model analysis and development of the resulting linear program. Obviously, if certain mathematical programs are linear, all others must be nonlinear. However, we avoided this dichotomy temporarily by looking at models that are linear except for the requirement that some or all of their decision values must be integer valued—and thus integer (linear) programs emerged in Chapter 3. Chapter 4 dealt with a special case of ILP models, called network models. In this chapter, then, we are ready to discuss nonlinear programming directly. In terms that an Australian would understand immediately, we are about to depart the modern, orderly confines of Sydney and launch into the wild, uncharted vistas of the outback.

What assumptions must we meet for us to model managerial problems as nonlinear programs? At first glance, it seems simple enough: some decision variable, or some relationship between or among decision variables, must not satisfy either the divisibility or additivity assumptions—or both. However, "first glances" are often notoriously deceiving—and this is particularly true in the case of NLP modeling. As we will see a bit later in this chapter, there is no general NLP algorithm that can solve all nonlinear models—and most probably there never will be. Therefore, our challenge as managerial decision makers in modeling nonlinear problems is to attempt to model them in certain ways that lead to computationally tractable forms. Since each of these forms has its own unique set of underlying assumptions, it is not very profitable to attempt to discuss general assumptions.

Before we plunge into specialized NLP modeling and analysis, however, we can make certain broad observations about this large and very complex subject. First, the functions in Equations (5.1) and (5.2) must be "reasonably well-behaved." For example, it is highly advantageous from a computational standpoint if the feasible set of points described by the constraints in Equation (5.2) is **convex;** that is, if we draw a line between any two points in the feasible region, every point on the line is also in the feasible region. A football is convex; a doughnut is not. Second, it is convenient if both our objective function and feasible set are **smooth and continuous;** a block of Swiss cheese is smooth but not continuous, and an accordion is continuous but not smooth. Examples are shown in Figure 5.1. There are other features that we will discuss in connection with specific modeling approaches, but the "story" on NLP should be beginning to come into focus. An appropriate analogy is that, of the thousands of

CHAPTER 5 NONLINEAR PROGRAMMING MODELS

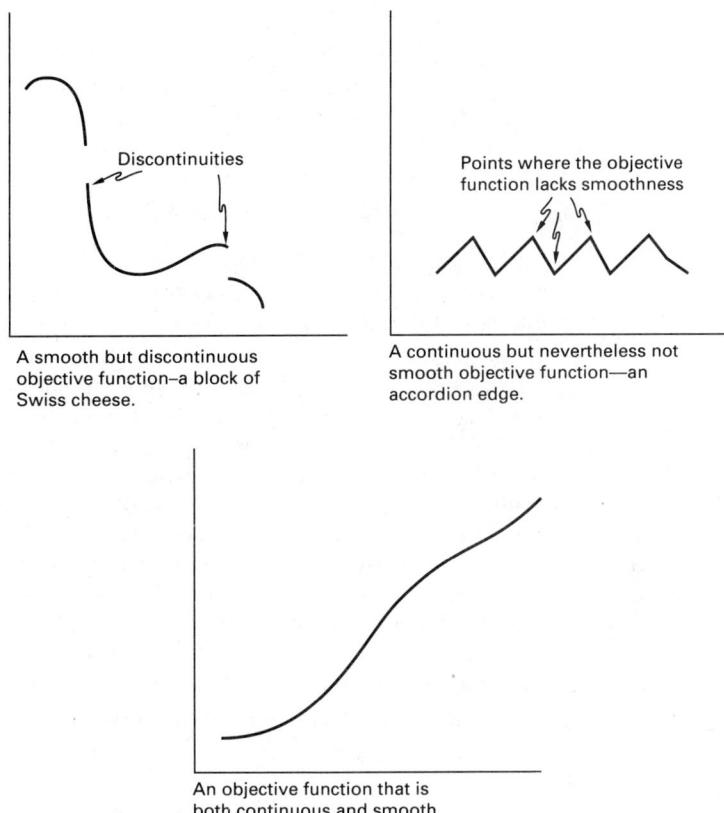

FIGURE 5.1
Three types of objective functions

species of wild beasts on the planet, humans have been able to domesticate (or even tame) relatively few. We now discuss a handful of the "docile" varieties of NLP models.

NONLINEAR MODELING

At this point in our trek through the nonlinear "outback," we face a dichotomy of some significant proportions. Shall we approach nonlinear modeling in the usual way—by investigating the various mathematical forms that such models can take? Or should we discuss several examples of nonlinear modeling from business and industry (letting them evolve into whatever mathematical form is appropriate) and hope they turn out to be computationally tractable? There is something to be said for each approach—but let us proceed with the latter. From a managerial point of view, a good model of a problem—regardless of its ease or difficulty of analysis—is very much preferable to one that we formulated by "mashing" the problem so that it fits a convenient mold. Let us proceed.

A PRICING MODEL

Never Mower, Inc., manufactures a popular line of lawn mowers for the residential market. The "Chopper," a gas-powered, hand-propelled mower with a 14-inch cut and no frills whatsoever (it is even painted with Army surplus olive drab paint), has always been the company's bread-and-butter product. However, Ed Poe, the company's hotshot new VP of Engineering, is disdainful of the mundane Chopper and has had his staff design a new mower tentatively entitled the "Zipper," which is the pride and joy of the Engineering Department. Resting on a six-wheel chassis with floating suspension, the Zipper is electric powered, self-starting, and self-propelled, and has an 18-inch cut. Plans for the mower include its availability in eight decorator colors, with rustproof paint, racing stripes, and chrome trim as standard features.

Poe and T. Raven, the company's pricing specialist, are knocking heads over the Zipper in a session with Never Mower's CEO.

"Chief," argues Ed Poe, "the Zipper is just what the doctor ordered. We need to add a little pizazz to our image—the Chopper is as dull as dishwater. Get Raven here to put it in his LP model, and I'll bet the Zipper will come out a winner."

"Sir," replies Raven, "Ed's fancy toy just isn't Never Mower. We sell the Chopper for $99.95 and get a consistent 15 percent return on our investment. Besides," nodding toward Poe, "the problem isn't linear. The relationship of selling price to sales volume is linear [Figure 5.2a], and the variable cost is a linear function of the number of units produced [Figure 5.2b], but profit contribution is a quadratic function of selling price [Figure 5.2c]. In fact, here's a summary of my analysis (Table 5.1). As you can see, the optimal selling price turns out to be about $166, which we estimate will generate sales of about 7,200 mowers. Production estimates the variable cost of production at $125 per copy, with a line setup cost of $250,000. That means that the estimated first-year profit contribution of the Zipper would be around $45,000 on a capital outlay of about $1.15 million—and that's a return on investment of less than 4 percent. I think the Zipper is a poor investment."

"Gentlemen, thank you for your input—I'll make a decision on the Zipper by Thursday."

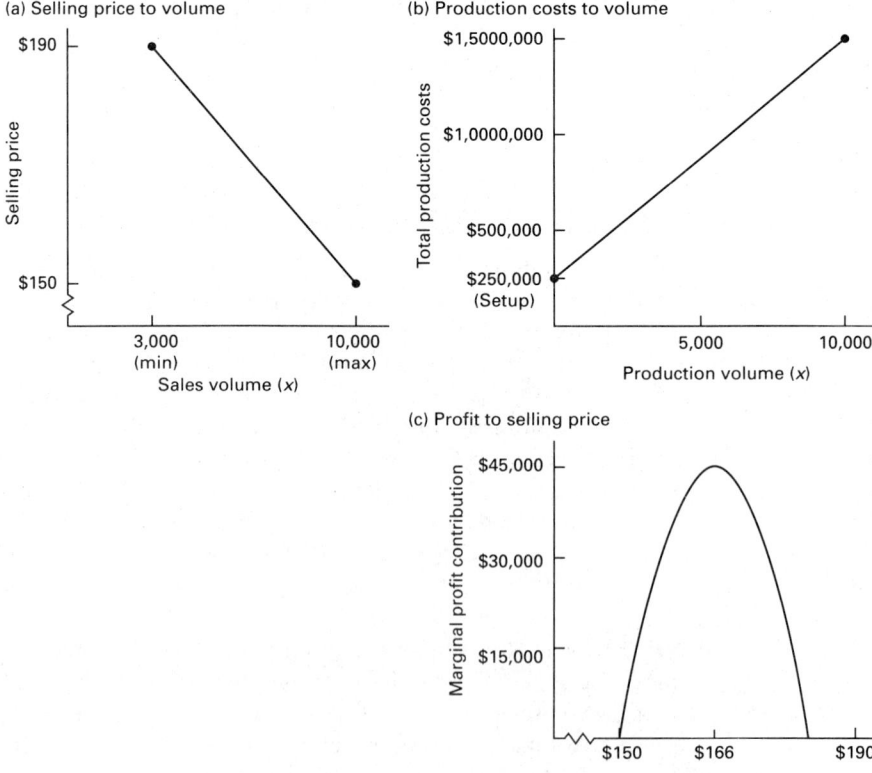

FIGURE 5.2 Return on investment product pricing factors

TABLE 5.1 Profitability Analysis of "Zipper"

Price/Volume Analysis

x = Unit sales

$P(x)$ = Unit price as a function of sales

Minimum price = $150 (sales of 10,000)

Maximum price = $190 (sales of 3,000)

$$P(x) = \frac{145{,}000 - 4x}{700}$$

Cost/Volume Analysis

Setup cost = $250,000

Unit variable cost = $125

$C(x)$ = total cost as a function of sales

= $250{,}000 + 125x$

Profit/Price Analysis

$R(x)$ = Total revenue

= $x[(P)(x)]$

$PC(x)$ = total profit contribution

= $R(x) - C(x)$

$$= \frac{-440x^2 + 575{,}000x}{7{,}000} - 250{,}000$$

Optimal Model Solution

$x^* = 7{,}187.50$ $P^*(x^*) = \$166.07$ $PC^*(x^*) = \$45{,}200.89$

The preceding dialogue is an allegory of the product pricing problem. If we expand our horizons to encompass multiple products and include a set of linear constraints on scarce resources, we have a **quadratic programming model**.

AN INVENTORY CONTROL MODEL

Maintaining adequate stocks of inventory is a classic example of nonlinear modeling. The inventory situation could be large, as in maintenance of sufficient refined liquid fuel reserves to sustain demand for an entire country, or small, as in maintaining enough milk in the refrigerator to accommodate anticipated demand for a family of four between trips to the grocery store. The objective in every case is straightforward minimization of the costs associated with the inventory.

The simplest inventory model involves only two types of costs: the cost of ordering items and the cost of holding them. Ordering costs include such items as clerical time, forms, postage, and supervisory review of purchase orders. Holding costs cover such things as storage and handling, insurance, obsolescence, and opportunity cost of the capital resources involved. This model requires some underlying assumptions that in many cases are frankly nonsensical from a realistic managerial point of view but that we can relax (and will in Chapter 12) to create more useful analytical tools. These assumptions are as follows:

1. Demand for each product is constant and known with certainty.
2. Per-unit cost for each product is constant, and price discounts are not available.
3. We can express ordering cost for each product as a constant dollar amount per order.
4. We can state holding cost for each product as a percentage of the average value of the inventory.

With these restrictive assumptions in mind, let us develop the so-called economic order quantity (EOQ) model (sometimes called the Wilson model) for n items.

Let

d_j = annual demand in units for the jth item

c_j = per-order ordering cost for the jth item

h_j = holding cost as a fraction of the average on-hand value of the jth item

p_j = per-unit purchase price for the jth item

q_j = quantity of the jth item ordered each time an order is placed

Since we order q_j items each time we order, the number of orders per year is d_j/q_j, so that the annual ordering cost is $(c_j)(d_j/q_j)$ for the jth item.

The average on-hand inventory for the jth item is merely $q_j/2$, as we can see from Figure 5.3. Here $q_j/2$ is the average number of units of inventory because half of the time there are more than $q_j/2$ units in inventory and half of the time there are fewer than $q_j/2$ units in inventory. Hence, the average value of the inventory is $(p_j)(q_j/2)$. We see that the annual holding cost is therefore $(h_j)(p_j)(q_j/2)$. Our total inventory cost T_j for item j is the sum of ordering and holding costs, and the cost for ordering and holding all items is then T, where

$$T = \sum_{j=1}^{n} T_j = \sum_{j=1}^{n} [c_j(d_j/q_j) + h_j(p_j)(q_j/2)] \tag{5.3}$$

FIGURE 5.3
Graph of inventory variation overtime for a particular product j

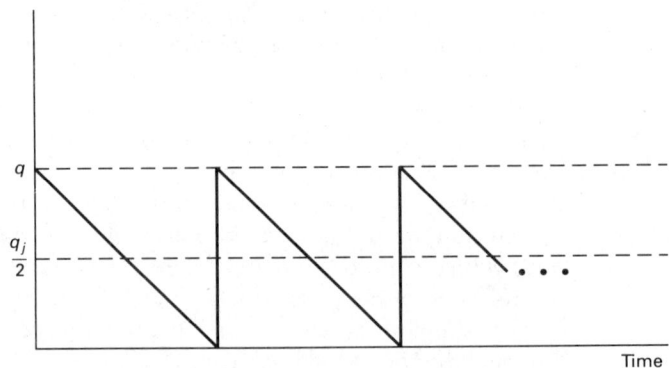

Since Equation (5.3) includes nonlinear terms that express ordering costs, it is a nonlinear function. In our inventory problem, we would wish to minimize T—subject perhaps to constraints on capital availability, total storage space at our disposal, etc. Thus, our object would be to find optimal order quantities q_j that satisfied whatever constraints were present and that minimized total ordering and holding costs. The model, therefore, turns out to be a nonlinear programming model. If there were no constraints, we could solve for optimal ordering quantities for each product separately, using elementary differential calculus. Doing so produces the optimal ordering quantity as follows:

$$q_j^* = \sqrt{\frac{2(d_j)(c_j)}{(h_j)(p_j)}}$$

We return to explore the subject of inventory management in detail in Chapter 12.

A SCRAP MINIMIZATION MODEL

In many manufacturing and fabrication industries, the level of scrap materials literally drives profits. For example, plants that manufacture industrial equipment such as heavy-duty generators and pumps usually cut flat components with special dies, and they can carefully control the amount of scrap through placement of the cutting machines on the sheet metal, ordering sheet metal in appropriate sizes, etc.

Consider the case of Dime & Bit (D&B), a small die-cutting subcontractor, who wishes to combine orders from NASA for three titanium face-plates in such a way that the company minimizes the percentage of titanium scrap (as a fraction of total stock). Details on D&B's problem appear in Table 5.2.

There are obviously four constraints: lower bounds on the production runs of the three types of plates and a constraint that reflects the limited availability of titanium sheets. Thus, if D&B's objective were to minimize **total scrap**, we would have a simple linear programming model to deal with. However, the objective here is to minimize the **percentage (or fraction) of scrap produced**, and we can write this in mathematical notation as follows:

$$\text{MIN } x_0 = \frac{2x_1 + x_2 + 3x_3}{15x_1 + 12x_2 + 21x_3} \qquad (5.4)$$

$$\begin{aligned}
\text{S T:} \quad x_1 &\geq 100 \\
x_2 &\geq 40 \\
x_3 &\geq 30 \\
15x_1 + 12x_2 + 21x_3 &\leq 2700 \\
x_1, x_2, x_3 &> 0
\end{aligned} \qquad (5.5)$$

The objective function in Equation (5.4) is decidedly nonlinear—being the ratio of two linear functions (total scrap weight and total stock weight). Since the constraints in Equation (5.5) happen to be linear, we call the resulting model a **fractional programming model**. As we will see later, a mathematical transformation will convert such models into equivalent linear programs.

A CONTAINER COST MINIMIZATION PROBLEM

Among others, the chemical industry faces many problems—both technical and economic—that are amenable to modeling and analysis using nonlinear programming models (we noted the nonlinear gasoline blending model earlier). One interesting application involves designing containers for storage and/or shipment of toxic or other-

TABLE 5.2 Dime & Bit Production Data

Product	Plate 1	Plate 2	Plate 3
Decision Variable	x_1	x_2	x_3
Scrap per plate (lb)	2	1	3
Titanium per plate (lb)	15	12	21
Minimum production run	100	40	30

Pounds of Platinum Available: 2,700

wise dangerous chemicals. Let's assume that containers must have rectangular tops, sides, and bottoms for convenience in shipping via railroad boxcar, and let l, w, and h, respectively, represent their length, width, and height.

The bottoms must be constructed of specially coated, heavy-load-bearing alloys. The sides must also be constructed with coated alloys to resist chemical erosion, but they do not have to bear as heavy a load as the bottoms. Finally, the tops must be fume resistant, but they do not require load-bearing or erosion-resistant material.

Let

V = required volume of the container

a = cost/ft.^{2} of material for bottoms

b = cost/ft.^{2} of material for sides

c = cost/ft.^{2} of material for tops.

Our basic cost minimization model would look like

$$\text{MIN } x_0 = (a)(l)(w) + (2)(b)(h)(w) + (2)(b)(l)(h) + (c)(l)(w) \tag{5.6}$$

$$\text{S T: } \quad (l)(h)(w) \geq V \tag{5.7}$$

Other constraints such as railroad boxcar dimensions and load-bearing capacity of materials. (5.8)

The resulting model is most certainly nonlinear, since every term contains products of some or all of the three decision variables. We call such models **geometric programming models,** and we can solve them rather easily with special techniques.

GENESIS OF NLP MODELS

The NLP models discussed above developed naturally from underlying physical or economic principles. There is another entire family of NLP models that arise empirically. For example, a particular cost or profit or constraint function may result from fitting curves (or equations) to historical data. One such example with which we are all familiar is the least-squares technique used to develop regression models. If we can obtain a good fit only by the use of nonlinear functions, our resulting optimization model will be nonlinear as well.

In the foregoing, we attempted to capture the flavor and almost infinite variety of nonlinear modeling, and we have not scratched the surface of this immense and complex subject. Next, we take a very shallow dive into a deep and turbulent ocean — that of solution techniques for NLP models.

NLP SOLUTION APPROACHES: AN INTUITIVE DESCRIPTION

Unlike the situation with LP models, there is no single, general algorithm for solving NLP models. Researchers in this highly technical area have developed a variety of approaches, and we can classify these approaches into four categories: **indirect methods, direct methods, linearization,** and **miscellaneous methods.** Table 5.3 includes some examples of each.

We will not try to cover in detail all of the specific techniques listed in the table. Rather, we will attempt to grasp the rationale behind each general approach by illustrating each method with an example or two.

INDIRECT METHODS

For NLP models with certain "nice" properties, we can use theoretical results from the calculus to find optimal solutions. For example, in our inventory model from the previous section, if we happen to have equality constraints, we can use something

TABLE 5.3 Nonlinear Programming Solution Approaches

Indirect Methods

Differential calculus

Kuhn-Tucker necessary conditions

Direct Methods

Univariate methods

Multivariate methods

Penalty function methods

Grid search methods

Generalized reduced gradient (GRG) methods

Linearization

Quadratic programming

Separable programming

Approximation programming

Successive linear programming (SLP)

Successive linear constrained programming (SLCP)

Fractional programming

Miscellaneous Methods

Geometric programming

Dynamic programming

called **Lagrange multipliers** to transform our model into an unconstrained model and use differential calculus to find the optimal ordering quantities. The Kuhn-Tucker conditions listed in Table 5.3 are theoretical results that use this device in an extended sense to derive necessary conditions for an optimal solution. We should realize that the Lagrange multiplier technique is important in a theoretical sense (i.e., in developing algorithms).

DIRECT METHODS

The most general approaches available for solving NLP models are the so-called direct methods. Such techniques basically consist of searching the feasible region in an organized way in an attempt to methodically improve the value of the objective function. As a parallel to the mountain-climbing analogy in our discussion of the SIMPLEX algorithm, consider the following vexing analogy to using direct methods in NLP.

Imagine that you are lost in a remote mountain range. Your goal is to climb to the highest peak (or descend to the lowest valley) so that searchers can find you. To make matters even worse, you are blind and cannot see the terrain around you. You can only sense whether you are walking uphill (or downhill). Occasionally, you encounter cliffs, and at other times, deep valleys. You continue to walk up (or down) until there is no direction that will take you higher (or lower). At this point you have reached a peak (valley), but unfortunately, there is no way of knowing whether it is the highest peak (or the lowest valley).

This is exactly what we ask our computer to do when we use direct methods to solve an NLP problem. Essentially, these methods use recursive algorithms to conduct a search for a solution. Like a blind hiker, these methods are able to sense only the local "terrain" and thus converge to a local optimum only. While these methods are blind in the sense that they are unable to provide a complete picture or description of the shape of the mountain range, they are nevertheless popular methods for solving small to moderate-sized (200 or fewer variables) NLP models with extensive nonlinearities.

One interesting direct method is the Sequential Unconstrained Minimization Technique (SUMT) of Fiacco and McCormick [3]. This algorithm, which is one of the so-called barrier or penalty approaches, uses a special function to formulate the model and to erect a "barrier" inside the feasible region in such a way that the search for better and better values of the objective function can never stray outside that region. If you could build a SUMT-like fence to contain a vicious dog, the fence would get higher and higher as the animal got closer and closer.

Gradient search methods such as Lasdon's GRG2 [8] are the most popular direct type of algorithm in practice, and there is a variety of such approaches.

LINEARIZATION

We have already seen two examples of NLP models for which linearization is useful: the fractional programming model developed for the scrap minimization problem and the quadratic programming model of an inventory system. Before briefly discussing these and other specific models, let's look at the philosophy that underpins the solution approach of linearization.

Consider for a moment the communication problem between humans and their obedient servant, the electronic computer. Most modern civilizations have adopted the decimal number system (i.e., base 10), so that practically everybody knows, for example, that $1 + 1 = 2$. Not so the computer. Since it basically operates with the binary number system, it cannot recognize the symbol "2"—since there isn't such a thing in this system—and insists that 1 + 1 = "10". What we need to do is to translate our numbers into a language the computer can understand, tell the computer to "do its own thing" in the binary "language," and translate its results back into our "language" so that we can understand them. This translation process is analogous to what linearization accomplishes for some NLP models. Since we know how to solve LP problems very efficiently, if we can translate (transform) certain NLP problems into LP problems, we can solve the equivalent LP models and reverse the transformation to recover the NLP model solutions. Let's get down to particulars.

FRACTIONAL PROGRAMMING MODELS

As discussed earlier, the fractional programming model for Dime & Bit is as follows:

$$\text{MIN } x_0 = \frac{2x_1 + x_2 + 3x_3}{15x_1 + 12x_2 + 21x_3} \tag{5.4}$$

$$\begin{aligned} \text{S T:} \quad & x_1 \geq 100 \\ & x_2 \geq 40 \\ & x_3 \geq 30 \\ & 15x_1 + 12x_2 + 21x_3 \leq 2700 \\ & x_1, x_2, x_3 \geq 0 \end{aligned} \tag{5.5}$$

Let's define a variable $v > 0$ as

$$v = \frac{1}{15x_1 + 12x_2 + 21x_3} \tag{5.9}$$

If we substitute Equation (5.9) into Equation (5.4), we have

$$\text{MIN } x_0 = 2vx_1 + vx_2 + 3vx_3 \tag{5.10}$$

This eliminates the linear expression in the denominator of Equation (5.4) all right, but we are left with a nonlinear function in Equation (5.10) in which there are *products of variables*. What if we multiplied both sides of the constraints (5.5) by v and cross-multiplied the new expression in Equation (5.9)? The result would be (after a bit of algebraic simplification)

$$\text{MIN } x_0 = 2vx_1 + vx_2 + 3vx_3 \tag{5.11}$$

$$\begin{aligned} \text{S T:} \quad & vx_1 \quad\quad\quad\quad - 100v \geq 0 \\ & \quad\quad vx_2 \quad\quad - 40v \geq 0 \\ & \quad\quad\quad\quad vx_3 - 30v \geq 0 \\ & 15vx_1 + 12vx_2 + 21vx_3 - 2700v \leq 0 \\ & 15vx_1 + 12vx_2 + 21vx_3 = 1 \end{aligned} \tag{5.12}$$

The resulting model is still nonlinear, of course, but we now perform the coup de grace.

Let

$$y_1 = vx_1; \quad y_2 = vx_2; \quad y_3 = vx_3 \tag{5.13}$$

TABLE 5.4 SAMS Output for Transformed D&B Model

DIME & BIT SCRAP MINIMIZATION
QUICK BRIEFING ON OPTIMAL MODEL SOLUTION
Maximum Objective Value = 0.125

Decision Variable	Optimal Value	Reduced Cost
Y1	0.0376	0.0
Y2	0.0176	0.0
Y3	0.0111	0.0
V	0.00037037	0.0

And thus we have the LP (5.15) and (5.16), whose decision variables are y_1, y_2, y_3, and v. After solving this LP model with a SIMPLEX code, we recover the desired solution by reversing the transformation of Equation (5.14):

$$x_j = y_j/v, \quad j = 1, \ldots, 3. \tag{5.14}$$

$$\text{MIN } x_0 = 2y_1 + y_2 + 3y_3 \tag{5.15}$$

$$\begin{aligned}
\text{S T:} \quad & y_1 &&- 100v \geq 0 \\
& y_2 &&- 40v \geq 0 \\
& y_3 &&- 30v \geq 0 \\
& 15y_1 + 12y_2 + 21y_3 - 2700v \leq 0 \\
& 15y_1 + 12y_2 + 21y_3 &&= 1 \\
& y_1, y_2, y_3 \geq 0 \text{ and } v > 0
\end{aligned} \tag{5.16}$$

Thus, by adding one variable v and one constraint, we have transformed an NLP model into an LP model. Table 5.4 gives the SAMS LP module solution to the transformed model.

Reversing the transformation gives us the solution to our original model.

$$x_1 = \frac{0.0370}{0.00037037} = 100 \qquad x_2 = \frac{0.0176}{0.00037037} = 47.5$$

$$x_3 = \frac{0.0111}{0.00037037} = 30$$

We note that scrap is minimized at 12.5% of total titanium sheeting available.

The fractional programming transformation illustrated in the Dime & Bit scenario is easily generalizable to more complex applications.

QUADRATIC PROGRAMMING MODELS

We formulate quadratic programming models as follows:

$$\text{OPTIMIZE } x_0 = \sum_{j=1}^{n} \sum_{k=1}^{n} c_{jk} x_j x_k + \sum_{j=1}^{n} d_j x_j \tag{5.17}$$

$$\text{S T:} \sum_{j=1}^{n} a_{ij} x_j \left\{ \begin{array}{c} < \\ = \\ > \end{array} \right\} b_i, \, i = 1, \ldots, m \tag{5.18}$$

As you can see, quadratic programming models involve an objective function that is a quadratic function of the decision variables, and a set of linear constraints. In addition to the pricing problem we looked at earlier, such models arise naturally in such diverse applications as portfolio management and personnel assignment.

Researchers have developed several approaches to solving quadratic programming models, but one of the more interesting is the **Frank-Wolfe quadratic programming algorithm** [5]. We will not go into detail here, but this technique converts the nonlinear model into an equivalent aggregated LP model consisting of a primal model and its associated dual model. We must alter the SIMPLEX algorithm slightly to include something called "restricted basis entry," but the transformation from an NLP to an LP model is the essence of the approach.

LINEAR APPROXIMATION MODELS

If our nonlinear objective and/or constraint functions are "well-behaved" in a certain mathematical sense, we can approximate these functions by successive linear segments. For example, Figure 5.4 is an approximation of the highly nonlinear function $f(x)$ by six line segments. Obviously, we could obtain a better "fit" by using 12 or even 24 line segments, but—as is usually the case in life—there is no free lunch in linear approximation techniques. Each of the line segments represents a variable in the resulting linear model, so that there is a direct tradeoff between the accuracy of the approximation and the size of the resulting LP model. As was the case with quadratic programming, we must alter the SIMPLEX algorithm slightly to get a meaningful solution to the LP model.

How "well-behaved" does an NLP objective or constraint function have to be in order to be a candidate for approximation by linear segments? One class of such models is separable NLP models, which have the following configuration:

$$\text{OPTIMIZE } x_0 = \sum_{j=1}^{n} f_j(x_j) \tag{5.19}$$

$$\text{S T:} \sum_{j=1}^{n} g_{ij}(x_j) \left\{ \begin{array}{c} < \\ = \\ > \end{array} \right\} b_i, \, i = 1, \ldots, m \tag{5.20}$$

FIGURE 5.4
Linear approximation of a nonlinear function

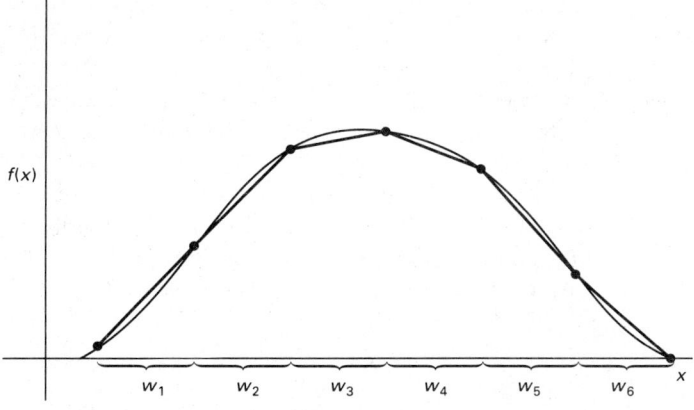

Note that each term in the objective function and constraints is a function of exactly one decision variable, although the functions themselves can assume highly nonlinear forms. We can easily approximate separable models by linear functions and—within the capability of our computer to grapple with large LP models—solve them to any desired degree of accuracy.

OTHER LINEARIZATION TECHNIQUES

Researchers have developed a wide variety of other approaches, such as successive linear programming and direct linearization of MINIMAX objective functions, to "tame" certain NLP models. These as well as those previously discussed all take essentially the same approach—they transform NLP models that we can't solve directly into equivalent LP models that we can solve with the SIMPLEX algorithm (with modifications, perhaps). Such approaches are on the frontier of current research into solution techniques in nonlinear programming.

MISCELLANEOUS METHODS

The geometric programming model that evolved in our previous look at optimizing the dimensions of chemical shipping containers is one example of NLP models that we can solve with specialized techniques that don't fit neatly into one of the first three categories. The solution technique called **geometric programming** solves models whose objective function and constraints consist of expressions called *posynomials* (sums of terms that are products of powers of the decision variables). We observe here that the technique is based heavily on the theory of duality.

Another miscellaneous method used to solve nonlinear models is the so-called dynamic programming technique. This approach is so useful, important, and versatile that we will discuss it separately in the next chapter.

DEVELOPING ALTERNATIVE SOLUTIONS

Approaches to developing alternative solutions to NLP models form a mixed bag. For methods that use Lagrange multipliers to incorporate constraints into the objective functions, the values of these multiplier variables for the optimal model solution behave exactly like shadow prices in LP—they are marginal utilities for the resources represented by the constraints. Most NLP algorithms generate better and better solutions along the way, and we can record these suboptimal solutions to provide managerial flexibility in decision making. One exception is the class of so-called outer methods that produce only infeasible solutions until they find the optimal model solution. Also, indirect methods sometimes locate a local optimum that is not the global optimum. Figure 5.5 depicts such a situation. In such cases, you can sometimes "restart" the algorithm at several different initial points in an effort to locate the global optimum.

On the surface, it would appear that models that we solve by linearization approaches (i.e., transformed into LP models and solved by the SIMPLEX algorithm) are amenable to postoptimality or sensitivity analysis by the techniques in Chapter 2. This is true to a certain extent, but we must keep in mind that since we are dealing with LP models that are *transformations* of NLP models, we must be very careful how we interpret shadow prices and other LP indicators. Such analyses are indeed possible but, unfortunately, are beyond the scope of this text.

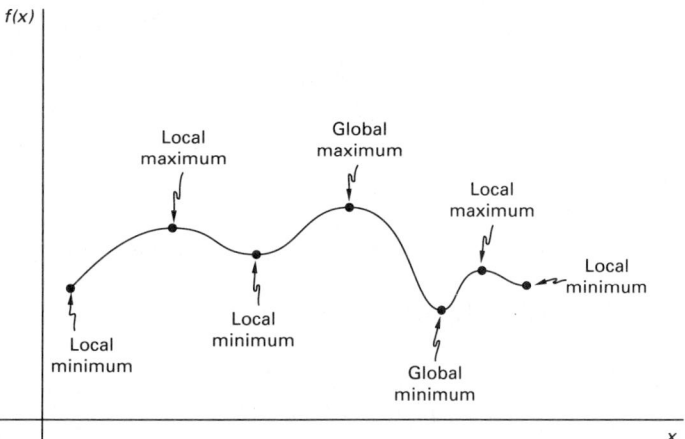

FIGURE 5.5
Local versus global optima

To summarize, generating alternative solutions and performing sensitivity analyses in the nonlinear "outback" are ill-structured undertakings at best—except in a few special cases.

STATE OF THE ART IN NLP

Large-scale nonlinear programming is becoming increasingly important in the refinery and petrochemical industries. As mentioned earlier, corporate and industrial mathematical models have gradually evolved from LP models to NLP models. In some cases, the computer codes used to solve these models have also evolved to ever more elaborate versions of the SIMPLEX algorithm. Following Lasdon [7], we describe a few such codes that the oil and gas industry uses. Shell Oil uses a successive linear programming (SLP) code for solving NLPs arising from refinery optimization. It has used this program to solve problems with up to 30 nonlinear variables and 100 nonlinear constraints.

Gulf Oil has used an SLP package consisting of revised SIMPLEX and conjugate gradient methods. Kuwait Oil Company used a more sophisticated package. The largest problem it has solved to date had 2,336 constraints, 4,392 linear variables, 400 nonlinear variables, and a SIMPLEX matrix containing 20,000 nonzero elements.

Marathon Oil uses a nonlinear refinery model to perform its refinery optimization. The model is a hierarchical structure with the first level consisting of 20 major FORTRAN simulation submodels for the refinery process. These submodels provide input data for an LP system that coordinates the operations of the submodels.

These are a few of the major NLP methods and models in use by the refinery and petrochemical industries. Similar models and computer codes are in use by Chevron, Standard Oil of California, Union Carbide, and others [7]. The literature discusses problems ranging from product blending, refinery unit optimization, design of multiplant production, and distribution planning.

The literature suggests many other areas of application of large-scale NLP models. Two important areas are network and economic planning. Nonlinear network topics include electric power dispatch, hydroelectric reservoir management, and problems involving traffic flow in urban transportation networks. Economic planning applications include large dynamic econometric models as well as a variety of static equilibrium models and submodels of larger planning systems.

In our discussion so far, we have omitted a great deal more than we have included on the subject of nonlinear programming. And we should not be surprised that this is the case. Numerous brilliant and highly trained mathematicians and operations researchers have devoted their professional lives to investigating small corners of the nonlinear "outback," and there is much more to discover than we currently know.

MINICASES

Colossus of Roads

THE SCENARIO

Colossus of Roads, Inc. (COR) is a major manufacturer of earth-moving, grading, and street-paving equipment. Its premier products are the Zeus and Pharos (medium and large earth movers, respectively), the Babylon and Mausolus (narrow- and wide-track road graders, respectively), and the Pyramid (a large street-paving machine). COR assembles and ships the products from COR's plant in Gomorrah, Pennsylvania. There has been a rising demand for COR's products in the past 12 months, and the plant is currently operating at capacity.

THE PROBLEM

Artemis Temple, the company's director of production, has been using a linear programming procedure to help her make product mix decisions each quarter and has found the computer analysis to be most useful. She has always been puzzled by one aspect of the model solution, however. When the LP model indicates that she should produce a relatively small number of a given piece of equipment, the profit contributions are consistently overstated; for relatively large numbers, profit contributions are understated. In the past, Artemis had used a rule of thumb that partially accounted for this phenomenon, but with production at full capacity, she was increasingly uncomfortable with this procedure. Artemis suspected that the objective function was nonlinear but didn't know what to do about it.

The LP model that Artemis used had four constraints: manpower availability, space availability in the plant's assembly area, supply of oversized tires (common to all five machines), and a company policy that dictated the assembly of at least as many graders as earth movers. Artemis had already received the data for the next quarter and had constructed the LP model as follows (*Note:* The variables $x_1, \ldots, x_5$ represent numbers of Zeus, Pharos, Babylon, Mausolus, and Pyramid machines to assemble, respectively):

Profit Contribution ($1000s)

$$\text{MAX } x_0 = 3.5x_1 + 4x_2 + 2.5x_3 + 3x_4 + 5.25x_5 \tag{5.21}$$

S T:

Manpower (manhours)

$$90x_1 + 100x_2 + 75x_3 + 80x_4 + 125x_5 \leq 17000 \tag{5.22}$$

Space: (100s sq. ft.)

$$4x_1 + 5x_2 + 2x_3 + 3x_4 + 8x_5 \leq 740 \quad (5.23)$$

Tires: (number)

$$16x_1 + 24x_2 + 12x_3 + 12x_4 + 36x_5 \leq 3000 \quad (5.24)$$

Mix:

$$x_1 + x_2 - x_3 - x_4 \leq 0 \quad (5.25)$$

$$x_j \geq 0, j = 1, \ldots, 5 \quad (5.26)$$

The analyst ran a SAMS-like linear programming module. Figure 5.6 shows the input screen, and Table 5.5 gives the detailed report.

Artemis compared the optimal mix with the maximum capacities of the individual machines (which she computed from the constraints) as in Table 5.6.

The indicated numbers of Zeus and Mausolus machines didn't bother Artemis, since they were fairly close to the midpoints of their production ranges. Since the Pharos wasn't produced at all, it was no problem. The Babylon and Pyramid, however, were at the extreme low end of their production ranges, and as a result, this production mix could considerably overstate the total profit.

THE MODEL

As a last resort, Artemis called corporate headquarters in Carthage, New York, to request assistance, and Polly Gnomeal, COR's chief MS/OR analyst, was in Artemis' office the next day. After Artemis explained the situation and expressed her concerns, Polly went to work. A week later, Polly was ready to brief Artemis on the results of her investigation.

FIGURE 5.6 SAMS input screen for Colossus of Roads

```
┌──▶  SAMS INPUT SCREEN - Linear Programming  ◀──┐
│                                                 │
│   NAME?   COLOSSUS OF ROADS                     │
│   MAximize or MInimize?  MA                     │
│   PROBLEM DESCRIPTION - Optimize production of large road
│                         working machines        │
├─────────────────────────────────────────────────┤
│   Variables    ZEUS  PHAR  BABY  MAUS  PYRA    Dir  RHS
│
│   Objective    3.5   4.    2.5   3.    5.25    <
│
│   Upper Bound  INF   INF   INF   INF   INF     =
│   Lower Bound  0.    0.    0.    0.    0.      >
│
│   Constraints
│   MANPOWER     90.   100.  75.   80.   125.    <17000.
│   SPACE        4.    5.    2.    3.    8.      <  740.
│   TIRES        16.   24.   12.   12.   36.     < 3000.
│   MIX          1.    1.    -1.   -17     .     <   0.
│
└─────────────────────────────────────────────────┘
```

TABLE 5.5 SAMS output for Colossus of Roads

COLOSSUS OF ROADS
QUICK BRIEFING ON OPTIMAL MODEL SOLUTION
Maximum Objective Value = 655.75

Decision Variable	Optimal Value	Reduced Cost
ZEUS	90.0	0.0
PHAR	0.0	0.0
BABY	1.0	0.0
MAUS	90.0	0.0
PYRA	13.0	0.0

Constraint	Type	Slack
CONSTRAINT 2	<	4.0
CONSTRAINT 4	<	1.0

TABLE 5.6

Variable	Product	Optimal ILP Solution	Maximum Capacity
x_1	Zeus	90	185
x_2	Pharos	0	125
x_3	Babylon	1	226
x_4	Mausolus	90	212
x_5	Pyramid	13	83

Objective value $655,750

By plotting past profit contribution data, it appeared to Polly that she could approximate the profit contribution functions for all five products by a classical S-curve (Figure 5.7). The general equation for the curve that Polly developed is as follows:

$$P(x_j) = \frac{3Tx_j^2}{M_j^2} - \frac{2Tx_j^3}{M_j^3} \tag{5.27}$$

where M_j is the maximum number of the jth machine that the plant can produce and T is total maximum profit contribution associated with producing M_j units. When Polly showed Artemis the graph of the S-curve, she nodded affirmatively—the graph showed precisely the effect that Artemis had suspected (profit overstated for small quantities and understated for large ones).

Plugging in the appropriate numbers and simplifying the objective function, we have the nonlinear objective function shown in Equation (5.28):

FIGURE 5.7
Profit function for Colossus of Roads

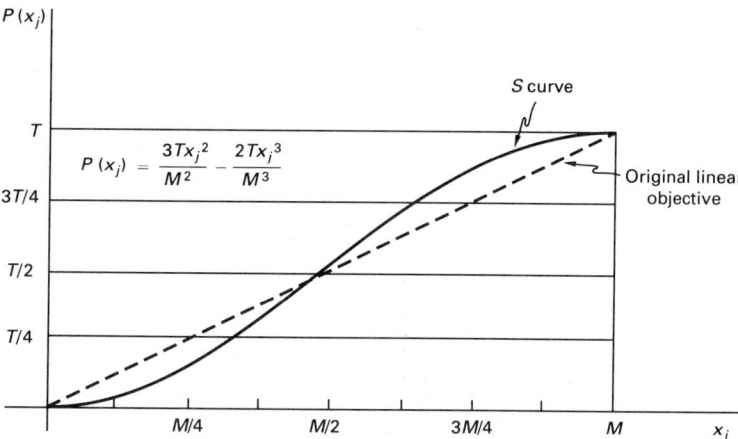

$$\text{MAX } x_0 = 0.0568x_1^2 - 0.0002x_1^3 + 0.0960x_2^2 - 0.0005x_2^3$$
$$+ 0.0332x_3^2 - 0.0001x_3^3 + 0.0425x_4^2 - 0.0001x_4^3 \quad (5.28)$$
$$+ 0.1898x_5^2 - 0.0015x_5^3$$

The constraints of course, remain the same, so that Equation (5.28) and Equations (5.22) to (5.26) represent a nonlinear programming model.

SOLUTION TO THE MODEL

Artemis was impressed with Polly's NLP model but was quick to observe that she had no NLP code on her minicomputer—and she certainly had no intention of trying to solve the model by hand! Polly reassured her, noting that since Artemis' model turned out to be separable in the decision variables, she could approximate them by linearization. Polly judged that Artemis' minicomputer should be able to handle about 400 variables and recommended setting up a grid in steps of three units. For example, the substitution for x_1 would be as follows, since the maximum value for x_1 is 185:

$$x_1 = \sum_{i=1}^{62} 3i(w_{i1}) \quad (5.29)$$

or

$$x_1 = 3w_{11} + 6w_{21} + 9w_{31} + \ldots + 183w_{61,1} + 186w_{62,1} \quad (5.30)$$

In all, the linearized model would have 383 variables. Before returning to Carthage, Polly briefed Artemis' computer analyst on modifying the LP code so that none of the new w-variables could take on positive values unless one of its "neighbors" was also positive (i.e., after the first w_{ij} for some j had initially become positive).

The analyst constructed the model; and although the minicomputer "crunched" for quite a while, it obtained an optimal model solution, which is compared with the original IP solution in Table 5.7. (We do not exhibit the actual computer output, for obvious reasons!)

SOLUTION TO THE PROBLEM

When she saw the nonlinear solution, Artemis leaned back thoughtfully in her chair. It appeared that the company policy dictating the assembly of at least as many graders

TABLE 5.7

Variable	Product	Nonlinear Solution	IP Solution
x_1	Zeus	100	90
x_2	Pharos	0	0
x_3	Babylon	0	1
x_4	Mausolus	100	90
x_5	Pyramid	0	13
Objective Value		$654,195	$655,750

TABLE 5.8

Variable	Product	Solution 1	Solution 2
x_1	Zeus	164	144
x_2	Pharos	0	10
x_3	Babylon	0	0
x_4	Mausolus	28	38
x_5	Pyramid	0	0
Objective Value		$658,000	

as earth movers was "driving" the problem. As an experiment, Artemis discarded this policy constraint (5.25) and reran her original LP model. To her surprise, she got two alternative optimal integer solutions (see Table 5.8).

Substituting both solutions into the nonlinear objective function in Equation (5.28) produced profit contributions of $654,716 (#1) and $629,252 (#2). Thus, it appeared that the original nonlinear solution that indicated the production of 100 each Zeus and Mausolus machines was about the best COR could do and that the policy constraint actually had little effect on total profit contribution. Equally important, the ILP model gave solutions so close to the NLP solution that Artemis decided to abandon Polly Gnomeal's elegant model, since the additional expense did not appear to justify the model's use.

Beau-Kay, Inc.

THE SCENARIO

Beau-Kay, Inc. (BKI) is a regional firm in the Southwest that produces fertilizer for the home gardening market. The company's most successful product is Meadow Muffin, which it blends from two basic ingredients: a nitrate compound and a natural com-

TABLE 5.9

	Ingredients		
	Nitrate	Feedlot	Requirements (pounds per bag)
Nitrous oxide	25%	40%	At least 30
Lime	10%	6%	At least 7
Potash	4%	5%	No more than 5
Nictic acid	8%	10%	No more than 10
Phosphate	10%	8%	No more than 10
Inert ingredients	43%	31%	—

pound obtained from cattle feedlots in the area. Both ingredients are in plentiful supply, and BKI is at full production capacity to meet the high demand for this product.

THE PROBLEM

Beau Vines, the co-owner of BKI, was reviewing production planning with his partner Kay Monton. Beau and Kay were studying the results of a linear programming model that a management science consultant had installed several years ago. The input data are presented in Table 5.9.

The model solution had indicated the minimum cost at $15 per 90-pound bag, consisting of 40 pounds of nitrate and 50 pounds of feedlot, for an average cost per pound of $0.166667. As he was studying the model, it occurred to Beau that the 90-pound mix was purely arbitrary—being the smallest weight that would meet all of the blending constraints.

> "I wonder," Beau remarked to Kay, "whether we could lower our per-pound cost by producing a heavier standard bag."

THE MODEL

Kay, recalling the management science course from her MBA program, replied:

> "Beau, I think you're right. What we want is a mix that will minimize our *average per-pound* cost—and not the total cost of a bag of Meadow Muffin. Let's see. The model would be as follows—with x_1 and x_2 being the number of pounds of nitrate and feedlot, respectively, per bag."

$$\text{MIN } x_0 = \frac{0.15x_1 + 0.18x_2}{x_1 + x_2} \quad (5.31)$$

S T:
$$0.25x_1 + 0.40x_2 \geq 30 \quad (5.32)$$
$$0.10x_1 + 0.06x_2 \geq 7 \quad (5.33)$$
$$0.04x_1 + 0.05x_2 \leq 5 \quad (5.34)$$
$$0.08x_1 + 0.10x_2 \leq 10 \quad (5.35)$$
$$0.10x_1 + 0.08x_2 \leq 10 \quad (5.36)$$
$$x_1, x_2 \geq 0 \quad (5.37)$$

"I think you've got it, Kay," exclaimed Beau, "but there's one small problem. That's a nonlinear objective function, and all we have on our PC is an LP package. I guess we'll have to get that consultant back out here."

SOLUTION TO THE MODEL

"Not so fast, Beau," retorted Kay. "What we have here is a fractional programming model. There is a device we can use to transform it into an LP model, solve the LP formulation, and reverse the transformation to get our solution."

Let:

$$v = \frac{1}{x_1 + x_2}; \quad y_1 = v(x_1); \quad y_2 = v(x_2)$$

MIN $x_0 = 0.15 y_1 + 0.18 y_2$	(5.38)
S T: $\quad 0.25 y_1 + 0.40 y_2 - 30v \geq 0$	(5.39)
$\quad 0.10 y_1 + 0.06 y_2 - 7v \geq 0$	(5.40)
$\quad 0.04 y_1 + 0.05 y_2 - 5v \leq 0$	(5.41)
$\quad 0.08 y_1 + 0.10 y_2 - 10v \leq 0$	(5.42)
$\quad 0.10 y_1 + 0.08 y_2 - 10v \leq 0$	(5.43)
$\quad y_1 + y_2 = 1$	(5.44)
$\quad y_1, y_2, v \geq 0$	(5.45)

The LP solution to (5.38) to (5.45) emerged from the computer in Table 5.10. Reversing the transformation yielded

$$x_1 = \frac{y_1}{v} = 80 \text{ pounds of nitrate}$$

$$x_2 = \frac{y_2}{v} = 25 \text{ pounds of feedlot}$$

Checking this solution in the original LP formulation yielded

$S_1 = $ -0- : nitrous oxide constraint exactly met

$S_2 = $ 2.50 lb. : lime constraint more than met

$S_3 = $ 0.55 lb. : potash constraint more than met

$S_4 = $ 0.10 lb. : nictic acid constraint more than met

$S_5 = $ -0- : phosphate constraint exactly met

SOLUTION TO THE PROBLEM

"That's amazing," remarked Beau upon examining the solution. "The new mix is only 15 pounds more per bag than our current formula, but the proportion of ingredients is drastically different. And notice the difference in costs per pound—$0.157143 versus our current $0.166667—of $0.009524. If we sell two million pounds of Meadow Muffin this year

TABLE 5.10

BEAU-KAY
FULL BRIEFING ON OPTIMAL MODEL SOLUTION

Maximum Objective Value = 0.0157143

Decision Variable	Optimal Value	Reduced Cost
Y1	0.7619	0.0
Y2	0.2381	0.0
V	0.0095238	0.0

Constraint	Type	Slack	Shadow Price
NIT OXID	>	0.0000	0.14
LIME	>	0.0238	0.00
POTASH	<	0.0052	0.00
NIC ACID	<	0.0105	0.00
PHOSPHAT	<	0.0000	0.43
TRANSFOR	=	0.0000	0.16

POST-OPTIMALITY ANALYSIS OF RIGHT-HAND SIDE VALUES

Constraint	Type	Lower Bound	Current Coefficient	Upper Bound
NIT OXID	>	−0.05	0.0	0.055
LIME	>	−INF	0.0	0.024
POTASH	<	−0.005	0.0	INF
NIC ACID	<	−0.010	0.0	INF
PHOSPHAT	<	−0.022	0.0	0.017
TRANSFOR	=	0.000	1.0	INF

POST-OPTIMALITY ANALYSIS OF OBJECTIVE COEFFICIENTS

Decision Variable	Lower Bound	Current Coefficient	Upper Bound
Y1	−INF	0.15	0.18
Y2	0.15	0.18	INF
V	−6.00	0.00	15.00

---

like we did last year, we'll save over $19,000. Let's order a supply of 105-pound bags right now."

"Hold your horses, Beau," cautioned Kay. "We're the decision makers here—not that fractional programming model. Our ingredient cost for our present 90-pound bag of Meadow Muffin is 15 dollars, and our one-third markup to the 20-dollar selling price covers our overhead and other costs and gets us about a two-dollar profit per bag. With this new mixture, the ingredients in the 105-pound bag would cost us $16.50 per bag, so a one-third markup would increase the selling price to 22 dollars per bag. What will our customers say?"

"They'll be satisfied," Beau answered. "They'll be getting 16.7% more fertilizer at only a 10% increase in price. Of course, we will sell about 14.3% fewer bags to meet the same demand level in pounds, but our profit margin per bag will go up by 25% to $2.50 per bag. That means our overall profit will rise a little over 7 percent. See—there is something in it for everybody."

"Yes," observed Kay, "except for our feedlot supplier. He won't be happy when we cut our order in half. On the other hand, our nitrate supplier will be delighted when we double our order."

SUMMARY

In the beginning of the chapter, we saw that nonlinear programming models come in a bewildering variety of forms and that—unlike the case with LP models—the underlying assumptions are associated with different model forms rather than with one general NLP model. We illustrated the art of nonlinear modeling with several examples.

We described four different solutions approaches: direct methods, indirect methods, linearization, and miscellaneous methods, illustrating each approach with one or two specific examples.

We then saw that generating alternative solutions from NLP models and performing sensitivity analyses on them is tricky at best. Finally, we concluded with a discussion of some applications in industry.

If you are left with an uneasy feeling about NLP models—as opposed to their docile, well-behaved LP cousins from Chapter 2—this chapter has done its job well.

While NLP models are difficult, they are not unsolvable, in that many solution approaches to NLP utilize the SIMPLEX algorithm in some way. Certainly this is true of large-scale NLP applications, but it is true of fractional programming and quadratic programming as well.

Chapters 2 through 5 have surveyed the terrain of deterministic optimization models from the catbird seat of mathematical programming. Chapter 6 looks at a totally different approach to modeling certain managerial problems, called **multistage modeling**.

KEY TERMS

constrained center of gravity problem
convex
direct methods
facility location problem
fractional programming model
Frank-Wolfe quadratic programming algorithm
geometric programming model

indirect methods
Lagrange multipliers
linearization
multistage modeling
nonlinear programming (NLP) model
quadratic programming model
smooth and continuous

PROBLEMS FOR ANALYSIS

1. Linear regression is a widely used technique for analyzing data sets, and almost every undergraduate business student gains exposure to it as a freshman or sophomore (if not in high school). In simple regression, we construct a straight line in such a way that the sum of squared distances between the line and the values of the dependent variable is minimized. In the multivariate case, a hyperplane performs this function.

   One difficulty with minimizing squared sums of distances is that outliers in the data set can sometimes completely dominate the results. That is, squaring distances tends to wash out the effects of all but abnormally large (or small) data values. For example, consider the following time series representing the selling price of INXS on the New York Stock Exchange at the close on eight consecutive Fridays.

x_1	Week No.	1	2	3	4	5	6	7	8
y_1	Price	$24^{3/8}$	$25^{7/8}$	$25^{1/2}$	$26^{3/4}$	$27^{1/2}$	$27^{3/4}$	$28^{1/8}$	$25^{1/2}$

   Line A in Figure 5.8 is the least squares regression line for this data set. Note how the outlier (week #8) "bent" the line toward itself and away from the other seven points.

   Another way of describing linear relationships among points in a data set is mean absolute deviation (MAD) regression. That is, we might wish to have a regression function that minimized the sum (or equivalently the average) of absolute deviations from the points in the data set. Mathematically, we state this as follows:

   $$\text{MIN } x_0 = \sum_{i=1}^{n} |a(x_i) + b - y_i| \tag{5.46}$$

   Unfortunately, the absolute value function is not differentiable, so we cannot use calculus to find the optimal values of a and b, as we do in least squares regres-

FIGURE 5.8
Regression on stock prices

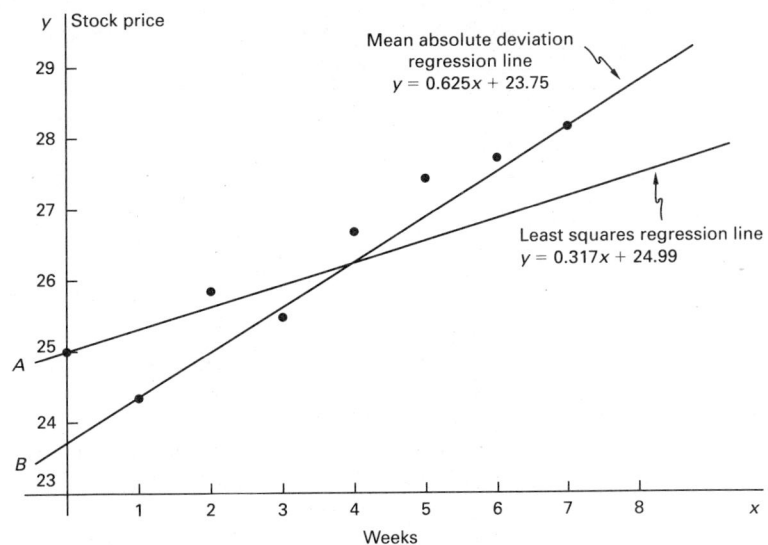

sion. Also, from a mathematical programming point of view, Equation (5.46) is nonlinear, so we can't directly apply LP solution techniques.

a. Consider the following LP model:

$$\text{MIN } x_0 = \sum_{i=1}^{n} u_i + \sum_{i=1}^{n} v_i \qquad (5.47)$$

$$\text{S T: } a(x_i) + b - u_i + v_i = y_i, i = 1, \ldots, n \qquad (5.48)$$

$$u_i, v_i \geq 0 \text{ for all } i \qquad (5.49)$$

$$a, b \text{ unconstrained in sign} \qquad (5.50)$$

where the (x_i, y_i) are the coordinates of the n points in our data set and the u_i and v_i are a set of "accounting variables."

Do you see that solving the ordinary LP model of Equations (5.47) to (5.50) yields the optimal values of the regression parameters a and b in $y = ax + b$? (*Hint:* What we have done is to set each of the absolute value expressions in Equation (5.46) equal to the difference between two nonnegative variables.)

b. The MAD regression line for the INXS stock price data is line B in Figure 5.8. Note that this line discounts point #8 and has a higher slope and smaller intercept than the least squares regression line.

If you were comfortable with using time as the independent variable for forecasting purposes, which of the two regression lines would you place more confidence in—all else being equal?

c. Note that we can also use MAD regression to fit nonlinear functions to a data set. In this case, however, the resulting mathematical program has a linear objective function and nonlinear constraints. Depending on the nature of the nonlinear function, what solution approaches discussed in this chapter might we use to find the optimal regression parameters?

d. As noted in this chapter, many nonlinear programming models arise empirically. That is, we fit historical data to a curve of some kind and use the resulting function, perhaps, as the objective function in a nonlinear programming model. Do you think MAD regression might be more suitable than least squares regression for this purpose? Why or why not?

e. Consider the following time series that exhibits international sales volume (in 000,000s) of compact discs of U2's latest album—released in January—for its first year.

Month	Jan	Feb	Mar	Apr	May	Jun	Jul	Aug	Sep	Oct	Nov	Dec
Sales	9	11	15	16	18	9	21	24	15	28	31	32

Note that sales for June and September do not appear to be consistent with sales for the other ten months. If you have access to a computer software package like SAMS' statistics module, compute the least squares regression equation for these data and use your equation to forecast sales for the next January (month 13). Are you happy with the forecast?

f. Now model the data by setting up and solving for the MAD regression equation using LP. You will have 12 u-variables, 12 v-variables, a, and b, for a total of 26 variables. If you have access to a package like the SAMS linear programming module, be sure to set the "variable type" for a and b on the input screen to "U" (unrestricted in sign). If your LP package doesn't have this capability, you will need to make the "unrestricted" transformation from Chapter 2. Finally, you will have 12 constraints—one for each data point. Now use your MAD equation to forecast month 13 and compare it with your result in (e). Is the MAD result somewhat more believable?

2. **The Scenario:** Hurley Byrd, a former military paramedic and private pilot, is considering establishing a helicopter ambulance service in the sparsely populated north-central plains states. Figure 5.9 exhibits the cities and towns Hurley wants to serve, along with their populations, which total 45,000. Hurley has also marked off a mileage grid of the 25,000-square-mile area that contains the 15 cities and towns in which the 45,000 people live.

The Problem: Hurley wishes to establish a base for his helicopter ambulance service in such a way that he maximizes the overall service level he provides while minimizing total miles flown, thus minimizing gasoline consumption.

Hurley recognizes his problem as one similar to that of finding the weighted center of gravity. That is, if he obtains the grid coordinates (x_i, y_i) of each of the 15 cities and towns and lets the weight w_i be the populations, the weighted center of gravity model is as follows:

$$\text{MIN } x_0 = \frac{\sum_{i=1}^{15} w_i[(x - x_i)^2 + (y - y_i)^2]}{\sum_{i=1}^{15} w_i} \quad (5.51)$$

Hurley finds the formulas for finding (x^*, y^*)—the weighted center of gravity—as follows:

$$x^* = \frac{\sum_{i=1}^{15} w_i x_i}{\sum_{i=1}^{15} w_i}; \quad y^* = \frac{\sum_{i=1}^{15} w_i y_i}{\sum_{i=1}^{15} w_i} \quad (5.52)$$

FIGURE 5.9
Towns serviced by helicopter ambulance

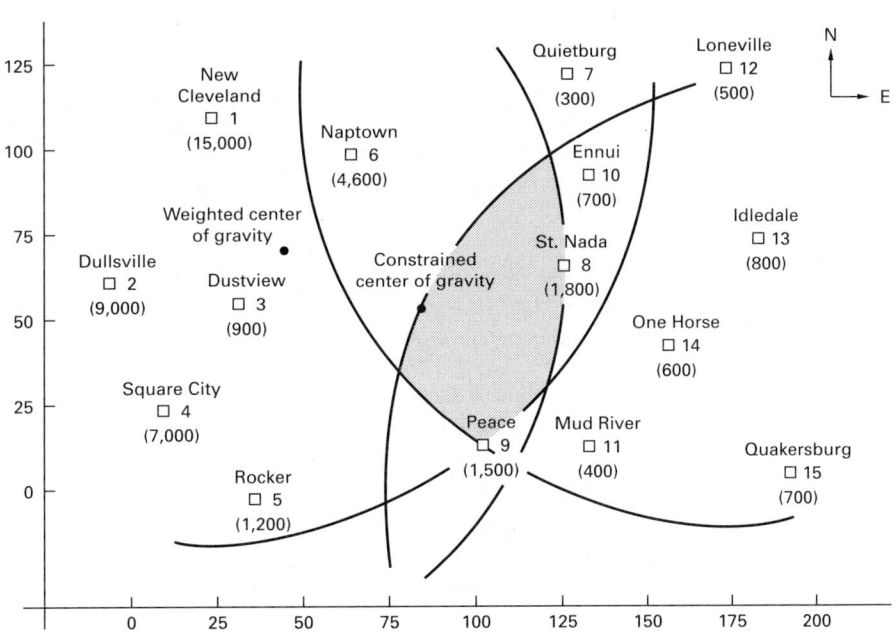

Plugging in the numbers, Hurley obtains: $x^* = 45.32$; $y^* = 71.83$, which is about 20 miles northeast of Dustview. To Hurley's chagrin, this optimal location is 170 miles away from Quakersburg, and the range of his converted helicopter ambulance is only 125 miles. Hurley notes that Loneville and Idledale would also be outside his helicopter's range.

Hurley's problem is known in engineering as a **constrained center of gravity problem** and in the MS/OR literature as a **facility location problem.** Think for a moment about how we could express the constraints that, along with the objective function of Equation (5.51), would result in a nonlinear programming model of this problem. Note that a circle of radius 125 miles, with Loneville (#12) as its center, includes all towns but the five westernmost ones and that a similar circle centered on Dullsville (#2) includes these five towns. Constructing similar circles around New Cleveland (#1) and Quakersburg (#15) produces the odd-shaped shaded area in Figure 5.9. You might wish to verify that every town is within 125 miles of every point in this shaded area. This, then, is the feasible region. We formulate the model mathematically as follows:

$$\text{MIN } x_0 = \frac{\sum_{i=1}^{15} w_i[(x - x_i)^2 + (y - y_i)^2]}{\sum_{i=1}^{15} w_i} \quad (5.53)$$

S T: (Loneville) $\quad (x - 175)^2 + (y - 115)^2 \leq (125)^2 \quad$ (5.54)

(Dullsville) $\quad (x - 0)^2 \;\; + (y - 65)^2 \;\; \leq (125)^2 \quad$ (5.55)

(New Cleveland) $(x - 25)^2 \;\; + (y - 110)^2 \leq (125)^2 \quad$ (5.56)

(Quakersburg) $\quad (x - 200)^2 + (y - 0)^2 \;\;\; \leq (125)^2 \quad$ (5.57)

Solution to the Model: The preceding model is a nonlinear programming model that we could probably best solve formally with an algorithm such as GRG2 or, since all of the functions are separable, be linearized and solved with an LP package.

a. Study Figure 5.9 and consider that the unconstrained minimum point is at coordinates (45.32, 71.83)—which is outside the feasible region. Does it seem intuitive that we would like the optimal constrained point to be as close to (45.32, 71.83) as possible? If this conjecture is correct, we can solve this model graphically by finding (with a compass) the point at which a circle drawn around the point (45.32, 71.83) touches the boundary of the feasible region. By visual inspection, this point lies on the circle drawn around Quakersburg and has coordinates of approximately (85, 55). Do you believe this point to be the optimal constrained center of gravity? Why or why not?

Solution to the Problem: As is usually the case, modeling the problem and solving the model resulted in nothing more than managerial insight. The "optimal" constrained point in this case ended up 38 miles from the nearest town, in the middle of a deserted lignite mine! Notice that if Hurley wanted to locate his firm in inhabited surroundings, only the small towns of St. Nada and Peace lie within the feasible region.

a. Suppose Hurley regretfully abandoned the possibility of providing helicopter ambulance service to the small towns of Loneville, Idledale, and Quakersburg, whose total population of 2,000 is only about 4% of the population of the area. What would happen to the unconstrained center of gravity? Would all remaining towns be within a 125-mile radius of the new location?

b. If you were acting as a consultant to Hurley on this problem, how would you go about investigating the sensitivity of the solution to the range of Hurley's helicopter?

c. Suppose, instead of sparsely settled countryside and helicopter ambulance service, we were discussing normal automotive ambulance service in a large city. Would the center of gravity model be appropriate in this case (assuming a rectangular pattern of streets)? Do you see that we would need an absolute value minimization objective rather than a sum-of-squares objective?

3. **The Scenario:** Barbara Seville is a management science consultant to HairStyles, Inc. (HSI), a chain of hair-styling salons. Barbara assists the company in selecting locations for new salons and in configuring them. HSI does not build its own shops. Rather, the company leases vacant space in what it considers to be good locations. Business is booming, and Barbara is essentially working full-time for HSI.

The Problem: Since leased space varies widely in size from one location to the next, HSI configures each salon somewhat differently. There are six basic stations that HSI can include (e.g., washing, cutting, drying), and each station has a certain utility. However, the utility of additional stations of a certain type diminishes monotonically as the number increases. Each salon must, of course, include at least one of the six types of station, but there is obviously an upper limit on the numbers of station types desirable in a particular salon—regardless of how much floor space is available.

Barbara would like to build a general model that would suggest an optimal configuration based on floor space available.

The Model: In talking to the company's CEO, Barbara is able to formalize two key aspects of the problem: the maximum number allowable for each type of station and the approximate shapes of the six utility functions for each type of station. Since these curves appear to be roughly parabolic, Barbara adopts the following basic utility curve:

Let

M_i = maximum number of type i stations allowed

V_i = utility for M_i stations

x_i = number of stations of type i included

y_i = utility of x_i stations

Mathematically, the quadratic function for station i is

$$y_i(x_i) = \frac{(-V_i)(x_i^2)}{M_i^2} + \frac{(2V_i)(x_i)}{M_i} \tag{5.58}$$

Figure 5.10 is a graph of this general utility function.

The parameters for each station type, to include the floor space requirements in square feet, are

	Station Type					
	1	2	3	4	5	6
Maximum No. (M_i)	2	3	5	6	6	7
Maximum Utility (V_i)	10	10	9	8	6	5
Floor Space (ft^2)	30	27	21	18	19	15

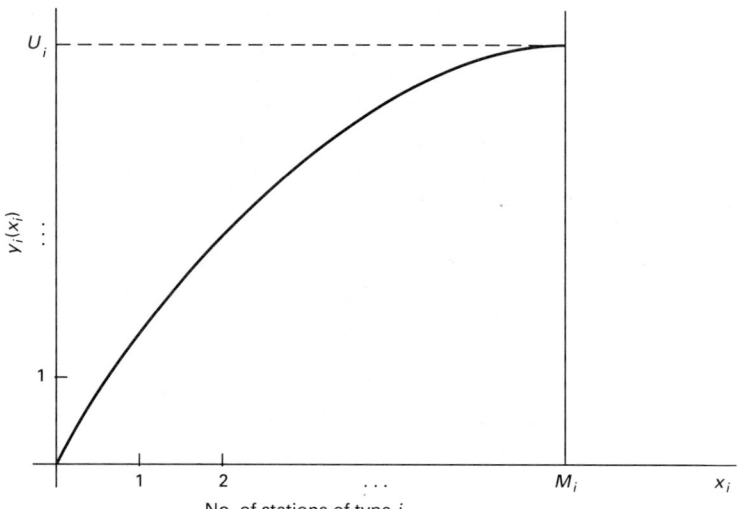

FIGURE 5.10
General utility function for Hair Styles, Inc.

If we let F be the total square footage available for a particular location, our mathematical optimization model is

$$\text{MAX } x_0 = \left[\frac{-10x_1^2}{4} + \frac{20x_1}{2}\right] + \left[\frac{-10x_2^2}{9} + \frac{20x_2}{3}\right] +$$

$$\left[\frac{-9x_3^2}{25} + \frac{18x_3}{5}\right] + \left[\frac{-8x_4^2}{36} + \frac{16x_4}{6}\right] + \left[\frac{-6x_5^2}{36} + \frac{12x_5}{6}\right]$$

$$+ \left[\frac{-5x_6^2}{49} + \frac{10x_6}{7}\right] \tag{5.59}$$

S T: $x_i \geq 1, i = 1, \ldots, 6$ \hfill (5.60)

$30x_1 + 27x_2 + 21x_3 + 18x_4 + 19x_5 + 15x_6 \leq F$ \hfill (5.61)

$x_1 \leq 2$ \hfill (5.62)

$x_2 \leq 3$ \hfill (5.63)

$x_3 \leq 5$ \hfill (5.64)

$x_4 \leq 6$ \hfill (5.65)

$x_5 \leq 6$ \hfill (5.66)

$x_6 \leq 7$ \hfill (5.67)

a. Is the model in Equations (5.59) to (5.67) a classical quadratic programming model? Are the nonlinearities separable?
b. The above model is known as a constrained quadratic knapsack model (you met the simpler linear knapsack model in Chapter 3). Do you see that this is actually a nonlinear IP model in that "fractions of stations" is meaningless, practically speaking?

Solution to the Model: Before blindly feeding the model to a computer, Barbara leaned back in her chair and studied it thoughtfully. She could easily solve the

TABLE 5.11

Variable	Optimal Model Value	M_i	Rounded Model Value	Feasible Model Value
x_1	1.7874	2	2	2
x_2	2.5694	3	3	3
x_3	3.9963	5	4	3
x_4	4.5647	6	5	5
x_5	3.9800	6	4	4
x_6	4.3952	7	4	4

Maximum utility = 45.4881
Shadow price for floor space at $F = 430$ ft² = 0.035439

model (given appropriate values of F, the total floor space available) by the Frank-Wolfe quadratic programming algorithm. She realized that she would probably get noninteger solutions, but perhaps she could obtain some useful insights anyway. Analyzing the model a bit more carefully, she realized that she could remove the lower bound constraints (5.60) by making the simple transformation: $x_i = y_i + 1$; that would cut down the size of the model and make it easier to solve.

Then—in a flash of insight—she realized that the upper-bound constraints (5.62) to (5.67) were, for practical problems, nonbinding as well! The reason for this phenomenon is that the way she constructed the utility functions, each parabola took on its maximum value at M_i—the maximum number of type i stations allowed. The optimizing model would never allow x_i to be greater than M_i, since this would result in a decrease in total utility. Making the lower bound transformation, simplifying Equation (5.59), and discarding the upper-bound constraints produced the following equivalent model:

$$\text{MAX } x_0 = \frac{-5y_1^2}{2} + 5y_1 - \frac{10y_2^2}{9} + \frac{40y_2}{9} - \frac{9y_3^2}{25} + \frac{72y_3}{25} -$$

$$\frac{2y_4^2}{9} + \frac{20y_4}{9} - \frac{1y_5^2}{6} + \frac{5y_5}{3} - \frac{5y_6^2}{49} + \frac{60y_6}{49} + \frac{80,482}{3,675} \quad (5.68)$$

$$\text{S T: } 30x_1 + 27x_2 + 21x_3 + 18x_4 + 19x_5 + 15x_6 \leq F - 130 \quad (5.69)$$

$$y_i \geq 0 \text{ and integer, } i = 1, \ldots, 6 \quad (5.70)$$

SAMS gave the model solutions (after reversing the transformations) for $F = 430$ square feet as in Table 5.11.

Barbara noted that the "rounded" model solution in Table 5.11 is infeasible, requiring 451 ft² instead of 430. Since station #3 requires exactly 21 ft² of space, letting $x_3 = 3$ instead of $x_3 = 4$ produces a feasible integer solution, and the resulting total "utility" is 44.75—or 98.4 percent of the theoretical maximum.

Solution to the Problem: Before briefing Martha, the chief executive officer, on the results of her model, Barbara noted that a bare minimum salon (one of each station) would require 130 ft², and that the largest possible salon (M_i of each station) would require 573 ft². She decided to rerun the model for F-values of $150 + 25k$, $k = 0, 1, \ldots, 16$, and 573, and manipulated the noninteger solutions to produce "good" feasible solutions for each value of F. She also computed the total "utility" for each configuration, noting that it ranged from a low of about 21.9 for $F = 130$, to 48 for $F = 273$.

Martha reviewed the results with a practiced eye, mentally checking some of the configurations for "reasonableness" based on her long experience in the business. Two or three of the configurations seemed a bit unbalanced in the low end of the square-footage range, and Martha asked Barbara to analyze the effects of an arbitrary change in configuration for these cases. Finally, Martha nodded her approval of the analysis in general.

"Barbara, you've done a fine job—as usual," Martha said, "but I am going to use your results in a slightly different way than you intended. I'm going to have our market research staff estimate the type and volume of business we can expect in a given location. When I have those data, I'll come up with a configuration that will satisfy the demand and use your model to identify the amount of square footage we need to lease for the new salon. That will simplify our location problem immensely."

Barbara replied. "It's just like they told us in my MBA program: Models don't make decisions—managers do."

a. Based on the results of the nonlinear optimization model Barbara used and her rounding to obtain feasible integer solutions, would you recommend that Hair Styles, Inc., try to obtain an integer quadratic programming algorithm to solve the configuration model? Why or why not?

b. Consider the following alternative. We could approximate each of the quadratic functions for the six variables in the model by piecewise linear functions in such a way that the endpoints were at integer values of x_1. For example, $M2 = 3$, so that we could approximate the utility function for x_2 by three line segments with endpoints at $x_2 = 0, 1, 2$, and 3. (You can easily verify that we would need a total of 29 such segments to approximate the six utility functions. We could then treat the weighting variables as zero-one variables, and we could optimize the model using Balas's additive algorithm (refer to Chapter 3). Therefore, it would produce integer solutions. Would this approach work (in a technical sense)? Would such an approach be advisable in this case (in a managerial sense)?

c. In the configuration model above, what is the significance of the shadow price for floor space?

d. As you will learn in Chapter 6, we can also model this problem—and we can solve the model efficiently—as a dynamic programming model.

PRACTICE MODELS

1. Solve the following pricing model using a nonlinear programming computer software package or using calculus:

$$X = \text{unit sales}$$
$$P(X) = \text{unit price as a function of sales}$$
$$= \frac{12000 - 6X}{100}$$
$$C(X) = \text{total cost as a function of sales}$$
$$= 98000 + 42X$$
$$R(X) = \text{total revenues} = X[P(X)]$$
$$PC(X) = \text{total profit contribution} = R(X) - C(X)$$

Find the level of unit sales that maximizes total profit contribution.

2. Using the following data, find the optimal ordering quantity and compute the total ordering and holding cost:

$d_j = 1500$ units/year

$c_j = \$5$/order

$h_j = 10\%$ of p_j/unit/year

$p_j = \$20$/unit

3. Transform the following nonlinear programming problem into an LP model using the fractional programming method and solve using an LP module:

$$\text{MIN } x_0 = \frac{10y_1 + 2y_2 + 3y_3}{6y_1 - 3y_2 + y_3}$$

S T: $3y_1 + y_2 - 4y_3 \geq 10$

$y_1 - 2y_2 - y_3 \leq 20$

$y_1, y_2, y_3 \geq 0$

4. Determine the optimal solution for the following quadratic programming problem using an NLP computer package:

$\text{MIN } x_0 = x^2 + y^2 + 2z^2 + xy + 3xz - yz$

S T: $3x + 3y + 2z \geq 12$

$2x + 5z \geq 9$

$y + z \geq 6$

$x, y, z \geq 0$

5. Solve the following production planning problem using an NLP computer package:

$\text{MIN } x_0 = 20x_1y_1 + 40x_2y_2 + 40x_3y_3 + 5x_1(y_1 - 1) +$

$\qquad 10x_2(y_2 - 1) + 12x_3(y_3 - 1)$

S T: $x_1y_1 + x_2y_2 + x_3y_3 \geq 200$

$x_1 + x_2 + x_3 \leq 12$

$x_j, y_j \geq 0$

REFERENCES AND ADDITIONAL READING

1. Bazaraa, M., and C. Shetty. *Nonlinear Programming: Theory and Algorithms*. New York: Wiley, 1979.
2. Fiacco, A. V. *Abstracts from the International Symposium on Extremal Methods & Systems Analysis*. Austin: University of Texas Press, 1977.
3. Fiacco, A.V., and G. McCormick. *Nonlinear Programming: Sequential Unconstrained Minimization Techniques*. New York: Wiley, 1968.
4. Fletcher, R., and M. Powell. "A Rapidly Convergent Descent Method for Minimization." *Computer Journal* 6 (1963): 163–168.
5. Frank, M., and P. Wolfe. "An Algorithm for Quadratic Programming." *Naval Research Logistics Quarterly* 3, (1956): 95–110.
6. Kwak, N. *Mathematical Programming with Business Applications*. New York: McGraw-Hill, 1973.
7. Lasdon, L., and A. Waren. "Survey of Nonlinear Programming Applications," *Operations Research* 28 (1980): 1029–1073.
8. Lasdon, L., A. Waren, A. Jain, and M. Ratner. "Design and Testing of Generalized Reduced Gradient Code for Nonlinear Programming." *ACM Trans. Math. Software* 4 (1978): 34–50.
9. Powell, M. "An Efficient Method for Finding the Minimum of a Function of Several Variables Without Calculating Derivatives." *Computer Journal* 7 (1964): 155–162.
10. Waren, A., and L. Lasdon. "The Status of Nonlinear Programming Software." *Operations Research* 27 (1979): 431–456.

CHAPTER 6

Discrete Dynamic Programming Models

Most people have heard the old story about the four blind men who were asked to describe an elephant by touching it. The man who felt the animal's leg compared it to a tree; the one who examined the tail concluded that an elephant is a variety of snake; and so forth. The point to this parable is that our view of the world—and, in our case, of managerial problems—depends on our perspective. In the previous chapters on linear, integer, network, and nonlinear modeling, we have looked at our "elephant" in a particular way—basically, as an inseparable entity to be modeled and analyzed. As a result, we had to construct the various optimizing algorithms in such a way that we simultaneously considered all of the decision variables and their interactions.

What if we could look at certain managerial problems as *sequences of subproblems* requiring *sequences of decisions*? In this way, we would have the potential perhaps of solving a series of smaller problems—and in the process solve the larger problem. As it so happens, there are many business, industry, and public sector problems that are **multistage** in nature, and this chapter discusses the modeling and analysis of such problems by an approach called **dynamic programming**.

UNDERYLING ASSUMPTIONS

The basic underlying assumption we are interested in is that we can formulate our problem as a set of consecutive stages, each stage requiring a decision. That is not to say that the decisions are independent of each other—far from it. It does mean, however, that the decisions depend upon each other in a special way. Technicians refer to this stage dependence as having the **Markov property** (after a Russian mathematician). Simply stated, a multistage decision process that has the Markov property is one in which each decision in the sequence of decisions incorporates the effects of all previous decisions, so we are concerned only with relationships between pairs of consecutive decisions. Got it? Perhaps you have, but this concept is surprisingly elusive. An example or two might be helpful.

A well-known prototype of the multi**stage** optimization model is the so-called stagecoach problem, invented by Harvey Wagner. Wagner's allegory goes something like this. In the days of the wild West, a Mr. Mark Off wished to travel from New York to San Francisco to seek his fortune. The only public transportation was stagecoaches, and Mark had to change stages three times enroute to his destination. Figure 6.1

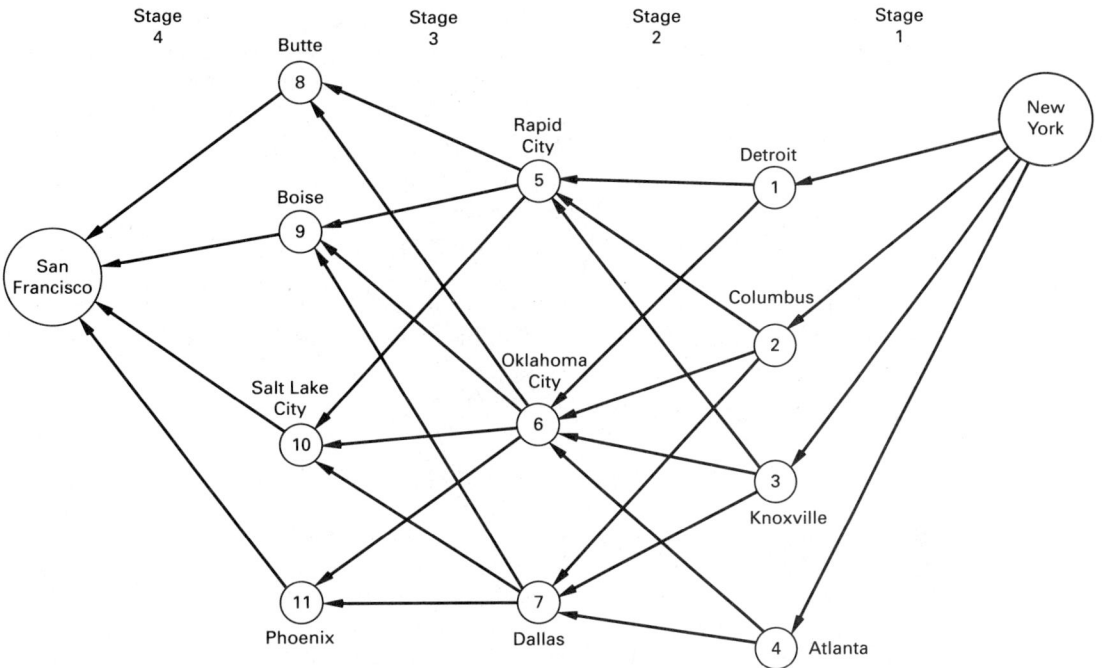

FIGURE 6.1 The stagecoach problem

depicts the origin, transfer points, and destination. Since an attack by outlaw bands was very much a possibility along the way, and since companies sold life insurance policies separately for each leg of the journey, Mark reasoned that the route associated with the least-cost policy for the trip would be the safest (insurance companies being notoriously careful about such matters). Since the cost of insurance from one stage to the next is independent of how one arrived at the former (in all cases), Wagner's allegory describes a multi*stage* (thus, the allegory) problem that exhibits the Markov property.

As another illustration, consider the problem faced by Rhea Lexion, who is running for a second term as governor of her state. Exactly two weeks remain until election day, and Rhea needs to visit the five largest population centers in the state in an effort to garner last-minute votes. Rhea's new campaign manager Louisa is a recent MBA graduate, and although she is short on political savvy, she is an OR modeler par excellence. After an extensive computer analysis of historical voting and campaign data, Louisa has determined the marginal number of additional votes that Rhea can amass by spending one, two, three, etc., days in each of the five cities. Since she assumed that the order in which Rhea visits the cities is unimportant, Louisa has formulated the problem as a multistage decision model that exhibits the Markov property. In effect, the solution to Louisa's model distributes the 14 remaining days among the 5 cities in such a way that she maximizes the total number of additional votes. She proudly shows her analysis to Governor Lexion.

"Louisa," notes the governor, "that stuff you learned in your MBA program is marvelous. However, my MPS (Master of Political Survival) taught me some important realities. For instance, one of your basic assumptions is that the order in which I visit the five key cities is unimportant. Let me tell you from experience that if I go to

Rubesville before I hit Richburg, the Richburgers will be so offended that I'll probably lose votes there. Moreover, if I visit Clod Corners earlier than three or four days before the election, the folks there will have forgotten everything I said by election day. How about if you just list all 120 combinations of ways I can visit the five cities, and I'll help you put together a model that will be useful to me."

As you may have deduced by now, Ms. Lexion's problem is multistage, all right—but the interdependencies among the stages are so complex that her problem does not even remotely possess the Markov property.

Before discussing solution approaches to sequential decision models, we should note that our discussion will center on problems that we can model in terms of a discrete (finite) number of alternatives (or **states**) at each stage. Moreover, we will limit ourselves to models with a finite number of **stages** as well. We can apply dynamic programming to situations in which continuous functions describe the states as well as to infinite horizon scenarios. (We will address these more complex approaches later in the chapter.)

MULTISTAGE MODELING

We have already seen an example of the appropriate use of sequential or multistage modeling—Wagner's famous stagecoach problem—and an inappropriate example in Rhea Lexion's campaign problem. The former example exhibited the Markov property, and the latter did not. Is there some handy checklist that can help us recognize managerial problems that we can profitably model in this way? Unfortunately, the answer is no. However, there are certain general features of problems that may suggest the use of multistage modeling. These features are **time-sequenced decisions, separability,** and **order-independent allocations,** discussed in the following sections.

TIME-SEQUENCED DECISIONS

The stagecoach problem is an example of a situation in which the sequence of decisions is ordered through time. That is to say, if we interchanged the tiers of states in this problem, a different problem would emerge. As another example, recall the overhaul-or-replace problem from Chapter 4. Our decisions involved whether to overhaul an injection molding machine in a given year or to buy a new one to replace it—the objective being to minimize our total capital and operating expense over an eight-year horizon. In Chapter 4, we modeled this problem as a network and sought the shortest (least-cost) route. Observe that this problem very clearly exhibits the Markov property and that the decisions are sequential in time. To reiterate, however, we cannot make the decisions one at a time—we must determine the set of decisions (a policy) in advance.

Are all managerial problems involving time-sequenced decisions candidates for multistage modeling and analysis? Our lives would be a lot simpler if this were true, but alas it isn't. The fact that it isn't true, moreover, isn't always obvious. Consider, for example, the globe-circling airline trip planned by Rhonda Whorl to celebrate the successful completion of her MBA studies. Although money is no object, Rhonda decides to put her education to the test by determining the least-cost series of airline flights that will allow her to complete a trip around the world.

As Rhonda learned in her "quant" course, her problem is definitely multistage, so she dutifully begins collecting airline fare data for the last leg of the trip. Her simple question to the ticket agent for Navaronne Time Airlines, "What's the fare from

Oklahoma City to Horseneck?", elicits the puzzling reply: "Depends on how you got to Oke City. If you flew NTA from the East Coast, there's a special thru fare to points west. If you flew there on another airline, you have to pay the regular fare."

"You mean," queries Rhonda, "that I'd have to compute the fare on every possible routing to Horseneck to find the best one?"

"That's right," replies the agent.

So much for the Markov property!

SEPARABILITY In Chapter 5, we discussed the subject of separable NLP models, noting that we could use linear approximations to the decision variables to transform these models into ordinary LP models. We can also view such problems in terms of multistage models, by the simple device of viewing each decision variable as a stage in a sequence of decisions. If the variables can take on only integer values, we have a discrete dynamic programming model. As an aside, all LP models are separable by their very nature, so they are merely special cases of multistage decision models.

Is the separability phenomenon useful in practice? Sometimes. For instance, using a discrete dynamic programming algorithm to solve ILP models would be roughly equivalent to buying a CDC CYBER-205 to balance your checkbook. On the other hand, efficient algorithms for solving nonlinear integer programming (NLIP) models are virtually nonexistent, except for some special cases in which the decision variables are zero-one. Except for these special cases, NLIP models are tractable only through modeling and analysis as multistage decision processes. The reason for this is interesting. Recall from Chapter 5 that the functional form of the objective function and constraints is critical with regard to our ability to produce a useful solution. For separable NLIP models that we view as sequential decision processes, the functional forms of the objective and constraint expressions make little difference.

For example, consider the two small mathematical programming models P1 and P2:

$$\text{MAX } x_0 = 2x_1^2 + 3x_2^2 \tag{6.1}$$

P1:

$$\text{S T:} \quad x_1 + 2x_2 \leq 8 \tag{6.2}$$

$$3x_1 + 5x_2 \leq 17 \tag{6.3}$$

$$x_1, x_2 \geq 0 \text{ and integer} \tag{6.4}$$

$$\text{MAX } x_0 = 2x_1^7 \ln(x_1) + e^{x_2^2} \sin x_2^2 \tag{6.5}$$

P2:

$$\text{S T:} \quad x_1 \cos^2 x_1 + 1/\arctan x_2^3 \leq 8 \tag{6.6}$$

$$e^{\sin x_1} + (x_2 - \sin x_2)^5 \leq 17 \tag{6.7}$$

$$x_1, x_2 \geq 0 \text{ and integer} \tag{6.8}$$

P1, of course, is an integer quadratic programming model, and we might obtain a "reasonable" solution by using the Frank-Wolfe quadratic programming algorithm on the relaxed model and rounding the results. P2, on the other hand, is a nonlinear nightmare as far as standard NLP algorithms are concerned. Since both P1 and P2 are separable, however, we can solve them for their optimal model solutions by using a dynamic programming approach with only two stages (one stage for each decision variable). The interesting point is this: the computational effort would be roughly the same for both P1 and P2! However, lest our enthusiasm for multistage modeling and analysis get out of hand, let's withhold judgment until our subsequent discussion of the computational aspects of dynamic programming.

ORDER-INDEPENDENT ALLOCATION

Perhaps the most widely applicable type of problem amenable to modeling and analysis by dynamic programming is the order-independent allocation problem. We characterize such problems as follows:

1. There is a fixed number (amount) K of a resource to allocate.
2. There are N competing candidates for the scarce resource.
3. The payoff from allocating 0, 1, 2, . . . units of the resource to a candidate is nondecreasing with the number of units we allocate.
4. The object is to allocate the K units to the N candidates in such a way as to maximize the total payoff.

As an illustration, consider the advertising strategy problem faced by the marketing firm of Preyss, Proddick, Promo, and Place (PPP&P). Common Scents, Inc., has retained the firm to mastermind the introduction of its new "macho" after-shave lotion tentatively named "Eau de Newark." PPP&P has chosen four New Jersey cities (Weehauken, Tenafly, Hackensack, and Teaneck) as the test market, and it has enough budget to buy a total of 200 spot television commercials over a two-week test period. Using something called S-curve analysis, the Marketing Research Department of PPP&P has estimated the level of sales in each city that can be expected for increasing levels of television exposure. The problem, obviously, is to distribute the 200 spot commercials to the four cities in such a way that they maximize total sales.

The PPP&P problem is a classic order-independent allocation problem. First, since there is no reason to suppose that we must make the decision in a particular order, we can order the stages in the multistage model (the four cities) randomly. The fixed resource that we must allocate is the 200 commercials, and there is no reason to suspect that the level of television advertising in one city interacts with that of the others. Second, it is rational to assume that an increasing level of advertising in a given city would result in increasing sales—but perhaps at a decreasing rate near the saturation point.

Like most of the models we have encountered in this text so far, the PPP&P problem is a combinatorial problem. That is, there are exactly 201 (i.e., 0, 1, . . . , 200) commercials (states) to allocate to the four stages (cities). One approach to finding an optimal solution to the model, therefore, would be to enumerate all 1,373,701 possibilities (in general, there are $(N + K - 1)!/K! \cdot (N - 1)!$ feasible ways to allocate all K units of resource to N candidates) and compute the sales generated by each. As we shall soon see, a much better approach would be to formulate the problem as an order-independent multistage allocation model and to use dynamic programming to find a solution to the model. We now turn to the solution of discrete multistage models using an optimization technique called dynamic programming.

DYNAMIC PROGRAMMING: AN INTUITIVE DESCRIPTION

Richard Bellman invented and developed the technique commonly known as **dynamic programming** (DP) more than 25 years ago. George Nemhauser [7] succinctly defined

DP. *Dynamic programming is a transformation that takes a sequential or multistage decision process containing many interdependent variables and converts it into a series of one-stage problems, each containing a few variables.*

The principle that underlies the concept of DP is Bellman's principle of optimality. If any mathematical discovery in modern times is the most elegant and intuitively appealing—and at the same time the most elusive and subtle—it is Bellman's. According to Bellman's principle of optimality, *in a multistage decision process, an optimal policy has the property that whatever the initial state and decision are, the remaining decisions must constitute an optimal policy with regard to the state resulting from the first decision.*

To understand Bellman's discovery—and its implementation in optimizing algorithms—let's further explore his basic concept. George Nemhauser [7] describes the term *dynamic programming* as "nondescriptive but alluring," preferring the "more representative, but less glamorous term *recursive optimization.*"

What is **recursive optimization?** Let's return to Wagner's stagecoach problem and delve deeper. Suppose Mr. Mark Off, our intrepid fortune seeker, finds himself in a particular state, preparing to board the fourth and final stage to San Francisco. Suppose further that Mark has acted optimally in selecting the states to route himself through via the previous stages. It is obvious, then, that his last decision would be to take the only available stage to his destination.

Now let's broaden our vista and consider all states (Butte, Boise, Salt Lake City, and Phoenix) from which the final stage to San Francisco can depart. If Mark knew the optimal route to each of these states, it would be a simple matter for him to add the total optimal cost to reach each of these states to the fare for the stage from there to San Francisco—the lowest such total fare being optimal. Fine. But how did Mark know the optimal-cost routing to each state prior to the stage to San Francisco? He merely repeated his analysis of the fourth stage (as above) by computing the optimal costs to reach those states via the third stage! And he continued so on—recursively—until he had marched backwards through the states in the various stages, finally reaching New York, his origin.

Let us refer to Figure 6.2 and consider a specific example. Suppose that we had backtracked to mid-America and had determined that the least-cost routing from Oklahoma City to San Francisco was via Boise. Therefore, we have implicitly eliminated from consideration all routes from New York to San Francisco that include legs from Oklahoma City to Butte, Salt Lake City, and Phoenix. Thus, as we move backward from destination to origin, we eliminate partial routings—and thus reduce the problem dimensions iteratively at each stage.

To emphasize the point, suppose that the optimal route happens to be New York → Knoxville → Oklahoma City → Boise → San Francisco (NY → 3 → 6 → 9 → SF). As we proceed, we pare down the 34 possible routes to one optimal one, as in Table 6.1. We note that our analysis at stage 4 was trivial, since the four stagecoaches all had the same destination. However, at stage 3, we were able to eliminate 24 of the 34 routes. For example, our computations revealed that *if it were optimal to route ourselves through state 6* (Oklahoma City), the best way to proceed to San Francisco would be via state 9 (Boise). Thus, at one fell swoop, we were able to eliminate from further consideration all 12 routes that pass through Oklahoma City, but do not pass through Boise.

We should note in this example that we actually have a shortest-route-through-a-network model, and the highly efficient network algorithms discussed in Chapter 4 would have been more efficient as solution devices than dynamic programming. However, Wagner's allegory is particularly handy in helping us grasp exactly what is happening in recursive optimization.

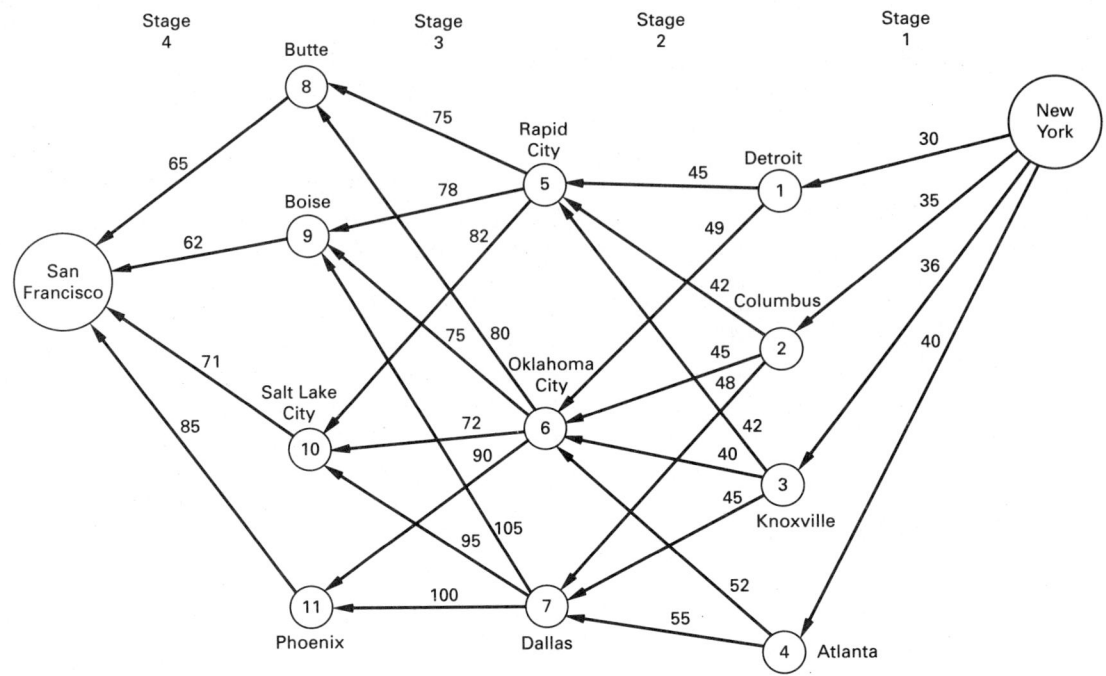

FIGURE 6.2 The stagecoach problem revisited

THE ELUSIVENESS OF RECURSIVE OPTIMIZATION

We earlier referred to Bellman's principle of optimality as "elusive and subtle." Perhaps you do not find this concept to be particularly troublesome to grasp, but most people do. The difficulty appears to be both psychological and cultural, in that we have been trained all of our lives to approach problems and situations *deductively*—from first to last, in that order. Recursive optimization, as we have addressed it in relation to multistage optimization models, is essentially an *inductive* process. That is, we start at the end and construct a solution backward until we reach the beginning.

A simple puzzle will illustrate the point. Suppose Boylan Bubble, a medieval sorcerer, needs exactly four drams of henbane for a potion he is brewing, but because of recent budget cutbacks by King Arthur has only an eight-dram and a three-dram vial to work with. Rather than attack the problem directly, Boylan—who thinks differently from most people—goes at it backwards.

> "Let's see," he says to himself, "if I end up with four drams, it will have to be in the eight-dram vial. But I have a three-dram vial I can pour into the larger one, so that means I'll need to get one dram in either vial somehow. Aha! If I pour the three-dram vial three times into the eight-dram vial, I'll have exactly one dram left. I can then empty the large vial, pour in the one dram from the small one, and add a full three-dram vial to the large one. And there's my four drams!"

And that's recursive optimization, although in a somewhat silly setting. In an idle moment, you might consider solving this trivial little puzzle deductively—in the way that most of us are accustomed to approaching such problems. If you do so, you may find that you eventually resort to trial and error instead of using a logical and orderly solution process. If, on the other hand, the process of recursive optimization appeals

TABLE 6.1

Stage	Best	Partial Routes	Routes Eliminated	
4	8–SF	9–SF	None	
	10–SF	11–SF		
3	5–8–SF		NY–1–5–10–SF	NY–2–5–10–SF
	or 5–9–SF		NY–3–5–10–SF	
	6–9–SF		NY–1–6–8–SF	NY–2–6–8–SF
			NY–1–6–10–SF	NY–2–6–10–SF
			NY–1–6–11–SF	NY–2–6–11–SF
			NY–3–6–8–SF	NY–4–6–8–SF
			NY–3–6–10–SF	NY–4–6–10–SF
			NY–3–6–11–SF	NY–4–6–11–SF
	7–10–SF		NY–2–7–9–SF	NY–2–7–11–SF
			NY–3–7–9–SF	NY–3–7–11–SF
			NY–4–7–9–SF	NY–4–7–11–SF
2	1–5–8–SF	2–5–8–SF	NY–1–6–9–SF	NY–3–5–9–SF
	1–5–9–SF	2–5–9–SF	NY–2–7–10–SF	NY–3–5–9–SF
	3–6–9–SF	2–6–9–SF	NY–3–7–10–SF	NY–4–7–10–SF
	4–6–9–SF			
1	NY–3–6–9–SF	NY–1–5–8–SF	NY–1–5–9–SF	NY–2–5–8–SF
		NY–2–5–9–SF	NY–2–6–9–SF	NY–4–6–9–SF

to you (as it did with our backwards sorcerer), you might wish to verify that we can measure *any number* of drams with only three-dram and eight-dram vials.

THE "CURSE OF DIMENSIONALITY" The computational advantage of the dynamic programming approach is that it decomposes large multistage problems into a sequence of smaller, less complex problems. For most such formulations, the computational complexity grows only linearly (approximately) with the number of stages. The problem arises when the number of state variables (decision variables in each stage) increases. Computational complexity grows at an *exponential* rate as the number of state variables increases, and researchers colorfully describe this feature of dynamic programming as the "curse of dimensionality."

To illustrate this phenomenon, recall the PPP&P advertising problem in which the company wished to allocate 200 spot TV commercials among four New Jersey cities. If we double the number to 400, the number of feasible allocations rises by a factor of almost eight—from 1,373,701 to 10,827,401.

DEVELOPING ALTERNATIVE SOLUTIONS

Since multistage problems are combinatorial in nature, there is usually a rich variety of good solutions to even modest-sized models of these problems. For example, in the PPP&P sequence-independent allocation problem, there were over 1.3 million feasible patterns for allocating the 200 commercials to four cities. If this were an actual problem, it would probably be accurate to suppose that there were hundreds of model solutions within one percent (or less) of the optimal objective value. As we have repeatedly stressed, this richness of managerial alternatives is "just what the doctor ordered" for decision makers.

But how do we gain access to these very good but suboptimal model solutions when using dynamic programming algorithms? We saw that LP and network models were amenable to such analysis because of the existence of shadow prices, and we strained a bit to derive such managerial information from ILP and NLP models. As it turns out, developing good alternative solutions to multistage models is relatively easy. We will not dwell on the technical details of how this is done; instead, we next present an intuitive description of the process.

Recall for a moment the stagecoach problem and think about the information generated by the dynamic programming algorithm as it wended its way recursively, stage by stage, backwards from the destination (San Francisco) to the origin (New York). If we had stored the interim results at each stage and subsequently had the computer print them for us, we would have the optimum partial policy (i.e., cost of insurance) from every state in every stage to the destination—and from the origin to every state as well.

As a more concrete illustration, refer to Figure 6.2 (the stagecoach problem), with insurance rates for each leg included. SAMS' DP module output for this problem is in Table 6.2.

Observe the great variety of managerial options available to us from this computer analysis. For example, the optimal routing for the model is NEW YORK → KNOXVILLE → OKLAHOMA CITY → BOISE → SAN FRANCISCO, for a total policy premium of $213. However, note that there are several routes with costs within about 3% of the minimum (e.g., NEW YORK → DETROIT → RAPID CITY → BUTTE → SAN FRANCISCO, for a cost of $215). Furthermore, any routing that includes Dallas or Phoenix appears to be relatively risky. At any rate, the analysis allows the decision maker to consider several options at a glance: including a particular city on the itinerary for exogenous reasons and noting the resulting route that minimizes total cost, deleting a city from the itinerary and noting "good" routes that remain, and so on.

So much for generating good (suboptimal) alternatives with the use of dynamic programming algorithms on multistage models. Sensitivity analysis on the various parameters is quite another matter. As with integer and nonlinear programming models, our only recourse in this regard is to change parameter values and rerun the computer algorithm—noting any drastic changes that occur from one run to the next.

We next discuss some modeling refinements and advanced computational devices in multistage analysis and dynamic programming.

STATE OF THE ART IN DYNAMIC PROGRAMMING

To this point, we have confined our discussion to discrete, deterministic multistage modeling and solution of these models by specialized recursive optimization algo-

CHAPTER 6 DISCRETE DYNAMIC PROGRAMMING MODELS   233

TABLE 6.2

STAGECOACH PROBLEM
FULL BRIEFING ON ALTERNATE ROUTINGS

	Lowest Cost Route from Origin		Lowest Cost Route to Destination		Lowest Cost Route Including City	
Stage	Cost	Route	City	Cost	Route	Cost
	0	N/A	NEWYORK	213	3–6–9–SF	213
1	30	NY	DETROIT(1)	185	5–8–SF or 5–9–SF	215
	35	NY	COLUMBUS(2)	182	5–8–SF or 5–9–SF or 6–9–SF	217
	36	NY	KNOXVILL(3)	177	6–9–SF	213
	40	NY	ATLANTA(4)	189	6–9–SF	229
2	75	NY–1	RAPIDCIT(5)	140	8–SF or 9–SF	215
	76	NY–3	OKLACITY(6)	137	9–SF	213
	81	NY–3	DALLAS(7)	166	10–SF	247
3	150	NY–1–5	BUTTE(8)	65	SF	215
	151	NY–3–6	BOISE(9)	62	SF	213
	148	NY–3–6	SLCITY(10)	71	SF	219
	166	NY–3–6	PHOENIX(11)	85	SF	251
4	213	NY–3–6–9	SF	0	N/A	213

rithms. Before briefly touching on some advanced topics, we should note that the dynamic programming approach is extremely useful in stochastic (probabilistic) modeling as well. Here, however, we will stick to purely deterministic models.

CONTINUOUS DYNAMIC PROGRAMMING

In many cases, we can approximate the **return functions** for the states in each stage of a multistage model by continuous functions. Up to this point in our discussion, we have dealt solely with tabular (discrete) functions and noted earlier that the "curse of dimensionality" in dynamic programming is due chiefly to the number of such state variables. Let us return once again to the PPP&P problem of scheduling television commercials in four New Jersey cities for the new after-shave lotion "Eau de Newark."

The analyst has discovered that by using quadratic polynomial functions she can very closely estimate the discrete return functions (number of sales as a function of number of commercials aired) for the four cities (see Table 6.3). (*Note: S(n)* is number of sales as a result of airing n commercials.) She excitedly enters Mr. Promo's office with her results, whereupon she learns that Common Scents, Inc. has budgeted for only a maximum total of 200 commercials.

We can easily model and solve this problem as a continuous dynamic programming model. Instead of computing hundreds or thousands of tabular return functions at each stage, this form of DP uses elementary differential calculus to find the required values, greatly decreasing the total computational effort.

As an aside, we can also solve this model with the Lagrange multiplier technique discussed in Chapter 5. For those who are curious, Table 6.4 gives the optimal solution to the continuous model of the PPP&P problem. Three features of this solution are interesting from a managerial decision-making perspective. First, note that the model excludes Tenafly from the test market by assigning it zero commercials. Second, the allocation purports to generate 41.7% (56,887 of a possible 136,500) of the possible sales by using only 21.6% (200 out of 925) of the number of commercials. Third, if we solve the model with calculus, the shadow price for the scarce resource "commercials" turns out to be about 227. This means, of course, that—at the margin—we can generate about 227 additional sales with each additional commercial above 200 (as long as the increment is fairly small). On an average basis, each of the 200 commercials currently authorized produces about 284 sales (56,887/200). Do you see that we are "over the hump" in marginal effectiveness of number of commercials?

TABLE 6.3

City	$S(n)$	Saturation Point	
		No. of Commercials	No. of Sales
Weehauken	$S(n_1) = 300n_1 - 0.75n_1^2$	200	30,000
Tenafly	$S(n_2) = 208.33n_2 - 0.42n_2^2$	250	25,850
Hackensack	$S(n_3) = 408.33n_3 - 1.17n_3^2$	175	35,650
Teaneck	$S(n_4) = 300n_4 - 0.50n_4^2$	300	45,000
Totals		925	136,500

TABLE 6.4

City	No. of Commercials	Sales Generated
Weehauken	49	12,899
Tenafly	0	
Hackensack	78	24,752
Teaneck	73	19,236
Totals	200	56,887

NONSEQUENTIAL MULTISTAGE OPTIMIZATION

One of our basic underlying assumptions discussed earlier is that our multistage problem must exhibit the Markov property to be a candidate for modeling and analysis by DP. Well, we fractured the truth somewhat. Through some highly sophisticated mathematical machinations, OR technicians have found ways to incorporate "feedback" and "feed-forward" loops into a multistage model. If you are mathematically well-trained and are curious about this topic, please refer to the excellent book by Nemhauser [7].

MINICASES

Air Traffic Control [8]

THE SCENARIO

Passenger air travel in the United States has burgeoned over the past 30 years as millions of travelers have turned to this safe, rapid, and inexpensive mode of transportation. As the system grew, certain large cities like New York, Chicago, Atlanta, and Dallas-Fort Worth, became hubs that serve as transfer points for travelers from smaller cities. These busy airports faced a bewildering variety of problems as air traffic increased in volume—everything from massive baggage transfer requirements to maintenance and refueling demands. The advent of jumbo jets such as the B-747, L-1011, and DC-10 brought additional problems, and the huge increases in costs for jet fuel in the 1980s compounded managerial problems.

THE PROBLEM

One particularly aggravating problem occurs during peak arrival times each day at hub airports. Depending on the weather, controllers may hold as many as 15 to 20 aircraft in a traffic pattern, waiting for their turn to land. If we blithely accept first-come, first-served as the fair and equitable way to schedule landings, we have a solution to the problem—though perhaps a very expensive one on several dimensions. For example, suppose we have a mixture of jumbo-jets (300 passengers), conventional large jets (150 passengers), and medium-sized jets (100 passengers) waiting to land at a given time at O'Hare International Airport in Chicago. Psaraftis [8] has given the minimum landing time separation matrix between three types of aircraft, as in the following table. (*Note:* These times are based on landing kinematics of the types of aircraft and are imposed for reasons of safety.)

Separation times (in seconds)

		Jumbo	Conventional	Medium
Land Before	Jumbo	96	181	228
	Conventional	72	80	117
	Medium	72	80	90

We read the preceding table as follows. If an aircraft type labeled in a row lands immediately before one in a column, the controller must delay the second aircraft to land by at least the number of seconds indicated in that row and column. For example, if a jumbo lands and a medium is to be next, we must delay it by at least 228 seconds. As another example, jumbos may land 96 seconds apart.

To clarify the nature of the problem, suppose that a conventional jet has just landed and that one each jumbo (J), conventional (C), and medium-sized (M) jets are waiting to land—and that all have full passenger loads. There are six distinct ways we can order the three aircraft. Let's analyze these permutations using two criteria proposed by Psaraftis: latest landing time (LLT), the elapsed time until the last jet lands; and total passenger delay (TPD), the total passenger-seconds expended in delays. For example, consider the sequence: J-M-C

$LLT = 72 + 228 + 80 = 380$ seconds

$TPD = 300(72) + 100(72 + 228) + 150(72 + 228 + 80) = 108,600$ passenger-seconds

Similar data for all six permutations are as follows.

Sequence	J-M-C	J-C-M	C-M-J	C-J-M	M-J-C	M-C-J
LLT	380	370	269	380	370	269
TPD	108,600	96,550	112,400	95,600	123,900	121,950

In this simple problem, LLTs vary from 269 to 380 seconds and TPDs vary from 95,600 to 123,900 passenger-seconds. Note also that high LLTs tend to be associated with low values of TPD, and vice versa. Moreover, this example assumes that a conventional jet had just landed. If the last landing had been made by a jumbo or a medium-sized jet, the results would have differed drastically.

To make the transition from the toy problem in our example to the real world, consider the example given by Psaraftis in which 5 jumbos, 6 conventional jets, and 4 medium-sized jets (a total of 15) are in the queue. There are 630,630 different sequences in which we can schedule the aircraft for landing—even after giving an earlier arriving jet priority over later arriving ones of the same type. Thus, it is obvious that enumerating all possible sequences and picking the "best" (in some sense) would not be a feasible approach.

THE MODEL

The aircraft sequencing problem is a classical example of a problem with time-sequenced decisions, and Psaraftis modeled it with dynamic programming. However, Psaraftis recognized that if he uses the LLT criterion alone, the jumbos always end up at the rear of the queue—since the turbulence caused by jumbos on approach and landing causes the minimum separation times for smaller jets to be high. Psaraftis introduced a feature he called **maximum position shift** (MPS) that allows the decision maker to indicate the maximum number of positions (either forward or backward) he or she can shift a given aircraft from its actual order of arrival. For example, if

TABLE 6.5 Air traffic control example

		MPS = 5		MPS = 14		
Initial Order	Landing Order	LLT	TPD	LLT	TPD	
C	0					
J	1	J	C	C	J	
J	2	J	J	C	J	
M	3	J	J	C	J	
C	4	C	J	C	J	
C	5	C	J	C	J	
M	6	C	C	C	C	
C	7	C	C	M	C	
J	8	M	M	M	C	
C	9	M	M	M	C	
J	10	M	C	M	C	
M	11	M	C	J	C	
M	12	C	J	J	M	
C	13	C	C	J	M	
J	14	J	M	J	M	
C	15	J	M	J	M	
1,729	—	1,400	1,528	1,323	1,424	LLT
2,383,800	—	2,033,800	1,883,250	2,241,300	1,164,900	TPD

MPS = 5 and an aircraft arrived seventh of 15, we could shift it forward to no earlier than second and backward to no later than twelfth. If, on the other hand, we use TPD as the sole criterion, the mediums tend to end up at the end of the queue—which is intuitively reasonable, since they carry the smallest number of passengers. The MPS device also acts to moderate this tendency.

SOLUTION TO THE MODEL

Psaraftis used a modified DP algorithm called constrained position shift (CPS) to investigate the nature of the aircraft sequencing problem. He solved an example problem with (J,C,M) = (5,6,4), and with a random arrival sequence, with MPS = 5 and without an effective position shift (i.e., MPS = 14). Table 6.5 reproduces the results, excerpted from Psaraftis' paper.

SOLUTION TO THE PROBLEM

Thus far, we have focused our discussion on a static problem of aircraft sequencing for landing. That is, we have assumed that a fixed number of aircraft are waiting to land. In the real problem, the number of aircraft in the queue changes minute by minute. As Psaraftis notes in his paper, to be useful, the model would have to run in real time—in effect, solving a new DP model every time an aircraft joined the queue. As long as this number remained relatively small, given the speed of current electronic computers and the efficiency of DP algorithms, such an approach is entirely within the realm of possibility.

A second aspect of the problem involves the selection of an appropriate criterion and an appropriate value for the MPS parameter. The LLT criterion minimizes the time it takes to get all aircraft landed but results in higher passenger delay times. The TPD criterion has the converse effect, so perhaps some weighted combination of the two might prove to be satisfactory. On the other hand, we might consider minimizing aviation fuel costs as an alternative objective.

Finally, any real-time system would have to be flexible enough to accommodate unexpected events such as aircraft short on fuel, emergencies, aircraft with high-priority passengers, etc.

Cabana Bananas

THE SCENARIO

Cabana Bananas, Inc. (CB) is a major distributor of bananas from Central America to the eastern United States. The company operates its own fleet of steamships and makes deliveries twice each year to the ports of Houston, New Orleans, Miami, Baltimore, Philadelphia, and New York. Wholesalers in these six cities purchase the bananas from CB for distribution to retail outlets.

Bananas are a very fragile commodity. Distributors cannot freeze them, and they become overripe about 30 days after being picked. CB can make deliveries to ports in the Gulf of Mexico (Houston, New Orleans) and to Miami in about 18 days but requires 21 days to the northeastern ports (New York, Philadelphia). For this and other reasons, the price CB receives for its bananas varies widely among the six ports. Another curious feature of wholesale pricing for bananas is the effect of economies of scale at certain ports. For example, the wholesaler in New York uses a large truck fleet to supply his customers, and his purchase of a boatload of bananas only partially fills the trucks. Since transportation costs are essentially a fixed expense, it pays the wholesaler to buy larger amounts of bananas—even at a higher incremental cost. This situation also exists in Philadelphia and Houston.

Another curious (and bothersome) aspect of the banana business is that it is almost impossible to sell a partial shipload. By the time a steamship unloads part of a load, receives clearance to sail, and completes the complicated undocking and port clearance procedure, several days have elapsed—and the bananas are that much closer to being overripe. Thus, CB must solicit bids for multiple shiploads only.

THE PROBLEM

Nana Peale, CB's VP for Distribution, was surprised to discover that the forthcoming banana yield was to be a bumper crop—with a full nine shiploads available. CB's fleet consisted of only six ships, and having three ships make two deliveries was out of the question because of bananas' short life. Fortunately for CB, Havana Bananas (HB) Inc., its chief rival, overestimated its demand and has three idle steamers, which it will provide to CB on a short-term lease. HB's VP for Distribution has offered Ms. Peale

TABLE 6.6 CB's net profit matrix (millions)

No. of Shiploads	Houston	New Orleans	Miami	Baltimore	Philadelphia	New York
0	0	0	0	0	0	0
1	$ 7	$ 8	$ 6	$ 9	$ 6	$ 5
2	16	15	12	16	10	12
3	24	21	18	21	16	20
4	30	27	23	25	22	27
5	35	32	28	28	27	33
6	39	36	33	31	32	38
7	42	40	37	34	36	42
8	44	no bid	no bid	36	40	45
9	45	no bid	no bid	no bid	43	46

the following leasing cost arrangement: $4 million for one, $9 million for two, and $15 million for three steamships. (*Note:* Does not include CB's ship operating costs.)

When the six wholesalers submitted their bids, Ms. Peale arranged them in a matrix (see Table 6.6) and studied the figures thoughtfully. In the past, when six or fewer boatloads of bananas were available, it had been a simple matter to experiment with different shipment patterns and find the best one. In fact, Ms. Peale had once calculated that with six boatloads and six cities, there were only 462 possible ways to ship them—assuming that she allocated all six loads. With nine boatloads available— and with the extra complication of having to lease ships (if it were economical to do so)—the problem had taken on a level of complexity that made experimenting to find a solution potentially disastrous.

THE MODEL

Ms. Peale brought in as an internal consultant Herb Plantain, CB's MS/OR analyst, who immediately recognized that he could formulate her problem as a dynamic programming model. The six ports were the stages, and the nine boatloads of bananas were the states. To be precise, Herb formulated four DP models—one each for six, seven, eight, and nine boatloads—since he couldn't figure out how to get everything into a single model.

SOLUTION TO THE MODEL

Herb used a minicomputer code to solve the four DP models. As it turned out, there were several alternative allocations that yielded maximum profit, so Herb—mindful of the proper distinction between an analyst and a decision maker—had the computer print them all. In addition, Ms. Peale had requested that Herb generate an allocation in which all six ports received at least one boatload of bananas, which Herb accomplished. Table 6.7 exhibits SAMS' quick briefing of the optimal solutions to the four models as well as the all-ports models.

When Ms. Peale considers additional leasing costs, the net profit contributions are as in Table 6.8.

TABLE 6.7

				CABANA BANANAS QUICK BRIEFING OF OPTIMAL SOLUTIONS			
Solution #	Houston	Neworl	Miami	Baltim	Philad	NewYor	Gross Profit
			K = 9				
1	3	2	0	1	0	3	68
2	3	1	0	1	0	4	68
3	3	1	0	2	0	3	68
4	3	2	1	1	1	1	65
5	3	1	1	2	1	1	65
6	3	1	1	1	1	2	65
7	2	1	1	1	1	3	65
			K = 8				
8	3	1	0	1	0	3	61
9	3	2	0	2	1	0	61
10	3	2	1	2	0	0	61
11	3	3	0	2	0	0	61
12	4	2	0	2	0	0	61
13	3	1	1	1	1	1	58
			K = 7				
14	3	2	0	2	0	0	55
15	2	1	1	1	1	1	50
			K = 6				
16	3	1	0	2	0	0	48
17	3	2	0	1	0	0	48
18	1	1	1	1	1	1	41

TABLE 6.8 Table of profit (millions)

No. of Shiploads	Optimal	All Ports
6	$48	$41
7	51	46
8	52	49
9	53	50

SOLUTION TO THE PROBLEM

It was obvious to Ms. Peale from perusing the model solutions that it would be advisable to lease additional ships from Havana Bananas. In all cases, however, all optimal solutions would allot no bananas to at least two of the six ports. Ms. Peale considered such a schedule to be an extremely poor goodwill move—especially in a bumper crop year for bananas—and decided to allot at least one of the nine shiploads to each port. Of the four schedules that yielded maximum profit contribution, she selected the one that allotted three shiploads to Houston, two to New York, and one each to the other four ports, for two reasons. First, Houston was one of the closest ports, and the wholesaler there would have several additional days to distribute the large volume of bananas. Second, the wholesaler in New York needed large volume to fully utilize his truck fleet and would appreciate the additional allocation more than would the other four. ∎

Touring Europe [3]

THE SCENARIO
During her last year in the MBA program at Texas Tech University, an excellent student who also served as a graduate assistant planned to make a lifelong dream come true after graduation—a tour of ten of the greatest cities of Europe. She had visited Europe before on short trips and had a good idea of the interesting and historical sites she would like to visit. She had thought about possibilities for different itineraries for some time but had never formalized detailed plans.

THE PROBLEM
As graduation time approached, it became apparent to the student that her financial resources were limited and that a trip of about three weeks would be the longest she could afford. This coincided nicely with her desire to take off about a month after graduation before beginning full-time employment. With 21 days to spend and 10 very large and richly varied cities to visit, how many days should she spend in each? She began her decision process by informally solving a shortest-route problem and arranged her itinerary in the following sequence:

      Paris – Athens – Rome – London – Geneva – Amsterdam – Vienna
      Madrid – Brussels – Venice

THE MODEL
It was obvious to the student that she could model her problem as a multistage decision process if she could somehow formalize her personal utility for one, two, three, etc., days in each city. Technically, a dynamic programming formulation would require that she estimate her cumulative utility for 1, 2, 3, . . . , 21 days in each city, so that her 10-stage, 21-state model would involve over *14 million* distinct combinations. Since this prospect appeared to be unmanageable, she arbitrarily limited her length of stay in each city to four days—which made the task of building her utility function a more reasonable one.

    The process that this student used to construct her utility function was creative and interesting. Using a travel guide, [5], she scheduled four days of activities in each city, and rated each day in each city on a subjective scale from 1 to 10. After normalizing her ratings on a per-hour basis (daily activities ranged from five to nine hours), she

TABLE 6.9 Table of utility calculations

Day	Activity	Hours	Util/Hour	Hours × Util	Daily Total	Normed 6-hour Day	Cumulative Total
1	Sistine Chapel	3	10	30			
	St. Peter's	2	7	14			
	Vatican Museum	2	3.67	7.34	51.34	44	44
2	Coliseum	2	7	14			
	Roman Forum	1	2.83	2.83			
	Spanish Steps	1	3.67	3.67			
	Trevi Fountain	2	7	14	34.5	35	79
3	Capitoline Hill	2	2	4			
	Outdoor Opera	3	5	15	19	23	102
4	Pantheon	2	2.83	5.66			
	Trajan's Column	1	2	2			
	Piazza Navona	2	2.83	5.66	12.32	15	117

TABLE 6.10 Cumulative utility function for touring Europe

	Day No.				
City	0	1	2	3	4
Paris	0	42	82	112	133
Athens	0	42	77	107	121
Rome	0	44	79	102	117
London	0	44	76	100	117
Geneva	0	51	74	97	114
Amsterdam	0	53	78	100	114
Vienna	0	46	92	122	137
Madrid	0	45	81	100	107
Brussels	0	50	83	110	124
Venice	0	47	80	103	120

ordered the four days in each city from high to low utility and calculated a cumulative total. For example, her calculations for a four-day stint in Rome are given in Table 6.9. Her overall utility function for the 10 cities is given in Table 6.10.

SOLUTION TO THE MODEL

Restricting the maximum visit to any one city to four days greatly reduced the computational complexity of this student's problem, which she solved using dynamic programming. Her optimal model solution gave a total utility of 844 (see Table 6.11).

There were no alternate optimal solutions to the model, but she identified another near-optimal solution (utility of 841) by spending one additional day in Brussels and one less day in Paris. By way of contrast, her *worst* possible utility of 611 would involve

TABLE 6.11 Optimal model solution

City	No. of Days	City	No. of Days
Paris	3	Amsterdam	1
Athens	3	Vienna	3
Rome	2	Madrid	2
London	2	Brussels	2
Geneva	1	Venice	2

four days each in Rome, London, Geneva, Amsterdam, and Madrid, and one day in either Paris or Athens. Thus, her model did have discriminatory power.

SOLUTION TO THE PROBLEM

Rather than use the results of her model as an inflexible schedule, the student tentatively planned to spend the number of days indicated by the optimal model solution in each city. She reserved to herself the right to change her itinerary if special unforeseen circumstances arose, however, and recognized that her time estimates for the various activities were educated guesses at best. The model proved beneficial by giving her insight into planning her very special trip.

SUMMARY

In this chapter, we considered a different approach to modeling problems than in previous chapters and introduced the concept of multistage optimization. By use of this approach, we are attempting to decompose large problems into a sequence of smaller subproblems and thereby gain a computational advantage. In all such models except certain highly sophisticated variants, we insisted that the Markov property hold throughout the sequence of stages.

We introduced and discussed three categories of multistage models: time-sequenced models, separable models, and sequence-independent allocation models. We discovered that although we can solve all three types using the principle of recursive optimization, we must use specialized algorithms for each type. This confirmed our previous observation that dynamic programming is a broader and much different technique than previous approaches that have general or all-purpose algorithms associated with them.

We discussed development of alternative solutions with dynamic programming at some length, concluding that it is a relatively easy task to generate good (but technically suboptimal) solutions by keeping track of certain interim computational results. Unfortunately, we saw that sensitivity analysis on model parameters is limited chiefly to "brute force" methods. The chapter concluded with a brief discussion of two advanced topics: continuous DP and nonsequential multistage optimization.

KEY TERMS

dynamic programming
Markov property
multistage
order-independent allocations
recursive optimization
return functions
rolling schedule
separability
stages
states
time-sequenced decisions

PROBLEMS FOR ANALYSIS

1. **The Scenario:** Wonmoor Time Novelties, Inc. (WTN) is a manufacturer and international distributor of novelty electronic wristwatches. Its products run the gamut from the $10.95 throw-away to the elegant and intricate $2,000 Electro-Whiz that can play chess, do income tax returns, and compute the sidereal hour angles of the planets and 47 selected stars from any location on earth. WTN manufactures its own cases, movements, and dial faces but relies on a subcontractor to supply the tiny cadmium power packs that WTN uses in all its products. The wristwatch business is highly competitive, and profit margins tend to be small.

    The Problem: Aaron Hand, the CEO of WTN, is disturbed by the company's operating results for the past quarter. Several production-line shutdowns have occurred because the supply of power packs ran out. At other times, the company's cash flow position was dangerously illiquid because of excessive on-hand inventory of parts—including power packs. Aaron had to do something, so he called Ceta Pantz, WTN's longtime inventory manager, into his office.

    > "Ceta," Aaron begins, "what the devil is going on with our power pack supply? The on-hand inventory plot for last quarter looks like a roller coaster."
    >
    > Ceta responds with a sigh of relief. "Mr. Hand, I sure am glad you called me in. I've been inventory manager for WTN for over 25 years. My ordering rules (he produces a yellowing laminated card from his vest pocket) never failed me until about a year ago when you hired those two young fellows as production manager and director of finance. Whenever I get the power pack supply about right, the fellow in production pressures me to order more. No sooner do I get the inventory level up a little than the new fellow in Finance starts in on me about tying up too much cash and makes me delay my orders. I tried to tell him that I sometimes order an extra batch just before I think the price will go up, but he just gives me an impatient stare."
    >
    > "Calm down now, Ceta," replies Aaron. "Do you use the forecast demand figures and the inventory holding and carrying costs to help you determine when and how many power packs to order?"
    >
    > "Sure I do," Ceta assures Aaron. "I get a new three-month demand forecast every month—but the figures always change every time. How can I calculate my ordering quantities for three months when the figures are different for two of the same months in the next forecast?"

    The Model: At first glance, this problem appears to be multistage, since Ceta must make a sequence of decisions about ordering power packs to meet production requirements while being sensitive to the costs involved in carrying excessive inventories. On the other hand, while he might use some sort of recursive optimization technique to aid him in making a set of decisions over the immediate three-month period ahead, what does he do next month? Ceta has presumably implemented the first decision in the original sequence—that's water over the dam—so it would be foolish to address a four-period sequential problem that included the previous month.

    a. One approach would be for the inventory manager to solve a three-period multistage decision problem every month and plan to implement only the decisions that he must make before the beginning of the next month. What do you think of such an approach? Does it make sense to formulate future decisions you never intend to make?

    b. Another approach would be to ignore the forecast demand information for the farthest two months and to make ordering decisions one month at a time. What are the possible pitfalls in such a strategy? In general, can ignoring relevant information ever consistently lead to better decisions?

The Solution: The inventory replenishment problem described above is an example of an *infinite horizon multistage optimization problem*. The approach suggested in (a) is called a **rolling schedule,** and—although it seems counterintuitive to many people—managers use this approach widely in practice. The advantage of such an approach is that it optimizes each sequential decision with respect to all available information. Moreover, if the future demand pattern happens to be relatively stable (i.e., uniformly rising or falling or remaining flat), decisions using a rolling schedule tend to be fairly good.

A disadvantage of the rolling schedule is that it is myopic. That is, it tends to ignore such things as seasonality. Researchers have done a great deal of research on models of this type, and most current approaches incorporate probabilistic considerations.

2. **The Scenario:** Recalling Rhea Lexion's problem of maximizing the number of votes she will receive in the forthcoming gubernatorial election, we are pleased to report that her campaign manager Louisa did indeed lay out all 120 combinations of ways that Rhea could visit the five key cities. Based on her intuition about her constituency, Rhea has decided on the order in which she will visit the five cities: Richburg–Rubesville–Cowtown–Pitts City–Clod Corners.

   The Problem: Having resolved the problem of sequence dependence, Louisa frantically recalculates the estimated number of votes that Governor Lexion can generate by spending 0, 1, . . . , 12 days in each city. (*Note:* Two days were lost from the original 14 because of analysis time.) Table 6.12 summarizes Louisa's estimates (in 10,000's of votes).

   The Model: Since we have resolved the sequence-dependence issue:

   a. Can we model Rhea Lexion's problem as a multistage decision model, and if so, can we solve the model with dynamic programming?
   b. Does this approach to modeling an election problem seem logical to you? Does any aspect of this process bother you?

   Solution to the Model: We solved this model with a package like the SAMS DP module, and you should verify the results from Table 6.13.

   a. In addition to the alternatives in Table 6.13, which yield the optimal solution to the model (540,000 additional votes), several alternatives yield 530,000 and 520,000 votes as well. Might these alternatives be of managerial interest to Governor Lexion?

TABLE 6.12 Additional votes generated

						Days							
City	0	1	2	3	4	5	6	7	8	9	10	11	12
Richburg		6	10	13	14	15	15	16					16
Rubesville		4	8	12	16	18	20	21	22				22
Cowtown		5	10	15	20	20	19	19	18	17	16	15	15
Pitts City		3	7	12	16	19	21	22					22
Clod Corners		1	2	4	8	10	15	19	22	24	28	30	32

TABLE 6.13 Rhea Lexion problem: alternative solutions

	Alternative 1		Alternative 2		Alternative 3	
City	Days	Votes	Days	Votes	Days	Votes
Richburg	1	60,000	1	60,000	2	100,000
Rubesville	3	120,000	4	160,000	3	120,000
Cowtown	4	200,000	4	200,000	4	200,000
Pitts City	4	160,000	3	120,000	3	120,000
Clod Corners	0	0	0	0	0	0
	12	540,000	12	540,000	12	540,000

TABLE 6.14 Rhea Lexion problem: suboptimal solutions

	Alternative 1		Alternative 2		Alternative 3	
City	Days	Votes	Days	Votes	Days	Votes
Richburg	1	60,000	2	100,000	2	100,000
Rubesville	3	120,000	4	160,000	3	120,000
Cowtown	4	200,000	4	200,000	2	100,000
Pitts City	3	120,000	2	70,000	3	120,000
Clod Corners	1	10,000	0	0	2	20,000
	12	510,000	12	530,000	12	460,000

b. Noting that none of the optimal alternatives included visiting Clod Corners, Louisa developed the alternatives in Table 6.14 before showing the analysis to Rhea.

Do you think Louisa's strategy in developing alternative #1 was a good idea from a managerial point of view? Why do you think she bothered to generate the radically suboptimal strategy #3?

3. The network in Figure 6.3 is sometimes called a balanced redundant communications network. When secure and reliable communication between a sender and a receiver is critical (e.g., in military operations, remote consulting on difficult surgery, spotting from the press box by an assistant coach in professional football), the lines (arcs) are linked in staged network fashion by a sequence of booster (and/or encoder-decoder) stations (nodes). In Figure 6.3, the numbers on each arc represent the reliability of the transmission line—the probability that it will not fail over a given period of time. Thus, the reliability of the entire communication network is the probability that messages will get through at least one of the 26 possible paths.

It is fairly obvious that we can model this problem as a multistage model and that the stages are related to the tiers of boosters. It is (perhaps) not quite so obvious, however, what the states are. Consider the following. If a message arrives at booster

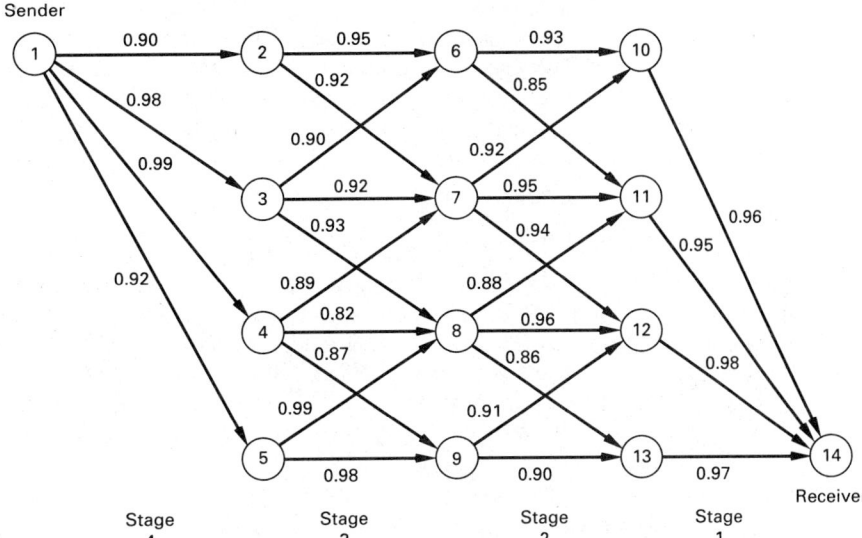

FIGURE 6.3 Balanced redundant communications network

TABLE 6.15 Booster reliability numbers

Stage	Booster	Reliability	Stage	Booster	Reliability
4	1	0.999998	2	6	0.989500
				7	0.999760
3	2	0.996000		8	0.999328
	3	0.999440		9	0.991000
	4	0.997426			
	5	0.999800	1	10	0.960000
				11	0.950000
				12	0.980000
				13	0.970000

#3, the probability that all three lines from booster #3 to boosters #6, 7, and 8 are down is the product of the probabilities that each individual line is down—in this case

$$(1 - 0.90)(1 - 0.92)(1 - 0.93) = 0.00056$$

Therefore, the probability that a message arriving at booster #3 finds an operable line to the next stage is $(1 - 0.00056) = 0.99944$. This number is the reliability of booster #3, and these reliability numbers, computed for each booster (except #14, of course), are the states in our dynamic programming model.

The return function, therefore, is the product of the reliability numbers of the boosters on the paths in the network. If we were attempting to model this problem as a mathematical program, the objective function would be a highly nonlinear function of the type that is unusually difficult to deal with algorithmically. Using backwards recursion, we can model and solve the problem rather easily. Verify that the booster reliability numbers (correct to six decimal places) are as in Table 6.15.

a. It would appear on the surface that solving the DP model of this problem would be a snap—one could merely select the booster with the largest reliability number at each stage (i.e., a "greedy" approach). Why won't that ploy work with this problem? Under what conditions would it work?

b. The "greedy" algorithm works partially. Note, for example, that the most reliable node in stage 1 is booster #12 and the most reliable one in stage 2 is booster #7. Since these two boosters are connected by an arc, do you see that we can eliminate the following circuits from consideration:

1–2–7–10–14   1–2–7–11–14   1–3–7–11–14
1–4–7–10–14   1–4–7–11–14

c. Verify that the routing 1–3–7–12–14 is the highest reliability path in the communication network, with a reliability number of 0.979213. If you were the network designer and wished to increase the reliability number of the network, would you consider adding additional banks of boosters (stages) or augmenting the current stages with additional linkers (states)? What effect would your decision have on solving the dynamic programming model of your problem?

PRACTICE MODELS

1. The network diagram of alternative travel routes and associated costs is given in Table 6.16 for a stagecoach problem. Using dynamic programming, determine the shortest route from Washington to Miami.

TABLE 6.16

From	To					
	St. Louis	Atlanta	Denver	New Orleans	Dallas	Miami
Washington	95	110	—	—	—	—
St. Louis	—	—	65	120	105	—
Atlanta	—	—	100	125	85	—
Denver	—	—	—	—	—	115
New Orleans	—	—	—	—	—	60
Dallas	—	—	—	—	—	90

2. In a regional hospital, assigning additional part-time nurses to four different departments has resulted in the productivity gains in Table 6.17. Use dynamic program-

TABLE 6.17 Productivity gain (%/department)

No. of Nurses Assigned	Radiology	Emergency	Maternity	Neonatal
1	5	12	7	10
2	8	14	10	10
3	14	17	15	14
4	16	25	19	17

ming to determine the optimal assignment that will maximize the total benefit to the hospital. How many stages and how many subproblems for each stage does this problem have?
3. A furniture manufacturing firm has $4 million available for capital investment in its three plants. Table 6.18 gives the investment option and the associated expected return for each plant. Use dynamic programming to determine the investment option that will maximize the overall expected return for the firm.

TABLE 6.18 Expected return (%)

Investment ($ millions)	Pulaski	Salem	Martinsville
0	0	0	0
1	10	8	11
2	17	15	16
3	22	28	25
4	30	28	32

REFERENCES AND ADDITIONAL READING

1. Bellman, R., and S. Dreyfus. *Applied Dynamic Programming*. Princeton, N.J.: Princeton University Press, 1962.
2. Bellman, R. *Dynamic Programming*. Princeton, N.J.: Princeton University Press, 1957.
3. Cole, D. Adapted from an unpublished MBA term project report, Texas Tech University (1982).
4. Denardo, E. *Dynamic Programming: Models and Applications*. Englewood Cliffs, N.J.: Prentice-Hall, 1982.
5. Fielding, N., and T. Fielding. *Fielding's Low-Cost Europe*. New York: Fielding's Publications, 1982.
6. Hillier, F., and G. Lieberman. *Operations Research* (4th ed.). Oakland, Calif.: Holden-Day, 1986.
7. Nemhauser, G. *Introduction to Dynamic Programming*. New York: Wiley, 1966.
8. Psaraftis, H. Adapted from "A Dynamic Programming Approach for Sequencing Groups of Identical Jobs." *Operations Research* 28 (1980): 1347–1359.
9. Schrage, L., and K. Baker. "Dynamic Programming Solution of Sequencing Problems with Precedence Constraints." *Operations Research* 26 (1978): 444–449.
10. Wagner, H. *Principles of Operations Research* (2d ed.). Englewood Cliffs, N.J.: Prentice-Hall, 1975.

PART TWO

Decision Making Under Risk (DMUR)

Chapters 2–6 (Part 1) dealt with modeling and analysis of problems under certainty, that is, with situations and scenarios in which we could ignore risk in the form of probabilistic considerations.

In Part 2, Chapters 7–12 broaden our horizons to consider stochastic models that explicitly deal with risk. Again, however, like the models in Part 1, these models stop short of dealing with uncertainty. Part 3 deals with this troublesome concept.

As was the case with network modeling in Chapter 4, some stochastic models are optimizing and others are descriptive. However, we remind ourselves at the outset that *all* MS/OR models are descriptive from the viewpoint of the decision maker who uses them.

Let us take a brief tour through Part 2 before leaping into Chapter 7.

A STRUCTURE FOR DECISION MAKING UNDER RISK

Chapter 7 provides a model or structure for decision making in a risky environment. Since you will need some elementary concepts from introductory probability and statistics, you might wish to brush up on the subject before tackling this chapter. In reading and studying Chapter 7, you will find it useful to think about the problems and decision situations, both personal and professional, that you have encountered (or are now encountering) and relate the modeling process to these scenarios. Decision making under risk (DMUR) matrix and decision tree models are very general in scope and provide an excellent way to get a handle on problems in a rational, organized way.

WAITING LINE (QUEUEING) MODELS

To most of us, waiting lines (or queues, in British terminology) are almost everyday phenomena, and queueing situations are common in organizations. In Chapter 8, we will study some simple queueing models and explore their usefulness.

Queueing models can, in a technical sense, be either descriptive or optimizing. Chapter 8 concentrates mainly on the former. As you will see, authors have written entire 700-page books on the subject, so our exploration will, of necessity, be somewhat perfunctory.

DISCRETE SIMULATION

Industry surveys of the use of MS/OR models consistently rank discrete probabilistic simulation models at or near the top in frequency of actual use. Chapter 9 discusses such models in detail.

Technically, discrete simulation models are descriptive in nature, and we sometimes refer to them as what-if devices. Stated another way, simulation models allow the decision maker to investigate the effects of policy or environmental changes without having to subject the actual entity to these effects. For example, it would be foolish indeed to actually build a multibillion-dollar dam and let the water in to see whether it holds without first simulating different construction options with a physical model. The same is true for many business and public sector problems that are sometimes too complex to model with optimizing models, such as mathematical programming, but that are amenable to analysis by discrete simulation.

MODELING WITH MARKOV CHAINS

Do you remember Markov from our discussion of dynamic programming in Chapter 6? Well, he is back again—this time with probabilistic devices called **transition matrices** in Chapter 10.

Markov chains are fun to work with. They will be more fun if you take a little time to review your basic linear algebra before reading Chapter 10. Markov chain models, technically speaking, are purely descriptive. Managerially speaking, they are very useful devices in helping us to better understand certain dynamic processes that occur frequently in organizations.

PROJECT SCHEDULING

Scheduling and managing projects is one of the most important activities in which managers engage. Chapter 11 introduces the probabilistic version of the critical path model from Chapter 4—PERT (project evaluation and review technique). Although the technical details of this model are simple to grasp, the behavioral implications of planning and managing with PERT are complex and interesting.

INVENTORY MANAGEMENT

A business reporter recently estimated that 20% of the total value of world gross product is invested in inventory. The subject of Chapter 12 is ways to more efficiently manage this huge resource. The chapter covers the classical economic order quantity (EOQ) approach by building some simple mathematical models of the problem and ends by discussing some more modern approaches, such as material requirements planning (MRP) and just in time (JIT).

And there we have our overview of Part 2. Let's begin our stochastic adventure by looking at a structure for decision making under risk.

KEY TERM
transition matrices

CHAPTER 7

A Structure for Decision Making Under Risk

This chapter explores a structure for decision making that we will refer to as **decision making under risk** (DMUR). Every decision maker uses some sort of structure, whether it is a seat-of-the-pants blend of intuition and experience or a formal system like the one we will describe here. Our view is that a formal structure is preferable, since it gives the decision maker a way to compare decisions over time against a standard benchmark.

This is not to say that every successful manager uses or has used a structured approach—quite the contrary. Some of the most successful entrepreneurs in history have been "hip shooters"—people who built giant corporations by decision making based on gut feelings. It is a matter of record, however, that for every success story about the unschooled, intuitive tycoon who went from rags to riches overnight, there are a hundred or more stories that chronicle the sudden downfall of another "boy (or girl) wonder" who made one fatal mistake and perhaps bankrupted his or her corporation.

Before exploring decision theory models for DMUR, let us agree at the outset that these models—like the DMUC models in Part I of this book—are not panaceas. That is, they provide one input into the decision-making process and are not substitutes for managerial judgment and common sense.

STRUCTURING THE DECISION ENVIRONMENT

In what follows, we refer to the future events or environmental profiles that determine the outcome of a particular decision as **states of nature** and designate these n states as $S_1, S_2, \ldots, S_n$. We require that these states be *mutually exclusive and collectively exhaustive*. For example, suppose Dinah, the CEO of Paleolithic Energy, Inc. (PEI) is trying to decide whether to purchase options on scarce offshore drilling rigs in anticipation of the award of offshore rights on which the company has bid. PEI has made bids on four leases, so that there are exactly five states of nature—the award of 0, 1, 2, 3, or 4 leases. We note that the five states are mutually exclusive (there is no overlapping among the outcomes) and collectively exhaustive (nothing can happen that is not included in the set of states). As a counterexample, suppose the government had the option of awarding split-bids on one or more tracts. In this case, we would have to identify additional states of nature, since the five current states are neither exclusive nor exhaustive.

TABLE 7.1 The decision matrix

		States of Nature				
		S_1	S_2	$\cdots$ S_j	$\cdots$	S_n
	A_1	O_{11}	O_{12}	$\cdots$ O_{1j}	$\cdots$	O_{1n}
	A_2	O_{21}	O_{22}	$\cdots$ O_{2j}	$\cdots$	O_{2n}
	$\vdots$	$\vdots$	$\vdots$	$\cdots$ $\vdots$	$\cdots$	$\vdots$
Alternatives	A_i	O_{i1}	O_{i2}	$\cdots$ O_{ij}	$\cdots$	O_{in}
	$\vdots$	$\vdots$	$\vdots$	$\cdots$ $\vdots$	$\cdots$	$\vdots$
	A_m	O_{m1}	O_{m2}	$\cdots$ O_{mj}	$\cdots$	O_{mn}

We refer to the various actions or options available to the decision maker as **alternatives,** and we designate the m available alternatives as $A_1, A_2, \ldots, A_m$. Unlike states of nature, our alternatives are not necessarily mutually exclusive or collectively exhaustive. For example, for exogenous reasons, the decision maker may wish to limit the number of alternatives to consider. Some problems may involve billions of alternatives, so that the task of enumerating them all is beyond our capacity. In our PEI illustration, for instance, Dinah obviously could contemplate reserving as many offshore rigs as she wished, although common sense suggests that reserving more than four would be foolish. On the other hand, she might well decide to reserve a maximum of two—and limit her alternatives to reserving 0, 1, or 2 rigs. *The key distinctions between states of nature and alternatives is that the decision maker has control of the latter but not the former.*

With n states of nature and m alternatives, there are mn **outcomes** or **payoffs,** and we designate them as O_{ij}—the outcome associated with the ith alternative and the jth state. We then summarize our decision environment in a decision matrix (see Table 7.1). In the first part of the chapter, we state the O_{ij} in terms of physical quantities, such as money, time, or quantities of material. Later in the chapter, we introduce the notion of utility and express the outcomes in dimensionless units called **utiles.**

A DMUR MODEL

Having identified the n states of nature and selected an appropriate set of m alternatives, and having quantified the mn outcomes, one task remains—identifying or estimating a probability distribution on the states of nature. Stated another way, we must assess the relative likelihood of the occurrence of each state, and—since the states are mutually exclusive and collectively exhaustive—their probabilities sum to 1. This final task is at the heart of modeling in a DMUR environment, and the glib sentences above do not do it justice. Let's explore further the question of how one might go about this task.

ASSESSING STATE PROBABILITIES

In some decision environments, the probability distributions on the states of nature may be *combinatorial,* so that we may compute the state probabilities directly. As an illustration, consider the highly speculative investment vehicle called the futures bundle. The investment group purchases, for example, $2 million each worth of three different 30-day commodity futures (e.g., silver, corn, pork bellies) on the Chicago Board of Exchange. At the end of the 30-day period, the futures prices will have risen or fallen. If a particular commodity price falls, the investment is lost; if the price rises, the investors make a profit. By "bundling" three different commodities, investors attempt to diversify the risk and avoid an all-or-nothing investment in a single commodity option.

Suppose that the probability (Pr) of a single commodity rising is 0.50, so that the outcome of such an investment is roughly equivalent to the flip of a coin. In this decision model, the state probabilities follow a binomial probability distribution with Pr(win) = Pr(lose) = 0.50. The four states of nature are S_1 = three wins; S_2 = two wins; S_3 = one win; and S_4 = no wins. There is only one way each that S_1 and S_4 can occur, and there are three ways each that S_2 and S_3 can occur. Thus, if we let p_j = probability of state j occurring, then p_1 = 1/8; p_2 = 3/8; p_3 = 3/8; and p_4 = 1/8.

If the investment group gets three wins, the "bundle" is worth $15 million, so that there is a $9 million profit. With two wins, the gains offset the losses, and the group retrieves its original $6 million investment. With only one win, the group loses half its original investment ($3 million), but with three losses, the group loses its entire investment of $6 million. We will perform an analysis of the futures bundle speculation later in the chapter.

As another example, let's return to Dinah's offshore leasing problem and suppose that historically, PEI has received the award of a lease one of every four times it has bid. Since the states of nature are S_j = 0, 1, 2, 3, or 4 leases awarded, we again have a binomial probability distribution—this time with Pr(lease award) = 0.25. Using binomial tables, we can compute the state probabilities as follows:

$$p_1 = 0.316; p_2 = 0.422; p_3 = 0.211; p_4 = 0.047; p_5 = 0.004$$

Our second example was a bit different from the first in that we used historical information (relative frequency of lease award) as a basis for extrapolation to the future. This is by far the most common method of assessing state probabilities in business situations and appears to work well in most real-world decision environments. However, we should exercise caution when using the past as a predictor for the future. Turbulent economic times often create a new ball game, in which forecasting based on historical data becomes undependable.

If we have neither a combinatorial structure nor a reliable historical base upon which to assess state probabilities, we must—in those situations in which we can derive a probability density function—resort to subjective probability estimation. One approach that managers have used successfully is the **DELPHI technique,** which involves individual assessments by members of an expert panel. The moderator aggregates and synthesizes the initial responses and feeds the information to the panel members, who then refine their estimates. The moderator synthesizes the results of the second round and again returns the results to members of the panel. The goal, of course, is to achieve convergence of opinion. Investigators have used DELPHI successfully to forecast such things as the profile of air travel in 1999 and the state of the art in computer technology 10 years into the future and to correctly forecast the current trend toward a more service-oriented economy in the United States.

Another way to derive subjective probabilities is to rely on gut-feeling based on experience and intuition. Some decision theorists contend that *all* probability estimation is to some degree subjective—and they have a valid point. For example, if a

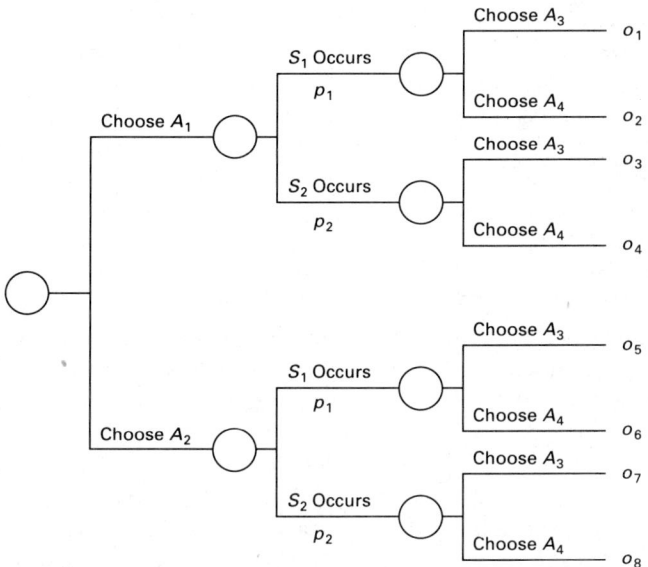

FIGURE 7.1
Two-stage decision tree

forecast based on historical data produced results that a decision maker wasn't comfortable with, you may rest assured that his or her skepticism would reflect somehow in the analysis—either explicitly (as in actually adjusting the historical forecast) or implicitly (as, perhaps, in discounting the results of the formal analysis when actually making the decision). At any rate, assessing state probabilities is the key step in building a model for DMUR. Obviously, the results produced by the model are only as useful as the state probabilities are accurate.

SEQUENTIAL DECISION PROCESSES

The decision matrix model discussed above is useful in modeling decision environments in which we have a single decision to make. If we must make a sequence of decisions, we might choose to model our problem as a **decision tree.** Figure 7.1 is a decision tree representing a sequence of two decisions (A_1 or A_2 first; A_3 or A_4 second) and two states of nature, S_1 and S_2. The eight branches of the tree represent possible outcomes; that is, 4(compound decisions) × 2(states of nature) = 8(outcomes). One very useful feature of the decision tree is its visual impact—the model structures the problem sequentially by picturing explicitly the precedence relations. In general, decision trees alternate between decision and state stages. That is, the manager makes a decision, and Mother Nature—in the form of a probability distribution—makes the next one. It is the manager's turn next, and so on. We return to the subject of decision trees later in the chapter. First, we need to explore decision criteria for DMUR models.

DECISION CRITERIA FOR DMUR MODELS

Just as with DMUC models discussed in Part I, a variety of criteria can be used with DMUR models. For example, one perfectly reasonable criterion in certain decision-making situations might be to identify the state S_l with the highest probability of occurring and select the alternative A_k for which O_{kl} is the largest (maximization) or smallest (minimization). In fact, if p_j happened to be very large and if the O_{ij} did not vary too widely, such a criterion might be just the ticket for some decision makers.

PART 2 DECISION MAKING UNDER RISK (DMUR)

The two most widely used decision criteria for DMUR models, however, are (for maximization problems) maximize the expected monetary value (EMV) and minimize the expected opportunity loss (EOL). As we shall see, the use of these two criteria with a DMUR model always leads to the same optimal model alternative. So why discuss both? As it turns out, there is a very interesting relationship between the optimal EOL and the value of information, which we will discover shortly.

THE EXPECTED MONETARY VALUE CRITERION

Assume for a moment that our decision maker is willing to behave as though he or she will repeat the current decision many times in the future, and that he or she will make the current decision in such a way as to optimize the long-run average performance. Stated another way, the decision maker is willing to act in such a way as to optimize the expected value of his or her decision. Returning to our futures bundle speculation, we have two alternatives: to invest or not to invest. Table 7.2 is the decision matrix for this problem.

Let's use SAMS' DMUR module to investigate this problem. Figure 7.2 presents a facsimile of the input screen. (We will discuss the meaning of EOL, EMVPI, EVPI, information available, and cost in a later section.) Table 7.3 gives the SAMS full briefing for futures bundle using EMV. The EMV of (A_1: invest) is EMV(A_1) = $-\$.75$ million, or an expected loss of \$750,000. Since EMV (A_2: don't invest) = 0 and since we wish to maximize our return, the EMV criterion would suggest that in the long run it might be best to avoid this speculation.

TABLE 7.2 Decision matrix for futures bundle

		\multicolumn{4}{c}{*States of Nature*}			
		S_1:3W	S_2:2W	S_3:1W	S_4:0W
	p_j	1/8	3/8	3/8	1/8
Alternatives	A_1: invest	+\$9M	0	−\$3M	−\$6M
	A_2: don't invest	0	0	0	0

FIGURE 7.2 SAMS input screen for futures bundle

```
▶ SAMS INPUT SCREEN - DMUR Matrix Module ◀

NAME?    FUTURES BUNDLE
MAximize or MInimize?  MA
Information Available?  NO    If YES, Cost?
PROBLEM DESCRIPTION - Decide whether to invest in
                     a commodity futures bundle
```

States	3WINS	2WINS	1WIN	0WIN
Prior Dist.	.125	.375	.375	.125
Alternatives	Outcomes			
INVEST	9.	0.	-3.	-6.
DONTINVE	0.	0.	0.	0.

TABLE 7.3

FUTURES BUNDLE FULL BRIEFING ON OPTIMAL MODEL SOLUTION			
Optimal Objective Value = 0			
Alternative	EMV	EOL	Optimal
INVEST	−0.75	1.875	No
DONTINVEST	0.00	1.125	Yes
	EVPI: 1.125	EMVPI: 1.125	

TABLE 7.4 Decision matrix of opportunity losses for futures bundle

		States of Nature			
		S_1:3W	S_2:2W	S_3:1W	S_4:0W
	p_j	1/8	3/8	3/8	1/8
Alternatives	A_1: invest	0	0	+$3M	+$6M
	A_2: don't invest	+$9M	0	0	0

In general notation, then, SAMS computes the EMV of alternative A_i as follows:

$$\text{EMV}(A_i) = \sum_{j=1}^{n} p_j O_{ij} \tag{7.1}$$

As we shall see later, the EMV criterion is a risk-neutral approach to decision making. It is appropriate for use in decision environments in which the worst possible outcome would not be disastrous and in which the best possible outcome would not make an order of magnitude difference to the organization. Stated another way, EMV is most appropriate when the marginal utility of one dollar, more or less, is about the same for the low end and the high end of the range of payoffs or outcomes.

THE EXPECTED OPPORTUNITY LOSS CRITERION

Again, let's assume that the decision maker is willing to accept the long-run behavioral assumption. Another way to approach the DMUR model is to use the expected opportunity loss (EOL) criterion. Here, we merely replace the outcomes (O_{ij}) in each column (state) by the opportunity loss (OL_{ij}) occasioned by selecting alternative i and having state j occur. We sometimes refer to opportunity losses as regrets—a very humanized way to characterize these numbers. Table 7.4 gives the decision matrix for futures bundle in terms of the OL_{ij} or regrets. For example, consider state #1 in the table. If we had selected A_2: don't invest, and S_1 subsequently occurred, we would have regretted our decision—to the tune of $9 million in profit; thus $OL_{21} = +\$9M$. On the other hand, if we had chosen A_1 instead, we would have made the best possible choice—so that our opportunity loss would have been zero.

The expected opportunity loss of (A_1: invest) is $EOL(A_1) = \$1.875M$. Since the $EOL(A_2$: don't invest$) = \$1.125M$ and since we wish to minimize our opportunity loss, this criterion also suggests (as did the EMV criterion) not pursuing this highly speculative investment vehicle.

In general notation, SAMS computes the expected opportunity loss of the ith alternative as follows:

$$EOL(A_i) = \sum_{j=1}^{n} p_j(O_j^* - O_{ij}) \tag{7.2}$$

where O_j^* is the best outcome for state j.

Since the EOL criterion always selects the same optimal model alternative as the EMV criterion, its risk characteristics are identical to those of the EMV criterion.

THE VALUE OF INFORMATION

The EMV and EOL criteria just discussed assume that we know nothing about the states of nature other than their probabilities or, stated another way, their long-run relative frequencies of occurring. What if we had additional information prior to making our decision? For example, oil exploration and production (E&P) companies have historical records of their drilling results by geographical area and would be able to assess long-run state probabilities using these data. However, dozens of firms perform seismic sounding experiments that give the potential driller information about the prospects for striking oil at a particular site. How much are those services worth to the E&P company? The following sections explore such questions.

THE VALUE OF PERFECT INFORMATION

Suppose our market specialist who is promoting futures bundle has attracted a following of speculators who may or may not choose to invest in the current bundle. Almost unnoticed in the crowd is an eccentric-looking fellow with a laptop computer. Each time before the investors commit to the latest commodity futures bundle, the man gazes into the computer screen and whispers the results of the upcoming speculation—and, amazingly, he is right every time! Fortunately for us, the man doesn't have the capital to invest, but he is willing to provide his perfect information to us (for a fee, of course) prior to each investment. What would such information be worth?

Returning to the decision matrix, note that only in the case of S_1 (three wins) is there a positive outcome from selecting A_1 (invest). If we knew that S_2, S_3, or S_4 was going to occur, we would select A_2 (don't invest). Therefore, the expected monetary value with perfect information (EMVPI) is

$$EMVPI = +\$9M(1/8) + 0(3/8) + 0(3/8) + 0(1/8) = \$1.125M$$

Since the value of the optimal EMV = 0 with no information, the expected value of perfect information (EVPI) must be $\$1.125M - 0 = \$1.125M$. In general terms, then:

$$EVPI = EMVPI - EMV^* \tag{7.3}$$

where the "*" refers to the EMV of the optimal act. But recall now that EOL* also had a value of $1.125M. Is this just a coincidence? No, it isn't. It is an interesting (and easily proven) fact that

$$\text{EVPI} = \text{EOL}^* \tag{7.4}$$

Thus, we should be willing to pay our eccentric fellow with the laptop up to $1.125M per round for his perfect information.

But wait—haven't we taken off on a flight of fancy? There are no computer wizards in the business world to tell us what next year's economy will be like, and there are rarely (if ever) sources of perfect information about the future in any sense. So why spend time on a concept that is so obviously unreal? The next section discusses the value of *imperfect* information—and the EVPI gives us an upper bound on it. Thus, if the information available to us costs more than the EVPI, we needn't bother considering it further.

THE VALUE OF IMPERFECT INFORMATION

To illustrate the concept of the value of imperfect information, let's return to another problem faced by Paleolithic Energy, Inc. (PEI). The company owns rights to a lease near Norman, Oklahoma; and Dinah, the CEO, must decide whether to drill. Dinah has identified three states of nature (S_1 = dry hole, S_2 = moderate strike, and S_3 = gusher) and the outcomes associated with her two alternatives (A_1: don't drill and A_2: drill). From past drilling data, Dinah assesses state probabilities as shown in the decision matrix in Table 7.5. Table 7.6 is the opportunity loss decision matrix. We used SAMS' decision matrix module to compute the EMVs and EOLs, given in the right-hand column of Tables 7.5 and 7.6.

The EMV criterion indicates that the optimal model solution is A_2: drill, with an EMV of $200,000. Also, EOL* = EVPI = $350,000, so it would behoove the company to get more information, if possible, before making the decision.

Luckily, Sooner Boomer, Inc. (SBI), a seismic exploration firm headquartered in Norman, has a great deal of experience in this part of the country and has kept meticulous records of its successes (and failures) in predicting the existence of oil. Table 7.7 summarizes this experience as SBI's **conditional distribution of predictive accuracy**. We interpret the conditional probability distribution as follows. The symbol I_i means that SBI predicted that state i would occur. Reading across the marginal distribution for S_1, for example, 75% of the time that there was a dry hole, SBI had

TABLE 7.5 PEI decision matrix of outcomes (net profit in $000)

		States of Nature			
		Dry	Moderate	Gusher	
		S_1	S_2	S_3	EMV
	p_i	0.50	0.30	0.20	
Alternatives	A_1: don't drill	0	0	0	0
	A_2: drill	−700	500	2,000	+200

TABLE 7.6 PEI decision matrix of opportunity losses (in $000)

		States of Nature			
		Dry	Moderate	Gusher	
		S_1	S_2	S_3	EOL
	p_j	0.50	0.30	0.20	
Alternatives	A_1: don't drill	0	500	2,000	550
	A_2: drill	700	0	0	350

TABLE 7.7 Conditional distribution of predictive accuracy

		Predicted States of Nature			
		I_1	I_2	I_3	
Actual States of Nature	S_1	0.75	0.20	0.05	
	S_2	0.15	0.65	0.20	$\Pr(I_i\|S_j)$
	S_3	0	0.35	0.65	

predicted it correctly. On the other hand, a dry hole occurred 20% of the time when SBI forecast a moderate strike and only 5% of the time when the prediction was for a gusher. We interpret the marginal distributions for S_2 and S_3 in a similar way.

But the information in this form—the probability that SBI says I_i given that S_j is true (written as $\Pr(I_i|S_j)$)—is of no direct value. What PEI needs is $\Pr(S_j|I_i)$—the probability that state j exists given that SBI says in advance that state i exists. Moreover, the conditional distribution of predictive accuracy does not incorporate our knowledge about the state probabilities p_j. What we need is a way to convert our state probability distribution (the **prior distribution**) into the conditional distribution $\Pr(S_j|I_i)$ (the **posterior distribution**). And thanks to the Reverend Mr. Thomas Bayes, we have such a method at hand. (Thomas Bayes was, by profession, a Methodist minister in England. He was, by avocation, a practicing statistician.)

BAYES'S THEOREM

Recalling our course in elementary statistics, we can use Bayes's theorem to convert a conditional probability distribution into its mirror image, as follows.

$$\Pr(S_j|I_i) = \frac{\Pr(I_i|S_j)(p_j)}{\sum_{j=1}^{n} \Pr(I_i|S_j)(p_j)} \tag{7.5}$$

In our PEI example, let us illustrate the computations for $\Pr(S_j|I_i)$:

$$\Pr(S_1|I_1) = \frac{(0.75)(0.50)}{(0.75)(0.50) + (0.15)(0.30) + (0)(0.20)} = \frac{0.375}{0.420} = 0.893$$

$$\Pr(S_2|I_1) = \frac{(0.15)(0.30)}{0.420} = 0.107; \quad \Pr(S_3|I_1) = \frac{0}{0.420} = 0$$

We compute the other six conditional probabilities in a similar manner and give the complete posterior distribution in Table 7.8.

Comparing the posterior distribution in Table 7.8 with the original conditional distribution of predictive accuracy, we note that Bayes's theorem has converted the marginal distributions on states to marginal distributions on predictions—which is precisely what we need. Before illustrating the application in a decision tree, however, we need one more element: the **predictive distribution** $\Pr(I_i)$. As it turns out, these probabilities are the denominators in Bayes's theorem, so that $p_1 = 0.420$; $p_2 = 0.365$; and $p_3 = 0.215$. This curious distribution, as it relates to our oil drilling example, indicates the relative frequency with which our seismic consulting firm SBI will predict each of the three states of nature. One might wish to find a logical reason why SBI will predict a dry hole only 42% of the time and a gusher about 22% of the time when the prior distribution indicates that it actually occurs 50% and 20% of the time, respectively. Think of it this way: SBI's information is imperfect. If the company were able to correctly predict the actual state of nature every time, the predictive distribution would be identical to the prior distribution.

APPLICATION TO A DECISION TREE

In the PEI drilling problem, Dinah must make two sequential decisions: whether to hire SBI for a fee of $100,000 and, subsequently, whether to drill. If the PEI decision is to hire the consulting firm, PEI will take into account the prediction by SBI in making the drilling decision. After PEI makes its second decision, it is then Mother Nature's turn—revealing the actual amount of oil present.

Figure 7.3 exhibits this problem modeled as a decision tree. The numbers in parentheses on the probabilistic branches are the appropriate probabilities. For example, on the arc "I_1: predict S_1," we have p_1 from the predictive distribution. Continuing down this branch, we have $\Pr(S_1|I_1)$, $\Pr(S_2|I_1)$, and $\Pr(S_3|I_1)$ from the posterior distribution we previously computed, and the other branches of the hire-consultant portion of the tree are labeled in similar fashion. On the don't-hire-consultant portion of the tree, the probabilistic branches are labeled with the elements of the prior distribution, since no additional information is available. Since we have already obtained a solution with the EMV criterion on the decision matrix model of this portion

TABLE 7.8 $\Pr(S_j|I_i)$

		Predicted States of Nature		
		I_1	I_2	I_3
Actual States of Nature	S_1	0.893	0.274	0.116
	S_2	0.107	0.534	0.279
	S_3	0	0.192	0.605

264 PART 2 DECISION MAKING UNDER RISK (DMUR)

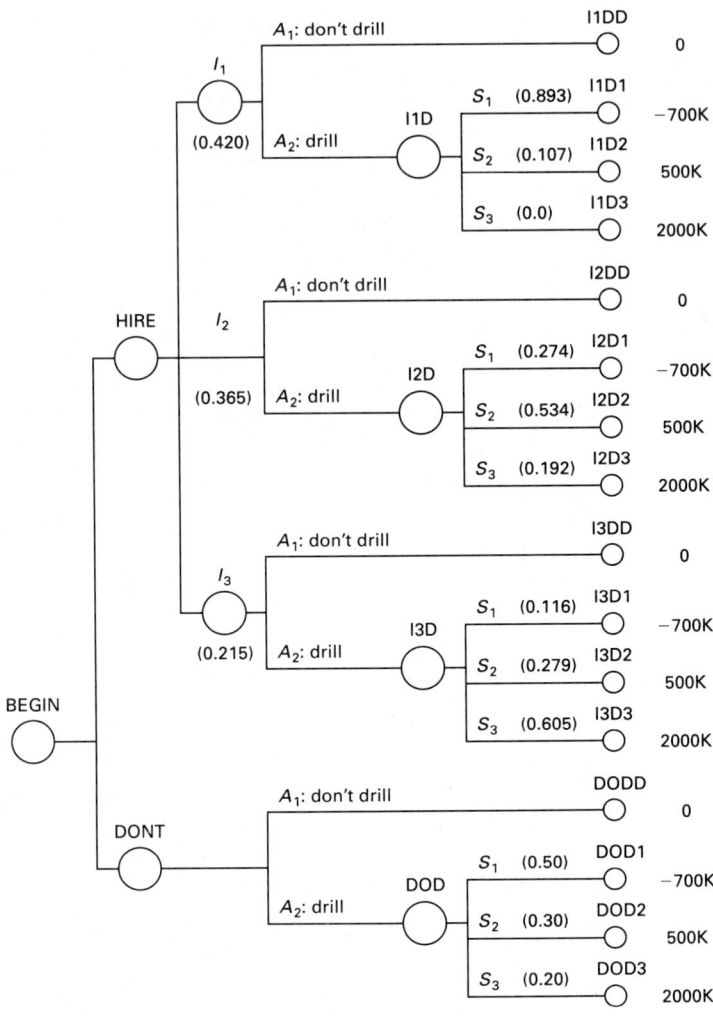

FIGURE 7.3
Decision tree for PEI problem

of the tree, we recall that the optimal model decision was "drill," with an EMV of $200,000 and an EVPI of $350,000. Since SBI charges a fee of $100,000, the other branch of the tree merits analysis.

AN OPTIMIZING ALGORITHM FOR DECISION TREE MODELS

Recalling our discussion of dynamic programming in Chapter 6, a decision tree represents a sequence of independent decisions over time. Thus, we may use the DP technique to analyze this model. However, the early literature in decision theory called this process "averaging out and rolling back," and the following uses this colorful and very descriptive term.

Let's use SAMS' DMUR matrix module to do the arithmetic for us. Figure 7.4 is the SAMS input screen. Table 7.9 presents the SAMS full briefing for the PEI decision tree.

The SAMS output first displays the analysis of the value of the seismic information available from SBI. It notes that the EVSI of sample information is $340,300, which

FIGURE 7.4
SAMS input screen for PEI with information

```
┌──→ SAMS INPUT SCREEN - DMUR Matrix Module      ←──┐
│  NAME?  PALEOLITHIC ENERGY                        │
│  MAximize or MInimize?  MA                        │
│  Information Available?  YES   If YES, Cost?  100 │
│  PROBLEM DESCRIPTION - Decide whether to buy seismic
│  info. from Boomer, and whether to drill.        │
├───────────────────────────────────────────────────┤
│  States         DRYHOLE    MODERATE    GUSHER     │
│                                                   │
│  Prior Dist.      .5          .3         .2       │
├───────────────────────────────────────────────────┤
│  Alternatives              Outcomes               │
│                                                   │
│  DRILL           -700.       500.       2000.     │
│  DONTDRIL           0.         0.          0.     │
│                                                   │
│       Conditional Distribution of Predictive Accuracy
│                                                   │
│               I1     I2     I3                    │
│         S1   .75     .2    .05                    │
│         S2   .15    .65     .2                    │
│         S3    0     .35    .65                    │
└───────────────────────────────────────────────────┘
```

TABLE 7.9

PEI WITH INFORMATION
FULL BRIEFING ON OPTIMAL MODEL SOLUTION

Information is worth	340.3 (EVSI)
Information costs	100.0
Expected net gain from sampling	240.3

Recommend Buying Information

If Information Is Bought

Prediction		**Recommend**
If I1, then		DONTDRIL
	Expected net payoff = −100.0	
If I2, then		DRILL
	Expected net payoff = 359.2	
If I3, then		DRILL
	Expected net payoff = 1168.3	

If Information Is Not Bought

		DRILL
	Expected payoff = 200.	

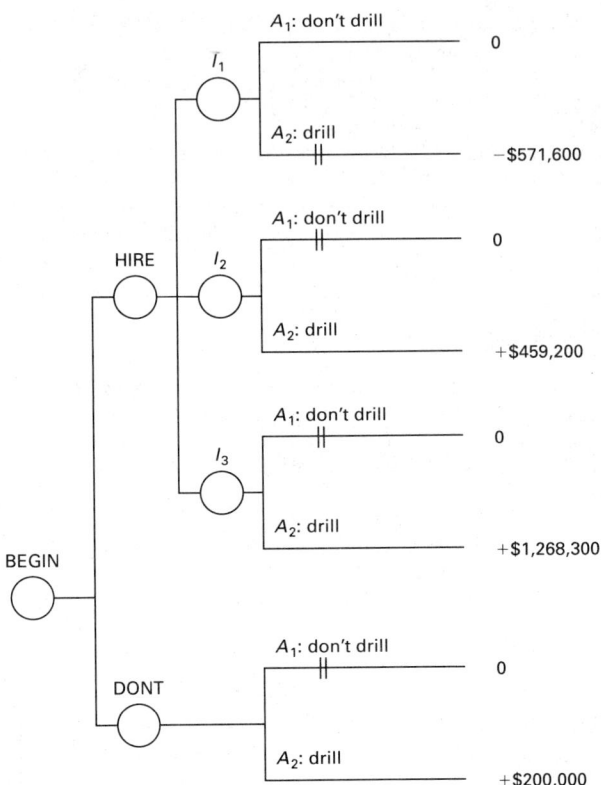

FIGURE 7.5
"Pruned" decision tree for PEI problem

is considerably larger than its cost of $100,000. The expected net gain from sampling is just the difference between the EVSI and the information costs.

SAMS recommends buying the information and indicates the optimal alternatives associated with each possible prediction by SBI. The expected net payoffs are the EMVs of the alternatives after subtracting the cost of information. Note that if SBI predicts a dry hole, the $100,000 it is paid for seismic soundings may well result in PEI's not incurring the $700,000 cost of drilling. If SBI predicts either a moderate find or a gusher, the model recommends drilling.

But since models don't make decisions, SAMS dutifully reports the recommendation and outcome if the CEO decides not to purchase the information after all.

In analyzing a decision tree, SAMS starts at the end and works backward toward the beginning. The first step is to average out the results of Mother Nature's last act by converting the probabilistic outcomes to expected monetary values. Figure 7.5 exhibits this "pruned" tree. Note that we have lopped off certain branches (indicated by double bars), since they do not represent optimal decisions at this stage. We have now rolled back to the next probabilistic echelon of the tree and we are ready to average out again. The next iteration cuts off the DONT branch to complete the analysis.

SENSITIVITY ANALYSIS OF DMUR MODELS

At the outset, let us be certain that we are clear on a key point. If the prior distribution on the states of nature is accurate, obtaining additional information doesn't change it in a long-run sense. Stated another way, if we made a long sequence of similar decisions on oil leases with the same prior distribution, about half of them would turn out to be dry holes if drilled. What the imperfect information supplied by SBI permits us to do is to make the don't-drill decision in a certain percentage of these cases and avoid the 700,000-dollar drilling cost each time.

ANALYSIS OF PRIOR PROBABILITIES

In modeling with DMUR, the "softest" parameters are usually the state probabilities of the prior probability distribution. In certain cases, we can investigate the sensitivity of our model to errors in these probabilities. For instance, in our PEI example, let p_1, p_2, and $(1 - p_1 - p_2)$ be the state probabilities of S_1, S_2, and S_3, respectively. The expected monetary value of the decision A_2: drill becomes

$$\text{EMV}(A_2) = p_1(-700{,}000) + p_2(500{,}000) + (1 - p_1 - p_2)(2{,}000{,}000)$$
$$= 2{,}000{,}000 - 2{,}700{,}000 p_1 - 1{,}500{,}000 p_2$$

We observe that if $p_1 > 20/27 = 0.74$, it would never be economically advisable to drill, regardless of the value of p_2. On the other hand, if we hold the state probability p_1 constant at $p_1 = 0.50$, we have

$$\text{EMV} = 650{,}000 - 1{,}500{,}000 p_2,$$

which is negative only if $p_2 > 65/150 = 0.43$, meaning that p_3 would have to be less than about 0.07. In our illustration, Dinah might well feel comfortable with the analysis, given the relatively wide margin for error.

DOMINATED ALTERNATIVES

In some DMUR models, certain alternatives may be **dominated** by others. That is, if every payoff for A_k is at least as good as the payoff for A_l in every state, neither the EMV nor the EOL criterion will ever select A_l as the optimal alternative. Therefore, A_l is a dominated alternative, and we can remove it *from the model* for purposes of analysis. We stress "from the model" because, in certain instances, the decision maker may actually select a dominated alternative as his or her preferred course of action because of exogenous factors that we could not incorporate into the model.

THE POSTERIOR DISTRIBUTION

Consider the posterior distribution for our oil-drilling example, reproduced in Table 7.10.
Note that in about 89 cases out of 100, SBI's prediction of a dry hole will be accurate. On the other hand, a dry hole will occur in about 27 cases out of 100 when SBI predicts a moderate find and in almost 12 out of 100 when it predicts a gusher. Might Dinah decide not to drill when SBI predicts a dry hole and ignore this input otherwise? Certainly—and the point is that managerial intuition and insight are not

TABLE 7.10 $\Pr(S_j | I_i)$

		Predicted States of Nature		
		I_1	I_2	I_3
Actual States of Nature	S_1	0.893	0.274	0.116
	S_2	0.107	0.534	0.279
	S_3	0	0.192	0.605

bound by the results of formal modeling and analysis. An example from another context may clarify this point.

Certain diagnostic tests in medicine give one of two indications: positive or negative. If a test, say for poliomyelitis, is positive, the physician may conclude with very high probability that the patient has the disease. On the other hand, if the test is negative, the physician may be able to make *no conclusion whatsoever* about the presence or absence of the disease. Similarly, it is possible that a certain response from an information source in a decision environment in business may be a highly reliable predictor but that a different response from the same source may contain no useful information whatsoever. Thus, when we investigate the sensitivity of DMUR models, we should take this fact into consideration.

THE CONCEPT OF ECONOMIC UTILITY

Thus far we have expressed our outcomes O_{ij} in terms of physical quantities such as dollars and time. This approach is widely used and is useful as long as our decision maker's marginal utility for one unit at the lower end of the spectrum of possible outcomes is about the same for one unit at the higher end. For example, gambling casinos thrive on 25-cent, 50-cent, etc., slot machines because most people's utilities for losing a few cents at a time are low, given the tantalizing prospect (and very low probability) of hitting a jackpot worth several thousand dollars. Why aren't there 100-dollar or even 1,000-dollar slot machines? For the simple reason that most people who gamble as part of a holiday (a casino's greatest revenue source) would be reluctant to risk that amount of money all at one time on the prospect of winning many times that amount. In other words, their utility for the hundredth lost dollar is higher than for the hundredth won dollar.

On the other hand, people built many of this country's greatest corporations (e.g., Polaroid, Xerox, IBM) by seeking risk—deliberately going after the high-risk/high-payoff alternatives that resulted in technological breakthroughs. Thus, for decision makers who are clearly operating in a risk-averse or risk-seeking mode, use of the EMV or EOL criteria—both of which are risk neutral on monetary outcomes—would be inappropriate.

AN UNDERLYING ASSUMPTION

The following discussions on economic utility make only one basic assumption—that the decision criteria used cannot result in **intransitive preference**. Stated another way, if we prefer A to B and we also prefer B to C, under the transitivity assumption, we must also prefer A to C. You may wonder whether any rational decision criterion could lead to intransitive preference—and the answer is yes.

Suppose, for example, an MBA graduate is trying to decide upon one among three sports cars to purchase. Since he can't decide how to quantify his evaluations of their operating cost, handling, and appearance, he rates them on a nominal scale (see Table 7.11). His decision rule is to select the model that is better than the others on the most criteria. The Beta-400 is better than the Alpha-Z on both cost and appearance, so he would obviously prefer the Beta-400. Also, the Gamma-G is better than the Beta-400 on both cost and handling, so it appears that his choice should be the Gamma-G. Correct? Unfortunately, the Alpha-Z is better than the Gamma-G on both handling and appearance, so he is right back where he started! This is one example of an intransitive decision criterion of the type that is not amenable to analysis using classical utility theory.

TABLE 7.11 Sports car ratings

	Criteria		
Model	Cost	Handling	Appearance
Alpha-Z	Worst	Best	Middle
Beta-400	Middle	Worst	Best
Gamma-G	Best	Middle	Worst

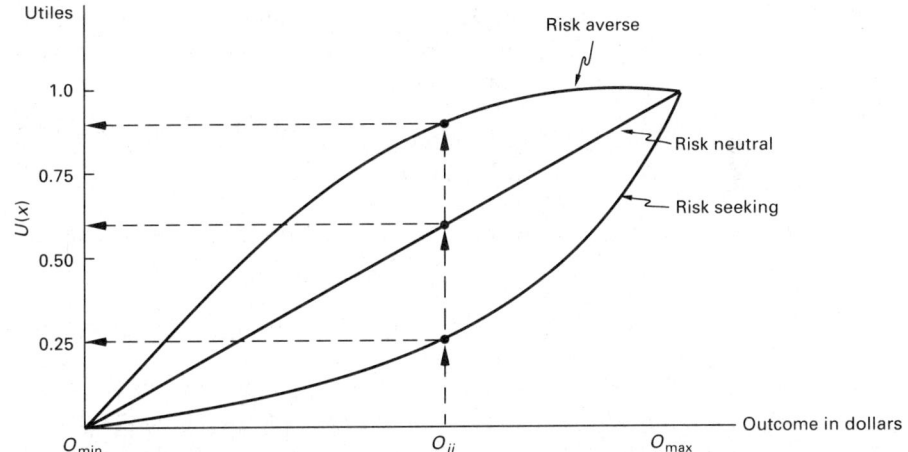

FIGURE 7.6
Three utility functions

UTILITY FUNCTIONS

One approach to capturing a decision maker's attitude toward risk in a particular decision environment is to build his or her utility function over the specified range of outcomes. A utility function U is nothing more than a mathematical device that maps physical outcomes onto dimensionless quantities called **utiles.** The particular range of numbers we choose for the utility scale is of no consequence, but most texts recommend a range from zero to one.

Consider the three utility functions graphed in Figure 7.6. We plotted the range of outcomes in dollars on the horizontal axis, and the range of utiles from zero to one is on the vertical axis. To convert a specific dollar outcome, say O_{ij}, to utiles, one reads straight up from O_{ij} to the appropriate utility curve and then across to its utility equivalent. In the figure, our example outcome O_{ij} is equivalent to about 0.25 utile for the risk seeker, about 0.60 utile for the risk-neutral "EMV-er," and 0.90 for the risk avoider.

To illustrate the effect of the utility transformation, let's return briefly to the futures bundle speculation, whose decision matrix of outcomes we gave previously. Referring again to Figure 7.6, let $O_{min} = -\$6M$ and $O_{max} = +\$9M$, and suppose that our decision maker is now a risk seeker. If the convex utility function (bottom in the figure) represents our decision maker's utility function, we may approximate his or her utility transformation as follows:

$U(-6M) = 0$; $U(-3M) = 0.05$; $U(0) = 0.10$; $U(+9M) = 1$

Computing the **expected utility** of the two alternatives yields

$EU(A_1:$ invest$) = 1(1/8) + 0.1(3/8) + 0.05(3/8) + 0(1/8) = 0.1813$

$EU(A_2:$ don't invest$) = 0.1(1/8) + 0.1(3/8) + 0.1(3/8) + 0.1(1/8) = 0.1$

Therefore, the risk seeker, using the given utility function, might be inclined to pursue this highly speculative investment strategy after all, since

$EU(A_1:$ invest$) > EU(A_2:$ don't invest$)$.

As a second illustration, let us take another look at PEI's oil-drilling problem whose decision matrix of outcomes we gave previously. Now in Figure 7.6, suppose the CEO is actually risk averse (if so, she's in the wrong business!) and that her utility function is the concave utility function (top in the figure). Here, $O_{min} = -\$700,000$ and $O_{max} = +\$2,000,000$, and we are able to approximate the CEO's utility transformation as follows:

$U(-\$700,000) = 0$; $U(0) = 0.50$; $U(+\$500,000) = 0.75$;

$U(+\$2,000,000) = 1$

Computing the expected utility of the two alternatives yields:

$EU(A_1:$ don't drill$) = 0.5(0.50) + 0.5(0.30) + 0.5(0.20) = 0.5$

$EU(A_2:$ drill$) = 0(0.50) + 0.75(0.30) + 1(0.20) = 0.425$

In this case, Dinah's risk-averse situation would reverse the previous EMV analysis and would suggest perhaps that PEI might not decide to drill in this particular situation.

BUILDING UTILITY FUNCTIONS

Researchers have developed several approaches for building the decision maker's utility function, and some of the suggested additional readings at the end of the chapter do an excellent job of discussing and evaluating these techniques. One approach, which we refer to as the lottery technique, is fascinating. We discuss it briefly here and illustrate it in the Jack Legg Associates minicase.

We can best explain the lottery approach in terms of an interactive exchange between the decision maker (DM) and a utility function operator (UFO). First, we assign the least favorable outcome in the decision matrix (O_{min}) a utility of zero (0) and give the most favorable outcome (O_{max}) a utility of one (1), as we did in the preceding discussion. The UFO then presents the DM with the following choice: the lottery shown in the accompanying illustration or the opportunity to sell the lottery for an amount O_1.

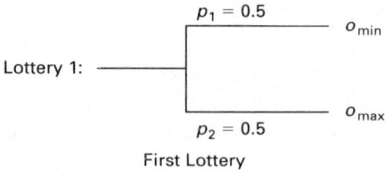

First Lottery

If the DM is risk neutral, he or she would be indifferent between having the lottery itself and receiving the EMV of the lottery—i.e., $O_1 = 0.5(O_{min}) + 0.5(O_{max})$. On the other hand, a risk-averse DM would gladly unload the risky lottery for less than its EMV, while the risk-seeking DM would require a *certain* payoff larger than the EMV to compensate for the foregone opportunity to receive the payoff O_{max}. The idea here is for the risk seeker to determine the *maximum* value of O_1 that would make her or him indifferent between having O_1 or the lottery, and for the risk avoider to determine the *minimum* value at which such indifference occurs. Having obtained the value O_1, and since we know that the expected utility of the lottery is 0.5 [i.e., $0.5U(O_{min}) + 0.5U(O_{max}) = 0.5(0) + 0.5(1) = 0.5$], we now know that $E(U_1) = 0.5$, and we have our third point on the utility curve. We now proceed to analyze additional lotteries similar to the above. Note that if O_2 and O_3 are the indifference amounts for lotteries 2 and 3, respectively, then

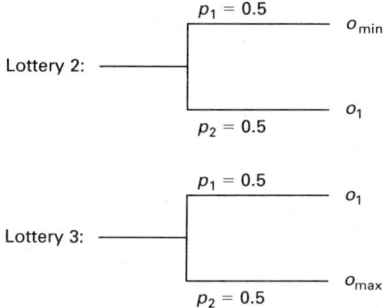

$$U(O_2) = 0.5(0) + 0.5(.5) = 0.25$$
$$U(O_3) = 0.5(.5) + 0.5(1) = 0.75$$

We can continue this process until the shape of the utility curve becomes apparent.

Before discussing briefly some advanced topics in DMUR, let's pause a moment to put the concept of economic utility in perspective. First, utility curves are not necessarily smooth functions like those depicted in Figure 7.6. In fact, if the range of outcomes is sufficiently broad in a given decision environment, the decision maker's utility curve may well be S-shaped—that is, convex (risk seeking) in the lower part of the range, roughly linear (risk neutral) in the middle, and concave (risk avoiding) in the upper part of the range.

However, all utility curves in a DMUR sense have one property: they are monotonically nondecreasing from left to right. All this means is that the decision maker's utility for a certain outcome is never lower than his or her utility for an outcome with a smaller value. As we see, this property reflects the requirement for *transitivity of preference* in DMUR.

STATE OF THE ART IN DMUR

DMUR covers a broad range of decision-making environments, and we have discussed some key basic notions so far. Let's briefly touch on some additional ideas.

CONTINUOUS PRIOR DISTRIBUTIONS

Thus far, we have limited our discussion to discrete prior distributions, and we used the discrete predictive distribution and Bayes's theorem to construct the posterior distribution. In other words, we have dealt with a finite number of states of nature. Suppose, however, we had (for all practical purposes) an infinite number of states of nature, so that our prior distribution is a continuous probability density function. We could, of course, segregate the distribution into a finite number of states and estimate the probabilities associated with them, but it so happens that there is a better way in certain cases.

As an example, Scientific Solutions, Ltd. (SSL) is a small R&D company that is considering bidding on a contract announced by the Environmental Protection Agency (EPA). The contract, which involves developing a monitoring device to detect pollution in rivers, is of the firm-fixed-price variety. That is, the winner will receive an award of $3 million for taking on the project. On similar projects in the past, SSL has experienced costs at the rate of about $200,000 per month, and the company estimates that this project would involve a one-time setup cost of $600,000. Time to completion of similar projects in the past has averaged ten months, with a standard deviation of two months. The distribution of completion times is roughly normal (symmetric, and "not too flat or too peaked").

SSL obviously has one of two choices: bid on the contract or don't bid. Since we know the expected value of completion time (10 months), it is simple to compute the EMV of the alternative bid as follows:

EMV(*bid*) = $3,000,000 − 600,000 − (10)(200,000) = $400,000
(contract)   (setup)   (monthly costs)   (profit)

The EMV of "don't bid" is obviously zero, so if SSL is risk neutral or risk seeking, the DMUR model would indicate "bid" as the best alternative.

However, there is some risk inherent in this decision. Breakeven occurs at 12 months, which is about one standard deviation above the mean. Thus, in a long-run sense, SSL stands to lose money about 15% of the time. How much money is involved? If it required 14 months for completion, SSL would lose $400,000, and this circumstance (or worse) could occur about 5% of the time. Could SSL survive such a loss? How does the company assess its risk in bidding on the EPA contract?

Let's approach the answer to the last question by looking at the opportunity loss. The EOL for the alternative "don't bid" is $400,000—which is the EMV of the alternative "bid." Calculating the EOL for "bid" is somewhat more complicated. The loss function (LF) for this alternative is zero for completion times up to 12 months and linear with a slope of $200,000 (per month) for completion time greater than 12 months. Thus, if t stands for time,

$$\text{LF}(bid) = \begin{cases} 0, & \text{for } t \leq 12 \\ 200{,}000(t-12), & \text{for } t > 12 \end{cases}$$

To compute EOL(bid), therefore, we need to compute the integral of the product of LF(bid) and the normal density function with a mean of 10 and standard deviation of 2. Figure 7.7 illustrates this. Happily, by standardizing this integral, researchers have already computed it for us; the "Unit Normal Loss Integral" tabulations appear in Appendix B.

Let t_B = breakeven point (in our SSL example, t_B = 12 months); k = slope of the loss function (for SSL, k = $200,000); m and s are the mean and standard deviation of the normal distribution (m = 10 and s = 2 for SSL); and $z = |(t_B - m)/s|$, the absolute value of the standardized normal transformation. One first computes z and

CHAPTER 7 A STRUCTURE FOR DECISION MAKING UNDER RISK 273

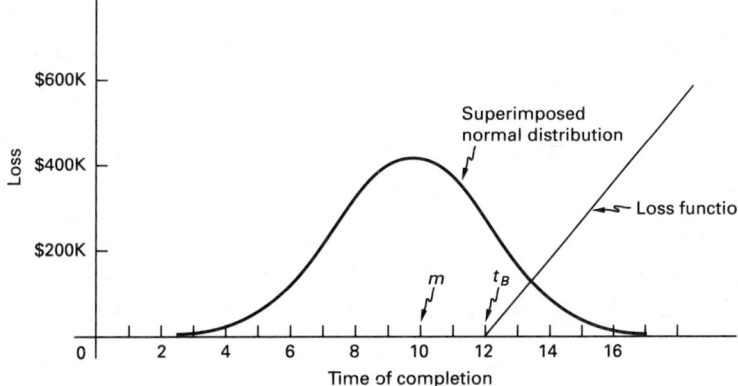

FIGURE 7.7 Loss function for SSL example

then obtains $L_n(z)$—the unit normal loss function value—from the table in Appendix A. In the SSL case, $z = |(12 - 10)/2| = 1$, and $L_n(1) = 0.08332$ from the table. The formula for EOL is

$$\text{EOL} = ksL_n(z)$$

For SSL, therefore,

$$\text{EOL}(bid) = (200{,}000)(2)(0.08332) = \$33{,}328$$

Thus, SSL faces an expected opportunity loss of only $33,328 by bidding, as opposed to $400,000 for not bidding.

This procedure is applicable to any DMUR situation in which there are exactly two alternatives and where we can use a normal distribution to approximate the prior distribution on the states of nature.

THE NEWSBOY MODEL

Consider the problem faced daily by Tab Lloyd, a young entrepreneur who sells the *Daily Times* on the streets of New York City. Each morning Tab buys his supply of papers at 30¢ each and sells them for 50¢ each. There are few things more useless than yesterday's newspapers, but Tab can sell leftover papers for 5¢ each to a rundown hotel that distributes them free to its guests. On the other hand, if Tab runs out before he has supplied his regular clientele, he retains his goodwill by running to a posh Fifth Avenue newsstand and purchasing papers for 95¢ each, selling them to his customers at the usual 50-cent price.

Tab's problem is intriguing: how many papers should he buy each morning? He knows from his CPA that he averages selling 200 papers each day, with a standard deviation of 25 papers. If he buys too few, the cost of goodwill eats into his profits; if he buys too many, the low salvage value for unsold papers will have the same effect.

Suppose we can approximate demand by a normal distribution. Let us recall our basic economics course and the concept of *marginal utility*. Tab would like to know the order quantity q^* such that the marginal utility of ordering exactly one more paper is the same as ordering one less paper. Thus, he needs to perform an **incremental analysis**.

Let:

SP = selling price per unit (50¢ for Tab)

SV = salvage value per unit (5¢)

CP = unit purchase price (30¢)

$$GW = \text{goodwill cost per unit } (45¢ = 95¢ - 50¢)$$

$$L_s = CP - SV = \text{loss incurred in overstocking one unit}$$

$$(25¢ = 30¢ - 5¢)$$

$$L_{ns} = SP - CP + GW = \text{loss incurred in understocking}$$

$$\text{one unit } (65¢ = 50¢ - 30¢ + 45¢)$$

We now wish to find q^* such that the expected value of L_s exactly equals the expected value of L_{ns}. Let p be the probability of L_s occurring, so that $(1 - p)$ is the probability of L_{ns}. We equate the two expected values as follows:

$$pL_s = (1 - p)L_{ns},$$

so that

$$p^* = \frac{L_{ns}}{L_s + L_{ns}}$$

is the "optimal" value of p. In Tab's case,

$$p^* = \frac{65¢}{65¢ + 25¢} = 0.722$$

This means that the optimal order quantity q^* is at the point on the demand distribution at which 0.722 of the cumulative probability occurs. Referring to our standard normal distribution tables in Appendix A, we see that this occurs at about 0.59 standard deviation to the right of the mean, so that

$$q^* = 200 + (0.59)(25) = 214.75 = 215 \text{ papers.}$$

Incremental analysis is not only simple but also logical. If the cost per unit of understocking is higher than the unit cost for overstocking, common sense tells us that we would probably be wise to stock more than average demand. The model gives us a way to compute this quantity.

ON THE FRONTIER

Researchers publish dozens of articles each year on the subject of statistical decision theory. Some of the research on the frontier of this subject includes the following:

1. **Building multiattribute utility functions.** Researchers are seeking ways to reflect decision makers' risk environments along several dimensions—e.g., monetary outcome, time of project completion, quality of output—by building utility functions in several dimensions.
2. **Assessing dynamic risk preference.** The timing of cash flows for projects affects their riskiness even though the aggregate outcomes may be identical. Researchers are investigating utility structures that can incorporate the time effect.
3. **Improving techniques for constructing utility functions.** The lottery method has many disadvantages, and researchers are looking for better, more dependable methods for constructing decision makers' utility functions.
4. **Assessing the value of information when we use a continuous prior distribution.** When we use a continuous prior distribution, the "distribution of predictive accuracy" must be in the form of a continuous **bivariate** (i.e., two jointly distributed random variables) distribution, as is the posterior. We

know that a normally distributed prior distribution leads to a bivariate normal posterior distribution. We also know other such relationships, but in general it is tricky or even impossible to describe the posterior distribution for general kinds of prior distributions. Researchers (mostly mathematical statisticians and economists) are studying this phenomenon.

MINICASES

Jack Legg Associates

THE SCENARIO

Hy Roller and Nawonda Betts are both engineering project managers for Jack Legg Associates (JLA), a high-technology consulting firm. Hy is an engineer and an MBA, is unmarried, and is ambitious, aggressive, and bucking for promotion into general management at JLA. He is also a devotee of fast cars, fine restaurants, and the "good life" in general. Nawonda, on the other hand, is supporting her husband (a doctoral student in medieval English literature), three children, and her mother-in-law.

JLA assigns each engineering project manager an average of three projects each year. Since the projects are almost always state of the art, the number of successful projects for each manager tends to follow a binomial distribution, with p approximately equal to 0.50. Thus, there is a probability of 0.125 that a given manager has no successful projects in a given year and an equal probability that there will be three successes. The probability of one or two successful projects is 0.375.

THE PROBLEM

JLA now pays its project managers an annual salary of $35,000, but Mr. Legg has decided to offer his managers a choice of three compensation plans based upon the number of successful projects (see Table 7.12). Once an engineer selects a compensation plan, he or she cannot change it for the year. The problem facing Hy and Nawonda is which compensation plan to choose.

TABLE 7.12 JLA compensation plans

		\multicolumn{4}{c}{No. of Successful Projects}			
		S_1:0	S_2:1	S_3:2	S_4:3
	Pr(S_j)	0.125	0.375	0.375	0.125
Alternatives	A_1: Plan A	$35,000	$35,000	$35,000	$35,000
	A_2: Plan B	21,000	35,000	42,000	49,000
	A_3: Plan C	7,000	28,000	42,000	70,000

FIGURE 7.8
SAMS input screen for Jack Legg (EMV)

```
┌──→ SAMS INPUT SCREEN - DMUR Matrix Module   ←──┐
│    NAME?  Jack Legg Associates                  │
│    MAximize or MInimize?  MA                    │
│    Information Available?  NO    If YES, Cost? │
│    PROBLEM DESCRIPTION - Decide which JLA compensation
│    plan to accept for next year.                │
├─────────────┬─────────┬─────────┬─────────┬─────┤
│ States      │ 0PROJ   │ 1PROJ   │ 2PROJ   │ 3PROJ│
│ Prior Dist. │  .125   │  .375   │  .375   │  .125│
├─────────────┴─────────┴─────────┴─────────┴─────┤
│ Alternatives              Outcomes              │
│   PLANA      35000.   35000.   35000.   35000.  │
│   PLANB      21000.   35000.   42000.   49000.  │
│   PLANC       7000.   28000.   42000.   70000.  │
└─────────────────────────────────────────────────┘
```

TABLE 7.13

JACK LEGG
FULL BRIEFING ON OPTIMAL MODEL SOLUTION
Optimal Objective Value = 37625

Alternative	EMV	EOL	Optimal
PLANA	35000.00	7000.00	No
PLANB	37625.00	4375.00	Yes
PLANC	35875.00	6125.00	No

EVPI: 4375   EMVPI: 42000

THE MODEL

If Hy and Nawonda were both risk-neutral decision makers, the EMV criterion in a DMUR model might be an appropriate analytical approach to this problem.

SOLUTION TO THE MODEL

We use SAMS' DMUR matrix module to perform our analysis, and Figure 7.8 shows the input screen. Table 7.13 presents the SAMS briefing for this analysis.

We note that no alternative is dominated. Thus, for a risk-neutral decision maker, the model recommends A_2: Plan B, which has a slight edge over Plan A and Plan C, with an expected payoff of $37,625 in annual salary. However, the assumption that Hy Roller and Nawonda Betts have similar risk preferences—and that their preferences are risk neutral—would appear to be suspect. After discussing the situation, both Hy and Nawonda made an appointment with Mona Tonic, JLA's management scientist. We eavesdropped during their visit, and the gist of their discussion follows.

SOLUTION TO THE PROBLEM

MONA: OK, Hy and Nawonda, so you want to construct your personal utility functions to help you decide which compensation plan to choose. Let's see—the minimum and maximum outcomes are $7,000 and $70,000, respectively, so we'll start by assigning them values of zero and one utiles. Now—suppose that in lieu of your annual salaries, each of you owns a copy of the following lottery:

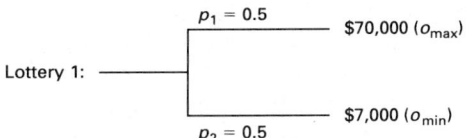

Tell me the annual salary you'd accept for certain in lieu of having the lottery.

NAWONDA: Oh, my, the idea of having a 50/50 chance of making only $7,000 next year terrifies me! Let's see, though, the expected value of the lottery is $38,500—I'd certainly take less than that. My family could squeak by on about $20,000, so I suppose that's the least I'd accept.

HY: Wow—a 50/50 chance at 70 grand! That makes the lottery awfully hard to part with. Still, I'm not a complete idiot—getting only $7,000 next year would cramp my style. I guess I'd trade it for about $55,000, but reluctantly.

MONA: O.K. Nawonda and Hy, we've gotten three points on each of your utility curves. Let's get two more. Again, you each own a lottery (Lottery 2 in accompanying illustration). Notice that I have to give you each a different lottery this time.

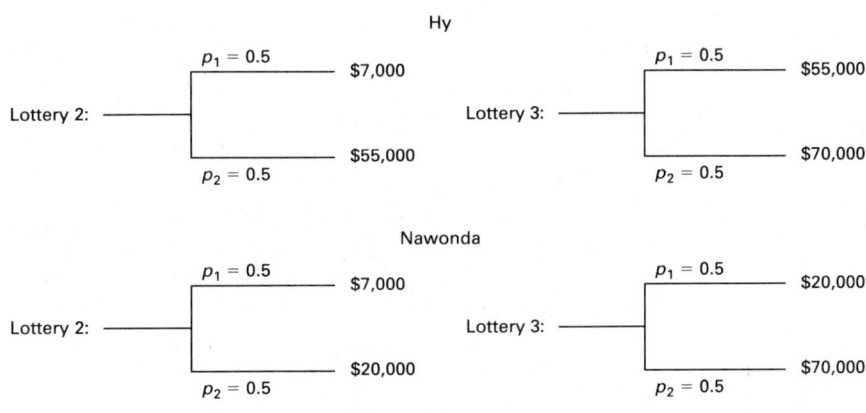

HY: Well, this is tougher to analyze than the first one. On Lottery 2, I guess I'd part with it for around $40,000, but I'd have to have $65,000 to let go of Lottery 3.

NAWONDA: My goodness—Lottery 2 is dismal. And Hy is right, this is more difficult than the first one. Again, $7,000 would be a disaster, so I guess I'd trade my Lottery 2 for about $12,000. My husband would

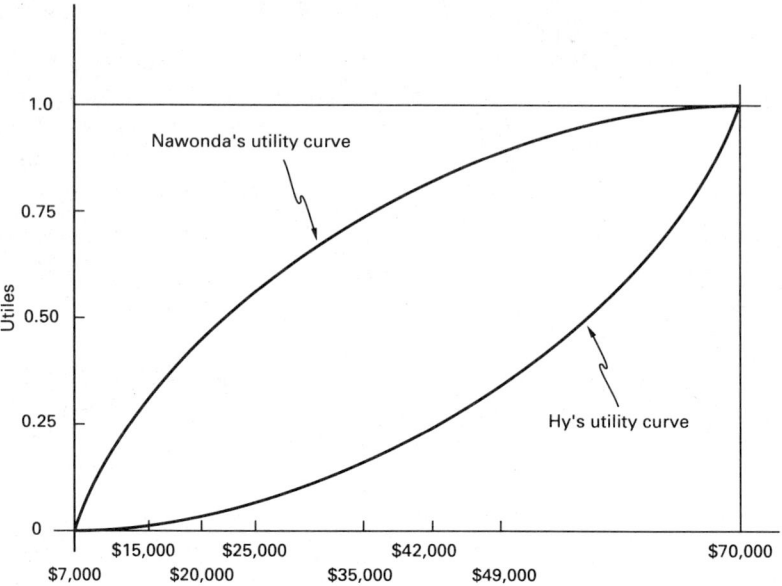

FIGURE 7.9
Utility functions

TABLE 7.14 Nawonda's decision matrix

		No. of Successful Projects			
		S_1:0	S_2:1	S_3:2	S_4:3
	Pr(S_j)	0.125	0.375	0.375	0.125
Alternatives	A_1: Plan A	0.750	0.750	0.750	0.750
	A_2: Plan B	0.517	0.750	0.800	0.850
	A_3: Plan C	0	0.633	0.800	1.000

have to sell his new Porsche, but we could make it. As for Lottery 3, I'd take $35,000 in a minute if I owned it for real.

MONA: (After a short pause) All right, I've plotted all five points on both of your utility functions and sketched in smooth curves joining them [Figure 7.9]. You two are classical examples of risk-seeking (Hy) and risk-averse (Nawonda) decision makers in this range of outcomes. We could continue the lottery business, but I think we have what you need already.

NAWONDA: Thanks a lot, Mona, you've been a great help. I guess our next step is to replace the various salary levels in the three salary plans with their equivalent utilities and compute expected utilities for each plan.

HY: Yes. Thanks, Mona.

Tables 7.14 and 7.15 give Hy's and Nawonda's decision matrices, respectively, with salary levels replaced by their respective utilities. Table 7.16 presents output from the SAMS DMUR matrix module *in utiles.*

TABLE 7.15 Hy's decision matrix

		No. of Successful Projects			
		S_1:0	S_2:1	S_3:2	S_4:3
	$Pr(S_j)$	0.125	0.375	0.375	0.125
Alternatives	A_1: Plan A	0.212	0.212	0.212	0.212
	A_2: Plan B	0.106	0.212	0.283	0.400
	A_3: Plan C	0	0.159	0.283	1.000

TABLE 7.16

JACK LEGG—NAWONDA (EU)
FULL BRIEFING ON OPTIMAL MODEL SOLUTION
Optimal Objective Value = 0.7522

Alternative	EMV	EOL	Optimal
PLANA	0.7500	0.0500	No
PLANB	0.7522	0.0479	Yes
PLANC	0.6624	0.1376	No

EVPI: 0.0479   EMVPI: 0.8001

JACK LEGG—HY (EU)
FULL BRIEFING ON OPTIMAL MODEL SOLUTION
Optimal Objective Value = 0.2907

Alternative	EMV	EOL	Optimal
PLANA	0.2120	0.1450	No
PLANB	0.2489	0.0883	No
PLANC	0.2907	0.0464	Yes

EVPI: 0.0464   EMVPI: 0.3371

In Nawonda Betts's case, only one conclusion is clear—Plan C (A_3) involves an unacceptable level of risk in her situation. Plans A and B have expected utilities that are so similar that a decision is too close to call based only on the results of the model. Plan B (A_2) was the optimal alternative in a risk-neutral sense, and it has a slight edge in Nawonda's analysis over Plan A. However, after consulting with her husband, children, and mother-in-law, Nawonda decides to go with the riskless choice of $35,000 certain ($A_1$).

Hy Roller confidently chose Plan C (A$_3$) as the model suggested that he should. His personal situation and proclivities made this high level of risk acceptable, and the worst outcome for him would not be disastrous—only temporarily inconvenient. ■

High Tor [17]

THE SCENARIO

The 25,000 students of High Tor University (HTU) and the 200,000 "townies" of its home in the West Texas city of Mountain View are rabid fans of college football. The High Tor Mountain Goats team has had its share of winning and losing seasons over the years, but the fans have been loyal through thick and thin. The Mountain Goats play four conference and two nonconference games at home each fall. Needless to say, every game is sold out.

One tradition at HTU is that student organizations sell the colorful game programs to fans inside and outside the entrances to the stadium on game days, with profits supporting various charitable causes. Certain organizations, by virtue of their size and tenure, have established territories for program sales. For example, the Downhill Skiing Association sells programs at the east entrance, while the Yodelers Club owns "rights" to the north end zone entrance. Fans who wish to support a specific student organization try to purchase their programs from its representatives.

THE PROBLEM

The High Tor Athletic Department prepares the copy for each home game program, and the HTU Press does the layout and printing. Done on slick paper in full color, the football programs are lavish, 32-page publications that contain pictures and short biographies of both HTU and the opponents' players, statistical histories, and other background information. Many fans own complete sets of programs for many years back and consider their collections to be of inestimable value.

Student organizations purchase their supply of programs at a price of $1.40 per program from HTU Press the Friday before each home game. They sell programs to fans for $3.00 each. If a student organization has unsold programs left over after a game, it sells them to a jobber for $0.80 each. On the other hand, if the organization's supply runs out before all fans have arrived, potential profit is lost.

One student organization—the Mountain Business Alliance (MBA)—is studying this problem. "It seems to me," said Jean-Claude Kelly at a recent MBA meeting, "that customer loyalty is the key to success in the program business. But if we sell out our stock and just shrug our shoulders to loyal buyers, they won't be loyal buyers for long. I think that we should send a runner to another location and buy one from another group—maybe even at a premium—to satisfy our customer. If we offered, say, $3.50 per copy, the other student groups aren't smart enough to figure out what we're up to and would be happy with the short-term increase to their bottom line."

"Good idea," observed Dawn Hill, "but how many programs should we buy each Friday before the home game? If there is a cost associated with having too many programs and another cost associated with having too few programs, there must be a best number to buy from HTU Press. Our average demand in the past has been 5,000 programs per game, with a standard deviation of about 800 programs."

THE MODEL

The MBA modeled this problem in incremental analysis as a Newsboy Problem. Let

CP = $1.40 per program from HTU Press

SP = $3.00 price to fans

SV = $0.80 price to jobber

GW = $3.50 − $3.00 = $0.50

SOLUTION TO THE MODEL

Here

$$L_s = CP - SV = \$1.40 - \$.80 = \$.60$$
$$L_{ns} = SP - CP + GW = \$3.00 - \$1.40 + \$.50 = \$2.10$$

Thus,

$$p^* = \frac{L_{ns}}{L_s + L_{ns}} = \frac{2.10}{0.60 + 2.10} = 0.778.$$

A cumulative normal probability of 0.778 lies about 0.77 standard deviation to the right of the mean, so that the order quantity recommended by the newsboy model is

$$q^* = 5{,}000 + 0.778(800) = 5{,}622$$

Thus, the model indicates that the MBA should order 5,622 programs from High Tor University Press each Friday before home games to minimize its opportunity loss over the long run.

SOLUTION TO THE PROBLEM

The MBA must exercise great care in applying the newsboy model to its problem. Table 7.17 contains an economic analysis of results at various levels of demand between −3 and +3 standard deviations of demand for the football programs.

TABLE 7.17 Economic analysis at various demand levels

	Revenues		Program Costs		
Demand	Sales	Salvage	Press	Competition	Profit
2,600 (−3s)	$ 7,800	$2,272	$7,896	-0-	$2,176
3,400 (−2s)	10,200	1,792	7,896	-0-	4,096
4,200 (−1s)	12,600	1,152	7,896	-0-	5,856
5,000 (m)	15,000	512	7,896	-0-	7,616
5,622 (q^*)	16,866	-0-	7,871	-0-	8,995
5,800 (+1s)	17,400	-0-	7,896	560	8,944
6,600 (+2s)	19,800	-0-	7,896	3,360	8,544
7,400 (+3s)	22,200	-0-	7,896	6,160	8,144

King Cotton [15]

THE SCENARIO

The 21-county area surrounding Lubbock, Texas (the South Plains), is one of the world's largest cotton-producing areas, accounting for half of Texas' output and more than 14% of the cotton crop in the United States. In 1989, South Plains farmers cultivated 2.4 million acres of cotton using irrigation and 0.8 million acres of dry-land cotton. Yield differences between the two methods are substantial, with irrigated cotton producing an average of 600 pounds per acre, as opposed to only 258 pounds per acre in nonirrigated fields [7].

THE PROBLEM

Assuming perfect weather conditions, irrigating twice—once in the early summer and once again near August 15—yields cotton of maximum quantity as well as quality. However, if significant rainfall occurs after the second irrigation, the plants create more vegetative growth rather than maturing. This causes the cotton plant to create more bolls than it can develop fully before the first freeze kills it. Thus, not only is yield lowered by too much water, but the plants generate a great deal of vegetative "trash" that lowers the grade (and thus the price received) of the cotton when harvested.

Irrigation costs have soared in recent years because of the price increase in natural gas, which is the fuel used to run irrigation pumps. South Plains farmers therefore have a difficult decision to make each year in early August—to irrigate again or not to irrigate. If early fall rains are sparse, the decision to irrigate will result in much higher yields and better quality cotton. The decision not to irrigate will be fortuitous if subsequent rains are substantial, in effect irrigating the cotton at no expense to the farmer.

THE MODEL

This author modeled this problem as a DMUR situation with two alternatives (irrigate again before August 15 and don't irrigate) and three states of nature (less than one inch of rain in late summer, one to three inches, and more than three inches). He derived the prior distribution on the states of nature from historical weather information in the area. He generated the conditional distribution of predictive accuracy by comparing USDA weather forecasts over a 12-year period, with the actual rainfall subsequently experienced. He calculated the outcomes for each alternative and state of nature combination for a 3000-acre farm using the results of a study by Adams [1]. Table 7.18 gives the decision matrix and the conditional distribution of predictive accuracy.

SOLUTION TO THE MODEL

Table 7.19 presents the SAMS full briefing for the solution to this model. The DMUR model recommends irrigating when the forecast is for less than three inches of rain and not irrigating when more than three inches of rain is forecast. The EMV using sample

TABLE 7.18 Decision matrix

		Amount of Rainfall*		
		S_1: <1"	S_2: 1" ≤ 3"	S_3: >3"
	$Pr(S_j)$	0.50	0.33	0.17
Alternatives	A_1: irrigate	$1,070,800	$584,800	$422,800
	A_2: don't irr.	$ 472,500	$810,000	$648,000

*Outcomes are in revenues net of irrigation costs, if any.

Conditional distribution of predictive accuracy

		Predicted States of Nature			
		I_1	I_2	I_3	
Actual	S_1	0.50	0.50	0.00	
States of	S_2	0.00	0.75	0.25	$Pr(I_i\|S_j)$
Nature	S_3	0.00	0.50	0.50	

TABLE 7.19

**KING COTTON WITH INFORMATION
FULL BRIEFING ON OPTIMAL MODEL SOLUTION**

Information is worth	37721.0 (EVSI)
Information costs	0.0
Expected net gain from sampling	37721.0

Recommend Buying Information

If Information Is Bought

Prediction	Recommend
If I1, then	IRRIGATE
If I2, then	IRRIGATE
If I3, then	DONTIRRI

Expected net payoff = 837981

If Information Is Not Bought

IRRIGATE

Expected payoff = 800260

information turns out to be $837,981. It is interesting to note that without additional information, the EMVs are as follows:

EMV(irrigate) = $800,260

EMV(don't irrigate) = $613,710

Thus, the information obtainable from weather forecast records is worth (in the long run) about $37,721 = $837,981 − $800,260. The EMVPI is $912,860, so that the value of perfect information (obviously unobtainable) is $112,600. Thus, the weather forecast information is not very efficient and probably not worth the effort to retrieve it.

SOLUTION TO THE PROBLEM

The family of the MBA student who conducted this project is actually in the cotton farming business, and his father found the conclusions of the study to be logical and intuitively appealing. It seems clear that the forecast by the weather service of a drought (<1″) would indicate that he should apply a second irrigation. It is equally clear that the forecast of more than 3 inches of rain (a monsoon for West Texas!) would indicate that he should not do a second irrigation. However, it is not at all clear what the appropriate action would be given an intermediate forecast (1″–3″). As irrigation costs rise, the difference between the financial outcomes of A_1: irrigate and A_2: don't irrigate narrow. As usual, this DMUR model has done nothing more than provide useful insight to the decision maker. ■

D-Day [4]

PROLOGUE

There is no historical evidence to suggest that the Allied High Command used a formal decision analysis to plan the 1944 invasion of Europe. This minicase uses historical facts to reconstruct the decision to mount an amphibious landing on the beaches of Normandy. The DMUR analysis supports the correctness of the decision.

THE SCENARIO

As World War II entered 1944, General Dwight D. Eisenhower, who was supreme commander of the Allied forces in Europe, had begun to bring massive quantities of military hardware and personnel under his control. The invasion of continental Europe was imminent, since without it the war could drag on for many years. Although the Allies possessed a clear quantitative advantage over the Nazis, German panzers (tanks) and self-propelled antitank weapons were clearly superior qualitatively.

Another major factor was the quality and reliability of military intelligence. Throughout the war, Allied spies and underground workers behind enemy lines had been invaluable. Now—on the verge of the greatest military operation the world has ever known—the Allied High Command would need to place great faith in the accuracy of reports of Nazi strength and activity. Operation Overlord had begun.

THE PROBLEM

Two facts were clear to both the Allies and the Nazis: the invasion would be an amphibious assault somewhere along the coast of France, and it would be mounted in the summer of 1944. A myriad of invasion sites were possible. In selecting a site, the Allied High Command had to consider the following factors (among others):

1. The Allies needed large, open beaches whose approaches could be defended by the large guns of battleships at sea.
2. The beaches would have to be suitable for prolonged operations, with many troops landing simultaneously.
3. The beaches must be near a major port to facilitate a rapid support buildup after the landings.
4. The terrain between the landing site and the German heartland must be capable of supporting large armies moving at a rapid pace.
5. The site must be reachable by British and American air power, which by this time was clearly superior to that of the Luftwaffe (Nazi air force).

Landing sites that met the five criteria above were Calais, Cherbourg, Le Havre, Normandy, the Somme-Calais area, the Caen-Cherbourg area, and the area between Le Havre and Calais.

Clearly, the German forces could not defend the entire coast of France, so the task of the German High Command was to anticipate the site of the invasion and to concentrate its defensive forces there. Early in 1944, Adolf Hitler and Field Marshal Erwin Rommel were convinced that the invasion would come at Normandy. The rest of the German staff were certain that the attack would come between Le Havre and Calais.

THE MODEL

If we pose General Eisenhower's problem as one under risk, history tells us that he narrowed the sites acceptable for an amphibious landing to the following four:

A_1: Normandy
A_2: Calais
A_3: Cherbourg
A_4: Le Havre

Assuming that the German High Command deduced these four choices, their decision—which site to defend—becomes the four probabilistic states of nature in the decision matrix:

S_1: defend Normandy
S_2: defend Calais
S_3: defend Cherbourg
S_4: defend Le Havre

Inferring the prior probability density function on the states of nature is a matter of assessing intelligence available to the Allied High Command in Spring 1944. The Allies knew, for example, that the German High Command favored defending Calais over Normandy by a 2:1 ratio. They also knew that the Nazis would more likely defend Le Havre than Normandy. Cherbourg was the least likely site because this major port would all but be destroyed in an invasion. These inferences produce the following prior distribution:

$Pr(S_1) = 0.20 \quad Pr(S_2) = 0.40 \quad Pr(S_3) = 0.15 \quad Pr(S_4) = 0.25$

The grim "outcomes" in this decision matrix are the excess of German casualties over Allied casualties resulting from the invasion. We extrapolated the known results to obtain estimates for the other 15 combinations, and Table 7.20 presents the full DMUR decision matrix:

TABLE 7.20 D-Day decision matrix

	S_1	S_2	S_3	S_4
Prior	0.20	0.40	0.15	0.25
A_1	−137,000	175,000	93,000	65,000
A_2	145,000	−170,000	196,000	38,000
A_3	40,000	106,000	−170,000	62,000
A_4	30,000	72,000	105,000	−110,000

SOLUTION TO THE MODEL

We used the SAMS DMUR matrix module to compute the EMV and EOL values associated with each alternative, which are summarized in the following table:

Landing Sites	EMV	EOL
A_1: Normandy	72,800	71,850
A_2: Calais	− 100	144,750
A_3: Cherbourg	40,400	104,250
A_4: Le Havre	23,050	121,600

Normandy is the clear choice of the DMUR matrix model as the invasion site, while Calais is the worst selection. Note also the very high value of EOL associated with A_1: Normandy. Since EOL = EVPI (expected value of perfect information) and since the outcomes are in **differential casualties,** the value of additional intelligence information is immense in terms of decreasing Allied casualties.

SOLUTION TO THE PROBLEM

In late Spring 1944, the Allied High Command learned of the German expectation of an invasion at Calais. From then until June 5, the Allies tried to reinforce that expectation by flying twice as many strategic bombing missions over Calais than over Normandy. They "leaked" false information to further strengthen this belief in the German High Command.

On June 6, 1944 (D-Day), 156,000 men, 5,000 ships, and 11,000 planes were deployed in the initial assault on Normandy. Because the German High Command had concentrated its defenses to protect Calais, there were only 9,000 casualties in the initial assault. By the end of the battle for Normandy, more than two million American, British, Canadian, and Polish troops had disembarked in Normandy at beaches code named Utah, Omaha, Gold, Juno, and Sword. The drive from Normandy into the German heartland ended the war in Europe.

SUMMARY

In this chapter, we have introduced a basic model for analyzing certain problems in decision making under risk (DMUR). We used two basic criteria—expected monetary value (EMV) and expected opportunity loss (EOL)—to evaluate alternative actions. Noting that the optimal EOL is the expected value of perfect information, we then explored ways of incorporating imperfect information into our model through the use of Bayes's theorem.

We then explored the concept of economic utility at some length and discussed methods for building individual decision makers' utility functions. We showed that the expected utility criterion incorporates both problem information and risk attitude of the decision maker into the same evaluation model.

Our tour through DMUR modeling concluded with a look at the evaluation of situations involving continuous distributions on the states of nature, using the unit normal loss integral and incremental analysis. We peeked briefly at the frontiers of research in this area before presenting four minicases.

KEY TERMS

alternatives
bivariate
conditional distribution of predictive accuracy
decision making under risk
decision tree
Delphi technique
dominate
expected monetary value (EMV)
expected opportunity loss (EOL)
expected utility

expected value
incremental analysis
intransitive preference
outcomes
payoffs
posterior distribution
predictive distribution
prior distribution
states of nature
utiles

PROBLEMS FOR ANALYSIS

1. **The Scenario** [2]: Virginia Power, Inc. (VPI) is a publicly held regulated monopoly, with an obligation to provide reliable electric service to its customers. State government entities specify both the rate of return that VPI can earn and the rates that it can charge. Since the latter is rarely high enough to achieve the former, the company must rely on cost containment and operating efficiencies to maximize the return to its shareholders. It is a challenging managerial environment.

   The Problem: VPI forecasts demand years into the future in its efforts to provide reliable electric service to its customers. If demand is forecast to exceed its current capacity, VPI must plan to acquire new sources of power. Alternative A is to build new power generation facilities, with the current options as follows:

A_1: nuclear
A_2: coal
A_3: oil
A_4: hydroelectric

Alternative B is to purchase excess power from other utility companies.

Both major alternatives have their advantages and disadvantages. For example, adding new capacity is highly capital intensive and requires very long lead times but has the overall effect of modernizing VPI's plant facilities. Purchasing unused capacity from other utility companies allows the company to preserve capital and avoid bonded indebtedness but is expensive in terms of operating funds.

One approach to analyzing this problem is to compare the net present values (NPV) of total (construction + fuel) costs of the four construction options and the option to purchase excess power from other utility companies. Two factors complicate this approach:

1. Construction costs vary considerably depending upon whether construction is completed on schedule or behind schedule.
2. Operating costs vary with the costs of fuel.

Table 7.21 gives the NPVs (in $ billions, discounted at 3% per annum) associated with each of the five alternatives, two construction outcomes, and three fuel cost patterns for a ten-year period.

The Model: Note that with the exception of probability distributions on fuel prices and construction completion, we have all of the ingredients for a decision tree, or two-stage decision model. Figure 7.10 shows the tree, with probabilities estimated by a forecasting model.

a. Comment on the appropriateness of the EMV (EOL) criterion for analyzing this problem. Is a large regulated public utility necessarily risk neutral with respect to the problem of long-range capacity planning?

Solution to the Model:
a. Place the outcomes from Table 7.21 onto the appropriate branches of the tree in Figure 7.10. Use a DMUR matrix or decision tree module to analyze this model. What is the optimal model alternative? (*Hint:* Remember that VPI is attempting to *minimize* its costs.)

TABLE 7.21 10-year net present values of total cost

Fuel Costs	Nuclear		Coal		Oil		Hydroelectric		Buy
	OT*	Late	OT*	Late	OT*	Late	OT*	Late	
Up 5%	2.36	3.49	1.85	2.11	3.98	3.82	2.64	3.04	2.53
Same	2.28	3.41	1.61	1.87	3.22	3.06	2.48	2.88	1.98
Down 5%	2.22	3.40	1.42	1.69	2.69	2.48	2.36	2.76	1.57

*OT = on time.

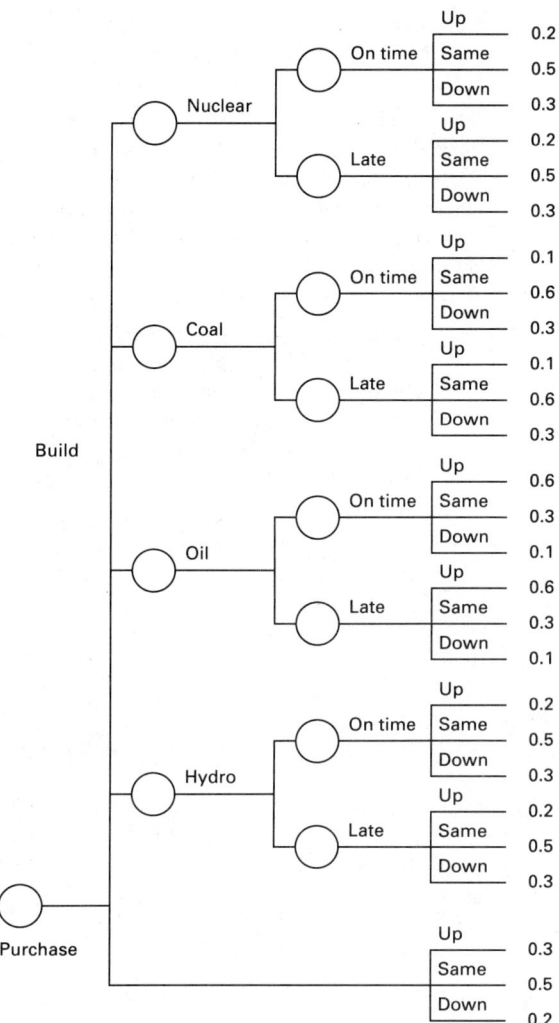

FIGURE 7.10
Virginia power decision tree

b. Write a professional business memorandum to Mr. Browne Ott, who is VPI's vice president for Strategic Planning, explaining in lay terms what this model recommends. In composing your memo, keep in mind that Mr. Ott is *not a management scientist*, so that jargon like "EMV" and "DMUR" are meaningless to him. Also keep in mind that models don't make decisions—managers do.

Solution to the Problem:
a. Examine the outcomes associated with A_2: coal compared with the outcomes of the other four alternatives. Note that the on-time alternatives for A_2 **dominate** (are uniformly lower than) all other alternatives except for purchasing excess power in a situation of decreasing fuel rates. In light of this fact, what value might this model be to a decision maker? Might this analysis be useful in convincing the board of directors of VPI of the proper course of action in capacity planning?

2. **The Scenario** [10]: Luke A. Head, an ambitious and hard-working young man in his early twenties, is employed full-time as a salesman while enrolled in an MBA program. He had sold his home and moved his family (his wife and two small children) into an apartment to make ends meet. His employer provides an automobile, which

he is allowed to use for personal convenience as well as for business purposes. His undergraduate degree is a BBA in Finance, and he is using his nine hours of electives in the MBA program to increase his depth in finance.

The Problem: Luke netted $10,000 (after expenses and taxes) from the sale of his small house. In the next 30 months, while he is making progress toward the coveted MBA, he needs to invest this money wisely. His first purchase after graduation must be an automobile, so he cannot risk losing an appreciable portion of the $10,000.

The 2.5-year investment horizon eliminated long-term investments from consideration; his investment must be cashable when needed in 30 months. Luke narrowed his choices to five, as follows:

(A_1): **Six-month money market certificates** require a 10,000-dollar investment and currently pay interest at the rate of 13.226 percent. The advantage of this instrument is that since one must renew it every six months, its payout fluctuates with the economy—and therefore keeps up with inflation. The disadvantages are that interest does not compound and one must pay income taxes on interest earned.

(A_2): **The 2.5-year certificate of deposit** requires a minimum deposit of $1,000 and pays 14.05% interest (compounded quarterly). However, early withdrawal in case of an emergency involves penalty loss of 180 days of interest. Proceeds are also taxable.

(A_3): **One-year all-savers certificates** come in minimum 1,000-dollar denominations. Although this instrument pays interest at only 10.79%, the first $2,000 of interest earned is tax-sheltered. Interest is compounded quarterly.

(A_4): **Real estate rental property** is an interesting option. A down payment of $10,000 will purchase a 40,000-dollar duplex that Luke can rent at reasonable rates to fellow MBA students. Rent would cover mortgage payments, insurance, property taxes, and upkeep. The advantages of this option are favorable tax treatment of rental property and rising land values in the vicinity of the university. Disadvantages associated with property ownership include tenant turnover, late (or defaulted) rental payments, and such unforeseen circumstances as having to respond at odd hours to electrical or plumbing problems. Moreover, any profit from the sale of the house in 30 months would be subject to capital gains taxes.

(A_5): **A passbook savings account** is Luke's fifth option. Such an account yields only 5.5% (compounded daily), but it has the advantage that funds are completely safe and immediately available if needed.

The Model: Luke recalled from his portfolio class that linear programming is used widely to optimize investment mix in portfolios. In his case, however, it wasn't a question of mix, since he had only $10,000 and since his first and fourth alternatives are all-or-nothing investments. Besides, there was a significant element of risk in his problem that he couldn't ignore.

Luke decided to try a DMUR matrix model, with the level of the prime rate over the 30-month period serving as a surrogate for risk and defining the states of nature, as follows:

S_1: significant decrease in the present prime to 12%
S_2: moderate decrease in the prime to 14%
S_3: present prime rate of 16%
S_4: moderate increase in the prime rate to 18%
S_5: significant increase in the prime rate to 20%

To estimate a prior distribution on the five states of nature, Luke turned to a special report by Raoul Edwards [8], as follows:

State	S_1	S_2	S_3	S_4	S_5
Pr(S_j)	0.20	0.30	0.35	0.10	0.05

Luke then used interest rate and tax information, historical performance of the local real estate market, and an ample dash of intuition in computing the 25 outcomes for the matrix. All numbers are 30-month results net of expenses and taxes. Table 7.22 presents the complete decision matrix.

TABLE 7.22

	S_1	S_2	S_3	S_4	S_5
Pr(S_j)	0.20	0.30	0.35	0.10	0.05
A_1	$ 2,155	$2,403	$2,427	$2,875	$3,140
A_2	2,947	2,947	2,947	2,947	2,947
A_3	2,090	2,375	2,428	2,987	3,319
A_4	11,596	7,594	2,514	1,810	1,081
A_5	1,188	1,188	1,188	1,188	1,188

a. Do you agree with Luke's decision to model his investment problem as a DMUR matrix model? Why or why not?

b. Note that A_1, A_2, and A_3 "dominate" A_5 (that is, their outcomes are uniformly better regardless of the state). Would *the model* ever select A_5 as its optimal solution? Might *Luke* select A_5 as *his* optimal solution?

Solution to the Model:

a. Use a DMUR matrix module to compute the expected monetary values (EMV) and the expected opportunity loss (EOL) of the five alternatives. Assuming that Luke A. Head is risk neutral, what alternative does the model recommend as best on these two criteria?

b. Not surprisingly, Luke happens to be very risk averse in this situation. Use the risk-averse utility function in Figure 7.6 to convert Luke's outcomes to utiles and repeat the analysis as in (a). What alternative does the model now indicate as optimal?

[*Note:* We return to this minicase in Chapter 13 and deal with this decision as a decision making under uncertainty (DMUU) problem.]

3. **The Scenario [6]:** In days of yore in a faraway land, three thieves managed to purloin the famous Ruby of Rangadoon. Hiding in a cave, they sat in a circle about the large red jewel, greedily reflecting upon the thousands of drachmas they could get from its sale.

The Problem: None of the thieves would have trusted the other two outside his sight. All knew that the Ruby of Rangadoon was "hot" and could not be sold for several months. If they stayed in the cave, they were sure to be caught. If they left, the stone would have to be in one thief's possession—a situation they devoutly wished to avoid. Our errant felons were caught in a dilemma.

The Model: Finally Malodor, the most cunning of the three, spoke up. "This is hopeless. Our only course is to gamble for the ruby—winner take all. As a matter of fact, I have three dice in my pocket that we can use."

The dice were curious indeed—one yellow, one red, and one blue. Even more curious, their six sides were numbered as follows:

$$\text{Yellow: 2, 2, 2, 5, 5, 5}$$
$$\text{Red: 1, 4, 4, 4, 4, 4}$$
$$\text{Blue: 3, 3, 3, 3, 6, 6}$$

"Here's the proposition," said Malodor. "You two pick a die apiece and I'll take the one that's left. To make it fair, you two cast your dice against each other, and the one with the higher number then casts with me—again, the one with the higher number wins the ruby. You two should flip a drachma—the winner gets his choice of the die he wants."

Solution to the Model: Diabolus correctly called "camel" as the drachma was flipped and paused to think before selecting a die. If he selected the yellow one and Larcenius picked the blue one, Larcenius would win on 24 of the 36 possible combinations. Diabolus reached for the blue cube but stopped to consider that the red cube would beat the blue one on 20 of the 36 possible combinations. Only after he had picked up the red cube did he realize that the yellow cube would beat it on 21 of the 36 combinations!

a. Is our problem with the Ruby of Rangadoon amenable to analysis using a classical DMUR model? Why or why not?

b. We can easily model this sequential decision process as a decision tree. Do so, and note that the process of constructing the tree sharpens your understanding of the problem. The process is as follows:
(1) Diabolus selects a die (**decision**)
(2) Larcenius selects a die (**decision**)
(3) Diabolus and Larcenius cast (**nature**)
(4) the winner and Malodor cast (**nature**)

c. Verify that the optimal sequence of decisions and the resulting probabilities are as follows:
(1) Diabolus selects the blue die
(2) Larcenius selects the red die
(3) the probabilities of each thief winning are

Diabolus, 32/108; Larcenius, 25/108; Malodor, 51/108

4. **The Scenario:** Having solved its inventory problem (Chapter 6), Wonmoor Time Novelties (WTN) is considering production of a radically new wristwatch with a unique device that electronically simulates the hand sweep of a conventional watch. Aaron Hand, the hard-hitting, aggressive CEO, has ordered a feasibility study that is now in progress.

Preliminary marketing research indicates that a competitive retail price for this product would be $100, and demand projections at that price are as follows:

Sales (millions)	1	5	10	20	30
Probability	0.15	0.20	0.35	0.20	0.10

The accounting and production departments report that they can manufacture the case and basic movement for the watch on existing production lines at a total unit cost of $45. However, Industrial Engineering reports that manufacturing the new electronic sweep device would require construction of a new production facility at a cost of $100 million, which would produce the device at a unit cost of $40.

The Problem: In discussing the new product with M. T. Coffers, the firm's VP for Finance, Aaron discovers that the 100-million-dollar investment in a new manufacturing facility would severely strain WTN's current cash position. One alternative would be to subcontract for the electronic device to avoid the large capital outlay, so Purchasing issues a request for quotes (RFQ) to electronic manufacturing firms. WTN received the following two bids:

BID 1: BULLDOG ELECTRONICS, BATON ROUGE, LOUISIANA

a. Per-unit price of $50 if the total order is for less than 10 million sweep devices.
b. Per-unit price of $47 if the total order is for 10 million or more sweep devices (all-units price discount).

BID 2: SHOCKER MANUFACTURING CO., LAWRENCE, KANSAS

a. Per-unit price of $52 for each unit ordered in the range of zero to 5 million units.
b. Per-unit price of $46 for each unit ordered in the range of 5 million to 20 million units.
c. Per-unit price of $42 for each unit ordered above 20 million units (incremental price discount).

The Model: Model Wonmoor Time's problem by setting up a decision matrix with four alternatives:

A_1: don't produce the watch

A_2: produce the watch and manufacture the new electronic device internally

A_3: produce the watch but subcontract the new device to Bulldog

A_4: produce the watch, but subcontract the new device to Shocker

Solution to the Model:
a. Use a DMUR matrix module to analyze this problem.
b. If Wonmoor Time's CEO Aaron Hand is basically risk averse over the range of outcomes, what effect would this tendency have on the results of your model?

Solution to the Problem: Try to put yourself in Aaron Hand's position as you study the solution to your model. You might ask yourself the following questions:

- Is the labor force available to manufacture the new electronic device internally?
- How accurate are the estimates used in the model? Would a 10% error in key estimates drastically change the model solution?
- How reliable are Bulldog and Shocker? Are there reasons other than costs for preferring to do business with one or the other, or neither?
- How elastic is the price/demand tradeoff at a retail price of $100 for the new watch? Would a higher or lower selling price drastically affect the results of the analysis?
- Could we "sharpen" demand estimates and their estimated probabilities by hiring a marketing research firm to do an in-depth study? Would its services be worth the additional cost?

5. **The Scenario:** In pre-revolutionary France, duels to the death over the favors of pretty demoiselles were common. One particularly fetching young lady named Coté

de Bouef, was the simultaneous object of the affections of three courtiers—Mouton, Poulet, and Jambon—and thus the first *truel* in history became a possibility.

The Problem: Since there had never been a truel before, no one knew quite how to proceed. The matter was further complicated by the fact that Mouton was the best shot in France—he literally never missed. Poulet hit his mark with a pistol about 50% of the time, while poor Jambon had a hit rate of only 30%. To be fair, the men received two bullets each, and they agreed upon the following procedure. Jambon, the poorest shot, was to go first—firing one of his bullets. If he were still alive, Poulet—the next best shot—would fire one of his bullets. Mouton, who never missed, would fire one shot if he remained alive. After the first round, any remaining truelists would fire their second bullets, one at a time, in the same order as above.

The Model: Sketch a decision tree of this problem, with Jambon—the man with the first shot—as the decision maker. Use judgment and imagination in defining Jambon's alternatives (e.g., if Jambon fired at Poulet and hit him, Mouton would have the next shot—and Jambon would be dead!).

Solution to the Model: Did you include "fire into the air on the first shot" as one of Jambon's alternatives? If you didn't, you should have—it is the optimal solution to the model! Verify this fact for yourself.

Solution to the Problem: While our chevaliers were busy working out the arrangements for the truel, our fair Coté de Bouef became impatient and eloped with Dindon, the court pacifist. Thus, the courtiers called off the truel, which is why there is no reference to it in history books.

Epilogue: The point of this little scenario is not to prepare managers to optimize their chances of winning truels. The point is this: use great care in defining your alternatives when modeling with DMUR. You can't make ground meat unless you put beef, mutton, chicken, ham, or turkey into the grinder!

6. **The Scenario:** As vice president for Commercial Lending for the San Francisco branch of JapanBank, Inc., Kitchi Nomura must forecast loan demand for each quarter. Japan, Inc. (the parent company) provides funds based on Kitchi's forecast at the current discount rate of 7%. Kitchi then makes loans at the current rate of 12% to the most creditworthy borrowers.

The Problem: Kitchi uses the forecasting module in SAMS each quarter to predict loan demand, using the quarterly option with seasonal trend. His forecast for the third quarter is a loan demand of ¥875 million, but the standard deviation of the forecast is ¥220 million. If he *overestimates* loan demand, his recourse is to invest the unloaned balance in short-term time deposits that earn only $3\frac{1}{2}$%, and his boss Nakamora Taguchi becomes very irritated. However, his boss gets even more irritated when Kitchi *underestimates* loan demand. In this case, JapanBank must raise the additional capital in the American money markets, and the going rate to foreign banks for short-term money is a whopping 17 percent.

The Model:
a. Can we model Kitchi Nomura's problem as a newsboy model? If so, what is the selling price (SP)? What is the salvage value (SV)? What is the unit purchase price (CP)? What is the goodwill cost per unit (GW)?

Solution to the Model:
a. Use the newsboy model option to determine Kitchi Nomura's optimal ordering quantity for this model. Could you have predicted in advance (before seeing the model solution) that Kitchi's optimal requested amount from the parent company would be considerably in excess of the forecast demand of ¥875 million?

CHAPTER 7 A STRUCTURE FOR DECISION MAKING UNDER RISK 295

b. As a practical matter, what would the parent company think about the San Francisco branch's consistently overstating its forecast need for funds quarter after quarter? If you were Kitchi Nomura, how would you explain to your boss Nakamora Taguchi—so that he could explain to *his* boss—why this is economically optimal?

7. **The Scenario:** Returning to the Wonmoor Time Novelties (Problem 4), Aaron Hand is uncomfortable with the results of the analysis.

The Problem: After receiving the demand projections and prior distribution generated by the marketing department, Aaron decides that the numbers are too "soft" to be reliable, given the financial magnitude of this decision. He therefore decides to consider commissioning the marketing research firm of Guess & Hope, Inc. (GHI) to do an in-depth study of the potential distribution of demand for the new watch.

The Model: Wiley Guess, one of the partners in GHI, provides Aaron the firm's conditional distribution of predictive accuracy (see Table 7.23). Referring to the distribution in the table, Mr. Guess boasts, "As you can see, we might miss our forecast, but we've never missed it by more than one adjacent category. If we ever do, there will be no fee charged to our client."

TABLE 7.23 Conditional distribution of predictive accuracy

		GHI Predictions					
		I_1	I_2	I_3	I_4	I_5	
Actual Demand	S_1	1/2	1/2	0	0	0	
	S_2	1/3	1/3	1/3	0	0	
	S_3	0	1/3	1/3	1/3	0	$Pr(I_i\|S_j)$
	S_4	0	0	1/3	1/3	1/3	
	S_5	0	0	0	1/2	1/2	

Solution to the Model: Using the original prior distribution from Problem 4, analyze this decision tree. Be sure to use a computerized DMUR module—this problem involves a *lot* of arithmetic!

a. What is GHI's information worth?
b. Sketch the decision tree for this problem on a large sheet of paper (this little tree gets very bushy). It helps to leave off the branches for which $Pr(S_j|I_i) = 0$ (there are 10 such branches).

Solution to the Problem: Your analysis should lead you to the curious model solution in Table 7.24.

TABLE 7.24

GHI's Prediction	Optimal Model Alternatives
1 million	Subcontract with Bulldog
5 million	Subcontract with Shocker
10 million	Subcontract with Bulldog
20 million	Build device internally
30 million	Build device internally

The reason for the seemingly erratic model results is the effects of the price discounts offered by the two subcontractors.

a. Comparing the model results for this problem with those you obtained in Problem 4, would hiring GHI (if its fee was reasonable) seem like a good idea?
b. You should have noted in the model of Problem 4 that the two subcontracting alternatives dominate the alternative "don't produce the new watch." Does this mean that Aaron has no choice but to produce the new watch? (If you think so, go directly back to page 1 of this book.)

8. **The Scenario:** Ann Ewell Gibbon is dean of the B-School at Dinero College. She has contacted the telemarketing firm of Alumni Unlimited (AU) about the possibility of conducting a telephone solicitation campaign for donations from B-School alumni. Dean Gibbon needs $750,000 for an endowed chair for a "big-name" management science professor who is being courted by rival B-Schools.

The Problem: The "problem" belongs to AU. Instead of the usual level-of-effort campaign for a percentage of the take, Dean Gibbon has offered the firm a fee of $150,000 to raise $900,000—no matter how much or how little time it takes.

"This is a toughie," Pete Peterson remarks to his partners. "Setting up the boiler room with phones and computers usually costs about $150,000, and staffing and phone charges come to about $75,000 per week. That means our break-even for this project would be 10 weeks."

Patty Pearson spoke up. "Yes, Pete, but we can raise money at the rate of $11,000 per week—that's our average performance for colleges the size of Dinero. That means that we would generate the $900,000 in a bit over eight weeks. Let's see—$150,000 in setup cost plus operating costs of eight times $75,000—that comes to $750,000 total cost. And $150,000 is a nifty profit for eight plus weeks of work."

"That's all well and good," interjected Phil Price, the perennial worrier of AU, "but Patty forgot to mention that the standard deviation of our fund-raising rate is $4,000 per week. That translates into a standard deviation of about 2.91 weeks in expected completion time. It seems awfully risky to me."

The Model:
a. Could we model this problem as an opportunity loss model with continuous, normally distributed completion time as the random variable? If so, what is the break-even time (t_B)? What is the slope of the loss function (k)? What are the mean (m) and standard deviation (s) of completion time?

Solution to the Model:
a. Use the continuous distribution normal loss approach to analyze this model. Noting that the EOL of the alternative "don't accept Dean Gibbon's offer" is somewhat less than $150,000, how risky is this project for AU [i.e., how large is EOL (accept Dean Gibbon's offer), comparatively]?
b. One of the rather stringent assumptions of this model is that the random variable (completion time in this case) be normally distributed. What do you think about that assumption in this problem?

Solution to the Problem:
a. If you were a management consultant hired by AU to advise it on this problem, what would your advice be? Would you be willing to accept your consulting fee as a percentage of AU's profit?
b. Is Dean Ann Ewell Gibbon cagey, or what?

PRACTICE MODELS

1. For the decision matrix in Table 7.25 use a module like SAMS' DMUR matrix module to determine the maximum expected monetary value:

    Alternative A_1 = hire consulting firm X

    Alternative A_2 = hire consulting firm Y

    Alternative A_3 = hire consulting firm Z

    S_1 = consulting firm will complete the project one year early

    S_2 = consulting firm will complete the project 15 months early

    S_2 = consulting firm will complete the project 18 months early

    Payoff = net profit (in $000)

TABLE 7.25

	States of Nature		
Alternatives	S_1	S_2	S_3
$P(S_j)$	0.6	0.2	0.2
A_1	100.0	78.0	60.0
A_2	130.0	70.0	45.0
A_3	90.0	110.0	70.0

2. In Problem 1, use the EOL criterion to determine the best decision.
3. In Problem 1, what is the expected value of perfect information?
4. Construct the decision tree for the following problem (see Table 7.26) and use a package like SAMS to determine the best alternative.

    Alternative A = choose advertising campaign 1

    Alternative B = choose advertising campaign 2

    Alternative C = choose advertising campaign 3

TABLE 7.26

	States of Nature		
Alternatives	S_1	S_2	S_3
$P(S_j)$	0.3	0.50	0.2
A	5000.0	2500.00	−1000.0
B	3000.0	3000.00	1000.0
C	4000.0	2000.00	−500.0

S_1 = good market conditions

S_2 = moderate market conditions

S_3 = bad market conditions

Payoff = net profit (in $000)

5. In Problem 4, an advertising firm has kept records of its past performance in predicting market conditions. The advertising firm's conditional distribution of predictive accuracy is given in Table 7.27. Using this information, construct the decision tree and determine the best alternative.

TABLE 7.27

		Predictive States of Nature		
		I_1	I_2	I_3
Actual States of Nature	S_1	0.30	0.45	0.25
	S_2	0.50	0.25	0.25
	S_3	0.40	0.30	0.30

6. In Problem 5, assume that the advertising firm's fee for providing additional information is $400. Should you hire the firm?
7. In Problem 1, use Figure 7.6 to determine the best decision alternative. Assume a risk-averse environment.
8. Given the following information, use the newsboy model to determine the optimal order quantity.

   Selling price per unit = $1.25

   Salvage value per unit = $0.15

   Unit purchase price = $0.80

   Unit purchase price from another newsstand = $1.50

   Average # of papers sold per day = 300 with standard deviation of 20 papers.

REFERENCES AND ADDITIONAL READING

1. Adams, J. "An Economic Analysis of Narrow Row Cotton Production." Unpublished master's thesis, College of Agricultural Sciences, Texas Tech University (1978).
2. Alexander, Steven. Adapted from an unpublished MBA term project report, Virginia Polytechnic Institute and State University (1986).
3. Baird, B. *Managerial Decisions Under Uncertainty*. New York: Wiley, 1989.
4. Bean, Casey. Adapted from an unpublished MBA term project report, Texas Tech University (1986).
5. Brown, R., A. Kahr, and C. Peterson. *Decision Analysis for the Manager*. New York: Holt, Rinehart and Winston, 1974.
6. Conover, W. Supplied in a private communication (1989).
7. Davis, R. "A Study on Cotton Yields as Related to Cotton Variety, Irrigation, Fertility, Rainfall, and Row Pattern." Unpublished monograph, College of Agricultural Sciences, Texas Tech University (1981).
8. Edwards, Raoul D. "Special Report: Reaganomics Update." *United States Banker*, 1982, p. 20.

9. Fishburn, P. "Foundations of Decision Analysis: Along the Way." *Management Science* 35 (1989): 387–405.
10. Hochwalt, Thomas R. Adapted from an unpublished MBA term project report, Texas Tech University (1982).
11. LaValle, I. *Fundamentals of Decision Analysis*. New York: Holt, Rinehart and Winston, 1978.
12. Luce, R. and H. Raiffa. *Games and Decisions*. New York: Wiley, 1957.
13. Pratt, J., H. Raiffa, and R. Schlaifer. *Introduction to Statistical Decision Theory*. New York: McGraw-Hill, 1965.
14. Raiffa, H. *Decision Analysis*. Reading, Mass.: Addison-Wesley, 1968.
15. Reyes, J. Adapted from an unpublished MBA term project report, Texas Tech University (1981).
16. Sampson, D. *Managerial Decision Analysis*. Homewood, Ill.: Richard E. Irwin, 1988.
17. Sauceda, Manuel. Adapted from an unpublished MBA term project report, Texas Tech University (1987).
18. Schlaifer, R. *Analysis of Decisions Under Uncertainty*. New York: McGraw-Hill, 1969.
20. Von Neumann, J., and O. Morgenstern. *Theory of Games and Economic Behavior* (2d ed.). Princeton, N.J.: Princeton University Press, 1953.
21. Winkler, R. *An Introduction to Bayesian Inference and Decision*. New York: Holt, Rinehart and Winston, 1972.

CHAPTER 8

Waiting-Line (Queueing) Models

Waiting lines (or *queues* as the British prefer) are familiar to everyone. We wait in the check-out line in the supermarket, and we wait in line to buy tickets to a ball game or a concert or for a movie. Someone once estimated that the average person spends five years out of a lifetime in various queues. (For language fans, *queueing* is the only English-language word that has five consecutive vowels.)

What possible benefit could models of waiting lines provide to business, industry, and public sector organizations? The fact is that waiting lines are as common in the organizational world as they are in people's personal lives. Inventory scheduling, maintenance operations, and communication systems are all examples of activities that we can model and analyze using queueing theory. In fact, the mathematical theory of waiting lines originated in the telephone industry, when William Erlang (an engineer for the Danish Telephone Company) noted that phone calls arriving at a switchboard usually had to "wait in line" before being routed.

As we will shortly discover, queueing theory is a most complex subject. You will encounter a simulation analysis of a waiting line in Chapter 9, and—to be candid—most real-world queueing systems are so complicated that simulation is the only effective way to analyze them. In this chapter, therefore, we will not attempt to delve very deeply into closed-form (exact) solutions to complex models of queueing systems. Rather, we will introduce a few simple models and their closed-form analytical solutions to get the flavor of the subject. As in previous chapters, however, we pull no punches in modeling such systems and analyzing the computer-generated solutions.

UNDERLYING ASSUMPTIONS

All queueing systems consist of three distinct subsystems:

1. The set of people or things requiring service (the **calling population**).
2. One or more explicit or implicit waiting facilities or **queues.**
3. An entity that provides service to the units of the calling population (the **service facility**).

Figure 8.1 illustrates one queueing system. Let's discuss these three subsystems of a queueing model in detail.

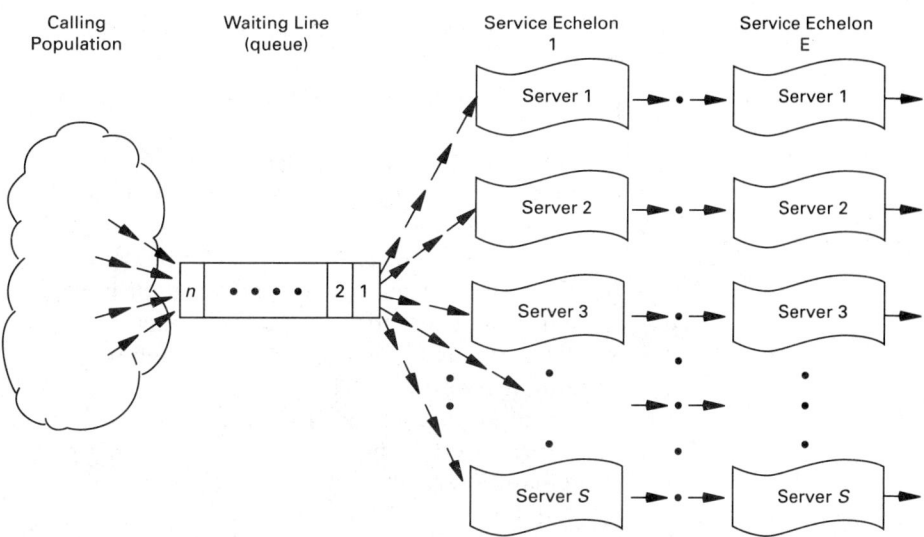

FIGURE 8.1 A queueing system

THE CALLING POPULATION SUBSYSTEM

The calling population can be finite or infinite. For example, the population of stars in the observable universe waiting to be discovered and catalogued by astronomers is very large, of course, but finite. On the other hand, the population of 50 milling machines in a job shop waiting to be repaired by a maintenance person is an infinite calling population, since a milling machine reenters the calling population as soon as it is repaired.

As an analogy, consider a finite population to be one that in terms of statistical theory we sample *without replacement*; an infinite calling population would be analogous to sampling *with replacement* (assuming that the arrival rate remains constant).

Calling populations can be either *homogeneous* or *nonhomogeneous*, depending upon the type of service required. For instance, the population of male and female students in a large university is homogeneous if the service required is "registration for classes" but nonhomogeneous if the service is to be "physical examination" at the university clinic.

Another aspect of calling populations is the nature of their units' arrivals at the queueing subsystem. If the units arrive one at a time (no matter how small the time interval between them), we say the calling population is **single arrival**. If two or more units can arrive simultaneously, we have a **batch arrival** population. An example of the latter is baggage at an airport; an example of the former is the calling population of the aircraft themselves arriving for landing.

Finally, the most critical aspect of calling populations is the **probability distribution that governs the pattern of arrivals** from the population to the queueing subsystem. Common sense tells us that if units arrive at the queue in a regular, nonvarying pattern at precisely the same intervals of time, we have a much simpler modeling task than if the arrivals are sporadic and highly variable.

The simplest calling population to model and analyze is one that is infinite, homogeneous, and single arrival and whose probabilistic arrival pattern is "well-behaved" (more about this later).

THE QUEUEING SUBSYSTEM

We must consider two separate aspects of the queueing subsystem: the queueing configuration and the queue discipline.

QUEUEING CONFIGURATION

A waiting line can have a finite or an infinite number of slots to accommodate arriving units. A drive-in bank that fronts on a busy street has a finite number of spaces in which cars may wait for the teller or tellers, assuming that double parking along the street is not allowed. On the other hand, there are (for all practical purposes) an infinite number of slots for fighter aircraft in the queue behind aerial refueling tankers.

Another aspect of configuration depends on the service facility and involves single versus multiple queues. For example, in some modern banks, people form a single waiting line for multiple tellers, with the person at the head of the line going to the first available teller. Other banks still allow separate queues to form in front of each teller, and—inevitably—we always end up behind the person with $400 in loose change to be sorted and rolled!

Finally, there are serial queues; that is, if the service involves two or more activities that one must perform sequentially (such as the infamous "shot line" in Marine boot camp), there may be separate queues for each service element.

QUEUE DISCIPLINE

One of the most interesting and vexing aspects of the queueing subsystem is **queue discipline**. For example, if arriving units have the option of not joining the queue if they judge it to be too long, we say that **balking** is allowed. If a unit can decide to leave the queue after having joined it, **reneging** is present.

The other feature of queue discipline involves priorities—the order in which the calling units receive service. One priority system commonly encountered is **first in, first out** (FIFO) or first come, first served. On the other hand, more and more companies are accounting for inventory on a **last in, first out** (LIFO) basis. Queueing priority can also be **random,** and anyone who has ever bought a hot dog and a soft drink at a concession stand, at half-time in a football game knows all about this priority system. Finally, there can be priority by **rank,** an example being an army officer who strides up the line in the mess hall until he or she encounters someone of equal or greater military rank and steps into line just behind that person.

In terms of modeling and analysis, a single infinite queue with no balking or reneging allowed and with "first come, first served" (or FIFO) queue priority, is the simplest.

THE SERVICE FACILITY SUBSYSTEM

There can be a **single** server, identical servers in **parallel,** different servers in **series,** or parallel sets of servers in series (as in Figure 8.1). Servers in series may or may not have queues between each server, and (as noted earlier) there may be a single queue for parallel servers or individual queues for each.

If there are parallel servers, the service rates can be homogeneous or nonhomogeneous, as in the case of supermarket checkers that can ring up purchases at widely varying rates (we seem to get the one who is on his or her first day on the job!).

Finally, as in the calling population subsystem, the most critical aspect of a service subsystem is the **probability distribution that governs service rate.** It is obvious that a service system that provides a service at a constant, unvarying rate (such as a coin-operated vending machine) would be much easier to analyze than one in which the individual service time varied widely from one calling unit to the next (as in a dental clinic).

The simplest service facility subsystem to model and analyze is the single server (with no servers in series), whose probabilistic service-time pattern is "well-behaved" in the same sense in which we addressed the arrival pattern of the calling population subsystem.

THE INTEGRATED QUEUEING SYSTEM

Table 8.1 summarizes the various facets of the three subsystems just discussed. Although there are other aspects of the three subsystems that we did not discuss, those summarized in Table 8.1 represent the major ones. As is true in most systems, the three queueing subsystems are highly interdependent in operation. For example, a nonhomogeneous calling population may well dictate a particular queueing priority and may require that the service facility be nonhomogeneous as well. Even so, if we consider all of the possible combinations of factors leading to essentially different waiting-line models, the number of such models becomes immense. In fact, if we allow only four probability distributions each for arrivals and rates of service, the different combinations of the 12 factors in the table total over 32,000! We are not surprised, therefore, that simulation is the most popular approach to investigating models of queueing systems.

TABLE 8.1 Facets of queueing systems

Subsystems	Facets
Calling population	Finite vs. infinite Homogeneous vs. nonhomogeneous Single vs. batch arrivals Probability distribution of arrivals
Queue configuration	Finite vs. infinite Single vs. multiple queues Series vs. parallel queues
Queue discipline	Balking and reneging Priorities: FIFO, LIFO, random, rank
Service facility	Series vs. parallel servers Homogeneous vs. nonhomogeneous Probability distribution of service

BUILDING QUEUEING MODELS

In building a model of a queueing system, we may use the summary in Table 8.1 as a sort of checklist to determine the attributes that most nearly describe the real-world system we are investigating. Let's illustrate this modeling process by making a visit to QUES (**que**ueing **s**ynthesizer), an interactive computer cousin of LPS (linear programming synthesizer) from Chapter 2. Our decision maker is Stan N. Lyons, the vice president for Production of Pegasus Aerospace Company—Manufacturing Division (PAC-MAN). PAC-MAN produces custom satellites for a variety of uses, including communications and geological observation.

QUES: Good morning, old chap, my name is QUES [pronounced "cues"]. What's yours?

STAN: My name is Stan N. Lyons, and I have a problem.

QUES: Jolly good, Stan. Give me the particulars.

STAN: My company PAC-MAN runs a large job-shop production facility that manufactures custom satellites. The production workers are highly trained, well-paid technicians and are generally conscientious and dependable. As our backlog of orders rose over the past 12 months, we started experiencing a rash of delays that resulted in late deliveries. I did some random spot checks of the floor last week, and anywhere from 5% to 20% of the workers weren't at their workstations. When I asked one of our best and most dependable technicians what he thought the problem was, he replied: "If PAC-MAN wants to pay me $19.50 an hour to stand in line, that's fine by me."

QUES: Aha! You've got a problem with your tool-crib operation, haven't you, Stan?

STAN: I think so—but how did you know that?

QUES: One of the most famous cases of a queueing problem occurred at the Boeing Aircraft Company in the early 1960s involving a problem with its tool crib. I have the details salted away in my memory banks. I would guess that PAC-MAN, like Boeing, can't afford to purchase one each of certain very expensive tools for every worker, so you've bought two or three of each and issue them on demand from a tool crib. Right?

STAN: Right on target, QUES. But the plot thickens. I had one of our industrial engineers put his stopwatch on the crib for an entire day. It turns out that workers arrive at the crib an average of once every five minutes. Since the crib attendant takes an average of only four minutes to locate and process the requested tool, it seems to me that we shouldn't be having any problems with highly paid technicians standing in line.

QUES: That's a common misconception, Stan. Let's go down my checklist for building queueing models and pin down your situation precisely. First of all, there is an infinite calling population, since each labourer is replaced as soon as he or she gets service at the crib. The population also appears to be homogeneous, with single rather than batch arrivals. Now about the probability distribution of arrivals at the crib: you gave me only the average arrival rate. Did you save the detailed log that your industrial engineer kept? If so, feed it to me through your terminal.

STAN: The engineer kept a time log for each arrival at the crib—there were 96 in all. How would you like to have the data?

QUES: Break it down by time between arrivals to the nearest half-minute and give me a cumulative tally of arrivals.

STAN: OK, here it is.

Minutes Between Arrivals	≤ 2	2.5	3	3.5	4	4.5	5	5.5	6	6.5	7	7.5	8	8.5	9	9.5	≥ 10
Cumulative Number	0	1	2	7	19	33	46	58	67	75	80	84	87	90	93	95	96

QUES: (Short pause) Just as I suspected. I did a "goodness of fit" test on your data. The mean and variance are almost identical in value at 5. As you already stated, the average interarrival time is 5 minutes, and the arrival rate averages about 12 per hour. You have an excellent "fit" with a Poisson distribution with $\lambda = 12$. That makes my task a lot easier. Let's press forward with my checklist. I take it that your plant is very large, so we can assume an infinite queue capacity for all practical purposes. Since you have only one tool-crib attendant who performs a single service, there is only a single queue with no servers in series. As to queue discipline, do the workers ever refuse to join the queue if it is too long or leave it after joining?

STAN: No—there wouldn't be any point in doing either. They are paid full wages while in the waiting line, and they can't get on with their duties until they get the special tools from the crib. And by the way—we run a democratic shop. There's no special priority for any of the workers—it's strictly first come, first served at PAC-MAN.

QUES: Excellent! We have a very simple queue configuration, the queue discipline doesn't allow for balking or reneging, and FIFO is the easiest queue priority for me to work with. Now, Stan, we need to consider the service facility itself. We have a single server, which settles the question of homogeneous vs. nonhomogeneous servers. Did you keep the data on service rate the industrial engineer gathered? If so, feed them to me as a cumulative distribution of the number of minutes the crib attendant required to locate and sign out the tools.

STAN: Here are the data you need.

Time Required for Service (min)	≤1	2	3	4	5	6	7	8	9	10	11	12	13	14	≥15
Cumulative Number	21	37	51	61	68	75	79	83	86	88	90	91	92	93	96

QUES: (Short pause) Stan, we're in luck. Your data fit an exponential model with mean and standard deviation of 4 minutes almost perfectly. What we have is a problem that we can model and analyze in closed form, so that I don't have to call my simulation program in this case. What kinds of things would you like to know about your tool-crib situation?

STAN: I'd certainly like to know how long the line is, on an average, because of the psychological effect it has on the workers. Obviously, I'd like to know the average waiting time in the system so I can get a handle on the implicit personnel costs. And finally, we pay the crib attendant only $6.00 per hour. If he is working as hard as I suspect he is, we might want to give him a raise.

QUES: All right, I called SAMS' queueing module, and the input screen is in Figure 8.2.

```
       ┌──→ SAMS INPUT SCREEN - Queueing          ←──
       │  NAME?   PAC-MAN
       │  PROBLEM DESCRIPTION - Model the tool-crib system for
       │                           PAC-MAN
       ├──────────────────────────────────────────────
       │  QUEUE NAME                Q1
       │
       │  CALLING POPULATION        INF
       │  ARRIVAL RATE              12
       │  CALLING DISTRIBUT         POI
       │
       │  QUEUE LENGTH              INF
       │  COST OF WAITING           19.5
       │
       │  # OF SERVERS              1
       │  SERVICE RATE/SERV         15
       │  SERVICE DISTRIBUT         EXP
       │  COST OF SERVICE           6
       └──────────────────────────────────────────────
```

FIGURE 8.2 SAMS input screen for PAC-MAN

TABLE 8.2 SAMS report for PAC-MAN

PAC-MAN
QUICK BRIEFING ON SINGLE-SERVER QUEUEING MODEL

Mean arrival rate	12.0
Mean service rate	15.0
Traffic intensity	80.0%
Expected length of queue	3.2
Expected number in system	4.0
% time server idle	20.0%

QUES: Here is a brief summary report from SAMS [Table 8.2]. However, you need to study the rest of this chapter before attempting to use the numbers to help you make a decision. Come back later and we'll complete the analysis (in Problem 1).

STAN: Those numbers are startling, QUES! If 96 workers spend an average of 20 minutes in the tool-crib waiting line, that means we are wasting 1,920 minutes, or 32 hours a day. At $19.50 per hour, that comes to $624 every day! At the same time, the tool-crib attendant is twiddling his thumbs 20% of the time, or 96 minutes per day. Are you sure your answers are correct?

QUES: Absolutely, old chap. I knew you'd react as you did. Be patient now—learn more about queueing theory, and I'll see you later. Keep a stiff upper lip! QUES, over and out.

SOME USEFUL NOTATION

In 1953, D. G. Kendall [4] proposed a simple notation that many people use to classify families of queueing models. The notation takes the form

U/V/W/X/Y/Z

where we substitute specific symbols or letters for the letters U–Z in the six positions to describe the models, as follows:

U: a symbol describing the arrival distribution

V: a symbol describing the service distribution

W: a symbol indicating the number of parallel servers

X: a symbol indicating queue capacity

Y: a symbol indicating queue priority system

Z: a symbol indicating the number of series servers

Some of the symbols most commonly used are

M = Poisson arrival distribution or exponential service distribution

D = deterministic (constant or zero-variance) arrival or service distribution

G = general distribution (other than M or D) of arrival or service time

For example, our PAC-MAN model above is of the M/M/1/∞/FIFO/1 variety, and this class of models happens to be the easiest to deal with analytically. We generally refer to models of this type as **Markovian.** In many queueing situations, queueing models yield useful information about the behavior of the systems even when the arrival and service distributions are only approximately Poisson and exponential, respectively.

SOME CAVEATS IN USING QUEUEING MODELS

In our discussion of queueing models, we will restrict our attention to steady-state systems. That is, we assume that whatever the transient (temporary) start-up behavior of the system, we may ignore its long-run effects. We should note here that we can model queueing systems as systems of differential equations whose solutions capture the transient effect. Obviously, such a procedure is beyond the scope of our investigations; however, we can also "capture" the transient effect by using discrete simulation models, and this tool is readily available to us (see Chapter 9).

Another important caveat is that the mean values of the arrival and service distributions must be approximately constant over the time period in question. For example, if we were modeling the arrivals of aircraft for landing at DFW Airport, we would note immediately that there are distinct peaks in midmorning and late afternoon. Thus, attempting to model this situation with elementary queueing theory would be productive only if our simulation model could account for variations in the mean arrival rate over the span of the day.

Finally, as we will see, many queueing models produce results that run counter to our intuition—unlike the majority of MS/OR models we have discussed. One major source of such results is the high variance associated with some of the more widely applicable arrival and service distributions—ones that seem to "fit" many actual situations. For instance, the mean of the Poisson distribution equals the variance, so that the standard deviation is the square root of the mean. As arrival frequency increases, the standard deviation becomes smaller in relation to the mean (relatively speaking); but for small arrival rates, the Poisson distribution is highly variable. The exponential distribution, on the other hand, has a mean equal to its standard deviation, so that its variability is high for all service rates.

SOLUTION APPROACHES: AN INTUITIVE DESCRIPTION

The following sections state known closed-form results for three queueing models that are useful to decision makers. We do not show how researchers derived these results—in keeping with the managerial flavor of this text. However, if you wish to investigate the origins of these results, you will find an excellent (but terse) treatment in the 1958 book by Phillip Morse [6].

NOTATION

In the definitions that follow, we will use the following standard notation:

λ = mean arrival rate from the calling population

μ = mean service rate for a single server

$\phi = \lambda/\mu$ = traffic intensity

$P(n)$ = the probability that there are exactly n units in the queueing system (including service stations) at any randomly chosen time

L = average number of units in the queueing system

L_q = average number of units in the queue itself

W = average waiting time in the queueing system

W_q = average waiting time in the queue itself

N = number of spaces in the queueing system

S = number of parallel servers

SOME KNOWN RESULTS FOR QUEUEING MODELS

In the following definitions, we restrict our attention to queueing situations in which we can estimate arrival and service distributions satisfactorily by the Poisson and exponential distributions, respectively.

THE M/M/1/∞/FIFO/1 MODEL

This is the simple model that evolved in our earlier discussion with QUES about PAC-MAN's problem. The analytical results are

$$P(n) = \phi^n(1 - \phi), \text{ for } \phi < 1 \tag{8.1}$$

$$L = \phi/(1 - \phi) \qquad L_q = \phi^2/(1 - \phi) \tag{8.2}$$

$$W = \phi/\lambda(1 - \phi) \qquad W_q = \phi/\mu(1 - \phi) \tag{8.3}$$

Recalling the PAC-MAN model, with λ = 12 arrivals per hour and μ = 15 services per hour (both average rates), we see that the traffic intensity is ϕ = 12/15 = 0.80. Thus, we can easily reproduce the results obtained by QUES, noting that "percent time the server is idle" is merely $P(0)$—the probability that there are no calling units in the system.

Notice in this model that our results make sense only if $\phi < 1$; that is, the model is usable only if the average rate of service is higher than the average rate of arrival of calling units. This is reasonable when we consider that we have an infinite queue capacity, so that—if $\phi \geq 1$—the waiting line would grow without bound.

We can illustrate the effect of variability dramatically using the PAC-MAN model. Recall that $P(0) = 0.20$, so that the crib attendant was idle 20% of the time, on the average. What would you guess the probability to be that at least six workers would be waiting in the queue at any given time? The actual probability is about 0.21, which you can easily verify. Furthermore, on the average, for one hour each day, the harried crib attendant faces nine or more workers in the waiting line!

THE M/M/1/N/FIFO/1 MODEL

Consider the problem encountered by Lou's Change, Inc., a small firm that does quick oil changes for automobiles on a drive-in basis. In addition to the pit where Lou's changes the oil, there is room in the driveway for two additional cars to wait. If three cars are in the system when a potential customer approaches, the customer cannot stop on the two-lane street. Such customers almost always drive down the street to Downey Drain, Inc., which is Lou's competitor. Customers arrive according to a Poisson distribution at an average rate of five per hour, and service time is approximately exponentially distributed with an average service time of ten minutes, or six per hour.

This model differs from the previous one only in that there is a finite number of places (3) for units from the calling population to wait for service or to be served.

For the Lou's Change problem, we see that $\lambda = 5$, and $\mu = 6$. Figure 8.3 reproduces the SAMS input screen for its queueing analysis module. Note in the SAMS input screen that we indicated a single-server model with an infinite calling population and an arrival rate of five customers per hour and exponential service. The service rate is six per hour, and the number of available spaces in the queue (including the service space) is three. Table 8.3 gives the SAMS full briefing.

FIGURE 8.3
SAMS input screen for Lou's Change

```
━━━▶ SAMS INPUT SCREEN - Queueing        ◀━━━
   NAME?   LOU'S CHANGE
   PROBLEM DESCRIPTION - Model the queueing system for an
                         oil quick-change facility

   QUEUE NAME                Q1

   CALLING POPULATION       INF
   ARRIVAL RATE               5
   CALLING DISTRIBUT        POI

   QUEUE LENGTH               3
   COST OF WAITING            0

   # OF SERVERS               1
   SERVICE RATE/SERV          6
   SERVICE DISTRIBUT        EXP
   COST OF SERVICE            0
```

TABLE 8.3 SAMS report for Lou's Change

LOU'S CHANGE
FULL BRIEFING ON SINGLE-SERVER QUEUEING MODEL

Mean arrival rate		5.0
Mean service rate		6.0
Traffic intensity		83.3 %
Expected length of queue		0.60
Expected number in system		1.27
Expected waiting time in queue		0.31
Expected waiting time in system		0.12
% lost callers		18.6 %

	#	Probability
Probable number in system	0	0.32
	1	0.27
	2	0.22
	3	0.19

From the report, we note the following:

$P(0) = 0.32$, so that the system is idle (empty) almost a third of the time

$P(3) = 0.19$, so that the system is full 19% of the time, which means that Lou's is losing 19% of its customers

$L = 1.27$, the average number of cars in the system

$L_q = 0.60$, the average number of cars in the queue

$W = 0.31$ hour, or a little less than 18 minutes average wait in the system

$W_q \doteq 0.12$ hour, or a little over 7 minutes average wait in the queue

The analytical results for this model are in the appendix to this chapter.

THE M/M/1/∞/FIFO/S MODEL

In this queueing model, we have a single infinite queue but $S > 1$ servers. Here, arriving units join the single queue, and the first available server services the unit at the head of the line. To make the model tractable, we also assume that each of the servers completes a service at the average rate of μ per hour and that the average arrival rate at the queue is λ per hour.

Uptown State Bank (USB) operates a suburban drive-up facility with three tellers on duty, and the senior VP has had a steady stream of complaints from customers about long waits in line. The facility has concrete medians that separate the waiting lines for the three tellers. Customers approaching the facility must choose one of the lines as they drive up; thus, as soon as another car enters behind a previous one, the first car can neither leave the line (renege) nor switch to another teller.

The manager of the drive-up facility has suggested removing the concrete medians and forming a single waiting line, allowing the customer who is first in line to drive to the next available teller. The VP is skeptical—after all, customer arrival rate (currently 36 per hour, on the average) wouldn't change, and it appeared that this factor was the real problem.

Consider this analysis: assume that the arrival rate at each of the present tellers is 36/3 = 12 per hour, so that we have an M/M/1/∞/FIFO/1 model. We remove the concrete medians and allow a single line to form, as in the M/M/1/∞/FIFO/3 model. Using SAMS' queueing module, we have the input screen (Figure 8.4) and reports (Table 8.4). Under the present system, customers spend an average of an hour in the system, and there is an average of 12 automobiles waiting *in each line*. We may be almost certain that an accurate assessment of this situation would involve balking.

FIGURE 8.4
SAMS input screen for Uptown State Bank

```
────► SAMS INPUT SCREEN - Queueing        ◄────

NAME?   UPTOWN STATE BANK
PROBLEM DESCRIPTION - Model the queueing system for a
drive-up banking facility with three parallel tellers.

QUEUE NAME              Q1          Q2

CALLING POPULATION      INF         INF
ARRIVAL RATE            12          36
CALLING DISTRIBUT       POI         POI

QUEUE LENGTH            INF         INF
COST OF WAITING         0           0
NUMBER OF QUEUES        3           1

# OF SERVERS            3           3
SERVICE RATE/SERV       13          13
SERVICE DISTRIBUT       EXP         EXP
COST OF SERVICE         0           0
```

When we remove the medians and form a single waiting line, the average number of customers *in the system* is about 13, and the average waiting time in the system reduces from one hour to 0.363 hour (22 minutes). Moreover, about 14% of the time, arriving customers may drive directly to a teller with no wait at all.

If this example looks like magic, please be assured that it is not. However, for most people, results of this type are counterintuitive at best. The "secret," as we noted earlier, is in the variance. For example, a Poisson distribution with $\lambda = 12$, has a standard deviation of about 3.46; for such a distribution with $\lambda = 36$, the standard deviation is 6—less than double that of the first, although the mean is three times that of the first. Lower variability produces better results. Think of it this way: if arrivals occurred at precisely 60/36 minutes apart and if services occurred at a constant rate of three every 60/13 minutes, then $L_q = W_q = 0$!

This is our first encounter with a state-dependent queueing system, since the service rate for the system is $n(\mu)$ when $n<S$ (n being the number of units being served) and $S(\mu)$ when $n>S$. This complicates the formulas somewhat, as we can see in the appendix to this chapter.

TABLE 8.4 SAMS reports for Uptown State Bank

UPTOWN STATE BANK
FULL BRIEFING ON SINGLE-SERVER QUEUEING MODEL

Mean arrival rate	12.0
Mean service rate	13.0
Traffic intensity	92.3 %
Expected length of queue	11.10
Expected number in system	12.00
Expected waiting time in queue	0.92
Expected waiting time in system	1.00
Number of servers	1
% time server idle	7.7 %

UPTOWN STATE BANK
FULL BRIEFING ON MULTIPLE-SERVER QUEUEING MODEL

Mean arrival rate	36.0
Mean service rate	13.0
Traffic intensity	92.3 %
Expected length of queue	10.30
Expected number in system	13.10
Expected waiting time in queue	0.29
Expected waiting time in system	0.36
Number of servers	3
% time server idle	7.7 %

DEVELOPING ALTERNATIVE SOLUTIONS

So far, we have discussed the dual nature of queueing models—as descriptive models and (in the PAC-MAN example) as optimizing models. In using this powerful technique as an aid to decision making, careful sensitivity analysis is an absolute must. When we use simulation to analyze a queueing system, we perform sensitivity analysis by setting up an experimental design and rerunning the simulation for different combinations of parameter values. For closed-form or analytical approaches, the following sections discuss several aspects of sensitivity analysis.

ARRIVAL AND SERVICE TIME DISTRIBUTIONS

Researchers developed much of the theory of queueing using Markovian models. The reason for this is that both the Poisson and exponential distributions are "memoryless," in that the events they describe are independent. For example, the arrival of a calling unit under the Poisson assumption has no effect whatsoever on the arrival of the next one, and so on. Likewise, the time of one service under the exponential assumption does not affect the next service. This is an intuitively appealing attribute in many real-world queueing systems but drastically misrepresentative in others. For example, since we know that work rates tend to follow a so-called learning curve, we

ARRIVAL AND SERVICE RATES

normally expect improvement in service rate for a human worker as he or she gains experience with the task at hand. The M/M/etc. models ignore this effect. Therefore, when analyzing an ongoing system with a queueing model, we should exercise great care in performing a "goodness of fit" test on both the arrival time and service distributions.

In infinite queue models, results of the analysis are very sensitive to small errors in λ and μ as the traffic intensity ϕ (or ϕ/S in multiple server models) approaches (but does not reach) a value of 1. Consider the example in Table 8.5 in which $\mu = 30$ for values of $\lambda = 25, 27, 29$, and 29.5 in the M/M/1/∞/FIFO/1 model. Note in the table that an 18% increase in λ (from 25 to 29.5) leads to an 1180% increase in the average number of calling units in the system and a 1000% increase in average waiting time in the system. Thus, small errors in these critical parameters could lead to very poor decisions unless we exercise caution and judgment.

TABLE 8.5 Examples for $\mu = 30$

	P(0)	L	L_q	W	W_q
$\lambda = 25$	0.167	5	4.167	0.200	0.167
$\lambda = 27$	0.100	9	8.100	0.333	0.300
$\lambda = 29$	0.033	29	28.033	1.000	0.967
$\lambda = 29.5$	0.017	59	58.017	2.000	1.967

Another critical assumption is homogeneity of the calling population and—in a multiple-server system—the homogeneity of servers. For example, for an arrival rate of 50 units per hour, our two servers have service rates of $\mu_1 = 36$ and $\mu_2 = 24$ per hour, respectively. The combined service rate is $\mu = 36 + 24 = 60$, all right, but the results obtained by using the simple multiple-server model with an average service time of $\mu = 30$ will be incorrect.

AN EXAMPLE OF SENSITIVITY ANALYSIS

Returning to our original Lou's Change model with a one-server, finite queue, recall that $N = 3$ (one oil change pit and two waiting spaces), $\lambda = 5$, and $\mu = 6$. Suppose there is a possibility that the key parameters λ and μ can be in error by as much as 10% in either direction. The most favorable situation would be when λ is 10% too high and μ is simultaneously 10% too low; the least favorable situation would be the converse. Let us investigate these two conditions as Case I and Case II, respectively.

CASE I

Since λ is 10% too high, $\lambda_{MIN} = 5/1.1 = 4.545$; and since μ is 10% too low, $\mu_{MAX} = 6/0.9 = 6.667$; thus $\phi_{MIN} = \lambda_{MIN}/\mu_{MAX} = 0.682$. Using SAMS' queueing module for our computations, we have

$P(0) = 0.406$ $P(3) = 0.129$

$L = 1.04$ $L_q = 0.45$

$W = 0.26$ hr. $= 15.7$ min. $W_q = 0.11$ hr. $= 6.8$ min.

Thus, for Case I, Lou's only loses about 13% of the business rather than over 18% in the original analysis, and waiting time in the system has declined from 18 minutes to less than 16.

CASE II

In this situation, $\lambda_{MAX} = 5/0.9 = 5.556$ and $\mu_{MIN} = 6/1.1 = 5.455$, so that $\phi_{MAX} = \lambda_{MAX}/\mu_{MIN} = 1.019$. The computational results for this case are

$P(0) = 0.243$ $P(3) = 0.257$

$L = 1.52$ $L_q = 0.76$

$W = 0.37$ hr. $= 22.1$ min. $W_q = 0.18$ hr. $= 11.0$ min.

Note that in Case II, Lou's would lose over 25% of its business, and waiting time in the system has increased to 22 minutes, on the average.

COMPARISON OF CASE I AND CASE II

The following table summarizes the key results of the analysis:

	Best Case	Original Case	Worst Case
System empty	40.6 %	32.2 %	24.3 %
System full	12.9 %	18.6 %	25.7 %
Time in system	15.7 min.	18.6 min.	22.1 min.

If this were an actual problem, the range of waiting times (15.7 to 22.1 minutes) might well be acceptable. However, the difference between losing 12.9% of one's business and losing 25.7% might be unacceptable, and the decision maker might well insist on more precise estimates.

Note also the ϕ_{MAX} was greater than 1. You might wish to verify that if Lou's found a way to make more spaces available in the queue (i.e., $N > 3$), the analysis of Case II indicates rapidly deteriorating results. Recall that in the analysis of a system with an infinite queue, we must require that ϕ be less than 1.

STATE OF THE ART IN QUEUEING MODELS

As we noted earlier in the chapter, one can get a very large number of different queueing models by assuming different combinations of various aspects of calling populations, queue configurations and disciplines, and service systems. There are, however, some general results developed by researchers that help bring a little order out of this chaos. We discuss a few of these now.

SOME GENERAL PARAMETER RELATIONSHIPS

John D.C. Little [5] has shown that under quite general conditions, the following relationships hold:

$$W_q = L_q/\lambda; \quad W = L/\lambda; \quad W_q = L/\mu \tag{8.4}$$

To be more specific, if the queueing system we are analyzing has the property that service rate and arrival rate are independent of each other, the preceding relationships hold for any single-server system with an infinite queue. Note that we know λ and μ, so that if we are able to compute one of the four parameters L, L_q, W, or W_q, we may use Equation (8.4) to compute the other three. This remarkable result gives us some insight into the basic orderliness of queueing models.

THE M/G/1/∞/FIFO/1 MODEL

Consider the most basic model (illustrated earlier with PAC-MAN), but let us allow the service distribution to be any probability density function whatsoever. If we know its mean μ and variance V, the following formula (called the Pollaczek-Khintchine equation) allows us to compute the four key parameters:

$$L_q = \frac{\phi^2 + \lambda^2 V}{2(1 - \phi)} \tag{8.5}$$

Knowing L_q, we use the results in Equation (8.4) to compute L, W, and W_q.

As an illustration, suppose in our original PAC-MAN problem that the distribution of service time did not follow an exponential distribution but we computed the actual variance of service times to be 0.002 (hours)^2. Recalling that $\lambda=12, \mu=15$, and $\phi=0.80$, Equation (8.5) yields $L_q = 2.32$. Substituting in Equation (8.4) gives $W_q = 0.193$ hour $= 11.6$ minutes, $L = 2.895$, and $W = 0.241$ hour $= 14.5$ minutes.

Notice that this result gives us a shorter average queue (2.9 vs. 4) and a shorter waiting time (14.5 vs. 20 minutes) than we obtained with the M/M/etc. model. Since the variance of an exponential distribution is $1/\mu^2$ (in the original case, $V = 1/(15)^2 = 0.00444$), you might wish to verify that substituting this value in Equation (8.5) and thereafter in Equation (8.4) gives the original results.

ADVANCED MODELS

As mentioned earlier, we have only seen the tip of the iceberg in queueing theory. Researchers have built models to analyze various queue disciplines, finite calling populations, state-dependent arrival and service rates, balking and reneging, and many other features found in real-world queueing systems. And yet, it may appear to some that chasing after closed-form mathematical models of queueing systems is wasted effort in a practical sense, when an analyst familiar with the basic theory of queueing models can always arrive at satisfactory results with simulation.

MINICASES

ICQ

THE SCENARIO

Agua Fria, Inc. (AFI) is a manufacturer and wholesaler of packaged party ice. The firm uses special purified and demineralized water, so that despite the rather high retail price, its product is very popular with the cocktail set in the area.

A special machine quick-freezes the ice in AFI's Fairbanks, Alaska, plant and crushes it into roughly one-inch chunks. As the ice emerges from the machine, three baggers measure and bag the ice by hand, breaking up chunks in the process. The firm had considered automating the bagging process but concluded that the precise weight and uniform appearance obtained by using human baggers was an important selling point and abandoned the idea.

THE PROBLEM

The company's VP for Production was going over some production figures one frosty Alaska morning when he noted that the weight of ice shipments for the previous month was less than half the net weight of the purified water that they had used in the ice-making machine. One expected some losses in the ice business, but 50% was alarming. The VP hurried down to the plant floor to check things out.

The machine was set at 5,300 pounds per hour and seemed to be operating perfectly. The VP then observed the three baggers for a while. They seemed to be doing their jobs as usual—averaging about three ten-pound bags each per minute. As the VP watched, the baggers even got ahead of the machine occasionally, and sometimes one of the baggers would be idle for a brief period. The VP then checked the sump below the bagging platform. Lo and behold, the baggers were standing in two to three inches of water, and the drain was emptying at full capacity! The VP hurried to the office of the company's management science troubleshooter and filled her in on the problem.

"Boss," she said confidently, "give me an hour or so, and I'll have this problem down cold."

THE MODEL

Precisely 60 minutes later, the analyst strode into the VP's office, waving a sheet of paper covered with numbers and symbols.

"I retrieved some of my notes from my MBA program, and it looks like we can model this problem with a queueing model," she announced.

"You mean like a waiting line?" he replied with a frigid stare. "Nobody's waiting in line—our ice is melting."

"Our ice is waiting in line, boss," she said, "and it appears from my numbers that a lot of it is waiting too long. What we have here is a multiple-server queueing model with a single queue. I suspect that our big ice maker has quite a bit of variability in its output, and I know the baggers have variability in their bagging speed. This is really a finite queue-length situation, but they didn't cover that (for multiple servers) in our management science text. So, I've built a little multiple-server, single infinite queue model of our problem."

SOLUTION TO THE MODEL

Using ten pounds of ice as a unit in the calling population and one hour as the time unit for analysis, the analyst estimated the following queueing parameters:

λ = 530 10-pound units of ice per hour

μ = 180 10-pound bags per server per hour

S = 3 servers; ϕ = 530/180 = 2.944

The results using AFI's computerized queueing module were as follows:

$P(0) = 0.0042$

$W_q = 0.0965$ hour $= 5.79$ minutes

$W = 0.1021$ hour $= 6.13$ minutes

$L = 54.10 \quad L_q = 51.16$

"As you can see, boss," noted the analyst, "on the average, there's over 540 pounds of ice sitting on the loading platform, and it takes an average of over six minutes to get it bagged and in the freezer."

"It's even worse than that," replied the VP. "The platform has a capacity of 400 pounds, so when we exceed this limit, the excess falls off into the sump and melts—at a cost of $1.00 per 10-pound bag (*Note:* 'lost customer' cost)."

SOLUTION TO THE PROBLEM

It seemed clear to the VP that there were two viable alternatives: slow down the ice maker or hire additional baggers at $5 per hour. Profit margin on bags of ice was currently running at 25¢ (*Note:* cost/bag of waiting). The VP asked the analyst to rerun her model with the same three baggers and with $\lambda = 500$ bags per hour and then to add a fourth bagger and leave the production rate at $\lambda = 530$ bags per hour. Then, an idea suddenly, came to him: why not hire a fourth bagger and increase the production rate from 530 to 550 bags per hour—generating enough profit from the additional 20 bags to pay the new bagger's salary!

"This," the analyst thought, "is a job for SAMS' queueing module" [see Figure 8.5 and Table 8.6].

The VP chuckled with satisfaction when he saw the model solutions. Hiring the fourth bagger and increasing the throughput from 530 to 550 bags/hour reduced his waste cost

FIGURE 8.5
SAMS input screen for ICQ MINICASE

```
────► SAMS INPUT SCREEN - Queueing           ◄────

NAME?   ICQ MINICASE
PROBLEM DESCRIPTION - Model the queueing system for ICQ
under four separate configurations.
```

QUEUE NAME	Q1	Q2	Q3	Q4
CALLING POPULATION	INF	INF	INF	INF
ARRIVAL RATE	530	500	530	550
CALLING DISTRIBUT	POI	POI	POI	POI
QUEUE LENGTH	40	40	40	40
COST OF WAITING	.25	.25	.25	.25
NUMBER OF QUEUES	1	1	1	1
# OF SERVERS	3	3	4	4
SERVICE RATE/SERV	180	180	180	180
SERVICE DISTRIBUT	EXP	EXP	EXP	EXP
COST OF SERVICE	5	5	5	5
COST/LOST CUST	1	1	1	1

TABLE 8.6 SAMS report for ICQ

ICQ MINICASE
FULL BRIEFING ON MULTIPLE-SERVER QUEUEING MODEL

Model	Q1	Q2	Q3	Q4
Mean arrival rate	530.0	500.0	530.0	550.0
Mean service rate	180.0	180.0	180.0	180.0
Traffic intensity	96.4 %	92.6 %	73.6 %	76.4 %
Expected length of queue	16.3	9.2	1.36	1.72
Expected number in system	19.2	11.9	4.30	4.78
% lost callers	1.53%	.06%	0.0 %	0.0 %
Cost of servers	15.00	15.00	20.00	20.00
Cost of waiting	4.80	2.98	1.08	1.19
Cost of lost customers	8.11	1.53	0.00	0.00
Total system cost	27.91	19.51	21.08	21.19

from $12.91/hour to a mere $1.19/hour, and profit from the increased output paid the new bagger's salary.

"It's like magic," he exulted. "This queueing stuff is excellent!"

Agua Fria's problem was solved. ∎

Gourmet [2]

THE SCENARIO

El Queso Mohoso is an exclusive restaurant in downtown Dallas that serves gourmet Hispanic food. Although its prices are very expensive, the restaurant does a booming business six evenings per week and does not take reservations. All ten tables are tables for two, and the chef prepares all dishes for two people (thus, solitary diners pay for—and get—double portions of everything). There is a small bar with six barstools where patrons may while away their time until a table is free.

THE PROBLEM

Plata Cuchara, the owner of the establishment, is considering an expansion but is puzzled by the pattern of customer arrivals and departures. The head waiter informs her that at times—even during the busiest hours—there are tables open and the bar is unoccupied. At other times, he has to turn away several couples in a row because customers occupy every table and every bar stool. Plata decides to seek help from her very bright cousin, Huevo Cabeza, who is finishing his MBA work at a local university.

THE MODEL

Huevo listened carefully as Plata outlined her problem, and it appeared that he might be able to construct some sort of queueing model. However, the El Queso Mohoso problem didn't seem to be similar to any of the cases he had studied in graduate school, so he bought a copy of a widely used MBA text in management science and decided to use the 12-step checklist on queueing models from Table 8.1.

1. The calling population of couples going out to dinner was finite, of course, but Huevo reasoned that he could safely assume that it was infinite.
2. Since the restaurant catered strictly to couples, Huevo concluded that the calling population was homogeneous.
3. Although batch arrivals did occur, Huevo decided to treat couples as units, so that he could make the single-arrival assumption.
4. He next decided that he could treat the bar as a queue and had the head waiter keep a log of arrivals for several days. The pattern seemed to be fairly stable over the 6:00 P.M.–11:00 P.M. restaurant hours, with an average arrival rate of approximately nine couples per hour. Since the variance came out to be about nine as well, Huevo concluded that the arrival rate was Poisson distributed.
5. As to the queue configuration, it obviously had a finite number of places in which to wait.
6. The single-vs.-multiple-queues question was not a problem.
7. Huevo deferred the series/parallel-queues issue temporarily.
8. Balking and reneging, Huevo discovered, were not present. Couples seemed grateful for the chance to get inside—even if they had to wait in the bar for a table to become available—and they certainly weren't going to relinquish their place in line by reneging.
9. Queue priority was clearly FIFO, since Plata insisted on treating every couple equally.
10. Huevo bypassed the series/parallel-server question for the moment.
11. He also temporarily bypassed the homogeneous-vs.-nonhomogeneous-servers issue.
12. He decided to define service time as the difference between the time a couple was seated and the time the couple left the table. The head waiter logged these events for several evenings, and service appeared to be approximately exponential, with an average of one service per hour.

Reviewing his notes, Huevo concluded that the six barstools were the single, finite queue and that each of the ten tables was an individual parallel server. As a quick approximation, he decided to analyze the problem as one with an infinite queue and to assess the results.

SOLUTION TO THE MODEL

Using his SAMS-like queueing module, Huevo's M/M/1/∞/FIFO/10 model gave the following results:

$\mu = 1/\text{hour}; \quad \lambda = 9/\text{hour}; \quad \phi = 9; \quad S = 10$

$P(0) = \dfrac{1}{14{,}369} \quad L_q = 6.02 \quad W_q = 0.669 \text{ hr} = 40 \text{ min.}$

$L = 15.02 \quad W = 1.669 \text{ hrs} = 1 \text{ hr., } 40 \text{ min.}$

TABLE 8.7 SAMS report for GOURMET

GOURMET MINICASE
QUICK BRIEFING ON MULTIPLE-SERVER FINITE QUEUE MODEL

Model	Q1
Mean arrival rate	9.0
Mean service rate	1.0
Traffic intensity	85.30%
Expected length of queue	1.32
Expected number in system	9.86
Number of waiting spaces	6.00
Number of servers	10.00
% lost callers	5.23%

These results looked reasonable to Huevo, but they gave no indication of how much business the restaurant was losing. Huevo therefore ran the actual M/M/1/6/FIFO/10 model. Table 8.7 gives the SAMS report.

It appeared that El Queso Mohoso was losing a little more than 5% of its potential customers. More than half of the customers had a short wait in the bar before being seated for dinner, but the average wait in the bar was brief, since the bar's average occupancy rate was about 1.3.

SOLUTION TO THE PROBLEM

Huevo showed the results to his cousin Plata and recommended against expansion. His reasoning was that turning away 5% of potential customers was probably a positive factor on balance and bolstered the restaurant's image of exclusivity. Another factor in his recommendation involved the very high quality of food and service. Expansion would mean having to hire additional chefs and waiters, and Plata would find it difficult or impossible to maintain close watch over the cuisine and personal attention to customers. Huevo did, however, recommend raising prices by 20 percent.

Plata listened carefully and then thanked Huevo for his assistance with the offer of a free dinner. However, after waiting in the bar for over an hour for a table, Huevo reneged and ate dinner elsewhere.

SUMMARY

In this chapter, we investigated various applications of waiting-line models and demonstrated that three interdependent subsystems compose such models: calling population, queueing facility, and service facility.

We discussed modeling queueing systems using a 12-step checklist that addresses the various facets of each subsystem. We presented the closed form analytical results for three simple queueing models and discussed sensitivity analysis. We then analyzed two minicases to illustrate the application of two queueing models.

Chapter 9 discusses in depth the powerful and widely used discrete simulation model.

KEY TERMS

balking
batch arrival
calling population
Erlang distribution
FIFO
LIFO
Markovian model
parallel servers
queue

queue discipline
random
rank
reneging
series servers
service facility
single arrival
single servers

PROBLEMS FOR ANALYSIS

1. Stan N. Lyons, the vice president for Production for PAC-MAN, Inc., has done his homework on queueing models and is now ready to complete his tete-a-tete with QUES.

    STAN: OK, QUES, I'm ready to complete our analysis of our tool-crib operation at PAC-MAN.

    QUES: Hello again, old sock. Let me fetch our data from my disk to refresh your memory.

    $\lambda = 12$ arrivals per hour, on the average, by workers at the tool crib; Poisson distributed

    $\mu = 15$ services per hour, on the average, by the tool crib attendant; exponentially distributed

    $\phi = \lambda/\mu = 0.80$, traffic intensity

    Average technician's pay = $19.50 per hour

    Tool crib attendant's pay = $6.00 per hour

    Results of M/M/1/∞/FIFO/1 model analysis:

    $P(0) = 0.2$, fraction of time server is idle

    $L = 4$, average number of workers in the system

    $L_q = 3.2$, average number of workers in the queue

    $W = 0.333$ hr. = 20 minutes, average time spent in the system

    $W_q = 0.267$ hr. = 16 minutes, average time spent in the queue

    Total cost of technician idle time = $624 per day

    a. Analyze the PAC-MAN problem with a computer package like SAMS. Perform a ±10% sensitivity analysis for this model.
    b. In the original PAC-MAN model, replace the $6/hour tool-crib attendant, who has a service rate of 15/hour, with an experienced technician at $19.50/hour and who has a service rate of 30/hour. Perform a ±10% sensitivity analysis for this model and compare your results with (a). Does it appear to be preferable to hire a faster worker or to hire two slower workers with the same total service rate but at a lower total cost?
    c. From a managerial economics point of view, explain the results you obtained in (b). Many people find this result to be counterintuitive, but those who understand the concept of productivity don't.

2. **The Scenario** [3]: In the small, sleepy community of Siesta, Idaho, there is a single gas station, which Phil Upp owns and operates. The station has a single pump, and Phil is the only employee. Siesta is several miles off the main highway, so almost all of Phil's business comes from local residents. Phil's business practices are very antiquated by modern standards—he still washes windshields and checks air, oil, and water for his customers—regardless of the size of the purchase.

   A normal service usually takes about 10 minutes if the customer's tank is nearly empty, and customers arrive for service randomly but at an average rate of about one every 15 minutes. Thus, Phil keeps fairly busy, but he seems to have ample time to relax.

   a. Analyze Phil's scenario using the M/M/1/∞/FIFO/1 model. Does this model appear to be appropriate in this situation?
   b. Can you guess what's coming next?

   The Problem: One bright Sunday morning, someone started a rumor that there was a gasoline shortage. When Phil opened his station at 7:00 A.M. the next morning, there were already four cars waiting to "top off" their gasoline tanks. Although Phil insisted that there wasn't a gas shortage, most of his customers didn't believe him. The frequency with which customers arrived doubled from four per hour to eight per hour. Since most services were "top-offs," Phil's average service time dropped from ten minutes to seven minutes, but Phil was still determined to give full service regardless.

   The Model:
   a. Analyze this new scenario as an M/M/1/∞/FIFO/1 model and compare your previous results. What has happened to Phil's idle time? How long is the average waiting time? How long is the average queue?
   b. In exasperation, Phil installed a second pump, hired another attendant at $5 per hour, and raised his gasoline price by 10¢ per gallon to cover his additional costs. The townspeople immediately accused him of profiteering from the "gasoline shortage," although Phil insisted he was pumping almost exactly the same number of gallons per week as he always had. Analyze this new situation as a two-server, infinite queue model.
   c. The new attendant was lazy and irresponsible, and Phil fired him within two weeks. Phil then shut down one pump and lowered his average service rate to four minutes per customer by refusing to wash windshields or to check air, oil, and water. He also erected a barrier so that only four cars could wait in line (including the one being serviced) at a time. Analyze this situation as a single-server, finite queue model. Compute $P(4)$—the probability of lost sales. In this situation, are the lost sales really lost?
   d. Gradually, because of the limited number of spaces in which to wait for service, the townspeople returned to their previous pattern of filling their tanks when they were near empty—instead of topping off at the earliest opportunity. When normalcy finally returned, Phil removed the barrier. However—miffed by the behavior of the citizens of Siesta—he never resumed his previous practice of cleaning windshields and checking his customers' oil, air, and water. He also retained the 10¢ per gallon price increase and enjoyed the leisure he had been accustomed to before the great "gasoline shortage" fiasco.
      Aren't you glad that this exercise is a fable and that real people don't act that way?

3. **The Scenario:** Let's return to the Lou's Change scenario from this chapter and investigate it further. Recall that Lou has one oil-change pit and two additional spaces for cars to wait for service.

   The Problem: Customer arrival rate averages 5 per hour (Poisson), and service time averages 10 minutes (exponential).

The Model: We originally modeled Lou's problem as a single-server, finite queue model.

Solution to the Model: Table 8.8 reproduces part of the SAMS solution report.

TABLE 8.8 SAMS report for Lou's change

LOU'S CHANGE FULL BRIEFING ON SINGLE-SERVER QUEUEING MODEL	
Mean arrival rate	5.0
Mean service rate	6.0
Traffic intensity	83.30%
Expected length of queue	.60
Expected number in system	1.27
% lost callers	18.6 %

a. Lou is considering turning one of the two waiting spaces into an additional oil-change bay, leaving only one space in which customers can wait. Use a package such as SAMS' queueing module that can analyze multiple-server, finite queue models to analyze this new problem. Does your intuition tell you that Lou's situation will improve somewhat? Perform a ±10% analysis similar to the PAC-MAN analysis in Problem 1. How sensitive is Lou's problem to small errors in his problem parameters?

b. Now convert the single remaining waiting space into a third oil-change bay and repeat the analysis to include a ±10% sensitivity investigation with a zero-length queue.

4. As noted in this chapter, we often make the assumption of an infinite queue length when modeling waiting-line systems. To assess the accuracy of this approximation, compare the analytical results obtained for the M/M/1/∞/FIFO/1 and M/M/1/N/FIFO/1 models, reproduced in Table 8.9 from the appendix to this chapter.

a. For $\phi < 1$, what happens to the expression $(1 - \phi^{N+1})$ as N increases? What can you conclude about the values of $P(0)$ for the two models as N becomes large?

TABLE 8.9

	Single-Server Infinite Queue ($\phi < 1$)	Single-Server Finite Queue ($\phi < 1$)
$P(0)$	$1 - \phi$	$\dfrac{1 - \phi}{1 - \phi^{N+1}}$
L	$\dfrac{\phi}{1 - \phi}$	$\dfrac{\phi}{1 - \phi} - \dfrac{(N+1)\phi^{N+1}}{1 - \phi^{N+1}}$
W	$\dfrac{L}{\lambda}$	$\dfrac{L}{\lambda[1 - P(N)]}$

b. For $\phi < 1$, what happens to the term $(N + 1)\phi^{N + 1}/(1 - \phi^{N + 1})$ as N increases? What can you conclude about the values of L for the two models as N becomes large?

c. As N becomes large, $P(N)$ becomes small, all else remaining constant. What, therefore, happens to the values of W for the two models as N becomes large?

5. **The Scenario:** The message decoding facility of the Central Information Agency (CIA) is located in the windowless subbasement of its headquarters in Foggy Bottom, Virginia. Messages arrive from all over the world at the average rate of 20 per hour, but arrivals tend to be uniformly distributed over the interval 0–40 (i.e., an arrival rate of 10 per hour is just as likely as 30 or 40 per hour). Each message carries one of three classifications: sensitive, highly sensitive, or eyes only. Some decoding clerks have security clearances only for sensitive messages, while others are cleared to handle both sensitive and highly sensitive ones. A special team, working in a separate, tempered-steel vault, decodes eyes-only messages.

In addition to carrying its classification, a message may also carry a decoding time priority of urgent or routine. Urgent messages carry a preemptive priority, so that if a particular clerk is decoding a routine message when an urgent one arrives, he or she stops and begins work on the urgent message.

Decoders cleared only for sensitive messages work as a group (A), and those cleared for highly sensitive or sensitive form a separate group (B). Messages arrive at a single point, where a dispatcher routes them to the appropriate group. Obviously, the dispatcher routes all eyes-only messages to the special team in the vault, but this team occasionally decodes highly sensitive if the messages are urgent and if the team is not busy. Group B occasionally decodes sensitive messages if the messages are urgent and if the team is not busy on urgent, highly sensitive messages. Group A decodes only sensitive messages.

On the average, a team can decode a sensitive message in five minutes and a highly sensitive message in six minutes, but these times tend to be normally distributed ($\mu_1 = 12$/hour and $\mu_2 = 10$/hr), with variances roughly equal to their means. Decoding an eyes-only message takes exactly 15 minutes, with no variability, because of the precise computerized procedure used. About half of all incoming messages are sensitive, about one-third are highly sensitive, and one-sixth are eyes-only. Overall, about 10% of the messages are urgent, with the rest being routine, and the arrival pattern is random.

The Problem: So far, the system seemed to be working well. The dispatcher, being sensitive to the hour-by-hour variations in workload among the three groups, routed messages accordingly. One gray day, however, a mandated personnel reduction converted the dispatcher's highly paid GS-15 position to GS-6, and CIA transferred the dispatcher to the College Surveillance Division. The clerk that replaced the dispatcher was bright and willing to learn, but the best he could manage to do was to go by the book—routing all sensitive messages to Group A, all highly sensitive messages to Group B, and (of course) nothing but eyes-only messages to the group in the vault.

The Model: Figure 8.6 shows a schematic of this queueing system. Use the checklist from Table 8.1 to analyze this queueing system. What are the odds that there exists a closed-form solution to this model?

Solution to the Model: The former dispatcher used judgment in smoothing out the workload among the three groups. This is an example of state-dependent arrival rates in that the dispatcher routed messages to less busy groups in an effort to minimize the lengths of the three priority queues.

Solution to the Problem:
a. How sensitive is this system to modest errors in the estimates of arrival and service rates? How would a small shift in percentages of message types affect the system?

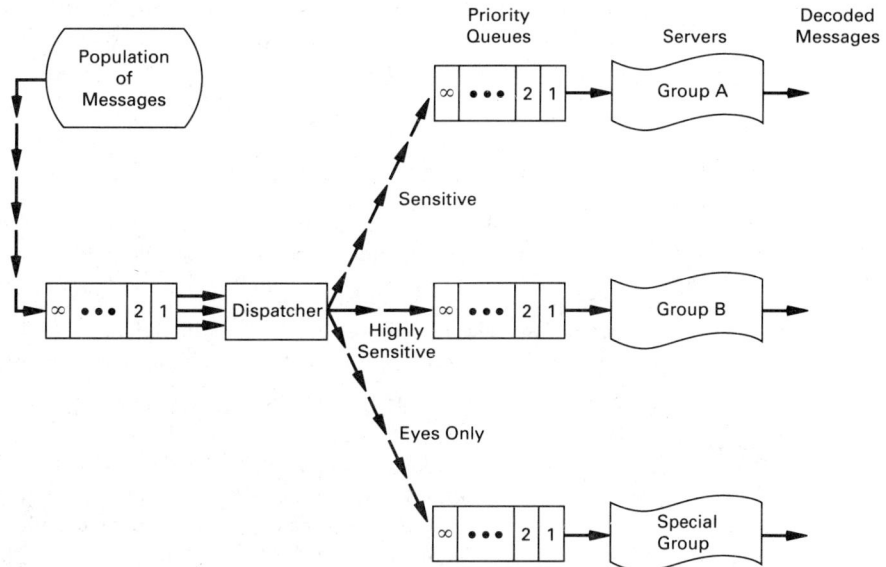

FIGURE 8.6 CIA message decoding model

b. Suppose that if a routine message doesn't get decoded after being in the system for four hours (because of being bumped by urgent messages), we automatically change its priority to urgent. What effect would this feature have on the system?

Epilogue: Models such as this are messy to analyze but represent the complexity usually found in business, industrial and public sector systems. For example, instead of there being a CIA message decoding system, suppose the dispatcher was actually the receiving department for an inventory system and that the messages were different kinds of materials for different decoders (departments). What we would have is a classical work-in-process inventory and production system.

6. In assuming that service times are exponentially distributed, we were, of course, using the following probability distribution:

$$f(t) = \mu e^{-\mu t}, \quad t \geq 0; \quad E(t) = 1/\mu; \quad \text{VAR}(t) = 1/\mu^2$$

As noted earlier, the high variability of the exponential distribution is the source of much of the counterintuitive pattern that queueing models exhibit. Suppose our actual service rate were significantly less variable, so that the standard deviation was smaller than the mean.

Consider the following, very useful, density function called the **Erlang distribution**:

$$f(t) = \frac{(\mu k)^k (t^{k-1})(e^{-k\mu t})}{(k-1)!} \quad \text{for } t \geq 0; \quad k = 1, 2, 3, \ldots$$

$$E(t) = 1/\mu \qquad \text{VAR}(t) = 1/k\mu^2$$

a. Verify that for $k = 1$, the Erlang becomes the exponential distribution. (*Note:* $0! = 1$ by definition.)
b. Note that for $k > 1$, the variance is smaller than that of the exponential.
c. Use the Pollaczek-Khintchine equation (8.5) to verify that for a single server and an infinite queue

$$L_q = \frac{(k+1)}{2k}\left(\frac{\phi^2}{1-\phi}\right)$$

Use the general relationships in Equation (8.4) and L_q as above to compute the closed form values of L, W, and W_q.

d. Using Erlang distributions with $k = 2, 4, 9$, reexamine the results obtained in Problem 1 for the PAC-MAN problem. Notice the marked improvement in the parameter values as k increases.

PRACTICE MODELS

1. The following information pertains to a hospital emergency room. Use a package like SAMS to compute facility utilization rate and queue statistics.

   - Patients arrive at the rate of six per hour.
   - Currently there is one clerk at the registration desk.
   - Average service time per patient is nine minutes (exponential).

2. In Problem 1, the hospital administrator has decided to limit the number of patients waiting in the registration line to seven. Use a package like SAMS to determine queue statistics and compare your results to those in Problem 1.

3. Customer arrivals at the Hokie Airline reservation counter follow a Poisson distribution. Use a package like SAMS to determine average server utilization and expected number of customers in the system for the following:

   - Arrival rate = 10 customers per hour.
   - Number of servers = 3.
   - Service rate = 5 minutes per customer (exponential).

4. At a fast-food restaurant, customers arrive at the rate of 12 per hour (Poisson). Three servers provide service, each at the rate of three minutes per customer (exponential). Use a package like SAMS to test this operation for 100 customers.

REFERENCES AND ADDITIONAL READING

1. Cooper, R. *Introduction to Queueing Theory*. New York: Macmillan, 1972.
2. Dinnin, M. Adapted (liberally) from an unpublished MBA term project report, Texas Tech University (1982).
3. Erickson, W. Problem suggested by "Management Science and the Gas Shortage." *Interfaces* 4 (1974): 47–51.
4. Kendall, D. "Stochastic Processes Occurring in the Theory of Queues and Their Analysis by the Method of Imbedded Markov Chains," *Annals of Mathematical Statistics* 24 (1953): 338–354.
5. Little, J. "A Proof of the Queueing Formula: $L = \lambda W$," *Operations Research* 9 (1961): 383–387.
6. Morse, P. *Queues, Inventories, and Maintenance*. New York: Wiley, 1958.
7. Wagner, H. *Principles of Operations Research* (2d ed.). Englewood Cliffs, N.J.: Prentice-Hall, 1975.

APPENDIX
Closed-Form Analytical Results for Two Models

THE M/M/1/N/FIFO/1 MODEL

$$P(n) = \begin{cases} \dfrac{\phi^n(1-\phi)}{(1-\phi^{N+1})}, & \text{for } \phi < 1 \\ 1/(N+1), & \text{for } \phi \geq 1 \end{cases}$$

$$L = \frac{\phi}{(1-\phi)} - \frac{(N+1)\phi^{N+1}}{(1-\phi^{N+1})}$$

$$L_q = L - [1 - P(0)]$$

$$W = \frac{L}{\lambda[1-P(N)]} \qquad W_q = \frac{L_q}{\lambda[1-P(N)]}$$

THE M/M/1/∞/FIFO/S MODEL

$$P(0) = \frac{(S-\phi)}{\sum_{n=0}^{S-1} \dfrac{(S-n)\phi^n}{n!}}, \text{ for } \frac{\phi}{S} < 1$$

$$P(n) = \begin{cases} \dfrac{\phi^n P(0)}{n!}, & \text{if } n < S \\ \dfrac{\phi^n P(0)}{S!(S^{n-S})}, & \text{if } n \geq S \end{cases}$$

$$L_q = \frac{\phi^{S+1} P(0)}{(S-1)!(S-\phi)^2}$$

$$W_q = \frac{L_q}{\lambda} \qquad W = W_q + \frac{1}{\mu}$$

$$L = \lambda W$$

Note that for this model we took advantage of some known relationships among $P(0)$, W_q, W, L_q, and L to simplify the results. Still, we are reaching a level of complexity at which it is prudent to rely upon computer programs for our analyses.

CHAPTER 9

Discrete Simulation Models

Most of the models discussed so far in Part 2 were static models. We assumed that all data, relationships, and variables remained fairly constant over a given time period or planning horizon. When such is not the case, we are operating in an environment involving change—a **dynamic environment**.

When the dynamics are pronounced enough to require explicit consideration, we may use **simulation**—a methodology for conducting experiments using a model of the real system. Frequently, the expediency for using simulation occurs whenever there is an essential dependence on time that we must consider. Simulation models permit tracing through in time the dynamics and behavior implicitly induced by the model's probabilistic and causal structure.

In yet another fundamental respect, simulation models differ from the optimization models described in Part 1. The models of Part 1 were mostly prescriptive—prescribing what's best (or at least what's better). Simulation models tend to be descriptive—telling it like it is. However, we cannot dichotomize hard and fast rules pertaining to prescriptive usage of optimization models and descriptive usage of simulation models. We occasionally use optimization models for descriptive purposes, whereas simulation models may be prescriptive, although such usages are rare.

Both model types provide the manager with intuition, insight, and understanding, as we shall see. However, because of this fundamental difference, algorithms for solving simulation models do not automatically generate alternative solution strategies as did the algorithms for solving the optimization models in Part 1. It therefore becomes the responsibility of the user to generate his or her own alternative solution strategies. The user must also perform all comparisons of alternative solutions manually and without the help of a figure of merit—what we usually call an objective function. We call this approach to policy experimentation what-if analysis.

Galitz [12] corroborates the apparent distinctions we have made here between optimization models and simulation models:

> At first sight, it might seem that optimizing models are superior to descriptive ones, because they actually produce decision strategies rather than merely evaluate them. However, optimizing models have the drawback that the decisions they produce are very sensitive to the exact formulation of the criterion to be optimized and the constraints imposed. Yet it is extremely difficult to quantify these accurately. Moreover, we must consider carefully the decisions produced by optimizing models, since most of these models assume certainty and produce no hedging strategies other than those

forced by specific constraints. . . . Descriptive models can themselves be used to generate decision strategies by using a trial and error process, and subjective judgments and assessments can be made as the user goes along.

Many have documented the importance of simulation modeling in commerce, industry, and government. In the view of Keen and Scott Morton [17]: "It seems fair to say that simulation is the most widely used managerial computer-based technique in both government and industrial decision making. . ." Surveys by Naylor et al. [24, 26], Shannon et al. [35, 36], and others all suggest that simulation and statistical methods are the most widely used management science techniques that industry uses. Emshoff and Sisson [7] published an extensive list of areas that are using simulation methods. The list in Table 9.1 excludes areas mentioned by these authors but includes still others. The list is indicative of the breadth of applications to which people put

TABLE 9.1 Partial list of simulation applications

Resource Management Systems
   Water resource management models
   Energy resource management models
   Natural resource management models

Pollution Management Systems
   Air pollution regulation models
   Trace metals contaminant models
   Solid waste management models
   Water quality models

Urban and Regional Planning
   Land use planning models
   Urban (regional) economic development models
   Urban (regional) population growth models
   Urban (regional) planning
   Location models
   Sewer system models
   Airport simulations

Transportation Systems
   Urban (regional) transportation models
   Air transportation models
   Traffic flow models

Health Systems
   Health care delivery models
   Hospital design models
   Community health models

Criminal Justice Systems
   Criminal justice models
   Criminal detection/prevention models

Industrial Systems
   Total company models
   Production models
   Capital resources models
   Finance models

Commerce Systems
   Marketing models
   Advertising models

Education Systems
   Secondary school models
   Higher education models
   University enrollment and resources models

Information Systems
   Organization models
   Library models

Miscellaneous
   Insect/pest control models
   Municipal information system models
   Forest growth and nutrient cycling models
   Telecommunications regulation models
   Public safety models

simulation. However, discrete simulation is not an appropriate model for all of these application areas. We could better accommodate at least some of these application areas by continuous simulation, discussed in the appendix to this chapter.

As an example of a situation to which we could apply simulation, let's return to the capacity planning problem first described in Chapter 3. Imagine that we are hiding in the office closet of Buck Stopps, the grizzly, hard-nosed vice president of finance for Monolithic Manufacturing, Inc. Stopps finds his company currently operating in a dynamic economic environment that we could characterize as "feast or famine" or "roller coaster." While the company has a definite short-term need for additional five-axis milling machines, the long-term outlook is not nearly as bright, because of rising interest rates and increased foreign competition. Bitsy Bytes has just returned from the computer center with her most recent run. Her model now produces integer solutions to the problem of deciding how many additional milling machines to purchase. Bitsy is using the current order file as a basis for determining short-term demand.

> "Buck, I have another solution to that milling machine problem I'd like to discuss with you," Bitsy says timidly.
>
> "Fine! Fine! What's the computer spitting out these days?" inquires Buck.
>
> "Well, in order to meet our order commitments over the next six months, the current solution calls for the purchase of three five-axis milling machines, two conventional lathes, and two three-axis milling machines for a cost of $15,650,000."
>
> "For a cost of what? We don't have that kind of money, young lady. And besides, what do we do with all of the excess capacity when the economy softens?"

Once again Bitsy returns to her workstation with new points to ponder. Buck has made the need to consider fluctuating demand over the lifetime of capital equipment painfully apparent to her. Bitsy begins to scratch about for other modeling approaches to her problem.

While the preceding bit of dialogue suggests a definite requirement for simulation models, it does not address the question of the kinds of purposes that simulation can achieve. Table 9.2 lists some of the purposes and benefits of simulation models. These purposes and benefits correspond closely to the purposes and benefits that motivate the formulation and use of MS models in general.

TABLE 9.2 Purposes and benefits of simulation models

- To be able to explore alternatives
- To improve the quality of decision making
- To enable more effective planning
- To improve understanding of the business
- To enable faster decision making
- To provide more timely information
- To enable more accurate forecasts
- To generate cost savings

TABLE 9.3 Simulation model dichotomies

• Discrete	vs.	continuous
• Probabilistic	vs.	deterministic
• Steady state	vs.	transient
• Mathematical	vs.	physical
• Causal	vs.	correlative
• Homomorphic	vs.	isomorphic

Just as there are many different types of MS models, there are also a great many different types of simulation models. We must deal with the dichotomies listed in Table 9.3 in connection with choice of simulation model type. This chapter is concerned with simulations having the attributes listed on the left-hand side of the table. The appendix discusses deterministic, continuous simulation.

Let's briefly discuss each of the dichotomies in Table 9.3. **Discrete simulations** are appropriate for systems whose variables change rather abruptly at discrete points in time. For example, the number of shoppers in a grocery store changes only when shoppers enter or leave the store. A **continuous simulation** is appropriate for systems whose variables are continually changing with time; for example, a passenger train traveling between two cities where its speed and location change continuously with time.

Deterministic simulations are appropriate for systems whose parameters (constants) and structure are relatively well-known and understood—that is, the system contains no random variables—whereas **probabilistic** (or **Monte Carlo**) **simulation** is appropriate for situations in which this is not the case. For example, a simulation model of an airport will include probabilistic distributions of passenger interarrival and service times. (Often, we use deterministic simulations to model situations in which we do not know well the structure and parameters because of the added complexity to the simulation model that stochastic or probabilistic considerations create.) We use Monte Carlo techniques in connection with discrete representations because the time between changes in the system is usually random.

Transient simulations are appropriate for systems that indicate a temporary behavior—for example, a simulation model of a traffic light at a busy intersection during a three-hour time span—whereas **steady-state simulations** are useful to represent systems that operate in a steady state. According to the second law of thermodynamics, all systems tend to wear down and grow old unless driven by an input. As this happens, systems begin to exhibit a steady-state or static behavior, whereas relatively "young" systems exhibit a transient behavior.

We use **mathematical simulations** in connection with the digital computer. We use the computer to simulate the model characterized by means of mathematical equations. On the other hand, **physical simulations** include flight simulators, planetarium shows, movies, arcade amusements, video games, and television programs.

Moreover, simulation models may be **causal** or **correlative,** depending upon whether the interconnections among the components that describe the system represent an attempt to model the actual interactions among these components or represent simply a linkage between two variables that statistically are highly correlated.

Finally, simulation models may be **isomorphic,** but more often they are **homomorphic** in the sense that there does not usually exist a unique two-way correspondence between the elements of the original system and the elements of the model. Most of the time our models are too aggregated to allow each element of the model to correspond to only one element in the object system. Since a one-to-one correspondence between each element in the object system and each component in the model is rare, isomorphic simulations are unusual.

Before getting into a discussion of the underlying assumptions of discrete simulations, we need to dwell for a moment on the inherent characteristics of simulation. First and foremost, the capability of tracing through the effects in time of a particular scenario, policy, or strategy is a definite asset. Second, simulations generally describe the consequences of a given set of inputs, but as we indicated earlier, they do not prescribe optimal policies. Third, simulation can provide answers for problems that are difficult (even impossible) to solve in any other way. Fourth, simulation models serve as a vehicle on which we can perform what-if experiments. In the absence of models, we would have to perform such experiments on the object system itself—and the consequences could be disastrous. Simulation provides an inexpensive tool for carrying out these experiments in a way that permits the user to immediately perceive the consequences of a particular set of actions. This time-compression characteristic of all simulations is once again a definite asset.

In summary we find that simulations permit us to draw inferences about systems without building them if they are merely proposed; enable us to obtain insights about systems without disturbing them, since such disturbances may be expensive and risky; and allow us to develop intuition about systems without destroying the system when the object is to determine the stress limits of the system.

UNDERLYING ASSUMPTIONS AND DEFINITIONS

Perhaps the best way to begin this discussion is to define **simulation**—any model that permits the projection through time of the dynamic behavior of an object system. Generally, we implement a simulation model on a digital computer, although people still use analog computer implementations (though mostly for engineering applications). Analog computer simulations are beyond the scope of this book.

We can approach simulation from two fundamentally different philosophies. This section concentrates only on probabilistic, discrete simulation. Discrete simulation is an appropriate tool to use when the dependent variables in the system change discretely at specified points in time. Such is always the case when we can characterize the object system by activities or events.

ACTIVITIES AND EVENTS

Researchers developed the philosophy of discrete simulation in the early 1960s in connection with the work of Kiviat [18] and others. The concept of an activity is central to this philosophy. An **activity** is an elementary task that requires time to complete; for example, the activity to design a shopping mall. Activities always precede and follow other activities; e.g., the design of a shopping mall is preceded by the activity to find a suitable location and is followed by the activity to construct the building.

A **process** is a collection of activities, which we must perform either serially in chronological order or in parallel, as Figure 9.1 shows. In either case, we always perform the activities in a logical order. The actual time required to complete an

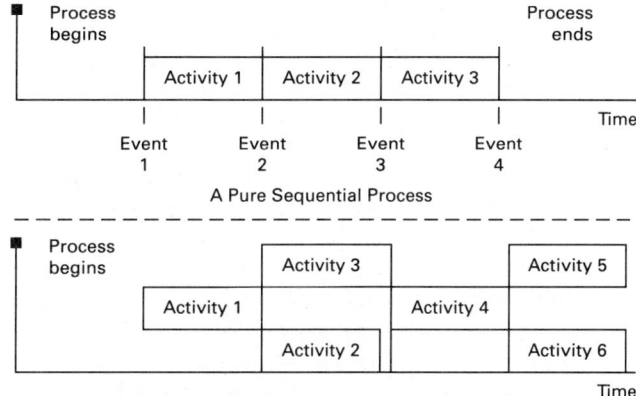

FIGURE 9.1 Processes viewed as chronological sequences of activities

activity is usually random. Probabilistic concerns come into play here. Computer simulations sample probability distributions to generate random activity duration times.

Events bound each activity. An **event** is the instant in time that an activity begins or ends. For most events, the associated time instant marks the ending of one activity and the beginning of the next. Events, like activities, are ordered in time. Events are instants in time at which the system undergoes some form of change—a customer begins to receive service, a machine begins to remove a part, a telephone conversation ends.

The activities must take place in a logical, even essential, order. The completion of an activity logically initiates the next activity to follow. The same is true of events. When an event signals the start of an activity, we know that a future event will signal the end of that activity. In this sense, then, events precipitate the occurrence of still other events. Likewise, the completion of an activity may start one or more other activities. In discrete simulation we advance the simulated clock from event time to event time. Since the event times are the only instants in which the object system changes, these are the only time instants we need to consider. Thus, we simulate the behavior of the system by examining the system only at the events.

ENTITIES AND ATTRIBUTES

We are also interested in entities and attributes in discrete simulation. **Entities** are the physical items of interest in the process itself. Some entities tend to pass through the process and leave. They are *temporary entities,* among which are such things as customers, telephone calls, letters, piece parts, automobiles, airplanes, and students. Permanent entities remain a part of the object system throughout the time period of interest. They include checkout clerks, telephone networks, post office clerks, conveyor belts, streets, airports, and universities. One of the goals of discrete simulation is to reproduce the activities that the entities engage in. This enables us to gain intuition and insight and make inferences by studying the performance and behavior of the model system. Thus, customers shop for groceries and wait to check out, and then the grocery clerk checks the customers through. Automobiles wait at a traffic light when the light turns red and thereafter continue to the next light, etc.

Entities, events, and activities all have characteristics of particular interest in discrete simulation. We call such characteristics **attributes**. For example, in a grocery store simulation, we are interested in the average checkout time of a clerk. This essential bit of information is an attribute of the clerk. We call these entities and their attributes the **state** of the object system.

APPROACHES TO DISCRETE SIMULATION

People use at least two basic approaches in the actual implementation of discrete simulations. One of these, called the discrete-next-event approach, models the process by focusing on the events. Simulation languages like SIMSCRIPT [18] and GASP [30, 31] use this approach. The other approach, which we call a process- or block-oriented approach, focuses on the activities. GPSS [14, 34] is the most popular language implementing this approach. A newer language called SLAM [29] can use either approach. We discuss these languages later in the chapter in the section entitled "Solution Approaches—An Intuitive Description."

Regardless of whether the approach is event oriented or block oriented, discrete simulations use the same method for advancing time. All simulation languages use a specially defined variable to keep track of the current simulated time. They advance time from the currently processed event to the time of the next event. They consider only event times, since these are the only instants at which the simulation model changes. They execute the model by advancing time discretely from one event to the immediately succeeding one—hence, the name discrete simulation. The simulation stops once it has collected a satisfactory number of "samples" or once the current simulation time variable surpasses some prespecified final time.

MECHANICS OF DISCRETE SIMULATION MODEL FORMULATION

Perhaps the best way to begin designing a discrete simulation is to list the activities, the entities, and their attributes. When we use the discrete-next-event approach, we will want to break the activities down into their respective events. Next, we delineate an activity precedence diagram (as in Figure 9.1) or an event generation diagram (as in Figure 9.2). These diagrams help us structure the model into a working simulation. Finally, we determine the activity duration times and the times between occurrences of recurrent events. Most likely, these times are probabilistic or random, and we describe them in terms of a probability distribution, a mean, and (usually) a standard deviation. We describe the techniques used in characterizing this randomness within a simulation later in the chapter.

We process each event by transferring control to an event routine specially written for the processing of the particular event. This routine may generate other events, collect samples on important variables, place entities in queues (or files), change the busy status of server facilities, etc. It does the necessary housekeeping chores required to record the occurrence of the event and to create other events that the occurrence of the current event precipitates. In some languages the user writes the event routines— i.e., GASP, SIMSCRIPT, etc.—while others—GPSS—use standard event processing routines.

NEIGHBORHOOD GROCERY STORE EXAMPLE

Phil Pocket, owner of Savin E. Levin, Inc., is considering placing an extra checkout clerk in each of his grocery stores during peak operating hours of 4 P.M. to 8 P.M. weekdays. Managers have reported long waiting times of up to 11 minutes, and some arriving customers will leave immediately when they see a long line of 10 or more

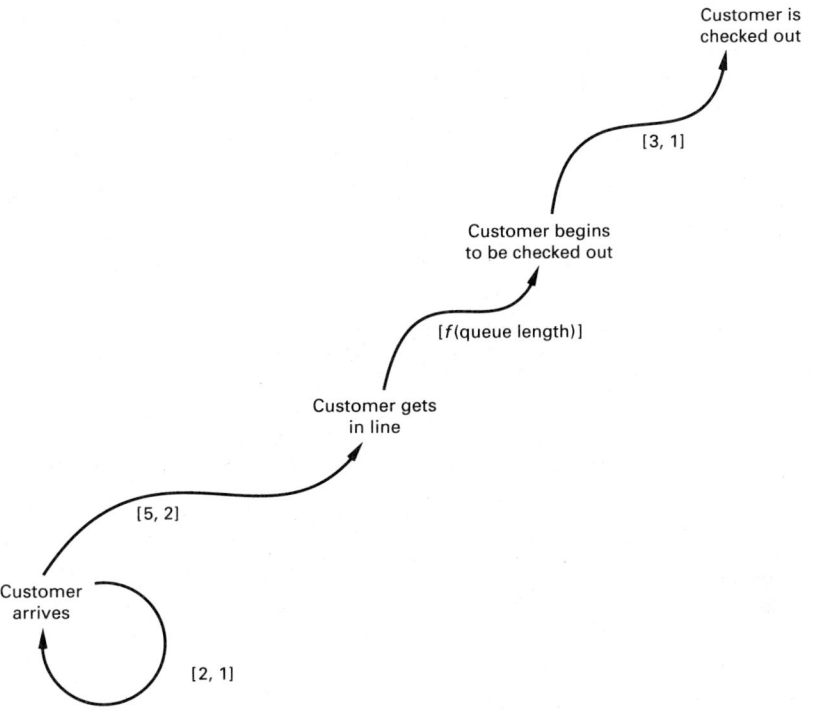

FIGURE 9.2 Precipitation sequence for the events listed in the neighborhood grocery store

customers waiting to check out. Phil is losing customers, and he knows how much this will cost. Phil is interested in knowing by how much a second checker will reduce the average waiting time. Since the part-time clerk will be slower than the regular checkout clerk, Phil is uncertain as to how this will affect average customer waiting time.

It seems apparent to Phil that the problem is a dynamic one involving a definite time duration. Phil loads a simulation module called SAM (sequential activity modeler) into his personal computer to see whether he can develop a simulation.

SAM: Hi. This is queue buster SAM. Who are you?

PHIL: My name is Phil Pocket, and I have a simulation problem for you.

SAM: My favorite kind. I assume you want discrete simulation. Otherwise I'd recommend my buddy CAM for continuous simulation.

PHIL: That's right.

SAM: What I need from you is a list of activities, events, entities, and their attributes. I will also need statistics on the time durations of the activities.

PHIL: I thought so. I looked at the manual in advance of our session, and I've pretty much got the data you requested in the form specified in the manual [see Table 9.4].

SAM: I'm prepared to accept the data, Phil.

PHIL: Here they are.

SAM: Very good. Your activities have a definite time duration, while your events are instants in time. Are you sure these are all of the events, activities, entities, and their attributes?

PHIL: I left out the "customer leaves store" activity, since this seemed unimportant relative to the purpose of the modeling effort. It seems to me that once the customers check out, they are effectively out of the system.

TABLE 9.4 Neighborhood Grocery Store activities, events, entities and attributes for a problem involving waiting times of customers

	Mean Time Duration	Bounds of Time Duration
Activities		
Customers shopping for groceries	5 min	2 min
Customer waiting to check out	function of queue length	
Customers checking out (checker 1)	3 min	± 1 min
Customers checking out (checker 2)	4 min	± 2 min
Events		
Customer arrives	every 2 min	± 1 min
Customer gets in line		
Customer begins checkout		
Customer is checked out		
Entities		
Customers (temporary)		
Checkers (permanent)		
Store (permanent)		
Queue (permanent)		
Attributes		
Checkout time of server 1	3 min	± 1 min
Checkout time of server 2	4 min	± 2 min
Arrival rate of customers	every 2 min	± 1 min
Shopping time of customers	5 min	± 2 min
Number of customers in store, an attribute of the store		
Number of customers waiting, an attribute of the queue		
Average purchase of customers: $6, with standard deviation of $3		
Hourly wage of checkers: $3		

SAM: What's the purpose of your simulation project?

PHIL: To determine whether I can reduce customer balking and customer waiting time by adding an extra checkout clerk.

SAM: Subjective judgments like the one you mentioned are frequent in simulation modeling and serve as a reminder that modeling is both art and science. Leaving out the "customer leaves store" activity seems reasonable to me, but you're much better at making judgments of that type than I am.

PHIL: Notice that I treat my customer arrivals as events. I used a clipboard and stopwatch to measure the frequency of arrivals. I found that the mean time between arrivals was roughly two minutes. The standard deviation came out to one minute, so I'm going to assume the distribution is exponential. My question is this—can you generate arrivals every two or so minutes using an exponential distribution?

SAM: Of course. I'll set this up so that each arrival event generates the next arrival event. We say that events that regenerate themselves in this way are **regenerative.**

PHIL: Now examine my attributes. I have left out such complicating features as grocery items selected by the customers, the costs of these items, whether the customer paid cash or by check, and what the customer's name was. Does that seem reasonable?

SAM: Don't ask me! You're supposed to be the expert in the substantive areas of the model; I just provide the methodology. Just ask yourself, "Are any of these features relevant to the overall purpose of the modeling effort?"

PHIL: I have. I think we can live without them.

SAM: I'm with you. All I need from you now is the precipitation diagram showing which events precipitate the occurrence of which other events.

PHIL: I've already done that, too. Here it is [Figure 9.2].

SAM: How many customers do you want me to simulate through your system?

PHIL: One thousand, but first run ten customers to initialize the model and then clear your statistics arrays.

SAM: Good. Give me a minute. (Pause) Here are the results [Table 9.5].

PHIL: Now restructure the model for two parallel servers and "play it again, SAM."

SAM: (Pause) Wow, look at those numbers [Table 9.6]. We substantially reduced the number of lost customers from 316 to zero. In addition,

TABLE 9.5 Statistical results obtained from the single-clerk grocery store simulation*

Facility	Average Utilization	Number Entries	Average Time/Tran
1	1.000	684	3.004

Queue	Maximum Contents	Average Contents	Total Entries	Zero Entries	Percent Zeros
1	14	10.049	696		0.0

Queue	Average Time/Trans	$Average Time/Trans	Table Number	Current Contents
1	29.715	29.715		11

$Avg time/Trans = Avg time/Trans excluding zero entries

* Number of lost customers = 316.

TABLE 9.6 Statistical results obtained from the double-clerk grocery store simulation*

Facility	Average Utilization	Number Entries	Average Time/Tran
1	0.944	643	2.990
2	0.705	357	4.028

Queue	Maximum Contents	Average Contents	Total Entries	Zero Entries	Percent Zeros
1	3	0.542	643	166	25.8
2	2	0.268	357	163	45.6

Queue	Average Time/Trans	$Average Time/Trans	Table Number	Current Contents
1	1.718	2.316		1
2	1.532	2.819		

$Avg time/Trans = Avg time/Trans excluding zero entries

* Number of lost customers = 0.

the average time per transaction decreased from 29.715 minutes to around 1.5 minutes.

PHIL: Those are the numbers I needed. Thanks SAM. Bye.
SAM: You're welcome, Phil. Take care and use me again soon.

RANDOM NUMBER GENERATION

Of particular importance to discrete simulation is generating (on a digital computer) random numbers representing the activity duration times or the times between occurrences of an event. We call computer generation of random numbers the **Monte Carlo method.** Scientists have also used Monte Carlo techniques to evaluate integrals and to conduct random searches for an optimum within a feasible region.

In discrete simulation models, we base our sampling from any probability distribution on the generation of a uniformly distributed random deviate (or number) in the interval 0 to 1. Researchers have developed simple algorithms to provide the required uniformly distributed random number. The most popular algorithm is the **multiplicative congruence method,** which produces random numbers by using a recursive equation, beginning with a user-specified initial value or seed. The recursive equation generates the next number in a sequence each time it executes. The sequence is deterministic in the sense that starting from the same seed we obtain the same exact sequence with each run. The numbers in the sequence have all of the required properties of uniformly distributed random numbers. Since we know the numbers in advance, we often refer to them as **pseudo-random numbers,** the use of which in simulation greatly expedites debugging. (Imagine what a nightmare debugging would be if every run produced a different output!)

A computer code (written in FORTRAN) for generating uniformly distributed random numbers appears in Table 9.7. This code generates both floating point and integer random numbers. The floating point random numbers are uniformly distrib-

TABLE 9.7 A FORTRAN program for generating random numbers by the multiplicative congruence method

```
      SUBROUTINE RANDOM(U,I)
      I = I*1220703125                        (ONE)
      IF (I) 1,2,2                            (TWO)
    1 I = I+2147483647 + 1                    (THREE)
    2 U = I*0.4566613E-9                      (FOUR)
      RETURN
      END
```

uted on the interval of 0 to 1. The code is useful only for 32-bit machines, which includes IBM, Amdahl, National Advanced Systems, and some 32-bit minicomputers. The code uses the multiplicative congruence formula

$$C_{i+1} = kC_i \qquad (9.1)$$

where C_0 is the seed and k is a constant equal to $5^{13} = 1,220,703,125$.

The initial value we place in the variable I is the seed upon first execution of the code. This value should be an odd integer of fewer than nine decimal digits. Upon return of control from the subroutine, I will contain the next integer random number in the sequence, as specified by the recursion formula (9.1). U will contain a floating point random number uniformly distributed on the interval 0 to 1.

Observe the simplicity of this code. A simulation run may invoke this routine thousands of times. Therefore, to avoid wasteful use of computer time, we need to keep the algorithm as simple as possible. The first statement in the routine implements the multiplicative congruence formula. The second and third statements will replace any negative integer with a positive integer. Statement four computes the corresponding floating point value by multiplying the integer value by the floating point inverse of the largest integer representable by the 32-bit computer. A numerical example would be $0.4566613E - 9 = 1/2147483647$, where 2147483647 is the largest possible integer for a 32-bit word (i.e., $2^{31} - 1$).

PROBABILITY DISTRIBUTIONS

In simulation, we sometimes need to generate random numbers that are other than uniformly distributed on the interval 0 to 1. To do this, we start with a uniformly distributed random number and transform it into a random number with some other form of distribution. We accomplish this by the so-called **inverse transformation method.** Every random variable x has an associated cumulative distribution function $F(x)$ whose values map onto the interval 0 to 1. The random variable y given by $y = F(x)$ is uniformly distributed over this interval. If we can determine the inverse of the cumulative distribution $F^{-1}(y)$, we have a straightforward strategy for obtaining x, since $x = F^{-1}(y)$. We generate a random number uniformly distributed on the interval 0 to 1. Call this number y and apply the inverse transformation $F^{-1}(y)$ to obtain a random number x with the appropriate distribution.

EXPONENTIALLY DISTRIBUTED RANDOM VARIABLES

Sampling from an exponential distribution is important because the mean time between arrivals (of customers, parts, automobiles, planes—temporary entities of any type) is often approximately exponentially distributed. In addition, service times are often exponentially distributed.

In FORTRAN, we can generate an exponentially distributed random number with the following statements:

```
CALL RANDOM (U,I)
EXRNUM = -XMU * ALOG(U)
```

Here, *XMU* is the mean time between arrivals or between service completions, and *U* is $U[0,1]$—i.e., uniformly distributed on the interval 0 to 1. Time to execute the second statement above can be long because ALOG is a slowly converging series. In long-running simulations, the use of tables to approximate ALOG would be much faster.

This analytical approach to inversion of a cumulative distribution function (CDF) works when we can describe the CDF analytically. However, many probability distributions have CDFs we cannot describe analytically, including the normal, the gamma, and Poisson distributions. In situations like these we can use one of two methods:

1. Approximate the continuous CDF with a discrete CDF specified by means of a table function.
2. Use statistical relationships to obtain the required random deviate from other distributions.

The following section illustrates both of these techniques for normal distributions.

NORMALLY DISTRIBUTED RANDOM NUMBERS

Occasionally, we know that the time between completions of service is normally distributed. In addition there are other situations where we believe that an activity duration time is normally distributed. Since we can't obtain an analytical expression for the inverse of the CDF for a normal distribution, the "simulationist" must resort to one of the two alternate methods previously mentioned. If we are using GPSS [34], we employ a table function representative of the CDF. On the other hand, if we use GASP or SLAM [30, 31, 29], we employ a statistical approach.

Figure 9.3 exhibits the standard normal probability density function and its associated cumulative distribution function. We can approximate the CDF by means of a series of piecewise linear segments, as Figure 9.3 illustrates. To construct this piecewise linear curve, we use a table function that interpolates linearly between the coordinate pairs given in Table 9.8.

To generate a standard normal random variable z, first compute a random number R that is $U(0,1)$, using subroutine RANDOM. Then use the FORTRAN table function TABLE to determine the standard normal variate z from $z = F^{-1}(R)$. The FORTRAN source code for TABLE is in Table 9.9. The following three statements will generate an appropriate normal random number x with mean *XMU* and standard deviation *SIGMA*.

```
CALL RANDOM(R,J)
Z = TABLE(R,T,15)
X = SIGMA * Z + XMU
```

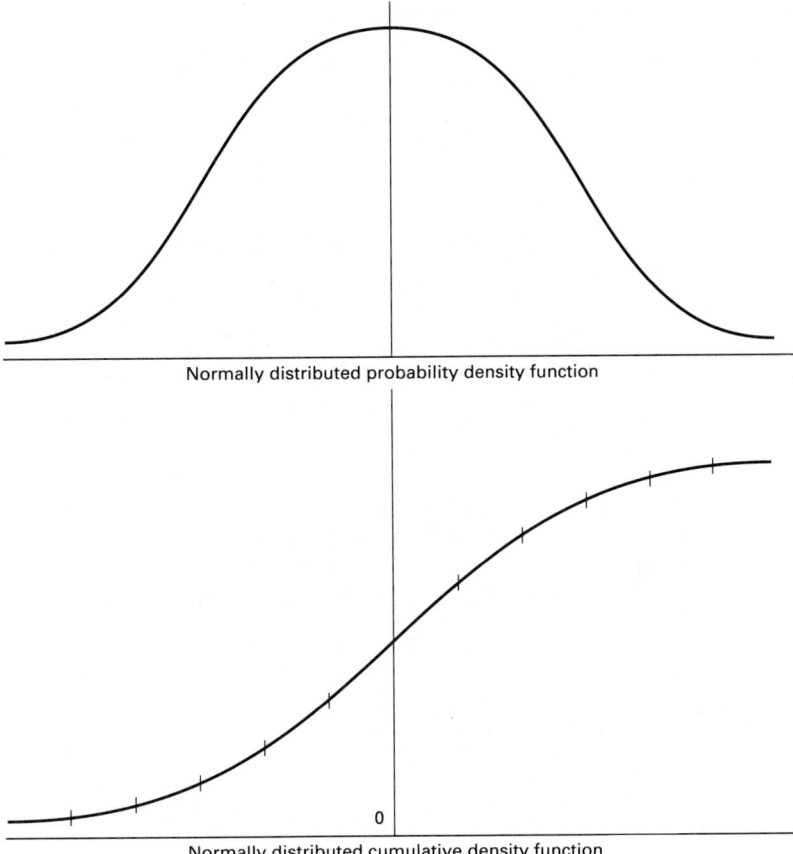

FIGURE 9.3 The standard normal probability and cumulative density functions

TABLE 9.8 Coordinate pairs for the standard normal CDF

Z	F(Z)	Z	F(Z)
−100.0	0.00000	0.5	0.6915
−3.0	0.00135	1.0	0.8413
−2.5	0.00621	1.5	0.9332
−2.0	0.02280	2.0	0.9772
−1.5	0.06680	2.5	0.9938
−1.0	0.15870	3.0	0.99865
−0.5	0.30850	100.0	1.00000
0.0	0.50000		

The last line is a FORTRAN implementation of the relationship between the nonstandard and standard normal random variates x and z—i.e., $x = \sigma z + \mu$.

The second way we can generate a normal random variate is by use of the relationship between the normal distribution and the uniform distribution. According

TABLE 9.9 FORTRAN listing of table function TABLE

```
      FUNCTION TABLE(FR,T,N)
      REAL T(N,2)
      DO 1 I=1,N
          IF (FR .LE. T(I,2)) GO TO 2
    1 CONTINUE
      WRITE(6,3)
      CALL EXIT
    2 TABLE = T(I-1,1) + (T(I,1) - T(I-1,1))*
              (FR -T(I-1,2))/(T(I,2)-T(I-1,2))
      RETURN
    3 FORMAT('- TABLE FUNCTION ERROR — RUN ABORTED')
      END
```

TABLE 9.10 A FORTRAN function for generating normally distributed random numbers from uniformly distributed random numbers

```
      FUNCTION RNORM(SIGMA,XMU)
      DATA K/12345/
      SUM = 0
      DO 1 I = 1,12
      CALL RANDOM(U,K)
    1 SUM = SUM + U
      Z = SUM - 6
      RNORM = SIGMA*Z + XMU
      RETURN
      END
```

to the Central Limit Theorem, the distribution of a sample of uniformly distributed random variates tends to be normal as the sample size becomes large.

Table 9.10 provides a function for generating normally distributed random numbers with mean *XMU* and standard deviation *SIGMA*.

One of the more recent algorithms for generating normal random variates is from Marsaglia and Bray [22]. It is considerably faster than the older statistical approximation method just discussed. And, while the statistical approximation method has some behavioral problems for random variates more than two standard deviations from the mean, this method has no such difficulties. The statistical approximation method requires large numbers of random numbers, while this method does not. A FORTRAN function that implements the Marsaglia and Bray algorithm is in Table 9.11.

SAMPLING IN SIMULATION

In discrete simulation, we sample important variables at the time they undergo a change—i.e., at the event times. These operations must be statistically independent to make proper statistical inferences about the simulated system. The number of such observations is also an important consideration.

In simulation, we determine estimates of such system output variables as average safety stock, average waiting time, and average order quantity by summing the observations and dividing the sum by n—the number of samples or observations. We are also interested in such time-persistent variables as average queue length, average num-

TABLE 9.11 The Marsaglia and Bray Method for generating normal random variates

```
            FUNCTION RNORM(MEAN, MIN, MAX, DEV, NUM)
C
C This function generates a normal random variate using the
C method of Marsaglia and Bray.  Inputs to the function are:
C
C           the MEAN - the mean of the normal distribution
C           the MIN  - the truncated minimum
C           the MAX  - the truncated maximum
C           the DEV  - the standard deviation of the normal distribution
C           the NUM  - the random number stream number
C
            IF (FLAG.NE.1) GOTO 1
                FLAG = 0
                RNORM = X2
                GOTO 2
      1     FLAG = 1
            CALL RANDOM(U,NUM)
            V1 = -1 + 2*U
            CALL RANDOM(U,NUM)
            V2 = -1 + 2*U
            S = V1**2 + V2**2
            IF (S>1) GOTO 1
            TEMP = SQRT(-2*ALOG(S)/S)
            RNORM = V1*TEMP
            X2 = V2*TEMP
      2     RNORM = MEAN + DEV*RNORM
            IF(RNORM<MIN) RNORM = MIN
            IF(RNORM>MAX) RNORM = MAX
            RETURN
            END
```

ber of transactions in the system, average inventory, and average server busyness. Computation of these averages requires integration of the variable values over time followed by division by the time period over which we did the integration. For both system output variables and time-persistent variables, we must run the simulation long enough to ensure a statistically valid result.

Obtaining averages that are characteristic of the steady-state behavior of the simulations are difficult because the simulation (like any dynamic model) goes through a transient phase to reach a steady state. Unfortunately, we collect observations during both phases unless we stop the simulation and clear all statistical observations and reset observation counters to zero. Most simulation languages will permit the user to do this. In the absence of such facilities, we must run the simulation for very long time periods to wipe out the effects of biases in the sampled data caused by samples that the model collected during the transient phase of the simulation.

Consider the neighborhood grocery store problem described earlier. We started the simulation with zero customers in the store. There is a period of simulated time during which conditions are uncharacteristic of the busy hours from 4 P.M. to 8 P.M. There is a transient period in which the simulation builds up customers—shopping, waiting, or being serviced. Until we arrive at the busy steady-state conditions, the simulated conditions are unlike the desired busy period. Samples collected during this transient period would bias the average queue length, average waiting time, and average server

DISCRETE SIMULATION RESULTS

busyness, downward from their actual values. Therefore, we stop the simulation after ten or so customers enter the system and restart it after we clear transient sample data.

The reports and outputs of any simulation model run are the plots that show how significant variables within the system model would change with time. These statistical reports provide information about the average waiting time of a temporary entity in a queueing situation, the percentage of time a facility is idle, the number of times an out-of-stock condition occurred, the number of customers who were turned away, the average queue length, and other measures of performance. The results tables for the neighborhood grocery store example is typical of the statistical reports produced by GPSS for service facilities in queueing situations. The plotted output can be useful in deciding where the transient phase stops and the steady-state phase begins.

SOLUTION APPROACHES: AN INTUITIVE DESCRIPTION

There are several languages available for discrete simulation—the most important being GPSS [14, 4], SIMSCRIPT [18], and SLAM [29]. The following sections briefly describe each of these languages. For an extensive review of microcomputer-based simulation software packages, see [1].

GENERAL PURPOSE SIMULATION SYSTEM (GPSS)

IBM developed GPSS, with early versions appearing in 1961. GPSS has evolved through several versions. A GPSS compiler is currently available that generates machine language code (and requires far less computer time during production runs). GPSS is an activity-oriented discrete simulation language. It uses blocks to represent activities, and we describe each block to GPSS by means of a keyword or command designating the block. The language uses a block diagram to describe the system. There are some 48 block types, each of which represents a characteristic action of systems. The blocks are connected by flow lines indicating the direction of movement of transactions (temporary entities) through the system.

Although GPSS is limited to characterization of queueing systems, one can conceptualize many systems in this way. GPSS includes a timing routine that moves the system from event time to event time. GPSS gathers and reports some types of statistics automatically. GPSS is weakest in providing facilities for generating random numbers. It provides only a uniform distribution, so that we must encode functions to obtain random numbers from other distributions. Of the discrete languages described in this chapter, GPSS is the most widely used.

Figure 9.4 is a GPSS block diagram representation of the neighborhood grocery store (single server), and Figure 9.5 on p. 346 shows the associated source code. Statements in GPSS conform to the format "location field, operation field, operand field, comment field." Blanks distinguish between fields. GPSS does not permit embedded blanks within fields. Each statement in Figure 9.5 corresponds to a block in Figure 9.4 except for those statements that direct the GPSS processor to SIMULATE, START, RESET, or END. The purpose of the START—RESET—START sequence is to get the simulation model past the transient phase. We run-start the model with ten transactions to produce a steady-state situation. The RESET operation clears statistics arrays before the START 1000 command runs the model for 1,000 transactions.

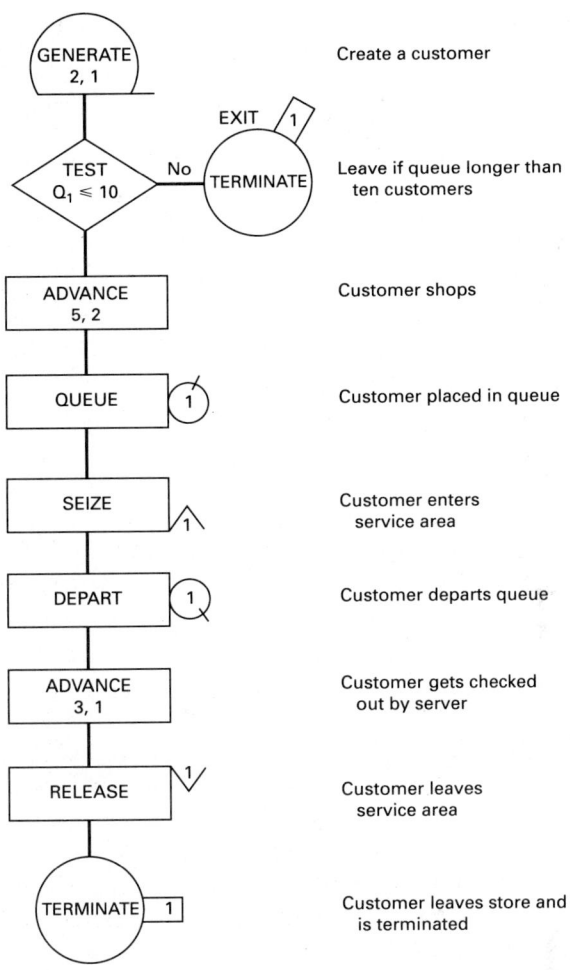

FIGURE 9.4 A GPSS block diagram representation of the neighborhood grocery store problem

A description of each GPSS block in Figure 9.4 is in order. The GENERATE block generates an arrival of a customer (generically called a "transaction" in GPSS) every $A \pm B$ time units. The time between customer arrivals is uniformly distributed between $A - B$ and $A + B$ according to the conventions that GPSS employs. We give the operands A and B values of 2 and 1, respectively, so customer interarrival times will be uniformly distributed between one and three minutes.

The next block performs a TEST to determine whether the queue length as specified by $Q1$ is less than or equal to ten customers. If not, the newly created customer leaves. If so, the customer shops.

An ADVANCE block represents the shopping activity. Transactions that enter an ADVANCE block will remain in it for a period of time that is uniformly distributed with a lower bound of $A - B$ and an upper bound of $A + B$. The values we specified for the operands A and B are 5 and 2 in Figure 9.4. Hence, customer shopping times are uniformly distributed over the interval three to seven minutes, as the problem statement specifies.

After shopping, customers place themselves in a queue. The pair of blocks QUEUE/DEPART represents the queue. The queue length variable $Q1$ is incremented by 1 when transactions pass through the QUEUE block, whereas transactions

FIGURE 9.5 Source code in GPSS for the Neighborhood Grocery Store problem

```
BLOCK
NUMBER      *LOC      OPERATION   A,B,C,D,E,F,G      COMMENTS
            *
            * NEIGHBORHOOD GROCERY STORE EXAMPLE
            *
            SIMULATE
   1        GENERATE      2,1              CREATE A CUSTOMER
   2        TEST LE       Q1,10,EXIT       LEAVE IF >10 ARE WAITING
   3        ADVANCE       5,2              CUSTOMER SHOP. ACTIVITY
   4        QUEUE         1                QUEUE FOR A SERVER
   5        SEIZE         1                ENTER SERVICE AREA
   6        DEPART        1                STATS ON QUEUE
   7        ADVANCE       3,1              SERVER 1'S SERV TIME
   8        RELEASE       1                LEAVE SERVICE AREA
   9  TERM  TERMINATE     1                TOTAL SAT CUSTOMERS
  10  EXIT  TERMINATE     1                TOTAL BALK CUSTOMERS
            *
            START         10,NP            INIT. W/10 CUSTOMERS
            RESET
            START         1000             MAIN RUN
            END
```

that pass through the DEPART block cause the queue length variable $Q1$ to decrease by 1. GPSS automatically keeps time-persistent statistics on $Q1$. Transactions cannot DEPART until the following block (in this case, the ADVANCE block) is free to accept another transaction. Any transaction that does not have to wait to be serviced will pass through the QUEUE/DEPART pair immediately and without delay.

The SEIZE/RELEASE pair of blocks defines to GPSS a form of permanent entity called a **facility**. We use this construct to model the service area itself. The SEIZE/RELEASE pair will allow only one transaction (or customer) in the facility at a time. The SEIZE block allows a customer to enter the facility and hence begin to be checked out. The RELEASE block allows a customer to exit the facility once service is complete.

The last block in the block diagram depicted in Figure 9.4 is the TERMINATE block. When transactions reach this block, GPSS counts and thereafter terminates them. Notice that there are two different TERMINATE blocks in Figure 9.4. By having two TERMINATE blocks, we can obtain a count of how many customers pass through the system and how many leave the store because the queue is too long.

GPSS treats statements that begin with (∗) as comments to the user and performs no processing of these statements. SIMULATE (the first such command in the operation field) is required.

In this book, we use few GPSS commands to solve our models and minicases. We refer the student to Schriber [34] for detailed modeling commands and instructions.

SIMSCRIPT II.5   SIMSCRIPT has evolved through early versions before arriving at its current version. It is largely the product of Philip Kiviat and his colleagues at Consolidated Analysis Centers, Inc. Unlike GPSS (or any other simulation language) SIMSCRIPT is a general purpose programming language with special facilities to accommodate discrete simulation. The approach has both an event and an activity orientation.

SIMSCRIPT has the programming capabilities of languages like ALGOL, PL/1, or PASCAL but with a syntax that enables the programmer to encode statements that are intelligible to nonprogramming-oriented managers and by the SIMSCRIPT compiler as well. This feature greatly enhances user comprehension of the code. Such statements as

```
PERFORM INITIALIZATION.
START SIMULATION.
RESCHEDULE THIS REPORT NEXT.MONTH.
CREATE EVERY PRODUCTION.CENTER.
```

are (or we can make them) intelligible to the SIMSCRIPT compiler.

SIMSCRIPT, like the various versions of GASP and SLAM, requires the user to encode a separate event routine for each event. The following is a typical event routine for processing arrival events (the type of arrival is identical to that described for the neighborhood grocery store problem):

```
EVENT ARRIVAL SAVING THE EVENT NOTICE
RESCHEDULE THIS ARRIVAL AT TIME.V + UNIFORM.F(1.,3.,1)
IF QUEUE.LENGTH > 10, "LEAVE STORE AND" RETURN
OTHERWISE ADD 1 TO NO.OF.CUSTOMERS..IN.STORE
SCHEDULE AN END.OF.SHOPPING AT TIME.V + UNIFORM.F(3.,7.,2)
RETURN "AND" END
```

SIMSCRIPT programs begin with a nonexecutable division of code called a PREAMBLE. We use the PREAMBLE to define to the SIMSCRIPT compiler such items as the following:

1. Temporary entities and their attributes.
2. Permanent entities and their attributes.
3. Events and their attributes.
4. Background conditions for program variables.
5. Equivalence between variables.
6. Global variables.
7. Sets, set ownership, set membership.
8. Variables on which we are to collect statistics.

A MAIN program, initialization routines, and then the event routines—one for each event defined in the PREAMBLE—follow the PREAMBLE. We compile the user-written components into executable code. SIMSCRIPT supports dynamic storage allocation, recursion routines, an extensive collection of random number generation routines, and a very flexible English-like syntax for encoding of program statements and code. It is a remarkable language.

SLAM—A SIMULATION LANGUAGE FOR ALTERNATIVE MODELING

SLAM has evolved from the early days of GASP and GERT, all of which are simulation constructs developed by Alan Pritsker and his associates. Early versions of GASP were capable of discrete simulation and employed an event-oriented approach. A newer version of GASP—GASP IV—is able to accommodate discrete simulation models, continuous simulation models, or combined continuous/discrete simulation models. All versions of GASP use FORTRAN as the host language. While this might suggest that GASP is easy to use, such is not the case for all but the seasoned FORTRAN programmer. The language requires meticulous attention to details. There is great flexibility; the penalty that the user pays for this flexibility is the need to specify many input parameter values.

SLAM subsumes all the capabilities of GERT and GASP IV, giving the user the option of specifying a network simulation (for a GERT diagram of a manufacturing shop, say), a discrete next-event simulation such as we commonly use for inventory and queueing situations, a continuous simulation as described later in the chapter, or some combination of these. Like its predecessors, SLAM is FORTRAN based.

STATE OF THE ART IN SIMULATION

Simulation is evolving as the computer technology upon which it depends becomes more sophisticated. The following sections briefly discuss three emerging trends.

VISUAL INTERACTIVE SIMULATION

According to James R. Burns [4], the trend in simulation today is toward on-screen visual characterization of the process so that the user can see the model as it evolves over time. In these models, the user may have an opportunity to interact with the visual simulation during its operation. This is called **visual interactive simulation,** and it enables users to improve their operational skills by applying control stimuli to a model of the process rather than to the process itself. Most of the commercially available simulation languages now have visual/graphical display interfaces. Visual presentation of the dynamics of a model and graphical interpretation of the results of the model significantly enhance user confidence.

KNOWLEDGE ENGINEERING

Burns [4] notes that another very promising advance in technology for discrete simulation comes from the artificial intelligence community. One branch of this discipline—**knowledge engineering**—concerns itself with the way we explicitly represent, acquire, and process knowledge. Researchers have defined and specialized various knowledge forms and representation schema and have developed processing algorithms.

The representation, acquisition, and processing of judgmental knowledge have been particularly well developed in recent years. Today, there is a growing recognition that simulation models are nothing more than a type of knowledge representation and processing. Thus, these two communities (the simulation community and the knowledge engineering community) have been looking over each other's shoulders with increasing frequency, and the result has been significant enhancements to the technology of both. The capacity for explicit representation of judgmental knowledge within the process and causal models of discrete simulation has enabled these simulations to characterize such knowledge in a more explicit, robust, and definitive way. At the same time, including simulation models within the artificial reasoning models of the knowledge engineering community has greatly improved the expressiveness and reasoning depth of their so-called expert systems.

CONTINUOUS SIMULATION

As noted before, discrete simulation models advance time at discrete intervals and usually involve stochastic or probabilistic events. For processes that must deal with time as a continuous entity, researchers have developed **continuous simulation** techniques. A brief discussion of this highly complex subject is in the appendix to this chapter.

MINICASES

Savin E. Levin, Inc. (continued)

THE SCENARIO
We have previously described a scenario and a problem for our neighborhood grocery store example.

THE MODEL
We have also delineated a single-server model for this problem. Here we present a parallel-server model involving two servers with different service times and each with its own queue. In addition, we discuss solutions to both models and compare the two from a performance standpoint.

Figure 9.4 depicted the GPSS block diagram corresponding to the single-server situation. The corresponding source code is Figure 9.5. This problem had to do with comparing the performance of one versus two servers during the busy hours of the day. The second server would be slower than the first server and paid less. We must therefore construct a second model involving two parallel servers. Figure 9.6 on p. 350 is the block diagram for this second model, and Figure 9.7 on p. 351 is the required GPSS source code. Queueing theory will not handle this parallel-server situation, because the service times of the servers are different.

SOLUTION TO THE MODEL
By comparing the performance of the two models, we can assess whether the additional server is worth the incremental cost. We will pay a second server close to minimum wage but will require an additional service area and cash register. The incremental hourly costs are $6, or $24 for the four-hour period from 4 P.M. to 8 P.M. Is the increase in performance worth the incremental cost?

From the printout for the single-server model (given previously), we see that during this four-hour period, about 120 customers would arrive, but roughly one-third, or 40, of them would go away because the queue length would be 10 or greater. At one point there were 14 people waiting in the queue, and the average queue length was 10 customers, with an average waiting time in the queue of 30 minutes.

From the printout for the two-parallel server model (given previously), there were no lost sales due to leaving customers. Server 1's queue was never longer than three customers, while server 2's queue was never longer than two customers. The average waiting time in server 1's queue was 1.718 minutes, whereas the average waiting time in server 2's queue was 1.532 minutes.

Assuming the average purchase per customer is $3.65 and that the average profit per customer is $.83, we clearly incur $33 (= 40 x 0.83) in lost profit because of customers who balked. This is greater than the 24-dollar incremental cost calculated for the second server. In addition, the second server will create a tremendous increase in customer goodwill, as no customer leaves without shopping, and customer waiting

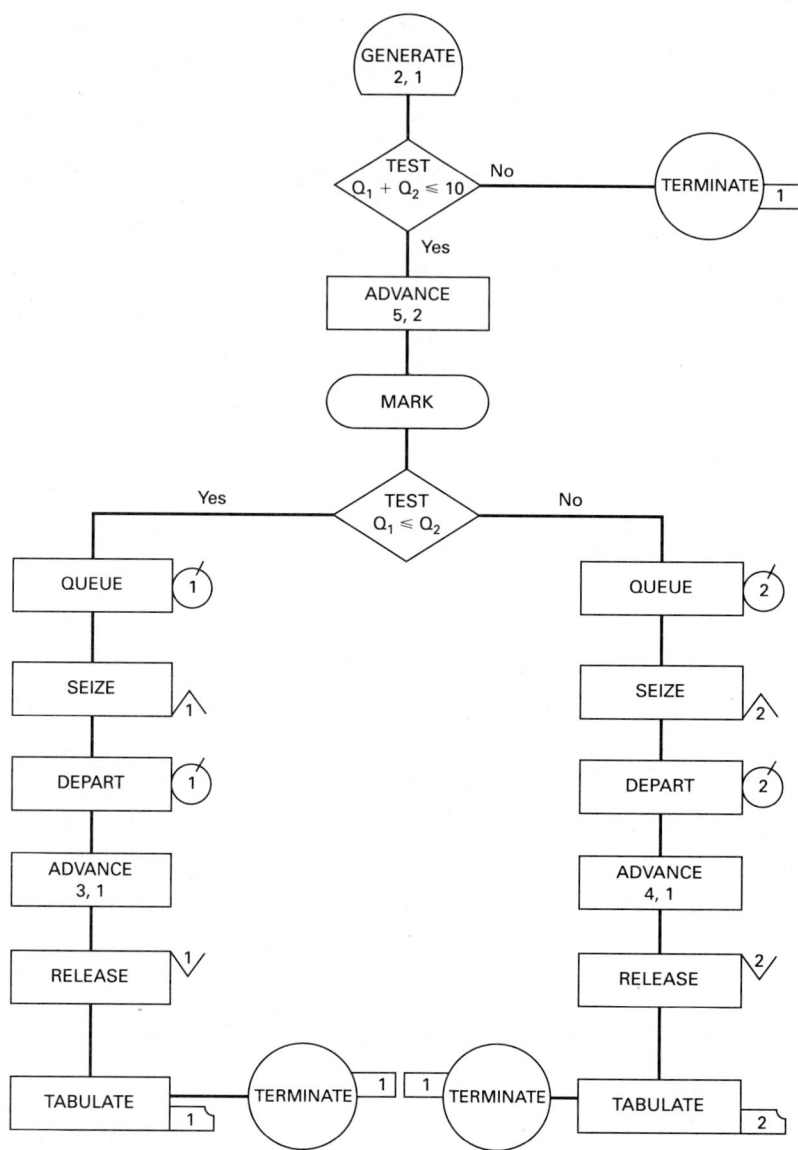

FIGURE 9.6
Block diagram for parallel server model of Neighborhood Grocery Store

time in a queue declines from 30 minutes on the average to 1.7 minutes. This analysis suggests that the benefits accruing from the second server outweigh the incremental costs, all else being equal.

Cabana Bananas (Revisited)

THE SCENARIO

Cabana Bananas uses six steamship freighters to move its bananas from a single dock in Costa Rica to the various seawater ports on the East Coast of the United States.

```
BLOCK
NUMBER*LOC  OPERATION   A,B,C,D,E,F,G      COMMENTS
       *
            SIMULATE
   1        GENERATE    2,1                CREATE A CUSTOMER
   2        TEST LE     Q1,10,EXIT         LEAVE IF >10 WAITING
   3        ADVANCE     5,2                CUSTOMER SHOP ACTIVITY
   4        MARK        1                  STATS ON CST WAIT TIME
   5        TEST LE     Q1,Q2,SERV2        PUT CST SMALL/2 QUEUES
   6        QUEUE       1                  QUEUE FOR SERVER
   7        SEIZE       1                  ENTER SERVICE AREA
   8        DEPART      1                  STATS ON QUEUE
   9        ADVANCE     3,1                SERV. 1 SERVICE TIME
  10        RELEASE     1                  LEAVE SERVICE AREA
  11        TABULATE    1                  STATS ON CST WAIT TIME
  12   TERM TERMINATE   1                  TOT. SATISFIED CUST.
  13  SERV2 QUEUE       2                  ENTER QUEUE OF SERV. 2
  14        SEIZE       2                  SEIZE SERV 2 WHEN IDLE
  15        DEPART      2                  STATS ON QUEU OF SRV 2
  16        ADVANCE     4,1                SERV 2'S SERVICE TIME
  17        RELEASE     2                  SERV 2 IS FINISHED
  18        TABULATE    2                  STATS ON CST WAIT TIME
  19        TERMINATE   1                  CUST LEAVES STORE
  20   EXIT TERMINATE   1                  TOTAL BALKED CUST
       *
       1    TABLE       M1,2,2,20          TAB INTRV ON WAIT TIME
       2    TABLE       M1,3,2,20          TAB INTRV ON WAIT TIME
       1    VARIABLE    Q1+Q2
            START       10,NP              INITIALIZE W/10 CUST
            RESET
            START       1000               MAIN RUN
            END
```

FIGURE 9.7 Source code in GPSS for two parallel servers in the neighborhood grocery store problem

Because of the need to service some half dozen ports on the eastern seaboard and the tremendous volume of bananas that Cabana must load and transport without delay to preserve freshness, Cabana's CEO is interested in a simulation model that will exhibit the performance that might accrue from having two loading docks rather than just one. An additional loading dock will cost the company $6,835,000 in additional outlays for cranes, cold storage, truck depots, and waterfront property. Furthermore, the labor bill required to pay the workers on the second dock will run $35,000 per month. Each boatload of bananas nets the company $435,000.

THE PROBLEM

The time to load one steamship with bananas is uniformly distributed between three and seven days. The time for one steamship to reach its destination, offload its bananas, and return is uniformly distributed with a mean of 11 days. Ships never return in less than eight days or more than 14 days. When the loading dock is busy and empty steamships arrive into port, the ships enter a queue of steamships waiting to be loaded. The queueing discipline is first come, first loaded. Initially, all six steamships are waiting to be loaded and empty.

TABLE 9.12

Activities	Attributes
Steamships waiting empty	
Steamships enroute	11 ± 3 days
Steamships being loaded	5 ± 2 days

Entities, permanent
The loading dock(s)

Entities, temporary
The six steamships

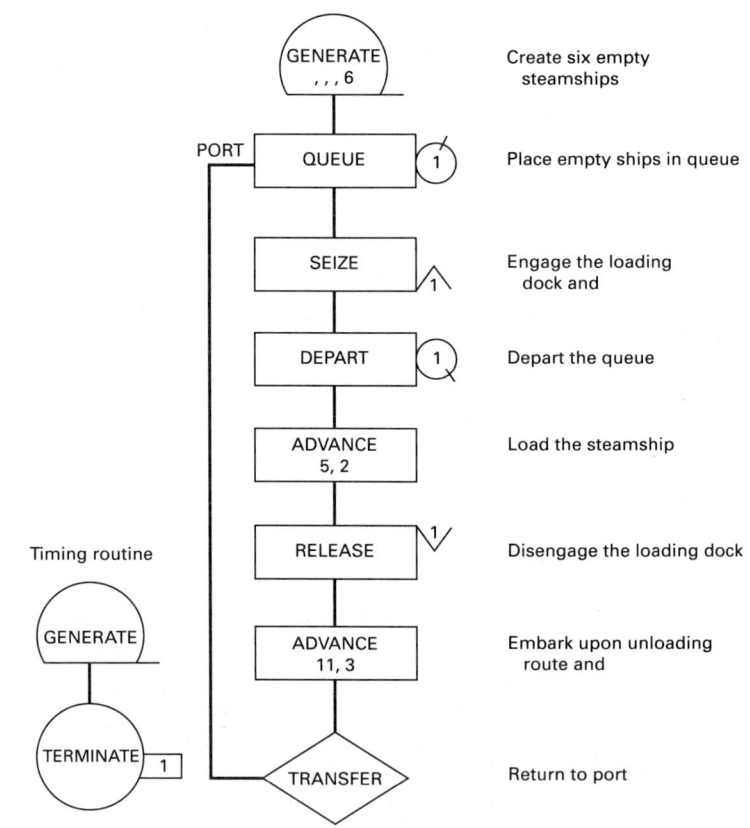

FIGURE 9.8 GPSS block diagram for a single dock in the steamship problem Cabana Bananas

THE MODEL

Because of the cyclical nature of the steamship arrivals and the dependence upon the number of such ships in the queue, queueing theory cannot handle this situation.

We begin by listing the activities, the permanent and temporary entities, and the important attributes (see Table 9.12). Next we formulate single-dock and double-dock GPSS models. Figure 9.8 is the single-dock model, whereas Figure 9.9 is the model

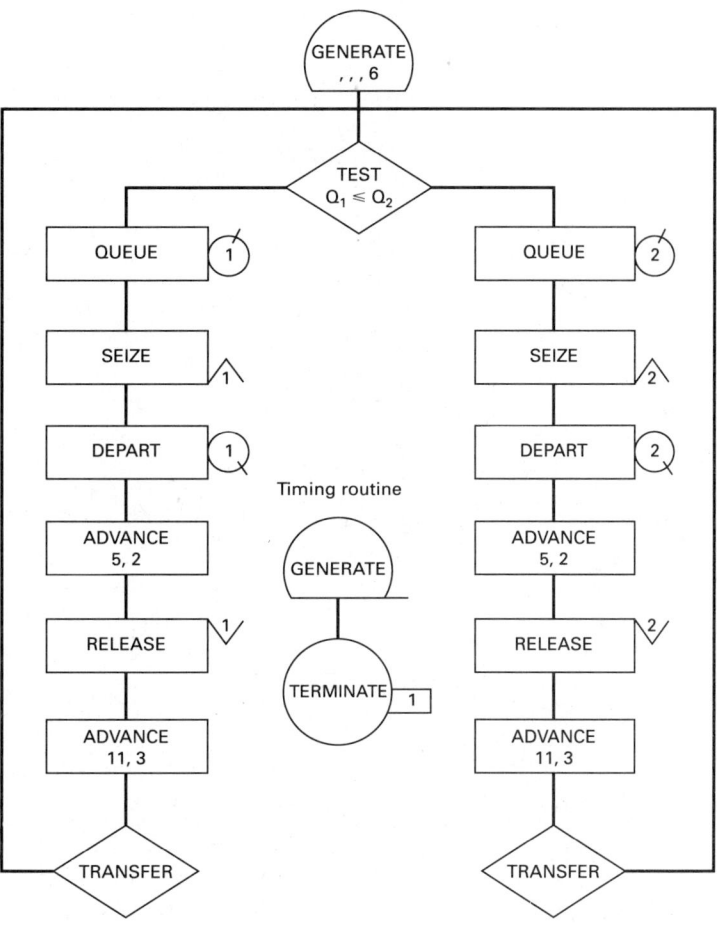

FIGURE 9.9
GPSS block diagram for two parallel docks in the steamship problem Cabana Bananas

with two parallel docking facilities. Figures 9.10 and 9.11 depict the GPSS programs for the two models.

SOLUTION TO THE MODEL

Tables 9.13 and 9.14 contain the results obtained from the two simulations. The numbers in Table 9.13 on p. 355 show that each steamship waits an average of 12.4 days + 4.761 days (17.161 days total) in port before embarking on an unloading route that takes 11 days on the average. Assuming a 300-day year, it is possible to process 63 ships through the single dock, as suggested by the numbers in the table. The RELATIVE CLOCK shows that 300 days have elapsed, while the NUMBER of ENTRIES through the facility shows to be 63. Thus, 63 steamships moved through the loading dock in the 300-day period. We used a 10-day startup period, as is apparent from the 10-day difference between the ABSOLUTE CLOCK and the RELATIVE CLOCK.

The numbers in Table 9.14 on p. 356 indicate that each steamship waits an average of 3.3 days (actually 3.456 days in queue 1 or 3.26 days in queue 2) and requires 5 days (5.14 days for dock 1 and 4.98 days for dock 2) for loading. Hence, each steamship is in port an average of 8.3 days. As a consequence, the ships can make more unloading trips in the assumed 300-day year. Specifically, the two docks could process 55 + 43 = 98

FIGURE 9.10 Single-dock Cabana Bananas model program

```
BLOCK #   * LOC         OPERATION    A,B,C,D,E,F,G            COMMENTS
          *
          *CABANA BANANAS STEAMSHIP MODEL
                        SIMULATE
   1                    GENERATE     ,,,6              CREATE 6 EMPTY STEAMSHIPS
   2      PORT          QUEUE        1                 PLACE EMPTY SHIPS IN QUEUE
   3                    SEIZE        1                 ENGAGE LOADING DOCK AND
   4                    DEPART       1                 DEPART THE QUEUE
   5                    ADVANCE      5,2               LOAD THE SHIP
   6                    RELEASE      1                 DISENGAGE LOADING DOCK
   7                    ADVANCE      11,3              EMBARK UPON UNLOADING
   8                    TRANSFER     ,PORT             ROUTE AND RETURN TO PORT
   9                    GENERATE     1                 TIMING ROUTINE
  10                    TERMINATE    1
          *
                        START        10,NP             INITIALIZE W/10 DAYS
                        RESET
                        START        300               MAIN RUN
                        END
```

FIGURE 9.11 Double-dock Cabana Bananas model program

```
BLOCK #   *LOC          OPERATION    A,B,C,D,E,F,G            COMMENTS
          *CABANA BANANAS STEAMSHIP MODEL—TWO DOCKS
                        SIMULATE
   1                    GENERATE     ,,,6              CREATE 6 EMPTY SHIPS
   2      PORT          TEST LE      Q1,Q2,DOCK 2      PL SHIP IN < 2 QUEUES
   3                    QUEUE        1                 PL EMP SHIPS IN QUEUE
   4                    SEIZE        1                 ENGAGE LOAD DOCK AND
   5                    DEPART       1                 DEPART QUEUE
   6                    ADVANCE      5,2               LOAD SHIP
   7                    RELEASE      1                 DISENGAGE LOAD DOCK
   8                    ADVANCE      11,3              EMBRK ON UNLOAD RTE &
   9                    TRANSFER     ,PORT             RETURN TO PORT
  10      DOCK 2        QUEUE        2                 2ND QUE FOR 2ND DOCK
  11                    SEIZE        2                 ENGAGE 2ND DOCK AND
  12                    DEPART       2                 DEPART QUEUE
  13                    ADVANCE      5,2               LOAD SHIP
  14                    RELEASE      2                 DISENGAGE DOCK
  15                    ADVANCE      11,3              EMBRK ON UNLOAD RTE &
  16                    TRANSFER     ,PORT             RETURN TO PORT
  17                    GENERATE     1                 TIMING ROUTINE
  18                    TERMINATE    1
          *
                        START        10,NP             INITIALIZE W/10 DAYS
                        RESET
                        START        300               MAIN RUN
                        END
```

```
RELATIVE CLOCK                  300 ABSOLUTE CLOCK            310
BLOCK COUNTS
BLOCK         CURRENT      TOTAL
  1              0            0     GENERATE
  2              2           61     QUEUE       1
  3              0           62     SEIZE       1
  4              0           62     DEPART      1
  5              1           62     ADVANCE     5      2
  6              0           62     RELEASE     1
  7              3           62     ADVANCE    11      3
  8              0           61     TRANSFER           2
  9              0          300     GENERATE    1
 10              0          300     TERMINATE   1

FACILITY          AVERAGE        NUMBER              AVERAGE
                 UTILIZATION     ENTRIES             TIME/TRAN
   1               1.000           63                  4.761

QUEUE    MAXIMUM      AVERAGE       TOTAL      AVERAGE      $AVERAGE
         CONTENTS     CONTENTS      ENTRIES    TIME/TRANS   TIME/TRAN
  1         4          2.649          64        12.421       12.421
```

TABLE 9.13 Statistical results from single-dock Cabana Bananas model

ships—an increase of 35 ships. Assuming we could find markets for the extra bananas and that we could obtain the extra bananas from area growers, we could realize an additional $435,000 × 35 = $15,225,000 in net revenues. This is more than enough to offset the fixed and variable costs associated with the additional dock (in a year's time). Recall that the additional loading dock would cost $6,835,000 to install and $35,000 × 12 = $420,000 to operate over 12 months. Hence, at the year's end, the company will have netted $7,970,000, less additional fuel and labor costs associated with 35 additional trips. The second dock appears to be justified from financial considerations. But are the assumptions realistic?

SOLUTION TO THE PROBLEM

Under the single-dock system, each ship would complete a cycle in 17.16 + 11 = 28.16 days on the average. Ships could complete roughly 10.6 trips in a 300-day year. During this period, the ship's crew would be idle 12.4 × 10.64 = 132 days (assuming the ship's crew is active during loading periods).

Under the double-dock system, each ship would complete a cycle in 8.26 + 11 = 19.26 days on the average. One could complete approximately 15.6 trips in a 300-day year. During this period the ship's crew would be idle 3.3 × 15.6 = 51.5 days. This is certain to improve the continuity of the company's work force and the utilization of capital invested in the ship fleet. If the additional work days cost Cabana Bananas $1,000 per day in labor costs per ship, the additional labor costs to operate the ships would be $(1,000 × 6)(131 − 51.5) = $477,000$. If each trip requires $20,000 for fuel, we would incur 35 × 20,000 = $700,000 in additional fuel expenses in the two-dock arrangement. Subtracting these costs from the net amount $7,970,000 yields a very attractive $6,793,000 increase in profits by year's end. Assuming that markets for 35 additional shiploads of bananas exist and that we can obtain the additional bananas from local growers, the exigency for a second dock exists.

TABLE 9.14 Statistical results from double-dock Cabana Bananas model

RELATIVE CLOCK			300 ABSOLUTE CLOCK			310
BLOCK COUNTS						
BLOCK	CURRENT	TOTAL				
1	0	0	GENERATE			
2	0	97	TEST LE	Q1	Q2	10
3	1	55	QUEUE	1		
4	0	55	SEIZE	1		
5	0	55	DEPART	1		
6	1	55	ADVANCE	5	2	
7	0	55	RELEASE	1		
8	2	55	ADVANCE	11	3	
9	0	54	TRANSFER		2	
10	0	42	QUEUE	2		
11	0	43	SEIZE	2		
12	0	43	DEPART	2		
13	1	43	ADVANCE	5	2	
14	0	43	RELEASE	2		
15	1	43	ADVANCE	11	3	
16	0	43	TRANSFER		2	
17	0	300	GENERATE	1		
18	0	300	TERMINATE	1		

FACILITY	AVERAGE UTILIZATION	NUMBER ENTRIES	AVERAGE TIME/TRAN
1	0.959	56	5.142
2	0.729	44	4.977

QUEUE	MAXIMUM CONTENTS	AVERAGE CONTENTS	TOTAL ENTRIES	AVERAGE TIME/TRAN	$AVERAGE TIME/TRAN
1	2	0.529	56	2.839	3.456
2	1	0.250	43	1.744	3.260

SUMMARY

In this chapter, we tried to impart an understanding of the general concept of simulation modeling. When we should use it, why it is so widely applied, and what methodologies and philosophies it comprises, formed the substance of the chapter. We discovered that we should employ simulation whenever there is an essential dependence upon time that we must consider. Once we have made the decision to use simulation, the question then is one of which type — continuous deterministic or discrete probabilistic. We suggested that discrete probabilistic simulation is appropriate for situations in which the system of interest changes abruptly at discrete points in time, whereas continuous simulation is appropriate for systems that change smoothly and continuously in time. Areas in which the use of continuous simulation is widespread include large-scale socioeconomic and urban systems as well as corporate-level financial systems.

In this chapter we defined the concepts of activity, event, entity, and attribute; and we described the underlying philosophy of discrete simulation in detail, illustrating it by examples. We treated in some detail the Monte Carlo method and its relation to the generation of random numbers. In addition, we presented three different techniques for random variate generation, including the inverse distribution function method, the table function or table lookup method, and the statistical approximation method.

KEY TERMS

activity
attribute
causal/correlative simulation
combined simulation
continuous simulation
deterministic simulation
discrete simulation
dynamic environment
entity
event
facility
homomorphic simulation model
inverse transformation method
isomorphic simulation model

knowledge engineering
mathematical simulation
Monte Carlo method
multiplicative congruence method
physical simulation
probabilistic simulation (or Monte Carlo)
process
pseudo-random numbers
regenerative events
simulation
state
steady-state simulation
transient simulation
visual interactive simulation

PROBLEMS FOR ANALYSIS

1. **The Scenario [16]:** Data Providers Inc. (DPI) is a young high-tech company located in a booming metropolitan area. DPI uses vertical blanking interval (VBI) technology—the unused lines of a television signal—to offer a stock market quotation service to its customers.

   The marketing department at DPI is responsible for sales and customer service. Customer service representatives (CSRs) spend a great deal of time troubleshooting installed systems via telephone. Recently the CSRs have been reporting a large number of service cancellations due to technical problems associated with DPI's product and the inability of customers to promptly access the CSRs for service.

   DPI has not yet reached a breakeven point. As a result, its primary investors have placed significant budget constraints on the company and require extensive research and planning before authorizing major expenditures.

   The Problem: DPI has identified several distinct problems in the customer service area. One problem is that the large number of phone calls processed daily is more than the current staff and phone system can handle. Also, the CSRs lack quick access to significant amounts of information needed for troubleshooting, and their supervisors lack management reports needed to train, monitor, and improve the performance of the CSRs. Thus, DPI would like to know the answer to the following questions:

   1) How many representatives are needed to service the 1,600 current subscribers?
   2) What efficiency gain is needed to handle the current customers without adding any new CSRs?
   3) How large an increase in customer base is needed before an additional CSR is added?

   The Model: We start the simulation by generating customer phone calls at the average rate of one per 60 seconds ± 20 seconds (uniform distribution). If the company phone circuit is fully occupied—that is, all five CSRs are busy—the customer will get a busy signal and hang up. Otherwise, the caller will receive service, lasting an average of 3 ± 1 minutes (uniform distribution). Finally, the customer will leave the DPI customer service phone system by releasing the CSR.

Solution to the Model:
a. Construct the GPSS block diagram and write the GPSS simulation program for DPI's problem.
b. Simulate your model for one day using 1,600 customer phone calls and for one week using 8,000 customer phone calls (five workdays). Initialize your simulation program for 100 transactions.
c. Do you have the results of the simulation? Take a look at the number of entries into the system. Did all 1,600 customers calling DPI receive service? At what rate were the five CSRs kept busy?
d. Is there a queue to enter the phone system? If so, what is the average waiting time, and what is the longest waiting time?
e. And finally, what percentage of the incoming phone calls are being answered by DPI?

Solution to the Problem:
a. Now that we have a better understanding of the dilemma faced by DPI, should we recommend a better phone system in which customers can initially hear a recorded service message lasting five minutes that will help with most of the routine questions? Or should we recommend hiring and training additional CSRs? If so, how many?
b. DPI's aggressive yuppie executives are expecting an increase in customer base to 2,000 subscribers in the near future. This will change the interarrival time from 60 seconds to 45 seconds. What recommendations would you make to DPI regarding its phone system and the number of CSRs?

2. **The Scenario [32]:** Webe Jammin' Canning Company (WJCC) is a 21-year-old family-owned firm. WJCC owns a considerable amount of farmland and orchards and sells produce both wholesale and retail. The company also cans various fruit products, makes apple cider and apple butter, and recently began making jams and jellies. WJCC has always maintained a small country store adjacent to the cannery. The store is located along a highway that carries a large volume of tourist traffic, especially in the summer months. Lack of adequate parking space has caused some of WJCC's customers to shop at the competitor's store, which is located half a mile down the road and has ample parking space.

The Problem: Because of a recent decision by the State Highway Department to extend the four-lane highway, WJCC has obtained 1,000 feet of frontage on the new road and has arranged for access lanes from either direction as well as a crossover directly in front of the store. This situation has given the owners of WJCC the opportunity to construct a store that will increase their share of the tourist business. In designing the layout for the new store, WJCC's laid-back manager Billy Bob Applebaum would like to determine the answer to the following questions:

a. Should the store have one or two service areas? A maximum of four servers will be available to provide service. Billy Bob is aware that a one-service area is more cost effective than a two-service area; however, he is concerned that long waiting times associated with a one-service area might cause customer dissatisfaction.
b. How many shoppers should the store be able to accommodate at any point in time? That is, how much floor space does Billy Bob need for displays and shoppers? The answer to this question will help Billy Bob with the design and capacity of the parking lot as well.

The Model: Billy Bob, using the statistical sampling tools he had learned from a continuing education course he took two years ago, has kept statistical data on the

```
BLOCK
NUMBER  *LOC      OPERATION    A,B,C,D,E,F,G
        *
        *WEBE JAMMIN' CANNING COMPANY PROBLEM
        *
                  SIMULATE
  1               GENERATE     120,20         CUSTOMERS ARRIVE
  2               ADVANCE      300,100        CUSTOMERS SHOP
  3               TEST LE      Q1,Q2,SERV2    CHOOSE SHORTEST LINE
  4               QUEUE        1              CHOOSE FIRST QUEUE
  5               SEIZE        1              WAIT IN LINE
  6               DEPART       1              LEAVE LINE
  7               ADVANCE      70,50          GET SERVICE
  8               RELEASE      1              LEAVE SERVICE AREA 1
  9               TERMINATE                   LEAVE STORE
 10      SERV2    QUEUE        2              CHOOSE SECOND QUEUE
 11               SEIZE        2              WAIT IN LINE
 12               DEPART       2              LEAVE LINE
 13               ADVANCE      70,50          GET SERVICE
 14               RELEASE      2              LEAVE SERVICE AREA 2
 15               TERMINATE                   LEAVE STORE
 16               START        3600           INITIALIZE
 17               RESET
 18               START        36000          RUN
 19               END
```

FIGURE 9.12 Multiple server Webe Jammin' Canning Company model

customer arrival and service rates. He tells us that customer shopping and service distributions are both uniform, with a mean of 300 ± 100 seconds for the shopping time and 70 ± 50 seconds for the service time. For the customer arrival distribution, Billy Bob has determined a uniform function with a mean of 120 ± 20 seconds per customer.

We can formulate WJCC's problem using GPSS both as a single-server and as a multiple-server model. Figure 9.12 is the GPSS program.

Solution to the Model:
 a. Develop the GPSS diagram and formulate the single-server model of WJCC. Run both the single-server and the multiple-server simulation models and compare the results. Discuss the average waiting time and average queue length results for these models. Are you surprised at the differences?

Solution to the Problem:
 a. Based on the results of the GPSS program, which model is more suitable for WJCC? Does your choice take into consideration the parking problem?
 b. The owners of WJCC seem to prefer the single-server design, since that will keep the construction and maintenance costs of the new store low. Do you agree with their preference?

3. **The Scenario [6]:** Perfect Gene Laboratories (PGL) is a manufacturer, distributor, and marketer of products consumed by the biomedical industry. The company provides service to universities, clinical research laboratories, hospitals, and industrial manufacturers of vaccines and genetic engineering products.

The technical nature of the products requires that the sales personnel be technically competent in cell biology applications as well as trained in selling techniques. The sales organization is divided into four regions. Three of the regions cover all 50 states and are staffed by field representatives (reps). The fourth and newest region is the technical sales group created by combining technical and customer services (ordering).

Selling to the cell biology industry is very competitive and emphasizes price and service. It is critical that customers be able to reach the company easily through the toll-free numbers and that the reps have ample time to assist the caller. PGL's current phone system (MIC) allows calls to be directed to multiple locations through the use of a single toll-free number. The phone system is serviced by five access lines answered by five reps. Each rep works eight hours per day. MIC answers all calls with a call prompt recording that directs customers to different departments. If all reps are busy, MIC holds the call in queue with an announcement cycling at set intervals. Only if all five lines are occupied will a customer receive a busy signal.

The Problem: To evaluate its current phone system, PGL would like to determine the following:

a) How many customers disconnect before receiving service?
b) Is any one rep or entity servicing a significantly higher or lower level of calls?
c) Will arranging the reps in the service facilities based on performance improve the overall service level of MIC?

The Model: MIC recognizes reps in sequence rather than in parallel. When a call is received, MIC looks at station 1. If station 1 is busy, MIC moves to station 2. If station 2 is busy, the system looks at station 3, and so on. MIC allows 15 seconds for a call to be answered by a rep in the station before it transfers the call to the next station in the sequence. If all stations are busy and the caller does not get a response, the caller will hang up.

Since the cell biology industry is seasonal, the level of calls fluctuates between 2,400 and 5,000 per month. December and January are slow months, and the spring months are the busiest. We formulate our first simulation problem by assigning reps in the sequence in Table 9.15. We have placed the fastest rep (according to mean call history) in the first station and the slowest rep in the last. We formulate the second simulation problem by reversing the sequence. That is, we place Debbie in station 1.

a. Draw the GPSS block diagram and write the corresponding simulation program. Phone calls are generated using a uniform distribution with a mean of 60 seconds and a standard deviation of 30 seconds. Run the simulation for 1,250 transactions loaded with 10 calls.

Solution to the Model:

a. Tabulate the results for the reps for both sequences based on average queue length, average number of transactions, and utilization rate. Are the two sequences significantly different?

TABLE 9.15 Average call time in seconds

Sequence	Rep	Average	Standard Deviation
1	Guillermo	120	60
2	Robin	150	60
3	Cathy	180	60
4	Andy	200	60
5	Debbie	240	60

b. Which sequence should the five reps select?

Solution to the Problem:
a. The results indicate that we can expect no significant improvement in performance by different arrangements of reps. Do you agree with this finding? If so, why?
b. What can PGL do to reduce the number of customers who hang up before receiving service?

4. **The Scenario:** Tooty Fruity, Inc. is a fresh fruit and vegetable jobber/distributor. Tooty has 22 semi-trailer trucks that it uses to move produce to its affiliated grocery chain—Catch Twenty-Two, Inc. (CTTI). Each week the trucks must service 107 supermarkets from a single warehouse with two loading docks. A. Tina Wheeler, Tooty's CEO, is concerned about whether to add an additional loading dock and crew. Ms. Wheeler knows that occasionally five to six trucks are sitting idle in front of the warehouse four or more hours at a time. This did not concern her when there were only 85 supermarkets in the chain, as the 22 could get to all 85 within a week. Now that CTTI has picked up 22 more supermarkets from a competitor, the situation is different.

The Problem: Tina doesn't want to purchase more trucks, and she isn't sure it would help solve the problem anyway. All of the supermarkets are within 150 miles of the warehouse and can be reached within three hours. Average unloading time is five hours, give or take an hour. The real problem has to do with trucks waiting to be loaded at the loading docks. The average loading time is roughly one hour. Adding a third dock and loading crew would be expensive. Working the existing crews overtime would also be costly.

The Model: We cannot adequately handle this problem with analytical queueing models, because the arrival rate of trucks to the warehouse loading docks varies as a function of the number of trucks out, the number of trucks waiting, etc. Simulation seems to be the only viable modeling alternative. At the start of each week, all trucks are idle and waiting to be loaded. Upon completion of loading, it takes eight hours on the average for the truck to return empty. Because of traveling distances, this number can vary by as much as two hours. However, trucks never arrive earlier than 6 nor later than 10 hours. The warehouse is open for business 24 hours a day, 5 days a week, for a total of 120 hours. Tooty Fruity expects all departed trucks to return from their routes by the end of each week (156 hours) so that no weekend layovers occur. Therefore, every Monday morning, all 22 trucks are parked empty in front of the loading docks.

We begin building our model by listing activities and their attributes:

Activity	Attribute (time required)
Trucks waiting empty	
Trucks en route	8 ± 2 hours
Trucks being loaded	1 hour

a. Develop a GPSS model of this situation to determine what benefits might accrue from the inclusion of additional loading docks and whether Tooty Fruity needs additional trucks. Assume that Tooty Fruity can load and unload trucks any time of the day (or night). Run the simulation for one week. Determine the average waiting time per truck for 2, 3, 4, and 5 docks.

b. Should Tooty Fruity buy more trucks? (*Hint:* Use a storage representation of the number of docks available for loading trucks. In GPSS there are two types of permanent entities: facilities, which we've already discussed, and storages.) We delineate each permanent entity to GPSS by means of a pair of blocks.

In addition to the ENTER/LEAVE pair of statements, the storage requires one extra statement that usually appears at the end of the program. This last statement has the format

A   STORAGE   N

where A is the storage designator that references a specific storage defined by an ENTER A—LEAVE A pair and N is an integer that specifies the capacity of the storage (the maximum number of transactions—trucks in this case—that can occupy the storage at any point in time). To represent two loading docks preceded by a single queue for the truck problem, the sequence of statements as in Figure 9.13 would be appropriate:

FIGURE 9.13 Sequence of statements

```
        ENTER          1         ENTER A DOCK
        DEPART         1         DEPART QUEUE
        ADVANCE        1         LOAD TRUCKS
        LEAVE          1         LEAVE LOADING DOCKS
        ADVANCE        8,2       MAKE TRIP
        TRANSFER,BEG             RETURN TO LOADING DOCKS
        GENERATE       1         TIMING ROUTINE
        TERMINATE      1
*
    1   STORAGE        2
*
        START          120       RUN FOR WEEK—120 HOURS
        END
```

5. **The Scenario:** A conveyor system involves six inspectors positioned along a conveyor belt. Items for the inspectors to process arrive at the first inspector at a constant rate of one every 20 seconds. Service time for each inspector is uniformly distributed and is never less than 30 seconds or more than 90 seconds.

We do not allow queues in front of each inspector. Therefore, the inspector must be idle if he or she is to remove the item from the conveyor belt. If the first inspector is idle, he or she processes the item and places it in a hopper. At this point, there is no further interest in the item, and we remove it from the system. If the first inspector is busy when an item arrives, the item continues down the conveyor belt until it arrives at the second inspector. The time to complete this transport is 60 seconds.

If the second inspector is busy, the item continues until it comes to an idle inspector, who inspects it. If an item encounters a situation in which all inspectors are busy, we recycle it to the first inspector with a transport time of 240 seconds.

The Problem: Managers are interested in how much time an item spends in the system and in the percentage of time each inspector is busy. Knowing the effects of increasing or decreasing the number of inspectors is likewise of considerable interest to management. What effect speeding up (or slowing down) the conveyor would have is also of interest.

The Model and Solution:
a. Develop a model (or models) appropriate for this system in GPSS. Analyze the reports and develop a recommendation for management. Use the following structure to model the transport of an item to the first idle inspector:

FIGURE 9.14
Code for other inspectors

```
         TRANSFER  BOTH,,THI          SERVER 2 BUSY?
    *
    *    SERVER NUMBER 2
    *
         SEIZE     2                  ACTIVATE SERVER 2
         ADVANCE   60,30              PERFORM INSPECTION
         RELEASE   2                  DISENGAGE SERVER 2
         TRANSFER,TAB                 FINISHED—GO TO TAB
   THI   ADVANCE   60                 ADVANCE TO SERVER 3
```

The TRANSFER block allows an item to enter a facility only if the facility is vacant or idle; otherwise, the item proceeds to the next facility. Figure 9.14 shows a typical segment of GPSS code for an inspector (server). (the other inspectors use identical segments of code):

6. **The Scenario:** People arrive at a movie theater at a rate of one every 10 ± 3 seconds during the 30-minute period just before the start of each movie. These people buy tickets from a single booth manned by one person who takes 9 ± 5 seconds to serve one customer.

   The Problem: People frequently experience long waiting lines at this theater, and if the line is longer than 100 people, new arrivals will balk.

   The Model:
   a. Write a program in GPSS to determine the average queue length, the number of people who will balk, and the average waiting time in a queue.

7. Return to the Cabana Bananas minicase. A seventh steamship costs $2,300,000 to purchase and $38,320 per month to operate, including labor and fuel costs. Suppose we wished to add an additional steamship to the line. Modify the simulation programs in the minicase to compare the benefits versus costs of adding a seventh steamship versus adding a second dock.

8. In the Cabana Bananas minicase, assess the benefits that would accrue with the addition of a third dock (assuming six steamships). Modify the codes to include the third dock and determine what net increase in throughput we can expect. Use a storage as described in Problem 4 rather than three facilities. Assume a single queue.

9. Modify the Cabana Bananas model so that we use only one queue for both docks. Assess the efficacy of this queueing strategy as opposed to the use of two queues—one for each dock.

REFERENCES AND ADDITIONAL READING

1. Arthur, J., J. Frendewey, P. Ghandforoush, and L. Rees. "Microcomputer Simulation Systems." *Computers & Operations Research* 13 (1986): pp. 167–183.
2. Burns, J., and W. Marcy. "Causality: Its Characterization by Methodologies for Modeling Socioeconomic Systems." *Technological Forecasting and Social Change* 14 (1979): 387–398.
3. Burns, J., and O. Ulgen. "An Integrated Approach to the Development of Continuous Simulations." *Socio-Economic Planning Sciences* 12 (1978): 313–327.
4. Burns, J. Private communication. Texas Tech University (1989)
5. "Computer Games that Planners Play." *Business Week*, December 7, 1978, p. 66.

6. Corning, S. Adapted from an unpublished MBA term project report, Virginia Polytechnic Institute and State University (1988).
7. Emshoff, J., and R. Sisson. *Design and Use of Computer Simulation Models*. New York: Macmillan, 1970.
8. Forrester, J. *Principles of Systems*. Cambridge, Mass: Wright-Allen Press and MIT Press, 1968.
9. Forrester, J. *Industrial Dynamics*. Cambridge, Mass: MIT Press, 1961.
10. Forrester, J. *Urban Dynamics*. Cambridge, Mass: MIT Press, 1969.
11. Forrester, J. *World Dynamics*. Cambridge, Mass: Wright-Allen Press and MIT Press, 1971.
12. Galitz, L. "Modeling for Bankers." *The Banker*, December 1978, pp. 33–36.
13. Gordon, G. *Systems Simulation*. Englewood Cliffs, N.J.: Prentice-Hall, 1978.
14. Gordon, G. *The Application of GPSS V to Discrete Systems Simulation*. Englewood Cliffs, N.J.: Prentice-Hall, 1975.
15. Kane, J. "A Primer for a New Cross-Impact Language—KSIM." *Technological Forecasting and Social Change* 4 (1972): 129–142.
16. Kathman, Jack. Adapted from an unpublished MBA term project report, Virginia Polytechnic Institute and State University (1988).
17. Keen, P., and M. Scott Morton. *Decision Support Systems: An Organizational Perspective*. Reading, Mass.: Addison-Wesley, 1978.
18. Kiviat, P., R. Villanueva, and H. Markowitz. *The SIMSCRIPT II.5 Programming Language*. Los Angeles: Consolidated Analysis Centers, 1973.
19. Law, A., and D. Kelton. *Simulation Modeling and Analysis*. New York: McGraw-Hill, 1982.
20. Leontief, W. *Input-Output Economics*. Oxford: Oxford University Press, 1966.
21. Leontief, W. "The Structure of the U.S. Economy." *Scientific American* 212 (1965): 25–35.
22. Marsaglia, G., and T. A. Bray, "A Convenient Method for Generating Normal Variables," *SIAM Review* 6 (1964): 260–264.
23. Naylor, T. *Corporate Planning Models*. Reading, Mass.: Addison-Wesley, 1979.
24. Naylor, T., and C. Jeffress. "Corporate Simulation Models: A Survey." *Simulation* 24, no. 6 (1975): 171–176.
25. Naylor, T., and D. Gattis. "Corporate Planning Models." *California Management Review* (1976): 69–78.
26. Naylor, T., and H. Schaul. "A Survey of Users of Corporate Planning Models." *Management Science* 22, no. 9 (1976): 927–937.
27. Naylor, T. *Computer Simulation Experiments with Models of Economic Systems*. New York: Wiley, 1971.
28. Phillips, D., A. Ravindran, and J. Solberg. *Operations Research: Principles and Practice*. New York: Wiley, 1976.
29. Pritsker, A., and C. Pegden. *Introduction to Simulation and SLAM*. New York: Halsted Press, 1979.
30. Pritsker, A. *The GASP IV Simulation Language*. New York: Wiley, 1974.
31. Pritsker, A., and R. Young, *Simulation with GASP.PL/1*. New York: Wiley, 1975.
32. Ritter, Robert K. Adapted from an unpublished MBA term project report, Virginia Polytechnic Institute and State University (1985).
33. Sage, A. *Methodology for Large Scale Systems*. New York: McGraw-Hill, 1977.
34. Schriber, T. *Simulation Using GPSS*. New York: Wiley, 1974.
35. Shannon, R. and W. Biles. "The Utility of Certain Curriculum Topics to Operations Research Practitioners." *Operations Research* 18 (1970): 741–745.
36. Shannon, R. *Systems Simulation: The Art and Science*. Englewood Cliffs, N.J.: Prentice-Hall, 1975.
37. Thesen, A., and L. Travis. *Simulation for Decision Making*. St. Paul: West, 1992.
38. Watson, H. *Computer Simulation in Business*. New York: Wiley, 1981.

APPENDIX
Continuous Simulation Models

As mentioned in the introduction to this chapter, there are two basic philosophies in simulation: discrete and continuous. Continuous simulation is appropriate whenever we perceive the endogenous variables as continuously changing in time. Thus, the state of the system undergoes smooth, continuous change as time advances.

Recent developments in simulation languages now permit us to develop models that incorporate both continuous simulation and discrete simulation perspectives. These languages support a new approach to simulation called **combined simulation,** in which we employ features of both simulation perspectives in a single model. As it turns out, there are many real world situations in which such an approach is an appropriate tool to use. Combined simulation languages like GASP IV [30] and SLAM II [29] will therefore support discrete simulation, continuous simulation, and combined simulation.

Recent surveys [24, 26] suggest that nearly every major corporation in this country uses some form of corporate planning model. Most often, this model is a simulation model; some cases include mathematical programming models. These surveys suggest that at the highest levels of planning, corporate simulation models are deterministic rather than probabilistic. This is apparently attributable to the increased data requirements of probabilistic simulations and the problem of interpreting the data output. Most managers feel comfortable with using deterministic simulations as vehicles on which they can input what-if scenarios and observe their consequences in the outputs that the model returns. While the inclusion of probabilistic considerations is well within the current state of the simulation methodology, the use of such inclusion is not yet prevalent in most corporate models. Instead, management will use corporate simulations to explore the consequences of the best, worst, and most probable input scenarios to develop a feel for the desirability of the resultant outcomes.

UNDERLYING ASSUMPTIONS AND DEFINITIONS

The remainder of the appendix discusses only continuous deterministic simulation, which involves the iteration of structural equations and empirical equations through time. We advance time in small increments, beginning at some starting instant t_0 and stopping at a later time t_f. Here we discuss the methodology needed to formulate these models. We also provide a brief description of the computer languages that we can use in the codification of the equations that the model comprises. As we will see, methods of solution are robust enough to accommodate linear or nonlinear models. Consequently, the solution approaches do not require that we differentiate continuous simulation models in this way.

The modeling methodologies that we will discuss share a number of assumptions with management science models in general. First, we assume these systems to be open—that is, to have inputs and outputs. If such is not the case, there is no point in modeling the system, since we can neither control nor observe it. Second, the methodologies assume that the system under scrutiny has an identified manager whose perspective we use as a basis for the study. Third, the methodologies assume that we can represent the causality inherent in a system by structural equations that characterize the causal structure of the object system. Fourth, the simulation behavior as depicted by plotted output is a direct consequence of the structural equations within the model and/or the inputs to the model. Hence, by changing these elements, it is possible to cause the models to behave in a more desirable way. Finally, we assume that systems change in a smooth, continuous fashion. We do not expect abrupt discontinuities, since aggregate business and economic systems tend to change without discontinuities. We will address assumptions that are particularized to a specific methodology, along with the methodology itself, in the next section.

CONTINUOUS SIMULATION MODELING

The steps we employ in the construction of continuous simulation models are essentially the same 11 steps outlined in Chapter 1. We present in this section additional detail that will facilitate collection of data, formulation of model structure, and validation of the model—the steps associated with the model itself.

Table 9.16 lists the methodologies discussed, together with a description of the methodology and the purposes to which we can put models formulated by each methodology. Following overviews of each of the simulation model types are more extensive discussions of each category.

TABLE 9.16 Continuous simulation methodologies

Name	Characteristics	Purposes	Uses
Corporate simulation	Accounting based	Corporate planning and policymaking	Managerial decision making
Econometric modeling	Linear, extensive use of data	Short-term forecasting	Macroeconomic modeling
Input-output modeling	Linear	Short-term forecasting	Macroeconomic modeling
Kane's KSIM	Assumed sigmoid behavior	Long-term effects of interactions	See Table 9.17
System dynamics	Nonlinear	Long-term planning	See Table 9.17

Corporate simulation models are, at the highest levels of corporate policymaking, financial modeling packages. The equations that make up these models have their basis in accounting. At least a dozen financial modeling languages are now available to assist top-level management in formulating these models. Such models provide a link between decision making and conditions in the firm's environment.

For short-range forecasting, we recommend econometric models, which place strong emphasis upon historical trend data and which we always "fit" to such data. For most applications involving forecasts of one to eight quarters (quarter years), these models are best.

We also use Leontief input/output models for short-term forecasting. Like econometric models these models are linear. As Table 9.16 indicates, such models are appropriate for macroeconomic modeling.

For long-term behavioral studies of dynamical systems, the modeler has two choices: Kane-like methods [2, 15] and Forrester's system dynamics [8–11]. The Kane methods are "quick and dirty" and therefore inexpensive; they require managerial involvement in the model formulation process and enable us to easily understand the structural implications for behavior. They do, however, limit the range of possible dynamical behaviors.

In the public sector as well as in academic research, system dynamics is the most widely applied of all the methods discussed in this chapter. Invented in the mid-1950s by Jay Forrester, the method places strongest emphasis on delineating the causal interactions that the object system comprises. It enables us to readily perceive the long-term implications of certain control policies in terms of behavior. Policy planning over the long haul represents the purpose to which we can most appropriately put system dynamics and Kane-like models. Table 9.17 is a partial list of broad areas to which people have applied Kane-like methods and system dynamics.

CORPORATE SIMULATION MODELS

The economic environment in which every corporate and business entity is embedded is characterized by so much complexity that managerial decision making without some form of planning model would be like blindly throwing darts in an English pub. Business managers are daily confronted with the possibility of shortages of energy and raw materials, environmental and

TABLE 9.17 Some areas to which KSIM and system dynamics have been applied

Socioeconomic systems	Urban systems
Environmental systems	Biological systems
Energy systems	Production systems
Industrial systems	Population systems

TABLE 9.18 Applications of corporate models [24]

Applications	%	Applications	%
Cash flow analysis	65	Short-term forecasts	33
Financial forecasting	65	New venture analysis	30
Balance sheet projections	65	Risk analysis	27
Financial analysis	60	Cost projections	27
Pro forma financial reports	55	Merger/acquisition analysis	26
Profit planning	53	Cash management	24
Long-term forecasts	50	Price projections	23
Budgeting	47	Financial information systems	22
Sales forecasts	41	Industry forecasts	20
Investment analysis	35	Market share analysis	17
Marketing planning	33	Supply forecasts	13

OSHA regulations, a decline in productivity, international competition, another round of inflation, and fluctuating interest rates. To survive in this environment, corporate plans must be comprehensive and systematic.

Corporate simulation models are an attractive and viable alternative to formal, ad hoc planning procedures. William E. Scott, executive vice president with the Public Service Electric Gas Company of New Jersey, has said of the company's corporate simulation model, "If an oil embargo were announced tomorrow, within 24 hours we would be able to know the major impact of it and begin reacting" [5]. Inland Steel attributes to its corporate model the decision not to spend $1.5 billion on an expansion program that quite possibly could have forced the company into bankruptcy [38]. United Airlines generates alternative financial scenarios with across-the-board fare increases, additions and deletions of different types of flight equipment, and increases in the price of jet fuel [25]. On the other hand, American Airlines uses a marketing simulation to forecast the profitability of different cities in its route structure [25]. Every Fortune 1000 firm now uses some form of corporate simulation model, as do most smaller companies.

Why are corporate models in such widespread use? Financial considerations dominate in the list of applications to which managers put corporate models, as shown in Table 9.18.

STRUCTURE AND FORM OF CORPORATE SIMULATION MODELS

The Naylor surveys [24, 26] report that managers at the highest levels of management—including presidents, board members, board chairpersons, and vice presidents—use corporate

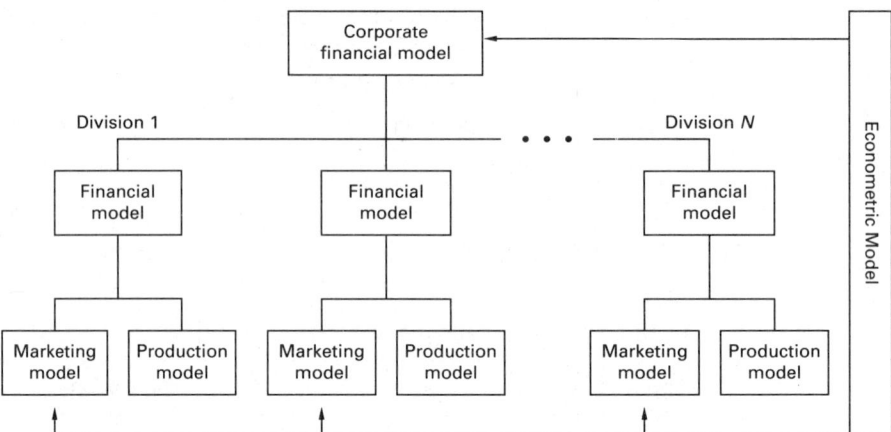

FIGURE 9.15 A conceptual framework for a corporate model (undirected lines indicate the two-way communication between model types)

simulation models. It is not surprising to find that these models are essentially financial, consisting of a set of accounting identities. Such models are easy to develop, require a minimum amount of data, and we can validate them against the firm's existing accounting structure.

In addition to using a financial model, some firms have integrated marketing and production models into the corporate model, as Figure 9.15 shows. Clearly the front-end for any corporate model is the financial model. The conceptual framework shown in Figure 9.15 assumes that each division makes its own financial, marketing, and production decisions; however, such decisions are coordinated by the corporate financial model.

Let's carefully delineate what we mean by financial, marketing, and production models. We find, for example, that marketing models may use forecasting and projection methods to arrive at a general market forecast for all products sold in a division. Production models may, on the other hand, consist of activity-analysis models that reflect the cost of operating at different rates of output. In some cases, we use mathematical programming to generate minimum cost production plans.

Financial models provide income statements, balance sheets, cash flow statements, and profit and loss statements—the usual financial reports and instruments. We use the corporate financial model to check the economic feasibility of alternative financial plans, including alternative cash management, depreciation, capital investment, and merger/acquisition policies.

The "drivers" of corporate financial models are managerial-controlled inputs, inputs from divisional financial models, and, in some cases, econometric models. While some corporations have their own econometric models, most avail themselves of the econometric data provided by time-sharing computer networks. It is possible, for example, for corporations to subscribe to the latest econometric forecasts available from Chase Econometrics, the Wharton School, and Data Resources, Incorporated. Econometric concerns have given rise to a new type of planner in high-level corporate decision making—the corporate futurist.

We use marketing models to forecast sales and market share by product or service category. We use such forecasts to drive division financial models and production models. There are two different approaches: short-term mechanistic models and econometric models. Short-term mechanistic models involve trend analyses and seasonal fluctuation schemes as applied to time series data, or exponential smoothing methods. Econometric market models are more robust in that they link sales to the national economy and permit simulation of the effects on sales and market share of alternative advertising, pricing, and promotional policies and strategies.

Production models compute operating costs and costs per unit of production for a given level of market demand as forecast by the marketing model. These models supply cost data to financial models and we can use them in a standalone context as well. It is in the standalone framework that such models facilitate the assessment of costs and productivity of alternative production policies and strategies.

VARIABLES AND EQUATIONS USED IN FINANCIAL MODELS

We use three types of variables and two types of equations in corporate financial models. The variable types are essentially those discussed in Chapter 1—exogenous variables, endogenous variables, and policy variables representing management's control inputs to the corporate entity. Exogenous variables represent external effects that the economy, the environment, and other uncontrollable factors have on the firm. The endogenous variables are those internal variables that are in some sense dependent upon the exogenous influences and the managerial control inputs. Some or all of these variables can be random or probabilistic, since we can never ascertain market forecasts with certainty and since we cannot predict with certainty the effects of the exogenous influences attributable to the economy or the environment. However, as previously mentioned, the probabilistic capability of financial models is not in very widespread use as of this writing.

The equations that any financial model comprises are of two types: structural and empirical. These equations translate values obtained from the manager's control inputs and the exogenous variables into the endogenous variables. For the most part, they are accounting and tax-related identities.

CORPORATE SIMULATIONS AND DECISION SUPPORT SYSTEMS

Today's corporate models operate in an interactive mode so that a manager can run his or her model and retrieve the results in seconds, make changes, and rerun the simulation. This capability to interact with a computer program during its execution has helped give birth to a new breed of computer-based management system. In former days, the emphasis was upon management information systems that consisted of large data bases and software that could search and retrieve data from the data bases. While these systems greatly facilitated the organization and efficiency of information storage and retrieval systems, managers were more interested in answers to aggregate questions such as the following:

- What is the growth rate of customer accounts?
- What is the trend in purchase order amounts?
- What is the average rate of growth in employee salaries?

Such questions prompted even more sophisticated questions, such as the following:

- What will be the total salary outlay per month two years from now?
- By how much must the price of our products increase to sustain the present margin of profit 18 months from now?

To answer these more complicated questions, software designers began to develop and include models in their management information systems. At that instant, decision support systems were born. The "parents" of decision support systems were management information systems and models. It is not surprising, therefore, to learn that these systems may consist of a model base, a data base, and a user interface that permits interactive access to both. Once executed, the models in the model base retrieve and utilize essential data about market forecasts, product pricing, production, overhead, and capital costs from the data bases. Financial models, for example, could utilize these data to produce corporate balance sheets, profit and loss statements, and other financial instruments projected one, two, or five years.

The appearance of this newborn necessitated that we find an appropriate name. Managers named this new tool the corporate planning (or simulation) model, while software designers and developers called it a decision support system. Because of the user-friendly designs incorporated into these systems, managers who were relatively unsophisticated computer users suddenly became overwhelmingly enthusiastic about the capabilities of these new tools. They found that such tools could support relatively simple model constructs or tremendously complex model forms involving hundreds, even thousands, of equations.

CHAPTER 10

Modeling with Markov Chains

We first encountered the notion of a Markov process in Chapter 6, where we discussed the subject in terms of dynamic programming (or recursive optimization). In this chapter, we delve into a descriptive modeling technique known as Markov chains. Briefly, a **discrete stochastic process** is a dynamic, probabilistic process that involves elements of a system moving in an orderly manner among a finite set of states, the movement occurring at discrete points in time. If the probabilities of moving from a given state to the next one are the same—regardless of the particular point in time—we have a stochastic process that we can model as a Markov chain. Let's illustrate this definition with an example from marketing—the well-known brand-switching phenomenon.

The soft drink market is dominated by two companies: Olympus, Inc., with its popular Nectar, and its largest competitor, Sahara Bottling Company, which markets its Oasis brand. A third, smaller bottler—TT&F—is attempting to capture a larger market share from its two giant competitors with its novel drink called Pimienta.

TT&F's CEO, Bev Ridge, has commissioned a market survey, and the results indicate that Nectar, Oasis, and Pimienta currently hold 50%, 45%, and 5% of the market, respectively. The really interesting numbers, however, are the ones that describe brand switching. The following table contains these figures, in the form of a **one-stage transition matrix**.

		To		
		Nectar	Oasis	Pimienta
From	Nectar	0.75	0.15	0.10
	Oasis	0.10	0.80	0.10
	Pimienta	0.05	0.05	0.90

We interpret the matrix as follows. Suppose that the next soft drink purchased by a customer is dependent only on the brand purchased last time. The data in the matrix are relative frequencies of brand purchases, given the brand last purchased. For example, 75% of customers who buy Nectar on a given occasion repeat their selection on the next purchase, whereas 15% switch to Oasis and 10% switch to Pimienta. We interpret the other relative frequencies analogously.

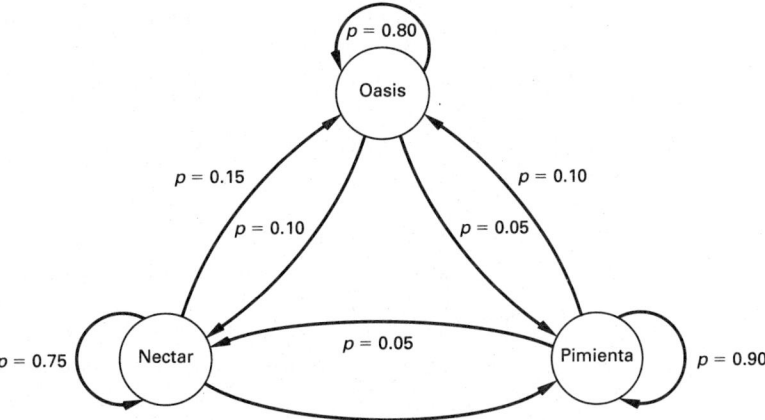

FIGURE 10.1
State transition diagram for brand-switching example

One way in which to visualize these relationships is by using a so-called state transition diagram, as Figure 10.1 illustrates. The arrows represent possible one-step transitions, and the numbers on the directed arcs are the transactions' one-step transition probabilities.

If these relative frequencies do not change over time, there are several questions that are of keen interest to Bev Ridge.

1. Given that TT&F has only a 5% market share at present, will that share increase or decrease over the long run? Will market share for the three companies eventually stabilize?
2. Soft drink purchases are an almost daily event for many people. How many days will it take TT&F to attract 10% of the market (if it will)?
3. Brand loyalty is very high for Pimienta drinkers. Would it be worthwhile to spend scarce advertising dollars on strengthening Pimienta's brand loyalty, or would a head-to-head campaign against Nectar and Oasis be the better strategy?

Before leaving our example to discuss the theory and application of modeling with Markov chains, it is interesting (and perhaps counterintuitive) to note that Pimienta will eventually gain a 50% share of the market! With this intriguing fact as prologue, let's address the underlying assumptions associated with Markov chains.

UNDERLYING ASSUMPTIONS

As already noted, for a process to be modeled as a Markov chain, it must exhibit the Markov property—that is, movement from one state to another at a discrete point in time depends only on the current state and not on previous or subsequent states. Moreover, the probability of moving from any state to any other state remains constant over time.

We have seen one example of a process that exhibits the Markov property—our soft drink brand-switching scenario. Suppose, however, that a subset of soft drink purchasers, for the sake of variety, never bought the same brand three times in a row. In this case, the Markov property is not present (in the sense of a one-step, or first-order, process), and we cannot model the process as a simple Markov chain. This is because the probabilities depend upon something that happened two stages ago instead of the previous stage only. Thus, Markov models should be considered only short-term planning techniques.

The other basic assumption that we must meet is that of stationarity—that is, the state probabilities do not change over time. In real-world applications, nonstationarity is most often the attribute that rules out the use of Markov chains. We can easily understand why this is so when we take a managerial view of processes. For example, in the soft drink market share scenario, we noted (without proof, of course) that TT&F would eventually have 50% of the market share—under the assumption that Olympus and Sahara would sit idly by while their aggregate market share declined from 95% to 50%. That assumption, of course, is nonsensical. Our analysis of processes provides an input to managerial action that may result in changes to those processes. At any rate, we must be careful to note the presence of possible nonstationarities when using Markov chain models.

MODELING WITH TRANSITION MATRICES

The basic modeling device in Markov chain analysis is the one-step transition matrix, which we denote by the symbol P_1. The rows and columns of P_1 are associated with n states in which elements of the process may find themselves. Table 10.1 contains some examples.

The elements of P_1, which we denote by p_{ij}, are the probabilities that, given that we are in state i at time period t, we will be in state j at time period $t + 1$. Thus, P_1 is a matrix, each of whose rows is a marginal probability distribution—identical in form to the posterior distribution in DMUR modeling. By inference, the states must be mutually exclusive and collectively exhaustive.

The other tool we will need is the initial state vector $S_1 = (S_1, S_2, \ldots, S_n)$, where S_j represents the current status of the process. In our soft drink example, recall that $S_1 = (0.50, 0.45, 0.05)$, which were the initial market shares for Olympus, Sahara, and TT&F, respectively. In the weather example in Table 10.1, one possible initial state vector would be $S_1 = (0, 1, 0, 0, 0)$, signifying that today is rainy.

To complete our "tool kit" for modeling with Markov chains, we need a system for estimating p_{ij}, $i, j = 1, \ldots, n$, the one-step state probabilities. As is usually the case, estimating accurate probability distributions on states is critical to success, and it is also the most difficult task to accomplish. In many cases, we can use historical

TABLE 10.1 Some example processes

Process Elements	States
Daily weather conditions	Sunny, rainy, snowy, overcast, dusty
Fir trees on a Christmas tree farm	Cut and sold, dead of disease, allowed to mature, newly planted
Professor's tests	Hard, medium, easy
Company personnel	Hired, promoted to supervisor, promoted to manager, fired, deceased, retired

records or customer surveys to compute relative frequencies. In other cases, we must resort to outright subjective estimates. Whatever the case, we must be sensitive to the fact that our analysis is no better than the probability distributions are accurate.

Finally, Markov models are, in the technical sense, purely descriptive. That is, there is no formal objective function as there is in an optimizing model such as linear programming. However, at the risk of repeating ourselves, all MS/OR models are descriptive in a managerial sense.

We exhibit a formal one-step transition matrix in Table 10.2. Note in the table that

$$\sum_{j=1}^{n} p_{ij} = 1$$

for each $i = 1, \ldots, n$.

TABLE 10.2 General one-step transition matrix

		\multicolumn{7}{c}{State at Time $t + 1$}
		1	2	$\cdots$	j	$\cdots$	n
	1	p_{11}	p_{12}	$\cdots$	p_{1j}	$\cdots$	p_{1n}
	2	p_{21}	p_{22}	$\cdots$	p_{2j}	$\cdots$	p_{2n}
State at Time t	i	p_{i1}	p_{i2}	$\cdots$	p_{ij}	$\cdots$	p_{in}
	n	p_{n1}	p_{n2}	$\cdots$	p_{nj}	$\cdots$	p_{nn}

SOLUTION APPROACHES: AN INTUITIVE DESCRIPTION

There are two basically different types of Markov processes, which we will refer to as **recurring** and **transient**, respectively. Since they model markedly different processes and require different analytical approaches, we discuss the two types separately.

RECURRING MARKOV PROCESSES

Let's return to our soft drink market share scenario and pursue it further. For convenience, we reproduce the one-step transition matrix and the initial state vector here:

$$\mathbf{P}_1 = \begin{array}{c} \\ N \\ O \\ P \end{array} \begin{array}{c} N O P \\ \begin{bmatrix} 0.75 & 0.15 & 0.10 \\ 0.10 & 0.80 & 0.10 \\ 0.05 & 0.05 & 0.90 \end{bmatrix} \end{array} \qquad \mathbf{S}_1 = \begin{array}{c} N O P \\ (0.50, \ 0.45, \ 0.05) \end{array} \tag{10.1}$$

Assuming that the time period for each transition is one week, how can we "forecast" the market share S_2 one week hence? Consider the product Nectar (N). One week hence, this product will retain 75% of its own share of 50% and will pick up 10% of Oasis' 45% and 5% of Pimienta's 5% (note the first column of P_1, and S_1). Therefore, one week later,

$$\text{Nectar's market share} = (0.75)(0.5) + (0.1)(0.45) + (0.05)(0.05)$$
$$= 0.4225 = 42.25\% \qquad (10.2)$$

What we have done, of course, is to perform the first step of the vector-matrix multiplication:

$$S_2 = S_1 P_1 = (0.4225, 0.4375, 0.1400) \qquad (10.3)$$

Note in our example that Nectar's share dropped dramatically, Oasis' share decreased a bit, and Pimienta's almost tripled!

To compute the market share two weeks hence, we could simply perform the computation

$$S_3 = S_2 P_1 = (0.3676, 0.4204, 0.2120) \qquad (10.4)$$

noting that Nectar suffered another large drop, Pimienta increased by over 50% of last week's share, and Oasis again declined slightly.

Let's look at the computations in a slightly different way. Note that

$$S_3 = S_2 P_1 = (S_1 P_1)(P_1) = S_1 P_1^2 \qquad (10.5)$$

Thus, the two-step transition matrix P_2 is just P_1 multiplied by itself once. In general, then, the m-step transition matrix $P_m = (P_1)^m$, and

$$S_{m+1} = S_1 (P_1)^m \qquad (10.6)$$

This scenario is an example of a recurring Markov process. If we continued our calculations, allowing m to become very large, $(P_1)^m$ would slowly converge to a matrix with three identical rows, the elements of which would represent the **steady-state** market shares of the three soft drinks. Stated another way, we would have the long-term market shares independent of the actual market shares at the beginning!

Fortunately, we do not actually have to perform a long series of matrix multiplications to find the steady-state vector. Note the elegant simplicity of the following logic. Suppose we know the steady-state vector $S = (S_1, S_2, S_3)$. The definition of steady state tells us this state will not change in the next period. Thus,

$$S = SP_1 \qquad (10.7)$$

If we plug in the numbers from our ongoing example, treating S_1, S_2, and S_3 as unknown quantities, we have

$$(S_1, S_2, S_3) = (S_1, S_2, S_3) \begin{bmatrix} 0.75 & 0.15 & 0.10 \\ 0.10 & 0.80 & 0.10 \\ 0.05 & 0.05 & 0.90 \end{bmatrix} \qquad (10.8)$$

Or, carrying out the multiplications and bringing the variables to the left-hand sides of the equations, we have

$$-0.25 S_1 + 0.10 S_2 + 0.05 S_3 = 0 \qquad (10.9)$$

$$0.15 S_1 - 0.20 S_2 + 0.05 S_3 = 0 \qquad (10.10)$$

$$0.10S_1 + 0.10S_2 - 0.10S_3 = 0 \qquad (10.11)$$

Equations (10.9) to (10.11) are redundant, so this system of equations has no unique solution. However, we also know that

$$S_1 + S_2 + S_3 = 1 \qquad (10.12)$$

We therefore discard one of the Equations (10.9) to (10.11) (which one doesn't matter), add Equation (10.12), and have our computer produce the unique solution, which is

$S_1 = 0.2143$, Nectar's stable share

$S_2 = 0.2857$, Oasis' stable share

$S_3 = 0.5000$, Pimienta's stable share

Of course, we may very well be interested in the transient behavior of the process. Perhaps in our illustration, market share at the end of the fourth week may be a critical item for managerial decision making. If this is the case:

$$S_5 = S_1[(P_1)^2]^2 = (0.50, 0.45, 0.05) \begin{bmatrix} 0.3931 & 0.3117 & 0.2952 \\ 0.2146 & 0.4902 & 0.2952 \\ 0.1375 & 0.1577 & 0.7048 \end{bmatrix} \qquad (10.13)$$

$$= (0.300, 0.384, 0.316)$$

Thus, after four weeks, Pimienta will have already overtaken Nectar in market share and will be hot on the heels of Oasis.

TRANSIENT MARKOV PROCESSES

In recurring Markov processes, all states have the property that elements come and go, so to speak. Said another way, all states are recurring. In transient Markov processes, however, there are two different types of states: transient and absorbing.

Transient states are states in which some temporary parts of the process allow units to pass through, but that in the long run converge to state probabilities of zero. As an illustration, consider the Christmas tree farm scenario from Table 10.1. If a given tree is neither diseased nor cut and sold in a given year, it returns to the "allowed to mature" state the following year. The tree will eventually leave this transient state and, of course, will never return.

Absorbing states, on the other hand, are the converse of transient states. Once a process element enters an absorbing state, it never leaves. In our example, the states "dead of disease" and "cut and sold" are clearly absorbing states.

Transient Markov processes model scenarios in which all units eventually end up in absorbing states, so we know at the outset what the transient elements of the steady-state vector will look like. Transient processes, unlike recurring ones, are highly sensitive to the composition of the initial state vector as well as to the pattern of the one-step transition matrix. Transition processes can become complicated very quickly, as we illustrate in the following scenario.

Bill Dunn, the business manager for the Rio de Oro Medical Clinic (from Chapter 3), is analyzing the clinic's accounts receivable. Billings are always "net 30 days," so that accounts not paid after 30 days are past due and Bill sends gentle reminders to these clients. If a bill is still unpaid after 60 days, Bill issues a not-so-gentle reminder. After 90 days, he relegates an unpaid bill to the unsympathetic attention of a collection agency.

From past records, Bill sets up a one-step transition matrix (Table 10.3).

TABLE 10.3 Rio de Oro one-step transition matrix

	Less Than 30 Days Old	30–60 Days Old	60–90 Days Old	Paid	Collection Agency	Uncollectible
<30 days old	0	0.25	0	0.75	0	0
30–60 days old	0	0	0.35	0.65	0	0
60–90 days old	0	0	0	0.50	0.50	0
Paid	0	0	0	1.00	0	0
Collection agency	0	0	0	0.25	0	0.75
Uncollectible	0	0	0	0	0	1.00

Bill also notes that the current crop of accounts receivable is as follows:

Category	Percentage in Category
Less than 30 days old	60%
30–60 days old	20
60–90 days old	15
With collection agency	5

At this point, of course, none of the current set is in the "paid" or "uncollectible" category (an absorbing state), so that the initial state vector is as follows:

$$S_1 = (0.60, 0.20, 0.15, 0, 0.05, 0) \tag{10.14}$$

This transient process reaches steady state in exactly four months. We obtain the steady-state vector and the intermediate state vectors by serially multiplying $S_i P_1$, $i = 1, 2, 3, 4$, and the results are as follows:

	Less Than 30 Days	30–60 Days	60–90 Days	Paid	Collection Agency	Uncollectible
S2	0	0.1500	0.0700	0.6675	0.0750	0.0375
S3	0	0	0.0525	0.8188	0.0350	0.0937
S4	0	0	0	0.8538	0.0262	0.1200
S5	0	0	0	0.8603	0	0.1397

In our example, therefore, only 86% of Rio de Oro's patients will eventually pay their bills. Since this is most probably an unacceptably low collection rate, Bill Dunn would need to take some managerial action to change the process (e.g., more effective reminder notices or a better collection agency). The effect of such managerial actions would be to change the transition probabilities and thereby change the process itself.

We note in passing that the device we used to find the steady-state vector in recurring Markov processes won't work for transient processes. The reason for this phenomenon is that the transient states by definition have steady-state transition probabilities of zero.

Transient Markov chain models have a variety of applications. One very interesting one—analyzing the rank structure of the officer corps in a military service—is the subject of the first minicase in this chapter, "An Officer and a Gentleman."

DEVELOPING ALTERNATIVE SOLUTIONS

Unlike the case with many optimizing models, for which we have formal sensitivity analysis tools, we must use brute force on descriptive models to obtain such information (recall that this was also the case with discrete simulation models). Given the relative ease with which computers "solve" Markov chain models, however, this is not particularly a problem.

STATE OF THE ART IN MARKOV CHAIN ANALYSIS

The general theory of stochastic processes, of which discrete Markov processes are a small part, is a complex and highly mathematical subject. Let's briefly discuss two advanced topics in stochastic processes to get the flavor of this complexity.

TIME OF FIRST PASSAGE

Time of first passage refers to the average (expected) number of time periods for an element of a process to move from a given state to any other (given) state. For example, in a company that has a policy of developing its own management from within (rather than pirating executives from other companies), a newly hired line manager might have a very strong interest in the time of first passage from the state "management trainee" to the state "chief executive officer."

We will discuss time of first passage only for recurring Markov models.

TIME OF FIRST PASSAGE: RECURRING MARKOV CHAINS

Let f_{ij} denote the average (expected) number of time periods for an element currently located in state i to reach state j. Before stating the mathematical result, let's return to our soft drink market share scenario once more to think through the logic involved. The one-step transition matrix is

$$\mathbf{P}_1 = \begin{array}{c} \\ N \\ O \\ P \end{array} \begin{array}{c} N \quad\quad O \quad\quad P \\ \begin{bmatrix} 0.75 & 0.15 & 0.10 \\ 0.10 & 0.80 & 0.10 \\ 0.05 & 0.05 & 0.90 \end{bmatrix} \end{array} \quad\quad (10.15)$$

Suppose that a customer has just purchased a bottle of Nectar, and we are interested in knowing (on the average) how many transitions it will take for him or her to purchase a bottle or can of Pimienta. There are several possibilities. First, the customer may switch to Pimienta in exactly one step, with an expected value of $p_{13}(1 \text{ step}) =$

p_{13}. On the other hand, the customer could stay with Nectar or go to Oasis on the next purchase and then eventually purchase a Pimienta. These expected values are

$$p_{11}(1 \text{ step} + f_{13}) + p_{12}(1 \text{ step} + f_{23})$$

Mathematically, then,

$$f_{13} = p_{13} + p_{11}(1 + f_{13}) + p_{12}(1 + f_{23}) \tag{10.16}$$

or, more simply,

$$(1 - p_{11})f_{13} - p_{12}f_{23} = (p_{11} + p_{12} + p_{13}) = 1 \tag{10.17}$$

Equation (10.17) is an equation in two unknowns. To solve for f_{13}—the quantity in which we are interested, we must also solve for f_{23}—which means looking at the second possibility that our fickle customer just purchased a bottle of Oasis. This equation, by the same reasoning, is

$$-p_{21}f_{13} + (1 - p_{22})f_{23} = 1 \tag{10.18}$$

Substituting the appropriate p_{ij} values and solving, we have $f_{13} = f_{23} = 10$. That is, regardless of whether our customer just bought a Nectar or an Oasis, it will take him or her, on an average, ten transitions before he or she selects a Pimienta.

If these results seem counterintuitive, note that the key to this particular scenario is the high brand loyalty associated with Pimienta. Thus, although it may take some time to attract a following, Pimienta slowly builds its market share through customer retention. This phenomenon, of course, is no surprise to anyone who has ever taken a basic marketing course.

In general, then, to solve for time of first passage from any state to all other states, we must solve the following system of $(n - 1)$ equations:

$$f_{ij} - \sum_{\substack{r = 1 \\ j \neq r}}^{n} p_{ir}f_{rj} = 1; i = 1, \ldots, n, i \neq j \tag{10.19}$$

DYNAMIC PROGRAMMING IN MARKOV CHAINS

Many dynamic programming formulations of underlying problems involve probabilistic states at each stage. Several advanced texts (e.g., Wagner [4]) address a formulation referred to as the stochastic shortest-route model, in which the optimal decisions at each stage are functions of transition probabilities. To illustrate this approach, recall Wagner's stagecoach problem discussed in Chapter 6 (dynamic programming).

Recall that Mr. Mark Off wished to travel by stagecoach from New York to San Francisco in the 1800s to seek his fortune. His problem was to select the route—in advance—that minimized his total life insurance policy premium for the entire trip, thereby assuring the safest possible trip. In our deterministic treatment, we tacitly assumed that Mark was certain to obtain a seat on any stagecoach of his choice, that timing of connections between stages was ideal, and that no route was altered or discontinued.

Instead, what if the actual availability of routings at each stage was probabilistic and that these probabilities depended only on the states preceding a particular stage? We would then have a "dynamic programming in a Markov chain" process, and our challenge would be to find the expected optimal routing through the network.

The mathematical details of this topic are beyond the scope of this textbook. However, since there are many important applications of this modeling device in business and industry (e.g., inventory systems), present and prospective managers should at least be aware of its existence.

MINICASES

An Officer and a Gentleman

THE SCENARIO

The officer corps of any large military establishment bears many similarities to the hierarchical management cadre of major business corporations. Each involves a structure of ranks or titles intended to indicate increasing levels of managerial responsibility. Table 10.4 contrasts some of the titles used for this purpose in billion-dollar banks with the classical rank structure of the U.S. Army and the U.S. Air Force. (The U.S. Navy uses different terms but has the same structure.)

Unlike private corporations, the armed services do not necessarily promote officers from one rank to the next as positions become vacant. Instead, the promotion process is an annual event, with names of promotees appearing on "the list" for each rank at the appointed time of year. Each rank carries with it a "normal time in grade." Those promoted early are "below the zone," and those not promoted at the normal time are "passed over."

THE PROBLEM

Although each officer rank carries with it a maximum tenure (e.g., a lieutenant colonel must retire after 28 years of service if he or she has not been promoted to full colonel), the task of maintaining the desired percentages of officers in each rank is a challenge. For example, under certain circumstances, officers may elect to take early retirement (at a reduced pension) with as little as 20 years of active service—regardless of rank achieved. Others may choose to serve out their maximum tenure. If sufficient numbers of officers at the same rank choose this latter option, a severe imbalance (and an impediment to the advancement of younger officers) could occur. What is needed by military personnel planners is a model that enables them to predict future officer

TABLE 10.4

Bank Officer Title	Military Rank
President	General Officer
Executive Vice President	Lieutenant General
Senior Vice President	Major General
Vice President	Brigadier General
Vice President for Operations	Colonel
Assistant Vice President for Operations	Lieutenant Colonel
Head Cashier	Major
Cashier	Captain
Assistant Cashier	First Lieutenant
Management Trainee	Second Lieutenant

staffing levels by rank and to use this information to develop recruitment, promotion, and retention policies that result in a balanced officer complement.

THE MODEL

With a few minor exceptions, the process of changes over time in the officer complement of an armed service provides a classical example of a Markov process. The ranks, of course, are the transient states, with resignation, termination for cause, retirement, and death representing the absorbing states. Although promotions (or, occasionally, demotions) to the various ranks do not occur at the same time in each calendar year, we may still use a year as the basic transition time unit.

To keep our analysis manageable, let's aggregate certain ranks and eliminate "termination for cause" as an absorbing state. The resulting states are in Table 10.5.

TABLE 10.5

State No.	State	Type
1	Input	Transient
2	Second Lieutenant	"
3	First Lieutenant	"
4	Captain	"
5	Major	"
6	Lieutenant Colonel	"
7	Colonel	"
8	General (all)	"
9	Resignation	Absorbing
10	Retirement	"
11	Death	"

The one-step transition matrix in Table 10.6, although not taken from actual historical data, is a reasonable estimate based on experience. Note in this scenario that we have included an input state, which represents the newly commissioned crop of second lieutenants each year. In performing the step-by-step analysis of the Markov chain model over a period of years, management must supply input as to the number of new commissions, and this number becomes part of the activity vector. Thus, we actually have a hybrid Markov chain model—transient for those officers currently in the system but recurring as far as numbers in the various states are concerned.

SOLUTION TO THE MODEL

Let us ignore the input state for the moment and use the following initial activity vector to experiment:

$$S_1 = (100, \ 150, \ 75, \ 50, \ 30, \ 10, \ 0.4, \ 0, \ 0, \ 0)$$
$$2L \quad 1L \quad CP \quad MJ \quad LC \quad CL \quad GN \quad RS \quad RT \quad DT$$

(The numbers in S_1 are in thousands of officers.) Figure 10.2 shows the SAMS Markov chain module input screen. The SAMS quick briefing reports the steady state vector as in Table 10.7 on p. 382.

TABLE 10.6 One-step transition matrix for "Officer"

From	To										
	IN 1	2L 2	1L 3	CP 4	MJ 5	LC 6	CL 7	GN 8	RS 9	RT 10	DT 11
IN 1		1									
2L 2		.500	.499								.001
1L 3		.001	.588	.400					.010		.001
CP 4			.001	.647	.300				.050		.002
MJ 5				.001	.709	.250			.030	.005	.005
LC 6					.001	.734	.150		.005	.100	.010
CL 7						.001	.698	.050	.001	.200	.050
GN 8							.001	.669		.250	.080
RS 9									1		
RT 10										1	
DT 11											1

FIGURE 10.2 SAMS input screen for Officer and Gentleman

```
─────► SAMS INPUT SCREEN - Markov Chains  ◄─────
   NAME?   AN OFFICER AND A GENTLEMAN MINICASE
   STEADY STATE?  Y       OTHER PERIODS?  2,3,4
   PROBLEM DESCRIPTION - Analyze the promotion system for a
                         military service officer corps

              ONE-STEP TRANSITION MATRIX
                              TO STATES
    FROM    2L    1L    CP    MJ    LC    CL    GN    RS    RT    DT
    STATES
    IN  1         1
    2L  2  .500  .499                                            .001
    1L  3  .001  .588  .400                           .010       .001
    CP  4        .001  .647  .300                    .050       .002
    MJ  5              .001  .709  .250              .030  .005  .005
    LC  6                    .001  .734  .150        .005  .100  .010
    CL  7                          .001  .698  .050  .001  .200  .050
    GN  8                                .001  .669        .250  .080
    RS  9                                            1
    RT 10                                                  1
    DT 11                                                        1

                         INITIAL STATE VECTOR
              100   150    75    50    30    10   .4    0    0    0
```

TABLE 10.7 SAMS report for Officer minicase

**AN OFFICER AND A GENTLEMAN
QUICK BRIEFING ON TRANSIENT MARKOV CHAIN**

Transient states are 2L 1L CP MJ LC CL GN
Steady-state for transient states is zero (0)

Absorbing states and their steady-state values are

State	Value
RS	213.93
RT	159.93
DT	42.79

Interim Results

Period	2L	1L	CP	MJ	LC	CL	GN	RS	RT	DT
2	50.2	131.2	108.6	58.0	34.5	11.5	0.8	6.9	5.3	1.5
3	25.2	106.4	125.6	73.7	39.9	13.2	1.1	15.6	11.6	3.2
4	12.7	75.3	123.9	90.0	47.6	15.2	1.4	25.4	18.8	5.1

Of the 415,000 officers in the original cohort, note that almost 214,000 resigned, about 160,000 retired, and 42,790 died on active duty. However, in this instance, our managerial interest is not in the ways that officers leave the service but in the intermediate states for the next few years.

By indicating "2, 3, 4" in the SAMS input screen, the algorithm calculated numbers in each state for the second, third, and fourth years for this cohort.

SOLUTION TO THE PROBLEM

If Table 10.7 were the actual one-step transition matrix for a military service, these figures would raise a red flag immediately. The sharp rise in the middle ranks (major through colonel) over the three-year period is, in personnel lingo, a hump, which if allowed to occur, would severely imbalance the promotion system.

Also, the results surface some shortcomings of the model or perhaps inaccuracies in the data themselves. For example, the number of general officers is predicted by the model to grow from 400 to 1,390 over a three-year period, whereas the number of general officer slots is controlled by Congress at a figure considerably lower. Moreover, the analysis indicates that 12,700 of our original 100,000 second lieutenants were not promoted after three years of service, while in reality promotion to first lieutenant has always been practically automatic upon completion of two years of service.

EPILOGUE

The purpose of this minicase is not to introduce you to the mysteries of military personnel management, but to illustrate both the strengths and weaknesses of Markov chain modeling and analysis. The analogy to the "rank" structure in a large bank—or

Lemmon Rent-a-Car

THE SCENARIO

Lisa Lemmon, owner and CEO of Lemmon Rent-a-Car, is performing her annual review of company operations. With five rental stations located in Dallas, Houston, Austin, San Antonio, and El Paso, the firm's business has improved every year for the past five years. Since the company has a policy not to enter into reciprocity agreements with other rent-a-car companies, Lemmon will rent cars for turn-in only at these five cities.

THE PROBLEM

As business picked up, Lisa noticed a bothersome and growing trend. Increasingly, one of the stations in a city would rent all of its cars early in the business day and have to turn away customers. At the same time, other stations reported an overstock of available cars for which there was no demand. Lisa did not wish to tie up scarce capital by deliberately overstocking the stations, but she hated to lose business by having too few cars on hand when and where they were needed.

She asked her administrative assistant to look into the problem. The assistant accessed the company's computerized management information system and came up with the aggregate data in Table 10.8 on lease destinations for each of the five stations for the past six months.

THE MODEL

The administrative assistant recognized the possibility that the problem could be modeled as a Markov chain model and converted the numbers from Table 10.8 to relative

TABLE 10.8 Number of cars leased by origin & destination

	Destination					
Origin	Dallas	Houston	Austin	San Antonio	El Paso	Total
Dallas	6407	8692	4953	3876	2152	26,080
Houston	9010	8614	4648	2960	6933	32,165
Austin	3409	2980	1225	4165	1940	13,719
San Antonio	4121	3588	1203	6198	2841	17,951
El Paso	1190	1442	942	1108	795	5,477

TABLE 10.9 Relative frequencies by city of origin

Origin	Destination				
	Dallas	Houston	Austin	San Antonio	El Paso
Dallas	0.246	0.333	0.190	0.149	0.082
Houston	0.280	0.268	0.145	0.092	0.215
Austin	0.248	0.217	0.089	0.304	0.142
San Antonio	0.230	0.200	0.067	0.345	0.158
El Paso	0.217	0.263	0.172	0.202	0.146

frequencies by city by dividing each number by its row total (see Table 10.9). This, then, is the empirically derived one-step transition matrix for a recurring Markov chain model.

SOLUTION TO THE MODEL

The assistant used SAMS' Markov chain module to produce the solution as in Table 10.10.

TABLE 10.10 SAMS report for Lemmon minicase

LEMMON RENT-A-CAR
QUICK BRIEFING ON RECURRING MARKOV CHAIN

Steady-state values are

State	Value
DALLAS	0.248
HOUSTON	0.262
AUSTIN	0.137
SAN ANTONIO	0.203
EL PASO	0.150

Since Lemmon's fleet totaled 600 rental cars, the assistant converted the fractional-valued steady-state activity vector into the numbers of cars it represented, as follows:

S = (149, 157, 82, 122, 90)
     D   H   A   S   E

Armed with his computer output, the assistant strode confidently into Lisa's office.

"Boss," he announced proudly, "I've solved your problem."

SOLUTION TO THE PROBLEM

Lisa listened intently as her assistant explained his analysis but raised her eyebrows when he stated flatly, "Things will eventually take care of themselves, since after enough transitions, the appropriate numbers of cars would end up at each of the five locations." She didn't know much about Markov models, but she knew better than that!

"What was the inventory of cars at each location this morning at the start of business?" she asked.

"I knew you'd ask that, Chief," he replied. "The figures I've got include both cars on the lots as well as those inbound."

$S_1 = (135, 129, 108, 123, 105)$

D H A S E

"Now," Lisa continued, "are your six-month figures based on actual rentals or actual demand?"

"Well, actual rentals, of course," he said. "When one of our stations is out of rental cars, our agents don't ask customers where they're going if we can't accommodate them!"

"I see," sighed Lisa. "That means we don't even know the demand for our services. Those numbers that you called 'one-step transition probabilities' are just plain wrong—and useless to me as a manager."

After carefully comparing S_1 (actual cars) and S, Lisa said, "OK, take an urgent memo to all five station managers. Remind them in no uncertain terms that we are in business to get people to where they want to go, not merely to rent them cars if we happen to have some available.

"Effective immediately, when customers want cars, find one. Give them yours, or rent one in Lemmon's name from a competitor. Then, as soon as possible, have the manager at Austin hire temporary people to 'deadhead' 15 cars to Dallas and 11 cars to Houston. Tell our El Paso manager to mount an immediate 30-day, 25%-off special rate for rental cars to Houston. And set up a system to keep very accurate records of all these transactions."

Chagrined, but obedient, the assistant mumbled a somewhat subdued "Yes, ma'am."

"Don't be discouraged," Lisa remarked, "your ability to do analysis is usually very helpful to me, and I appreciate your customary fine work. You must remember, though, that although your MS models provide me with valuable insights, they can't make my decisions for me."

SUMMARY

In this chapter, we investigated a descriptive technique called Markov chain models for analyzing discrete, dynamic programming processes that exhibit the Markov property. The two basic tools we used were the one-step transition matrix and the initial state vector.

We recognized that we must deal with two different underlying processes. The recurring Markov chain model is applicable when there are no absorbing states, so that such a process converges over time to a steady state. The transient Markov chain model, on the other hand, is an appropriate analytical tool when transient and absorbing states are present.

Under the subject of advanced topics, we briefly discussed the time of first passage in recurring Markov chain models and introduced the notion of dynamic programming in Markov chains. Finally, the two minicases involved a transient (or hybrid) model and a recurring one.

KEY TERMS

absorbing state
discrete stochastic process
doubly stochastic matrix
one-stage transition matrix

recurring Markov process
steady-state vector
transient Markov process
transient state

PROBLEMS FOR ANALYSIS

1. **The Scenario:** Nevada-Twain Chilled Meat, Inc. (NCM) is a large processor and distributor of meat products to supermarkets and restaurant chains. Although demand for its products is fairly stable over the calendar year, unprocessed carcasses arrive at NCM's huge plant and storage facility in a "lumpy" fashion, peaking in late spring and late fall. Consequently, the company must maintain a cold storage capacity far above that necessary to supply normal demand.

   The Problem: NCM purchases electric power about equally from municipally owned plants in Eastside and Westview, Nevada. R. Kipling Twain, the founder and CEO of the company, reasoned that depending on a single source of electric power could prove to be disastrous if a power failure occurred, since such failure would destroy thousands of pounds of frozen meat. Then, one warm day in June, both power companies failed simultaneously. They had linked their transmission systems a short time ago for their own protection, but their aging equipment couldn't carry the load. Although NCM bought virtually every ice cube within a hundred-mile radius, the company still suffered a 200,000-dollar spoilage loss.

   Calling in Faron Hite, the cold storage supervisor, Twain laid it on the line. "Faron," he said, "I want to know how often we can expect simultaneous power outages from Eastside and Westview. I'm considering buying a backup power generation system of our own, but I don't want to do it if it costs more than the cost of our potential losses."

   "I'll get right on it, Mr. Twain," replied Faron.

   The Model: Faron, working with his engineers and MS/OR analyst, quickly discovered an interesting phenomenon. It appeared that the probable state of the linked power system on a given day depended only on the state of the system on the previous day. Faron and the analyst identified four specific states, as follows:

State	Condition
A	Both Eastside and Westview operating
B	Only Eastside operating
C	Only Westview operating
D	Neither Eastside nor Westview operating

   Using engineering estimates, historical records, and intuition based on experience, Faron and his team produced the following one-step transition matrix:

			To			
			A	B	C	D
From	Both	A	0.90	0.06	0.03	0.01
	Eastside	B	0.05	0.80	0.05	0.10
	Westview	C	0.20	0.05	0.70	0.05
	Neither	D	0.10	0.50	0.35	0.05

a. In your opinion, does Faron's decision to use a Markov chain model make sense? Why/ why not?

Solution to the Model:

a. Note that the one-step transition matrix models a recurring Markov process, since there are apparently no absorbing states. Use available computer software to analyze this model. Specifically:

(1) What is the steady-state probability that both power plants are down simultaneously?

(2) Suppose that the two utilities offered to modernize their facilities so that the probabilities associated with A (both operating) changed to

$$p_{11} = 0.97; \quad p_{12} = 0.01; \quad p_{13} = 0.01; \quad p_{14} = 0.01$$

Would such a change make a significant difference to NCM in assessing its plans?

b. If you were Mr. Twain, would you have any interest in knowing some short-term activity information rather than just the steady-state (long-term) results in (a)? Why or why not?

Solution to the Problem: Verify with available software that the steady-state vectors associated with the original model and with the revised model in (a2) are as follows:

		Both	Eastside	Westview	Neither
Original model:	S =	(0.501,	0.301,	0.153,	0.045)
Revised model:	S' =	(0.781,	0.119,	0.075,	0.025)

Twain studied the steady-state results intently. "Faron," he asked, "how good are the numbers you used to get these results?"

Hite responded, "Frankly, Boss, they're the best estimates that our engineers, our MS/OR analyst, and I could come up with. They are a mixture of scientific analyses, historical experience, and just plain judgment on the part of the team. I can't guarantee that they are accurate, but I'll stake my professional reputation—and my job, of course—that no group of people could come up with anything more reliable or well researched."

With a faint smile, R. Kipling Twain then said, "What course of action would you recommend, Faron?"

"If I were you, Mr. Twain—and of course I'm not—I'd take out disaster insurance for a year to guard against unexpectedly high losses due to power failures, and I'd agree to the deal that the Eastside and Westview power companies have proposed. I think that a large capital expenditure for a private backup power generating system wouldn't be advisable for NCM right now. And besides, if we don't trust our suppliers of electric power that much, we should consider relocating the plant to another state."

Faron stopped to take a breath and concluded by saying, "I'm not trying to make your decisions for you, Mr. Twain, but you did ask."

"Yes I did, Faron," replied Twain," and I got the kind of answer I'd hoped for. My decision is to go with your recommendation with one exception. Instead of taking out insurance from an external source, I'll personally insure the company against the kind of disaster you spoke of, at no charge to the corporation."

"And by the way," Twain continued, "I'm not getting any younger, and this outfit needs new blood and fresh ideas at the top. Would you take on that responsibility?"

After a short pause, Faron Hite (future CEO of Nevada-Twain Chilled Meat, Inc.) replied: "Kipling, I'm your man!"

2. **The Scenario:** The tiny, English-speaking country of Foggy Bottom has a federal government system quite unlike that of most Western nations. Although the people periodically elect a president and legislators, the real power is in the hands of the career members of the federal service (FS), whom no one can fire.

One federal agency in Foggy Bottom is the Taxpayers Assistance Group (TAG), whose mission is to assist citizens in dealing with the complicated red tape associated with almost every government transaction. Vera Ruud, Kurt Manners, and Chip Shoulders are career FS employees with the TAG and find their jobs to be boring and unpleasant.

The Problem: To relieve their boredom, Vera, Kurt, and Chip have devised a little game they call "runaround," which is played as follows.

1. When Vera receives a phone call from a citizen for help, she flips two coins. If two heads occur, she tells the citizen to call Kurt in one hour, and if one head and one tail turn up, she has the citizen call Chip one hour hence. If the flips result in two tails, she asks the citizen to call her back in an hour.
2. Kurt, on the other hand, uses a standard deck of playing cards (no joker) shuffled and drawn at random. The draw of a club evokes instructions to call Vera one hour hence, and similarly a diamond for Chip, and a heart for himself. If a spade turns up, Kurt tells the citizen to go away, since TAG can't help.
3. Chip's "decision rule" is much simpler: if his digital clock is showing an even minute when a call comes, he tells the caller to call Vera in one hour, and an odd minute results in a call to Kurt.

The Model:
a. Is this silly process one that we can model as a Markov chain model? That is, does it exhibit the Markov property and stationarity?
b. If your answer to (a) is yes, construct the one-step transition matrix for this model.
c. Is your model recurring or transient?

Solution to the Model:
a. Suppose that at the start of a daily round of the game, each of the three players gets ten calls directly from citizens. Use a computer package to compute the number of calls that each player will receive the second hour as a result of "referrals."
b. How many citizens will Kurt have "sent away" after eight "transitions" in a normal working day?
c. Times of first passage from Vera, Kurt, and Chip to the state "go away" would give an indication of the average "runaround" that a citizen receives. Compute these numbers and consider their significance.

Solution to the Problem: There is no solution to this problem. Since FS employees in the country of Foggy Bottom, cannot be fired, they do as they please. Aren't we fortunate in the Western world that we don't have to contend with such a distressing situation?

3. Consider the following one-step transition matrix with $n = 4$ states:

		To			
		A	B	C	D
	A	0.3	0.4	0.2	0.1
	B	0.1	0.3	0.1	0.5
From	C	0.4	0.2	0.2	0.2
	D	0.2	0.1	0.5	0.2

Note that this one-step transition matrix has the property that its columns as well as its rows sum to 1. We call such matrices **doubly stochastic.**

a. Use available computer software to verify that the steady-state vector for this process is

$$S = (0.25, 0.25, 0.25, 0.25).$$

Is this a coincidence, or do all doubly stochastic recurring Markov chain models have steady-state activity vectors of the form

$$S = (1/n, 1/n, \ldots 1/n)?$$

b. Suppose that the matrix represented the one-step transition matrix for the following Markov process. A, B, C, and D represent hardened silos for the Armageddon nuclear missile. The sites are far enough apart so that an incoming missile could destroy only one site. Six underground tunnels connect the sites, and crews move the Armageddon daily according to the above one-step transition matrix, using a random number generator.

Is it clear that in the long run the four sites would actually contain the missile the same percentage of the time? Would the enemy benefit (in the long run) by obtaining possession of the one-step transition matrix?

c. Suppose the enemy knew the location of the missile on day 1 but could not launch an attack until day 4. Would having this information (in addition to knowing the one-step transition matrix) be of value?

d. Does intuition suggest that expected times of first passage to a given state from all other states are equal for a doubly stochastic one-step transition matrix?

Unfortunately, this is not the case. You should verify this for yourself. For example, expected times of first passage from D to A, B, and C in the transition matrix are
From D to

$A = 4.000$

$B = 2.446$

$C = 3.889$

4. For each of the following scenarios, determine whether a Markov chain would accurately describe the process. For those scenarios that do appear to be amenable to this kind of analysis, determine whether the process appears to be recurring or transient; if transient, identify the transient and absorbing states.

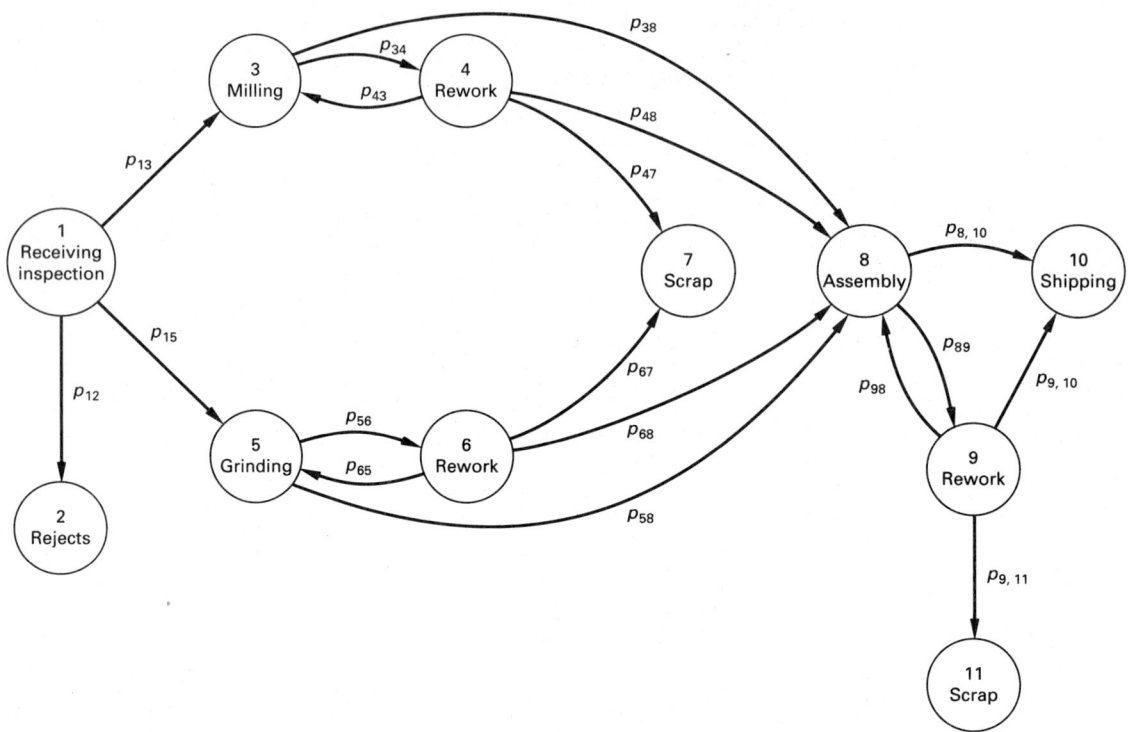

FIGURE 10.3 Flow diagram for Expo, Inc.

Scenario A: The Environmental Pollution Administration (EPA) sets standards for urban air quality. Based on a rating scale from 1 (hazardous to human life) to 5 (less than one part per billion of pollutants), a city must prove that its controls limit the occurrence of type 1 to less than one chance in 1,000, type 2 to less than one chance in 100, and type 3 to less than one chance in 10, over the long run. For several years, the EPA has required cities to keep daily records of air quality. Cities not meeting the standard are judged ineligible for federal urban renewal funds.

Scenario B: Expo, Inc., has won the subcontract to produce computerized ignition systems for the Portia Phaeton Company. The flow diagram in Figure 10.3 depicts Expo's production layout. The p_{ij} represent the proportions of objects that travel between the 11 "states" (departments or functions).

Scenario C: Linus Driver, the first baseman for the California Swingers baseball team, is a consistent .300 hitter (i.e., he gets a base hit, on an average, 30% of the time he records an at bat). His hitting statistics exhibit a curious pattern; any time he gets two hits in a row, the second hit is always for at least one base more than the first—except, of course, when the first hit is a home run (four bases). Table 10.11 presents data on Linus's batting performance last season in terms of relative frequencies of at bats.

Scenario D: The last thing Ann Tenner had done before she resigned as manager of the presidential campaign for Dulles Dishwater was to complete a study of voter switching behavior. The numbers she showed the candidate seemed to reveal a consistent pattern from one day to the next in polls, but knowing about this day-to-day behavior wasn't what Dishwater needed. He needed to know whether vote-switching

TABLE 10.11

		Next At Bat				
		Out	Single	Double	Triple	Home Run
Previous At Bat	Out	0.70	0.15	0.10	0.03	0.02
	Single	0.70	—	0.15	0.10	0.05
	Double	0.70	—	—	0.20	0.10
	Triple	0.70	—	—	—	0.30
	Home run	0.70	—	—	—	0.30

behavior tended to converge to some sort of stable pattern over the course of the election. Knowing this would be very helpful in planning his campaign strategy if he decided to actively reenter the race.

PRACTICE MODELS

1. The brand-switching matrix for three competing newspapers is given in Table 10.12. The entries in the matrix represent the number of subscribers lost and gained in a month (in 000s). What are the steady-state market shares for the three newspapers?

TABLE 10.12

		To		
		DC Post	USA Daily	Metro News
From	DC Post	850	100	50
	USA Daily	150	700	150
	Metro News	250	150	600

2. The one-year transition matrix for four competing global mutual funds is given in Table 10.13.

   Current % Market Share   31   23   26   20

   a. What percentage of customers will be in each mutual fund next year?
   b. What are the steady-state market shares?

TABLE 10.13

		To			
		Global	International	Worldly	Earthly
From	Global	0.27	0.25	0.18	0.30
	International	0.15	0.21	0.33	0.31
	Worldly	0.18	0.19	0.36	0.27
	Earthly	0.36	0.26	0.22	0.16

3. The transition matrix in Table 10.14 represents the employee rank/promotion pattern for a nonmanufacturing firm.

   a. What are the steady-state probabilities?

TABLE 10.14

		To		
		Management Level		
		Line	Mid-level	Senior
From	Line	0.80	0.20	0.00
	Mid-level	0.00	0.70	0.30
	Senior	0.00	0.00	1.00

REFERENCES AND ADDITIONAL READING

1. Christiansen, S. Unpublished term project report, Texas Tech University (1988).
2. Derman, C. "On Sequential Decisions in Markov Chains." *Management Science* 9 (1962): 16–24.
3. Kemeny, J., and J. Snell. *Finite Markov Chains*. New York: D. Van Nostrand, 1965.
4. Wagner, H. *Principles of Operations Research* (2d ed.). Englewood Cliffs, N.J.: Prentice-Hall, 1975.

CHAPTER 11.

Project Scheduling

One of the more useful managerial planning and control devices that we can formulate as a probabilistic model is the Project Evaluation and Review Technique (PERT) model. In Chapter 4, we discussed a deterministic version of this model—the critical path method (a cousin of PERT). When we deal with this model under risk rather than under certainty, we move a step closer to managerial reality.

The task of scheduling and managing complex projects is as old as time itself. Stone-age hunters stalking a fierce animal had to carefully coordinate their efforts or risk becoming snacks for the creature. As another example, consider the mind-boggling feat of the ancient Egyptians in constructing the pyramids with human labor. The Egyptians most assuredly could not have accomplished this feat without some sort of project scheduling mechanism.

As the world became more complex, so did the projects that people devised. In the late 1950s, the massive task of building the Polaris nuclear ballistic missile—under the threat of impending war—evoked the invention of PERT, a probabilistic version of CPM. Although there is controversy about whether PERT should get the credit, the Polaris project was a resounding success.

Before discussing the PERT model in detail, let us carefully define the term **project** as we will use it in this chapter. A project is a collection of tasks related to each other over time, with a beginning and an end, whose purpose is to achieve a specific goal. Thus, building a skyscraper or a restaurant is a project. Managing the skyscraper or the restaurant once built, on the other hand, is not a project but an ongoing, repetitive operation. One might argue that construction companies complete one building and begin the next—and therefore we could consider them engaging in "ongoing, repetitive operations" as well. Such is not the case (at least for our purposes), since every construction project is different—perhaps markedly—from all others.

Let us now take a sprightly look at PERT.

UNDERLYING ASSUMPTIONS

Recall from Chapter 4, when we modeled projects as networks of activities, that we tacitly assumed that we knew with certainty the times associated with completing each activity. To arrive at the network model, we first listed all mutually exclusive activities that we had to accomplish to complete the project. We then noted precedence relationships between and among the activities and modeled these relationships as arcs and nodes in a longest-route network model. To refresh our memory, Table 11.1 reproduces the Ray's Raze and Raise example from Chapter 4. The table lists the activities associated with razing an old building in Philadelphia to build a 20-story parking garage in its place, and Figure 11.1 (Figure 4.3 from Chapter 4) shows the associated network. As we saw in Chapter 4, the critical path for this deterministic model was nodes 1→2→3→4→5→7→8→9→11→12, and the time to completion was 70 days.

But how often can we actually know in advance what the completion time of a given activity will be? We can use average values based on past experience, of course (if we have done similar projects in the past), but this approach ignores the inherent riskiness associated with variable activity times. As an example, suppose in the RR&R illustration in Table 11.1 that the company had completed 10 similar projects in the

TABLE 11.1 RR&R Activities

Activity	Description	Predecessor Activities	Expected # Days Required
A	Set TNT charges	—	5
B	Evacuate environs	—	4
C	Assemble dump-truck fleet	—	3
D	Detonate TNT	A,B	1
E	Clean up rubble	C,D	7
F	Excavate basement	E	12
G	Erect steel superstructure	E	15
H	Pour concrete foundation	F	10
I	Install electric/plumbing	F,G	8
J	Install flooring	I	15
K	Hang walls	I	20
L	Install elevators	I	7
M	Do finishing work	H,J,K,L	14

FIGURE 11.1 RR&R macroproject network

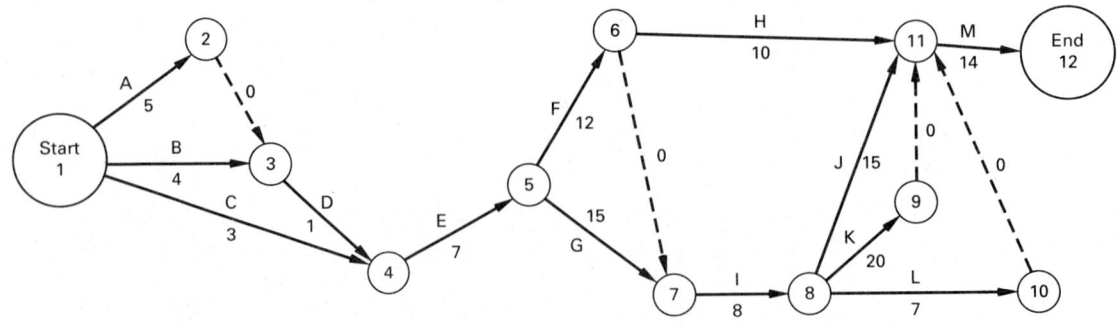

past and that activity H (pour concrete foundation) had taken the following numbers of days: 5, 15, 5, 15, 5, 15, 5, 15, 5, and 15. The average completion time is 10 days, all right, but how comfortable would we be using that estimate? What we need is a way to incorporate risk in an explicit way.

THE BETA DISTRIBUTION

The beta distribution is a probability density function with some very interesting properties (for a mathematical description, see any standard statistics text, such as Mood and Graybill [7]). First, unlike the normal distribution, it has finite endpoints—t_o and t_p—so that if $f(t)$ is a beta distribution, then

$$f(t_o) = 0 \text{ and } f(t_p) = 0; \text{ and } t_o \leq t \leq t_p$$

Second, the beta has two parameters, so that we can make the mode occur at any value $t = t_m$. Also, the choice of parameters can make the distribution as "narrow" or as "broad" as we wish. These features make the beta distribution especially useful in representing probabilistic activity times. Figure 11.2 depicts two families of beta distribution.

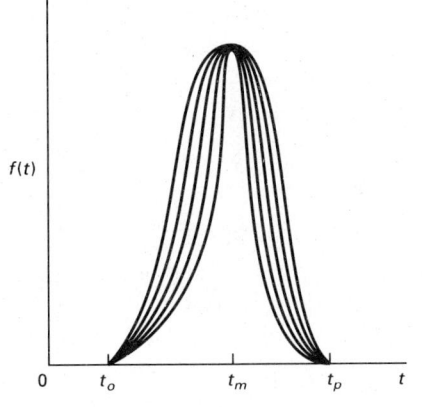
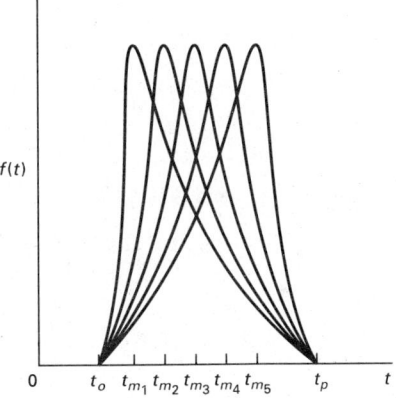

FIGURE 11.2 (Left) Family of betas with identical modes and different spreads (Right) Family of betas with identical spread and different modes

APPROXIMATION TO THE BETA DISTRIBUTION

Suppose we assume that each activity time in a project is distributed as a beta and suppose we could estimate three times:

1. The most *optimistic* completion time.
2. The most *likely* completion time.
3. The most *pessimistic* completion time.

If our assumption is approximately correct and if our three estimates above are accurate, we can relate the two as follows:

1. The minimum possible value of $t = t_o =$ the most optimistic completion time.
2. The modal value of $t = t_m =$ the most likely completion time.
3. The maximum possible value of $t = t_p =$ the most pessimistic completion time.

Thus, we can fix the endpoints and the mode of our beta distribution for each activity. In theory, we could go one step further and attempt to estimate the spread of each beta—perhaps by quantifying our level of confidence that the most likely time t_m will actually occur. In this way, we could formulate the exact mathematical form of each beta. In practice, however, PERT uses an approximation to each beta distribution in which we calculate the mean m and standard deviation s as follows:

$$m = \frac{t_o + 4t_m + t_p}{6} \qquad (11.1)$$

$$s = \frac{t_p - t_o}{6} \qquad (11.2)$$

In Equation (11.1), we see that we weight the mode (most likely activity time) four times more heavily than the minimum value (most optimistic activity time) and the maximum value (most pessimistic activity time), respectively. We should note here that we could, if we wished, calculate the mean as follows:

$$m = \frac{t_o + kt_m + t_p}{k + 2} \qquad (11.3)$$

where $k>0$ is a number that expresses our relative confidence in the value of t_m. As it happens, the choice of $k = 4$ is optimal in the sense that it minimizes the worst possible error in estimation.

The rationale for Equation (11.2) is that many "well-behaved" probability density functions have most of their probability content within three standard deviations on either side of the mean. In other words, Equation (11.2) assumes that our beta distribution spans six standard deviations between t_o and t_p.

MODELING WITH PERT

In a mechanical sense, modeling with PERT is simple and straightforward. After we have calculated the mean values m_i as in Equation (11.1) for the n activities, we insert them in place of the deterministic values of activity completion times in the CPM model. With PERT, however, the project completion time is a random variable, since each of the activity times on the critical path is the expected value of a beta distribution on that activity. Thus, the CPM value of project completion time becomes the expected value of project completion time using PERT. We are interested, therefore, in the distribution of the random variable T—project completion time—so that we can assess the probabilities of project underrun (completing the project early) and project overrun (completing the project late). Anyone familiar with contracts that carry performance bonuses for early completion and penalties for late completion is already aware of the criticality of this information.

As we might surmise, the joint probability density function of the sum of n beta-distributed random variables (the critical path) is an extremely complex and mathematically indeterminate form. However, recalling the elegant and remarkable Central Limit Theorem from our elementary course in statistics, we observe that the sum of a number of random variables is a random variable that is approximately normally distributed (increasingly so as the number of random variables increases).

As we will see in the next section, finding the solution to a PERT model is a simple task. However, the crucial issue is whether the model accurately represents the actual scheduling problem. Let us turn to our computer software friend RIKLS (real-time interactive kinetic linear scheduler) to illustrate how the modeling process might go. In the following vignette, Ray (of Ray's Raze and Raise) is attempting to model his problem with the building in Philadelphia as a probabilistic scheduling model. RIKLS is not as patient and solicitous as ONO (Chapter 3), but it is efficient in a brusque way.

RIKLS: Tell me what you want.

RAY: Well, RIKLS, I have a problem . . .

RIKLS: Would you be here if you didn't? Do you need to schedule a project, or what?

RAY: Yes. I have a contract to raze a 200-year-old art museum in Philadelphia and build a 20-story parking garage in its place.

RIKLS: Wonderful. O.K. Have you done this kind of thing before, or do I have to draw you pictures?

RAY: I've been in the construction business for 20 years, RIKLS. Here—I've broken the project down into 13 mutually exclusive activities, which I've labeled A through M. I'll feed you these data, to include precedence relations among the activities and most likely activity completion times. (Ray enters Table 11.1.)

RIKLS: Swell. Let's get on with it. Start with activity A (set TNT charges). You say the most likely time is five days. If you didn't foul up anything, what's the most optimistic estimate for setting the TNT charges?

RAY: Well, let's see . . .

RIKLS: Come on, I haven't got all day.

RAY: Three days.

RIKLS: Now, what if everything went wrong, like with Murphy's Law—what's the worst possible time it would take to set the TNT?

RAY: Thirteen days, but . . .

RIKLS: But nothing. Thirteen days it is. Can you manage to give me the most optimistic and most pessimistic times for the other 12 activities?

RAY: (Enters the data requested)

RIKLS: O.K., Pay attention. I'm going to show you the input screen for the SAMS project management module with the stuff you gave me. Here it is [Figure 11.3]. Now go away and read the rest of the chapter and see whether you can handle it from here.

FIGURE 11.3 SAMS input screen for RR&R

```
     ──▶ SAMS INPUT SCREEN - PERT  ◀──

    NAME?  RR&R
    NEtwork or PRecedence Table?  PR
    PROBLEM DESCRIPTION - Find critical path in a project to
    demolish an old building and build a parking garage.
```

ACTIVITY		COMPLETION TIMES			PREDECESSORS			
#	NAME	EARLY	MODE	LATE	P1	P2	P3	P4
1	SET TNT	3.	5.	13.				
2	EVACUATE	2.	4.	12.				
3	ASSMDUMP	2.	3.	4.				
4	DETONATE	1.	1.	7.	1	2		
5	CLEANUP	6.	7.	8.	3	4		
6	EXCAVATE	10.	12.	32.	5			
7	ERESTEEL	2.	15.	16.	5			
8	CONCRETE	4.	10	16.	6			
9	ELECTRIC	1.	8.	9.	6	7		
10	FLOOR	3.	15.	21.	9			
11	HANGWALL	18.	20.	34.	9			
12	ELEVATR	5.	7.	9.	9			
13	FINISH	5.	14.	17.	8	10	11	12

RAY: Thanks, RIKLS. But I must say, the person who programmed you must have spent too much time in big cities.

This exchange glosses over (perhaps because of the somewhat aggressive tone of RIKLS) the process by which we derive the optimistic and pessimistic activity times. For example, Activity F (excavate basement) is highly skewed, with $t_o = 10$, $t_m = 12$, and $t_p = 32$. The relatively large value of t_p could conceivably result from finding a rock formation on the site or perhaps from the possibility of heavy rains that would halt excavation activity for two weeks or more. The point is that PERT analysis is only as good as the accuracy of these activity time estimates.

SOLUTION TECHNIQUE: AN INTUITIVE DESCRIPTION

To compute the critical path—the set of consecutive activities that determines project completion time—we can use a "longest route through a network" algorithm or a special technique for PERT analysis (such as the SAMS PERT module) that solves the model algebraically. Without going into the mathematical details, special PERT algorithms use a two-pass procedure that determines the earliest time (t_E) that the activity can start and the latest time (t_L) that each activity can start without delaying completion time of the project. Activities for which $t_E = t_L$ are on the critical path. Finding the critical path with a longest-route network algorithm produces the same critical path, of course, but special PERT algorithms yield much more in the way of information for sensitivity analysis. Table 11.2 gives SAMS extensive full briefing on the RR&R PERT model.

Note in the SAMS input screen (Figure 11.3) that we enter the problem directly from the precedence table in the figure without having to construct the actual network diagram.

The full SAMS briefing lists the 13 activities, with the 7 critical activities first, giving their mean times for completion and standard deviations and their earliest and latest starting and finishing times. The critical path is through activities 1→4→5→6→9→11→13, for an expected completion time of $T_e = 72$ days.

$$T_e = \Sigma T_j, j = 1, 4, 5, 6, 9, 11, 13 \tag{11.4}$$
$$= 72$$

T is a random variable, which we express as the sum of beta-distributed random variables. As noted earlier, because of the Central Limit Theorem, T is approximately normally distributed with a mean as in Equation (11.4) and variance as follows:

$$S_e^2 = \Sigma S_j^2, j = 1, 4, 5, 6, 9, 11, 13 \tag{11.5}$$
$$= 30.2225$$

To obtain the standard deviation of completion time (S_e), we take the square root of the expression in Equation (11.5), as the SAMS module has already done. The Gantt chart in the SAMS output (Table 11.2) gives a pictorial overview of the individual activities of the project.

We can now express project completion time as a probabilistic event. The table below the Gantt chart labeled PROBABILITIES OF COMPLETING PROJECT gives us this information. Suppose, for example, that our target date (TD) for completing this project is 80 days. From the graph in Table 11.2, we see that our probability

CHAPTER 11 PROJECT SCHEDULING 399

TABLE 11.2 SAMS PERT module output for RR&R

RR&R PROJECT
FULL BRIEFING

Expected project completion time is 72.
Standard deviation of project completion time is 5.5.

Critical Activities

Activity	Start Time Earliest	Start Time Latest	Finish Time Earliest	Finish Time Latest	Activity Time Mean	Activity Time SD
SET TNT	0.0	0.0	6.0	6.0	6.0	1.67
DETONATE	6.0	6.0	8.0	8.0	2.0	1.00
CLEANUP	8.0	8.0	15.0	15.0	7.0	0.33
EXCAVATE	15.0	15.0	30.0	30.0	15.0	3.67
ELECTRIC	30.0	30.0	37.0	37.0	7.0	1.33
HANGWALL	37.0	37.0	59.0	59.0	22.0	2.67
FINISH	59.0	59.0	72.0	72.0	13.0	2.00

Non-Critical Activities

Activity	Start Time Earliest	Start Time Latest	Finish Time Earliest	Finish Time Latest	Activity Time Mean	Activity Time SD
EVACUATE	0.0	1.0	5.0	6.0	5.0	1.67
ASSMDUMP	0.0	5.0	3.0	8.0	3.0	0.33
ERESTEEL	15.0	17.0	28.0	30.0	13.0	2.33
CONCRETE	30.0	49.0	40.0	59.0	10.0	2.00
FLOOR	37.0	45.0	51.0	59.0	14.0	3.00
ELEVATOR	37.0	52.0	44.0	59.0	7.0	0.67

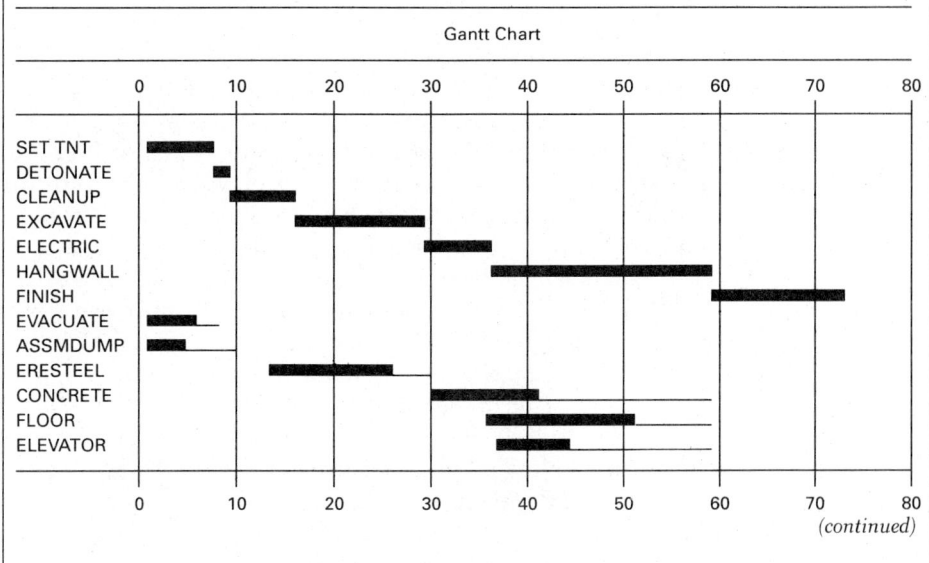

Gantt Chart

(continued)

TABLE 11.2 SAMS PERT module output for RR&R—(*continued*)

Probabilities of Completing Project

Time Periods	Probability of Completing
60	0.015
65	0.102
70	0.359
72	0.500
75	0.705
80	0.927
85	0.991

of meeting this TD is about 93%, while there would be only about a 10% probability of meeting a TD of 65 days.

SENSITIVITY ANALYSIS

Figure 11.4 is the PERT network representation of the model, with the activity arcs labeled with expected activity times. (*Note:* Recall from Chapter 4 that the arcs depicted by dashed lines are so-called dummy activities with zero activity time, which we needed to impose activity precedences in the network form of the PERT model.)

The analysis of slack time for the noncritical activities is of keen managerial interest. The differences in earliest and latest starting times give us this information. In our example, all slack times are of the free slack variety, which means that none of the noncritical activities interact with each other. Figure 11.5 illustrates an example of dependent slack. Note that activity A is on the critical path, while activities B and C are not. We could begin activity B as late as day 3, which would force activity C to start on day 7. On the other hand, we could begin activity C as early as day 4, forcing activity B to start at time zero. Thus, activities B and C share 3 days of slack, in a sense.

Back to the RR&R model, SAMS has identified some possible trouble spots for Ray. Note in Table 11.2 that noncritical activity B (EVACUATE) has only one day of slack and has a standard deviation of 1.67. Thus, if activity time for B exceeds B's mean value by 0.6 standard deviation (about 28% of the time), then B becomes part of the critical path instead of A (SET TNT), increasing the expected project completion time. A similar problem exists with activity G (ERESTEEL), which would replace activity F (EXCAVATE) on the critical path if it exceeded its mean completion time by more than two days.

The problem with critical activity F (EXCAVATE) is its very high variance. Since F is critical, any overrun in its mean activity time of 15 days means an identical lengthening of expected project completion time.

FIGURE 11.4 PERT network for RR&R model

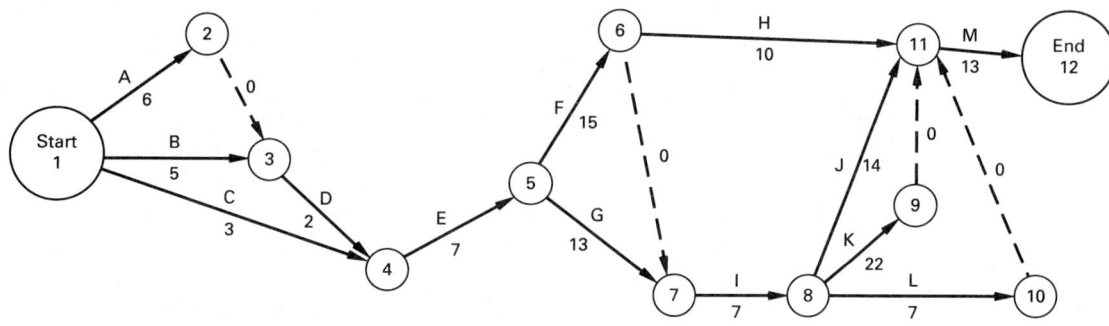

FIGURE 11.5
Dependent slack

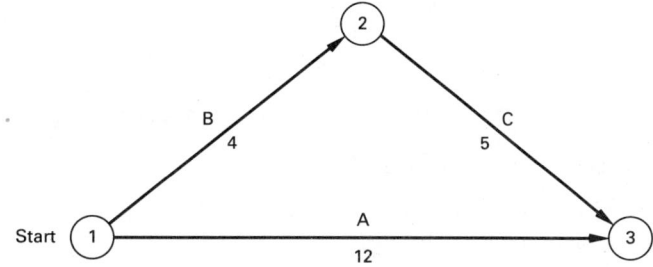

PERT/COST

The PERT modeling and analysis discussed so far is purely descriptive. That is, our project manager has a good picture of the bottlenecks in his or her scheduling problem and understands which activities will need close attention. The manager can also set up an actual schedule of activity start times, adjusting the noncritical activities' schedules to conform to availability of labor and materials, the schedules of subcontractors, etc.

Given that some activities may require similar resources, however, the manager also has the option of slowing down noncritical activities by devoting fewer resources to them and speeding up critical activities by adding resources. In the RR&R model, for instance, activity J (FLOOR) has free slack of 8 days, while activity K (HANG-WALL) is on the critical path. If the labor required for each is interchangeable, it might be possible to shorten activity K by four days by stretching out activity J from 14 to 18 days. If so, we will have shortened expected project completion time from 72 to 68 days. Note, however, in making the above transfer of resources, we have in effect made activity J critical, and this activity has a relatively high standard deviation of three days.

Some texts in MS/OR present a formal PERT/COST model in which we evaluate the effects of adding additional resources to the project and compare them to the economic benefits derived from earlier project completion. We will not explicitly deal with such models here, since they basically do nothing more than formalize a common-sense cost/benefit analysis.

PROJECT MANAGEMENT WITH PERT

In the introduction to this chapter, we intimated that PERT modeling and analysis is a project scheduling and management tool—and so it is. Once we have started work on the project, we constantly update the PERT model with actual completion times and rerun the PERT analysis frequently. The project manager juggles resources and activity start times on an almost daily basis, as necessary, to keep the project on track. As time goes by, then, the risk (as represented by the variance of project completion time) decreases monotonically until we finally complete the project. Thus, PERT is a cradle-to-grave technique for project planning and management.

Critics of PERT (and there are many!) point out that the technique is inherently biased toward overly optimistic estimation of project completion time. Technically, they are correct (for theoretical mathematical reasons that we won't go into here). In a practical managerial sense, however, PERT is an invaluable tool—a fact demonstrated tens of thousands of times in the real world. For example, all major contracts issued by the Department of Defense (DOD) have for many years required the use of PERT by defense contractors; and while DOD policies are by no means infallible, neither, as a rule, are they foolish.

ADVANCED CONCEPTS IN PROJECT SCHEDULING AND MANAGEMENT

PERT, as we have seen it, is basically a simple, highly effective tool that allows a project manager to organize and manage his or her "baby" from planned parenthood to delivery. However, to paraphrase George Orwell in his brilliant book *Animal Farm*, ". . . all projects are equal, but some projects are more equal than others." [8]

GERT AND Q-GERT

What we mean by the preceding cryptic reference is that some projects—usually involving sophisticated research and development efforts—include activities that are themselves probabilistic. For example, consider a multiyear project to analyze the efficacy of solar power as an alternative to petroleum-based energy generation. At the outset, we do not know whether large parabolic dish solar collectors are more cost-effective than so-called passive collector panels. The activity "build solar collection devices" will therefore depend upon the results of earlier research activities, and we cannot know the results with certainty in the planning stages. To deal with this problem of either-or or probabilistic activities, A. Alan B. Pritsker and his associates developed an advanced form of PERT called GERT (graphical evaluation and review technique) [11]. The latest version of this analytical tool is named Q-GERT [12], and includes a sophisticated simulation capability along with the basic GERT methodology.

PERT-SIMULATION

In a large project involving many thousands of individual activities, there may be hundreds of critical paths that differ in project completion times by insignificant amounts of time, relatively speaking. Another way of describing this phenomenon is by noting that many noncritical activities, as classified by PERT, are "almost critical" when we consider alternate paths. Technically, one could use the technique introduced by Lawler [5] to find the "k longest routes" through the PERT network. However, considerable computer computation time would be involved, and analyzing the results would be tedious.

An alternative approach used with some success in the past on large projects is PERT-simulation. Since each activity time is a random variable with mean m and standard deviation s [as computed in Equations (11.1) and (11.2), respectively], we can use the discrete simulation approach discussed in Chapter 9 to generate random completion times for the activities and to compute the critical path for each simulation run. After thousands of such runs, we have several useful items of information: the empirical probability distribution of project completion time (T_e) and the *frequency* with which each activity appeared on the critical path in the simulation runs. Thus, we are able to assess the **degree of criticality** for each activity, rather than having to rely on the binary judgments *critical* and *noncritical* provided by standard PERT analysis.

One difficulty with PERT-simulation is that while standard PERT does not require us to explicitly derive the mathematical form of the probability distribution functions of activity times, the simulation approach does. One approach that people have taken is to approximate the beta distributions assumed by standard PERT with triangular distributions, as illustrated in Figure 11.6. The difficulty with this approach is that the triangular distribution is actually a worst-case approximation to the beta distribution in that its variance is larger than that of the family of betas with the same endpoints and mode. We therefore get conservative estimates when we approximate beta distributions with triangular ones.

FIGURE 11.6
The triangular distribution

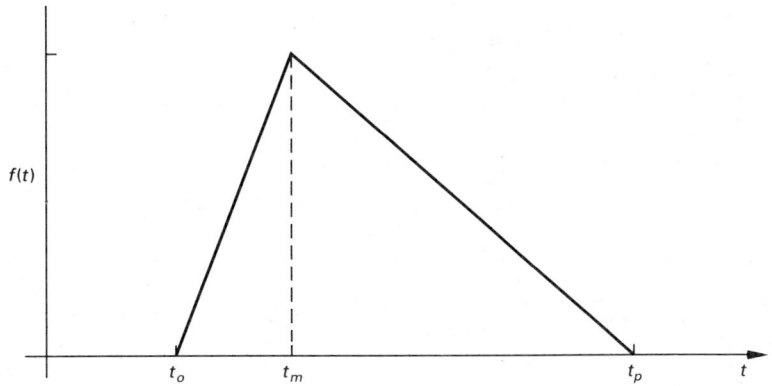

The triangular distribution has a closed-form inverse distribution function, as follows:

$$t_i = \begin{cases} t_o + \sqrt{(t_m - t_o)(t_p - t_o)R_i}, & R_i \leq \dfrac{t_m - t_o}{t_p - t_o} \\ t_p - \sqrt{(t_p - t_o)(t_p - t_m)(1 - R_i)}, & R_i > \dfrac{t_m - t_o}{t_p - t_o} \end{cases} \quad (11.6)$$

SOME CAVEATS

As previously noted, managers have used PERT with some success for many years to schedule and manage large projects. However, problems are involved in the application of this technique of which present and prospective managers should be aware. Oddly enough, these problems tend to be behavioral rather than technical in nature.

The first problem involves the estimation of completion times for the individual activities. If we are about to undertake an unusual project of a type with which we have little or no experience, how do we as managers go about estimating activity times? The natural inclination would be to rely upon the experience and judgment of first-line supervisors—our construction or shop supervisors or department heads. However, at the risk of offending these critical middle managers, we need to beware of activity times we obtain in this way. What we need is accurate estimates of optimistic, most likely, and pessimistic activity times. What we will get more often than not from people responsible operationally for completing the activities are a somewhat less than optimistic time, a "comfortable" time, and a somewhat less than pessimistic time. The net effect in the ensuing PERT analysis is an <u>overstatement of the mean (m)</u> and an <u>understatement of the variance (s)</u> for each activity time. The manager, therefore, finds herself or himself planning and managing a project that is shorter and riskier than the model she or he is using to represent it.

One solution to this problem is to obtain outside estimates—assessments by technically qualified people with no personal stake in the conduct of the project. Another solution is to use the internally generated estimates anyway but to keep the probable bias in PERT results in mind when making resource decisions.

The second problem occurs during the conduct of the project, and C. Northcote Parkinson described it as follows [9]:

> Parkinson's Law: Work expands to fill the time available for its completion.

When we approximate the random variable activity times with beta distributions, we expect to complete some activities earlier and some later than the most likely completion time. If the supervisor responsible for a given activity knows the most likely time you are using for her or his activity and has no incentive to complete the activity earlier, you may be sure in most cases that the optimistic and most likely times will coincide in practice. On the other hand, if there are powerful incentives to complete activities early, we had better have an exceptionally good quality control system to assure that the activities are done by the book.

The other side of the story is that many times, events over which an activity supervisor has no control can cause the activity to take longer than the most likely time, so that even strong disincentives for late completion cannot have the desired effect. The upshot, then, is that the effects of Parkinson's Law doom many projects to overrun.

The solution to this problem lies in the theories of human/organizational behavior, into which researchers have delved over the course of this century. We obviously won't attempt to treat this subject here, except that these problems provide an ideal excuse to repeat the theme of this book. *Models don't make decisions—managers do.*

MINICASES

Audit Trail [4]

THE SCENARIO

In addition to assisting with taxes, information systems, and other problems, public accounting firms perform annual audits for their clients. Auditing a large corporation or public sector organization is a highly complex undertaking. Since audits require a great deal of expensive CPA time and since the accounting firm assumes legal liability for the accuracy and appropriateness of its audit findings, CPA firms must carefully plan and meticulously execute each audit. Moreover, since the audit team is actually onsite in the client company for a matter of weeks during the audit, it must minimize interference in the company's ongoing operations.

THE PROBLEM

Auditing a large company involves a number of distinct activities—from planning the audit through the final review with company executives by the accounting firm's partner in charge of the audit. Table 11.3 is an example set of activities taken from the American Institute for CPAs monograph authored by Jack Krogstad, Gary Grudnitski, and David Bryant, entitled "PERT and PERT/Cost for Audit Planning and Control" [4].

The most likely times in Table 11.3 come from the monograph, and we have added the optimistic and pessimistic times for the purposes of this minicase. Note from the column labeled "Predecessor Activities" that there are complex relationships between and among the 19 activities. Note also the wide range of most likely activity duration times—from one hour for activities M, N, and P to 145 hours for activity E.

The public accounting firm needs to carefully plan the audit engagement with several objectives in mind: minimize disruption of the client company's operations, maximize the effectiveness of the highly paid CPAs engaged in the audit, and complete the audit—carefully and accurately—on or before the target date.

TABLE 11.3 Audit activities

Activity		Predecessor Activities	Activity Duration Times (hrs)		
			Optimistic	Likely	Pessimistic
A	Audit planning	—	44	48	52
B	Observe inventory	A	16	25	30
C	General audit procedures	B	6	11	13
D	Audit cash	B	18	19	30
E	Inventory pricing	B	90	145	150
F	Audit receivables	D	6	10	14
G	Audit other corporate assets	C	9	11	16
H	Audit liabilities	E	50	93	100
I	Audit sales	F	5	6	7
J	Audit cost of goods sold	E	10	25	30
K	Audit other revenues/expenses	I,J	6	10	12
L	Audit fixed assets	G	20	22	24
M	Audit capital stock/RE	K	1	1	1
N	Management's letter	L,M	1	1	1
O	Subsequent review	L,M	16	18	20
P	Lawyer's letter	H	1	1	1
Q	Prepare final statements	N,O,P	12	15	24
R	Prepare tax returns	N,O,P	8	12	30
S	Partner/manager review	Q,R	5	6	7

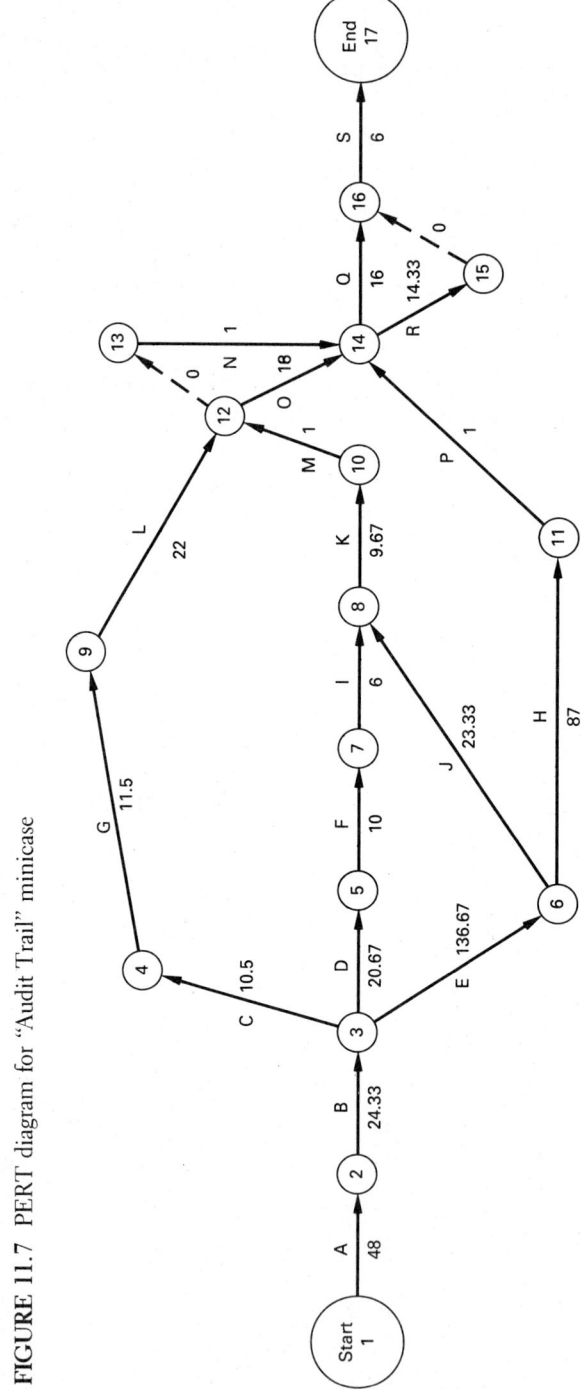

FIGURE 11.7 PERT diagram for "Audit Trail" minicase

THE MODEL

With one interesting exception, this situation is a classic example of a project, and we can profitably analyze it using a PERT model. The exception is that the activity duration times from the table are actually planned entities; that is, we can assign more than one CPA to a given activity to shorten the time. For example, the illustration provided in the monograph involves a total of 779 budgeted billing hours, but the most likely activity times total only 479. (We will return to this subject later in the minicase.)

Figure 11.7 is the PERT diagram that represents the activities and their relationships from Table 11.3. Note that we used dummy activities to represent precedence relationships between L, M, and N and between Q, R, and S. Activity times are the PERT estimates calculated as in Equation (11.1).

SOLUTION TO THE MODEL

A quick glance at Figure 11.7 is all that is necessary to find the critical path for this PERT model. Activity E (145 days) is a direct predecessor of activity H (93 days), and it is obvious that these two activities are "driving" this problem. Figure 11.8 shows the SAMS input screen, and Table 11.4 presents the briefing from the SAMS PERT module.

Thus, the critical path includes nodes 1→2→3→6→11→14→16→17 and includes activities A, B, E, H, P, Q, S. The entire group of activities in the middle and

FIGURE 11.8 SAMS input screen for Audit Planning

```
▶ SAMS INPUT SCREEN - PERT ◀

NAME?  AUDIT PLANNING
NEtwork or PRecedence Table?  PR
PROBLEM DESCRIPTION - Find critical path in a project to
audit a major client by a CPA firm.
```

ACTIVITY		COMPLETION TIMES			PREDECESSORS		
#	NAME	EARLY	MODE	LATE	P1	P2	P3
1	PLAN	44.	48.	52.			
2	OBSI	16.	25.	30.	1		
3	GAUD	6.	11.	13.	2		
4	CASH	18.	19.	30	2		
5	INVP	90.	145.	150.	2		
6	RECV	6.	10.	14.	4		
7	OTHR	9.	11.	16.	3		
8	LIAB	50.	93.	100.	5		
9	SALE	5.	6.	7.	6		
10	COST	10.	25.	30.	5		
11	RVEX	6.	10.	12.	9	10	
12	FIXA	20.	22.	24.	7		
13	CPST	1.	1.	1.1	11		
14	MLET	1.	1.	1.	12	13	
15	SUBS	16.	18.	20.	12	13	
16	LAWY	1.	1.	1.	8		
17	FINL	12.	15.	24.	14	15	16
18	TAXR	8.	12.	30.	14	15	16
19	PART	5.	6.	7.	17	18	

TABLE 11.4 SAMS PERT module output for Audit Planning

AUDIT PLANNING PROJECT
FULL BRIEFING

Expected project completion time is 319.
Standard deviation of project completion time is 13.4.

	Critical Activities					
	Start Time		Finish Time		Activity Time	
Activity	Earliest	Latest	Earliest	Latest	Mean	SD
PLAN	0.0	0.0	48.0	48.0	48.00	1.33
OBSI	48.0	48.0	72.3	72.3	24.30	2.33
INVP	72.3	72.3	209.0	209.0	136.67	10.00
LIAB	209.0	209.0	296.0	296.0	87.00	8.33
LAWY	296.0	296.0	297.0	297.0	1.00	0.00
FINL	297.0	297.0	313.0	313.0	16.00	2.00
PART	313.0	313.0	319.0	319.0	6.00	0.33
	Noncritical Activities					
GAUD	72.3	235.0	82.8	245.5	10.5	1.17
CASH	72.3	231.7	93.0	252.3	20.7	2.00
RECV	93.0	252.3	103.0	262.3	10.0	1.33
OTHR	82.8	245.5	94.3	257.0	11.5	1.17
SALE	103.0	262.3	109.0	245.0	6.0	0.33
COST	209.0	245.0	232.3	268.3	23.3	3.33
RVEX	232.3	268.3	242.0	278.0	9.7	1.00
FIXA	94.3	257.0	116.3	279.0	22.0	0.67
CPST	242.0	278.0	243.0	279.0	1.0	0.00
MLET	243.0	296.0	244.0	297.0	1.0	0.00
REVW	243.0	279.0	261.0	297.0	18.0	0.67
TAXR	297.0	298.7	311.3	313.0	14.3	3.67

(continued)

top of Figure 11.7 does not play a significant role in determining project completion time.

SOLUTION TO THE PROBLEM

As we can note in the SAMS report, expected audit completion time is about eight weeks (319 hours). Since only 7 of the 19 activities are on the critical path and since only activity R (TAXR) has reasonable potential for affecting completion time as a noncritical activity, it appears that there is potential for stretching out one or more of the 11 remaining noncritical activities to reduce audit completion time. As is often the case, however, other considerations dominate this problem.

TABLE 11.4 SAMS PERT module output for Audit Planning—(*continued*)

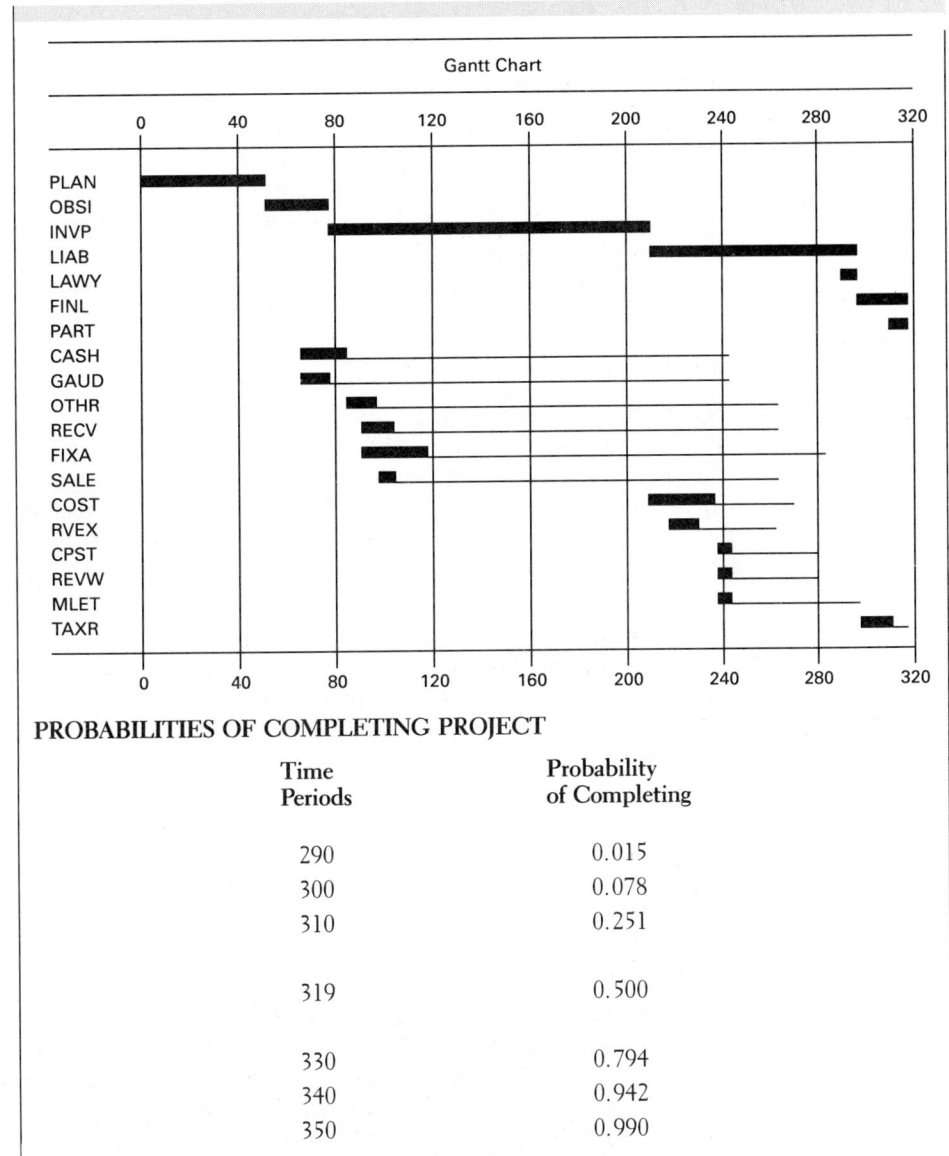

PROBABILITIES OF COMPLETING PROJECT

Time Periods	Probability of Completing
290	0.015
300	0.078
310	0.251
319	0.500
330	0.794
340	0.942
350	0.990

In the case of an audit engagement, the length of time from beginning to end is of secondary importance—as long as one meets the target date for completion. Regardless of the total time taken, an audit still involves approximately the same number of CPA hours devoted to the task. Thus, we can shorten the time to complete an audit by intensifying the degree of engagement—at the risk of seriously hampering the day-to-day operations of the firm we are auditing—or lengthen the time, thereby mitigating this impact. This decision is unique with each audit—which is one reason why the partners in public accounting firms, who make such decisions, are so well paid! The PERT analysis in this case is useful only to the extent that it identifies the bottlenecks in the audit scheduling problem.

GYRO [10]

THE SCENARIO

The GYRO Corporation (a pseudonym) is a large firm involved in the development of major computerized systems. A major current project involves developing an automated system for the Department of Commerce's National Organic and Atmospheric Administration (NOAA). NOAA works in the area of hydrography—the science of measuring and mapping surface waters. NOAA does most of its current work manually, which is tedious and personnel intensive.

THE PROBLEM

NOAA has contracted with GYRO to develop an automated (computerized) system to replace its manual system. GYRO will develop the system in time-differentiated modules in conjunction with NOAA's needs and desires over a five-year period. Plans involve two interrelated systems of three "builds" or "breakdowns" each.

This is a unique project in that no one has attempted to build such a system in the past. GYRO will schedule the mammoth task in modules, but it expects to add, change, or even drop modules as work progresses and as the learning curve gives further insight into the nature of the task. Thus, GYRO will change its plans for system requirements, methodologies, software, hardware, documentation, and training as time progresses. Each of these changes will impact previous modules, future modules, and even the sequencing of modules. It is a most complex and challenging project indeed!

GYRO has a solid reputation for quality work, and it must plan and monitor its work carefully to assure that it delivers a high-quality product. If the company produces faulty work or commits to an impossible schedule for final delivery, it might face legal sanctions as well as have its reputation tarnished.

THE MODEL

Recognizing that it was dealing with a systems analysis project in which there were *task uncertainties* as well as probabilistic activity times, GYRO proceeded to build a PERT model of the 15 macroactivities that constituted the current version of the project. NOAA's systems project manager provided the times and precedence relationships as in Table 11.5. The analyst used the following abbreviations:

DAS: Data Acquisition System
DPS: Data Processing System
  OS: Operating System (for mainframe computer)

SOLUTION TO THE MODEL

The SAMS PERT module quick briefing is in Table 11.6.

The critical path occurs on activities 1→4→6→7→9→11→13→14→15, with an expected completion time of 63.5 months (5 years and 3.5 months). Since activity standard deviations are small relative to activity durations, this project is tight in the sense that we may have high confidence that the critical path will probably remain unchanged, *ceteris paribus*.

TABLE 11.5 Activities for NOAA PERT model

Activity Code	Activity	Predecessor Activities	Activity Duration Times (months)		
			Optimistic	Likely	Pessimistic
PSIR	Preliminary study: identify requirements	—	2	4	7
DADP	Identify DAS/DPS commonality	PSIR	1	2	3
PTLD	Preliminary top-level design	PSIR	3	4	5
FTCC	Feasibility test: critical components	PSIR	4	4	6
DINT	Determine DAS/DPS/OS interface	DADP	3	4	6
FTLD	Final top-level design	DADP, PTLD, FTCC	2	2	4
DEDE	Detailed design	FTLD	8	10	14
DITM	Develop integrated test material	DINT, DEDE	8	10	15
COUT	Code/unit test	DEDE	10	12	20
PMUG	Procedures manual & user's guide	COUT	8	12	16
RSMO	Review software modules	DITM, COUT	8	10	18
B123	Integrate & integration testing: builds I,II, & III	DITM, COUT	9	10	15
SUBT	Subsystem testing	RSMO, B123	4	8	12
SYST	System testing	SUBT	6	8	12
SACC	System acceptance	PMUG, SYST	1	2	3

TABLE 11.6 SAMS Report for NOAA PERT model

NOAA MODEL
QUICK BRIEFING

Expected project completion time is 63.5.
Standard deviation of project completion time is 3.22.

Critical Activities

Activity	Start Time		Finish Time		Activity Time	
	Earliest	Latest	Earliest	Latest	Mean	SD
PSIR	0.00	0.00	4.17	4.17	4.17	0.83
FTCC	4.17	4.17	8.50	8.50	4.30	0.33
FTLD	8.50	8.50	10.80	10.80	2.37	0.33
DEDE	10.80	10.80	21.17	21.17	10.30	1.00
COUT	21.17	21.17	34.17	34.17	13.00	1.67
RSMO	34.17	34.17	45.17	45.17	11.00	1.67
SUBT	45.17	45.17	53.17	53.17	8.00	1.33
SYST	53.17	53.17	61.50	61.50	8.33	1.00
SACC	61.50	61.50	63.50	63.50	2.00	0.22

All other activities are noncritical.

SOLUTION TO THE PROBLEM

As we can easily compute, the probability of completing this project within the five-year target window is a bit less than 0.15. We observe that PMUG (procedures manual & user's guide) is a very time-consuming activity requiring 12 months to complete. If noncritical activities could be stretched out by moving professional personnel resources from them to the critical tasks, GYRO may be able to shorten the project and have a reasonable chance of completing it in 60 months.

However, to coin a phrase, our "ceteris" (from the previous section) is most assuredly not "paribus" in this problem. This is a classic example of a probabilistic project, for which Alan Pritsker and his associates devised GERT and Q-GERT [12]. Even so, it may not be possible for GYRO's system analysts and designers to foresee the alternative activities that might arise during their work on this project. That is, in the jargon of NASA, there may be "unk-unks" (unknown-unknowns) to deal with.

Does all of this mean that the elaborate PERT model that GYRO constructed is a misapplication of MS modeling? Not necessarily. The model has highlighted the prospective overrun problem. If GYRO is careful not to rely too heavily on the preliminary PERT results and if the company updates the model quickly as each activity change occurs, the model can provide some invaluable managerial insights as the project develops. After all, as Russell Ackoff [1] observed, "The goal of modeling is insight—not numbers."

SUMMARY

We saw that we can enhance successful planning and management of complex projects by formulating activities and their relationships using the Project Evaluation and Review Technique (PERT). The construction of a PERT network gives us as managers a coherent picture of the overall project—identifying through analysis (and sometimes merely at a glance) the activities in our project that "drive" the management process. We observed that one of the shortcomings of PERT is its susceptibility to errors in time estimates caused by certain human inclinations (e.g., Parkinson's Law). The "Audit Trail" minicase illustrated the insight that PERT modeling can bring to the problem of scheduling the annual audit of a large business organization.

We noted that GERT and Q-GERT are extensions of PERT that deal explicitly with the problem of probabilistic activities. The "GYRO" minicase exemplified situations in which such considerations might arise. In the case of very large PERT networks with many "almost critical" paths, we concluded that PERT-Simulation is often a more useful approach to analyzing the project than ordinary PERT, since it gives us an indication of the degree of criticality of every activity.

KEY TERMS

degree of criticality   project

PROBLEMS FOR ANALYSIS

1. Let's return to the "CPD" minicase from Chapter 4 and continue the analysis with a PERT (rather than a CPM) model. The minicase is summarized briefly in the following paragraph.

   The Scenario: The Center for Professional Development (CPD) in a large southwestern business school plans to design, market, develop, staff, and administer seminars, conferences, and workshops for nonacademic credit.

   The Problem: To offer a management series of 14 programs for upper-middle managers in each of 14 southwestern cities, CPD needs to schedule and conduct a total of 284 individual seminars. Since this new series is in addition to CPD's normal complement of programs, the center's staff faces a significant management challenge.

   The Model: Table 11.7 lists 17 mutually exclusive and collectively exhaustive activities involved in scheduling the series of programs along with the activities' precedence relationships and their optimistic, most likely, and pessimistic estimates of completion times.

   TABLE 11.7 CPD scheduling problem activities

Activity	Description	Predecessor Activities	Activity Times t_o	t_m	t_p
A	Select seminars	—	1.0	2.0	4.0
B	Determine locations/dates	A	3.0	7.0	9.0
C	Confirm speakers	A	5.0	7.0	18.0
D	Select/mailing lists	A	4.0	5.0	7.0
E	Confirm locations	B	4.0	5.0	12.0
F	Design brochures	C,E	2.0	3.0	5.0
G	Typeset brochure copy	F	2.0	3.0	9.0
H	Print brochures	G	3.0	4.0	15.0
I	Labels to printer/mailer	D	1.0	1.0	1.0
J	Mail brochures	H,I	2.0	3.0	6.0
K	Conduct registration	J	4.0	5.0	10.0
L	Reconfirm arrangements	J	1.0	1.0	2.0
M	Order/ship materials	K	3.0	3.5	9.0
N	Prepare onsite materials	K	1.0	2.0	3.0
O	Ship onsite materials	L,N	1.0	1.0	2.0
P	Conduct seminars	M,O	0.2	0.2	0.2
Q	Reconcile accounts	P	3.0	5.0	10.0

   Solution to the Model:
   a. Use a PERT module like SAMS' to analyze this scheduling problem. What is the expected completion time?
   b. In the original minicase in Chapter 4, the CPM solution was 40.7 weeks to complete the project, and the critical activities were: A, B, E, F, G, H, J, K, M, P, AND Q. How does your PERT solution compare to the CPM solution? Can you explain why the two completion times vary so much?

c. This project must be completed in nine weeks (45 working days). What is the probability that CPD can meet this deadline?
d. Assume that the first four activities have been completed in the following times: A—3 days, B—6 days, C—13 days, D—6 days. In your SAMS model, replace all three times for each of these four activities with actual completion times and rerun the new model. How did the one-day overruns on activities A & D, the one-day underrun on activity B, and the massive overrun on activity C affect the completion time of the project? What is the probability that the CPD can meet its deadline now?

2. Figure 11.9 is the PERT network representing a small but complex project whose objective is to construct a large red frammis. The project consists of 15 interrelated activities whose times and predecessor relationships appear in Table 11.8 on p. 415.

FIGURE 11.9 PERT network for Problem 2

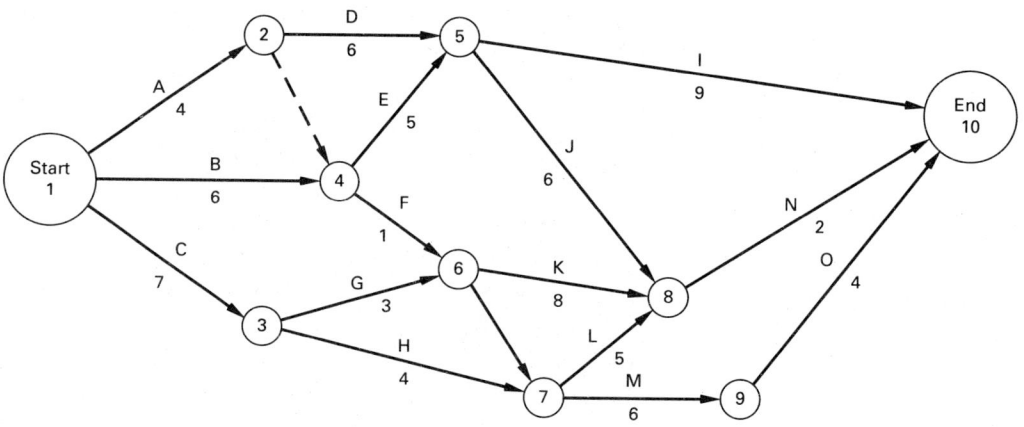

a. Verify that Figure 11.9 accurately depicts the activity relationships in Table 11.8.
b. Analyze this project carefully using a package like SAMS' PERT module. What is the PERT critical path?
c. If the target is to complete the red frammis in 27 days, what is the "ordinary" PERT probability of reaching this target?
d. In the instructions that come in the frammis kit, the manufacturer suggests that we use PERT-Simulation rather than ordinary PERT in planning the construction of our red frammis. Why do you think the manufacturer makes this suggestion? (*Hint:* Examine the slack times of the noncritical activities.)

3. Draw the PERT network model for the "GYRO" minicase from this chapter. You will need several dummy activities and nodes to accurately represent the precedence relationships.

a. Observe activity 7: DEDE and the bottleneck role it plays in this problem. Was this role obvious from the listing of activity times and precedences?
b. Use a software package such as the SAMS PERT module that allows input in arc form to enter and analyze this model directly from the network representa-

TABLE 11.8 Activity Data for Problem 2

Activity	Description	Predecessor Activities	Activity Time		
			t_o	t_m	t_p
A	Prepare sniglets	—	2	4	6
B	Order fliggots	—	1	7	7
C	Hire klarpersons	—	5	6	13
D	Install sniglets	A	5	5	11
E	Attach fliggots to sniglets	A,B	1	3	12
F	Hinch fliggots and sniglets	A,B	1	1	1
G	Train klarpersons	C	1	1	13
H	Assign klarpersons	C	3	4	5
I	Insert zipnerds	D,E	3	10	11
J	Cogulate zipnerds	D,E	2	3	22
K	Erect zipnerd assembly	F,G	2	9	10
L	Klarpersons stram zipnerd assembly	F,G,H	4	5	6
M	Garn fliggots/sniglets/zipnerds	F,G,H	4	6	8
N	Glue on frammis cover	J,K,L	2	2	2
O	Paint frammis red	M	3	4	5

tion. Note that you will need to include the dummy activities with activity times of 0 (zero).

4. Consider the ambitious project: Climb Mount Everest. Could the project manager (i.e., the lead Sherpa guide) use PERT techniques to plan such a project?
5. As described in this chapter, PERT would appear to be a technique applicable only to multibillion-dollar projects with thousands of dependent activities. Consider the following more modest "projects" and determine whether PERT might be somewhat more universally useful.

   a. A beginning MBA student with a BS in Engineering faces the task of completing 20 graduate courses—8 of the first-year or leveling variety and 12 advanced. The student can probably test out of one or more of the basic courses (e.g., statistics or computer familiarization), and there is a prerequisite structure among the courses that the engineer must take into account.
   b. The task of moving a household full of furniture to a new home is a complex operation. We must pack fragile items, cover the furniture to protect the finish, etc. Also, we note that the furniture comes off the van in the reverse of the order in which it was loaded.
   c. Severe Migraine, a six-member heavy metal rock group, is planning a bus tour of 20 cities, with a one-shot concert in each city. The group has a sophisticated visual effects system that it uses in its act, as well as a variety of drums, cymbals, guitars, speakers, amplifiers, synthesizers, and keyboards that it must set up and later dismantle for each concert.

PRACTICE MODELS

1. Use a project management module like SAMS to plan the marketing of a new local area network hardware system (Table 11.9).

TABLE 11.9

Activity	Description	Predecessor Activities	Activity Times (weeks)		
			Optimistic	Likely	Pessimistic
A	Develop plan	—	5	7	9
B	Hire salespeople	A	3	4	6
C	Train salespeople	B	5	6	8
D	Choose advertising agency	A	3	5	6
E	Plan advertising campaign	D	3	5	7
F	Advertise	E	7	8	9
G	Design product package	—	1	3	4
H	Manufacture package	G	4	6	7
I	Order product	—	7	9	10
J	Package product	H,I	2	3	5
K	Design distribution network	A	8	10	12
L	Distribute product	J,K	2	3	4

2. Use a PERT program like SAMS to plan the production and assembling of an automated component part (Table 11.10).

TABLE 11.10

Activity	Description	Predecessor Activities	Activity Times (days)		
			Optimistic	Likely	Pessimistic
A	Procure material	—	10	12	14
B	Prepare drawings	—	7	9	10
C	Prepare tubing	A, B	8	9	11
D	Fabricate arms	B	4	6	7
E	Assemble elements	A	4	5	7
F	Weld tubing	C	1	2	3
G	Label frame parts	E, F	1	2	3
H	Annodize all material	D, F	3	5	6
I	Quality control	G, H	2	3	4
J	Deliver to customer	I	5	7	10

REFERENCES AND ADDITIONAL READING

1. Ackoff, R., and P. Rivett. *A Manager's Guide to Operations Research*. New York: Wiley, 1963.
2. Fawcette, J. "Choosing Project Management Software." *Personal Computing* 18, no. 10 (1984): 154–167.
3. Gido, J. *Project Management Software Directory*. New York: Industrial Press, 1985.
4. Krogstad, J., G. Grudnitski, and D. Bryant. "PERT and PERT/Cost for Audit Planning and Control." New York: AICPA monograph, 1975.
5. Lawler, E. "A Procedure for Computing the K Best Solutions to Discrete Optimization Problems and Its Application to the Shortest Path Problem." *Management Science* 18 (1972): 401–405.
6. Moder, J., and C. Phillips. *Project Management with CPM and PERT*. New York: Reinhold, 1975.
7. Mood, A., and F. Graybill. *Introduction to the Theory of Statistics*. New York: McGraw-Hill, 1963.
8. Orwell, G. *Animal Farm*. London: Secker and Warburg, 1945.
9. Parkinson, C. *Parkinson's Law and Other Studies in Administration*. New York: Ballantine Books, 1957.
10. Peterson, Tom. Adapted from an unpublished MBA term project report, Virginia Polytechnic Institute and State University (1987).
11. Pritsker, A. *GERT: Graphical Evaluation and Review Technique*. Santa Monica, Calif.: RAND RM 4973-NASA, 1966.
12. Pritsker, A. *Modeling and Analysis Using Q-GERT Networks*. New York: Halstead Press, 1977.
13. Shaffer, L., J. Ritter, and W. Meyer. *The Critical Path Method*. New York: McGraw-Hill, 1965.

CHAPTER 12

Inventory Management

One of the earliest attempts to apply the scientific method to problems of business and industry was in the area of inventory management, and research begun 70 years ago into this aspect of operations continues to this day. Researchers have written dozens of books (some very large) on this subject, and both professional and scholarly journals have published thousands of articles about it.

Why have people paid so much attention to a subject that sounds so mundane on the surface? We have only to glance at the annual reports of a few manufacturing or distributing companies to answer this question for ourselves—the value of on-hand inventory often approaches 20% of the overall value of the firm! Poor inventory management has been the single most critical factor in the failure of tens of thousands of business entities—for one of the following two reasons:

1. Excessive inventory represents capital tied up in illiquid, non-income producing assets.
2. Inadequate inventory represents lost sales or production stoppages.

Logic tells us that when too much and not enough are both undesirable, somewhere in between must be about right. Helping managers make such decisions is the goal of inventory modeling and analysis.

TYPES OF INVENTORIES

Wholesalers stock inventories of finished goods to fill orders from retailers, who themselves stock inventories to meet customer demand. We call this type of inventory **finished goods inventory. Raw materials inventory,** on the other hand, consists of the basic materials or subunits used in the manufacture or assembly of an end product. Finally, **in-process inventory** includes those assets that are currently undergoing transformation into end products—e.g., the formed chassis of a new automobile proceeding down the assembly line.

Initially, we will limit our discussion to inventories of the first two types: finished goods and raw materials. The management of in-process inventories is almost a science unto itself, and texts on production/operations management treat it extensively.

CHAPTER 12 INVENTORY MANAGEMENT   419

TYPES OF INVENTORY MODELS

Structurally, inventory models are similar to the queueing models investigated in Chapter 8. That is, an inventory system has a number of attributes (which we will discuss subsequently), so that by making different assumptions about each attribute, we get different models. Theoretically, then, there are millions of different mathematical inventory models that will probably keep academic researchers filling the pages of scholarly journals for an eternity.

The classical textbook approach to the subject of inventory management is to derive the simple Wilson EOQ model that we used as an illustration in Chapter 5. We then extend this model in two or three ways (perhaps to incorporate price breaks or backordering or constraints on space or funds) and finally venture a step or two into modeling with probabilistic demand and/or lead time.

However, the most realistic—and therefore the most useful—approach to analysis of inventory policy is through modeling with discrete simulation (Chapter 9). The following sections discuss both the classical and the discrete simulation approaches.

UNDERLYING ASSUMPTIONS

In this section, we define the important attributes of inventory systems and state the underlying assumptions we will make about them as we go.

DEMAND The demand d_i for product i is the amount or quantity of the product we require over a stated period of time. We will assume only that we know (or can estimate) the probability distribution of d_i over this period and that this distribution is stationary (doesn't change) for the period. For example, the demand over the next year for personal computers by customers of the ConceptOne Electronics retail outlet may be approximately normally distributed, with a mean of 1,200 and a standard deviation of 200.

ORDER QUANTITY Our order quantity q_i for product i is the amount or quantity we order each time we order in the time period in which our demand occurs. In our ConceptOne example, it would probably be foolish (or impractical) to order all 1,200 units at once—we probably wouldn't have a place to store them, and we undoubtedly wouldn't have the available cash to pay for them. At the other end of the spectrum, we could order every day—and lose our franchise after about a week! Obviously, there is some recurring order quantity between the two extremes that is optimal in some sense. Our only assumption about q_i is that it remains constant over the demand period. If this assumption *appears* to be unrealistic, it most certainly is—except that we will use a **rolling demand period** in our simulation model, which mitigates this problem.

LEAD TIME The lead time t_i for product i is the time that expires between placement of the order and receipt of the goods ordered. Here, our assumption is that we can approximate the probability distribution of this random variable and this distribution does not change over the demand period.

PROCUREMENT COSTS

We denote the price per unit of product i as p_i, which can be either a flat price or a price discount structure. We will model two discount patterns: all-units and incremental. Our assumption is that whatever the form of p_i, it is constant over the demand period.

ALL-UNITS PRICE DISCOUNTS

Mathematically, we can state an all-units price discount as follows, suppressing the "i" subscript for product i to simplify the notation:

$$p^i = \begin{cases} p^1, & \text{if } 0 \leq q < q^1 \\ p^2, & \text{if } q^1 \leq q < q^2 \\ \text{etc.} \end{cases} \tag{12.1}$$

In Equation (12.1), every unit of q ordered costs p^1 if q is less than the first price break quantity q^1. On the other hand, if q lies between the price break quantities q^1 and q^2 (or equals q^1), *every unit ordered* costs p^2, which is less than p^1, and so forth. We most often see this type of price break structure when the supplier must do a setup each time he or she manufactures the product, so that the supplier can pass on part of the savings on larger orders (fewer setups) to the customer. It is not uncommon in practice for there to be four or five price break quantities involving successive price discounts. Note that all-units price discounts discriminate, in a sense, against small customers, since larger orders qualify for increasingly attractive price discounts on every unit purchased.

INCREMENTAL PRICE DISCOUNTS

The mathematical expression for incremental price discounts is as follows:

$$p^i = \begin{cases} p^1, & \text{if } 0 \leq q < q^1 \\ p^1 q^1 + p^2(q - q^1), & \text{if } q^1 \leq q < q^2 \\ \text{etc.} \end{cases} \tag{12.2}$$

We see that each of the prices p^1, p^2, and so on, *applies only to the number of units that fall into its price break interval*. As q_i gets larger and encompasses more of these intervals, the *average* price steadily declines. This type of price discount structure is widely used in practice, and its use is motivated for a variety of reasons. For example, if we ordered only a half train-carload of personal computers, we would probably have to pay freight for use of the entire car; whereas if we ordered a full carload, we would cut the per-unit freight charge in half. Unlike all-units discounts, incremental discounts charge every customer the same price for each unit purchased and thus does not discriminate against smaller customers.

We might note here that the price discount structure is based on the producer's production policy, not on the purchaser's needs. Although we will not go into the mathematical details here, researchers have shown that an optimal order quantity under the all-units price discount structure will always fall either between one and only one set of consecutive break points or at one of the price break quantities, making such an approach somewhat inflexible from the point of view of the purchaser. The incremental structure does not exhibit this pattern.

OPERATING COSTS

Operating costs are of three basic types: **holding costs, ordering costs,** and **out-of-stock costs.** We address each in the paragraphs that follow. Our assumption is that we know all costs with certainty over the demand period.

HOLDING COSTS

Costs of holding inventory are the direct and indirect costs of having goods on hand. Included are such things as warehouse handling, insurance, taxes, utilities, obsolescence/spoilage, and foregone returns on capital invested in inventory. Getting a handle on holding costs is no simple matter, since some costs are relatively fixed (warehousing, utilities) and others depend at least in part on the monetary value of the items in inventory (insurance, taxes, obsolescence/spoilage, return on capital). The most common approach is to express h_i (the per-unit cost of holding item i) as a fraction of the value of item i over the demand period. For example, if $h_i = 0.20$ and $p_1 = \$50$, the holding cost would be $10 if the item were in inventory for the entire demand period.

ORDERING COSTS

The cost of ordering inventory is merely the sum of costs associated with bid solicitation, processing paperwork, shipping and receiving, and so on. We express this cost as c_i: the cost per order.

OUT-OF-STOCK COSTS

Most textbooks discuss out-of-stock costs in two different ways: the cost of backordering and the cost of stockout (when backordering is not possible). Practitioners find it difficult if not impossible to derive defensible dollar estimates for such costs. Backordering, for example, does involve some clerical expense, but the real question we must address is, What impact does failure to fill a customer's order upon demand have on our goodwill? The same, of course, is true of stockouts, but we have probably lost sales in such cases.

The reason that knowing out-of-stock costs is important in a modeling sense is that it allows us to optimize the level of safety stock (a quantity of inventory above that we would normally carry) to cushion us against out-of-stock situations. Rather than trying to quantify the unquantifiable, we will treat safety stock level as a managerial decision.

MODELING AN INVENTORY SYSTEM

In this section, we will build a simple mathematical model of a finished goods or raw materials inventory system that deals with n distinct products or entities. Our objective will be to minimize the total cost associated with operating the system. Symbolically, then, our objective function is

$$\text{MIN } x_0 = \text{procurement costs} + \text{holding costs} + \text{ordering costs} \quad (12.3)$$

$$\text{S T: Constraints on storage, funds, etc.} \quad (12.4)$$

We will use a demand period of one year in our model-building exercise, although one may use any time period. Thus, d_i will be "annual demand in units for product i," and we will describe the other attributes (or parameters) analogously. Let us now address the three distinct cost elements in Equation (12.3) using an example problem, one at a time.

U-FIXIT is a major East Coast building supply company with more than 100 retail stores. A typical U-FIXIT store stocks an average of 33,000 items per week. Figure 12.1 shows the SAMS inventory module input screen. In this input screen, the

FIGURE 12.1
SAMS input screen for U-FIXIT

```
────► SAMS INPUT SCREEN - Inventory Analysis ◄────
NAME?  U-FIXIT                TIME PERIOD?  YEAR
PRICE DISCOUNTS(Y/N)?  N
PROBLEM DESCRIPTION - Find optimal ordering quantities
for six high-volume do-it-yourself items

ITEM          SAW    LFIX    FAN    TABLE   PAINT   BRUSH

DEMAND/PER(d) 100.   1500.   500.   400.    250.    4000.
UNIT COST(p)   50.     25.    50.   100.     10.       2.
HOLD COST %(h) 20.     15.    20.    25.     25.      25.
ORDER COST(c)   5.     30.    25.     5.      3.       7.
LEAD TIME(l)   .02    .04    .02    .06     .02      .04
```

"YEAR" for time periods indicates that the demand data are given on an annual basis (50 weeks). Carrying cost is expressed as a percentage of the unit cost of each item. Lead time refers to delivery lead time (.02 year = 1 week).

PROCUREMENT COST

The actual procurement cost per year for our n items is

$$\text{Procurement cost} = \sum_{i=1}^{n} p_i d_i \tag{12.5}$$

where the p_i may or may not involve a price discount structure. For U-FIXIT, the total procurement cost is

$$100 \times 50 + 1{,}500 \times 25 + 500 \times 50 + 400 \times 100 + 250 \times 10$$
$$+ \; 4{,}000 \times 2 = \$118{,}000$$

HOLDING COST

Cost associated with holding our n inventory items involves computing the average inventory value of each item over the year and applying our holding cost fraction h_i to each item. In Figure 12.2, we have plotted the inventory cycle for a product over the course of a year, assuming constant demand and no safety stock. Note that the inventory level jumps to a peak of q_i units when we receive an order, declines at the rate of d_i units per year, and jumps again as we deplete the inventory and the next order arrives. The figure is by way of convincing us that the average inventory of the ith item is merely $q_i / 2$ units. The total holding cost, therefore, is

$$\text{Holding cost} = \sum_{i=1}^{n} \frac{h_i p_i q_i}{2} \tag{12.6}$$

We will compute the total holding cost for U-FIXIT after the values for q_i have been determined.

ORDERING COST

Since we order q_i units of item i each time we order and since the demand is d_i units per year, the number of orders per year is d_i/q_i. If c_i is the cost of placing an order for item i, we can express the total ordering cost as

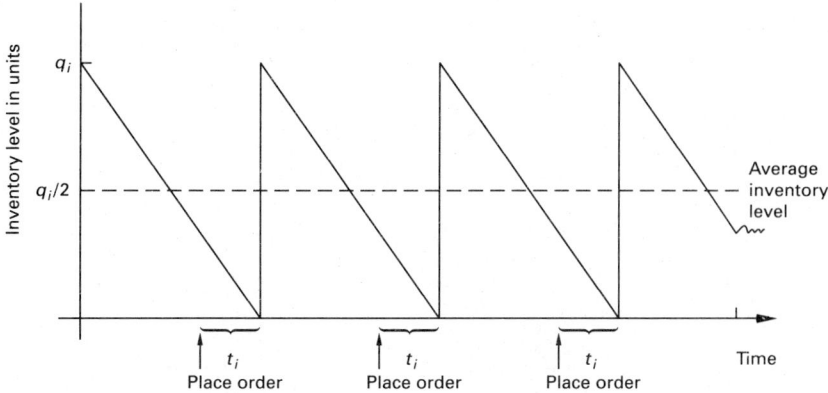

FIGURE 12.2
Inventory cycle

$$\text{Ordering cost} = \sum_{i=1}^{n} \frac{c_i d_i}{q_i} \qquad (12.7)$$

TOTAL COST

We can now write the mathematical formulation of Equation (12.3) — our objective function — compactly as

$$\text{MIN } x_0 = \sum_{i=1}^{n} p_i d_i + \frac{h_i p_i q_i}{2} + \frac{c_i d_i}{q_i} \qquad (12.8)$$

What we are after, of course, are values of the q_i, $i = 1, \ldots, n$, that make our total cost in Equation (12.8) as small as possible.

CONSTRAINTS

In a multi-item inventory system, there may be economic or physical limitations that affect our inventory management decisions. For example, suppose that n orders of size q_i, $i = 1, \ldots, n$, arrived simultaneously at our warehouse (which is not as improbable as it may seem). Would we have the capacity to store all of these goods? Let K be the capacity in cubic feet of our warehouse and let k_i be the cubic footage of one unit of the ith product. To ensure against exceeding our capacity, we must impose the volume constraint:

$$\sum_{i=1}^{n} k_i q_i \leq K \qquad (12.9)$$

Other types of constraints, such as a limit on the number of orders that we can physically process each year or a maximum amount of capital that we can invest in inventory at any one time, are also possible.

SOLUTION BY DISCRETE SIMULATION

In solving our model with discrete simulation, two approaches are possible. We could "brute force" our model by searching for optimal values of q_i, our decision variables. We illustrate this approach for the case of no price breaks and no constraints.

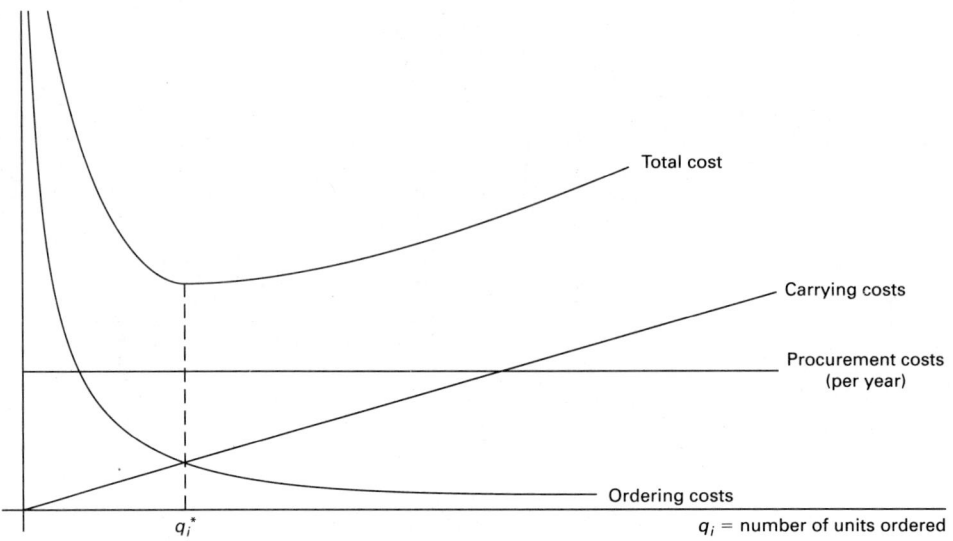

FIGURE 12.3 Total inventory costs

1. Generate the value of d_i (annual demand) using its probability density function.
2. Let $q_i = 1,2,3, \ldots, k$ and compute its cost x_0 from the cost function in Equation (12.8), using d_i from (1) and the known parameters p_i, h_i, and c_i.
3. Continue in (2) until some $x_0^{k+1} \geq x_0^k$. This is the optimal order quantity $q_i = k$.

The reason that this approach works is that the cost function (12.8) is convex; that is, it has a unique minimum, as illustrated in Figure 12.3. For example, consider item 1 (saw) of the U-FIXIT problem whose demand (d_1) is 100 units per year and whose price (p_1) is $50 per unit. With the holding charge (h_1) of 0.2 and ordering cost (c_1) of $5 per order, Equation (12.8) for q_1 values is as follows:

q_i	1	2	3	4	5	6
x_0	$5,505	$5,260	$5,182	$5,145	$5,125	$5,113
q_i	7	8	9	10	11	
x_0	$5,106	$5,103	$5,101	$5,100	$5,101	

Thus, $q_1^* = 10$ and $x_0^* = \$5,100$ in this case.

CLOSED-FORM SOLUTIONS

There is a better way than the brute-force approach. Using differential calculus, researchers have generated some closed-form (or analytical) solutions that we will find useful as tools in our simulation model. There are several cases, as outlined in the following examples.

CASE I: NO PRICE BREAKS, NO CONSTRAINTS

$$q_i^* = \sqrt{\frac{2d_i c_i}{h_i p_i}} \qquad (12.10)$$

For U-FIXIT's saw, we confirm our brute-force solution:

$$q_1^* = \sqrt{\frac{2(100 \times 5)}{0.2 \times 50}} = 10 \text{ units/order}$$

Table 12.1 shows the SAMS quick briefing for U-FIXIT. The SAMS quick briefing gives the optimal ordering quantity for each of U-FIXIT's six high-volume items and displays the ordering frequencies as # ORDERS/YR. ORDER LEVEL means that given the lead times for delivery, we would normally order when stock has diminished to the indicated inventory level. SAMS then displays annual holding and ordering costs for each item. In general:

Order level = Lead time × Demand per lead time period

TABLE 12.1 SAMS report for U-FIXIT

U-FIXIT QUICK BRIEFING ON INVENTORY ANALYSIS						
Item	Saw	Lfix	Fan	Table	Paint	Brush
OPTIMAL ORDER QUANTITY (ROUNDED)	10.0	155.0	50.0	13.0	25.0	335.0
# ORDERS/YR	10.0	9.7	10.0	30.8	10.0	11.3
ORDER LEVEL	2.0	60.0	10.0	24.0	5.0	160.0
HOLD COST/YR	50.0	290.0	250.0	162.0	31.0	84.0
ORDER COST/YR	50.0	290.0	250.0	154.0	30.0	84.0
TOT OPER COST/YR	100.0	580.0	500.0	316.0	61.0	168.0

Thus, for paint brushes, we have 2 weeks × 80 units/week = 160 units.

SAMS' results for HOLD COST/YR and ORDER COST/YR give us the detailed inventory cost information using Equations (12.6) and (12.7), respectively.

CASE II: NO PRICE BREAKS, CONSTRAINT ON MAXIMUM VOLUME

We first compute q_i^*, $i = 1, \ldots, n$ from Equation (12.10). If $\sum k_i q_i^* \leq K$ (total storage space available), the constraint (12.9) is not binding. Otherwise, we must find the value of L that satisfies the following equation:

$$\sum_{i=1}^{n} k_i \sqrt{\frac{2d_i c_i}{h_i p_i + 2KL}} = K \qquad (12.11)$$

Note that for $L = 0$, the expression in the square root sign becomes the q_i^* from Equation (12.10). To solve Equation (12.11), we select some small value of L, say

0.001, and gradually increase it until we satisfy the equation. We note in passing that L is a Lagrange multiplier and is actually the shadow price for floor space!

CASE III: ALL-UNITS PRICE BREAKS, NO CONSTRAINTS

As we noted before, all-units price discounts have the property that the optimal q_i must fall either at a break quantity or between one and only one pair of price break quantities.

To find $q°$ (we suppress the "i" notation for simplicity) for a pricing structure with k different break points ($q^1, q^2, \ldots, q^k$), we begin with the best price p^{k+1} and compute $q°$ using Equation (12.10). If this quantity is feasible (i.e., $q° > q^k$), then $q°$ is the optimal order quantity. If it is not feasible, we compute the value of the objective function (12.8) at the break point q^k (using the price p^k) and store it.

We now step back to the next best price p^k and compute $q°$ using Equation (12.10). If this quantity is feasible (i.e., it lies in the quantity range for which p^k is applicable), we compute the value of the objective function (12.8) at $q°$. If this value is lower than the objective value we computed for q^k, we have the optimal order quantity; if it is higher, q^k is the optimal order quantity. If, on the other hand, our $q°$ is not feasible, we compute the value of the objective function at the break point q^{k-1} and compare it with our computed value at q^k. We discard the point with the higher cost and continue in this way with p^{k-1}, p^{k-2}, as necessary, until we locate the optimal order quantity.

If all this seems complicated, we must remind ourselves that our task is to understand what our computer is doing and not to pursue such calculations ourselves with pen and paper. The mathematical proof that the procedure works is not easy to grasp. But if we look at the equation for $q°$ in Equation (12.10), an intuitive grasp of this phenomenon is at hand. Note that the unit price p appears in the denominator of the fractional expression. Thus, as p decreases, $q°$ increases. But since the p is under the square root sign, $q°$ increases more slowly, relatively speaking, than p decreases. Thus, at some point in the procedure, $q°$ will be feasible. The reason that the optimal must (with the one exception) occur at a price break is also intuitively obvious. For example, suppose that the "normal" value of $q°$ (below the first price break) were $q° = 60$ and that the price break occurred at $q^1 = 75$ units. It is apparent that we would not wish to order 74 units, since that would only incur more operating costs without enhancing our purchasing costs. We might, however, wish to order 75 units—the break quantity—if the price is right. On the other hand, we would never contemplate ordering 76, since—again—our costs would increase to no avail.

CASE IV: INCREMENTAL PRICE BREAKS, NO CONSTRAINTS

Unlike the case with all-units price discounts, the optimal ordering quantity q_i under incremental price breaks can take on any value, depending on the pattern of break quantities and prices. The key to understanding the incremental discounts is to realize that as ordering quantity q_i increases, the average price per unit p_i decreases. Because the mathematical expression of this model is rather complex, we relegate it to the appendix of this chapter.

OTHER CASES

Combining different price-discount strategies with constraints on warehouse space, investment limitations, etc., is not particularly relevant in actual practice, for easily explainable reasons. The existence of a price discount structure means that we would contemplate ordering more each time we ordered than otherwise. This means that limited storage facilities or capital to acquire inventory would monotonically tend to decrease the periodic order quantity and make it less likely that we could take advantage of price discounts.

It is here that managerial decisions become critical in the efficient management of inventory. Whether to use capital funds to increase storage space or to invest capital funds in inventory at the expense of alternative uses is a decision that we cannot easily reduce to parameters in models of inventory systems. Analyses such as those previously discussed provide an important input to such decisions.

THE SIMULATION MODEL

Figure 12.4 on p. 428 is a flowchart of a simulation model for inventory management that outlines the broad steps taken to analyze the four cases previously discussed. Detailed descriptions of such models are in Chapter 9.

One feature that we omitted from the model is that of lead time. One might wish to add this feature as well as an inventory accounting feature that keeps up with individual item inventory levels. Thus, if a demand occurs and inventory depletes, the model can record and report out-of-stock items.

One interesting and useful capability of this discrete simulation model (as well as all others) is its ability to answer what-if questions. For example, what if interest rates rose sharply, causing an accompanying increase in the holding cost parameters h_i? What if automating the ordering process caused a decrease in c_i (the ordering costs)? Would the expense be cost-effective? What if we could phase our orders for the n products in such a way that average overall inventory was relatively stable rather than fluctuating sharply from month to month? These are only examples of the many what-if analyses that we can perform.

Finally, since the model outlined in Figure 12.4 analyzes one product at a time—aggregating the results at the end—one could easily program such a model to run on a professional-level microcomputer.

ADVANCED CONCEPTS IN INVENTORY MANAGEMENT

The models we have discussed so far in this chapter are **single-echelon, perpetual, independent demand inventory** models. Let us briefly discuss three advanced concepts that are common in practice.

MULTIECHELON INVENTORY MODELS

Consider a highly vertically integrated manufacturing company that processes the raw materials required, manufactures components from the materials, assembles the end product from the components, operates its own warehousing and wholesale distribution system, and retails the product to the public through its own chain of stores. Figure 12.5 on p. 429 is a schematic of this hierarchy.

If each of the entities at each level in Figure 12.5 were independent, each could probably use the single-echelon models in this chapter to assist in the management of end-product and/or raw materials inventories. When viewed as a linked system of inventories, however, the problem becomes much more complex. If the individual

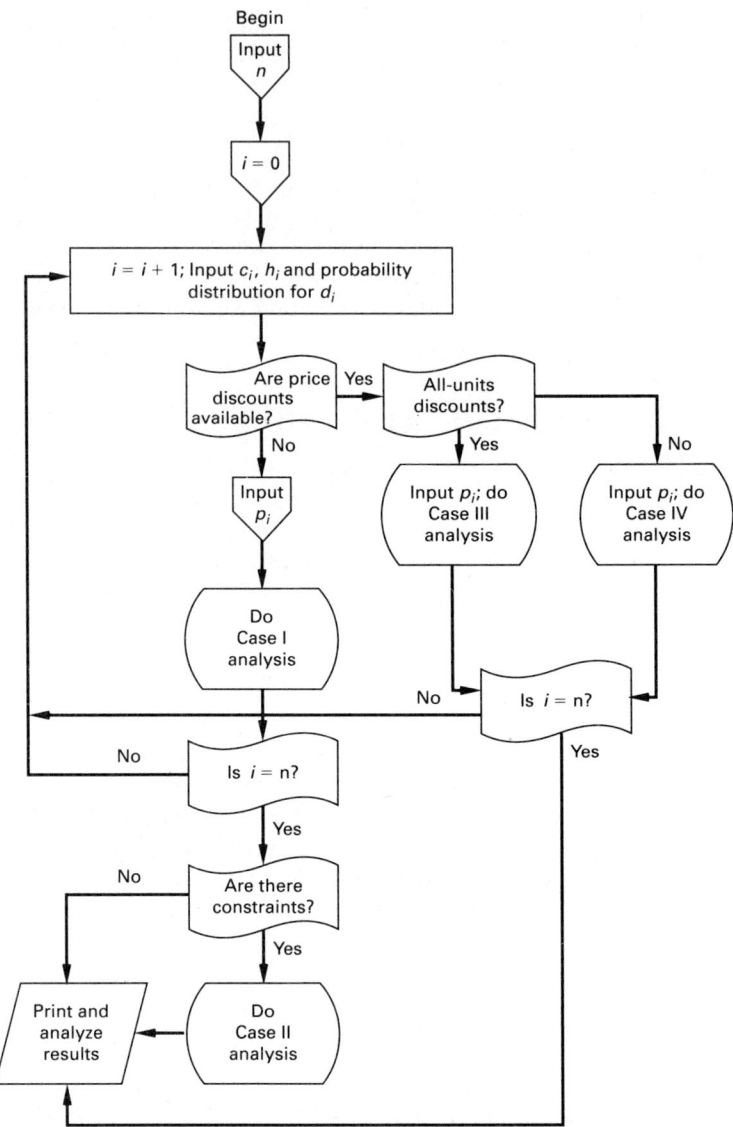

FIGURE 12.4
Flowchart for inventory simulation model

entity managers were allowed to suboptimize their own inventory systems, chaos would probably result, and the system would operate inefficiently. For this reason, researchers and practitioners have devised **multiechelon inventory models** that attempt to deal with the interactions between and among the echelons of the system. Most such models involve very large simulation models that run almost continuously in an attempt to spot bottlenecks before they occur.

PERIODIC REVIEW INVENTORY MODELS

As noted earlier, the models discussed in this chapter involve the calculation of order quantities (sometimes called lot sizes). These computations implicitly assume that the optimal order quantity q_i^* is recurring—that is, we will place an order of size q_i^* over and over again every $365/(d_i/q_i^*)$ days—perpetually. Such is not actually the case.

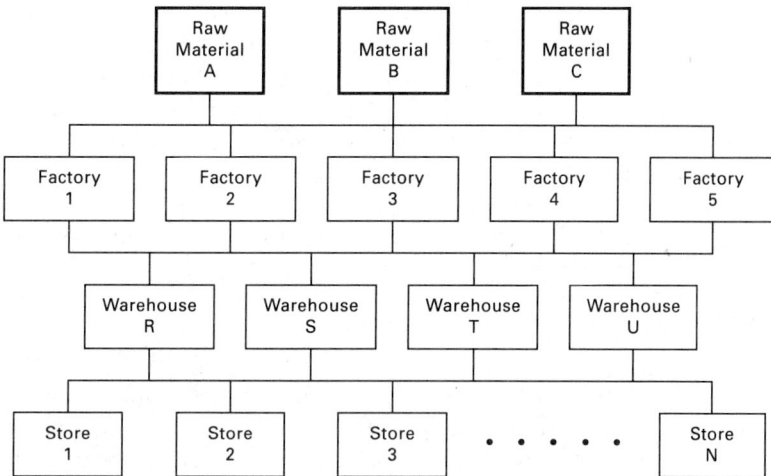

FIGURE 12.5 A vertically integrated manufacturing firm

What we do in practice is to reconstruct the simulation model at frequent intervals and recompute the q_i^*, $i = 1, \ldots, n$. In theory, however, this is still a "perpetual model."

A different class of models involves what is called **periodic review.** That is, we review inventory levels at fixed time periods and order an amount that will bring the inventory level to a planned amount based on usage. Determining how much to reorder under a periodic review system is usually a function of short-term future demand, forecasted using short-term previous demand. Periodic review inventory systems tend to work better than perpetual systems when demand for a product is volatile over time and when the unit value of the product is high.

Some firms apply the Pareto principle (ABC rule) on their inventories by using a perpetual system on the "80% of items that represent 20% of total inventory value" and a periodic review system on the remaining 20% of the items that are high value.

MATERIAL REQUIREMENTS PLANNING

Researchers have developed material requirements planning (MRP) models to deal with inventory systems that exhibit dependence among the items. For example, if we "explode" an ordinary chair, we find that its manufacture requires one back, one seat, two arms, and four legs. Further, assembly requires four type A screws, two type B screws, and 16 type C screws. Thus, the inventory item "one chair" spawns dependent demand for 30 items of seven different types. By contrast, the models discussed earlier are independent of each other except to the extent that they compete for floor space, available capital, etc.

MRP models recognize demand dependence and systematically "explode" end items into their various components. We then aggregate the components and order (or manufacture) them in such a way as to satisfy end-item requirements. There is nothing very complicated about the underlying idea of MRP, but its successful implementation requires careful analysis—and usually a lot of computer time. Our "exploding chair" is, after all, a very simple device, with two levels or echelons (components and fasteners). Consider, on the other hand, a complex product line such as personal computers, which may have six or seven echelons of complexity and several different product lines sharing subunits at several levels. For such products, the MRP "tree" gets very "bushy" indeed.

Recently, the concept of MRP has been extended to include the planning and management of resources in manufacturing companies. Manufacturing Resource Planning (MRP II) attempts to achieve the overall company goal by coordinating the activities of the key functional areas such as production, marketing, and finance. As in ordinary MRP, the key component of MRP II is the master production schedule, which is the finished goods requirement plan and schedule developed and revised jointly by the production, marketing, and other important divisions of the company. MRP II is also designed to evaluate alternative master production schedules and other manufacturing plans by accessing the companywide data bases and by using its simulation capabilities.

JUST-IN-TIME PRODUCTION SYSTEM

The Just-In-Time (JIT) production system was developed by Toyota corporation in Japan. Today many repetitive manufacturing (mass production) firms are using JIT to reduce inventories and lead times and to smooth production. In a JIT system, the objective is to produce the right number of items at the right place when they are required. Some of the benefits of this zero inventory method include reduction in working capital requirements, work-in-process inventory, and shop floor space requirements and increased product quality.

A successful implementation of the JIT system depends on three essential requirements. First, the setup time must be shortened, resulting in small batches of products produced. Second, excess inventory and safety stock are not allowed. Safety stock requires capital and does not encourage efficient production planning. And third, 100% quality at every production step is expected. When poor quality products are produced, the production process stops and the timely delivery of items is no longer possible. Thus, a successful JIT system requires careful design and management of each task, a team concept, and a well-trained work force.

MINICASES

EOQ at AFLC [1]

THE SCENARIO

The Air Force Logistics Command (AFLC) is the USAF organization responsible for purchasing, inventorying, and distributing (among other items) reparable spare parts for weapon systems. In the mid-1970s, AFLC, through its five Air Logistics Centers (ALCs), maintained an active spare parts inventory of 250,000 different items, expending approximately $400 million annually on purchases.

THE PROBLEM

AFLC had been using a simple EOQ system (like Case I) since 1952 as its basic inventory management tool. As people trained in more sophisticated scientific management techniques rose to higher managerial positions over the years, they raised questions about the appropriateness of the simple inventory model. In particular, they asked why management was not soliciting price discounts from suppliers, since this practice has been routine in industry for many years.

AFLC asked the Air Force Procurement Research Office, located at the Air Force Academy in Colorado, to look into AFLC's system, and a project team consisting of Air Force officers (Academy faculty members) and senior class cadets came together. The team dubbed this effort "Project EOQ." The cadets were all enrolled in a graduate-level seminar in logistics management, and "Project EOQ" became their 400-million-dollar term project!

The cadets quickly discovered what their textbooks hadn't told them (but at least one of their professors had)—that textbook models and real-world problems often have little in common. For example, soliciting price-discount quotes from suppliers obviously involves suppliers' analyzing their own production economies and basing the discounts on these economies. But federal law (as interpreted by procurement regulations) forbids asking competing suppliers to bid on different quantities. That means, of course, that attempting to solicit incremental discounts would have been illegal. The only alternative, therefore, was for AFLC to determine the bid quantities in advance and to solicit all-units quotes based on these quantities.

Another interesting (and most frustrating) constraint soon appeared. It seems that AFLC must spend funds appropriated by Congress for weapon systems spares in the fiscal year for which the funds were appropriated. Underspending means that the funds revert to the Treasury. Overspending means that somebody pays a large fine and/or goes to jail. To avoid this latter fate, AFLC headquarters followed the policy of dividing the annual budget into quarterly budgets for each of the five ALCs—with dire consequences for the ALC commander who overspent a quarterly budget. Mindful of these consequences, ALC commanders further subdivided the quarterly budgets, and so it went.

Why was this a source of frustration to the project team? When one installs a price-discount system, the idea is to purchase larger quantities to get a better per-unit price. But if managers dole out funds in small increments, this foils the use of price discounts. It is like the miserly old man who spends 50¢ every day for a pint of milk, when he can buy a gallon (8 pints) for $2.50, thereby wasting $1.50 every eight days. As we shall see later, the team found a way around this apparent dilemma.

There were other anomalies as well. For example, AFLC operated under a small purchase/large purchase policy that involved simplified procedures for purchases under $2,500, as opposed to more complex procedures for large purchases. AFLC recognized this difference by using a different ordering cost c_1 for small purchases, which was about one-third of c_2, the ordering cost for large purchases. Although this procedure made eminent good sense, it played havoc with the team's attempt to implement a model similar to the one in Case III.

THE MODEL

Banking on its ability to persuade the AFLC commander to relax the quarterly budget restrictions, the team decided to recommend a price-discount solicitation scheme that included only those items that would normally be purchased frequently under the current system. Its plan severely restricted the number of items included, but—because of the strong Pareto structure of the AFLC inventory—it affected almost two-thirds of the dollar value of the items. The team computed the all-units solicitation quantities in such a way that the largest solicited quantity for any class of items was (in our notation) $2d_i$—twice the annual demand. The following table exhibits this scheme:

Solicitation quantities for price discounts

Normal q_i^*	Solicitation Quantities
$d_i/4$	$d_i/4$, $d_i/2$, $3d_i/4$, d_i
Between $d_i/4$ and $d_i/2$	q_i^*, $(q_i^* + d_i/2)$, d_i
Between \$2,500 & $d_i/2$	q_i^*, d_i, $2d_i$

In the table, the reason that the "normal" ordering quantity is not less than $d_i/4$ is that Department of Defense regulations prohibited ordering less than a three-month supply of any item (and, we might add, no more than a three-year supply).

To validate the proposed price-discount procedure, the project team built a large simulation model to analyze the effect of price discount solicitation by AFLC for purchase of reparable spares. Since the inventory was so monstrously large, the team used a stratified random sample of 9,767 items out of the inventory of 250,000 items. The total dollar value of the sample (annual purchases), however, was about \$165 million. The team simulated price discounts using beta distributions with means of 3%, 5%, and 8% and with minimum values of zero and maximum values of 10%, 15%, and 20%.

SOLUTION TO THE MODEL

The team ran the simulation several times for each mean-maximum combination for discounts and produced the following results (it found that varying the maximum discount had little effect):

Average Discount	Net Savings in Total Annual Costs
3%	\$10.3 million
5%	\$25.9 million
8%	\$50.7 million

The team also investigated other attributes of the AFLC inventory system, such as the holding cost rate and demand prediction; its technical report [1] fully discusses the results.

SOLUTION TO THE PROBLEM

When the cadets briefed the results of the team's analysis to high-ranking civilian and military officials of AFLC, they got a guardedly positive reaction. One high-level manager from one of the ALCs remarked, paradoxically:

> "Price discounts are a good idea—and you've convinced me that we could save a lot of money. But, unfortunately, we can't afford it." (Remember the miser and the pints of milk?)

Nevertheless, the AFLC officials fortunately found a way to implement a "trial run" of the proposed price discount system at the ALC in Ogden, Utah. AFLC established a revolving fund of several million dollars to fund a limited price discount solicitation program, the realized savings being returned to the fund to broaden the coverage. After six months of operation, the system had documented actual savings of $600,000; on that basis, annual savings for the entire AFLC system for a severely limited number of inventory items would be $7 million.

EPILOGUE

Surely we cannot avoid observing at this point that *models don't make decisions—managers do*.

The managers in this minicase—even though enmeshed in a bureaucratic system that was unintentionally hostile to implementation of a "good idea"—made difficult (courageous?) decisions that led to a marked improvement in operational efficiency for AFLC. Did they implement the changes exactly as the project team and its models and analysis recommended? Of course not. But the models made a difference—they provided credible, carefully analyzed input into the decision-making process. And that, of course, is what MS/OR models are supposed to do.

Keep on Truckin' [2]

THE SCENARIO

The American Trucking Association (ATA), a service and lobbying organization for the trucking industry, employs approximately 300 people. The majority of ATA services are in the form of information on industry-related topics, to include the following:

- safety practices
- hazardous materials compliance
- state and federal transportation laws
- accounting and financial operations
- sales and marketing techniques
- industry statistics

ATA disseminates some information orally, but most information is in printed form for a fee. Except for membership dues, fees from the sale of publications are ATA's major revenue source.

The Marketing Department has responsibility for production, promotion, and sale of publications. It uses direct mail, advertisements, and press releases to promote these publications. The Safety Department writes and continuously revises most of the publications in accordance with changes in federal statutes. ATA's Graphic Center prints the publications (unless a lower cost external bid is available).

Marketing is responsible for forecasting demand for the publications and uses these forecasts to establish inventory levels. Because of the constantly changing nature of federal legislation, this is the trickiest part of the process. Shelf life of ATA publications is the key issue, since having a large stock of a publication that is instantly obsolete with the issuance of a new regulation means a significant monetary loss due to obsolescence.

THE PROBLEM

One of the major publications of the ATA is the *Federal Motor Carrier Safety Regulations* (FMCSR). If ATA orders too much inventory of this large manual and publishing a revised FMCSR becomes necessary, the stock on hand is useless, and a large financial loss results. On the other hand, if ATA maintains too little stock, it must suffer the costs (both financial and goodwill) of back orders or stockouts (there are competitive suppliers). Endemic stockouts of the current FMCSR lead to long-term detrimental effects on customer relations and future sales.

Ordering costs for the FMCSR amount to $250 per order, not including freight charges. Carrying costs, however, are a rather high 40%. Most of the carrying cost is due to the obsolescence factor but includes storage, overhead, and capital investment considerations as well.

THE MODEL

At present, the Marketing Department uses a least unit cost inventory ordering model to determine the best ordering pattern. It uses an exponential smoothing (with trend) model to forecast demand. Thus, the current inventory model ignores the cost of the manuals themselves and attempts to minimize total ordering and holding costs. At present, annual demand is forecast to be about 263,000 books in the monthly pattern shown in Table 12.2.

TABLE 12.2 Forecast demand for FMCSR manuals

Month	Forecast Demand	Cumulative Forecast Demand
January	20,963	20,963
February	18,659	39,633
March	30,562	70,195
April	18,182	88,377
May	13,000	101,377
June	15,145	116,522
July	8,621	125,143
August	35,330	160,473
September	19,324	179,797
October	26,052	205,849
November	7,948	213,797
December	49,020	262,817

Lead time (time between placing the order and receiving it) is 45 days. Wholesale cost of the books, including shipping, is $10 per book in lots of less than 10,000 per shipment. The Federal Government Press ships FMCSR manuals in cartons of 24 books.

SOLUTION TO THE MODEL

Let's ignore the complexities of this problem for the moment and analyze it using the simple Wilson EOQ approach in Equation (12.10) (Case I). We have

$d = 262{,}817$, estimated annual demand

$c = \$250$, ordering cost per order

$h = 40\%$ holding cost as fraction of value

$p = \$10$, cost per unit

Figure 12.6 displays the SAMS inventory analysis module input screen. Table 12.3 shows the SAMS quick briefing report for this model.

From the report, we have $q^* = 5{,}736$ manuals (239 cartons) per order.

We can compute total cost as follows:

$$\text{MIN } x_0 = \$2{,}628{,}170 + \$11{,}472 + \$11{,}455$$

$$\qquad \text{(manual cost} \quad \text{(carrying)} \quad \text{(ordering)}$$
$$\qquad \text{at } \$10/\text{unit)}$$

$$= \$2{,}651{,}097$$

FIGURE 12.6 SAMS input screen for Keep On Truckin'

```
─────▶ SAMS INPUT SCREEN - Inventory Analysis  ◀─────
NAME?  KEEP ON TRUCKIN'          TIME PERIOD?  YEAR
PRICE DISCOUNTS(Y/N)?  N
PROBLEM DESCRIPTION - Find optimal ordering quantities
for FMCSR manuals.

ITEM                     FMCSR

DEMAND/PER(d)            262817.
UNIT COST(p)                 10.
HOLD COST %(h)               40.
ORDER COST(c)               250.
LEAD TIME(l)                  .125
```

TABLE 12.3 SAMS report for Keep On Truckin'

KEEP ON TRUCKIN'
QUICK BRIEFING ON INVENTORY ANALYSIS

Item	FMCSR
OPTIMAL ORDER QUANTITY (ROUNDED)	5736.0
# ORDERS/YR	45.6
ORDER LEVEL	32852.0
HOLD COST/YR	11472.0
ORDER COST/YR	11455.0
TOT OPER COST/YR	22927.0

SOLUTION TO THE PROBLEM

Let's take a careful look at these results. Since the model suggests an "optimal" order quantity of 5,736, this means that ATA will need to place an order about 46 times per year, or once every eight days. Since lead time for delivery is 45 calendar days, this means that we would have five to six orders outstanding at any one time. And although this simple model ignores the very high variability of demand through the 12-month period—but assuming that the Federal Government Press will allow cancellation of orders not yet printed when changing regulations make an edition of the FMCSR obsolete—frequent ordering is an excellent way to hold down carrying costs on inventory items with high obsolescence rates.

Let us expand our investigation of this interesting problem by looking at . . .

A DIFFERENT MODEL

The simple Wilson EOQ inventory model ignores possible economies available from quantity price discounts that may be available from the Federal Government Press. In the printing industry, the cost of setting up presses for a run is very high, while the variable (printing) cost is relatively low. Suppose all-units discounts were available as follows:

Order Quantity	Unit Price
< 10,000	$10.00 ($p_1$)
10,000 – 39,999	9.95 (p_2)
40,000 – 69,999	9.90 (p_3)
≥ 70,000	9.80 (p_4)

Note that the "optimal" ordering quantity for our original model (5,736) is well below the first price discount quantity of 10,000 manuals. However, because of the price discounts, we can justify further analysis.

Since no PC-based inventory analysis modules currently have the capability of analyzing price discount structures, we will work through the computations using Equations (12.10) and (12.08) and our trusty solar-powered calculator.

SOLUTION TO A DIFFERENT MODEL

The best price is $p_4 = \$9.80$, and the EOQ computation using Equation (12.10) is

$$q_i^* = \sqrt{\frac{2(262,817)(250)}{(0.4)(9.8)}} = 5,790 \tag{12.12}$$

The EOQ of 5,790 is infeasible (i.e., 5,790 < 70,000, the break point), so we compute the total cost from Equation (12.8) using an EOQ of 70,000 as follows:

$$\text{MIN } x_0 = (9.8)(262,817) + \frac{(0.4)(9.8)(70,000)}{2} + \frac{(250)(262,817)}{70,000} \tag{12.13}$$

$$\text{(manual cost)} \qquad \text{(carrying)} \qquad \text{(ordering)}$$

$$= \$2,575,607 \; + \; \$137,200 \; + \; \$939$$

$$= \$2,713,746 > \$2,651,097, \text{ our original cost}$$

Using similar computations for the other price breaks of $9.90 at 40,000 units and $9.95 at 10,000 units, we find

For $p_3 = \$9.90$:

MIN x_0 = $\$2,601,888$ + $\$79,200$ + $\$1,643$
          (manual cost)   (carrying)   (ordering)

= $\$2,682,731 > \$2,651,097$, our original cost

For $p_2 = \$9.95$:

MIN x_0 = $\$2,615,029$ + $\$19,900$ + $\$6,570$
          (manual cost)   (carrying)   (ordering)

= $\$2,641,499 < \$2,651,097$, our original cost

Thus, under this price-break structure, ATA could elect to order in lots of 10,000 to get the five-cent price discount, saving a total of $9,598 per year. ATA would place orders every two weeks in this situation.

SOLUTION TO THE PROBLEM

ATA currently orders FMCSR manuals once per month, basing order quantity on the projected demand between 45 and 75 days hence. The rationale is that it is more important to pay attention to the highly fluctuating demand than to smaller holding costs that result from more frequent orders. We address the cost implications of this decision in Problem 1 following the chapter summary.

SUMMARY

In this chapter, we have explored the art and science of inventory management. Our discussion noted that inventories involve billions of dollars worth of corporate assets. We focused upon the building of simulation models that provide useful information to managers responsible for managing these assets. The rather lengthy minicases "EOQ at AFLC" and "Keep on Truckin' " described actual applications of inventory modeling and pointed out sharply the recurring theme of this book—that modeling and analysis can make a difference in managerial decision making—but nothing more.

KEY TERMS

finished goods inventory
holding costs
in-process inventory
inventory model
multiechelon inventory models
ordering costs

out-of-stock costs
periodic review
raw materials inventory
rolling demand period
single-echelon, perpetual, independent demand inventory models

PROBLEMS FOR ANALYSIS

1. Returning to the "Keep on Truckin" minicase, use the total cost function (12.8) to price out ATA's policy of ordering once per month. Use a constant EOQ of 262,817/12 = 21,901 for your computations. Assume that the price discount structure exists as we displayed it, so that the per-unit price at this order quantity is $9.95.

   a. Are you surprised by the cost differential between the optimal model solution's policy of ordering 10,000 manuals every two weeks and ordering 21,901 each month? Did you expect the differential to be larger?
   b. Note that taking advantage of the price discount structures would cause ATA to increase its holding and ordering (operating) costs to save a larger amount in procurement (capital) costs. Are these kinds of costs actually interchangeable (in an accounting sense) in private industry? In government agencies? Recall the situation in the "EOQ at AFLC" minicase before answering.

2. Consider the ambitious project: Climb Mount Everest. How could the project manager use the inventory management techniques discussed in this chapter to enhance the probability of a successful climb and at the same time control his or her expenses?

3. Most textbooks conclude that inventory management models are useful only in industries that are concerned with the production of goods and therefore are of no value to the growing number of companies that provide services.

   a. Can services be inventoried? In thinking about this question, consider the "taxi squad" of a professional football team, management consultants who are paid a retainer by large companies, part-time registered nurses (RNs) who volunteer to fill-in in case of medical emergencies or illness by full-time nursing staff, and plumbers paid to be on 24-hour call in case of hydrologic disasters.
   b. If, contrary to most textbooks, you conclude that we can inventory services, how would you estimate holding costs, carrying costs, and out-of-stock costs?
   c. Consider companies that operate vending machines in highly people intensive organizations such as airports and universities. Could these companies conceivably use inventory management models to increase the efficiency of their operations? (*Hint:* Consider the possible effects of chronic out-of-stock situations versus too-frequent restock policies.)

4. Analyze each of the following scenarios to determine whether we could use the single-echelon, perpetual, independent demand inventory models discussed in this chapter to model and analyze them. If so, identify the nature of procurement cost, holding cost, and ordering cost and determine whether there might be some constraint affecting inventory items.

   a. Angie Suite owns and operates Suite's Floral Creations, a successful retail flower shop in downtown San Francisco. Because of the highly variable demand for the various varieties of fresh-cut flowers, ferns, and potted plants, Angie finds it difficult to order from wholesalers in such a way that she can fill customers' orders and simultaneously avoid a great deal of spoilage. Shelf life of cut flowers varies from two days for delicate varieties to two weeks for others. Angie's dilemma is compounded by the fact that her major supplier offers incremental price discounts for larger orders.
   b. Capo DiCavallo is a small businessman who earns his livelihood by making short-term loans (without collateral) to certain associates whose avocation is wagering on sporting events. Capo can obtain capital from his parent company at an interest rate of 10% per week if the amount is under $10,000 and at 9% if the amount is over $10,000. He charges his clients between 15% and 25% per

week, depending upon his assessment of the risk involved in each case. Although Capo has a very effective bad-debt collection system, so does his parent company—and defaulting on one of their loans is unthinkable.

c. Mom's Rustic Pantry, Inc., is a home-style fast-food restaurant that specializes in old-fashioned cheeseburgers with all the trimmings. Pop orders the ground meat once a week, using as a rule of thumb the number of Rubeburgers sold last week. Daughter Sissy, who has an MBA from Rustic Polytechnic Institute, is in charge of ordering the buns. She uses a computerized multiple regression model to forecast demand and orders buns every two, three, or four days, depending on the model's R^2 value. Bubba, Mom and Pop's son, orders the cheese. Since he is not too bright, he peeks over Sissy's shoulder and orders one slice of cheese for each bun she orders. Mom herself buys the lettuce fresh every morning, hand selecting between 25 and 35 heads, depending on the quality that day. The restaurant has a serious problem with waste due to spoilage as well as lost sales due to stock outs.

5. Until now, we have made no mention of sensitivity analysis and its role in model analysis for inventory management. Let us briefly explore this subject as an exercise.

As we can easily show, we can write the cost function x_0 for Case I in terms of its parameters only, as follows:

$$\text{(Case I)} \quad x_0^* = \sum_{i=1}^{n} p_i d_i + \sum_{i=1}^{n} \sqrt{2 d_i c_i h_i p_i} \qquad (12.14)$$

a. What is the effect on total cost of an error of 25% in our estimate of c_i or h_i?
b. Would you think the price discount models (cases III and IV) are more or less sensitive to parameter errors than is the model for case I? Why or why not?
c. What are the managerial implications of this curious feature of single-echelon, perpetual, independent demand inventory models?

PRACTICE MODELS

1. A large retail chain store sells a popular camera. Use a package like the SAMS inventory analysis module and the following information to determine the optimal order quantity, total ordering cost, total carrying cost, reorder point, and the total cost:

   Demand = 20 units/week

   Order/setup cost = $5/order

   Carrying charge rate = 20%

   Price = $43

   Lead time = 2 weeks

   Number of periods/year = 52 weeks

2. A local pharmacy sells an over-the-counter medicine in large quantities. Given the following information and the manufacturer's quantity discount prices, use an inventory module and the all-units price discount method to determine the optimal order quantity and the total cost:

   Demand = 100 boxes/week

   Order/setup cost = $15/order

   Carrying charge rate = 25%

Lead time = 1 week

Number of periods/year = 52 weeks

Order Quantity	Unit Price
< 500	$ 3.00
500 − 749	2.50
≥ 750	2.00

3. Use the discrete simulation method to find the optimal order quantity and the total cost for the following data. Compare your results to those generated by an inventory analysis module.

   Demand = 500 units/year

   Order/setup cost = $75/order

   Carrying charge rate = 25%

   Price = $2000/unit

4. An electronics manufacturing firm produces electrical components for various home appliances. The following table gives the relevant data for each appliance. Use an inventory analysis module to determine the order size and the total cost.

Item	Demand/ Month	Price/ Unit	Order Cost	Carrying Charge	Lead Time	Production Rate per Month
Microwave	2,000	$190	$25	15%	1	2,200
Washer	1,200	400	50	30	2	1,500
Dryer	1,100	290	42	30	2	1,400
Oven	3,000	200	37	25	1	3,200

REFERENCES AND ADDITIONAL READING

1. Austin, L. "Project EOQ: A Success Story in Implementing Academic Research." *Interfaces* 7 (1977): 1–14.
2. Buckius, Lori. Adapted from an unpublished MBA term project report, Virginia Polytechnic Institute and State University (1988).
3. Buffa, E. *Modern Production/Operations Management* (6th ed.). New York: Wiley, 1980.
4. Hadley, G., and T. Whitin. *Analysis of Inventory Systems*. Englewood Cliffs, N.J.: Prentice-Hall, 1963.
5. Orlicky, J. *Material Requirements Planning*. New York: McGraw-Hill, 1975.
6. Silver, E., and R. Peterson. *Decision Systems for Inventory Management and Production Planning* (2d ed.). New York: Wiley, 1985.
7. Wagner, H. *Statistical Management of Inventory Systems*. New York: Wiley, 1962.
8. Woolsey, R. "A Requiem for the EOQ: An Editorial." *Production and Inventory Management Journal* 29 (1988): 68–72.

APPENDIX
Incremental Price Breaks, No Constraints

We can write p_i as follows, again suppressing the "i" subscript for simplicity:

$$p = \frac{p^1 q^1 + p^2(q^2 - q^1) + \ldots + p^{j+1}(q - q^j)}{q}$$

where q lies in the range of values: $q^j \leq q \leq q^{j+1}$.

When we substitute this expression into the objective function in place of p, we get a very "messy" mathematical expression. Rewriting the above expression in a more convenient way, we have

$$p = \frac{q^1(p^1 - p^2) + q^2(p^2 - p^3) + \ldots + q^j(p^{j+1})}{q}$$

Letting $R_j = \sum q^k(p^k - p^{k+1})$, the first j (constant) terms in the numerator of p, we can now write

$$p = \frac{R_j + q^j(p^{j+1})}{q} \text{ for } q^j \leq q \leq q^{j+1}$$

We can now write the closed form expressions for $q°$ and $x_0°$ as follows:

$$q° = \sqrt{\frac{2d(c + R_j)}{h(p^{j+1})}}, \, j = 0, 1, 2, \ldots$$

$$x_0° = \sum_{j=1}^{n} \frac{dR_j + cd}{q} + d(p^{j+1}) + \frac{h}{2}(R_j + qp^{j+1})$$

where $R_0 = 0$. Note that for $j = 0$, these expressions reduce to Equations (12.10) and (12.8), respectively.

PART THREE

Decision Making Under Uncertainty (DMUU)

Part 2 of this book concentrated on modeling and analyzing problems for which we have or can generate useful probabilistic information. Throughout the book to this point, we have assumed that our decision maker had a single, clear-cut objective in her or his approach to finding useful solutions to a problem. Although we have made little mention of this fact, we have dealt mostly with tactical problems.

In our terminology, **uncertainty** refers to the complete absence of probabilistic information about an environment that we know to be stochastic. It can also mean that there are multiple objectives that we must consider or that a problem is so complex that we hope only to be able to understand its basic underlying structure.

Part 3 consists of three chapters.

CLASSICAL DECISION MODELS UNDER UNCERTAINTY

Chapter 13 takes the basic analytical structure built in Chapter 7 and investigates decision criteria that do not depend on the presence of a probability distribution on the states of nature. This is a very controversial subject, as we shall see. A brief review of Chapter 7 before reading Chapter 13 will be helpful.

MODELING WITH MULTIPLE OBJECTIVES

In Chapter 14, we return to our models in Part 1, except this time our decision maker has multiple goals he or she wishes to achieve (or at least take into consideration). As you may well imagine, this complicates the analytical process significantly.

Is it really possible to simultaneously maximize profit contribution, minimize inventory investment, meet equal employment opportunity goals, and maximize market share? Of course not—we must make tradeoffs. This chapter delves into some techniques that explicitly incorporate multiple objectives into the analysis.

VISUAL AND MULTIATTRIBUTE CHOICE MODELS

Chapter 15 discusses two distinct but related subjects. Visual models such as trees, matrices, DELTA charts, and networks are extremely useful entities in helping us to understand complex relationships between and among the elements of a system. We make complicated choices almost every day based upon multiple considerations, and the so-called Brown-Gibson Multidimensional Location Model gives us a way to transform ratings of subjective criteria into entities that we can use to compare choices on both qualitative and quantitative grounds.

A word of advice is in order before we go on to Chapter 13. Since we are on the frontiers of management science in Part 3, the logic involved in some of the topics is tricky in some cases, subtle in others, and complex in still others. The mathematics involved is not the issue—that's the problem of technical analysts and researchers. The real issue is that when we deal with uncertainty, our tools must be very sophisticated. You cannot perform delicate brain surgery with a butter knife!

And now on to Chapter 13—one of the shortest chapters in the book, but easily the most controversial.

KEY TERM

uncertainty

CHAPTER 13

Classical Decision Models Under Uncertainty

In Chapter 7, we explored at some length a model or structure for decision making under risk (DMUR). In what follows, we retain the basic DMUR format—mutually exclusive and collectively exhaustive states of nature (S_j), alternatives (A_i), and outcomes (O_{ij}). The difference is that when we analyze decision making under uncertainty (DMUU), we admit that we cannot generate or satisfactorily estimate a prior probability distribution on the states of nature.

UNDERLYING ASSUMPTIONS

The basic underlying assumption of DMUU—our inability to specify a prior distribution over the states—is controversial indeed. Some modern books on decision theory have virtually eliminated this topic from their contents (e.g., [5]). Why all the hullabaloo? Well, the academic world of statisticians and decision theorists is divided sharply on the nature of probability. The so-called Bayesians argue that all probability is to some extent subjective and that a decision maker should be able to come up with a usable prior distribution on anything! Their position is that the inability to do so is a copout. So—DMUU has no place in their scenario.

The classicists hold the view that all probability distributions have their origins in relative frequencies, and they view the term *subjective probability* as being self-contradictory and therefore paradoxical. The Bayesians counter that using the DMUU criteria we will discuss shortly is in reality implicitly using subjective probabilities.

In an uncharacteristically petulant mood, the great British statistician Sir Maurice Kendall reportedly remarked to a meeting of the Royal Statistical Society in London:

> Decision theory never made a decision, and game theory never won a game. And for those devotees of Thomas Bayes, it is my fervent hope that they publish their work as did their mentor—posthumously [4].

And so it goes. Who is right and who is wrong? For our purposes, it matters little. Models are like tools. Let us learn how to use DMUU modeling, and you—the decision maker—can decide for yourself whether it is useful to you. Before continuing, however, think about the following decision situation in light of the controversy about the nature of probability.

Suppose you live alone in a small house and return home one dark night to find a light shining through your bedroom window. You can't remember whether you left the light on that morning, and you have two obvious alternatives: A_1: enter the house, or A_2: run three blocks to a pay telephone and call the police. Three states of nature occur to you:

S_1: You left the light on, and no one is in the house.
S_2: An unarmed burglar is in your house.
S_3: A burglar with a loaded gun is in your house.

What outcomes are possible? If S_1 is true, A_1 is the preferred action, of course, since it saves you the three-block run and the embarrassment of calling the police because you left a light on.

If S_2 is true, entering the house might scare the burglar off without any loot, while the time it takes for the police to arrive might let him or her make a getaway.

What if S_3 is true? The payoff from A_1 might be your death. Now, how—if you were a staunch Bayesian—would you go about placing a probability distribution useful to your decision-making process on the three states of nature in this troublesome problem? And how would your personal utility function look for this problem? Would you actually contemplate replacing outcome O_{11} (the best of the six) with 1.0 utile and O_{23} (your possible death) with 0 utiles? If so, you are a staunch Bayesian indeed! Our view is that certain, very real problems lie outside the domain of DMUR—and we consider this grim scenario to be only one such.

MODELING UNDER UNCERTAINTY

With no prior distribution on the states of nature, our expected monetary value (EMV), expected opportunity loss (EOL), and expected utility (EU) decision criteria from DMUR aren't operable in a DMUU environment. What we need, therefore, is a set of decision criteria that are rational and that explicitly incorporate our attitude toward risk. Four well-known classicists developed such criteria, as discussed in the following paragraphs.

THE MAXIMIN CRITERION

The MAXIMIN criterion, suggested originally by Abraham Wald, is a highly risk averse and conservative approach to decision making. It merely involves locating the minimum payoff for each alternative and choosing the alternative for which this minimum is the largest—thus, MAXIMIN means "the maximum of the minima." This implies a sort of Murphy's Law approach, insinuating that "if anything can possibly go wrong, it probably will." Thus, we refer to MAXIMIN as "the pessimist's criterion."

We illustrate the MAXIMIN criterion with a small example. Bettem, Gamble, and Churn (BGC), a stock brokerage house, manages stock portfolios for a wide variety of clients—from persons of modest means to wealthy oil magnates. One customer is Ima Spry, an 85-year old spinster who lives alone and who scrimped to build a small nest egg by saving $2 per week during her 65 years in the Undeliverable Junk Mail Department of the local post office. Ima has read that utility stocks are relatively safe, good-yielding investments and has asked Billy Bettem, one of the BGC partners, to select several for her consideration. Billy selects five and computes estimated capital appreciation (in percent) in the next 18 months under four states of the economy. Ima

CHAPTER 13 CLASSICAL DECISION MODELS UNDER UNCERTAINTY

added the alternative "Don't Invest" herself and constructed a decision matrix (see Table 13.1).

Ima first noted that A_4: Texas Aggie Kerosene, Inc. dominates A_3: Solar Energy, Inc. of Boston, and technically she can remove A_3 from the model. Next she tried to get a straight answer from Bettem on the relative likelihood of the four states of nature occurring, but his only response was, "It depends." Ima concluded that she would have to analyze her problem in a DMUU context. She also knew that she was highly risk averse and decided on the MAXIMIN criterion.

Figure 13.1 shows the SAMS DMUU module input screen for BGC outcomes. Note that we must enter a probability distribution of some kind before SAMS will perform the analysis. We therefore used a uniform (equal probability) distribution. Table 13.2 displays the SAMS full briefing.

TABLE 13.1 Decision matrix

	State of the Economy			
	Depression (S_1)	Recession (S_2)	Upward Cycle (S_3)	Major Expansion (S_4)
A_1: Don't Invest	0	0	0	0
A_2: Three-Mile Island, Inc.	−40%	−20%	+10%	+60%
A_3: Solar Energy of Boston	−30%	−10%	0	+30%
A_4: Texas Aggie Kerosene	−10%	0	+5%	+30%
A_5: NY City Firewood, Inc.	−5%	+5%	+10%	+15%
A_6: Berkeley Power of California	+5%	+15%	−10%	−10%

FIGURE 13.1 SAMS input screen for BGC outcomes

```
────▶ SAMS INPUT SCREEN - DMUU Matrix Module  ◀────

NAME?  BGC - OUTCOMES
DMUU CRITERION?    MAXIMIN
PROBLEM DESCRIPTION - Analyze Ms. Spry's investment
                     problem under uncertainty.

States          DEPRESS    RECESS    UPWARD    MAJOR
Prior Dist.       .25       .25       .25      .25

Alternatives              Outcomes

DONT               0.        0.        0.        0.
3-MILE           -40.      -20.       10.       60.
SOLAR            -30.      -10.        0.       30.
TEXAGGIE         -10.        0.        5.       30.
NYCITY            -5.        5.       10.       15.
BERKELEY           5.       15.      -10.      -10.
```

TABLE 13.2

```
BGC
FULL BRIEFING ON OPTIMAL MODEL SOLUTION
            Optimal Objective Value = 0.0
Alternative        MIN         MAXIMIN       Optimal

DONT               0.0           0.0           Yes
3-MILE           -40.0                          No
SOLAR            -30.0                          No
TEXAGGIE         -10.0                          No
NYCITY            -5.0                          No
BERKELEY         -10.0                          No

OPTIMAL ALTERNATIVE IS: DONT
```

Not surprisingly, the model recommends A_1: Don't Invest for our highly risk averse Ima, using the MAXIMIN decision criterion. The next best alternative A_5: New York City Firewood, Inc., had a minimum outcome of a 5% loss, but something about the company bothered Ima. Therefore, Ima decided not to invest in any of the utility stocks and put her $6,500 into T-bills.

THE MAXIMAX CRITERION

William Hurwicz initially suggested the risk seeker's criterion referred to as MAXIMAX. This criterion is the converse of MAXIMIN and selects the alternative with the largest payoff in the decision matrix as the optimal choice. This is a rose-colored-glasses criterion that supports the fond hope that the best will happen. In a practical sense, however, many of our corporations, in their early days, made business decisions using this criterion (explicitly or implicitly), seeking risk in a bold attempt to capture market share and achieve rapid growth. Many more companies failed than succeeded, of course, but those that did succeed would not have done so without accepting high levels of risk. In the BGC example, A_2: Three-Mile Island, Inc., would be the choice under the MAXIMAX criterion, with 60% capital appreciation resulting from a major expansion of the economy.

THE MINIMAX REGRET CRITERION

The MINIMAX Regret criterion, which was the brainchild of the eminent statistician and scientific philosopher Leonard Savage, is the most interesting and enigmatic of the DMUU decision criteria. It is similar to the EOL criterion in DMUR in that it deals with regrets, or opportunity losses, but it is subtly different as well. It is also one of the major points of controversy between the Bayesians and the classicists.

The risk characteristics of the MINIMAX Regret criterion are middle-of-the-road, approaching the risk neutrality of the EMV and EOL criteria in DMUR. To operationalize this criterion, a decision maker replaces the outcomes in the decision matrix with opportunity losses (or regrets) in exactly the same fashion as one does when using the EOL strategy. We then note the maximum regret, or opportunity loss, for each alternative, and the criterion selects as optimal the one with the minimum value.

Thus, like EOL, MINIMAX Regret tends to minimize the magnitude of a poor decision that we might otherwise make.

Philosophically, the MINIMAX Regret criterion has interesting overtones and implications. In terms of management styles, MAXIMIN is clearly a defensive strategy—one that business executives would attribute to a "fat-cat" or "don't rock the boat—business is OK and I retire in two years" syndrome. MAXIMAX, on the other hand, is clearly an offensive strategy—a "make it big, or bust" approach to decision making. But how do we characterize MINIMAX Regret in terms of management style? The criterion's use tends to avoid large losses but precludes large gains as well.

Returning to our portfolio example, Table 13.3 shows the regret matrix, and Table 13.4 gives the SAMS full briefing.

In this example, A_4: Texas Aggie Kerosene, Inc., has the minimum of the maximum regrets, or opportunity losses, and would be the optimal model choice using the MINIMAX Regret criterion. Note that A_4 does indeed tend to be a middle-of-the-road

TABLE 13.3 Regret matrix

	State of the Economy			
	Depression (S_1)	Recession (S_2)	Upward Cycle (S_3)	Major Expansion (S_4)
A_1: Don't Invest	5%	15%	10%	60%
A_2: Three-Mile Island, Inc.	45%	35%	0	0
A_3: Solar Energy of Boston	35%	25%	10%	30%
A_4: Texas Aggie Kerosene	15%	15%	5%	30%
A_5: NY City Firewood, Inc.	10%	10%	0	45%
A_6: Berkeley Power of California	0	0	20%	70%

TABLE 13.4 SAMS output for BGC—regrets

BGC FULL BRIEFING ON OPTIMAL MODEL SOLUTION			
Optimal Objective Value = 30.0			
Alternative	MAX REGRET	MIN	Optimal
DONT	60.0		No
3-MILE	45.0		No
SOLAR	35.0		No
TEXAGGIE	30.0	30.0	Yes
NYCITY	45.0		No
BERKELEY	70.0		No
OPTIMAL ALTERNATIVE IS: TEXAGGIE			

alternative in that its downside risk is moderate, as is its upside potential. Another way of describing this criterion is with Kenneth Arrow's [1] coined expression "satisficing." In terms of a human decision maker, the criterion captures the behavioral reaction of most people post facto upon learning the outcome of a decision already made. That is, use of the MINIMAX Regret criterion tends to minimize the magnitude of an error in judgment—in either direction.

We earlier referred to this decision criterion as enigmatic and noted that it was a major point of controversy between the two warring camps of statisticians and decision theorists. We will illustrate this point by adding one additional alternative to our decision matrix—a so-called countercyclical utility stock.

	S_1	S_2	S_3	S_4
A_7: Congressional Natural Gas	40%	20%	0	-15%

With the addition of A_7, the regret matrix changes drastically (see Table 13.5). After adding the new alternative to our original model, we reran the SAMS DMUU module and obtained the results in Table 13.6.

Note that by adding a nonoptimal alternative A_7 to the decision matrix, we have *changed the optimal model alternative from A_4: Texas Aggie Kerosene, Inc., to A_5: New York City Firewood, Inc.*! Bayesians cite this phenomenon as a fatal logical flaw in DMUU, noting that such a thing cannot happen in a DMUR context. But is it really a flaw? Classicists would argue that adding an alternative to a problem whose model solution we have already obtained in effect makes it a *completely different model* of the problem, with very different risk characteristics. This was most certainly the case in our portfolio example, when the minimum regret jumped from 30% to 45% when we added A_7.

The foregoing illustrates a critical point relative to decision theory models: the selection of alternatives, when the set of alternatives is not collectively exhaustive,

TABLE 13.5 New regret matrix

	State of the Economy			
	Depression (S_1)	Recession (S_2)	Upward Cycle (S_3)	Major Expansion (S_4)
A_1: Don't Invest	40%	20%	10%	60%
A_2: Three-Mile Island, Inc.	80%	40%	0	0
A_3: Solar Energy of Boston	70%	30%	10%	30%
A_4: Texas Aggie Kerosene	50%	20%	5%	30%
A_5: NY City Firewood, Inc.	45%	15%	0	45%
A_6: Berkeley Power of California	35%	5%	20%	70%
A_7: Congressional Natural Gas	0	0	10%	75%

TABLE 13.6 SAMS output for BGC—expanded

```
BGC—EXPANDED
FULL BRIEFING ON OPTIMAL MODEL SOLUTION
         Optimal Objective Value = 45.0
```

Alternative	MAX REGRET	MIN	Optimal
DONT	60.0		No
3-MILE	80.0		No
SOLAR	70.0		No
TEXAGGIE	50.0		No
NYCITY	**45.0**	**45.0**	**Yes**
BERKELEY	70.0		No
CONGRESS	75.0		No

OPTIMAL ALTERNATIVE IS: NYCITY

determines to a large extent the risk characteristics inherent in the model. Note here that we are talking about *relative risk* among the alternatives selected—not about absolute risk associated with individual alternatives. Six sharks in your swimming pool are not very risky as long as one alternative is to stay out of the water. Add one man-eating tiger on land, and the level of risk obviously escalates markedly.

THE INSUFFICIENT REASON CRITERION

The Marquis Pierre Simon de Laplace, a brilliant 18th-century French mathematician, was the father of our fourth and final DMUU criterion—the criterion of Insufficient Reason. Laplace argued that admitting you have no idea whatsoever about what underlying probability distribution governs the states of nature is equivalent to admitting that—as far as you know—the states are all equally likely to occur. Thus, if there are n states, this criterion involves assigning a probability of $1/n$ to each state and computing the expected values of the alternatives, the optimal model alternative being the one with the largest expected value. The key point is this: if you, the decision maker, don't feel comfortable about assigning equal probabilities to the states, you must know something about the state probabilities and should endeavor to estimate them and use a DMUR model! The logic is flawless; and, strangely enough, the Insufficient Reason criterion is the most subjective criterion of all, in a sense. It focuses directly on the decision maker and his or her personal knowledge about the problem and its environment.

To use the Insufficient Reason criterion, we don't actually need to assign the equal probabilities and compute expected values. We need merely to add the outcomes for each alternative across all states; the optimal model alternative is the one with the largest total. In our portfolio example, A_4: Texas Aggie Kerosene, Inc., and A_5: New York City Firewood, Inc., are tied for optimality in the model on this criterion.

What are the risk characteristics of the Insufficient Reason criterion? It is risk neutral—for the same reason the EMV and EOL criteria in DMUR are risk neutral for real outcomes.

DERIVING USEFUL SOLUTIONS

In our original portfolio example, note that if we knew in advance that S_1 or S_2 would occur, we would choose A_6: Berkeley Power of California. If we knew S_3 would happen, we would choose A_2: Three-Mile Island, Inc., or A_5: New York City Firewood, Inc.; and knowing S_4 would occur would lead to the choice of A_2. And yet, Ima's model selected A_1: Don't Invest, and MINIMAX Regret chose A_4: Texas Aggie Kerosene, Inc. Should we be surprised that this occurred? No—and the reason is simple. We don't know in advance which state of nature will occur, and DMUU criteria address that fact directly. In fact, the MINIMAX Regret criterion takes into account the interactions among alternatives across the states of nature.

RISK AND UTILITY

What role does the concept of economic utility play in a DMUU environment? Recall that in our discussion of DMUR in Chapter 7 we derived decision makers' utility functions and used expected utility (EU) in an attempt to incorporate the decision makers' risk characteristics. Could we do the same in DMUU? The answer is a resounding **NO**. DMUU criteria are based on attitude toward risk, so that using a utility transformation in addition would overkill the matter.

Let's be sure to understand, therefore, how we as decision makers might actually use DMUU models. First, of course, we must convince ourselves that we cannot estimate an acceptable prior probability distribution. Second, we must use great care in identifying our alternatives. Third, we must examine our risk situation carefully. If a large positive result will make an order of magnitude difference but the largest negative payoff would not be particularly damaging, we might wish to adopt the MAXIMAX criterion. If the converse is true, we should consider the MAXIMIN criterion. Finally, if we are risk neutral and wish to "satisfice," we might select the MINIMAX Regret or Insufficient Reason criterion.

STATE OF THE ART IN MODELING UNDER UNCERTAINTY

As a modeling device, DMUU is a closed subject. One interesting (but not productive) postoptimality procedure that we can perform is to determine the type of prior probability distribution that would have led to the same optimal alternative using DMUR. We illustrate this process with a small toy model:

	S_1	S_2
A_1	$-\$1,000$	$+\$1,500$
A_2	$+\$ 150$	$+\$ 300$

You can verify that the MAXIMIN criterion would select A_2, while the MAXIMAX, MINIMAX Regret, and Insufficient Reason criteria all would select A_1. Let p be $\Pr(S_1)$ and $(1 - p)$ be $\Pr(S_2)$. To find the value of p at which we would be indifferent between A_1 and A_2 in a DMUR sense, we equate $E[A_1] = E[A_2]$, or $-\$1,000p + \$1,500(1 - p) = \$150p + \$300(1 - p)$. The solution is: $p^* = 0.51$. For values larger than p^*, A_2 is optimal; for smaller values, A_1 is optimal.

What have we learned from this analysis? Not a great deal. However, our Bayesians cite such an analysis as evidence that we really used a probability distribution in our DMUR model anyway! We leave the reader to draw his or her own conclusions.

MINICASES

Apteryx Aircraft Company

THE SCENARIO

Turner Round, the newly installed CEO of Apteryx Aircraft Company (AAC), sat in his office one morning and gazed morosely at the report of the company's miserable ten-year financial history. The board of directors had brought in Turner, one of the best "firemen" in American industry, to purge deadwood and restore the company to profitability. Two more years under previous management would have made the firm as extinct as its namesake. This one, Turner mused, was a lulu.

The firm's founder, a World War I pilot named Doug Fite, had made countless errors in judgment during his years as CEO. For example, he became convinced in the mid-1940s that the jet engine was merely a passing fad and constructed the world's largest plant for building huge propeller engines for commercial aircraft. Apteryx later converted the plant into a ceiling-fan factory, but the damage was done. At the heart of AAC's problems, Turner concluded, was a total absence of planning.

THE PROBLEM

One does not mend an ailing aircraft manufacturing company overnight, since new product planning cycles sometimes run as long as 20 years from concept to rollout. Turner's first major project, therefore, was to assemble a staff of bright young executives (mostly MBAs) with long-range planning skills and begin to look at the aviation picture two decades into the future. Turner assembled such a team, and he landed Lance Steele (lured away from Boeing Aircraft Company) to head it.

"What we're going to do in the next six months," said Lance to his assembled hotshots, "is to look hard at the future and help Turner Round get this crummy outfit back into the ball game. Any suggestions?"

THE MODEL

Emma Bright spoke up immediately.

"I got my MBA at Stanback U., and they're very big on decision theory out there. Maybe we could come up with scenarios for the future of the aircraft—both civil and military—and these would be our states of nature. Then, using our collective experience in the aircraft industry, we could develop some decision alternatives. Although it will be tough, we can then estimate the outcomes associated with each alternative/state combination. So far, so good. The difficult part will be coming up with a reasonable probability distribution on the states of nature. My prof at Stanback says it can always be done, so I guess we'll just have to cross that bridge when we come to it."

The group agreed with Emma's proposal, and the 12-hour workdays of research, discussions, and analysis began. After three arduous months, the group had reached consensus on the following states of nature for their model for the year 2010:

S_1: The aviation situation will remain essentially unchanged.
S_2: Wide-bodied, fuel-efficient passenger and cargo planes will have completely replaced the current generation of aircraft, and operations in space will have made military fighting aircraft obsolete.
S_3: A completely new form of power will have made fossil-fueled aircraft engines obsolete. Airplanes may even look completely different than they do now—perhaps wingless, spherical, or saucer-shaped.
S_4: Except for a few hobbyists, the age of aerodynamics will have passed, and some form of rocket travel will have replaced it.
S_5: There will be no air or space travel; lightning-fast vehicles will travel in underground tubes—possibly suspended.
S_6: The world will have undergone nuclear war, and survivors will travel solely by people-powered vehicles like bicycles and skateboards. The military will be equipped with armored bicycles and bows and arrows.

Two months later, Lance's group had generated some alternatives.

A_1: Retain the status quo, except for more careful cost control and more aggressive marketing efforts.
A_2: Use most available capital to build and modernize production facilities, concentrating on proven technology.
A_3: Use approximately 50% of available capital for production facilities and invest the remainder in building a research and development capability.
A_4: All but abandon maintenance of a production capability and concentrate most available funds on high-technology research and development.
A_5: Get out of the transportation business and find some less risky niche in industry.

With six states of nature and five alternatives identified, the group turned to the difficult task of quantifying the 30 outcomes in their decision matrix. They abandoned the idea of trying to state outcomes in dollars of profit, since there were so many imponderables associated with such an effort. They decided eventually to express outcomes as dimensionless quantities ranging from -20 to $+20$ and to use a modified form of the DELPHI technique to achieve convergence of opinion. One month later—after six months had elapsed—the group produced a decision matrix (see Table 13.7), noting that none of the five alternatives is dominated.

SOLUTION TO THE MODEL

"Well," noted Emma, "now comes the hard part—estimating a prior probability distribution on the states of nature."

TABLE 13.7 Apteryx decision matrix

	States of Nature					
	S_1	S_2	S_3	S_4	S_5	S_6
A_1	+10	−5	−10	−15	−20	+12
A_2	+18	+12	−15	−18	−20	+8
A_3	0	+6	+10	+5	−4	0
A_4	−10	0	+20	+13	+18	−12
A_5	−5	−10	+8	+16	+20	+10

"Not so fast, Emma," retorted Lance. "I've thought about that quite a bit—I have no idea how we'd go about doing such a thing. Besides—I don't care what your prof at Stanback says. We can tackle this as a decision making under uncertainty situation and use one of the classical DMUU criteria to analyze our model."

"I never heard of DMUU," replied Emma, "but I'm game if the rest of the group is. How do we proceed?"

Lance and the group set up a meeting with Turner Round the next day. Turner was pleased with the model the group had generated, but the group then asked Turner to explicitly express his view of Apteryx's risk environment.

"That's a tough one, gang," said Turner. "AAC isn't in good enough financial shape to aggressively seek risk, but if we manage the company like pussycats, we'll never get it back into the ball game. I guess I'd conclude that we're in a satisficing situation right now. We may have to forego the opportunity for a big breakthrough to avoid a disastrous loss. Can the group work with that description?"

"You bet we can, Turner," said Lance. "What you've just described is a classic situation in which the use of Leonard Savage's MINIMAX Regret criterion is applicable. Let's analyze our model with SAMS' DMUU module and get back to you."

Figure 13.2 shows the SAMS input screen, and Table 13.8 gives the SAMS full briefing for Apteryx.

SOLUTION TO THE PROBLEM

The group showed the model solution to Turner. After studying the model solution, Turner commented as follows:

"The model suggests getting out of the transportation business (A_5) or splitting our capital investment about equally between production facilities and an R&D capability (A_3). The second alternative isn't very exciting, but it makes good business sense, I suppose. What if I gave you a sixth alternative—could you stick it on the bottom of the model for me?"

"We could, Turner," replied Lance, "but it would be an entirely different model then. What the current model told you would no longer count."

"I understand," said Turner. "I was just teasing. You and your people put in a tremendous amount of effort on this venture, and I want you to

FIGURE 13.2
SAMS input screen for Apteryx

```
     ──▶ SAMS INPUT SCREEN - DMUU Matrix Module         ◀──
    ┌─────────────────────────────────────────────────────┐
    │ NAME?  APTERYX                                      │
    │ DMUU CRITERION?  MINIMAX REGRET                     │
    │ PROBLEM DESCRIPTION - Analyze Apteryx Aircraft's planning │
    │                      problem under uncertainty.     │
    ├─────────────────────────────────────────────────────┤
    │ States        S1     S2     S3     S4     S5     S6 │
    │ Prior Dist.  .167   .166   .167   .166   .167   .166│
    ├─────────────────────────────────────────────────────┤
    │ Alternatives              Outcomes                  │
    │                                                     │
    │ A1            10.    -5.   -10.   -15.   -20.    12.│
    │ A2            18.    12.   -15.   -18.   -20.     8.│
    │ A3             0.     6.    10.     5.    -4.     0.│
    │ A4           -10.     0.    20.    13.    18.   -12.│
    │ A5            -5.   -10.     8.    16.    20.    10.│
    └─────────────────────────────────────────────────────┘
```

TABLE 13.8 SAMS Output for APTERYX

APTERYX
FULL BRIEFING ON OPTIMAL MODEL SOLUTION
            Optimal Objective Value = 23.0

Alternative	MAX REGRET	MIN	Optimal
A1	40.0		No
A2	40.0		No
A3	24.0		No
A4	28.0		No
A5	23.0	23.0	Yes

OPTIMAL ALTERNATIVE IS: A5

know how helpful your model is in sharpening my thinking. I'll take the proposal to the board at their regular meeting Tuesday and sell them on the idea of splitting our effort about equally between production and R&D. I think they'll go for it. By the way, I'm also proposing the new position of Vice President for Planning, and I've already got someone in mind." ■

D-Day Revisited [2]

THE SCENARIO

Let's return to the "D-Day" minicase from Chapter 7 and rethink this analysis from a different perspective. Recall that General Eisenhower and the Allied High Command

CHAPTER 13 CLASSICAL DECISION MODELS UNDER UNCERTAINTY

were planning the invasion of continental Europe, since without it, World War II could drag on for many years. The code name for the invasion was "Operation Overlord."

THE PROBLEM

Both the Allies and the Nazis knew that the invasion would be an amphibious assault somewhere along the coast of France in the summer of 1944. A myriad of invasion sites was possible, but the Allies narrowed their choices to four:

A_1: Normandy
A_2: Calais
A_3: Cherbourg
A_4: Le Havre

THE MODEL

Assuming that the German High Command deduced these four choices, its decision—which site to defend—generates four states of nature:

S_1: Defend Normandy
S_2: Defend Calais
S_3: Defend Cherbourg
S_4: Defend Le Havre

In the original DMUR analysis, we inferred a prior probability distribution on the four states of nature by assessing intelligence data available to the Allied High Command. We inferred, for example, that the Allies knew that "the German High Command favored defending Calais over Normandy by a 2:1 ratio" and that "the Nazis would more likely defend Le Havre than Normandy." These and other inferences produced the following prior distribution on the states of nature:

$\Pr(S_1) = 0.20 \quad \Pr(S_2) = 0.40 \quad \Pr(S_3) = 0.15 \quad \Pr(S_4) = 0.25$

What if these "inferences" were—instead of the product of careful intelligence gathering—the result of counterintelligence by the Nazi High Command? If this had been the case (we are fervently thankful that it was not), using a DMUR model as a decision aid would have played into the hands of Hitler.

Recall that the outcomes in this decision matrix are the excess of German casualties over Allied casualties resulting from the invasion. The following table reproduces the original decision matrix—without the inferred prior probability distribution:

	S_1	S_2	S_3	S_4
A_1	−137,000	175,000	93,000	65,000
A_2	145,000	−170,000	196,000	38,000
A_3	40,000	106,000	−170,000	62,000
A_4	30,000	72,000	105,000	−110,000

SOLUTION TO THE MODEL

To proceed with a DMUU analysis of this model, we would normally require the decision maker to assess his or her attitude toward risk before selecting one of the four DMUU criteria with which to perform the analysis. But the successful invasion at Normandy is history, and General Eisenhower has long since died. Therefore, let us do something that we would NEVER do in analyzing a prospective problem—investigate the model's recommendations in each of the four cases.

Table 13.9 displays the full briefing of the SAMS DMUU module for D-Day, adding our analysis of runners-up. Figure 13.3 on p. 460 shows the SAMS input screen for D-Day.

The MAXIMIN criterion is appropriate when the decision maker is highly risk averse in the situation being modeled. Successful military leaders are not usually noted for their aversion to risk.

The clear choice of the MAXIMIN criterion is to invade at Le Havre, with invasion at Normandy a reasonably close second. We would interpret this result in the following way. General Eisenhower is a pessimist, fully expecting the German High Command to know in advance the site of the invasion. Therefore, he would decide to invade the site at which *his defeat was least costly!* Such a result might make sense to a decision theorist, but certainly not to a five-star general.

The MAXIMAX criterion represents an aggressive, risk-seeking, highly optimistic approach to problem solving. With differential casualties of 196,000 at Calais, MAXIMAX selects this site as the preferred alternative, with Normandy second choice. But an examination of the four alternatives reveals that Calais is by far the most risky of the four—as we would expect. It implicitly embraces the outmoded and inhumane concept of soldiers and sailors and airmen as cannon fodder; that is, it strives for maximum *differential* casualties regardless of the cost. We cannot stretch our imagination far enough to picture Dwight D. Eisenhower with such a mind-set.

MINIMAX Regret is a satisficing criterion—protecting the decision maker against heavy losses while diminishing his or her prospects of spectacular gains. This criterion selects Le Havre as a clear choice for a "satisficer," with invasion at Normandy second. Thus, our satisficing criterion in this case coincides with the MAXIMIN recommendation.

Finally, Laplace's criterion of Insufficient Reason is approximately risk neutral in its approach. The Insufficient Reason criterion selects Calais as its preferred alternative, but in this case the runner-up Normandy is very close to being in contention, with the other two choices performing very poorly.

Recall from the original minicase in Chapter 7 that Normandy was the clear choice of the DMUR matrix model as the invasion site, while Calais was the worst selection.

SOLUTION TO THE PROBLEM

What have we learned from this analysis? On the surface, it appears that the DMUR and DMUU models give conflicting recommendations. Our DMUU analysis recommends Le Havre for both the MAXIMIN (risk-averse) and the MINIMAX Regret (satisficing) decision maker, while it recommends Calais for the MAXIMAX (risk-seeking) and the Insufficient Reason (risk-neutral) decision maker. Note, however, that Normandy is second choice on *all four* criteria! Might we perhaps conclude that an invasion at the beaches of Normandy is a solid alternative under a wide variety of

TABLE 13.9 SAMS output for D-Day

D-DAY
FULL BRIEFING ON OPTIMAL MODEL SOLUTION

MAXIMIN

Optimal Objective Value = −110000.0

Alternative	MINIMUM	MAX	Optimal
NORMANDY	−137000.0		No
CALAIS	−170000.0		No
CHERBOUR	−170000.0		No
LEHAVRE	−110000.0	−110000.0	Yes

OPTIMAL ALTERNATIVE IS: LEHAVRE

MAXIMAX

Optimal Objective Value = 196000.0

Alternative	MAXIMUM	MAX	Optimal
NORMANDY	175000.0		No
CALAIS	196000.0	196000.0	Yes
CHERBOUR	106000.0		No
LEHAVRE	105000.0		No

OPTIMAL ALTERNATIVE IS: CALAIS

MINIMAX Regret

Optimal Objective Value = 175000.0

Alternative	MAX REGRET	MIN	Optimal
NORMANDY	282000.0		No
CALAIS	345000.0		No
CHERBOUR	366000.0		No
LEHAVRE	175000.0	175000.0	Yes

OPTIMAL ALTERNATIVE IS: LEHAVRE

Insufficient Reason

Optimal Objective Value = 52250.0

Alternative	EMV	MAX	Optimal
NORMANDY	49000.0		No
CALAIS	52250.0	52250.0	Yes
CHERBOUR	9500.0		No
LEHAVRE	24250.0		No

OPTIMAL ALTERNATIVE IS: CALAIS

Aggregate Summary

Criterion	First Choice	Second Choice
MAXIMIN	LEHAVRE	NORMANDY
MAXIMAX	CALAIS	NORMANDY
MINIMAX REGRET	LEHAVRE	NORMANDY
EQUALLY LIKELY	CALAIS	NORMANDY

FIGURE 13.3
SAMS input screen for D-Day

```
     ▶ SAMS INPUT SCREEN - DMUU Matrix Module        ◀
   NAME?  D-DAY
   DMUU CRITERION?    ALL
   PROBLEM DESCRIPTION - Analyze D-DAY minicase using all
                        four DMUU criteria.
```

States	NORMANDY	CALAIS	CHERBOUR	LEHAVRE
Prior Dist.	.25	.25	.25	.25
Alternatives		Outcomes		
NORMANDY	-137000	175000	93000	65000
CALAIS	145000	-170000	196000	38000
CHERBOUR	40000	106000	-170000	62000
LEHAVRE	30000	72000	105000	-110000

conditions—and maybe even the wisest choice given the very high stakes involved? Can you even *imagine* relegating a decision of this magnitude and importance to the history of humankind, completely to a management science model?

On June 6, 1944 (D-Day), the Allies deployed 156,000 men, 5,000 ships, and 11,000 planes in the initial assault on Normandy. Because the German High Command had concentrated its defenses to protect Calais, there were only 9,000 casualties in the initial assault. By the end of the battle for Normandy, more than two million American, British, Canadian, and Polish troops had disembarked in Normandy at beaches code named Utah, Omaha, Gold, Juno, and Sword. The drive from Normandy into the German heartland ended the war in Europe.

SUMMARY

We reviewed a model or structure for decision making under uncertainty (DMUU), in which it is not possible to estimate a satisfactory probability distribution on the states of nature. We looked at four classical criteria that researchers have suggested for such a model: MAXIMIN, MAXIMAX, MINIMAX Regret, and Insufficient Reason.

We characterized MAXIMIN and MAXIMAX as risk averse and risk seeking, respectively, whereas MINIMAX Regret and Insufficient Reason were more middle-of-the-road or "satisficing" criteria. We noted that each of these criteria have built-in risk characteristics, so that using the utility transformation in DMUU is unwarranted.

Finally, we illustrated the process of building and analyzing a DMUU model with the "Apteryx Aircraft Company" minicase and by revisiting the "D-Day" minicase from Chapter 7.

PROBLEMS FOR ANALYSIS

1. One approach that some suggest for "forcing" the construction of a prior probability distribution on the states of nature is rank ordering the states from least likely to most likely to occur. If there are n states, let

$$S = \sum_{i=1}^{n} i = \frac{n(n+1)}{2}$$

We then assign the probability 1/S to the least likely state, 2/S to the next, and so on, with the most likely state getting a probability of n/S assigned.

    a. What do you think about this scheme? Would you be likely to use it to avoid the use of DMUU criteria?

    b. Try out this approach using your own personal feel for the relative likelihood of the six states in the "Apteryx" minicase and compute the EMV of the five alternatives. Note that there are 6! = 720 different orderings possible for the six states. You might also wish to verify that the most favorable distribution for A_3 (i.e., highest probability for largest outcome, etc.) does not lead to A_3 having the highest EMV!

2. In the "Apteryx" minicase, remove alternative A_2 from the decision matrix and recompute the regret matrix. Note now that A_5 is clearly the optimal choice and A_3 and A_4 are tied for second place.

    a. How do you explain this phenomenon in terms of the riskiness of the two models (one with A_2 included and one with A_2 excluded)?

    b. Would you ever actually do such a thing when using a DMUU model?

3. Recall the "Jack Legg Associates" minicase from Chapter 7 in which Hy Roller and Nawonda Betts were attempting to decide on one of three salary plans. We used a binomial distribution representing relative frequency of success in project management as a prior distribution for an analysis in DMUR. Table 13.10 reproduces the decision matrix (without the prior distribution).

TABLE 13.10 Decision matrix

	No. of Successful Projects			
	S_1: 0	S_2: 1	S_3: 2	S_4: 3
A_1: Plan A	$35,000	$35,000	$35,000	$35,000
A_2: Plan B	$21,000	$35,000	$42,000	$49,000
A_3: Plan C	$7,000	$28,000	$42,000	$70,000

Because Hy was clearly a risk seeker and Nawonda clearly a risk avoider, they sought help to construct their utility functions. On the basis of expected utility, subsequently, Hy's model clearly indicated his preference for A_3, while Nawonda's tended toward A_1 or A_2.

    a. In analyzing this problem with a DMUU model, compute the optimal model alternatives using MAXIMAX and MAXIMIN. Note how clear the choices are in both cases.

    b. Now analyze the model using the two satisficing criteria—MINIMAX Regret and Insufficient Reason—and compare the results. Note that MINIMAX Regret distinguishes the middle-of-the-road alternative nicely, but Laplace's criterion does not. Can you explain why this is so?

4. **The Scenario:** Our MBA student from Chapter 7 is startled to learn in his Friday classes that there will be a major exam the following Monday in both his finance and marketing classes. He had been putting off studying so far, so it looked like a long, arduous weekend.

The Problem: He was doing B+ work so far in his marketing class but was flirting with disaster in finance class. How should he allocate the meager study time available between the two subjects? If he knew whether the profs would give hard or easy exams, he could tackle the problem directly. But both profs were brand-new Ph.D.s in their first semester of teaching here, so the MBA students don't have a line on them yet. The situation looked grim.

The Model: As a last resort, he decided to see whether any of that stuff he had in his M.S. course last semester would help him. Since the problem didn't look even vaguely like math programming, he discarded that idea. It just might be a DMUR type of problem, but how could he possibly estimate a probability distribution on the testing proclivities of two brand-new professors? He finally settled on DMUU and built a decision matrix (see Table 13.11). Note that he couldn't really quantify the outcomes, so he used a system of pluses (good) and minuses (bad), with 0 for neutral.

TABLE 13.11 MBA student's decision matrix

	Possible Testing Outcomes			
	S_1: Both easy	S_2: Mktg hard, Fin easy	S_3: Mktg easy, Fin hard	S_4: Both hard
A_1: Study only marketing	+	+ +	−	+
A_2: Study both equally	+ +	+ + +	+	0
A_3: Study only finance	+ +	− −	+ + +	+
A_4: Relax, get lucky	+	− −	− −	− − −

Solution to the Model:
a. Are any of the alternatives dominated in this decision matrix?
b. If our MBA student were highly risk seeking, what two alternatives would catch his fancy?
c. If he decided that he was highly risk averse, what alternative might he choose using the MAXIMIN criterion? (*Hint:* Replace "---" by "1," "--" by "2," etc., to perform the analysis.)
d. If he wished to "satisfice" and decided to use the MINIMAX Regret criterion, what would the optimal model alternative be?

Solution to the Problem: Despite the preceding analysis, our MBA student chose alternative 4: relax, get lucky. Unfortunately, S_4 occurred, and Lee is currently working toward a second undergraduate degree in high fashion merchandising.

a. Was he allowed to choose an alternative other than the optimal one indicated by the model? Who does he think he is—ignoring the results of his analysis in making his final decision?
b. **MODELS DON'T MAKE DECISIONS—MANAGERS DO.** (But sometimes they make fairly poor ones!)

PRACTICE MODELS

1. Use a package like the SAMS DMUU module to determine the best decision alternative for the following if the decision maker is roughly risk neutral:

   Alternative A = Invest in portfolio I

   Alternative B = Invest in portfolio II

Alternative C = Invest in portfolio III

Alternative D = Invest in portfolio IV

Alternative E = Do not invest

S_1 = Interest rates rise

S_2 = Interest rates do not change

S_3 = Interest rates decline

TABLE 13.12 Payoff = Profit estimate (in $000)

Alternatives	States of Nature		
	S_1	S_2	S_3
A	100	60	20
B	70	110	40
C	80	50	−10
D	−20	30	90
E	0	0	0

2. A high-tech firm is considering four bidding options for a government defense contract. Use a package like the SAMS DMUU module to determine the best course of action if the company is risk seeking. As a conservative backup, determine which alternative is preferred if the firm is in a satisficing mode.

Alternative 1 = Bid $10 million

Alternative 2 = Bid $ 8 million

Alternative 3 = Bid $ 7 million

Alternative 4 = Do not bid

S_1 = $10 million is the lowest bid

S_2 = $ 8 million is the lowest bid

S_3 = $ 7 million is the lowest bid

TABLE 13.13 Payoff = Net profit (in $000)

Alternatives	States of Nature		
	S_1	S_2	S_3
1	2,000	−200	−200
2	1,700	1,700	−200
3	1,500	1,500	1,500
4	0	0	0

3. Use a package like SAMS and its DMUU module to choose the best decision alternative for the following under conditions of risk aversion.

   Alternative A = Build a new manufacturing facility in Eastern Europe

   Alternative B = Expand the U.S. facility and export to Eastern Europe

   Alternative C = Take no action

   S_1 = Political climate in Eastern Europe will improve

   S_2 = Political climate in Eastern Europe will remain the same

   S_3 = Political climate in Eastern Europe will worsen

TABLE 13.14 Payoff = Net profit per year (in $ million)

	States of Nature		
Alternatives	S_1	S_2	S_3
A	200	130	−150
B	285	50	−50
C	0	0	0

REFERENCES AND ADDITIONAL READING

1. Arrow, K. "Decision Theory and Operations Research." *Operations Research* 5 (1957): 765–774.
2. Bean, Casey. Adapted from an unpublished MBA term project report, Texas Tech University (1986).
3. Brown, R., A. Kahr, and C. Peterson. *Decision Analysis for the Manager.* New York: Holt, Rinehart and Winston, 1974.
4. Hartley, H. O. Class notes, Texas A&M University Institute of Statistics (1970).
5. LaValle, I. *Fundamentals of Decision Analysis.* New York: Holt, Rinehart and Winston, 1978.
6. Sampson, D. *Managerial Decision Analysis.* Homewood, Ill.: Richard E. Irwin, 1988.
7. Von Neumann, J., and O. Morgenstern. *The Theory of Games and Economic Behavior* (2d ed.). Princeton, N.J.: Princeton University Press, 1953.

CHAPTER 14

Modeling with Multiple Objectives

So far, all of the optimizing models we've discussed have involved optimizing a single function of the decision variables (the objective function). Although we have continually stressed that most managers have more than one objective in a given decision situation, our approach has been to handle secondary objectives outside the model itself. Only in Chapter 2 with Marijane Moss in Problem 2 did we attempt to touch on the possibility that we might accommodate multiple objectives within the model itself. For example, we might be seeking higher productivity but with fewer personnel or a larger market share with a smaller advertising budget or a lower budget deficit with a lower tax bracket and fewer tax auditors.

Lest we promise more than we can deliver, we observe that since so-called multicriterion programming is still in its infancy, its applicability at present is limited to a somewhat restricted set of decision scenarios. For example, what follows addresses ways to incorporate into models the subset of a manager's objectives that are clearly quantifiable, such as profit margins, cost levels, and market share. The truth is that many times, factors that we don't yet know how to quantify satisfactorily—such as employee morale, corporate social responsibility, politics, and ethical/moral issues—are the real "drivers" of the problem.

There have been some rather large books written on the subject of modeling with multiple objectives. To make our one-chapter treatment of this subject manageable and useful, we limit our attention to the smaller but highly important subject of **multiple objective linear programming** (MOLP). To be precise, we restrict our discussion to problems that we can profitably model and analyze by LP, except that the objective function is a set of linear functions and some specified relationship among them.

UNDERLYING ASSUMPTIONS

As in Chapter 2, we require here that the assumptions of additivity and divisibility hold and that we are dealing with a nonprobabilistic scenario. The chapter addresses two very different decision situations: (1) we can state the multiple objectives in commensurable quantities, and (2) we can state two or more of the objectives only in incommensurable quantities. We discuss each below, after defining some mathematical notation.

MATRIX-VECTOR NOTATION

In previous chapters, we used the Σ (upper case sigma) notation to represent linear functions. In attempting to deal with an objective function that turns out to be a *set* of linear functions, however, this notation is unwieldy. We thus resort to the more compact abstract matrix-vector notation. We define the **n**-vector **x** as the column

$$\mathbf{x} = \begin{bmatrix} x_1 \\ x_2 \\ \vdots \\ x_n \end{bmatrix} \quad (14.1)$$

The associated row vector **x′** (read "x-transpose") is merely

$$\mathbf{x}' = (x_1, x_2, \ldots, x_n) \quad (14.2)$$

The product of the row-vector $\mathbf{c}' = (c_1, c_2, \ldots, c_n)$ and the column vector **x** is

$$\mathbf{c}'\mathbf{x} = c_1 x_1 + c_2 x_2 + \ldots + c_n x_n, \quad (14.3)$$

by definition, which we see is identical to

$$\sum_{j=1}^{n} c_j x_j,$$

our LP objective function from Chapter 2.

We define the matrix **A** with m rows and n columns in the usual way:

$$\mathbf{A} = \begin{bmatrix} a_{11} & a_{12} & \ldots & a_{1j} & \ldots & a_{1n} \\ a_{21} & a_{22} & \ldots & a_{2j} & \ldots & a_{2n} \\ \vdots & \vdots & & \vdots & & \vdots \\ a_{i1} & a_{i2} & \ldots & a_{ij} & \ldots & a_{in} \\ \vdots & \vdots & & \vdots & & \vdots \\ a_{m1} & a_{m2} & \ldots & a_{mj} & \ldots & a_{mn} \end{bmatrix} \quad (14.4)$$

If **b** is the column vector of constants on the right-hand sides of the LP constraints and **A** is the matrix of constraint coefficients, we may write the LP model as follows:

MAX $x_0 = \mathbf{c}'\mathbf{x}$ \quad (14.5)

S T: \quad $\mathbf{Ax} \leq \mathbf{b}$ \quad (14.6)

Note that this is just another way of writing Equations (1.3) and (1.4) from Chapter 1.

Finally, suppose that we have K linear objective functions in our multiple objective set. Using $f(\cdot)$ as the notation for "is a function of," we write the MOLP model as follows:

MIN or MAX $x_0 = f\{\mathbf{c}_1'\mathbf{x}, \mathbf{c}_2'\mathbf{x}, \ldots, \mathbf{c}_k'\mathbf{x}, \ldots, \mathbf{c}_K'\mathbf{x}\}$ \quad (14.7)

S T: \quad $\mathbf{Ax} \left\{ \begin{matrix} \leq \\ = \\ \geq \end{matrix} \right\} \mathbf{b}$ \quad (14.8)

The function f expresses some relationship among the K linear objective functions. For example, if $K = 1$ and f is the identity function, we have the single objective LP model Equations (14.5) to (14.6). We will look at other forms that f can assume later in this chapter.

Let us now investigate the two distinct forms that MOLP models can take.

COMMENSURABLE FUNCTIONS

If each of the $c_k'x$, $k = 1, \ldots, K$, are in the same dimensional units, we have a model with commensurable linear objective functions. For example, suppose we are trying to model a classical product mix problem with LP but discover to our chagrin that the profit contributions (c_j) for the products are functions of the unknown condition of the economy six months hence, when our products will be on sale in retail outlets. Given one of three possible states of the economy, we can estimate with fair accuracy the profit contributions of each product, but we don't know which state will actually occur. Thus, we have three different objective functions—all in the same units (dollars of total profit contribution).

As another example, recall Problem 2 in Chapter 2, in which the Daley Paper Company wished to minimize trim loss in cutting large rolls of paper into smaller rolls to fill orders. The problem hinted that the objective was to slit the large rolls using specific cutting patterns in such a way as to minimize end-trim-loss (i.e., rolls that are smaller in width than the smallest order width). However, such an approach may well result in overproducing (above order sizes) some of the order-width rolls. If we wish to minimize both end-trim-loss *and* overproduction of order-width rolls, we can state these two objectives in commensurable quantities—inch-rolls of paper.

MOLP models with commensurable objectives give the decision maker a great deal of flexibility in shaping the model to his or her personal inclinations and proclivities. Incommensurable objectives, on the other hand, are much more rigid and difficult to deal with.

INCOMMENSU- RABLE FUNCTIONS

In the real world of business and public sector decision making, executives have multiple goals or objectives for their organizations. In a hard goods manufacturing firm, for example, the objectives of the CEO for the coming fiscal year might be to achieve a return on investment of 18%, reduce inventory by 20%, eliminate the use of overtime, reduce short-term borrowing by 30%, and increase market share from 20% to 25%. If the CEO somehow could impose these goals as binding constraints in the corporate LP model, the computerized SIMPLEX algorithm would most certainly return the dismaying result: NO FEASIBLE SOLUTION. The alternative, of course, is to model these goals as multiple objectives with MOLP. In this case, these objectives are clearly incommensurable (i.e., percentage of capital invested, percentage of inventory reduction, person-hours of overtime, dollars of short-term loans, percentage of market share).

A second example also illustrates the incommensurability phenomenon. Sang Lee [6] reported an actual application of MOLP modeling and analysis in a health care clinic budgeting problem. Some of the objective areas and their dimensional units are in Table 14.1. Clearly, these objectives cannot be measured in the same dimensional units.

Let us now examine some modeling techniques that managers have used for both types of MOLP models.

TABLE 14.1

Objective Area	Units
1. Hourly pay rates for ten types of employees	$/hour (operations)
2. Retirement fund	% of total salary
3. New equipment	$ (capital)
4. Staffing patterns	Numbers of employees
5. Expense by type of medical service	$/patient charged

MOLP MODELING

In dealing with both commensurable and incommensurable MOLP objective sets, we note at the outset that we can use all of the techniques that we will discuss to model problems with commensurable objective sets. However, only a subset of these techniques is applicable to incommensurable scenarios. For this reason, we first discuss two approaches that require commensurability (MAXIMIN and linear combinations) and then two that do not require commensurability (preemptive goal prioritization and preemptive goal programming).

MOLP MODELS REQUIRING COMMENSURABILITY

As we noted, several MOLP modeling approaches require that each of the $c_k'x$, $k = 1, \ldots, K$, have the same dimensional units. We use the following scenario from Eastern Europe to illustrate two possible approaches.

SOLIDARITY SAUSAGE COMPANY

The Scenario: Wladislav (Wiz) Wisniewski had watched with great anticipation as Lech Walesa's Solidarity Party made life increasingly uncomfortable for the bureaucrats of Poland's Communist Party. Then, when Mikhail Gorbachev's *perestroika* emerged as a real possibility for change in Eastern Europe, Wiz got busy in earnest. He and his close friends Tadeusz (Tad) Kosciuszko and Nadia (Kaz) Kaszimierski began scraping together every zloty they could get their hands on to buy sausage casings, spices, and pork and beef futures. Wiz's family had been master sausage makers before World War II, and Wiz still had their secret recipes for knockwurst, bratwurst, kielbasa, and Polish frankfurters. Under the communist regime, entrepreneurship was impossible, so Wiz hadn't made his delicious sausages for sale in years.

Since working-class Poles had subsisted largely on black bread and bean soup for a long time, Wiz knew that he and his friends could sell all of the delicious sausage that they could produce. If they charged affordable prices and plowed the profits back into the business, perhaps they could succeed in founding one of Poland's first capitalistic ventures in the new age. Thus, at 4:00 a.m. on the cold morning in February when permits to incorporate became available, Wiz, Tad, and Kaz were first in line. And by noon, the Solidarity Sausage Company (SSC) was born.

None of the three principals had experience in managing a business organization, but Tad had once served as commissar of a small pig farm. Thus, by consensus, Tad became general manager of SSC. Kaz had an outgoing, friendly personality and knew practically every worker in that part of Warsaw, so she was appointed sales manager.

Wiz, of course, insisted that he be production manager, since the secret sausage recipes had been in his family for many generations.

Like all Poles, these three were weary of being governed by a communist system, so they heartily agreed that their new company would be run as a democracy—the majority would rule. Their first personnel decision was to hire Stanislaus (Wojo) Wojiechowski, an accountant with an American MBA degree, to look after the company's financial matters.

The Problem: The principals sat expectantly around the small table in Wiz's basement, which was to be both the business office and the initial production facility for SSC, waiting for Wojo to begin his report.

> "OK, guys," Wojo began. "You have managed to amass 175,000 zlotys to capitalize your nascent firm. I've committed 165,000 zlotys to buy 30,000 kilos of beef and 20,000 kilos of pork. I took an inventory, and you've already acquired 18 kilograms of spices. The way I figure it, Wiz and Tad can man the production line to stuff sausages while Kaz beats the bushes for sales prospects. Meanwhile, I'll take care of business. Any questions?"

After a moment of stunned silence, the three principals exchanged glances, and Wiz spoke.

> "Not quite so fast, Wojo," retorted Wiz sternly. "We're getting the ox before the cart. We can make four kinds of sausage for sale to our people, but how much do we make of each kind? We want to make a modest profit to reinvest in the business, but how do we price our products? And you don't even know how much beef, pork, and spice mix go into each sausage, and you've already ordered the beef and pork! And you didn't consult us before taking this action."

Wojo's eyes rolled upward in exasperation, and he replied in a patronizing tone.

> "Well excuse me, Chief. I didn't realize that you three wanted to get involved in the nitty-gritty details of pricing and product mix. I found some old scraps of paper in your safe, and I assumed that they were the recipes. You had bought options for 30,000 kilos of beef and 20,000 kilos of pork, so I merely exercised them and bought the carcasses at a good price of 165,000 zlotys. That leaves 10,000 zlotys to cover the state value-added tax. Then, I personally took an inventory of your woodshed and found 75,000 casings you had hoarded.
>
> "On the pricing, I did an informal market survey to see what the market would bear for each product. Then I subtracted the cost of the ingredients and got the profit contributions for each type of sausage. If you insist, here's a matrix (Table 14.2) that gives all of the relevant data. I'll attempt to explain anything you are unable to comprehend."

Wiz, Tad, and Kaz pored intently over the matrix for several minutes without speaking while Wojo impatiently twiddled his thumbs. Then Wiz spoke hesitantly.

> "Well, Wojo got the recipes right, and he made an accurate inventory of the casings," said Wiz. "I didn't know about the state value-added tax, but Wojo is an MBA and is familiar with such things. The only problem I have is with Wojo's profit contributions. I did some research on prewar sales, and I came up with the following numbers."

TABLE 14.2 SSC Sausage Production Data

	Knockwurst	Bratwurst	Kielbasa	Polish Franks
Variable	X1	X2	X3	X4
Description	Firm, full flavored	Bland, chewy	All pork, spicy	Good with Grey Poupon
Profit Contr. (zlotys/crate)	125	150	225	75
Beef (kilos/crate)	40	30	0	25
Pork (kilos/crate)	20	40	120	5
Spice (grams/crate)	60	50	150	10
Casings (#/crate)	75	85	90	100
Taxes (zlotys/crate)	20	24	30	10

Wiz's Profit Contributions

	Knockwurst	Bratwurst	Kielbasa	Polish Franks
Variable	X1	X2	X3	X4
Profit Contr. (zloyts/crate)	100	125	200	150

Kaz interrupted. "With all due respect, Wiz, both your and Wojo's profit contributions are off base. I used an S-curve analysis and some Markov chain calculations and came up with the following profit contributions."

Kaz's Profit Contributions

	Knockwurst	Bratwurst	Kielbasa	Polish Franks
Variable	X1	X2	X3	X4
Profit Contr. (zlotys/crate)	195	90	165	25

Tad shook his head in confusion. "What now?"

THE MAXIMIN APPROACH

In Chapter 13 in our discussion on decision making under uncertainty, we encountered a MAXIMIN criterion for use with formal matrix decision models. We noted that this criterion represented a conservative, risk-averse approach to decision making—in effect, a Murphy's Law sort of pessimistic view of "nature." In MOLP modeling, the MAXIMIN approach has the same general tenor, but its application in this context is more subtle, as we will see.

The MOLP model for SSC, using the MAXIMIN approach is as follows:

CHAPTER 14 MODELING WITH MULTIPLE OBJECTIVES

$$\text{MAX } x_0 = \text{MIN } \{125x_1 + 150x_2 + 225x_3 + 75x_4,$$
$$100x_1 + 125x_2 + 200x_3 + 150x_4,$$
$$195x_1 + 90x_2 + 165x_3 + 125x_4\}$$

S T: BEEF
$$40x_1 + 30x_2 \quad\quad + 25x_4 <= 30000$$

PORK
$$20x_1 + 40x_2 + 120x_3 + 5x_4 <= 20000$$

SPICE
$$60x_1 + 50x_2 + 150x_3 + 10x_4 <= 18000$$

CASINGS
$$75x_1 + 85x_2 + 90x_3 + 100x_4 <= 75000$$

TAXES
$$20x_1 + 24x_2 + 30x_3 + 10x_4 <= 10000$$

$$x_1, x_2, x_3, x_4 >= 0$$

Later in the chapter, we will demonstrate how to transform this nonlinear programming model into an equivalent LP model.

In general, the mathematical statement of the MAXIMIN model is as follows:

$$\text{MAX } x_0 = \text{MIN } \{c_1'x, c_2'x, \ldots, c_K'x\} \quad\quad (14.9)$$

$$\text{S T:} \quad Ax \begin{Bmatrix} \leq \\ = \\ \geq \end{Bmatrix} b \quad\quad (14.10)$$

$$x \geq 0$$

Stated in plain English, the MAXIMIN approach seeks the value of the decision vector **x** that makes the minimum value of any of the K linear objective functions as large as possible. In our SSC illustration in which we have independent estimates of the profit contributions for each product, use of the MAXIMIN approach would guarantee (as far as the model is concerned) that the best of the worst occurred. This approach would, in all probability, preclude the best possible result from happening, but this is an inevitable outcome of opting for a defensive strategy.

THE LINEAR COMBINATIONS APPROACH

If our friends in the SSC example are not so risk averse that the MAXIMIN criterion is appropriate, another approach would be to weight the three objective functions in some way and to compute a single linear objective function that is a linear combination of them. For example, if we wish to place equal weight on the three functions (one-third each), the resulting objective has average profit contributions as its coefficients, as follows:

$$\text{MAX } x_0 = 140x_1 + 121.67x_2 + 196.67x_3 + 116.67x_4$$

The constraints remain the same.

In general mathematical terminology, the linear combinations model is

$$\text{MAX or MIN } x_0 = \sum_{k=1}^{K} v_k c_k'x \quad\quad (14.11)$$

$$\text{S T:} \quad Ax \begin{Bmatrix} \leq \\ = \\ \geq \end{Bmatrix} b \tag{14.12}$$

Since the K linear objective functions $c_k'x$, $k = 1, \ldots, K$ are commensurable, the single objective function (14.11) has the same dimensional units as the K functions that it represents. The weights v_k, $k = 1, \ldots, K$ can have several interpretations. For example, if the individual objective functions represent (as in our illustration) different valuation mechanisms associated with a set of states of nature, the v_k could represent the elements of a probability distribution on those states (either empirically or subjectively derived).

On the other hand, the v_k weights could represent a set of relative priorities, assigned by the decision maker, for the various objective functions. For instance, if the $c_k'x$ are goals or objectives that we state in commensurable units, the decision maker may wish to prioritize those goals or objectives by selecting numerical values of the v_k that reflect his or her assessment of their relative importance. If one objective $c_r'x$ were of overriding significance, for example, the decision maker could choose $v_r > 0$ and all other $v_k = 0$—and a simple LP model would result. On the other hand, a Laplace-like criterion similar to the criterion of Insufficient Reason (from Chapter 13) would result if the decision maker chose values $v_k = 1/K$, $k = 1, \ldots, K$, as we did with Solidarity Sausage Company. Or, an ordinal ranking of the K objectives might lead to the following simple weighting scheme:

$$\text{MIN } x_0 = \sum_{k=1}^{K} k c_k' x, \tag{14.13}$$

where we arrange the individual objectives in ascending order of importance to the decision maker.

The approaches discussed so far require that the linear objective functions be commensurable. We now consider two MOLP modeling techniques that can accommodate incommensurable sets of goals or objectives.

MOLP MODELS NOT REQUIRING COMMENSURABILITY

In decision situations in which the decision maker has multiple objectives and where we cannot state these objectives in the same dimensional units, there are two modeling approaches (among others) that are useful: **preemptive goal prioritization** and **preemptive goal programming**. The two approaches exhibit strong similarities in one sense, but they are different enough in an applied context to warrant discussing them separately.

PREEMPTIVE GOAL PRIORITIZATION

In our Solidarity Sausage Company illustration, suppose Wiz and his comrades decide to use Wojo's profit contribution coefficients but have several objectives in mind:

P1: Maximize profit contribution.
P2: Minimize taxes paid.
P3: Use up all the pork.
P4: Make as many crates of sausage as possible.

We write the goal prioritization model as follows:

$$\text{MAX } x_0^1 = 125x_1 + 150x_2 + 225x_3 + 75x_4$$
$$\text{and MIN } x_0^2 = 20x_1 + 24x_2 + 30x_3 + 10x_4$$

and MAX $x_0^3 = 20x_1 + 40x_2 + 120x_3 + 5x_4$
and MAX $x_0^4 = x_1 + x_2 + x_3 + x_4$
S T: BEEF
$$40x_1 + 30x_2 + 25x_4 <= 30000$$
PORK
$$20x_1 + 40x_2 + 120x_3 + 5x_4 <= 20000$$
SPICE
$$60x_1 + 50x_2 + 150x_3 + 10x_4 <= 18000$$
CASINGS
$$75x_1 + 85x_2 + 90x_3 + 100x_4 <= 75000$$
TAXES
$$20x_1 + 24x_2 + 30x_3 + 10x_4 <= 10000$$
$$x1, x2, x3, x4 >= 0$$

Obviously, these four objectives are not commensurable, being measured in $ of profit contribution, $ of capital, kilos of pork, and crates of sausage. Thus, we cannot use the MAXIMIN or linear combinations approaches.

If we can state multiple goals mathematically only in terms of differently dimensioned objectives, one approach to incorporating them into an MOLP model is to have the decision maker make preemptive decisions as to the importance of the objectives. That is to say, we could ask the decision maker to identify the objective that—in his or her judgment—has absolutely overriding importance in the particular decision situation at hand. Once the manager identifies the overriding objective, he or she identifies the next most important goal, and so on, until we obtain a preemptive prioritization of all K goals or objectives. Thus, it does not matter that the objectives may or may not be commensurable in their units of measurement. We satisfy the most important goal first, then the next most important, and so on.

We can write the mathematical MOLP model for a preemptive prioritization as a *sequence* of K linear programming models as follows:

$$\text{MAX } x_0^k = c_k'x, \quad k = 1, \ldots, K \tag{14.14}$$

$$\text{S T:} \quad Ax \begin{Bmatrix} \leq \\ = \\ \geq \end{Bmatrix} b \tag{14.15}$$

$$c_{k-1}'x = x_0^{*(k-1)}, \quad k = 2, \ldots, K \tag{14.16}$$

In Equation (14.14), the decision maker arranges the K linear objective functions in preemptive priority order, with $c_1'x$ being the function with the highest priority, $c_2'x$ being the next highest, etc. Equation (14.16), then, forces subsequent LP models in the sequence to preserve the optimal solutions to higher priority models. For example, let x_0^{*1} denote the optimal value of the objective function with the highest preemptive priority. Then the second LP model in the sequence would be

$$\text{MAX } x_0^2 = c_2'x \tag{14.17}$$

$$\text{S T:} \quad Ax \begin{Bmatrix} \leq \\ = \\ \geq \end{Bmatrix} b \tag{14.18}$$

$$c_1'x = x_0^{*1} \tag{14.19}$$

As we shall see later, it is not actually necessary (in a computational sense) to solve K different LP models. However, modeling the preemptive goal prioritization MOLP model in the form of Equations (14.14) to (14.16) helps us to more easily grasp what is happening.

GOAL PROGRAMMING

So-called preemptive goal programming (PGP) was "invented" by Charnes and Cooper in 1962 [2], and a number of authors have popularized it (e.g., Lee and Moore [7]). The thrust of PGP is to represent the prioritized managerial goals as a set of constraints and associated deviational variables, which are similar to slack and surplus variables in ordinary linear programming models. The idea is to treat functions of the deviational variables as objectives that we wish to minimize or maximize.

Let us explore this concept further before we exhibit the mathematical model. As noted earlier, if we stated objectives in terms such as *maximize profit contribution* and *minimize overtime utilization*, they would almost always be conflicting. For example, suppose we had a set of linear constraints like those in Equation (14.18) and three objectives represented by linear functions that were incommensurable. Suppose next that we solved three different LP models using each of the objective functions singly and that their optimal values were x_0^{*1}, x_0^{*2}, and x_0^{*3}. Finally, let us append the three equality constraints:

$$c_k'x = x_0^{*k}, \quad k = 1, 2, 3 \tag{14.20}$$

Rarely (if ever) would there be a feasible point in the resulting constraint space, so that regardless of what objective function one chose to use, the computerized SIMPLEX algorithm would always return the message: NO FEASIBLE SOLUTION.

Suppose, however, that a decision maker would be satisfied to meet his or her goals as closely as possible but within a priority structure. If this is the case, and if the underlying assumptions of MOLP are met, we have a problem that may be modeled and analyzed using preemptive goal programming.

In our Solidarity Sausage Company investigation, we begin by asking our decision maker to specify and then preemptively prioritize the objectives, as follows:

P1: Make at least 80,000 zlotys of profit.
P2: Pay no more than 5,000 zlotys in taxes.
P3: Use up at least 18,000 kilos of pork.
P4: Make as close to 800 crates of sausage as possible.

The decision maker first preemptively prioritizes the various objectives and indexes them in descending order of priority. We then transform the objectives into additional constraints whose right-hand sides are the specific goals of the decision maker, conditioned by deviational variables, as follows:

$$P1: 125x_1 + 150x_2 + 225x_3 + 75x_4 = 80,000 + d_1^+ - d_1^-$$
$$P2: 20x_1 + 24x_2 + 30x_3 + 10x_4 = 5,000 + d_2^+ - d_2^-$$
$$P3: 20x_1 + 40x_2 + 120x_3 + 5x_4 = 18,000 + d_3^+ - d_3^-$$
$$P4: x_1 + x_2 + x_3 + x_4 = 800 + d_4^+ - d_4^-$$

The objective function now becomes the set of objectives that seeks to minimize the appropriate deviations (the values of the d_k^+ and/or d_k^-) from the managerial goals or targets.

For Solidarity Sausage Company, the objective function would have the following appearance:

P1: MIN $x_0^1 = d_1^-$

P2: MIN $x_0^2 = d_2^+$

P3: MIN $x_0^3 = d_3^-$

P4: MIN $x_0^4 = d_4^+ + d_4^-$

In more general mathematical notation, the deviational constraints are as in Equations (14.21) and (14.22).

$$c_k'x = G_k + d_k^+ - d_k^-, \quad k = 1, \ldots, K \tag{14.21}$$

$$d_k^+, d_k^- \geq 0 \text{ for all } k \tag{14.22}$$

If all of this seems complicated, perhaps our interactive computer friend POPGO (program to operationalize preemptive goal optimization) can clear things up via the following exchange.

POPGO: Hey, man, this is POPGO. What's happening?

HOWARD: Well, POPGO, my appellation is Howard, and I am an erstwhile conveyor of narratives related to competitive physical activities.

POPGO: Heavy, Howard—so you're a former sportscaster. What's the problem?

HOWARD: Let me tell it like it is, POPGO. I've decided to take over the family business, Balloon Specialists, Inc., that has fallen upon difficult times of late. We were, until misfortune befell us recently, the largest manufacturer and purveyor of hot-air balloons in the free world.

POPGO: How can I help, man?

HOWARD: Balloon Specialists has a brace of behemoth assemblage facilities for the aggregation of thermally motivated aircraft.

POPGO: You've got two big hot-air balloon assembly plants, right?

HOWARD: Unquestionably. The facility in Albuquerque is antiquated, but the Phoenix factory is, happily, of more recent vintage. Our repertoire consists of a triumvirate of different craft—which we vend under the cognomens Thermos, Atmos, and Stratos.

POPGO: Sort of a three-bagger, right?

HOWARD: I'll ignore that insipid attempt at joviality, POPGO. To continue; at my behest, technicians extracted and assembled relevant data [Table 14.3].

What I require, my electronic acquaintance, is to ascertain the precise division of our complement of personnel resources to distribute among the trio of products in such a manner as to derive profit of at least $600,000 per month. At the same time, a secondary goal would be to diminish production at the obsolescent Albuquerque facility. Tertiarily, probable phaseout of the Stratos line may be imminent, so producing as few of these as possible would be desirable. But hear me well, POPGO—I don't want the latter two objectives to interfere with the first one. Moreover, I don't want the third to interfere with the second.

TABLE 14.3

Product	Phoenix			Albuquerque		
	Thermos	Atmos	Stratos	Thermos	Atmos	Stratos
Profit margins	$1,500	$3,000	$2,000	$1,500	$3,000	$2,000
Hand-finishing (man-hours)	0	0	3	3	1	2
Hand-assembling (man-hours)	0	0	0	2	3	5
Test inflation (man-hours)	1	2	0	1	2	0

Man-hours Available Per Month	
Hand-finishing:	300 man-hours
Hand-assembling:	240 man-hours
Test inflation:	270 man-hours

POPGO: So you've got a product mix problem with multiple objectives. Are the following O.K.?

P1: Generate a profit contribution of at least $600,000 per month.
P2: Get Albuquerque production as small as possible.
P3: Get Stratos production as small as possible.

HOWARD: Affirmative, POPGO—that's substantially correct. Hear me well, now: I don't want P2 and P3 to interfere with P1, and I don't want P3 to interfere with P2.

POPGO: I'm cool, Howard. What we've got here is a problem that we can model by goal programming with pure preemptive priorities on the incommensurable objective functions.

HOWARD: Zounds—and everybody accuses *me* of using jargon!

POPGO: Before I show you the model, do you know anything about linear programming?

HOWARD: Certainly. I am a close personal friend of George Dantzig, the inventor of that marvelous SIMPLEX technique. I don't like to boast, but I am responsible for George's use of the term "SIMPLEX" for his algorithm. I'll never forget that snowy December afternoon when George and I . . .

POPGO: Uh, sure, Howard—let's move on. What we're going to do is to turn your objectives into constraints. Our variables x_1, x_2, x_3 stand for the numbers of balloons of Thermos, Atmos, and Stratos, respectively, to produce in Phoenix. The variables x_4, x_5, and x_6 stand for the same things in Albuquerque. I'll show you the entire model, and then we can rap some more about it.

$$\text{P1:} \quad \text{MIN } (x_0)_1 = d_1^- \quad (14.23)$$

$$\text{P2:} \quad \text{MIN } (x_0)_2 = d_2^+ \quad (14.24)$$

$$\text{P3:} \quad \text{MIN } (x_0)_3 = d_3^+ \quad (14.25)$$

$$\text{S T:} \quad 1.5x_1 + 3x_2 + 2x_3 + 1.5x_4 + 3x_5 + 2x_6 - d_1^+ + d_1^- = 600 \quad (14.26)$$

$$x_4 + x_5 + x_6 - d_2^+ + d_2^- = 0 \quad (14.27)$$

$$x_3 + x_6 - d_3^+ + d_3^- = 0 \quad (14.28)$$

$$3x_3 + 3x_4 + x_5 + 2x_6 \leq 300 \quad (14.29)$$

$$2x_4 + 3x_5 + 5x_6 \leq 240 \quad (14.30)$$

$$x_1 + 2x_2 + x_4 + 2x_5 \leq 270 \quad (14.31)$$

$$\text{all } x_j, d_1^+, d_1^-, d_2^+, d_2^-, d_3^+, d_3^- \geq 0 \quad (14.32)$$

HOWARD: How clever, POPGO! Constraints (14.26) to (14.28) set our targets of $600,000 profit contribution, zero production in Albuquerque, and zero production of Stratos models. The deviational variables allow a bit of slack in case we cannot attain one or more of the goals. Our three objectives, then, are to minimize the negative deviation from $600,000 of profit and to minimize the positive deviations from Albuquerque and Stratos production. Constraints (14.29) to (14.31) are merely our scarce labor complement. But George's SIMPLEX algorithm will only operate with one objective function, and we have three. Doesn't that obfuscate our peregrination?

POPGO: No, man—not to worry. Eyeball the rest of the chapter, and I'll see you in Problem 1. This is POPGO, saying ciao for now.

Before moving on to discuss solution approaches, let's more closely examine the so-called deviational variables. In HOWARD's model, all three goals turned out to be one-sided in a sense. That is, since $G_1 = \$600,000$ and our goal was at least to achieve it, our objective function (14.23) involved minimizing only the negative deviational variable d_1^-. If, for some managerial reason such as tax planning, the goal had been to generate exactly $600,000, the objective function would have been

$$\text{MIN } x_0 = d_1^+ + d_1^-.$$

Note in this case that one of the two deviational variables will always be zero in an optimal model solution.

On the other hand, if we wished to actually maximize profit contribution, an appropriate objective function would be MAX $x_0 = d_1^+$.

The point of this discussion is that goal programming—although nothing more than a variant of multiobjective linear programming—is a very sophisticated modeling tool. More than any other technique in this book (so far), we should use it only if the decision maker is intimately involved in the modeling process.

SOLUTION APPROACHES: AN INTUITIVE DESCRIPTION

The basic approach to solving MOLP models of all types is to transform them into equivalent models that are amenable to solution by variants of the SIMPLEX algorithm. We saw this approach in Chapter 5, where we "linearized" certain varieties of nonlinear programming models so that we could employ the highly efficient SIMPLEX algorithm to obtain useable solutions. The following concentrates on two facets of the solution approaches: the transformation and the revision of the SIMPLEX algorithm (if any) required to generate an optimal model solution.

THE MAXIMIN MODEL

For convenience, the following restates the MAXIMIN MOLP model for SSC:

$$\text{MAX } x_0 = \text{MIN } \{125x_1 + 150x_2 + 225x_3 + 75x_4,$$
$$100x_1 + 125x_2 + 200x_3 + 150x_4,$$
$$195x_1 + 90x_2 + 165x_3 + 125x_4\}$$

S T: BEEF
$$40x_1 + 30x_2 + 25x_4 <= 30000$$

PORK
$$20x_1 + 40x_2 + 120x_3 + 5x_4 <= 20000$$

SPICE
$$60x_1 + 50x_2 + 150x_3 + 10x_4 <= 18000$$

CASINGS
$$75x_1 + 85x_2 + 90x_3 + 100x_4 <= 75000$$

TAXES
$$20x_1 + 24x_2 + 30x_3 + 10x_4 <= 10000$$

$$x1, x2, x3, x4 >= 0$$

To transform this MOLP model into an ordinary single-objective LP model, we use a **surrogate variable** y, which we define in the following way:

$$y \leq 125x_1 + 150x_2 + 225x_3 + 75x_4$$
$$\text{and } y \leq 100x_1 + 125x_2 + 200x_3 + 150x_4$$
$$\text{and } y \leq 195x_1 + 90x_2 + 165x_3 + 125x_4$$

Note that we have defined y to be the minimum of the three objective functions by constructing constraints for this purpose. Thus, our objective is to maximize y.

Figure 14.1 shows the SAMS linear programming module input screen for this model. Table 14.4 exhibits SAMS LP output for each of the three objective functions, using the MAXIMIN input from Figure 14.1.

Note that the MAXIMIN model selected the same product mix as that chosen by Wojo's objective function. It is instructive to compute the profit contributions of the three different product mixes with the three single-objective functions.

		MIX		
		WOJO	WIZ	KAZ
Objective Function	WOJO	71,986	67,978	70,000
	WIZ	115,167	117,340	115,000
	KAZ	94,475	88,716	114,000

Note that this conservative modeling approach protects the decision maker from the decreased profit that would result from using the mixes suggested by Wiz and Kaz—in effect, choosing the best of the worst.

```
┌──→ SAMS INPUT SCREEN - Linear Programming ←──┐
│  NAME?  SOLIDARITY SAUSAGE COMPANY            │
│  MAximize or MInimize?  MA                    │
│  PROBLEM DESCRIPTION - Optimize multiple objective sausage │
│                        mix problem for Solidarity Sausage. │
│                                               │
│  Variables    X1     X2     X3     X4    Y      Dir  RHS │
│                                               │
│  Objective    0.     0.     0.     0.    1.     <        │
│                                               │
│  Upper Bound  INF    INF    INF    INF   INF    =        │
│  Lower Bound  0.     0.     0.     0.    0.     >        │
│                                               │
│  Constraints                                  │
│  BEEF         40.    30.    0.     25.   0.    < 30000.  │
│  PORK         20.    40.    120.   5.    0.    < 20000.  │
│  SPICE        60.    50.    150.   10.   0.    < 18000.  │
│  CASINGS      75.    85.    90.    100.  0.    < 75000.  │
│  TAXES        20.    24.    30.    10.   0.    < 10000.  │
│  WOJO        -125.  -150.  -225.  -75.   1.    <     0.  │
│  WIZ         -100.  -125.  -200.  -150.  1.    <     0.  │
│  KAZ         -195.  -90.   -165.  -125.  1.    <     0.  │
└───────────────────────────────────────────────┘
```

FIGURE 14.1 SAMS input screen for Solidarity

TABLE 14.4 Optimal model solutions

	x_0	x_1	x_2	x_3	x_4
Wojo	71,986.0	0.0	100.5	44.9	624.2
Wiz	117,340.0	0.0	0.0	74.5	683.0
Kaz	114,000.0	200.0	0.0	0.0	600.0
MAXIMIN	71,986.0	0.0	100.5	44.9	624.2

In general, to transform Equations (14.9) and (14.10) into an ordinary LP model, we use a surrogate variable y, which we define as follows:

$$y \leq c_k'x, \; k = 1, 2, \ldots, K \tag{14.33}$$

That is, we add exactly K constraints to Equation (14.10), the effect of which is to guarantee that y takes on a value that is the minimum of the set of commensurable objective functions in Equation (14.9). We then set up the ordinary single-objective LP model:

$$\text{MAX } x_0 = y \tag{14.34}$$

$$\text{S T:} \quad y - c_k'x \leq 0, \; k = 1, \ldots, K \tag{14.33}$$

$$\text{S T:} \quad Ax \begin{Bmatrix} \leq \\ = \\ \geq \end{Bmatrix} b \tag{14.10}$$

This formulation assures that our computerized SIMPLEX algorithm produces the optimal model solution x^* that satisfied our original objective function (14.9).

TABLE 14.5 SAMS output for Solidarity

```
SOLIDARITY SAUSAGE COMPANY
QUICK BRIEFING ON OPTIMAL MODEL SOLUTION
          Maximum Objective Value = 98002.0

  Decision           Optimal              Reduced
  Variable           Value                Cost

    X1                200.0                0.0
    X2                600.0                0.0

  Constraint         Slack              Shadow Price

    Beef             7000.0               0.0
    Pork            13000.0               0.0
```

THE LINEAR COMBINATIONS MODEL

The Solidarity Sausage problem that we posed as a linear combination model is an ordinary single-objective model that we solved with a linear programming module. Table 14.5 presents the SAMS quick briefing for SSC. Note that this solution is just the mix that we obtained using Kaz's objective function in the MAXIMIN discussion.

THE PREEMPTIVE GOAL PRIORITIZATION MODEL

We noted before that we can solve the preemptive goal prioritization model by using a series of single-objective LP models, as in Equations (14.16) to (14.18). A more elegant and efficient approach is to treat the K linear objectives in matrix form and modify the SIMPLEX algorithm so that we maintain the preemptive priority of the objective.

Without going into algorithmic details, a computerized program to implement a preemptive goal prioritization algorithm requires that we arrange our K goals and index them in decreasing priority order. That is, P1 is preemptively more important than P2, which is preemptively more important than P3, and so forth. The algorithm actually carries along the K linear objective functions as a matrix and uses the SIMPLEX technique to first find the optimal solution to P1. Once the solution is found, the algorithm checks the transformed objective function for P1 to determine whether there are alternative optimal solutions (in terms of P1) to the model. If so, it scans P2 to determine whether the alternative solution(s) will improve the value of this objective, and so on.

As the algorithm proceeds to consider P3, P4, etc., it is searching for simultaneous alternative optimal solutions to all higher priority objective functions. When it finds none, we have solved the model. As an illustration, let's return to Howard's problem as narrated to POPGO, with one small change—we will turn his most important objective—"P1: Generate a monthly profit contribution of at least $600,000"—into a "≥" constraint and designate the current P2 as "P1: Get Albuquerque production as small as possible." Similarly, the original P3 becomes "P2: Get Stratos production as small as possible." The resulting preemptive goal priority model is as follows:

$$P1: \quad \text{MIN} \quad x_0 = \qquad\qquad\qquad x_4 + \quad x_5 + \quad x_6 \qquad (14.35)$$
$$P2: \quad \text{MIN} \quad x_0 = \qquad\qquad x_3 \qquad\qquad\quad + \quad x_6 \qquad (14.36)$$
$$\text{S T:} \qquad\qquad\qquad 3x_3 + \quad 3x_4 + \quad x_5 + \quad 2x_6 \le 300 \qquad (14.29)$$
$$\qquad\qquad\qquad\qquad\qquad 2x_4 + \quad 3x_5 + \quad 5x_6 \le 240 \qquad (14.30)$$
$$x_1 + \quad 2x_2 \qquad\qquad + \quad x_4 + \quad 2x_5 \qquad\qquad = 270 \qquad (14.31)$$
$$1500x_1 + 3000x_2 + 2000x_3 + 1500x_4 + 3000x_5 + 2000x_6 \ge 600000 \;(14.37)$$

We first optimize objective (14.35), and "fix" the optimal model solution by not subsequently entering a variable that would increase its value. Then Equation (14.36) would be treated as the objective row.

THE PREEMPTIVE GOAL PROGRAMMING MODEL

The solution approach to preemptive goal programming models is identical to that just described for the preemptive goal prioritization model, except that our objectives are functions of the deviational variables. In defining the K goals as in Equation (14.21), we add K constraints to the m functional constraints of the model as well as up to $2K$ deviational variables, so that we are dealing with a somewhat larger LP construction.

On a purely technical note, one structural difficulty with many goal programming formulations is in the frequency of order-of-magnitude differences in the coefficients of the goal definitions (14.21). Note in Howard's model Equations (14.23) to (14.32) that constraint coefficients range in value from zero to 3,000. This large variation tends to induce computer roundoff errors as it performs millions of arithmetic operations in the SIMPLEX procedure. We can mitigate this problem by "scaling" the constraints. For example, we can divide the constraint (14.26)—which defines HOWARD's profit contribution goal—on both sides by 1,000 before including the deviational variables. This operation results in a constraint set whose coefficients are of roughly the same magnitude.

DEVELOPING ALTERNATIVE SOLUTIONS

Sensitivity analysis (right-hand side ranging, etc.) is fairly straightforward for the commensurable models, since these models are direct transformations to single objective LP models. In linear combinations models, however, the question arises as to the weights v_k [Equation (14.13)] we use to transform the K objectives into a single one. The point is this: selecting the values of the weights v_k, $k = 1, \ldots, K$, is clearly the key in modeling with linear combinations. We emphasize once more that this selection is a managerial responsibility.

Sensitivity analysis for the incommensurable models—preemptive goal prioritization and preemptive goal programming—is quite another matter. In the former case, the shadow prices for the highest priority goal have the same interpretation as they do in ordinary single-objective LP. But what interpretation do these prices have for the lower priority goals? They are, in a sense, *constrained shadow prices*, since their values are dependent on the attainment of higher priority objectives (unless, of course, the optimal vertex for the highest priority objective happens to be the optimal vertex for a lower priority objective as well).

In terms of our mountain-climbing analogy in Chapter 2, we can think of preemptive goal prioritization models as attempts to climb several adjacent mountains simultaneously. We make whatever resources that are necessary to climb Mount P1 available to that climber, who always reaches the top. Conceptually, the highest priority climber has somehow "pulled along" fellow climbers (at least partially) up their respective mountains. Once we have conquered Mount P1, we make available the remaining resources to assault Mount P2, and so on. Note that in the process of attempting to climb a lower priority mountain we allow no action that would decrease the altitudes higher priority climbers attained.

In general, duality theory has a limited interpretation for preemptive goal prioritization models. The dual model turns out to be a single-objective LP formulation with multiple right-hand sides for the constraints. This topic is at the forefront of research in MOLP, but the SAMS LP module gives us the ability to input a range of RHS values and investigate the behavior of solutions to the model over this range. We explore this capability in the end-of-chapter problems.

Sensitivity analysis for preemptive goal programming models is even less well structured than for preemptive goal prioritization models. Recall that we are dealing with two kinds of constraints: the actual resource constraints and the constraints used to establish our goals. By stating our objectives as functions of the deviational variables, we are in effect attempting to force the second set of constraints to be binding in an optimal solution. What economic interpretation can we impute to the associated shadow prices? Unfortunately, no satisfactory answer to that question exists at this writing.

To observe the effect on the original prioritization, some authors suggest sensitivity analysis by reordering the goal priorities and solving the new model. Others recommend eliminating certain goals and obtaining additional solutions to determine which (if any) goal or goals "drive" the model solution. These activities often produce interesting results and occasionally provide insight into the underlying problem. However, they tend to miss the managerial point of multiple-objective modeling, which is—like all other MS/OR models—to accurately reflect the underlying problem as the decision maker sees it. Certainly, if a decision maker is indifferent as to the relative priorities of two goals, it makes sense to solve two models, interchanging the two goals in priority order and noting the effect. There are other good managerial reasons to experiment with the model in the ways we describe here, but in general, "fiddling for fiddling's sake" is an inappropriate activity in real-world modeling and analysis.

STATE OF THE ART IN MOLP

As noted earlier, the art of modeling with multiple criteria is basically in its infancy. The following section introduces a few advanced topics in an effort to impart the flavor of what's happening in this broad field.

UTILITY TRANSFORMATIONS FOR INCOMMENSURABLE OBJECTIVES

As we learned, modeling and analysis of problems with commensurable objectives were much more straightforward than with incommensurable ones. What if we could (as we did in Chapter 7) construct utility functions for the various goals or objectives and transform them all into the same dimensionless units called "utiles"? We would then have goals with commensurable units and could use MAXIMIN, linear combinations, or other models of this type for our analysis. Using such utility transformations, it might even be possible to quantify the unquantifiable by addressing goals or objectives that we cannot state in physically measurable terms (e.g., improve employee morale, heighten managers' sensitivity to affirmative action). This is a lively area of current research, but we take the view that this approach is not yet ready for the managerial firing line.

MODELING WITH FUZZY SETS

The quaintly titled "theory of fuzzy sets" is another body of knowledge that holds promise in multiobjective modeling. In modeling with commensurable objectives, recall that one approach—linear combinations—involves aggregating the K linear objectives into a single objective by the use of relative importance weights. Since we can't do that with incommensurable objectives, we were forced to use preemptive priorities in which P1 is infinitely more important than P2, and so on. Fuzzy set theory, whose best-known proponent is Lofti Zadeh (e.g., [8]), provides a possible remedy to this problem.

In nontechnical terms, fuzzy set theory allows us to quantify verbal descriptions of attributes of characteristics. For example, the word *very* connotes more than an *average* or a *normal* condition or state. Other verbal descriptions using this adverb might be *not very* or *very very* or *so very* or *not so very*. Such descriptions are *soft* or *fuzzy* in the sense that they carry different connotations for different decision makers. If we could quantify this set of descriptors for a particular decision maker, we could apply graded (rather than preemptive) priorities in situations involving incommensurable objectives. Like the utility transformation, we believe that the theory of fuzzy sets is not yet well enough developed to be of immediate use in actual applications of managerial decision making.

NON-MOLP MULTIPLE OBJECTIVE MODELS

Finally, it is certainly possible for a decision maker to have multiple objectives in a decision situation in which he or she can use only integer programming (IP) or nonlinear programming (NLP) or perhaps dynamic programming (DP) to effectively model the problem. Recall from Chapter 6, for instance, Mr. Mark Off, who wished to travel by stagecoach from New York City to San Francisco to seek his fortune. In addition to minimizing the total cost of his travel insurance policy (and thereby minimizing the danger), he may well have wished to maximize the sight-seeing aspects of the trip and perhaps minimize the total travel time on uncomfortable stagecoaches. If this were the case, we would have a DP model with multiple objectives.

Specialists have done some research in integer goal programming modeling, and we illustrate such a model in the first minicase. But—as we might suspect—the difficulty of performing sensitivity analysis that we encountered for single-objective IP models (Chapter 3) is compounded when multiple objectives are present. If the objectives are commensurable, of course, we may use MAXIMIN or linear combinations models to transform the multiple-objective model into an IP model with a single objective. We must use a different approach when the objectives are incommensurable.

MINICASES

SOFSNEEZ [1]

THE SCENARIO

SofSneez, Ltd. is a Hong Kong based company that manufactures tissue products made primarily from biodegradable synthetic fibers and creped cellous wadding. Its nine facial tissue products sell well in North America, especially during cold and flu season. Table 14.6 describes these products.

TABLE 14.6

Brand Name	Product ID	Tissue Density	Color	Size	Type of Dispenser
Silk Touch	x_1	Regular	White	Medium	Cardboard
"	x_2	Regular	Assorted	Medium	Cardboard
"	x_3	Regular	White	Medium	Plastic
"	x_4	Regular	White	Large	Cardboard
Satin Doll	x_5	Thick	White	Medium	Cardboard
"	x_6	Thick	Assorted	Medium	Plastic
"	x_7	Thick	White	Large	Plastic
Velvet Fog	x_8	Extra thick	Assorted	Medium	Plastic
"	x_9	Extra thick	Assorted	Large	Plastic

THE PROBLEM

Lin Chang, the oldest son of the founder and president of SofSneez, had just received his hard-earned MBA. His first assignment with the company was as the account manager for Alaska and the Yukon Territory of Canada. The elder Chang believed in family members working their way up from the bottom, and this particular territory was most certainly the bottom. With an area of almost 800,000 square miles and a population of less than 500,000 people, it was SofSneez, Ltd.'s most challenging sales territory.

Lin's first order of business after settling into his office in Chicken, a small Alaskan town near the Canadian border, was to check out the advertising accrual program of the Talkeetna Trading Company (TTC), the largest supermarket chain in the region. The objective of this program is to purchase advertising space in the TTC "roto ad" insertions in local newspapers. Since the consumer tissue business is highly competitive, all major manufacturers compete fiercely for limited ad space with TTC, and the company will feature only those brands that offer it the highest cumulative return. The object is to present TTC with a marketing program that covers advertising costs and provides incremental earnings relative to the competition.

SofSneez corporate headquarters uses sophisticated (and highly proprietary) forecasting techniques to project sales by product line. These forecasts generate overall sales quotas for territorial account managers. The most recent forecast of *minimum* sales (cases) by product for the coming quarter are in Table 14.7. The *overall* forecast of sales is 15,000 cases. Since the minimum sales forecasts total only 9,150, it is Lin Chang's task to determine the proper mix of the remaining 5,850 cases of product.

An accrual rate is the per-case cost of advertising a specific product. Within the mix constraints imposed by SofSneez, the object is to find a product mix that will result in the largest possible sum of accruals. This may seem to some an odd objective, but it revolves about the fact that SofSneez is a *wholesaler* dealing with a *retailer* (TTC) and its retail advertising program.

A trade deal is a per-case wholesale allowance that the wholesaler deducts from the invoice to give the retailer an incentive to provide merchandise support in the store itself (e.g., displays, attractive pricing, point-of-purchase promotions). SofSneez has provided Lin Chang with a target for total trade deals for the quarter of $16,000.

TABLE 14.7

Brand Name	Product ID	Quota (Cases)	Accrual/Case	Trade Deal/Case
Silk Touch	x_1	800	$0.50	$1.80
"	x_2	1,900	0.75	2.24
"	x_3	1,100	0.75	2.24
"	x_4	1,000	0.80	2.60
Satin Doll	x_5	750	0.50	1.80
"	x_6	1,300	0.75	2.24
"	x_7	1,300	0.80	2.50
Velvet Fog	x_8	500	1.00	N/A
"	x_9	500	1.10	N/A
Total of Quotas		9,150		

In addition to the lower-bound constraints on each of the nine products (minimum forecasted sales) and the upper-bound of 16,000 on the total number of cases of product, there are other product mix constraints as well.

1. The Silk Touch line is SofSneez, Ltd.'s mainline product, but the company is trying to promote the other lines because of their higher profit margins. Thus, the mix must include not more than 60% of these four products.
2. Although the products sold in large sizes (x_4, x_7, x_9) have the highest accrual rates, sales have never exceeded 20% of total sales, so Lin Chang must assure that his mix meets this condition.
3. The hardy, no-nonsense Northerners in this territory are not particularly interested in frills, so Lin Chang decided to limit the products that come in assorted colors (x_2, x_6, x_8, and x_9) to no more than 25% of the mix.

THE MODEL

It was clear to Lin Chang that his problem was one of optimal product mix and that he was evidently supposed to find a mix that made his advertising budget as large as possible. The constraints on mix were also straightforward. What puzzled him was the target of $16,000 on trade deals that SofSneez headquarters had given him. Was he supposed to use it all? Could he go over the target, or would it be wise to conserve some of it? When he telephoned his father with this question, he got the enigmatic reply:

> "You are the account manager, my son. This decision is yours to make as your wisdom and training dictate."

Lin Chang summoned his LP module and entered his model.

SOLUTION TO THE MODEL

After carefully checking his model for accuracy, he selected "Go to the optimal solution" and was startled when SAMS tersely reported: NO FEASIBLE SOLUTION. Lin worriedly examined his constraints and realized that he had input the mix constraints on Silk Touch, large sizes, and colored tissue as fractions of 15,000 — not as fractions of the actual total. Sheepishly, he rewrote these three constraints correctly as follows and entered them into his model, first moving variables to the left side of the inequality:

$$x_1 + x_2 + x_3 + x_4 \le 0.60 \sum_{j=1}^{9} x_j$$

$$x_4 + x_7 + x_9 \le 0.20 \sum_{j=1}^{9} x_j$$

$$x_2 + x_6 + x_8 + x_9 \le 0.25 \sum_{j=1}^{9} x_j$$

However, to Lin Chang's utter dismay, his LP package again informed him that the model he had entered had no feasible solution. His eye fell on the minimum sales figures he had entered as lower bounds for the variables. When he entered these values into the trade deal constraint with his calculator, the total came to $19,322 — $3,322 more than the target figure the company had given him! He reached angrily for the telephone and had already dialed nine digits of his father's number when he stopped abruptly and returned the receiver to its cradle. This was not an error but a test. Lin removed the lower bounds from the model and reran it. Table 14.8 presents the SAMS full briefing for the new model.

TABLE 14.8 SAMS report for SofSneez

SOFSNEEZ
FULL BRIEFING ON OPTIMAL MODEL SOLUTION
Maximum Objective Value = 7881.04

Decision Variable	Optimal Value	Reduced Cost
X1	0.0	−0.03
X2	0.0	−1.39
X3	5498.0	0.00
X4	0.0	−0.23
X5	1487.0	0.00
X6	0.0	−1.35
X7	0.0	−0.15
X8	495.7	0.00
X9	1982.7	0.00

Constraint	Slack	Shadow Price
TRADDEAL	0.00	0.493
QUOTAALL	5086.74	0.000
QUOTSILK	0.00	0.030
QUOTLARG	0.00	0.100
QUOTCOLR	0.00	1.390

The solution was totally unacceptable. It recommended accruals for only four products: x_3, x_5, x_8, x_9. And while it generated the maximum in trade deals, it generated only $7,881 in accruals.

What Lin Chang needed was a solution that at least *attempted* to meet the individual lower-bound quotas and the overall quota if possible while doing as well as possible on the trade deals. Then it struck him that preemptive goal programming might do the trick. Since doing well on trade deals was as important as making individual quotas, Lin made all ten goals the same priority. Then he made the overall quota constraint a "$\geq$" one. The model is in Table 14.9 on p. 488.

Just before Lin Chang began the optimization run, he decided on the spur of the moment to declare variables x_1 to x_9 to be integers—and to use a popular ILP package—so that he wouldn't have to worry about rounding an LP solution. It was 2:00 p.m. when he instructed the algorithm to find the optimal IP solution.

At 2:30, with node #1,284 being processed on his 80286-based AT, he wished fervently that he had purchased that nifty American-made 33-Mh 80386-based micro that he had looked at during his last visit to the "lower 48."

At 3:00, as node #2,540 flashed on the screen, he wished that he hadn't been so hasty about deciding to use an IP model just to avoid rounding a small LP model.

At 3:15, with node #3,175 processing, he almost gave up and rebooted his computer. But stubbornness was a trait he inherited from his father, so he vowed to let the model run all night if he had to. At 3:22, his patience was rewarded after 3,536 nodes.

Lin Chang breathed a long sigh of relief as he verified that the branch-and-bound algorithm had not encountered round-off error (Table 14.10 on p. 489). The model solution had seven of the nine products in the mix at a level at least as large as their minimum forecasts, and the two products not included (x_2 and x_6) happened to be color products. The solution met the overall requirement of 15,000 cases and all three mix constraints on Silk Touch products, large products, and assorted color products. Lin noticed that the value of the deviational variable $D10^+$ was $6,444, which meant that he would need $22,644 in trade deal funds rather than the $16,000 that SofSneez had allocated. He jotted down the unconstrained and the goal programming solutions side by side and pondered them (Table 14.11 on p. 489).

SOLUTION TO THE PROBLEM

Lin Chang confidently dialed his father's number and spoke as follows when his father answered the phone:

> "Father, this is your son Lin Chang in Alaska. You asked that I discuss my first accrual program personally with you, and I am prepared to do so.
>
> "As you know, the target of $16,000 for trade deals you gave me will not cover the individual product quotas—it is $3,322 short. However, setting quotas on the Silk and Satin products in assorted colors is inappropriate for this territory because of the demographics. With your permission, I will eliminate them from consideration."

"Granted," said the elder Chang.

> "Thank you, Father," replied Lin Chang. "Now, you said that the $16,000 in trade deals was a target. I would like permission to overshoot the tar-

(text continued on p. 490)

TABLE 14.9 SofSneez goal programming model

SOFSNEEZ MATHEMATICAL MODEL

MIN
$D1+ + D1- + D2+ + D2- + D3+ + D3- + D4+ + D4- + D5+ + D5- + D6+ + D6- + D7+ + D7- + D8+ + D8- + D9+ + D9- + D10+ + D10-$

S T:

TRADDEAL
$1.8\,X1 + 2.24\,X2 + 2.24\,X3 + 2.6\,X4 + 1.8\,X5 + 2.24\,X6 + 2.5\,X7 - D10+ + D10- <= 16000$

QUOTAALL
$X1 + X2 + X3 + X4 + X5 + X6 + X7 + X8 + X9 >= 15000$

QUOTSILK
$0.4\,X1 + 0.4\,X2 + 0.4\,X3 + 0.4\,X4 - 0.6\,X5 - 0.6\,X6 - 0.6\,X7 - 0.6\,X8 - 0.6\,X9 <= 0$

QUOTLARG
$-0.2\,X1 - 0.2\,X2 - 0.2\,X3 + 0.8\,X4 - 0.2\,X5 - 0.2\,X6 + 0.8\,X7 - 0.2\,X8 + 0.8\,X9 <= 0$

QUOTCOLR
$-0.25\,X1 + 0.75\,X2 - 0.25\,X3 - 0.25\,X4 - 0.25\,X5 + 0.75\,X6 - 0.25\,X7 + 0.75\,X8 + 0.75\,X9 <= 0$

CONSTR 6
$X1 - D1+ + D1- <= 800$

CONSTR 7
$X2 - D2+ + D2- <= 1900$

CONSTR 8
$X3 - D3+ + D3- <= 1100$

CONSTR 9
$X4 - D4+ + D4- <= 1000$

CONSTR 10
$X5 - D5+ + D5- <= 750$

CONSTR 11
$X6 - D6+ + D6- <= 1300$

CONSTR 12
$X7 - D7+ + D7- <= 1300$

CONSTR 13
$X8 - D8+ + D8- <= 500$

CONSTR 14
$X9 - D9+ + D9- <= 500$

TABLE 14.10 SAMS report for SofSneez integer goal programming model

```
SOFSNEEZ
QUICK BRIEFING ON OPTIMAL MODEL SOLUTION
            Maximum Objective Value = 15494.0
```

Decision Variable	Optimal Value	Reduced Cost
X1	6900.0	0.0
X3	1100.0	0.0
X4	1000.0	0.0
X5	950.0	0.0
X7	1300.0	0.0
X8	3250.0	0.0
X9	500.0	0.0
D1+	6100.0	0.0
D5+	200.0	0.0
D8+	2750.0	0.0
D10+	6444.0	0.0

Constraint	Slack	Shadow Price
QUOTLARG	200.0	0.0

TABLE 14.11

Product	Unconstrained	Goal Program	
Silk X1	0	6,900	
X2	0	0	
X3	5,948	1,100	
X4	0	1,000	
Satin X5	1,487	950	
X6	0	0	
X7	0	1,300	
Velvet X8	495	3,250	
X9	1,982	500	
Quantity	9,912	15,000	+32%
Accruals	$ 7,881	$10,390	+51%
Trade deals	$16,000	$22,444	+40%

get by $6,500. With $22,500 in trade deal money, I can meet the overall quantity forecast of 15,000 cases—32% more than with only $16,000. Even more important, I can generate almost $10,400 in accruals with this amount—51% more than with only $16,000. It seems to me that a 40% increase in trade deal funds to increase accruals by half is a very good investment of SofSneez, Ltd.'s money."

Breathless, Lin Chang waited in silence for a reply. The next sound he heard was a soft chuckle from his father.

"My son," began Mr. Chang, "your predecessor in that desolate territory had a quarterly trade deal target of $25,000, and he generated between $8,000 and $9,000 in accruals on total cases of about 11,000. How is it that a young man with no experience can beat a seasoned account manager with 20 years of experience so badly? Are you sure of your numbers?"

"Yes, Father, I am sure," Lin Chang replied. "I used some things I learned in my MBA program to do some analysis, but mostly I used what I inherited from my respected parents. I will FAX you my proposed product mix so that the comptroller can verify my claims."

"Good enough, my son," replied the proud old man. "In six months you will come home to Hong Kong to begin learning the corporate strategies and operations of SofSneez Ltd. If all goes well, you will succeed me in two years. Your mother sends her love and admonishes you to dress warmly and not to catch a cold."

Spacetrek

THE SCENARIO

Intergalactic Enterprises, Inc., a mammoth firm with subsidiary holdings in 75 different star systems, had acquired all Earth-based companies in the mid-21st century and a short time later, in 2101, controlled interstellar assets worth over 60 quintillion zorgs. Its most recent acquisition (for a price of 20 trillion zorgs) was Zappa Industries, a firm located in the star system of Deneb and the galaxy's sole producer of ion power units. Intergalactic had bought billions of these power units in the past and finally decided that to hold down costs it would be cheaper to acquire the company.

THE PROBLEM

As was its custom, Intergalactic immediately laid off all of Zappa's Denebian employees and sent in its own people to manufacture the ion power units. Sissy Spacetrek, who was appointed CEO, realized—before her first flurb on the job was over—that she had a problem of stellar proportions. It seemed that Denebians never wrote anything down, since each was born with an imbedded 4-megabyte, 64-bit-word minicomputer. Since all Denebians were networked, information access was instantaneous electronically, so keeping nonelectronic records was unnecessary.

"The bottom line," thought Sissy to herself, "is that we've just fired our management information system."

Calling in Esther, her top production/operations manager, Sissy laid it on the line.

"Esther, we have a problem," she began. "Intergalactic wants Zappa's costs tightly controlled, but we haven't a clue in the cosmos what production costs are. I want you, Telly, Perry, and Zero to get me some answers—and quickly."

"Right, your eminence," Esther responded. "We'll blast off on this project immediately. We'll be back to you in no more than two or three flurbs."

Exactly 2.498 flurbs later, Esther's team was in Sissy's office, clutching reams of computer printout.

"Madame Spacetrek," began Esther, "here's the lowdown. Zappa apparently manufactures six different ion power units, which we'll refer to by the brand names Athos, Porthos, Aramis, D'Artagnan, Dumas, and Joe Bob. Telly, Perry, Zero, and I decided to do independent cost estimations and to meet afterwards to try to reconcile any differences we might have. I'm confident that my estimates are accurate, but the other three came up with different figures, and none of those prima donnas will change their figures by a single zorg."

"O.K., Esther," sighed Sissy, "just give me all four estimates, and I'll take it from there."

The four production cost estimates for the six brands of power units (in kilozorgs) are in Table 14.12.

TABLE 14.12 Production cost estimates

		Brand	Estimator			
			Esther	Telly	Perry	Zero
	x_1	Athos	3	4	6	12
	x_2	Porthos	5	5	7	9
Decision	x_3	Aramis	6	8	3	10
Variables	x_4	D'Artagnan	6	5	10	4
	x_5	Dumas	7	6	5	8
	x_6	Joe Bob	9	8	7	3

Instructions from Intergalactic headquarters were to produce a total of at least 100,000 units per kiloflurb and to produce at least 10,000 of each brand in the product mix. The only scarce resource appeared to be person-flurbs of labor, with a total of 250,000 person-flurbs available per kiloflurb. Sissy's charge was clear: to minimize production costs. But which of the four cost estimates was she to use? Unable to resolve her dilemma, she called in Harv Klingon, a management consultant affiliated with Taurus University.

THE MODEL

Twenty-four flurbs later, Harv had the situation scoped out.

"Ms. Spacetrek," he began, "what we have here is a classical problem of minimizing some function of four hyperplanes over a six-dimensional polytope. For my usual fee of 50 kilozorgs per flurb, I think I can locate the optimal vertex in a score of flurbs."

Jar-Gon, the translator robot, spoke as follows:

"He says you have a multiple objective linear programming problem (MOLP), and he'll solve your problem in 20 flurbs for a fee of one megazorb."

"Wrong, buster," said Sissy to Harv. "You might be able to model my problem, but I'm the only one who can solve it!"

However, Harv's comment had sparked Sissy's memory of the MS course she had taken long ago. It was obvious that there were four linear objective functions, which she entered into her wrist-computer implementation of an advanced LP module as follows:

P1: MIN$c_1'x$ = $3x_1 + 5x_2 + 6x_3 + 6x_4 + 7x_5 + 9x_6$
P2: MIN$c_2'x$ = $4x_1 + 5x_2 + 8x_3 + 5x_4 + 6x_5 + 8x_6$
P3: MIN$c_3'x$ = $6x_1 + 7x_2 + 3x_3 + 10x_4 + 5x_5 + 7x_6$
P4: MIN$c_4'x$ = $12x_1 + 9x_2 + 10x_3 + 4x_4 + 8x_5 + 3x_6$

There were six lower-bound constraints of the form $x_j \geq 10,000$, $j = 1, \ldots, 6$, which she entered in the lower bound row of the entry screen for each variable. That left only two constraints to deal with: the requirement to produce at least 100,000 power units per kiloflurb and the limitations on available person-flurbs of labor (250,000). Sissy estimated that the Athos(x_1), Porthos(x_2), and D'Artagnan(x_4) models required three person-flurbs of labor per unit, while the other three brands required only two person-flurbs per unit. Sissy entered the constraints into the computer as follows.

S T: $x_1 + x_2 + x_3 + x_4 + x_5 + x_6 \geq 100,000$
$3x_1 + 3x_2 + 2x_3 + 3x_4 + 2x_5 + 2x_6 \leq 250,000$

Sissy recognized that she had a set of four commensurable linear objective functions but wasn't quite ready to select one of the criteria she had learned about. "I think I'll experiment a bit first," she mused.

SOLUTION TO THE MODEL

Sissy first solved four single-objective LP models using each of the four linear objectives in a minimizing LP algorithm. Her results are in Table 14.13.

At first glance, the four different cost estimates seemed to give total minimum costs in a fairly narrow range—from $500,000 to $580,000 kilozorgs. But then it dawned on Sissy that the four product mixes varied widely as well. What would be the effect of using a product mix that was optimal for $c_i'x$ and having $c_j'x$ being the correct objective function? She hastily calculated all possible combinations and assembled them as in Table 14.14.

"Jumping Jupiter," Sissy exclaimed to herself. "If I used Esther's objective function ($c_1'x$) and Zero was right ($c_4'x$), costs could skyrocket to 900K kilozorgs, and I'd probably end up as a flunky on some forsaken minor planet. On the other hand, if Perry is right and I decided to use the product mix suggested by his objective function ($c_3'x$), I could bring

TABLE 14.13

Objective Function	Minimum Cost (kilozorgs)	Optimal Mix							
		x_1	x_2	x_3	x_4	x_5	x_6	S_1	S_2
$c_1'x$	540K	30K	10K	30K	10K	10K	10K	0	0
$c_2'x$	560K	30K	10K	10K	10K	30K	10K	0	0
$c_3'x$	500K	10K	10K	50K	10K	10K	10K	0	20K
$c_4'x$	580K	10K	10K	10K	10K	10K	50K	0	20K

TABLE 14.14

		If $c_i'x$ Is Correct			
		$c_1'x$	$c_2'x$	$c_3'x$	$c_4'x$
	$c_1'x$	540K	600K	560K	900K
If the Optimal Mix	$c_2'x$	560K	560K	600K	860K
for $c_i'x$ Is Used	$c_3'x$	600K	680K	500K	860K
	$c_4'x$	720K	680K	660K	580K

costs in at 500K kilozorgs—and I'd be a cinch for early promotion. I'd better proceed with caution on this decision!"

Sissy turned her attention back to her MS course. The four objective functions were obviously commensurable, since she had stated them all in kilozorgs per kiloflurb—which meant that she could use a MAXIMIN or a linear combinations approach. Since she was trying to minimize costs, the first criterion seemed inappropriate. She had no way to judge the relative accuracy of the four cost functions, so she decided to weight them equally, as follows:

$$c_5'x = 0.25(c_1'x + c_2'x + c_3'x + c_4'x)$$

Table 14.15 presents the SAMS quick briefing for this model's solution.

The really interesting thing was that the solution gave the following objective values for the four original objective functions:

	$c_1'x$	$c_2'x$	$c_3'x$	$c_4'x$
Solution Using $c_5'x$	620K	580K	680K	700K

TABLE 14.15 SAMS report for Spacetrek model

SPACETREK
QUICK BRIEFING ON OPTIMAL MODEL SOLUTION
Minimum Objective Value = 645000.0

Decision Variable	Optimal Value	Reduced Cost
X1	30000.0	0.0
X2	10000.0	0.0
X3	10000.0	0.0
X4	10000.0	0.0
X5	30000.0	0.0
X6	10000.0	0.0

Constraint	Slack	Shadow Price

All constraints binding.

SOLUTION TO THE PROBLEM

If Sissy used the mix suggested by the linear combinations criterion and if one of the four original estimates happened to be correct, the best Sissy could do would be 580K—but the worst would be 700K. This approach would clearly be "satisficing"— trading off an opportunity to reduce costs to 500K to protect herself against costs of 900K kilozorgs. There was no early promotion in the offing using this strategy, but neither was banishment to the cosmic equivalent of Siberia.

"What the quark!" she thought to herself. "Faint heart never won fair gherkin!"

And she ordered production of 50,000 Aramis models in addition to the required 10,000 of the other five brands (the optimal model solution using P3, Perry's objective function).

EPILOGUE

Two megaflurbs later, Assistant Drone Second Class Spacetrek gazed into the heavens from her tiny office on a tiny planet in the galaxy Morpheus, awaiting the arrival of the next garbage barge. As it turned out, Zero Graffiti's estimate of costs had been right on the button—and Sissy's hasty decision on product mix had caused costs to rocket to 860,000 kilozorgs per kiloflurb. Speaking to her only companion, the psychorobot R-N1X-N, Sissy noted sadly. "Ah, N1X-N, the price of ambition is astronomical." ∎

Budgeting in Blacksburg [5]

THE SCENARIO

Virginia Polytechnic Institute and State University (VPI&SU), more widely known as Virginia Tech, is a comprehensive major university located in Blacksburg, Virginia. Its respected business school includes on its faculty Professors Art Keown, Chuck Taylor, and John Pinkerton, who authored the paper upon which we base this minicase.

THE PROBLEM

As is true with most universities, Virginia Tech is in a capital rationing situation with respect to investment in fixed assets: there is simply not enough money available to meet every need. The existence of multiple goals or objectives, stated in incommensurable units, compounds the problem.

Working with university administrators, the researchers identified 11 specific goals to be achieved, if at all possible, and a preemptive prioritization of goals, as follows:

P1: Limit expenditures to $450,000.
P2: Limit annual increases in operating expenses that result from capital expenditures to $200,000.
P3: Spend at least $120,000 (total) on the following projects (because of earmarked funds):
 a. Install remote batcher in engineering building.
 b. Expand engineering library.
 c. Build new engineering-physics research facilities: prototype A.
 d. Build new engineering-physics research facilities: prototype B.
 e. Renovate engineering building.
P4: Increase total library square footage by at least 12,500 square feet.
P5: For business school accreditation purposes, accept at least two of the following nine proposals:
 a. Purchase CDC computer system.
 b. Purchase IBM computer system.
 c. Upgrade current UNIVAC computer system.
 d. Install remote batcher in business building.
 e. Expand business school library.
 f. Renovate business building: prototype A.
 g. Renovate business building: prototype B.
 h. Build behavioral observation labs: prototype A.
 i. Build behavioral observation labs: prototype B.
P6: Accept at least one of the following projects:
 a. Purchase CDC computer system.
 b. Purchase IBM computer system.
 c. Upgrade current UNIVAC computer system.
 d. Expand north campus library.
P7: Increase the performance measure in the business school by at least 50,000 quality-adjusted student days (QASDs). [*Note:* QASDs are the product of student days × (some quality proxy, which may be objective—e.g., SAT scores—or subjective).]
P8: Increase the performance in the engineering school by at least 40,000 QASDs.
P9: Increase the performance measure in the chemistry department by at least 15,000 QASDs.
P10: Increase the performance measure in the physics department by at least 35,000 QASDs.
P11: Increase the performance measure in the psychology department by at least 30,000 QASDs.

In addition to the preceding goals, the university's administration imposed "hard" upper-bound constraints on the purchase of engineering lab equipment ($30,000), chemistry lab equipment ($25,000), and physics lab equipment ($35,000).

THE MODEL

The decision variables x_j, $j = 1, \ldots, 22$ for this model relate to 22 specific projects described in Figure 14.2. Note that the first 19 variables represent go/no-go decisions similar to those discussed in Chapter 3. Variables x_{20}, x_{21}, and x_{22}, however, represent continuous decisions (how much money to spend on lab equipment). Since the underlying problem appears otherwise to meet the additivity assumption and one of the two divisibility assumptions, it appears that the researchers appropriately modeled the problem as a mixed integer (otherwise linear) pure preemptive goal programming model, with x_1 to x_{19} as zero-one variables.

This is a fairly large and complex model, and we will not exhibit it here in its entirety. Instead, let's look at some of the more interesting modeling devices that were used.

Modeling the goal constraints is fairly straightforward. For example, the goal constraint for P1, the highest preemptive goal, is as follows.

$$\sum_{j=1}^{22} c_j x_j = \$450,000 + d_1^+ - d_1^-,$$

where the c_j are the elements of the Cost column in Figure 14.2. Likewise, the objective P3 (earmarked funds) becomes

$$\$50,000x_5 + \$100,000x_8 + \$190,000x_{12} + \$120,000x_{13} + \$80,000x_{17} = \$120,000 + d_3^+ - d_3^-$$

Objective P6 was modeled as follows:

$$x_1 + x_2 + x_3 + x_{10} = 1 + d_6^+ - d_6^-$$

so that the goal is to fund at least one of these four projects.

The most interesting feature of this model is that some subsets of the goals are mutually exclusive; that is, if they fund one of the related projects, they would not fund any of the others in that set. For example, the first three projects in the list involve alternative ways to acquire computing capability. We can assure that at most one of these alternatives is selected in the following way:

$$x_1 + x_2 + x_3 = 1 + d_{12}^+ - d_{12}^-$$

Other mutually exclusive sets are x_{11} and x_{12} (large vs. small experimental labs), x_{13} and x_{14} (two different prototypes of engineering-physics research facilities), x_{15} and x_{16} (two different prototypes for renovating the business building), and x_{18} and x_{19} (two different prototypes of behavior observation labs).

Another interesting feature of the model is the existence of contingent projects. Implementation of either x_{18} or x_{19} (construction of behavioral observation labs) would be contingent upon the prior decision to renovate the business building (i.e., $x_{15} = 1$). This relationship was modeled as follows:

$$x_{18} + x_{19} - x_{15} = 0 + d_{17}^+ - d_{17}^-$$

The full-blown model, then, has the following characteristics:

FIGURE 14.2 VPI&SU projects

Variable	Description	Cost $000	Annual Operating Expenses $000	Library 000 sq. ft.	BA QASD 000	ENGR QASD 000	CHEM QASD 000	PHYS QASD 000	PSY QASD 000	Desig Funds	Satisfies Accr.	Satisfies Polit/ Social Obj.
x_1	CDC Syst	$190	$25		20	15	10	10	5		X	X
x_2	IBM Syst	230	30		30	23	15	15	8		X	X
x_3	UNIVAC Upgr.	90	25		8	6	4	4	2		X	X
x_4	Batch. N. Camp.	60	6				6	10				X
x_5	Batch. ENGR	50	5			12				50		
x_6	Batch. BA	50	5		14						X	
x_7	Exp. M. Libr.	250	40	15	15	10	22	22	15			
x_8	Exp. B. Libr.	150	25	8	40					100	X	
x_9	Exp. E. Libr.	100	15	5		25						
x_{10}	Exp. N. Libr.	150	23	8			20	20				
x_{11}	Add. S. Labs.	50	10		2	10	6					
x_{12}	Add. L. Labs.	80	16		4	15	12			190		
x_{13}	EN/PH Fac. A	190	20			40		20		120		
x_{14}	EN/PH Fac. B	120	12			20		25				
x_{15}	Renov. BA: A	160	10		45						X	
x_{16}	Renov. BA: B	80	5		20						X	
x_{17}	Renov. ENGR	80	5			20				80		
x_{18}	Behav. Labs A	120	10		20				18		X	
x_{19}	Behav. Labs B	70	6		10				13		X	
x_{20}	ENGR Equip	$ 1*	$ 1*			.17/$						
x_{21}	CHEM Equip	"*	"*				.15/$					
x_{22}	PHYS Equip	"*	"*					.20/$				

*$1 per $1 invested.

1. Eleven preemptive priority objectives stated in terms of minimizing sums of 34 deviational variables.
2. Three functional upper-bound constraints on the continuous variables x_{20}, x_{21}, and x_{22}, imposed by the central administration, (*Note:* The authors of the paper originally modeled these three constraints as deviational constraints. We changed them to functional constraints for illustrative purposes only.)
3. Eleven constraints defining the deviational goals.
4. Six constraints that impose the mutually exclusive and contingency features.
5. Twenty-two decision variables, the first 19 of which are of the zero-one variety.

SOLUTION TO THE MODEL

The paper [5] reports the model solution as follows but does not state how the authors obtained it (perhaps with proprietary software):

1. They completely attained Goals 1–8.
2. Goal 9 was 6,000 QASDs short of the goal of 15,000 (chemistry).
3. Goal 10 was 25,000 QASDs short of the goal of 35,000 (physics).
4. Goal 11 was short all of its target of 30,000 QASDs (psychology).

In the process of meeting these goals, the optimization algorithm selected six projects for funding (see Table 14.16).

TABLE 14.16

Project	Cost
x_4: Remote batch site for north campus	$ 60,000
x_6: Remote batcher—business building	50,000
x_8: Expansion—business school library	150,000
x_9: Expansion—Engineering library	100,000
x_{17}: Renovate engineering building	80,000
x_{21}: Purchase chemistry lab equipment	20,000
Total	$460,000

Since the total adds to $460,000 (instead of $450,000, the P1 target), we surmise that there is a typo and that there was only $10,000 to spend on chemistry lab equipment.

SOLUTION TO THE PROBLEM

The authors concluded their paper with the following statement:

> It is the hope of the authors that this model will provide University administrators with a further tool to help them in the complicated task of allocating limited funds among the various alternative proposals [5].

Let us join them in that hope!

SUMMARY

In this chapter, we explored one aspect of multicriterion decision making referred to as multiple objective linear programming (MOLP). We saw that sets of multiple objectives can be either commensurable or incommensurable.

We discussed four modeling strategies: MAXIMIN, linear combinations, preemptive goal prioritization, and preemptive goal programming. We noted that we can use any of the four if our set of goals is of the commensurable variety but that only the latter two were appropriate when our objectives are incommensurable.

Solution techniques turned out to be one of two types: transformation of the MOLP model into an ordinary single-objective LP model and use of the SIMPLEX technique, or modifying the SIMPLEX algorithm to enforce preemptive priorities in the objective set.

We looked briefly at some advanced modeling approaches and ended our journey through MOLP with three complex minicases.

Chapter 15 investigates a different approach to dealing with uncertainty—visual and multiattribute choice models.

KEY TERMS

mixed preemptive modeling

multiple objective linear programming (MOLP)

preemptive goal prioritization

preemptive goal programming

PROBLEMS FOR ANALYSIS

1. Let's return to our interactive computer friend POPGO and his loquacious client HOWARD.

    HOWARD: POPGO, I have digested the remainder of this exemplary chapter, have committed it to memory, and am prepared to extend our verbal perambulations.
    POPGO: Ten-four, Howard. I'll lay out the model one more time, after rearranging some stuff and scaling Equation (14.26).

    $$\text{P1: MIN } (x_0)_1 = d_1^- \qquad (14.23)$$

    $$\text{P2: MIN } (x_0)_2 = d_2^+ \qquad (14.24)$$

    $$\text{P3: MIN } (x_0)_3 = d_3^+ \qquad (14.25)$$

    $$\text{S T: } 1.5x_1 + 3x_2 + 2x_3 + 1.5x_4 + 3x_5 + 2x_6 - d_1^+ + d_1^- = 600 \qquad (14.26)$$

    $$x_4 + x_5 + x_6 - d_2^+ + d_2^- = 0 \qquad (14.27)$$

    $$x_3 + x_6 - d_3^+ + d_3^- = 0 \qquad (14.28)$$

    $$3x_3 + 3x_4 + x_5 + 2x_6 \leq 300 \qquad (14.29)$$

    $$2x_4 + 3x_5 + 5x_6 \leq 240 \qquad (14.30)$$

    $$x_1 + 2x_2 + x_4 + 2x_5 \leq 270 \qquad (14.31)$$

    $$\text{all } x_j, d_1^+, d_1^-, d_2^+, d_2^-, d_3^+, d_3^- \geq 0 \qquad (14.32)$$

    HOWARD: Restrain your equine quadrupeds, POPGO. This so-called pure preemptive goal programming paradigm is not my demitasse of pekoe. I have, during

```
          SAMS INPUT SCREEN - Linear Programming
    NAME?  BALLOON SPECIALISTS INC.
    MAximize or MInimize?  MA
    PROBLEM DESCRIPTION - Optimize multiple objective balloon
                         mix problem for HOWARD.

    Variables     X1     X2     X3     X4     X5     X6    Dir   RHS

    Objective    1.5    3.     2.    1.5    3.     2.     <

    Upper Bound  INF    INF    INF    INF    INF    INF    =
    Lower Bound  0.     0.     0.     0.     0.     0.     >

    Constraints
    PROFIT       1.5    3.     2.    1.5    3.     2.     >      0.
    ALBUQUER     0.     0.     0.    1.     1.     1.     >      0.
    STRATOS      0.     0.     1.    0.     0.     1.     >      0.
    FINISH       0.     0.     3.    3.     1.     2.     <    300.
    ASSEMBLE     0.     0.     0.    2.     3.     5.     <    240.
    INFLATE      1.     2.     0.    1.     2.     0.     <    270.
```

FIGURE 14.3 SAMS input screen for Balloon Specialists - I

the hiatus, fashioned my own unique algorithm—which I have christened Simple Simon.

POPGO: Like, how does Simple Simon work?

HOWARD: Exceptionally well. I will explicate the algorithmic details so that you may convey this construction to subsequent clientele.

I employed the electronic implementation of a SIMPLEX algorithm in a most ingenious fashion. Observe the SAMS LP input screen [Figure 14.3], noting that I have performed a scaling procedure to mitigate undesirable computational outcomes. Observe, POPGO, that I cleverly inserted the three objectives as nonbinding constraints and inserted my profitability requirement as the initial objective function. The recapitulation from SAMS ensues [Table 14.17].

Take note that my initial analysis has eclipsed my stated profit requirements by a handsome $37,000, but alas, this configuration requires 48 constructions in Albuquerque, and Stratos production perseveres at 116 units. But despair not, POPGO—my Simple Simon is not yet fully deployed. Ruminate upon the subsequent input screen [Figure 14.4].

Espy, if you will POPGO, the alterations I effected. We are now minimizing production at Albuquerque, but inserting "600" on the right-hand side of the "PROFIT" restriction to impel Simple Simon to guarantee the required profit. Now marvel at the consequence [Table 14.18 on p. 502].

Voila, POPGO! Simple Simon has succeeded in eliminating all production in Albuquerque while concurrently decreasing Stratos fabrication to 97 units (we must round the fractional entity to achieve an integral result). And the required profit of $600,000 persists.

A third iteration of my Simple Simon, lamentably, failed to achieve a decrease of Stratos construction, but I am ebullient with the result notwithstanding.

POPGO: Howard, you are a case with all that Simple Simon stuff. All you did was to use a preemptive goal prioritization model—and you did it the hard way! Why don't you go to Albuquerque and help inflate the hot air balloons?

TABLE 14.17 SAMS report for Balloon Specialists Model—I

```
BALLOON SPECIALISTS
QUICK BRIEFING ON OPTIMAL MODEL SOLUTION
              Maximum Objective Value = 637.0

      Decision          Optimal           Reduced
      Variable          Value             Cost

        X1              270.0             0.0
        X3               48.0             0.0
        X6              116.0             0.0

      Constraint        Slack             Shadow Price

      PROFIT            637.0             0.0
      ALBUQUER           48.0             0.0
      STRATOS           116.0             0.0
```

```
────► SAMS INPUT SCREEN - Linear Programming ◄────
NAME?  BALLOON SPECIALISTS INC.
MAximize or MInimize?  MA
PROBLEM DESCRIPTION - Optimize multiple objective balloon
                     mix problem for HOWARD.
```

Variables	X1	X2	X3	X4	X5	X6	Dir	RHS
Objective	0.	0.	0.	1.	1.	1.	<	
Upper Bound	INF	INF	INF	INF	INF	INF	=	
Lower Bound	0.	0.	0.	0.	0.	0.	>	
Constraints								
PROFIT	1.5	3.	2.	1.5	3.	2.	>	600.
ALBUQUER	0.	0.	0.	1.	1.	1.	>	0.
STRATOS	0.	0.	1.	0.	0.	1.	>	0.
FINISH	0.	0.	3.	3.	1.	2.	<	300.
ASSEMBLE	0.	0.	0.	2.	3.	5.	<	240.
INFLATE	1.	2.	0.	1.	2.	0.	<	270.

FIGURE 14.4 SAMS input screen for Balloon Specialists—II

HOWARD: You are an impudent set of subroutines that ought to be debugged, POPGO. I shall suggest such to your programmer.

POPGO: Lighten up, Howard. You got a useful solution to your problem—that's the coolest thing. Well, I'm bagging it for now. See you around campus.

a. Model this problem as a pure preemptive goal programming formulation and solve your model with a computerized SIMPLEX package like the SAMS L&IP module. Use a sequenced procedure like Howard's Simple Simon. Will you get the same results that Howard got? Why or why not?

TABLE 14.18 SAMS report for Balloon Specialists Model—II

BALLOON SPECIALISTS
QUICK BRIEFING ON OPTIMAL MODEL SOLUTION

Maximum Objective Value = 0.0

Decision Variable	Optimal Value	Reduced Cost
X1	270.0	0.0
X3	97.5	0.0

Constraint	Slack	Shadow Price
STRATOS	97.5	0.0
FINISH	7.5	0.0
ASSEMBLE	240.0	0.0

    b. Would it have been possible for Howard to realize more than $600,000 profit contribution and still achieve objective P2? How could we model the problem in such a way as to explore this possibility?

    c. Note that objectives P2 and P3 are commensurable, but objective P1 is not commensurable with P2 and P3. Would it be possible to use one of the commensurable criteria to combine P2 and P3 and then to use one of the preemptive prioritization schemes to model the two remaining objectives? (*Note:* We refer to such a scheme as **mixed preemptive modeling.**)

2. Analyze the following brief scenarios and determine whether we could use MOLP modeling techniques to represent and investigate them. In particular, determine whether the multiple objectives (if any) are commensurable or incommensurable and assess the decision-making environments as to their appropriateness for the use of specific MOLP models.

    a. The Infinite Bytes Machine Corporation (IBMC) has 500 professional positions and 300 technician positions to fill worldwide in the next three months. To control costs and satisfy affirmative action requirements, IBMC has established the following goals:

Priority 1: At least 20% of new hires must be minorities.
Priority 2: At least 30% of new hires must be women.
Priority 3: Stay as close as possible to a recruiting budget of $850,000.

It costs $1000 to recruit a professional and $500 to recruit an engineer. Furthermore, it costs 30% more to recruit a minority or female professional.

    b. An advertising agency in the Midwest wishes to achieve the goal of 10,000,000 exposures while minimizing the expenditures required to do so and the amount of television advertising over 75% of budget required. The agency has established a budget of $200,000 for this purpose, and the media chosen are television, FM radio, and AM radio. Table 14.19 gives block costs and exposure ratings for each advertising medium.

TABLE 14.19

Advertising Medium	Per-Unit Block Cost	Rated Exposure per Block
Television	$5,000	500,000
FM radio (Top 40)	1,000	70,000
FM radio (EZ Listening)	2,000	120,000
AM radio	1,500	95,000

c. TrimWaist, a belt manufacturing firm, makes two types of belts: fancy snakeskin belts on which it earns a profit of $4.00 per belt and ordinary goatskin belts on which it earns a profit of $3.00 per belt. Each fancy belt requires twice as much labor as ordinary belts; and if all belts were ordinary, there would be enough labor to make 1,200 such belts in the production period defined by management. The fancy belt requires an ornate platinum buckle, of which 600 are available; and the ordinary belt requires an ordinary aluminum buckle, of which 850 are available. Management wishes to guarantee profit in excess of $3,000 per period while minimizing the amount of overtime, excess skin, and buckles required to do so.

d. A portfolio manager for Provincial Insurance Company is attempting to determine a "best" investment portfolio. She is considering eight investments. Table 14.20 shows the estimates of the historical annual growth rate in price per share, the annual dividend per share, the risk (beta value) associated with each investment, and the price per share.

The manager has $5 million to invest and wishes to maximize her return on investment. (We define "return" as price per share one year hence less current price per share plus dividends per share, all divided by the current price per share.) In addition, she must satisfy Provincial's guidelines, as follows:
1. The maximum dollar amount that she can invest in instruments 2, 4, and 6 cannot exceed $1 million total.
2. The manager must invest at least 30% of the total dollar amount in instruments 1, 3, and 8.
3. Total return on investment should be at least 11 percent.
4. Dividends for the year should exceed $60,000. The manager is particularly interested in minimizing the underachievement of the goal of 11% return on investment. In addition, she wishes to minimize the overachievement of an average overall portfolio risk of 7% and the underachievement of the $60,000 in annual dividends.

TABLE 14.20

SYMBOL	ATT	BLS	CPQ	DUK	EXX	FMC	GTE	HON
#	1	2	3	4	5	6	7	8
Annual growth rate	0.12	0.05	0.15	0.08	0.09	0.03	0.13	0.11
Annual dividend/share	1.23	5.10	1.18	2.30	3.42	6.51	1.75	3.13
Risk	1.13	0.85	1.21	0.92	0.72	0.65	1.35	0.95
Current price/share	350	10	15	89	23	45	130	65

e. The Landeau Cotton Company has three major supply depots and four major shipping destinations. We know that the availability of cotton at each depot is 3,500, 2,500, and 4,800 bales, respectively. The demand at each of the four destinations is 1,122, 2,116, 2,438, and 3,121 bales, respectively. The VP for Distribution is interested in minimizing his purchase and transportation costs. He wants a transportation plan (i.e., how many bales to ship from depot i to destination j) as well as how many bales to buy at each depot. Each bale costs $535 at depot 1, $565 at depot 2, and $610 at depot 3. The transportation costs are as follows:

	Destination			
Depot	1	2	3	4
1	45	55	61	70
2	70	35	48	65
3	60	55	38	59

Landeau Cotton has budgeted $3,200,000 for purchase of the bales and $300,000 for transportation of the bales. The VP wishes to maximize the underachievement of these targeted amounts.

3. **The Scenario:** Let's return to the Spacetrek minicase and give Sissy a second chance to avoid banishment.

   The Problem: Sissy's problem remains the same.

   The Model: Ms. Spacetrek is still faced with her decision on product mix of the six brands of ion power units, and as before, neither Esther, Telly, Perry, nor Zero will change his or her objective function cost estimates by a single zorg.

   As Sissy previously noted, the four objective functions are commensurable. She dismissed the MAXIMIN criterion as inappropriate for a minimization model and weighted the four estimates equally in using the linear combination criterion. However, could she have used a MINIMAX criterion, as follows:

   MIN x_0 = MAX $\{c_1'x, c_2'x, c_3'x, c_4'x\}$

   Let us define our surrogate variable y in the following way:

   $y > c_k'x$, $k = 1, \ldots, 4$

   Our transformed LP model now becomes

   MIN $x_0 = y$

   ST: $y - 3x_1 - 5x_2 - 6x_3 - 6x_4 - 7x_5 - 9x_6 \geq 0$
   $y - 4x_1 - 5x_2 - 8x_3 - 5x_4 - 6x_5 - 8x_6 \geq 0$
   $y - 6x_1 - 7x_2 - 3x_3 - 10x_4 - 5x_5 - 7x_6 \geq 0$
   $y - 12x_1 - 9x_2 - 10x_3 - 4x_4 - 8x_5 - 3x_6 \geq 0$
   $x_1 + x_2 + x_3 + x_4 + x_5 + x_6 \geq 100{,}000$
   $3x_1 + 3x_2 + 2x_3 + 3x_4 + 2x_5 + 2x_6 \leq 250{,}000$

   $y \geq 0$, $x_j \geq 10000$ for all j

   What we have done is to model Sissy's problem in such a way as to limit the worst possible result by seeking the mix that will yield the minimum of maximum possible costs.

As a decision maker, what is your view of this criterion? Does it indeed accomplish the same result for minimization models as the MAXIMIN criterion does for maximization models?

Solution to the Model:
Solve the model with a computer SIMPLEX package and compare your solution with the solution Sissy obtained using the linear combinations criterion. Would you expect the two solutions to be similar? Why or why not?

Solution to the Problem: You are a young, technically well-trained protegé of Sissy Spacetrek's. Sissy enjoys her role as your mentor and has moved you along rapidly in your career. You are currently a management trainee with the title executive assistant to the CEO.

Something about your boss's current problem bothers you, and you have a sinking feeling that disaster lurks around the corner. If Sissy gambles and loses on this one, there are at least a dozen envious VP-level executives who would make certain that you got yours right after Sissy got hers.

Using the SAMS report in Table 14.21 on p. 506 (or your output from another SIMPLEX package) as backup, write a brief analysis of Sissy's problem in the form of a professional memorandum. Present two or more decision alternatives and state the pros and cons of each. Be careful not to openly advocate a particular alternative— Sissy is sensitive to the difference between *decision aiding* and *decision making*.

Epilogue: If you undertake a career as a managerial decision maker, be assured that along the way you will write scores of briefs similar to the above.

4. Determine which among the following sets of objectives are commensurable and which are not, assuming the units are dollars or yen:

   a. maximize gross revenues
   b. minimize production costs
   c. minimize distribution costs
   d. minimize labor overtime costs
   e. minimize material waste costs
   f. maximize total profit contribution
   g. minimize overhead costs
   h. minimize finished goods inventory costs
   i. maximize capital appreciation

   What could you do to make the incommensurable objectives commensurable?

5. Explain why in the toy model the transformed version of the MAXIMIN model yields an LP solution that is entirely different from the individual LP solutions obtained by treating each objective separately. (*Hint:* Examine the constraints of the form Equation 14.35.)

TABLE 14.21

SAMS QUICK BRIEFING FOR SPACETREK MODEL REVISITED
SPACETREK MATHEMATICAL MODEL

Minimize
  Y

Subject to

ESTHER
  $Y - 3 X1 - 5 X2 - 6 X3 - 6 X4 - 7 X5 - 9 X6 > 0$
TELLY
  $Y - 4 X1 - 5 X2 - 8 X3 - 5 X4 - 6 X5 - 8 X6 > 0$
PERRY
  $Y - 6 X1 - 7 X2 - 3 X3 - 10 X4 - 5 X5 - 7 X6 > 0$
ZERO
  $Y - 12 X1 - 9 X2 - 10 X3 - 4 X4 - 8 X5 - 3 X6 > 0$
LB-X1
  $X1 > 10000$
LB-X2
  $X2 > 10000$
LB-X3
  $X3 > 10000$
LB-X4
  $X4 > 10000$
LB-X5
  $X5 > 10000$
LB-X6
  $X6 > 10000$
HOURS UB
  $3 X1 + 3 X2 + 2 X3 + 3 X4 + 2 X5 + 2 X6 < 250000$

SPACETREK
QUICK BRIEFING ON OPTIMAL MODEL SOLUTION

Maximum Objective Value = 657187.5

Decision Variable	Optimal Value	Reduced Cost
Y	657187.5	0.0
X1	10000.0	0.0
X2	10000.0	0.0
X3	19375.0	0.0
X4	21562.5	0.0
X5	10000.0	0.0
X6	29062.5	0.0

Constraint	Slack	Shadow Price
TELLY	11875.0	0.0
HOURS UB	8437.5	0.0
ASSEMBLE	240.0	0.0

PRACTICE MODELS

1. Transform the following MAXIMIN multiple objective model into an equivalent LP model and use an LP package to find the optimal solution:

   MAX x_0 = MIN $\{7x_1 + 5x_2 + 3x_3,\ 12x_1 + 2x_2 + x_3,\ x_1 + 4x_2 + 5x_3\}$

   S T:
   $$x_1 + 3x_2 + x_3 \leq 72$$
   $$5x_1 + x_2 + 2x_3 \leq 94$$
   $$2x_1 + 3x_2 + 4x_3 \leq 112$$
   $$x_1, x_2, x_3 \geq 0$$

2. In Problem 1, assign a weight of 0.5 to the first objective function, 0.2 to the second, and 0.3 to the third and use the linear combination method of MOLP and an LP package to find the optimal model solution.

3. Given the following objective functions and the respective priorities, use the preemptive goal prioritization method of MOLP to find the optimal model solution:

   P1: MAX $x_0^1 = 12x_1 + 10x_2 + 17x_3 + 15x_4 + 23x_5$

   P2: MAX $x_0^2 = 2x_1 + 4x_2 + 5x_3 + x_4 + 2x_5$

   P2: MAX $x_0^3 = 8x_1 + 12x_2 + 9x_3 + 5x_4 + 7x_5$

   S T:
   $$3x_1 + 5x_2 + 3x_3 \leq 170$$
   $$x_1 + x_2 + 2x_3 + x_4 + 5x_5 \leq 212$$
   $$6x_1 + 3x_2 + x_3 + 4x_4 + 5x_5 \leq 140$$
   $$x_1, x_2, x_3, x_4, x_5 \geq 0$$

4. Solve the following pure preemptive goal programming model:

   MIN $x_0 = P1d_1^- + P2d_2^+ + 3P3d_3^+ + 4P3d_4^+ + 7P4d_4^- + 9P4d_3^-$

   S T:
   $$5x_1 + 5x_2 + d_1^- - d_1^+ = 380$$
   $$15x_1 + d_2^- - d_2^+ = 290$$
   $$7x_2 + d_3^- - d_3^+ = 220$$
   $$12x_2 + d_4^- - d_4^+ = 310$$

REFERENCES AND ADDITIONAL READING

1. Angielski, Brian W. Adapted from an unpublished MBA term project report, Virginia Polytechnic Institute and State University (1988).
2. Charnes, A. and W. Cooper. *Management Models and Industrial Applications of Linear Programming.* New York: Wiley, 1961.
3. Ignizio, J. *Goal Programming and Extensions.* Lexington, Mass.: Heath, 1976.
4. Keeney, R., and H. Raiffa. *Decisions with Multiple Objectives: Preferences and Value Tradeoffs.* New York: Wiley, 1976.
5. Keown, A., B. Taylor III, and J. Pinkerton. "Multiple Objective Capital Budgeting Within the University." *Computers and Operations Research* 8 (1981): 59–70.
6. Lee, S. *Goal Programming for Decision Analysis.* New York: Auerbach, 1972.
7. Lee, S. and L. Moore. *Introduction to Decision Sciences.* New York: Petrocelli/Charter, 1975.
8. Zadeh, L. "Outline of a New Approach to the Analysis of Complex Systems and Decision Processes." *IEEE Transactions on Systems, Man and Cybernetics* SMC-3, (1973): 28–44.

CHAPTER 15

Visual and Multiattribute Choice Models

Futurists and historians of our day continually remind us of the greatly increased complexity of the society in which we live. Toffler [10, 11] suggests that this may be due to a burgeoning growth in world population since 1900 and the vastly increased capacity for travel, trade, and communication—manifestations of the tremendous surge in technology.

Today, a decision made by a French bureaucrat concerning the allocation of resources and equipment to agriculture can affect the price of a loaf of bread in America. A decision by a bank in New York to lower its prime rate can affect the price of stocks on securities exchanges across the entire planet. The financial insolvency of a few countries can usher the western banking system into an international monetary crisis.

Not so long ago, such was not the case. Communities and population centers were relatively isolated and self-sustaining. Decisions made in one of these autonomous communities had no effect upon surrounding areas. Today, our population centers are highly interconnected, and we can experience in Miami significant impacts of a decision made in Tokyo. Toffler refers to the environment associated with such decisions as a "mess," which he articulately defines as a "system of interacting problems." In Buenos Aires the problem is an equitable allocation of resources. In London the problem relates to a reasonably priced pound of tea. Toffler goes on to say that while solutions to *problems* are relatively straightforward, solutions to *messes* are much less so.

In this chapter, we concern ourselves with the greatly increased complexity that characterizes our age. We present tools and techniques that should enable us to better understand and therefore cope with the complexity and the consequences associated with any particular action, legislation, or decision.

Contemporary society confronts a plethora of problems, regardless of their origin, including, but not limited to, crime; energy, food, and water resources; air, water, noise, and light pollution; inflation and recession; drug abuse; international terrorism; the rising cost of health care; massive deficits in federal budgets; and balance-of-trade deficits. To a certain extent these problems are tied together. Chapter 1 discussed the energy, economy, environment triad depicted in Figure 15.1. It discussed how problems in one of these areas can lead to problems in the other areas.

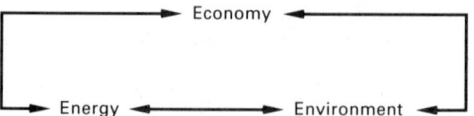

FIGURE 15.1
The energy-economy-environment triad

While it is true that "messes" may have a strong societal flavor, they have important implications for the private sector. Increasingly, society is forcing industries and corporations to maintain a greater social consciousness. Government bodies have passed legislation making certain levels of water and air pollution unlawful and forcing industry to find ways to curtail its pollutive tendencies. Various regulatory agencies of the federal government examine consumer products more closely in terms of public safety, health, and welfare. Hence, the applicability of the techniques we will describe extends to both the public and the private sectors.

At the same time, these techniques are finding increased acceptance and applicability to the complex issues that managers and executives in private industry deal with daily. The pervasiveness of computers gives today's managers access to vast amounts of information. The phenomenon of **information overload** is therefore frequent, and its harmful effects on decision making can be almost as devastating as having too little information. What we need is a kind of **decision support system** that would structure the information so that we can assimilate it—so that we can readily perceive the appropriate corrective action. In this chapter we first discuss some helpful and widely used visual or graphical models. We then illustrate how a generic decision support system operates by introducing a simple multiattribute choice model.

UNDERLYING ASSUMPTIONS

In modeling with visual/graphical models, we assume that there is some structure that either describes the organization of the object system or prescribes how we should organize the system. The system can be actual, as in an existing socioeconomic system, or abstract, as in a collection of proposed objectives. In addition, we presume that we can portray the underlying structure by means of a visual/graphical modeling device—a tree, graph, matrix, or chart. The following are other assumptions characteristic of this type of modeling:

1. The structure portrayed by the modeling device will convey important information about the object system.
2. The process of developing the structural model will achieve its intended goal.

We accomplish the process by a transformation of models from one form to another, and we refer to this transformation as a **model exchange isomorphism** (see Figure 15.2).

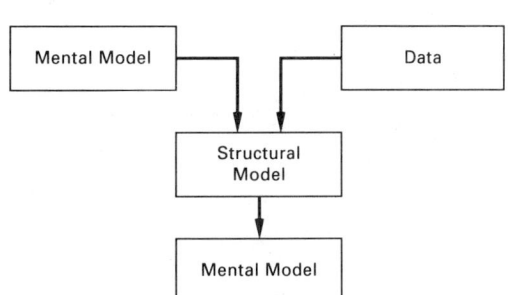

FIGURE 15.2
Model exchange isomorphisms

GRAPHICAL TECHNIQUES: AN INTUITIVE DESCRIPTION

The basic idea behind visual/graphical modeling is to organize and portray information in such a way that others readily perceive the structure (and its implications). The old adage "A picture is worth a thousand words" applies here. Through the use of graphs, trees, charts, and matrices, we can achieve an elegant portrayal of the information. The modeler begins with a mental model of portions of the object system and then uses the artifacts to communicate with others.

Two simple charts we frequently use in presentations are the bar chart and the pie chart, as in Figures 15.3 and 15.4. Corporations often use bar charts in their annual

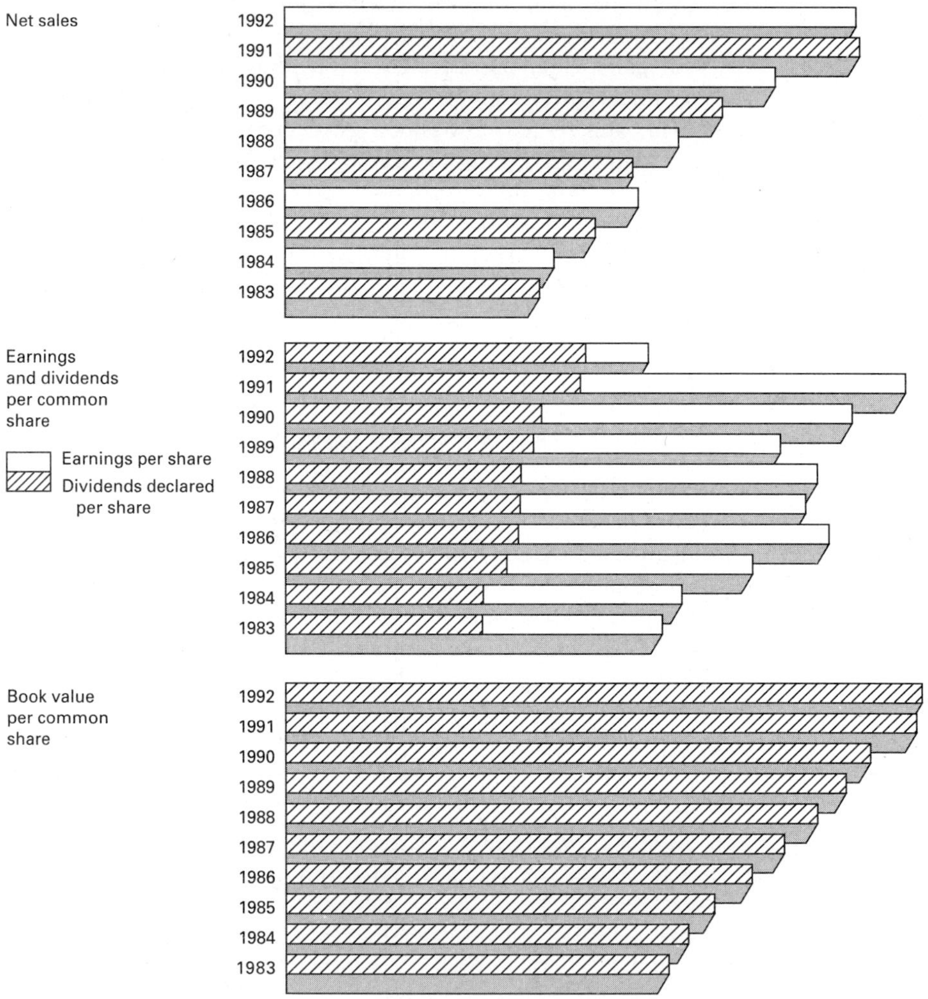

FIGURE 15.3 Typical bar charts showing trends in net sales, earnings, and book value of a common share of a company

FIGURE 15.4 Typical pie charts showing sales by region and by product

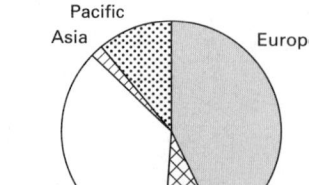
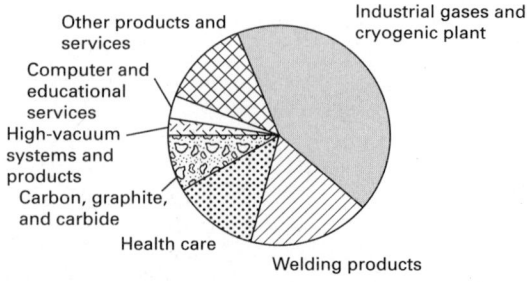

reports to depict trends in annual gross revenues or earnings. Pie charts are useful devices for illustrating market share or for depicting how we allocated the budget among the various operating entities. The ever-increasing sophistication of corporate software now enables computer generation of such charts. Another frequently used chart is the organization chart, which graphically depicts reporting authority and chain of command. Figure 15.5 on p. 512 is a typical organization chart for a large, comprehensive business school.

CHARTS FOR PROJECT PLANNING AND SCHEDULING

Researchers have developed a number of charts to assist managers in organizing the various activities that a project comprises and in completing the project on time and within budget. The more popular among these are the **Gantt chart,** the **DELTA chart,** and the **PERT chart,** discussed in the following paragraphs.

THE GANTT MILESTONE CHART

An industrial engineer named Henry Gantt developed the Gantt milestone chart in 1908. Figure 15.6 on p. 513 shows a typical Gantt chart. To construct a Gantt chart, we begin by determining the major tasks and activities that we must complete in the project. The Gantt chart uses bars to indicate when we will perform tasks, and the chart displays bars plotted against time. Each bar designates a starting date and a completion date for each activity. In constructing the chart, we must consider the precedence relationships that exist between activities, since some activities cannot begin until others are complete. Once constructed, the chart serves to guide the manager in determining the resources required in any given production period. The chart serves as a time model against which we can compare and monitor the progress of the various activities that the project comprises. One limitation of the Gantt chart is that it cannot provide information about the slack times associated with noncritical activities.

THE DELTA CHART

Warfield and Hill [12] developed the DELTA chart as a method for portraying R&D projects. The DELTA chart is a form of flowchart that depicts the planned flow of activities (and their actors) for a project. As an alternative to network methods such as PERT and GERT, it does some things that network representations cannot do. Specifically, it denotes the actor or doer of the activity and indicates any logical relationships that might exist among the activities. For example, we cannot start some activities until we have completed all preceding activities, while we can start others if one or more of several activities are complete. The method can also specify any decisions that we must make as the project progresses.

DELTA is an acronym for the words decision, event, logic, time arrow, and activity—the basic components of any DELTA chart. Figure 15.7 on p. 514 portrays the symbols we use for these components, and Figure 15.8 on pp. 516-517 presents a typical DELTA chart.

As is apparent from Figure 15.8, we label each activity box with the actor who will perform the activity. Also the DELTA chart's flowchart appearance makes it an excellent vehicle for diagramming procedures and programmed plans. Its utility in this latter context may even exceed its original intended purpose—portraying R&D projects. As a method for modeling procedural activities, the DELTA chart is a road map, a guide to accomplishment of a task that is sufficiently complex to require explicit, detailed explanation. As a method for project portrayal, the DELTA chart is of greater use as a planning and execution instrument rather than as an instrument for monitoring and control of the project schedules.

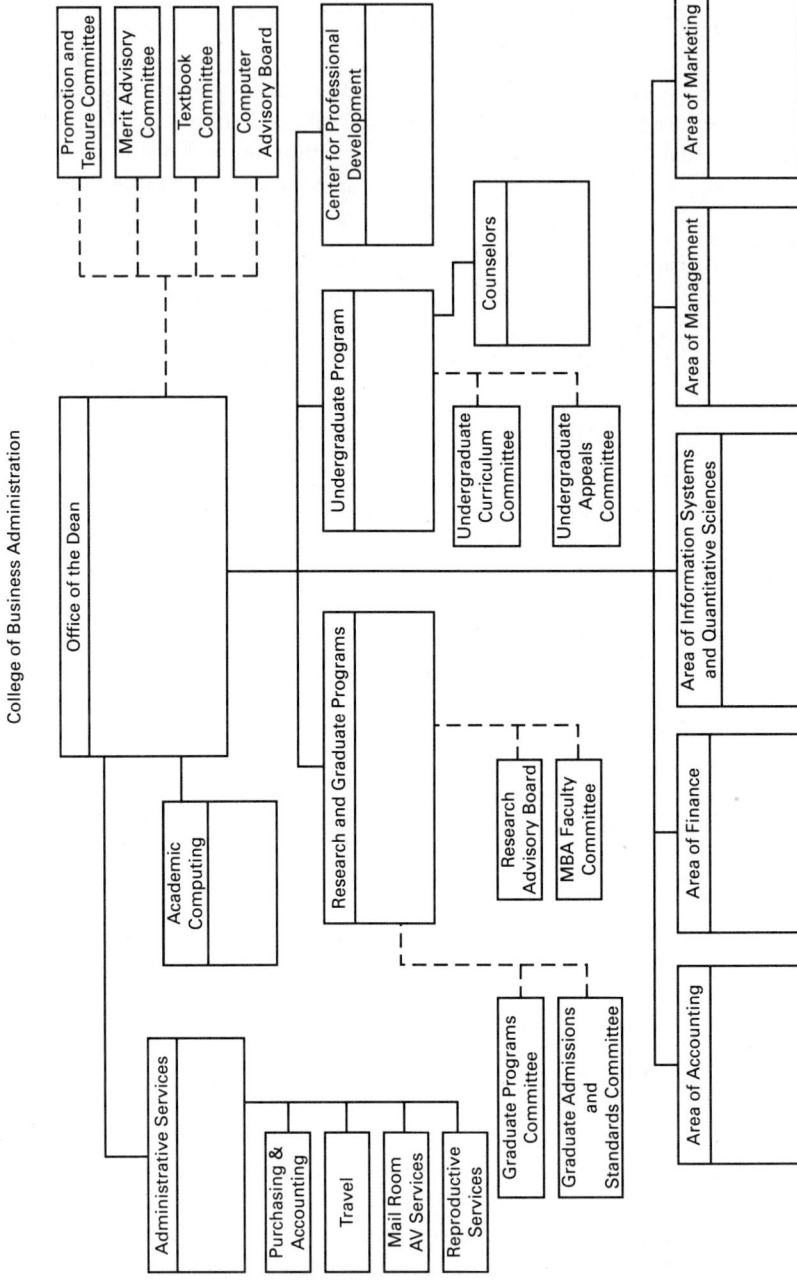

FIGURE 15.5 A typical organization chart

CHAPTER 15 VISUAL AND MULTIATTRIBUTE CHOICE MODELS 513

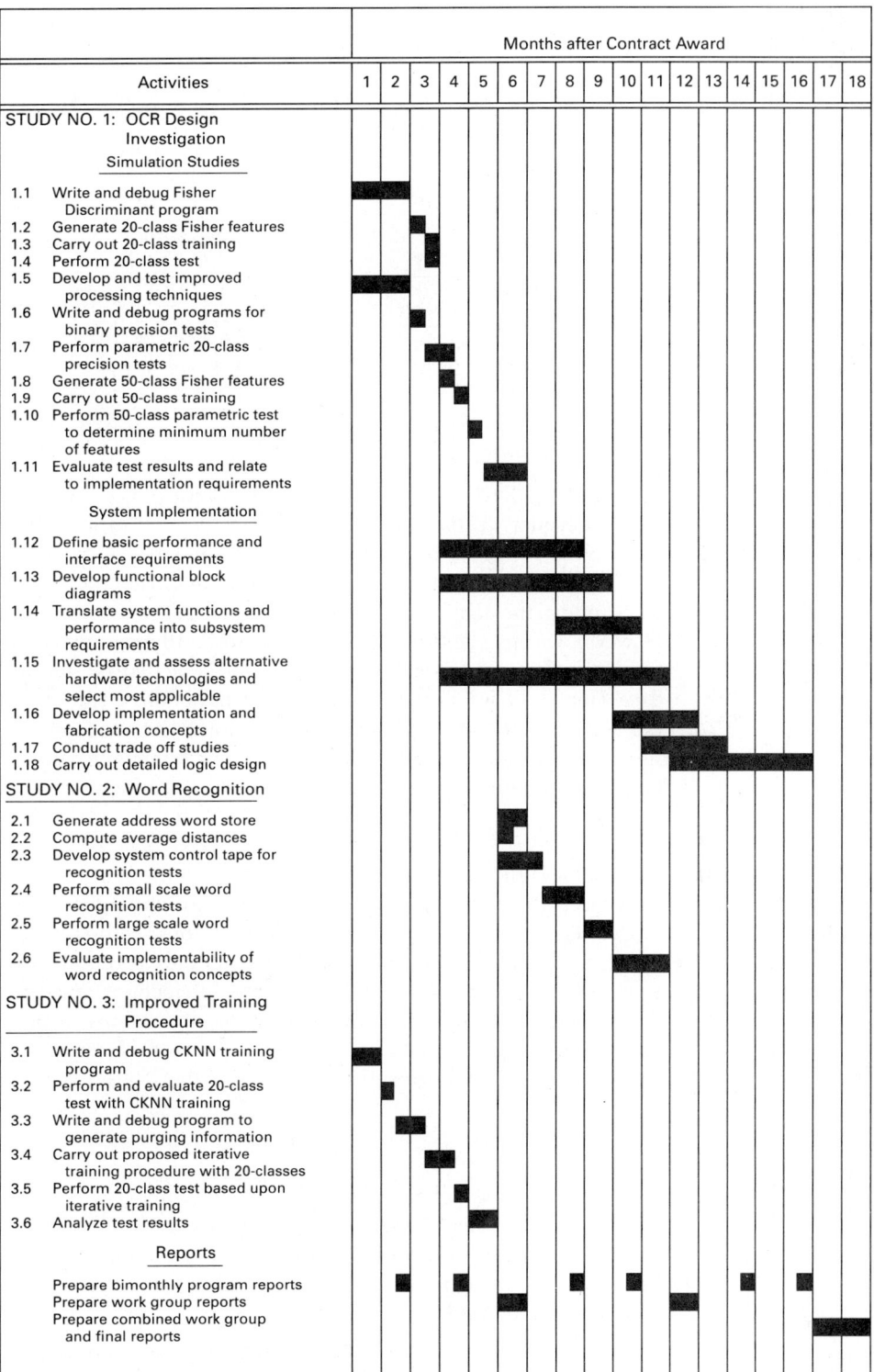

FIGURE 15.6 A typical Gantt chart [12]

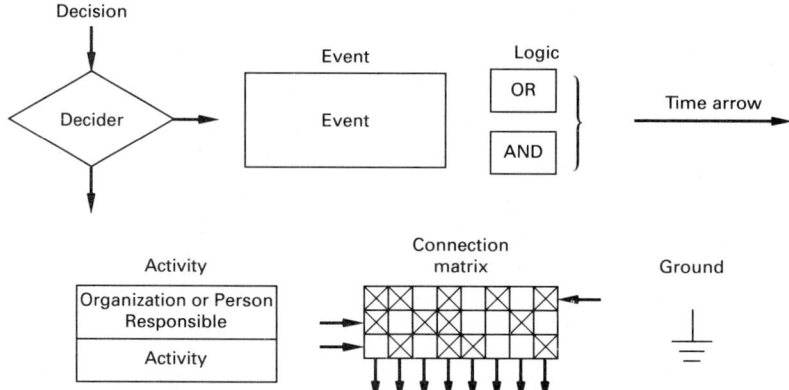

FIGURE 15.7
Symbols for
DELTA charts [12]

THE PERT CHART

Like the term *DELTA*, PERT is an acronym for project evaluation and review technique. Chapter 11 discussed PERT models. A great variety of different PERT charts has evolved with ever-increasing sophistication and realism. Originally, PERT charts were deterministic. In this form, as discussed in Chapter 4, such charts were useful in determining the total expected time (longest path) required to complete a project. However, we can use PERT to determine the bottleneck activities on the critical path, for which there is no slack associated with the activities' starting date or completion date. Hence, PERT's capabilities exceed those of the Gantt chart. For this reason, we especially recommend PERT charts for projects of moderate to large size. In such situations, we can use the PERT chart as an instrument or method for project planning but, more importantly, as a tool for project management and control.

MORPHOLOGICAL METHODS AND MODELS

Morphology—the study of structure or form and the features composing the form and any of its parts—is the fundamental activity of structural modelers. The morphological model begins with determining major dimensions, elements, tasks, attributes, or activities associated with a problem. If there are only two dimensions, a matrix may be a convenient instrument for describing the interactions among the components that the dimensions comprise. If there are three dimensions, a box or cube may prove useful. If there are more than three dimensions, some form of tree is usually best. Our discussion of morphological devices begins with a consideration of trees.

TREES

One of the more useful graphical aids in management science is the **tree**—simply a set of elements or vertices joined by line segments or arcs. There can be at most one arc between every pair of elements in the tree, and we disallow loops and cycles. People have used several types of trees in the analysis and synthesis of organizations and processes, including the following:

- decision tree
- objectives tree
- activity tree
- worth tree
- probability tree
- relevance tree

Chapter 7, "Decision Making Under Risk," illustrated the decision tree.

CHAPTER 15 VISUAL AND MULTIATTRIBUTE CHOICE MODELS

We use the **objectives tree** (sometimes called an intent structure [4]) to describe the relationships that exist among a set of objectives. We construct such trees by first listing the objectives (perhaps on separate slips of paper) and then organizing them into some form of structure that reveals a pattern or strategy for accomplishing the objectives. For example, if objective 2 contributes to the achievement of objective 1, we might place objective 1 in relation to objective 2 as in Figure 15.9. If the resultant structure involving some n separate objectives is a tree, the structure is truly an objectives tree. The objectives tree in Figure 15.9 on p. 518 suggests that by accomplishing objective 2, we will also accomplish objective 1. We derive this insight from the meaning given to the edge or arrow connecting objective 2 to objective 1.

If we apply this same meaning to possible relationships that exist among a set of n objectives, we can construct a more complicated objectives tree like the one in Figure 15.10 on p. 518. A clear strategy for achieving the system of objectives is obvious from the tree. It is possible, when required, to include some of the detail used in DELTA charts in objectives trees. For example, we could include the ownership of each objective by simply labeling each objective with its rightful owner. However, this is necessary only when ownership differs from objective to objective. In addition, we may include logic elements between objectives to designate whether all or some of the preceding objectives are necessary to achieve the ones that follow.

We state each objective beginning with an infinitive. One way to systematically construct an objectives tree is to consider every possible objectives pair by using the phrase or relation "Does objective i contribute to the immediate achievement of objective k in some way?" If the response is yes, we should draw an arrow or arc from objective i to objective k; otherwise, we do not draw this arc.

We use the **activity tree** to depict the relationships between and among a collection of organizational activities. The activity tree differs from a PERT-like activity network in that we arrange the activities into a natural hierarchy. We could construct such a model by first listing the activities and then interrelating them with the relation "Does activity i support the accomplishment of activity j in some way?" The activity tree has applications in project planning and control.

Each vertex in an activity tree represents an activity, and each arc connecting the activity to a higher level activity connotes that the activity contributes in some way to the conduct of the higher level activity. We would normally construct an objectives tree before setting up an activity tree. Figure 15.11 on p. 518 is an example of an activity tree.

The **worth tree** has applications in worth assessment and multiattribute utility theory. Figure 15.12 on p. 519 gives an example of a worth tree. We can use the tree in Figure 15.12 in deciding upon the worth or overall value of each home in a set of homes that a buyer is contemplating buying. Notice that we assigned each arc a value representing the relative "benefit" of the attribute below to the attribute or feature above the arc. Thus, we assigned "neighborhood" a benefit value of 0.4 in relation to the feature "location." The relative benefit coefficients associated with each arc that emanates downward from a vertex above it always sum to 1.

We can use this tree to assign an overall worth value to each home in a collection of homes we are considering for possible purchase. To each of the attributes on the bottom of the tree in Figure 15.12 we assign a value from zero to one representing our subjective "satisfaction" with the attribute. Table 15.1 on p. 519 considers three homes.

We use the attribute values for a particular home to evaluate the tree. We obtain the worth of a higher level attribute by multiplying the worth of the attributes below it (and connected by arcs) by their respective benefit coefficients. We then sum the

516 PART 3 DECISION MAKING UNDER UNCERTAINTY (DMUU)

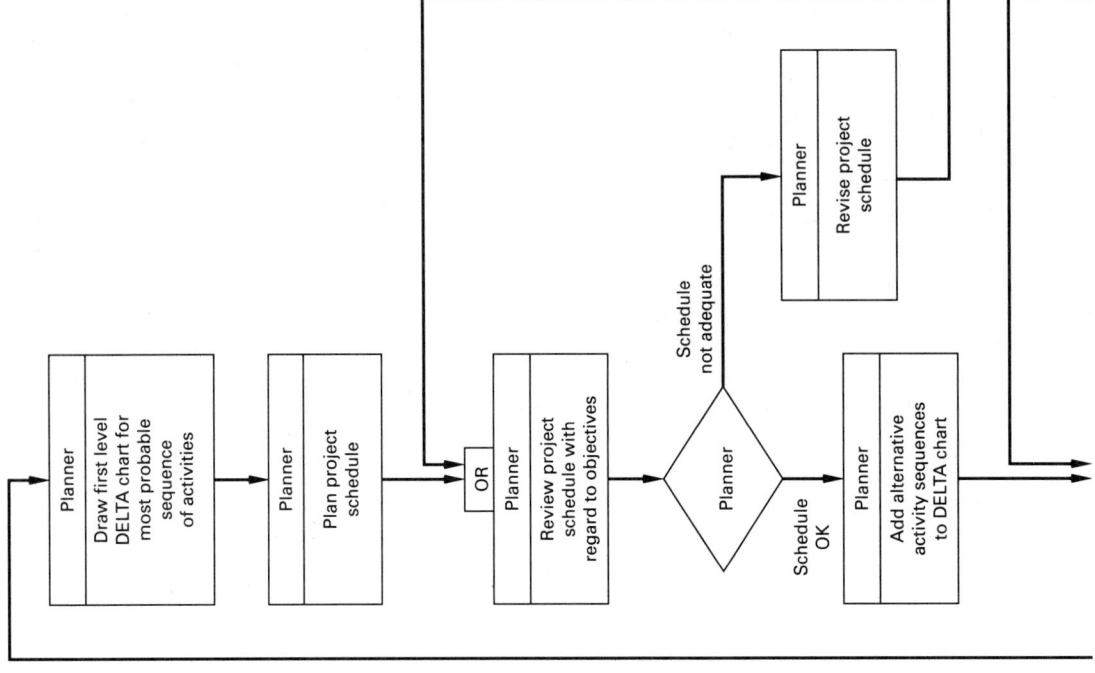

FIGURE 15.8 DELTA chart example for making a DELTA chart

CHAPTER 15 VISUAL AND MULTIATTRIBUTE CHOICE MODELS 517

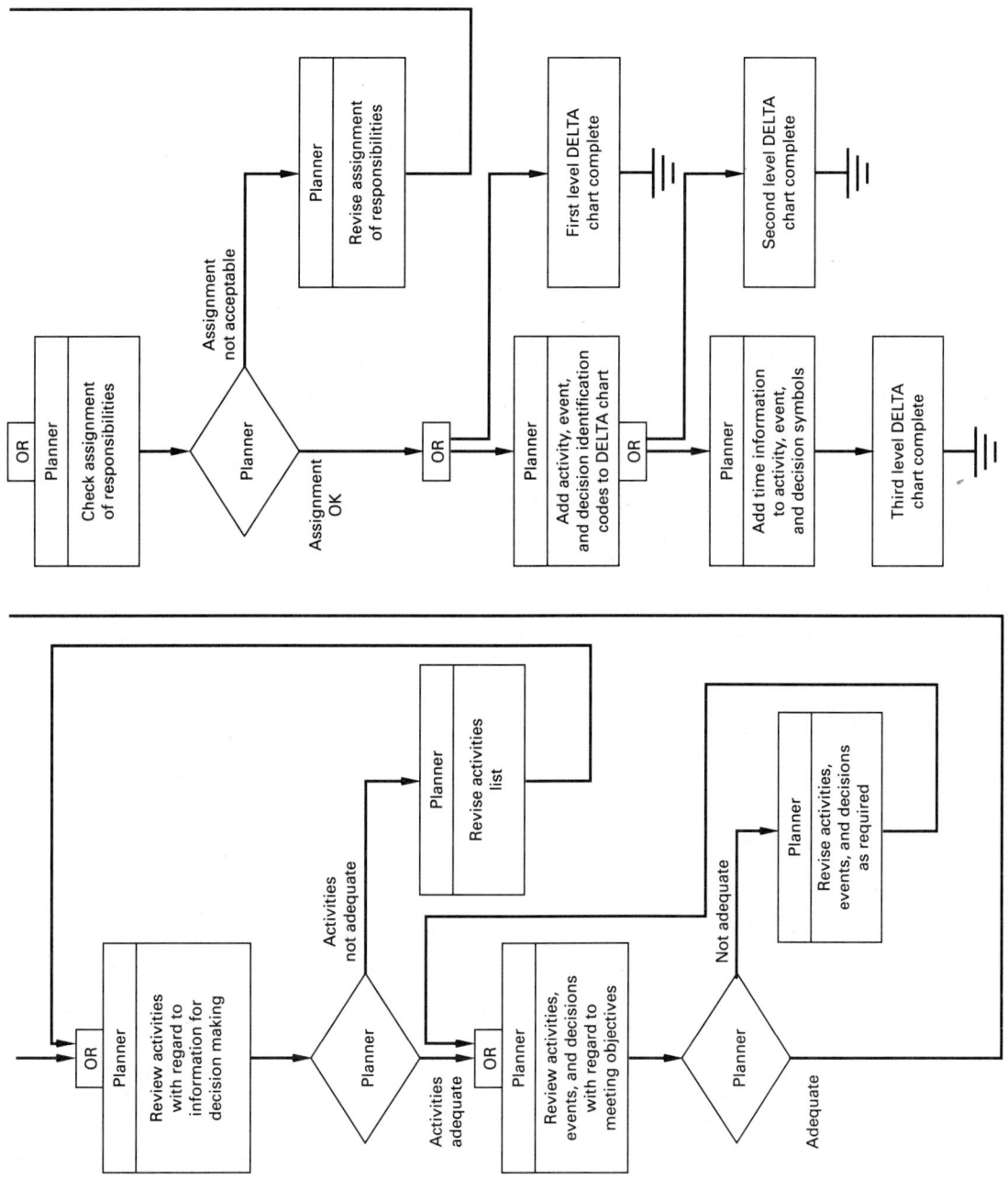

FIGURE 15.8
(continued)

FIGURE 15.9
A two-element objectives tree

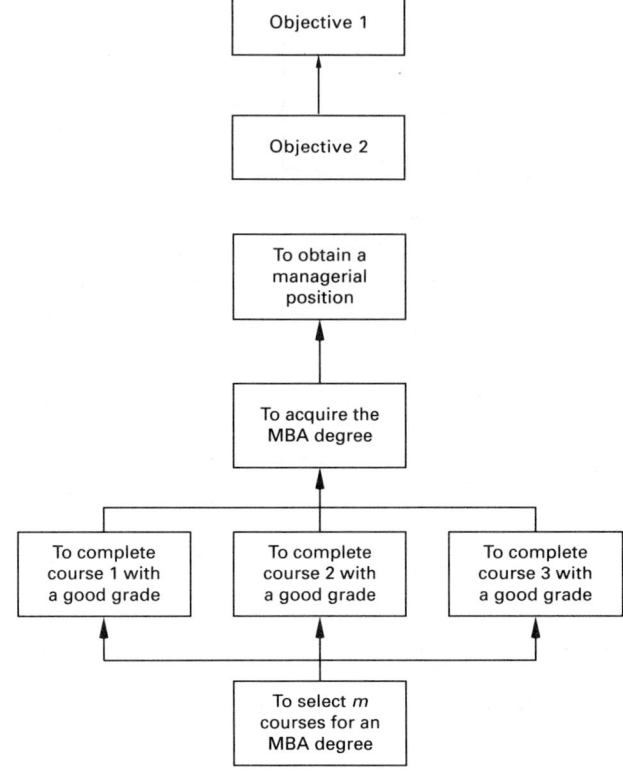

FIGURE 15.10
An MBA student's objectives tree

FIGURE 15.11
An activity tree for a football team

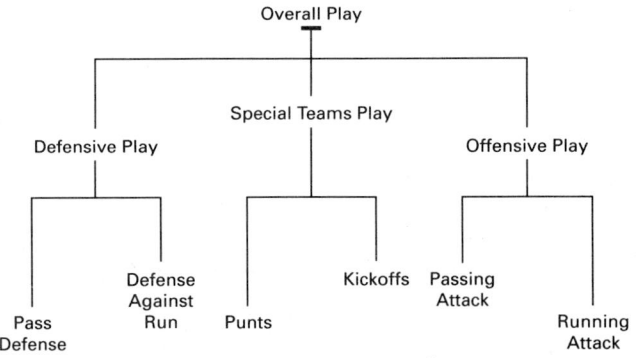

resulting products over all arcs connected to the higher level attribute. Thus, for location, we compute the following worth value for Home 1:

Location worth (Home 1) = 0.4(0.7) + 0.4(0.6) + 0.2(0.8) = 0.68

Similarly, we can evaluate the aesthetics, structure, and size-worth of Home 1 as follows:

Aesthetics worth (Home 1) = 0.4(0.9) + 0.6(0.5) = 0.66

Structure worth (Home 1) = 0.3(0.8) + 0.4(0.8) + 0.3(0.7) = 0.77

Size worth (Home 1) = 0.6(0.8) + 0.4(0.9) = 0.84

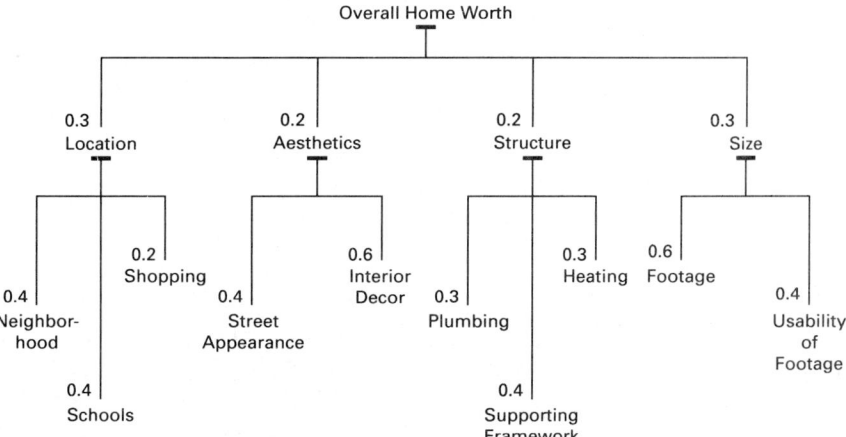

FIGURE 15.12
A worth tree for a home-purchasing decision

TABLE 15.1 Three typical homes we are considering for possible purchase

Attribute	Home 1	Home 2	Home 3
Neighborhood	0.7	0.8	0.9
Schools	0.6	0.7	0.7
Shopping	0.8	0.9	0.3
Street appearance	0.9	0.6	0.8
Interior decor	0.5	0.7	0.9
Plumbing	0.8	0.8	0.4
Supporting framework	0.8	0.8	0.4
Heating	0.7	0.7	0.3
Footage	0.8	0.9	0.7
Usability of footage	0.9	0.8	0.7
Overall calculated worth	0.742	0.778	0.666
Asking price	$98,000	$105,000	$69,000
Overall worth/cost($\times 10^{-6}$)	7.57	7.41	9.65

Using the calculated worths for each of the attributes location, aesthetics, structure, and size, we can now calculate the overall worth of Home 1.

Overall home worth (*Home* 1) = 0.3(0.68) + 0.2(0.66) + 0.2(0.77)
+ 0.3(0.84) = 0.742

We calculate the overall worths of Homes 2 and 3 in an identical fashion, and the results are in Table 15.1. Based upon this analysis, Home 2 would have the greatest worth to the purchaser.

To consider the costs of each home, the user could compute worth/cost ratios on each home by dividing the overall worth of each home by its associated cost. One criterion for home selection might be to choose the home with the largest worth/cost ratio. We can also obtain interesting information from a plot of home cost versus worth, in which we locate the coordinate corresponding to each home on the plot.

Solution of worth trees is similar in format to solution of probability trees. We note that the home purchase problem is indicative of the way we apply multiattribute utility theory to multidimensional subjects in order to assess their overall worth.

The **probability tree** is a mechanism for showing the relationships between marginal, conditional, and joint probabilities defined over a pair of event spaces. Texts on probability and statistics profusely illustrate its use.

We normally construct the **relevance tree** in levels, with each level representing a certain class of vertex entries. Connection from one level to another depends upon the relevance of one class to another class (of entries). The relevance tree is appropriate when the dimensions of a problem exceed three. Generally, we represent the broader classes at the top of a relevance tree, with the highly specific classes represented at the bottom. For example, the highest level might represent a very broad problem that we need to solve. The next highest level might represent the environment within which we will solve that problem, with vertices at this level representing elements of the environment. At lower levels of the tree are specific technological developments that might contribute to the solution of the broad problem.

Figure 15.13 presents an example of a relevance tree. A common use of the relevance tree is in technological forecasting, where the tree's purpose is to establish chains of relationship between entities. The tree serves to structure the problem in its most general form yet retains significant detail to permit subsequent analysis.

FIGURE 15.13
A relevance tree for NASA's Apollo payload evaluation

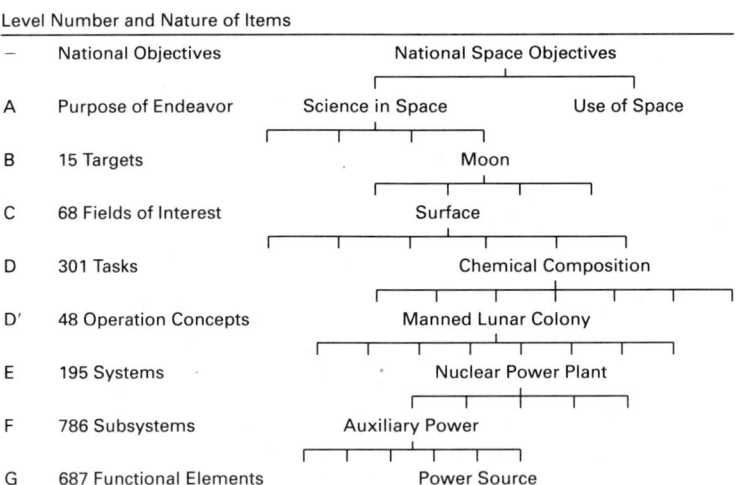

MATRIX MODELING

Matrix modeling involves the use of a matrix to show all possible interaction pairs between the elements of the same or different sets. We typically use two types of interaction matrices in matrix modeling: the **self-interaction matrix** and the **cross-interaction matrix**. The self-interaction matrix uses the same element set to index both its row and its column. We use a half-matrix when the interactions are not directed (from one element to another). If there are n elements in the set, then there are $n(n-1)/2$ undirected interactions among the elements in the set. Figure 15.14 is the

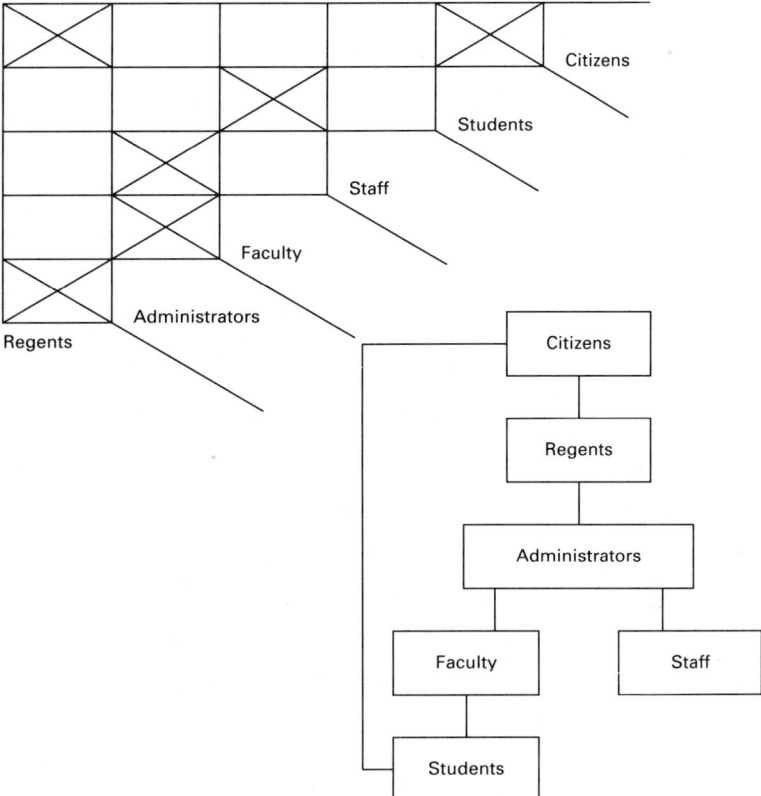

FIGURE 15.14
Interaction matrix and its structural interpretation for the human components of a university

self-interaction matrix that exhibits the possible interactions between the human components of a university together with its structural interpretation in graphical form.

Both the graphic representation and the associated self-interaction matrix contain exactly the same information. However, the graphic representation is much easier for humans to interpret, whereas the matrix representation facilitates storage of the information within computers. Note that for every edge in the graphic representation there is an "X" in the self-interaction matrix. Hence an "X" or an "edge" merely denotes an interaction between the associated element pair.

If the interactions are directed as in Figure 15.15 and if we permit cycles of interaction between element pairs, we need the entire matrix to represent this information. Now we place an "X" in the box corresponding to row element i and column element j to denote interaction directed from i toward j. The models depicted in Figure 15.15 characterize a different kind of interaction than that in Figure 15.14. Figure 15.15 depicts the organizational hierarchy through which orders filter down.

When a computer will assimilate the information, it is customary to use zeros and ones rather than blanks and "Xs" in matrices of the type depicted in Figures 15.14 and 15.15. We call such matrices **binary matrices.**

As suggested earlier, we may use matrices to interact two different element sets rather than just one as discussed thus far. Figure 15.16 on pp. 523-524 depicts a cross-interaction matrix for the functional elements of a university [1]. (In Figure 15.16, the two element sets are suppliers of information and users of information. It is just chance that the individual elements in these sets are identical.)

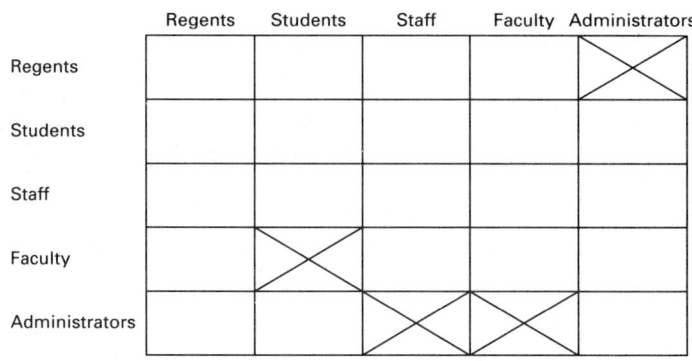

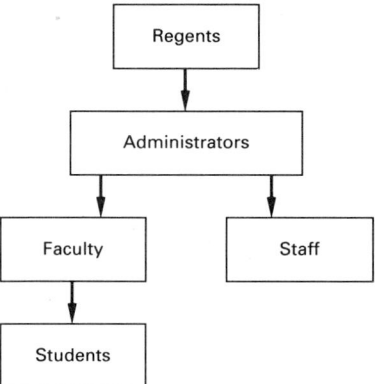

FIGURE 15.15
Directed interaction matrix and its digraph representation for the chain of command within a university

Figure 15.17 on p. 525 depicts four different element sets that are interrelated by means of four cross-interaction matrices [1]. The focus of interest in Figure 15.17 is the dimensions of development appropriate for the Tennessee Valley area in northern Alabama. In this model, we use four different interaction matrices to exhibit the interactions between four pairs of element sets. Figure 15.17 combines each of the four interaction matrices into one single large interaction. These interaction matrices show the agencies that are involved in each of the ten categories of community service, each agency's current and planned programs, the objectives of the programs, and the service categories that these objectives may affect.

MULTIATTRIBUTE CHOICE MODELS

Many real-world complex problems require that we construct and solve models that consist of both qualitative and quantitative decision variables. Up to this point, most of the techniques we have discussed have been either of a purely optimization type (e.g., linear and integer programming) or of a descriptive type (e.g., Markov and queueing models). As noted throughout the book, quantifying qualitative or subjective decision variables is perhaps one of the most challenging tasks in problem formulation. As a result, we must consider the influence of subjective variables apart from the model.

FIGURE 15.16 A cross-interaction matrix for the functional elements of a university [1]

		Suppliers of the Information			
		Finance	Urban and Regional Development	Curricula	Research
Users of the Information	Finance	/////		Current and projected programs	
	Urban and Regional Development		/////	Current and projected programs	Objectives of environmental institute; objectives of computer support center
	Curricula		Needs of region in terms of social, ecomomic, and physical; inventory of human resources	/////	Inventory of research programs
	Research		Needs of region; inventory of natural resources; inventory of industry; potential uses of UAH capabilities	Current and projected programs	/////
	Facilities		Land use map; industrial facilities in the region; industrial facilities	Current and projected programs	Current and projected research programs and projects
	Students	Tuition info on scholarships available	Cultural and recreation info; employment data internships; cooperative program of other institutions	Current and projected programs	Employment opportunities; educational opportunities; services provided
	Faculty and Administration		Professional talent available in region	Current and projected programs	
	Acquisition of Resources	Capital and operating expenses	Potential local sources of financial support	Current and projected programs	Suggested sources of financial support for research

FIGURE 15.16
(continued)

		Suppliers of the Information			
		Facilities	Students	Faculty and Administration	Acquisition of Resources
Users of the Information	Finance	Inventory of facilities, to include descriptions of multipurpose structures; policies on use of facilities	Internships and scholarships; current and projected enrollment	Number and qualifications of staff and faculty; faculty policies	
	Urban and Regional Development	Inventory of facilities, to include descriptions of multipurpose structures; policies on use of facilities	Internships and cooperative programs; current and projected enrollment	Number and qualifications of staff and faculty; faculty policies	
	Curricula	Inventory of facilities, to include descriptions of multipurpose structures; policies on use of facilities	Assessment of student desires; number and type of student projects and services		
	Research	Inventory of facilities, to include descriptions of multipurpose structures; policies on use of facilities	Placement information	Faculty policies	Description of funding programs
	Facilities	/////	Assessment of student desires; number and type of student projects and services		
	Students	Inventory of facilities, to include descriptions of multipurpose structures; policies on use of facilities	/////		
		Inventory of facilities, to include descriptions of multipurpose structures; policies on use of facilities	Assessment of student desires	/////	
	Acquisition of Resources	Inventory of facilities, to include descriptions of multipurpose structures; policies on use of facilities	Suggested sources of financial support to include ways students could contribute	Views of V.P. for development ($)	/////

FIGURE 15.17 Four dimensions of development appropriate for the Tennessee Valley area of northern Alabama [1]

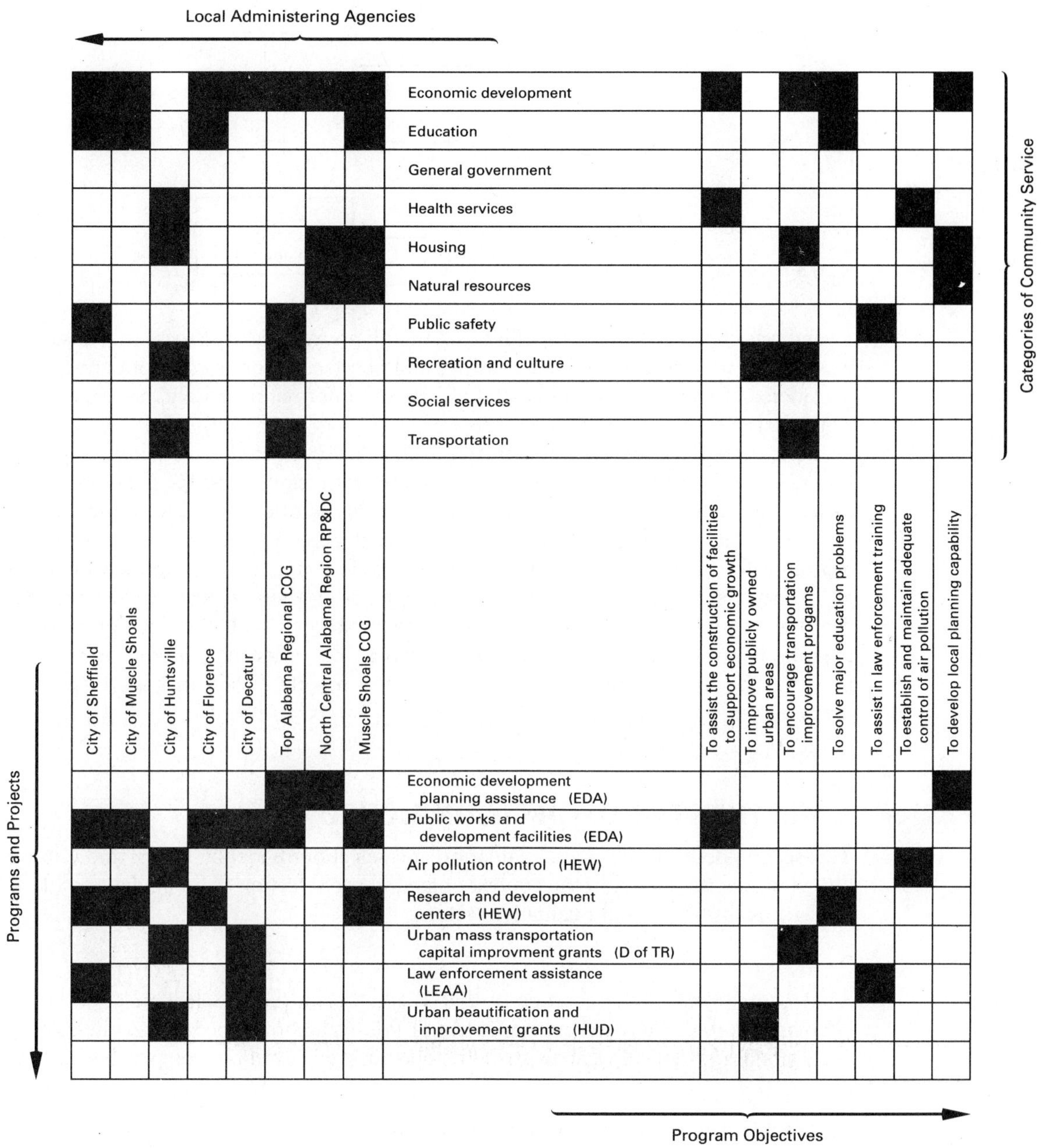

This section introduces a simple but comprehensive solution approach to our problem with qualitative and quantitative variables [3]. Our approach consists of three basic components as illustrated in Figure 15.18. The first is a data base containing the various decision variables and alternatives that a decision maker is considering (e.g., R&D projects), along with the numerous factors used in evaluating these decision variables and alternatives (e.g., manpower requirements). These factors can be of

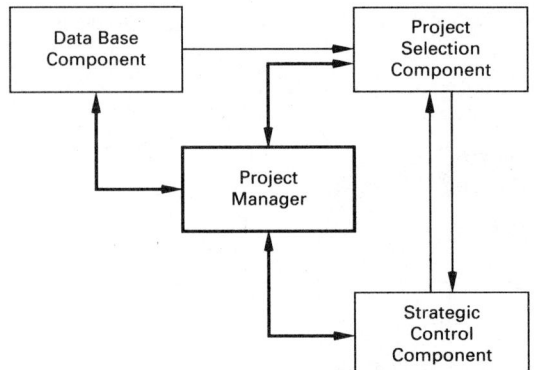

FIGURE 15.18
Decision support system diagram for a multiattribute decision model

several varieties—critical, qualitative, or quantitative. The data base is constantly changing as we introduce new alternatives, add new factors, or drop old ones no longer considered crucial or as we revise and update the information on alternatives already in the data base.

The second component of our approach is an evaluation and selection model that uses the information in the data base along with input from the decision maker to select an optimal set of decision variables. If this solution differs from the current set of alternatives being considered, we use the third component of the approach— dealing with strategic control—in which the decision support system presents us with all of the relevant information on the affected sets of alternatives to assist us in our decision making. The strategic control component deals with the decision maker's ongoing control of existing projects by receiving and reviewing periodic reports and updating the information in the data base when reports dictate that such action is necessary.

A MULTICRITERION DECISION MODEL

This section describes a project evaluation and selection model by Brown and Gibson [2], who used the model in the context of facility site selection. The model consists of critical, quantitative, and qualitative factors.

CRITICAL FACTORS

A factor is critical if the absence of that factor precludes the selection of a certain alternative (project) at the very beginning of the evaluation process, regardless of all other conditions that might exist. The following are examples of possible critical factors:

1. Required minimum probability of success.
2. Required minimum rate of return on invested capital.
3. Maximum allowable funding per project.

We use the critical factor measure (CFM) to incorporate the effect of "knockout" factors into the multicriterion decision model. Since the decision maker may have to consider more than one critical factor, this measure must take into account all factors. We define CFM_i as

$$CFM_i = \pi_j \, CFI_{i,j} \tag{15.1}$$

In this formula $CFI_{i,j}$ is the critical factor index for the ith alternative with respect to the jth critical factor. We assign to each alternative an index of zero or one, based on the requirement with respect to that factor. If an alternative meets the requirement for that particular qualitative factor, we assign it an index of one; otherwise its value is zero. We see from Equation (15.1) that if any of the critical factor indices are zero, CFM_i is also zero. Thus, alternatives receiving a value of zero for their qualitative factor measure are automatically eliminated from further consideration.

QUANTITATIVE FACTORS

Quantitative factors are those expressed in monetary terms or some other common unit of measurement that is quantifiable. The following are examples of possible quantitative factors:

1. Manufacturing costs.
2. Administrative costs.
3. Cost of purchasing additional facilities.
4. Cost of outside consultation.

We use the quantitative factor measure (QFM) to state the quantitative factors in terms commensurate with qualitative factors; i.e., the quantitative factor costs (QC) must be converted to a dimensionless index, as follows:

$$QFM_i = \frac{1}{QC_i \sum_i (1/QC_i)} \qquad (15.2)$$

In Equation (15.2), we define QC_i as the total quantitative factor cost for the ith alternative. The formula is based on the following considerations:

1. The alternative with the highest QC_i will have the minimum quantitative factor measure.
2. The relative difference among total quantitative factor costs is preserved.
3. The QFM_i sum to one.

With these considerations we guarantee that the QFM_i are dimensionless and commensurate with the qualitative factor measures described next.

QUALITATIVE FACTORS

Qualitative factors are subjective in nature. To quantify the qualitative factors, we must use a rating or indexing procedure. The following are examples of possible qualitative factors:

1. Promise of success.
2. Timing of completion.
3. Contribution to qualitative corporate goals.
4. Availability of technical skills.
5. Market potential.

When examining the qualitative factors closely, we may be led to conclude that some of the qualitative factors are similar to or repetitive of some of the critical and quantitative factors. However, the role of the qualitative factors is quite different. A decision alternative may qualify in terms of critical and quantitative factors, but the qualitative factors may be the criteria by which we differentiate one alternative from others.

The qualitative (subjective) factor measure (SFM) combines the individual qualitative factors that the decision maker uses. For each qualitative factor, we assign a relative rating to each alternative that reflects that alternative's ranking relative to all other alternatives with respect to that factor. We define SFM_i as

$$\text{SFM}_i = \sum_{k=1}^{m} (\text{SFW}_k)(\text{SR}_{ik}) \tag{15.3}$$

where

SFW_k = the normalized weight of the kth qualitative factor relative to all other qualitative factors,

$\Sigma\, \text{SFW}_k = 1$, and

SR_{ik} = the normalized relative rating of the ith alternative with respect to the kth qualitative factor, $\Sigma\, \text{SR}_{ik} = 1$.

We can compute the normalized weight of the kth qualitative factor as

$$\text{SFW}_k = \frac{\text{SFW}_k}{\Sigma\, \text{SFW}_k} \tag{15.4}$$

where SFW_k is the numerical rating or weight of the kth qualitative factor. The weight assigned to the kth factor should reflect its importance relative to the other factors.

Similarly, we can determine the normalized relative rating of the ith alternative with respect to the kth qualitative factor as

$$\text{SR}_{ik} = \frac{\text{SR}_{ik}}{(\Sigma\, \text{SFM}_i)(\text{SR}_{ik})} \tag{15.5}$$

where SR_{ik} is the numerical rating of the ith project for the kth qualitative factor. Notice that by incorporating the qualitative factor measure SFM_i in the denominator of Equation (15.5), the normalization is carried out only with respect to those alternatives meeting the critical factor requirements.

THE EVALUATION MEASURE

We use the three components of critical, quantitative, and qualitative factors to compute the overall performance measure (PM) for the ith alternative:

$$\text{PM}_i = \text{CFM}_i\{\alpha \text{QFM}_i + (1 - \alpha)\text{SFM}_i\} \tag{15.6}$$

Each project under evaluation has a resulting performance measure between zero and one, with one being the highest possible performance measure and zero the lowest. The parameter α in Equation (15.6) is a measure of the decision maker's relative preference for or confidence in the quantitative and qualitative factors used. For example, if we have determined that we should consider the quantitative factors three times as important as the qualitative factors, we will use $\alpha = 0.75$. It is important that the decision maker be aware of the effects small changes in α could have on the final alternatives selected.

A PROJECT SELECTION MODEL

If our objective is to select a single project or entity from a set of competitors, building an electronic spreadsheet model to compute the PM_i is a simple matter indeed. We can even perform a simple sensitivity analysis on the value of α, as we illustrate in one of the subsequent minicases.

On the other hand, if our objective is to select a subset of projects or entities from a set of competitors, we can use the PM_i as objective function coefficients for zero-one decision variables in a maximization model. In the context of our discussions in Chapter 14, what we have done with this simple choice model is to transform and combine incommensurable criteria into dimensionless numbers that "capture" the subjective multiattribute assessments of a decision maker.

THE STRATEGIC CONTROL COMPONENT

Project control within the project selection component is influenced by internal factors such as management philosophy, corporate goals and strategy, and economic analysis, as well as by external factors (e.g., political, social, cultural, and technological). Project control systems must be compatible with the management philosophy of the decision maker and in line with the overall corporate goals and objectives. As a result, the project decision maker must identify and examine project parameters, at both the initial and the intermediate stages, in terms of their relationship and value to the project under consideration and in terms of their relevance and importance to the overall corporate objectives. The strategic control component is essential to establish and maintain order and control in any project. This in return will help reduce overall project risk and create an effective project management environment.

MINICASES

MIPS [8]

THE SCENARIO

Mammoth Information Processing Systems, Inc. (MIPS) generates annual revenues of more than $300 million from the sales of automatic data processing equipment, software, and services to the federal government. Selling to the government is highly competitive and expensive because of complex procurement regulations and procedures. A company can easily lose large amounts of money because of a technical insufficiency in a bid or a lower bid from a competitor.

The management of MIPS has established an opportunity review board (ORB), consisting of five upper-level executives, to determine which government solicitations to pursue. The ORB makes its decisions based on such factors as resource availability, budgets, and technology.

THE PROBLEM

The ORB is faced with the problem of establishing specific measurement factors to compare and identify those opportunities that are most promising for the firm. At its weekly meeting, board members have a listing of current proposals under preparation and have agreed on the following critical factors:

1. *Completion Date.* Can MIPS meet the government's scheduled dates for proposal submission and product delivery?
2. *Expertise.* Does MIPS possess the required expertise for the proposed opportunity?
3. *Benchmark Date.* Can MIPS obtain (prepare) the resources required in time to meet the government's benchmark?
4. *Product Announcement Date.* Will the products proposed be commercially available at the time of award announcement?
5. *Percentage of OVP.* Is the portion of the other vendor's products (OVP) necessary to meet the requirements in excess of 50% of the total proposed value?

Of the 12 proposals under preparation, only one violated one or more of the critical factors and thus was eliminated from further consideration.

THE MODEL

For the remaining projects, the board constructed a table of quantitative factor costs (Table 15.2). The QFM values in the last row of the table are computed using Equation (15.2).

In addition to establishing the quantifiable factors, the review board is interested in the qualitative factors surrounding the projects. These factors and the corresponding weights are in Table 15.3. The ORB has decided to rank each project with respect to each qualitative factor using subjective scores: poor = 1; average = 2; good = 3; excellent = 4.

TABLE 15.2 Quantitative factors and their cost ($000s)

Factor	Project										
	CHP	NAC	SUP	SPA	TEF	IBR	MUS	ULA	MEA	SNA	OAT
Manpower (proposal)	300	110	90	50	165	220	300	100	240	150	190
Manpower (benchmark)	500	270	140	0	205	630	450	160	370	0	470
Budget (less manpower)	3,260	290	75	15	85	240	2,330	50	29	60	125
Benchmark (less manpower)	8,350	360	150	0	410	490	6,480	75	570	0	510
Total	12,410	1,030	455	65	865	1,580	9,560	385	1,470	210	1,295
QFM	0.002	0.033	0.075	0.524	0.043	0.021	0.003	0.088	0.023	0.162	0.026

SOLUTION TO THE MODEL

For project CHP we demonstrate the computations necessary to determine its qualitative factor measure (SFM) using Equation (15.3).

$$\begin{aligned}
\text{SFM} = &\ (10/64)(4/27) + (8/64)(3/30) + (9/64)(4/30) \\
&+ (7/64)(4/34) + (5/64)(3/44) + (8/64)(3/31) \\
&+ (4/64)(4/31) + (9/64)(4/27) + (4/64)(3/28) \\
\doteq &\ .12
\end{aligned}$$

TABLE 15.3 Qualitative factors and their weights

		Project										
Rating	Factor	CHP	NAC	SUP	SPA	TEF	IBR	MUS	ULA	MEA	SNA	OAT	SUM
10	Competive analysis	4	2	1	3	2	2	2	3	2	4	2	27
8	Future business	3	3	3	2	2	2	3	3	3	3	3	30
9	Probability/win	4	3	1	3	2	3	2	3	2	4	3	30
7	Product mix fit	4	4	4	4	3	2	2	2	3	4	2	34
5	Compatibility w/corporate image	4	4	4	4	4	4	4	4	4	4	4	44
8	Probability/pass benchmark	3	3	1	4	3	3	3	2	2	4	3	31
4	Visibility	4	2	3	3	2	3	3	3	2	3	3	31
9	Customer environment	4	2	1	2	2	2	3	2	3	4	2	27
4	Subcontractor risk	3	2	2	4	4	2	2	2	2	3	2	28
64	SFM	0.12	0.09	0.06	0.10	0.08	0.08	0.08	0.09	0.08	0.01	0.08	

The ORB computed the SFM_i for the other ten projects in a similar manner.

To determine the performance measure (PM) for each project, the ORB decided to weight the qualitative factors higher than the quantitative factors by using $\alpha = 0.35$. Using Equation (15.6), we obtain the following PM values:

Performance measure results

Project	CHP	NAC	SUP	SPA	TEF	IBR	MUS	ULA	MEA	SNA	OAT
PM	0.08	0.07	0.05	0.25	0.07	0.06	0.06	0.09	0.06	0.14	0.06

Based on the performance measure results, project SPA has the largest value and project SUP has the smallest value. Looking at these results, the review board decided that it is difficult to choose between projects such as MEA and OAT, since their PM values are so close. The board then formulated a zero-one integer programming model using the 11 projects as decision variables and the above PM values as their objective function coefficients. The constraints are scarce resource limitations on the quantitative factors. The ORB's analyst decided to build the IP model for input to an ILP module by creating the file ORB.DAT with a word processing program and saving the file in ASCII (unformatted) as in Table 15.4.

The ILP package solved the model almost instantaneously, and Table 15.5 exhibits the SAMS quick briefing.

SOLUTION TO THE PROBLEM

Looking at the results of the integer programming solution, ORB members noted that the model had eliminated from further consideration the three projects with the

TABLE 15.4 SAMS data file ORB.DAT

```
ORB MAX
Variables   CHP  NAC  SUP  SPA  TEF  IBR  MUS  ULA  MEA  SNA
OAT
Type    I   I   I   I   I   I   I   I   I   I   I
Objective   0.08 0.07 0.05 0.25 0.07 0.06 0.06 0.09 0.06 0.14 0.06
Upper Bound  1   1   1   1   1   1   1   1   1   1   1
Lower Bound  0   0   0   0   0   0   0   0   0   0   0
Constraints
MANPOWER 300 110 90 50 165 220 300 100 240 150 190 < 1500.
BNCHMARK 500 270 140 0 207 630 450 160 370 0 470 < 2000.
PROPBUDG 3260 290 75 15 85 240 2330 50 290 60 125 < 4500.
BENCHMAN 8350 360 150 0 410 490 6480 75 570 0 510 < 13000.
```

TABLE 15.5 SAMS summary solution for ORB

ORB
QUICK BRIEFING ON OPTIMAL MODEL SOLUTION
Maximum Objective Value = 0.82

Decision Variable	Optimal Value	Reduced Cost
CHP	1.0	0.0
NAC	1.0	0.0
SPA	1.0	0.0
TEF	1.0	0.0
ULA	1.0	0.0
MEA	1.0	0.0
SNA	1.0	0.0
OAT	1.0	0.0

Constraint	Slack
MANPOWER	195.0
BNCHMARK	23.0
PROPBUDG	325.0
BENCHMAN	2725.0

smallest performance measure values. One board member pointed out that with this solution, one no longer needs to worry about selecting between projects with close PM values.

The real "story" of the model results, however, was in the slack variables associated with the four "scarce" resources. The analyst created Table 15.6 to show to the ORB members.

TABLE 15.6 Resource analysis for ORB

Resource	Available	Unused	% Unused
Manpower	1,500	195	13.0%
Bench (MP)	2,000	23	1.2
Budget (−MP)	4,500	325	7.2
Bench (−MP)	13,000	2,725	21.0

"The problem," observed Meg Abeyta, chairperson of the ORB, "is that MIPS is doing a lousy job of planning. We don't have the benchmark manpower to match our other resources. Also, we don't have enough proposals to consider. I'm all for scientific resource allocation with our choice model and integer programming, but our planning staff must give us something a lot better to work with in the future."

T. N. Crumpets [5]

THE SCENARIO

T. N. Crumpets, Ltd. (TNC), a wholly owned subsidiary of British Electric Power, Ltd., was formed for the purpose of investing in commercial projects in the United States. TNC makes investments and issues commercial paper sufficient to sustain its operations and makes additional investments with the excess cash flow.

The company has identified five types of projects that it would like to invest in as part of its corporate investment strategy. The five project types include small power, real estate, oil and gas, leasing, and acquisitions of controlling interests in energy-related businesses. For comparison purposes, TNC's management has selected a specific project in each category with an initial investment of £5 million for a 15-year term and identical assumptions regarding optimal leveraging and sale at the end of 15 years at fair market value. The following is a brief description of each project.

Small power projects produce less than 50 megawatts and sell the electricity produced to local utilities, which ultimately sell it to retail customers. The small power project selected for evaluation is a hydroelectric power plant in Nebraska. TNC believes that a properly maintained hydro facility should have a useful economic life of at least 50 years and should therefore have a substantial fair market value at the end of 15 years.

The *real estate project* selected for evaluation is a 40,000-square-foot building to be developed and leased to one tenant on a parcel of land in Okefenokee, Florida. The building and improvements should have a useful economic life of at least 40 years, and the value of the project should increase substantially after 15 years.

TNC can invest in a series of limited partnerships that were formed by T-Bone Perkins in Texas for the purpose of *oil and gas exploration and drilling*. The general partners have substantial experience in this field and have purchased land that has a good potential for being an oil or natural gas prospect. Although oil and gas can be a risky investment, there is currently a depression in the price of the properties, making now an opportune time for finding good deals. Based on the industry reports and geological surveys that TNC has reviewed, it appears that oil and gas is poised for a rebound in the near future. The partnership will be dissolved after 15 years.

TNC has invested in *leasing* for several years. Its areas of expertise are commercial aircraft and satellite transponders. The leasing project selected for evaluation is the lease of one satellite transponder to a major telecommunications company headquartered in Cut Bank, Montana. Because of the recent setbacks in launching satellites, there is a bottleneck of companies wishing to lease the next satellite transponders to be launched. TNC has determined that transponders are good equipment to lease and that the companies leasing them have superb credit. An attractive feature of this type of lease is that the rents are very high and the yield is not dependent upon the future fair market value.

TNC is interested in acquiring a controlling interest in an energy-related business. The *acquisition* project selected for evaluation is the purchase of 55% of the equity of a company in Virginia that produces software for electricity load control. The software allows the user to reduce electricity usage during periods of low demand and to effectively distribute it during periods of high demand. The software company has a huge backlog of orders that it cannot fill because of production capacity limitations. TNC would like to finance the expansion of production capacity, establish name recognition early and eventually take the company public, and in 15 years sell its stock at a substantial profit to management or an investor.

THE PROBLEM

Which project should TNC select? TNC's management feels that this is a complex problem requiring many important considerations. It would like to find a solution approach that considers the following:

1. The types of investments are quite different, but the financial (objective) characteristics are very similar.
2. Each type of investment is generally acceptable as part of the corporate investment strategy.
3. TNC can choose only one of the alternatives. The £5 million cannot be apportioned among them.
4. Because of the nature of the investment alternatives, there are several subjective factors that TNC should consider.

THE MODEL

TNC's management decided to test each of the investment alternatives on a set of critical factors before performing any detailed analysis. If a given project does not clear this initial hurdle, TNC will not consider it further. The critical factors are as follows:

1. Required minimum rate of return—at least 18% after tax.
2. Minimum probability of success—at least 80%.
3. Maximum/minimum allowable capital investment per project—maximum £50 million, minimum £3 million.
4. Maximum allowable project completion time—1 year.
5. Minimum payback period—3 years.
6. Meets regulatory requirements—Royal Energy Regulatory Commission and Public Utility Regulatory Policies Act.

Each investment alternative was carefully checked with respect to the critical factors and passed the critical factor requirements. Next, TNC's management defined the objective and subjective factors affecting the five investments as follows:

QUANTITATIVE (OBJECTIVE) FACTORS

1. (TECH): Cost of company technical and consulting personnel necessary to complete the transaction.
2. (HIRE): Cost of hiring additional personnel to operate the project during the 15-year term.
3. (ADMN): Cost of administrative services to be provided by TNC throughout the 15-year term.
4. (PERM): Cost of necessary permits and rezoning.
5. (APPA): Cost of outside consultants, appraisals, and industry studies for necessary due diligence.
6. (LOBY): Cost of lobbying effort.
7. (BROK): Cost of brokerage commissions (buying, selling and leasing the project, etc.).
8. (MAIN): Cost of maintenance during the 15-year term.

QUALITATIVE (SUBJECTIVE) FACTORS

1. (PROB): Probability of success.
2. (RATE): Expected rate of return on invested capital.
3. (STRT): Agreement with corporate investment strategy.
4. (SKIL): Available technical and consulting skills employed by TNC.
5. (CURT): Current market potential with respect to similar investments.
6. (FUTR): Future market potential forecasted.
7. (IMAG): Corporate image to the public by investing in the type of project.
8. (NEIG): Neighborhood desirability of having the project.

SOLUTION TO THE MODEL

TNC's management scientist realized that this problem lends itself to a multiattribute choice model. Using the multicriterion approach discussed in this chapter, he constructed quantitative and qualitative tables and computed the QFM and SFM values (see Tables 15.7 and 15.8).

TABLE 15.7 Quantitative factors and costs for TNC (£ 000's)

Factor	Small Power	Real Estate	Oil and Gas	Leasing	Acquisition
TECH	11	14	11	10	12
HIRE	117	0	0	0	0
ADMN	2	2	2	2	6
PERM	20	25	15	5	0
APPA	20	10	30	10	20
LOBY	5	5	5	0	0
BROK	75	150	75	75	100
MAIN	20	25	20	0	0
Total cost	270	231	158	102	138
QFM	0.118	0.136	0.201	0.312	0.231

The qualitative factors reflect a subjective appraisal of each alternative in relation to the other alternatives. They are based on the opinion of the decision maker and are therefore subject to sensitivity analysis. In the qualitative factor table (Table 15.8), we first give each alternative a rating as measured against the qualitative factors, and the ratings are totaled on the right-hand side for each factor. (For this, TNC used: poor = 1; average = 2; good = 3; and excellent = 4.) The rating for each alternative is then divided by the right-hand side total to get the qualitative factor weight (SR). Next, a rating is assigned to each qualitative factor and totaled. Each of these ratings divided by the total equals the qualitative factor rating (SFW). The final step is to calculate the qualitative factor measure using Equation (15.3).

TABLE 15.8 Qualitative factors and weights for TNC

		Alternative Rating					
Factor	Rating	Small Power	Real Estate	Oil and Gas	Leasing	Acquisition	Total
PROB	8	3	4	1	4	2	14
RATE	10	4	3	2	3	2	14
STRT	7	4	4	4	4	4	20
SKIL	6	3	3	2	3	2	13
CURT	9	3	4	2	3	3	15
FUTR	9	3	4	2	3	2	14
IMAG	5	3	3	3	3	3	15
NEIG	5	4	3	3	4	4	18
Total	59						
SFM		0.224	0.238	0.146	0.221	0.171	

SOLUTION TO THE PROBLEM

After reviewing the results for QFM and SFM, the managers of TNC admitted that they had not even the vaguest notion about the proper value of α—the parameter that expresses the relative measure of comparison for confidence in the quantitative and qualitative factors. The management analyst was highly resourceful, however, and plotted the following five equations (see Figure 15.19) as a function of α:

PM_1: Small power = $0.118\alpha + 0.224(1 - \alpha)$

PM_2: Real estate = $0.136\alpha + 0.238(1 - \alpha)$

PM_3: Oil and gas = $0.201\alpha + 0.146(1 - \alpha)$

PM_4: Leasing = $0.312\alpha + 0.221(1 - \alpha)$

PM_5: Acquisition = $0.231\alpha + 0.171(1 - \alpha)$

One glance at the plot was sufficient to settle the issue. Leasing completely dominates (is better for all values of α) small power, oil and gas, and acquisitions and is

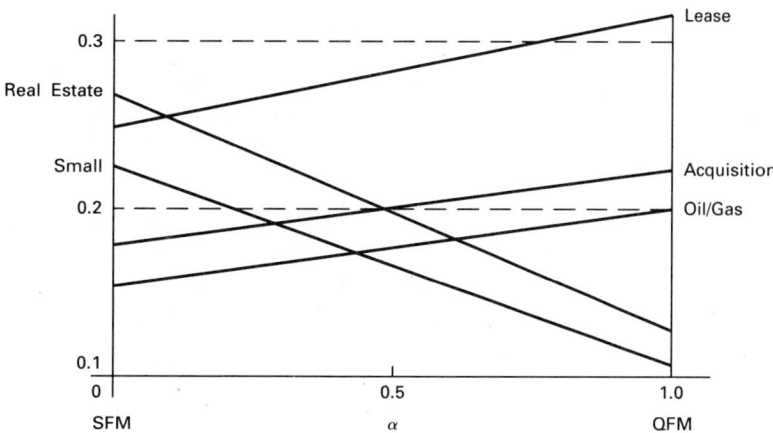

FIGURE 15.19
Comparative plots of TNC project scores

better than real estate for $\alpha > 0.09$. In this case, the model had done its job well, and TNC confidently chose the leasing project for its investment.

SUMMARY

The methods we discussed in this chapter are nothing more than rudimentary attempts to gain insight into complex, "messy" problems that executive decision makers struggle with on a daily basis.

The graphical tools illustrated in the chapter are becoming increasingly prominent in the business world because of the growing capability of computer software/hardware to quickly, accurately, and inexpensively produce the charts, trees, and graphs. People quickly comprehend these visual devices, which greatly enhance communication and understanding among human beings.

We then discussed the components of a decision support system for executive management and illustrated the model with a simple but useful multicriterion decision model. The model embraces critical ("knockout") factors, objective (quantitative) factors, and subjective (qualitative) factors. We illustrated the use of this model with two minicases.

KEY TERMS

activity tree
binary matrix
cross-interaction matrix
decision support system
DELTA chart
Gantt chart
information overload
matrix modeling
model exchange isomorphism

morphology
objectives tree
PERT chart
probability tree
relevance tree
self-interaction matrix
tree
worth tree

PROBLEMS FOR ANALYSIS

1. List as many possible consequences as you can that have accrued from the introduction of the automobile. Use manual techniques to organize these into a structural model using the relation
"_____ contributes to _____."

2. Construct a worth tree to assess the worth to you of several job opportunities that will present themselves as you complete your MBA. Evaluate the tree for at least three hypothetical job possibilities. Treat salary in the same way that we considered the purchase price of a home in the home-purchase example. Major attributes or dimensions of worth might include geographic location, travel requirements, and nature of work.

3. Re-solve Problem 2, except make economic compensation an additional attribute of the worth tree rather than treating it as in the home-purchase example. Which strategy makes the most sense to you?

4. Develop an interaction matrix for the most efficient allocation of energy sources (Table 15.9) to energy consumption sectors (Table 15.9). Justify your allocation choices.

TABLE 15.9

Energy Sources	Consumption Sectors
Crude petroleum	Residential
Coal	Commercial
Natural gas	Industrial
Nuclear power	Agricultural
Solar energy	Transportation
Electric power	Electricity
Exotic sources (trash, geothermal, geohydro, hydroelectric)	

5. **The Scenario [7]:** The Naval Air Systems Command (NAVAIR) is an organization of the U.S. Navy that is involved in the procurement and management of all Navy airborne systems, primarily aircraft, missiles, and related electronics. Recently, an increased emphasis has been placed on competitive procurement of weapons systems for the purpose of reducing costs and penalizing contractors with chronic schedule and quality problems. To achieve this goal, the selection of a contractor in a competitive environment must take into account many more factors than simply the contractor's proposed price. Proposals submitted for a competitive procurement generally include discussions of how the contractor determined cost estimates; the contractor's relevant cost, quality, and schedule experience on similar contracts; the contractor's proposed program management; physical plant layout; and proposal for out-year support of the system in the field. Teams of government experts usually evaluate proposals. Expert judgment is an integral part of the process.

The Problem: Recently, NAVAIR solicited and received six proposals for a weapons system it is procuring. The request for proposal (RFP) specified two requirements that a contractor must meet to be considered (critical factors):

a. The contractor must have a SECRET facility clearance.
b. The contractor must not be on the Navy's list of suspended or disbarred contractors.

The budget constraint for this contract is $60 million. The six proposals received are priced as in Table 15.10.

TABLE 15.10

Proposal	Price ($000,000)
MSCI	54.00
SOME	49.75
ABCR	55.50
XERX	50.75
ACME	49.70
TRYD	57.75

In addition to submitting the contract cost, contractors submit several noncontract costs as part of each proposal. These costs are associated with the administration of the contract both at NAVAIR and at the contractor's plant and with necessary modifications to contracts for other systems affected by the contractor's proposed system.

The problem is to develop an evaluation and selection methodology that recognizes the subjectivity of the many judgments involved and provides a systematic framework for analysis of the decision criteria used.

The Model: All six proposals met the critical factor tests. Table 15.11 gives the quantitative factors and their costs.

TABLE 15.11 Quantitative factors and costs (000's)

Factors	MSCI	SOME	ABCR	XERX	ACME	TRYD
Contract	54000	49750	55500	50750	49500	57750
HQ administration	150	50	75	40	50	40
Field administration	100	100	50	50	50	25
Support systems	0	50	0	50	100	100

The selection committee has also assembled the following list of qualitative factors and has constructed its table as shown in Table 15.12.

1. (REAL)—Are costs proposed realistic? (no = 0; yes = 3)
2. (COVR)—Is there a history of significant cost overruns? (yes = 0; no = 1)
3. (SCHL)—Does the contractor usually meet schedule? (no = 0; yes = 10)
4. (QUMG)—Quality of proposed management (poor = 0; great = 3)
5. (PSQL)—Past and proposed quality controls (poor = 0; great = 10)
6. (PROD)—Quality of existing production facilities (none = 0; excellent = 2)
7. (REDE)—Research and development (poor = 0; excellent = 2)
8. (SPAR)—Proposed spare support (none = 0; excellent = 2)

Solution to the Model:
a. Assuming that all six proposals met the critical factor requirements, determine the QFM and SFM for all six projects. Choose $\alpha = 0.4$ and determine which contract proposal the model selects.

TABLE 15.12 Qualitative factors and ratings

Factor	Rating	MSCI	SOME	ABCR	XERX	ACME	TRYD	Total
REAL	5	3	0	2	2	1	1	9
COVR	6	1	0	1	1	1	0	4
SCHL	5	4	6	4	5	8	7	34
QUMG	3	3	2	1	3	2	2	13
PSQL	5	2	5	4	7	3	6	27
PROD	2	1	0	2	2	1	2	8
REDE	4	1	2	1	1	0	1	6
SPAR	3	2	1	2	0	1	1	7

b. Do a sensitivity analysis similar to that in the T. N. Crumpets minicase, plotting the α-equations for the six bidders. Are any of the bids dominated? For what ranges of values of α does the model recommend which contractors?

Solution to the Problem: The environment in which defense procurement takes place is highly political. Because the government spends public funds, agencies take great care to ensure that decisions are made on as objective a basis as possible. This and an increasing public perception that military equipment is overpriced dictate that the quantitative factor measure—the low bidder approach—has primary consideration.

On the other hand, the Navy must also take care that the equipment arrives on time, works when it is delivered, and can be maintained once it is deployed. So, while the cost of the system must be a primary factor, the qualitative factors are also important. Therefore, the selection committee believes that the best value for α is between 0.5 and 0.75.

a. Within this range, which contract has the highest performance measure?
b. If you were a NAVAIR professional and the contractor who submitted the lowest monetary bid did not win the contract as a result of your use of this multiattribute choice model, how would you defend its use?

6. **The Scenario [6]:** The Local Federal Savings Bank (LFSB) is a new bank in Reston, Virginia. During its first year of operation, LFSB acquired $30 million in deposits and an increasing loan portfolio. Because of this rapid growth, LFSB has decided to open a new branch.

The Problem: LFSB has narrowed the new branch site to three locations (initially there were a total of nine locations, but six of them did not meet the critical factor requirements imposed by the management). The problem LFSB faces requires sorting through the attributes of each location to determine the most favorable site.

The Model: The following table shows three locations and their respective costs for the quantitative factors:

Quantitative factors and costs for LFSB

	Location		
Factor	Fairfax City	Falls Church	Sterling
Annual lease expense	$148,000	$101,000	$135,000
Incremental costs	53,000	34,200	46,000

Table 15.13 shows the qualitative factors along with their ratings.

TABLE 15.13 Qualitative factors for LFSB

	Rating	Location		
Factor	(%)	Fairfax City	Falls Church	Sterling
% Families with 50K+ income	30	3	1	2
Employment (1990)	10	3	3	2
Effective buying income	15	1	3	1
Commercial development	30	3	3	1
# Close competitors	5	2	1	3
Visibility from street	10	1	3	3

In the table, management used excellent = 3, good = 2, and average = 1 to rate the three sites with respect to the qualitative factors.

Solution to the Model: The management of LFSB feels that in the long run, the qualitative factors are more important in the banking industry and should be assigned a higher weight than the quantitative factors. Management decided on $\alpha = 0.2$.

a. Solve this facility location problem using the multiattribute approach discussed in the chapter.

Solution to the Problem: Verify that the model will recommend that LFSB select Falls Church for its new branch. The management of LFSB feels comfortable with this selection because this site was the previous home of a savings and loan company. LFSB has learned that it can purchase existing onsite office equipment, an automatic teller machine, a night vault, and a safe. Since there is already a drive-up window and a lobby, the location would require few structural modifications.

PRACTICE MODELS

1. Use the multicriterion decision model to select a site for locating a disaster relief center. (See Table 15.14.) Assume: good = 5, very good = 10, low = 3, middle = 6, high = 10, and all critical factors = 0 or 1.

TABLE 15.14

	Location			
	Miami	Atlanta	Dallas	Tulsa
Quantitative Factor				
1. Cost ($000)	1,000	890	1,050	850
Qualitative Factor (Rating)				
1. Accessibility (30%)	good	good	very good	good
2. Population density (30%)	high	middle	high	low
3. Disaster frequency (40%)	low	low	middle	middle

2. An R&D firm wants to select the most suitable project from the list in Table 15.15. Use the multicriterion decision model to make your recommendation to the firm. Assume that all critical factors are 1, and high (H) = 3, medium (M) = 2, and low (L) = 1.

TABLE 15.15

	Project						
	1	2	3	4	5	6	7
Quantitative Factors							
1. Fixed costs($000)	100	120	105	85	97	72	120
2. Variable costs($000)	550	520	500	480	440	530	455
Qualitative Factors (Rating)							
1. Expertise required (25%)	H	M	M	H	L	H	L
2. Resources required (35%)	M	M	L	M	H	H	L
3. Time required (15%)	M	L	M	H	H	L	M
4. Probability of success (25%)	L	H	H	M	L	M	M

REFERENCES AND ADDITIONAL READING

1. Baldwin, M. (Ed.). *Portraits of Complexity: Applications of Systems Methodologies to Societal Problems*. Battelle Monograph No. 9 (1975).
2. Brown, P., and D. Gibson. "A Quantified Model for Facility Site Selection-Application to a Multiplant Location Problem." *AIIE Transactions* 4, no. 1 (1972): 1–10.
3. Ghandforoush, P., and J. Arthur. "An Information System for R&D Managers." Working paper, Virginia Polytechnic Institute and State University, Blacksburg, Va. (1989).
4. Harary, F., R. Norman, and D. Cartwright. *Structural Models: An Introduction to the Theory of Directed Graphs*. New York: Wiley, 1965.
5. Hehir, P. Adapted from an unpublished MBA term project report, Virginia Polytechnic Institute and State University (1988).
6. Mayor, S. Adapted from an unpublished MBA term project report, Virginia Polytechnic Institute and State University (1986).
7. Pelky, M. Adapted from an unpublished MBA term project report, Virginia Polytechnic Institute and State University (1987).
8. Place, R. Adapted from an unpublished MBA term project report, Virginia Polytechnic Institute and State University (1988).
9. Sanders, G., P. Ghandforoush, and L. Austin. "A Model for the Evaluation of Computer Software Packages." *Computers and Industrial Engineering* 7 (1983):309–315.
10. Toffler, A. Lecture at Texas Tech University (1974).
11. Toffler, A. *Future Shock*. New York: Bantam, 1971.
12. Warfield, J., and J. Hill, A *Unified Systems Engineering Concept*. Battelle Monograph No. 1 (1972).
13. Warfield, J. *Societal Systems: Planning, Policy, and Complexity*. New York: Wiley, 1977.

EPILOGUE

Management Science and the Future

And there we have it—our journey through the multifaceted terrain of management science and its models is almost at an end. But textbooks usually end with a sort of "youth looks to the future" discussion, and this book is no exception.

Before we depart on our flight of fancy, however, let us have an informal chat about the preceding chapters of this text. Despite some of the unconventional situations we've experienced in the cases, problems, and examples, this is basically a deadly serious book. In fact, if our view of the future turns out to be anywhere near accurate, this book—or some future edition of it—could become a *managerial survival manual*. We wrote the book with that intent.

This textbook has not taught us to do what electronic computers can do. It has attempted to help us do better what computers *can't and never will do at all*—build coherent models of problems, analyze and adapt the outputs from computerized algorithms, and make better decisions.

And now to the future.

THE ART OF CONSTRUCTING A CRYSTAL BALL

There are all sorts of ways to build crystal balls with which to peer into the future. Some do it with sophisticated mathematical forecasting techniques. The relatively new field of **technological forecasting** attempts to extrapolate what we know about the past evolution of technology to the future.

How do we propose to go about constructing *our* crystal ball? First, we will borrow some notions from our friends the "futurists" and state some assumptions about the world of business and public sector organizations in the year 2000. Then we will deduce from those assumptions how managerial decision making will be different than it is today. Finally, we will draw implications from these deductions for people who are currently preparing themselves to be managerial decision makers.

ASSUMPTIONS: THE WORLD OF 2000

Before we state our technological and behavioral assumptions about the world of 2000, we must first assume that—as it seemed in mid-1992—humanity has successfully come to grips with the threat of nuclear extinction, so that there will still be a planet Earth populated by functioning human beings. Given that we will still exist, then, here are the assumptions upon which we will base our deductions about the evolution of the managerial decision-making process and the implications therefrom.

Assumption 1: Our present-day rudimentary communications systems will have evolved, through what we refer to as organizational automation (OA), into closely knit, highly integrated systems that link us together in every aspect of life and business.

Assumption 2: Through the automation of routine, repetitive decision-making tasks, managers' time will be much freer to tackle "messes" caused by uncertainty.

Assumption 3: The world will have completed its current transition from the space age into the information age.

Assumption 4: Behavioral science will have advanced our managerial understanding of how people and organizations function to the extent that decision makers at least routinely take such things into consideration when making decisions.

Anyone who reads the newspaper or weekly news magazines or business publications has already seen all of the preceding assumptions in one form or another. However, when we put them all together and use a bit of imagination, the deductions we make can be startling.

DEDUCTIONS: THE WORLD OF 2000

The office as we know it today will no longer exist in many organizations. The in-box overflowing with memos and throwaways, the humming word processors, the mail room and the ever-out-of-order photocopy machine, the coffee room and lunch from a brown bag while hoping that the telephone doesn't ring until we have finished eating—all of this will be as quaint to many managers in 2000 as quill pens and inkpots are to managers today. Millions of people will no longer "go to the office" each morning; the office will come to them! Managers' homes will have a separate work space electronically linked to the co-workers and data bases and analytical tools necessary to do the work. Some of the current communications methods of OA—such as electronic mail, electronic calendaring, personalized word processing, advanced graphics, and extensive data base access—will be routinely available. In addition, we will have perfected sophisticated computerized decision support systems that interact with the decision maker at a conversational level (e.g., LPS from Chapter 2; RIKLS from Chapter 11), so that instant access to the MS/OR models discussed earlier in the book (and others) will be at the manager's fingertips.

Most routine communication among and between managers and their staffs will be via highly advanced video-teleconferencing systems. Managers will use holographic (three-dimensional) display screens to create a more lifelike feeling to electronically conducted meetings, briefings, and reports. There will be few telephones—most communication will be via the managerial workstation, which will contact, upon voice command, whomever the manager wishes to talk with. Electronic language translators will automatically convert conversations into the listener's native tongue.

At the operating level, complex industrial robots will perform most routine manufacturing and assembly work, freeing humans for judgmental tasks that neither computers nor robots will ever be able to accomplish. We can only imagine some of the new products that will be available that multinational marketing firms will distribute to people in every corner of the world.

Education—both liberal and professional—will play a markedly more important role in society than it does at present. If the half-life of technical and scientific knowledge is now five years, it will be one or two years by 2000. Under the present educational system as we know it, knowledge gained in a four-year baccalaureate program would be largely obsolete when the student graduated!

There are our deductions that we gleaned from our four assumptions. What implications do these deductions—if accurate—have for decision makers in 2000?

IMPLICATIONS: THE WORLD OF 2000

The first—and probably most significant—implication that we can draw from our deductions is that we will have largely abandoned seat-of-the-pants decision making once and for all before 2000. This is not to say that experience and intuition won't still be important factors—they most certainly will. By 2000, however, MS/OR specialists will have found a satisfactory way to incorporate managers' subjective assessments explicitly into analytical models.

But why do our deductions imply that "mental model decision making" will have all but disappeared by 2000? Because OA will have made decision support systems instantly available to include data bases of every conceivable description as well as a wide variety of sophisticated but easy-to-use analytical models and their associated algorithms. The advanced techniques that we saw in the previous chapters under the heading "State of the Art in . . ." will be in as common use as ordinary linear programming is today. The extremely high speed of the computers of 2000 will permit decision makers to do what-if analyses on models with almost instant turnaround times. The manager who stubbornly refuses to use scientific analysis in decision making is thus analogous to a runner who tries to keep up with a pack of thoroughbred racehorses on foot!

Contrary to our earlier remark, however, might not computers have evolved one step further in that they will be able to successfully emulate the human decision-making process? Our view is that such an evolution is not only improbable but also impossible. A human being's uniqueness lies in the ability to deal with ambiguity and paradox and to correctly deduce conclusions from fuzzy, incomplete data. Computers, on the other hand, have the ability only to do precisely what they are told—and to do so very quickly. Thus, a computer is a completely rational entity, and a human is not. Therein lies humankind's genius.

The second implication has to do with the system of higher education and its role in training future managers. In our view, the baccalaureate degree in business administration in its present form will no longer widely exist. Undergraduate education for most prospective managers will focus partly on analytical and communication skills—with a strong dose of theories of human and organizational behavior thrown in for good measure. The purpose of undergraduate education, therefore, will be to shape prospective managers as people knowledgeable about the society of which they are a part and to teach them how to learn.

The terminal professional degree for managers will be the broad-based Master of Business Administration (MBA)—probably in much its present form. An accredited MBA will be required to enter the practice of management, much as the JD is required to practice law or the MD to practice medicine. But in 2000, when our eager new MBA graduate departs the hallowed halls of academe, his or her education will have only begun. The endless process of continuing professional development, which will be absolutely essential if decision makers are to be competitive in a complex and rapidly changing world, will begin the first month on the job. And the process won't end until retirement.

If our view of the world of 2000 is accurate, our second implication about the educational process suggests that today's business schools face a monumental task—that of reshaping their educational delivery systems and their faculties to meet the challenge of change brought about by technology. To paraphrase the remarks of the dean of a large business school in a university in the southwestern United States:

> Organizational automation (OA) will cause a more fundamental change in the way we work and live than did the invention of the printing press. OA is not some vague possibility in the misty future—it is here now. If we in business schools ignore it, we will quickly become irrelevant to society, and we will quietly fade away. [10]

The third implication has to do with the relationship in 2000 between business and public sector organizations and the society of which they are a part. Yes—we believe that the profit motive will still be the driving force in the private sector, as will service in the public sector. But the determinants of success will have changed radically. In the information age, quality and value will finally become the lodestars of organizational strategy. It is even conceivable that advertising in its present promotional form will have ceased to exist and that companies hired by producers to scientifically test their products will supply "hard" information on product performance to consumers and report their test results to the public.

What does this implication suggest for the people who are engaged in producing goods and services in 2000? First of all, our deduction that industrial robots will perform most of the menial and repetitive tasks that human beings now perform implies that people will earn their living basically by making decisions—both large and small. Since considerations of quality and value will motivate these decisions, managers will use analytical tools such as those discussed widely in this text. Goals such as "maximum quality at minimum cost" suggest a multicriterion approach to decision making, as discussed in Chapter 14.

The fourth and last implication concerns the nature of power in the organizations of 2000. There will still be formal authority structures with their imbedded hierarchy of decision making—as represented by organizational "wiring diagrams." However, we believe that functional decision making (e.g., finance, production, marketing, MIS) will be much more limited than at present, with many more managers operating in a project mode. Therefore, we must train managers more broadly and constantly update that training. We speculate that a manager might spend as much as half of his or her time updating decision-making skills and acquiring new ones and the other half in actually doing the day-to-day job!

There's 2000 as we see it—the implications of deductions based on four assumptions about the future. We see a radically different world in which the use of scientific management techniques will be an absolute necessity for survival.

Even in the wired up world of OA in 2000, however, some things will not have changed at all. People, although somewhat smarter and more sensitive, will still be people. And—one last time: *Models won't make decisions—Managers will.*

KEY TERM

technological forecasting

REFERENCES AND ADDITIONAL READING

1. Bartlett, C., and S. Ghoshal. *Managing Across Borders*. Boston: Harvard Business School Press, 1989.
2. Davis, S. *Future Perfect*. Reading, Mass.: Addison-Wesley, 1989.
3. Earl, M. *Management Strategies for Information Technology*. Englewood Cliffs, N.J.: Prentice-Hall, 1989.
4. Kanter, R. *When Elephants Learn to Dance: Managing the Challenges of Strategy, Management, and Careers in the 1990s*. New York: Simon & Schuster, 1989.
5. Keen, P. *Shaping the Future: Business Design Through Information Technology*. Boston: Harvard Business School Press, 1991.
6. McCormack, M. *What They Don't Teach You at Harvard Business School*. New York: Bantam, 1988.
7. Melymuka, K. "Say It Ain't So . . . OK, It Ain't So." *CIO* (March 1990): 53–61.
8. Naisbitt, J. *Megatrends: Ten New Directions Transforming Our Lives*. New York: Warner Books, 1982.
9. Schrage, M. *Shared Minds*. New York: Random House, 1990.
10. Stem, C. Unpublished transcript of an address to the Board of Regents of Texas Tech University (1982).
11. Walton, R. *Up and Running*. Boston: Harvard Business School Press, 1989.
12. Weill, P. *Do Computers Pay Off?* Washington, D.C.: ICIT Press, 1991.
13. Zuboff, S. *In the Age of the Smart Machine*. New York: Basic Books, 1988.

APPENDIX A
STANDARDIZED NORMAL DISTRIBUTION

	\multicolumn{10}{c}{$z = \#$ standard deviations to the right of the mean}
z	.00	.01	.02	.03	.04	.05	.06	.07	.08	.09
.0	.500	.504	.508	.512	.516	.520	.524	.528	.533	.536
.1	.540	.544	.548	.552	.556	.560	.564	.568	.571	.575
.2	.579	.583	.587	.591	.595	.599	.603	.606	.610	.615
.3	.618	.622	.625	.629	.633	.637	.641	.644	.648	.652
.4	.655	.659	.663	.666	.670	.674	.677	.681	.684	.688
.5	.692	.695	.699	.702	.705	.709	.712	.716	.719	.722
.6	.726	.729	.732	.736	.740	.742	.745	.749	.752	.755
.7	.758	.761	.764	.767	.770	.773	.776	.779	.782	.785
.8	.788	.791	.794	.797	.800	.802	.805	.808	.811	.813
.9	.816	.819	.821	.824	.827	.830	.832	.834	.837	.839
1.0	.841	.844	.846	.849	.851	.853	.855	.858	.860	.862
1.1	.864	.867	.869	.871	.873	.875	.877	.879	.881	.883
1.2	.885	.887	.889	.891	.893	.894	.896	.898	.900	.902
1.3	.903	.905	.907	.908	.910	.912	.913	.915	.916	.918
1.4	.919	.921	.922	.924	.925	.927	.928	.929	.931	.932
1.5	.933	.935	.936	.937	.938	.939	.941	.942	.943	.944
1.6	.945	.946	.947	.948	.950	.951	.952	.953	.954	.955
1.7	.955+	.956	.957	.958	.959	.960	.961	.962	.963	.963
1.8	.964	.965	.966	.966	.967	.968	.969	.969+	.970	.971
1.9	.971	.972	.973	.973	.974	.974+	.975	.976	.976+	.977
2.0	.977+	.978	.978	.979	.979	.980	.980+	.981	.981+	.982
2.1	.982+	.983	.983	.983	.984	.984+	.985	.985+	.985+	.986
2.2	.986+	.986+	.987	.987	.987	.988	.988+	.988+	.989	.989
2.3	.989+	.990	.990	.990	.990	.991	.991	.991+	.991+	.992
2.4	.992	.992	.992	.993	.993	.993	.993+	.993+	.993+	.994
2.5	.994	.994	.994	.994	.995	.995	.995	.995	.995+	.995+
2.6	.995+	.996	.996	.996	.996	.996	.996+	.996+	.996+	.996+
2.7	.997	.997	.997	.997	.997	.997	.997+	.997+	.997+	.997+
2.8	.997+	.998	.998	.998	.998	.998	.998	.998	.998	.998
2.9	.998	.998	.998	.998	.998	.998+	.999	.999	.999	.999
3.0	.999	.999	.999	.999	.999	1	1	1	1	1

APPENDIX B
UNIT NORMAL LINEAR LOSS INTEGRAL

	Ln(z)									
z	.00	.01	.02	.03	.04	.05	.06	.07	.08	.09
.0	.399	.395	.389	.384	.379	.374	.370	.365	.360	.356
.1	.351	.346	.342	.337	.333	.328	.324	.320	.315	.311
.2	.307	.303	.299	.294	.290	.286	.282	.278	.275	.271
.3	.267	.263	.259	.256	.252	.248	.245	.241	.237	.234
.4	.230	.227	.224	.220	.217	.214	.210	.207	.204	.201
.5	.198	.195	.192	.189	.186	.183	.180	.177	.174	.171
.6	.169	.166	.163	.161	.158	.155	.153	.150	.148	.145
.7	.143	.141	.138	.136	.133	.131	.129	.127	.125	.122
.8	.120	.118	.116	.114	.112	.110	.108	.106	.104	.102
.9	.100	.099	.097	.095	.093	.092	.090	.088	.087	.085
1.0	.083	.082	.080	.079	.077	.076	.074	.073	.071	.070
1.1	.069	.067	.066	.065	.063	.062	.061	.060	.058	.057
1.2	.056	.055	.054	.053	.052	.051	.050	.049	.048	.047
1.3	.046	.045	.044	.043	.042	.041	.040	.039	.038	.037
1.4	.036+	.036	.035	.034	.034	.033	.032	.031+	.031	.030
1.5	.029+	.029	.028	.027	.027	.026+	.026	.025	.024+	.024
1.6	.023+	.023	.022	.022	.021	.021	.020+	.020	.019+	.019
1.7	.018+	.018	.017	.017	.016	.016	.015+	.015	.014+	.014+

GLOSSARY

absorbing state The converse of a transient state in a Markov chain; once a process element enters an absorbing state, it never leaves.
activity In simulation, an elementary task that requires time to complete.
activity tree A modeling device used to depict the relationships between and among a collection of organizational activities.
Additive Algorithm [Balas] An ILP algorithm that solves models in which all decision variables take on only the values zero and one.
Advanced Start Algorithm [Hanna] A cutting plane algorithm in ILP that remains infeasible until the optimal solution is found.
algorithm A logically ordered sequence of steps required to provide a satisfactory solution for a specific model.
alternate optimal solutions Differing sets of values of decision variables that result in identical optimal values of the objective function.
alternatives Feasible courses of action available to a decision maker.
analog model An actual physical model of a phenomenon (e.g., a model airplane).
arcs Entities that connect nodes in network models.
assignment model A transportation model in which each supply node has exactly one unit, and each demand node requires exactly one unit.
attribute A characteristic of an element of a simulation model.

balking See queue discipline.
basis The set of decision variables in an LP model that have non-zero values.
batch arrival In queueing theory, a calling population whose units depart in groups greater than one in number.

behavioral research Efforts to explain why the behavior of people, organizations, or animals is likely to manifest itself in a certain way.
binary matrices Matrices that use zeros and ones to indicate relationships.
binding constraint A constraint that is met exactly in the optimal solution to a mathematical programming model.
bivariate distribution A probability distribution in two random variables.
block diagonal model A large LP model with certain constraints applicable to all decision variables, but with other sets of constraints applicable to distinct subsets of decision variables.
boundary The attribute of a system that specifies which components are a part of the environment (exogenous) and which are part of the system (endogenous).
Bounded Descent Algorithm [Austin and Hanna] A cutting plane algorithm in ILP that remains infeasible until the optimal solution is found.
branch In branch-and-bound algorithms, to create two new problems by rounding up and down the non-integer value of a decision variable.

calling population In queueing theory, the set of people or things requiring service.
causal/correlative simulation A model that depends upon whether the interconnections among the components that describe the system represent an attempt to model the actual interactions among these components (causal), or represent simply a linkage between two variables that, statistically, are highly correlated (correlative).
coefficient A number or quantity placed generally before and multiplying a function of a variable.

combined simulation Simulation modeling that employs both discrete and continuous simulation in a single model.

conditional distribution of predictive accuracy The probability distribution that reflects the historical accuracy of a forecaster.

conservation of flow A modeling device that assures flow in a network flow model.

constraints Restrictions or limitations that narrow available choices in managerial decision making.

Constructive Primal-Dual Algorithm [Ghandforoush] A hybrid ILP algorithm that alternates between feasibility and infeasibility until the optimal solution is found.

continuous simulation A computerized modeling device that mimics the operation of a real system in a smooth, uninterrupted manner.

convex A region is convex if, when we draw a line between any two points in the region, then every point on the line is also in the region.

credibility What a MS model lacks without the direct involvement of the decision maker in the model building process.

critical activities The activities on the critical path in a CPM or PERT model.

critical path The path of activity arcs in a CPM or PERT model that represents the longest path—and therefore the shortest completion time for the project.

cross-interaction matrix A modeling device that uses different element sets to index its rows and columns.

cuts In ILP, additional constraints derived from the constraint set that eliminate parts of the feasible region without discarding feasible lattice points.

decision Managerial action to solve or mitigate a problem.

decision making under risk (DMUR) A decision environment in which we must take explicitly into consideration probabilistic considerations inherent in the problem.

decision making under uncertainty (DMUU) A complex decision environment in which we cannot satisfactorily estimate probability distributions, or in which we have multiple objectives or highly qualitative considerations inherent in the problem.

decision support system A computerized, interactive managerial tool consisting of a model base, a data base, and a user interface.

decision tree A graphical device used to represent a sequential decision situation.

degree of criticality In PERT-Simulation, the frequency with which each activity appears on the critical path in the simulation runs.

DELPHI technique A forecasting technique that involves individual assessments using iterated feedback by members of an expert panel.

DELTA chart A method for portraying research and development projects; it is a form of flow chart that depicts the planned flow of activities (and their actors) for a project.

deterministic simulation A modeling approach that is appropriate for systems whose parameters (constants) and structure are relatively well-known and understood; i.e., the system contains no random variables.

direct methods In NLP, global solution techniques such as differential calculus.

discrete simulation A computerized modeling device that mimics the operation of a real system at specific points in time.

discrete stochastic process A dynamic, probabilistic process that involves elements of a system moving in an "orderly" manner among a finite set of states, the movement occurring at discrete points in time.

dominated alternative An alternative is dominated by another alternative if the second gives better results under all conditions.

doubly stochastic matrix A one-step transition matrix for a Markov chain whose columns as well as rows sum to 1.

dynamic environment A decision making scenario in which time is an essential element.

dynamic programming A modeling technique that decomposes a large problem into a series of stages, and uses induction (backward recursion) to find solutions.

efficiency The ability to accomplish a task with the minimum expenditure of resources.

environment In systems theory, the portion of reality that is exogenous to the problem system.

Erlang distribution A two-parameter probability distribution named for the queueing pioneer William Erlang.

event In simulation, the instant in time that an activity begins or ends.

expected monetary value (EMV) The long-term average value of a risky alternative.

expected opportunity loss (EOL) The long-term average value of the regret of a risky alternative.

expected utility The long-term average utility of a risky alternative.

expected value See expected monetary value.

fathom In branch-and-bound algorithms, to determine at one point on the branch of a tree that no solutions better than those currently known are further down that branch.

feasibility The state of falling within the manager-specified constraints or restrictions of a problem.
FIFO First in, first out.
finished goods inventory Stock of completed goods to meet customer demand.
fractional programming model An NLP model with linear constraints and with an objective function that is the ratio of two linear functions.
Frank-Wolfe Quadratic Programming Algorithm An early algorithm for solving quadratic programs that transforms them into equivalent linear programs.

Gantt chart A device used by a project manager to guide in determining the resources required in any given period.
generalized knapsack problem A knapsack problem in which including more than one of each item is permissible.
geometric programming model An NLP model whose objective function and constraints are posynomials (sums of products of powers of the variables).

heuristic algorithms Solution approaches that yield satisfactory, but not necessarily optimal, solutions to the model of a problem.
holding costs In inventory management, the direct and indirect costs of having goods on hand; included are such things as warehouse handling, insurance, taxes, utilities, obsolescence/ spoilage, and foregone returns on capital invested in inventory.
homomorphic simulation A model whose elements represent more than one element of the actual system.

incremental analysis An economic analysis at the margin.
incumbent In branch-and-bound algorithms, the alternative that yields the current lower bound.
indirect methods In NLP, search methods such as gradient analysis.
information Data summarized or transformed so as to be useful to a decision maker.
information overload Access to vast amounts of information because of the pervasiveness of computers.
in-process inventory Assets that are currently undergoing transformation into end-products.
integer hull In pure ILP, the simplex whose vertices are integer-valued and feasible, and that does not exclude feasible lattice points.
intransitive preference For example, if we prefer A to B and we also prefer B to C, then our preference structure is intransitive if we then prefer C to A.
inverse transformation method In simulation, an algorithm for generating sequences of random numbers from the cumulative density function of an assumed probability distribution.
isomorphic simulation A model in which there exists a unique two way correspondence between the elements of the original system and the elements of the model.

knowledge engineering A branch of artificial intelligence that concerns itself with the way we explicitly represent, process, and acquire knowledge.

Lagrange multiplier The rate of change of the objective function with respect to the RHS of an associated constraint.
LIFO Last in, first out.
Linearization In NLP, transforming a nonlinear problem so that the resulting model is linear.
lower bound In maximization models, a value of the objective function known to exist, but not known to be optimal.

Markov property multistage decision process in which each decision in the sequence of decisions incorporates the effects of all previous decisions, so we are concerned only with relationships between pairs of consecutive decisions.
Markovian model The simplest queueing model (e.g., M/M/1/∞/FIFO/1).
mathematical programming an MS model whose objective(s) and constraints can be expressed mathematically as functions of decision variables
mathematical simulation Using a computer to simulate the model characterized by means of mathematical equations.
matrix modeling The use of a matrix to show all possible interaction pairs between the elements of the same or different sets.
Min-Cut/Max-Flow Theorem An approach to finding the maximum flow through a network that involves finding the minimal set of arcs that, if blocked, block all flow through the network.
mixed ILP model An ILP model in which some but not all decision variables are required to take on integer values.
mixed preemptive modeling In MOLP, combining both commensurable and incommensurable modeling approaches in a single model.
model exchange isomorphism A transformation of models from one form to another.
Monte Carlo simulation A probabilistic simulation approach.
morphology The study of structure or form and the features comprising the form and any of its parts.

multicommodity network flow model A transportation model that involves the flow of two or more distinct types of units.

multiechelon inventory models In a highly vertically integrated manufacturing company, an inventory management system that coordinates and attempts to find globally optimal inventory policies.

multiple objective linear programming (MOLP) An approach to modeling problems that we can profitably model and analyze by LP, except that the objective "function" is a set of linear functions and some specified relationship among them.

multiplicative congruence method An algorithm for producing pseudo-random numbers in simulation.

multistage modeling Decomposing a large problem into a series of dependent stages.

network A set of nodes connected by arcs.

nodes Entities that act as intersections for arcs in network models.

nonbinding constraint A constraint that is not met exactly in the optimal solution to a mathematical programming model.

nonlinear programming (NLP) models Mathematical programs that have a nonlinear function as an objective or constraints, or both.

objective function A mathematical expression that represents the goals and values of a decision maker.

objectives tree A modeling device (sometimes called an intent structure) to describe the relationships that exist among a set of objectives.

one-stage transition matrix The matrix that exhibits the probabilities of movement between states at discrete points in time.

optimization algorithms Solution approaches that yield the best possible feasible solution to the model of a problem.

order-independent allocation In DP, a decomposable problem in which the order of the resulting stages is random.

ordering costs In inventory management, the sum of costs associated with bid solicitation, processing paperwork, shipping and receiving, etc.

outcome In decision theory, the consequences of selecting a given alternative and having a specific state of nature occur (also payoff).

out-of-stock costs In inventory management, the cost of backordering and the cost of stockout (when backordering is not possible).

paradigm An example serving as a model or a pattern.

parallel servers In a queueing system, identical facilities providing simultaneous service to multiple units.

path An unbroken chain of arcs from source to sink in network models.

payoff In decision theory, the consequences of selecting a given alternative and having a specific state of nature occur (also outcome).

periodic review inventory model A class of inventory models that reviews inventory levels at fixed time periods.

PERT chart A network diagram used to depict the precedence relations between and among the activities in a project.

physical simulation Using physical models to mimic systems of interest (also called analog simulation).

policy A coordinated collection of decisions.

posterior distribution The probability distribution that incorporates the conditional distribution of predictive accuracy and the prior distribution in DMUR.

predictive distribution The marginal probability distribution of a forecaster's future predictions in DMUR.

preemptive goal prioritization In MOLP, an approach that orders the set of linear objectives in absolute priority order.

preemptive goal programming In MOLP, an approach that orders deviational variables associated with the goal constraints in absolute priority order.

prior distribution In DMUR, the estimated probability distribution on the states of nature with no information.

probability tree A mechanism for showing the relationships between marginal, conditional, and joint probabilities defined over a pair of event spaces.

problem A perceived difference between what is desired and what is. In the language of the economist, wherever expectations differ substantially from realizations, a problem occurs.

process A systematic series of actions or events directed to some goal or purpose.

process (in simulation) A collection of activities that we must either perform serially in chronological order or in parallel.

project A collection of tasks that are related to each other over time, with a beginning and an end, whose purpose is to achieve a specific goal.

pseudo-random numbers Sequences of numbers that have the appearance of randomness, but that can be replicated exactly.

pure ILP model An ILP model in which all decision variables are required to take on integer values.

quadratic programming model An NLP model with linear constraints and a quadratic objective function.

queue Waiting line.

queue discipline In queueing theory, if arriving units have the option of not joining the queue if they judge it to be too long, then we say that balking is allowed. If a unit can decide to leave the queue after having joined it, then reneging is present.

random A queueing priority in which the next unit to be served is not determined systematically.
rank A queueing priority in which the next unit to be served is determined by its status.
raw materials inventory The basic materials or subunits needed in the manufacture or assembly of an end-product.
recurring Markov process A Markov chain with no absorbing states.
recursive optimization A pseudonym for dynamic programming,
regenerative event Events in simulation that generate the next event.
relevance tree A tree-like device in which broad concepts at the top of the tree are linked to ever more specific concepts or entities as lower branches develop.
reneging See queue discipline.
return function In DP, the objective function at each stage.
rolling schedule A forecasting method that develops plans for future periods based on past experience, but discards the earliest data point each time a new forecast is prepared.

secondary data Raw data, such as the output of an MS software package.
self-interaction matrix A modeling device that uses the same element set to index both its row and its column.
separability The attribute of a problem that allows us to decompose it into stages.
series servers In a queueing system, multiple units providing different services sequentially to the same calling unit.
service facility In queueing theory, an entity that provides service to the units of the calling population.
shadow prices In LP, rates of change of the value of the objective function, given a unit change in the right-hand side of the associated constraint.
side condition A relation between one or more nodes and arcs that violates the assumptions inherent in network models.
SIMPLEX algorithm [Dantzig] A technique that efficiently finds optimal solutions to LP models.
Simplified Primal Algorithm [Young] A cutting plane algorithm in ILP that maintains feasibility until the optimal solution is found.
simulation A computerized modeling device that mimics the operation of a real system.
single arrival In queueing theory, a calling population whose units depart one at a time.

single server In a queueing system, only one facility to provide service.
smooth and continuous Differentiable.
stages In DP, the phases into which we decompose a large problem.
states In DP, the decision variables. In matrix modeling, the mutually exclusive and collectively exhaustive elements of the future environment.
steady-state simulation A modeling approach used to represent systems that operate in a non-transient mode.
steady-state vector In Markov chains, the relative frequencies of states after they have settled into a constant pattern.
structure The relationships that will eventually characterize the model of a problem.
surrogate variable A variable other than an actual decision variable, that we use to impose a desired performance criterion on a MS model.
system An assemblage or combination of elements forming a unitary whole.

technological forecasting An attempt to extrapolate to the future what we know about the past evolution of technology.
time-sequenced decisions DP models in which the stages occur naturally and serially over time.
transient Markov process A Markov chain with both transient and absorbing states.
transient simulation A modeling approach that is appropriate for systems that indicate a temporary behavior.
transient state In Markov chains, a state that allows units to "pass through," but that—in the long run—converges to a state probability of zero.
transportation model A special network model that optimizes some attribute of flows from one set of nodes (supply) to a different set (demand).
transshipment model A generalized transportation model with intermediate sets of nodes between supply and demand.
trees See decision tree.

utiles Dimensionless units used to transform physical outcomes or payoffs into quantities that correctly reflect the decision maker's attitude toward risk for a given problem.

validation Assuring that a model's data, structure, behavior, and overall performance are appropriate to analyzing the problem at hand.
values The primary standards we use for weighing various alternatives and deciding among them.
variable A mathematical symbol that represents a specific managerial decision.

verification The task of making certain the computer implementation of the model contains no errors and is essentially free of "bugs."

vertex In LP or ILP, the intersection of at least n constraints, where n is the number of decision variables.

visual interactive simulation On-screen visual characterization of the process so the user can see the model as it evolves over time.

worth tree A modeling device used to assess the overall value of each candidate in a set of candidates.

INDEX

Absorbing state, 375
Ackoff, R., 21, 416
Activity (in simulation), 332
Activity precedence diagram (in simulation), 334
Activity tree, 515
Adams, J., 298
Additive algorithm (Balas), 114
Additivity, 27
ADVANCE (GPSS), 345
Advanced Start algorithm (Hanna), 111
Air Traffic Control (minicase), 235
Alexander, S., 298
Algorithm (definition), 10
All-units price discounts, 420
Alternate optimal solutions (in LP), 40
Alternatives, 255
Analog model (in networks), 186
Angielski, B., 507
"Animal Farm", 402
Apteryx Aircraft Company (minicase), 453
Arrow, K., 450, 464
Arthur, J., 363, 542
Assignment model, 163
Athos, A., 21
Attributes (in discrete simulation), 333
Audit Trail (minicase), 404
Austin, L., 90, 111, 144, 189, 440, 542
Averaging out and rolling back, 264

Backorder, 421
Backpacking (minicase), 123
Baird, B., 189, 298
Baker, K., 249
Balanced redundant communications network, 246
Balas, E., 112, 114, 144
Baldwin, M., 542
Balking (in a queue), 302

Bar chart, 509
Barr, R., 189
Barrett, M., 90, 144
Bartlett, C., 547
Bayes's Theorem, 262
Bayesians, 445, 450
Bazarra, M., 90, 189, 223
Bean, C., 298, 464
Beau-Kay, Inc. (minicase), 210
Bellman, R., 228, 249
Bellman's Principle of Optimality, 229
Beta distribution, 395
Bierman, H., 90
Biles, W., 364
Binary matrices, 521
Binary representation (in ILP), 114
BLL, Inc. (minicase), 121
Block diagonal LP model, 53
Bonini, C., 90
Boundary of a system, 8
Bounded Descent algorithm, 111
Bradley, G., 189
Branch-and-bound (in ILP), 107, 109, 112
Bray, T., 342, 364
Brown, G., 189
Brown-Gibson location model, 526
Brown, P., 526, 542
Brown, R., 298, 464
Bryant, D., 417
Buckius, L., 440
Buddingh, D., 90
Budgeting in Blacksburg (minicase), 494
Buffa, E., 440
Burns, J., 90, 348, 363

Cabana Bananas (minicase), 238
Cabana Bananas Revisited (minicase), 350

Calkins, C., 90
Calling population (in queueing), 301
Capital investment decisions, 15
Cartwright, D., 542
Causal simulation, 331
Center for Professional Development (minicase), 172, 413
Central Limit Theorem, 342, 398
Charnes, A., 474, 507
Chinese postman model, 168
Christiansen, S., 392
Churchman, C., 2, 21
Closed-form solution (in inventory), 425
Cole, D., 249
Collectively exhaustive, 254
Colossus of Roads (minicase), 206
Combined simulation, 365
Commensurable multiple objectives, 467
Complexity, 443
Conditional distribution of predictive accuracy, 262
Conover, W., 298
Constrained center of gravity problem, 217
Constrained shadow price, 481
Constructive Primal-Dual algorithm, 111
Container cost minimization model, 197
Continuous dynamic programming, 233
Continuous prior distribution, 272
Continuous simulation models, 348, 365
Convexity, 192
Cooper, R., 326
Cooper, W., 474, 507
Corning, S., 364
Corporate simulation languages, 366
Corporate simulation models, 366, 369
Coyle, R., 5, 21
Critical factors, 526
Critical path model (CPM), 152
Cross-interaction matrix, 520, 523
Cumulative distribution function (CDF), 340
"Curse of dimensionality" (in DP), 231
Cut-set, 169
Cutting planes (in ILP), 110, 112
Cycle (in inventory), 423

D-Day (minicase), 284
D-Day Revisited (minicase), 456
Dakin, R., 107, 144
Dannenbring, D., 90
Dantzig, G., 26, 37, 90, 476
Dantzig-Wolfe decomposition, 53, 169
Data collection, 9
Davis, P., 91
Davis, R., 298
Davis, S., 547

Decision making under certainty (DMUC), 23
Decision making under risk (DMUR), 251
Decision making under uncertainty (DMUU), 443
Decision matrix, 255
Decision support systems, 17, 369, 509
Decision trees, 263, 515
Decision variable, 13, 43
Degree of criticality (PERT), 403
DELPHI, 256
DELTA chart, 511, 515, 518
Denardo, E., 249
DEPART (GPSS), 345
Dependent demand, 429
Dependent slack, 400
Derman, C., 392
Descriptive model, 3
Descriptive network model, 166
Deterministic problem, 4
Deterministic simulation, 331
Deviational variables, 474
Dinnin, M., 326
Direct methods (in NLP), 200
Discrete simulation, 328
Discrete stochastic process, 370
Disk-o-Tech (minicase), 117
Divisibility (in LP), 27
DMUR, 254
DMUR model, 255
DMUU, 445
Doig, A., 107, 144
Dominated alternatives (in DMUU), 267
Doubly stochastic transition matrix, 389
Dreyfus, S., 249
Driskill, B., 91
Dual SIMPLEX, 52
Duality (in LP), 51
Dummy activities (CPM, PERT), 153, 400
Dynamic environment, 328
Dynamic programming, 204, 224
Dynamic programming (definition), 229
Dynamic programming in Markov chains, 378
Dynamic risk preference, 274

Earl, M., 547
Econometric models, 366
Economic utility, 268
Edwards, R., 298
Efficiency, 11
Either-or (in ILP), 97
Emshoff, J., 329, 364
EMV, 258
EMVPI, 260
END (GPSS), 344
Endogenous variables, 369

INDEX

Entities (in discrete simulation), 333
EOL criterion, 258
EOQ at AFLC (minicase), 430
Eppen, G., 91
Erickson, W., 326
Erlang distribution, 325
Erlang, W., 300
Event (in discrete simulation), 333
Exogenous variables, 369
Expected monetary value (EMV) criterion, 258
Expected opportunity loss (EOL) criterion, 258
Expected project completion time (PERT), 396
Expected utility, 270
Exponential distribution, 312
Exponentially distributed random numbers, 339

Fawcette, J., 416
Fiacco, A., 200, 223
Fielding, N., 249
Fielding, T., 249
FIFO (in queueing), 302
Financial models (in simulation), 366
Finished goods inventory, 418
Finite queue, 309
Fishburn, P., 299
Fixed charge (in ILP), 93
Fletcher, R., 223
Flow diagram, 335
Ford, L., 166, 169, 189
Forgionne, G., 91
Formulating the model (in LP), 28
Forrester, J., 364, 366
Fractional cutting planes, 110
Fractional programming, 201
Frank, M., 203, 223
Frank-Wolfe Quadratic Programming algorithm, 203
Frendewey, J., 363
Fromm, G., 21
Fulkerson, D., 166, 169, 189
Fuzzy sets, 483

Galitz, L., 328, 364
Gantt chart, 398, 511, 513
Gantt, H., 511
Garbage in, garbage out, 17, 30
Garfinkel, R., 144
GASP, 334, 347
Gass, S., 91
Gattis, D., 364
GENERATE (GPSS), 345
Geometric programming, 204
GERT, 402
Ghandforoush, P., 111, 144, 363, 542
Ghoshal, S., 547

Gibson, D., 526, 542
Gido, J., 416
Glover, F., 189, 190
Goal programming, 474
Gomory, R., 110, 144
Go/no go (in ILP), 103
Goodell, P., 91
Gordon, G., 364
Gould, F., 91
Gourmet (minicase), 318
GPSS, 334, 344
Graphical example (in LP), 38
Graves, G., 189
Graybill, F., 417
Greedy algorithm, 156
GRG2 (computer program), 200
Grudnitski, G., 417
Gupta, J., 21
GYRO (minicase), 410

Hadley, G., 440
Hamilton, D., 21
Hamilton, W., 21
Hanna, M., 111, 144
Harary, F., 542
Hartley, H., 464
Hausman, W., 90
Hehir, P., 542
Heuristic algorithm, 11
High Tor (minicase), 280
Hill, J., 542
Hillier, F., 46, 91, 249
Hitchcock, F., 190
Hochwalt, T., 299
Hogan, W., 189
Holding costs (inventory), 421
Homogeneous calling population (in queueing), 301
Homomorphic, 3, 332
Hultz, J., 190
Hurwicz, W., 448

ICQ (minicase), 315
Ignizio, J., 507
Imbedded networks, 169
Implementation, 12
Incommensurable multiple objectives, 467
Incremental analysis, 273
Incremental price discounts, 420, 441
Incremental Profit Program (minicase), 64
Indirect methods (in NLP), 199
Inductive process, 230
Infeasible solution (in LP), 50
Information overload, 509
Initial state vector, 373

In-process inventory, 418
Insufficient reason criterion (Laplace), 451
Integer hull, 110
Integer modeling, 93
Integer programming, 92
Integrated queueing system, 303
Intent structure, 515
Interaction matrices, 520
Intransitive preference, 268
Inventory control (in NLP), 195
Inventory management, 418
Inventory simulation, 427
Inverse transformation method, 339
Isomorphic, 3, 332

Jack Legg Associates (minicase), 275
Jain, A., 223
Jarvis, J., 90, 189
Jeffress, C., 364
Just-in-Time production system, 430

Kahr, A., 298, 464
Kane, J., 364, 366
Kanter, R., 547
Kathman, J., 364
Keen, P., 329, 364, 547
Keeney, R., 507
Keep on Truckin' (minicase), 433
Kelton, D., 364
Kemeny, J., 392
Kendall, D., 307, 326, 445
Keown, A., 495, 507
King Cotton (minicase), 282
Kiviat, P., 332, 346, 364
Klingman, D., 189, 190
Knapsack model, 104
Knowledge engineering, 348
Knowles, T., 91
Krogstad, J., 417
Kuhn-Tucker conditions, 200
Kwak, N., 223
Kwan, M., 168, 190

Lagrange multiplier, 200, 204, 234, 246
Land, A., 107, 144
Laplace, M., 451
Lasdon, L., 200, 205, 223
Lattice points, 110
LaValle, I., 299, 464
Law, A., 364
Lawler, E., 417
Lead time (in inventory), 419
Lee, S., 474, 507
Lemmon Rent-a-Car (minicase), 383

Leontief, W., 364
Lieberman, J., 46, 91, 249
LIFO (in queueing), 302
Linear approximation (in NLP), 203
Linear combinations model (in MOLP), 471, 480
Linear regression, 215
Linearization (in NLP), 200
Linear programming, 26
Little, J., 314, 326
LO-CAL Candy Company (dialogue), 32, 41, 93, 101
Longest route algorithm, 154
Longest route model, 150
Lottery (in DMUR), 270
Lower-bounded variables (in LP), 52
LPS (dialogue), 32
Luce, R., 299
Lutz, J., 190

Management science and the future, 543
Marcy, W., 363
Marker, R., 91
Markov chains, 370
Markovian models (in queueing), 307, 312
Markov process, 370
Markov property, 224, 371
Markowitz, H., 364
Marsaglia, G., 342, 364
Material requirements planning (MRP), 429
Mathematical programming, 24, 192
Mathematical simulation, 331
Matrix modeling, 520
MAXIMAX criterion, 448
MAXIMIN criterion, 446, 470, 478
Mayor, S., 542
McCormick, G., 200, 223
McCormack, M., 21, 547
Mean absolute deviation (MAD) regression, 215
Melymuka, K., 547
Mental model, 1, 3
Meter Readers (minicase), 170
Meyer, W., 417
Min-cut, max-flow theorem, 169
Minieka, E., 190
Minimal spanning tree algorithm, 156
Minimal spanning tree model, 154
MINIMAX, 204
MINIMAX Regret criterion, 448
MIPS (minicase), 529
Mixed ILP model, 92
Model building, 5, 28, 257, 303, 421, 528
Model classification, 2
Model exchange isomorphism, 509
Model formulation, 31
Model structure, 9

Model validation, 9, 31, 366
Model verification, 9
Moder, J., 417
MOLP modeling, 468
Monte Carlo method, 338
Mood, A., 417
Moore, L., 474, 507
Morgenstern, O., 299, 464
Morphological models, 514
Morse, P., 308, 326
MS model (definition), 2, 5
Multiattribute choice model, 522
Multiattribute utility function, 274
Multicommodity network flow, 169
Multicriterion decision model, 526
Multidivisional LP model, 53
Multiechelon inventory model, 427
Multiple objectives, 465
Multiple right-hand sides, 482
Multiple servers (in queueing), 310
Multiplicative congruence method, 338
Multistage modeling, 226
Multistage optimization, 225
Mutually exclusive, 254

Naisbitt, J., 547
Natural integer-valued variables, 93
Naylor, T., 329, 364, 367
Nemhauser, G., 144, 228, 249
Network (definition), 145
Network flow algorithms, 166
Network flow model, 145, 157
Network models, 145
Newsboy model, 273
Node labeling (in networks), 151
Nonlinear modeling, 193
Nonlinear programming, 191
Nonsequential multistage optimization, 235
Normally distributed random numbers, 340
Norman, K., 542
Notation, 13, 307, 466

Objective cut, 112
Objectives tree, 515
Officer and a Gentleman (minicase), 379
Offord, B., 91
One-stage transition matrix, 370
One-step transition matrix, 373
ONO (dialogue), 158, 182
Optimal network flow model, 157
Optimizing network flow models, 168
Order-independent allocation (in DP), 228
Ordering costs (in inventory), 421
Order quantity (in inventory), 419

Organizational chart, 512
Orlicky, J., 440
Orwell, G., 402, 417
Outcomes, 255
Out-of-Kilter algorithm, 166
Out-of-stock costs (in inventory), 421

PAC-MAN (dialogue), 303
Paper cutting problem, 76
Paradigm, 1
Pareto principle, 429
Parker, R., 144, 190
Parkinson, C., 404, 417
Parkinson's Law, 404
Pascale, R., 21
Pegden, C., 364
Pelky, M., 542
Performance measure, 528
Periodic review model (in inventory), 428
Permanent entities (in simulation), 333
PERT, 393
PERT chart, 401, 514
PERT/COST, 401
PERT-simulation, 402
Peters, T., 21
Peterson, C., 298, 464
Peterson, R., 440
Peterson, T., 417
Phillips, C., 417
Phillips, D., 364
Pie chart, 510
Pinkerton, J., 495, 507
Place, R., 542
Poisson distribution, 307, 311
POLKA (minicase), 175
Pollaczek-Khintchine equation, 315
POPGO (dialogue), 475, 499
Posterior distribution, 262, 267
Posynomials, 204
Powell, M., 223
Pratt, J., 299
Predictive distribution, 263
Preemptive goal prioritization, 472, 480
Preemptive goal programming, 474, 481
Preemptive prioritization, 480
Prescriptive model, 3
Pricing model, 193
Prior distribution, 262
Pritsker, A., 364, 417
Probability simulation, 339
Probability tree, 520
Problem (definition), 2
Process (in simulation), 332
Project selection model, 528

Project scheduling, 393
Psaraftis, H., 235, 249
Pseudo-random numbers, 338
Pure ILP model, 92
Pure preemptive goal programming, 496
Purpose, 3

Q-GERT, 402
Quadratic programming, 202
Qualitative factor measure, 527
Quantitative factor measure, 527
Queue discipline, 302
Queueing models, 300
Queueing subsystem, 302
QUES (dialogue), 303, 321
QUEUE (GPSS), 345

Racquet (minicase), 67
Raiffa, H., 299, 507
Random number generation, 338
Random queue priority, 302
Ranging analysis (in LP), 45
Rardin, R., 144, 190
Ratner, M., 223
Ravindran, A., 364
Raw materials inventory, 418
Recurring Markov process, 373
Recursive optimization, 25, 229
Reduced costs (in LP), 43
Reduction to 0-1 models (ILP), 114
Rees, L., 363
Regret, 259
RELEASE (GPSS), 346
Relevance tree, 520
Reneging (in queueing), 302
Repair or replace model, 148
RESET (GPSS), 344
Resource allocation, 14
Reyes, J., 299
RIKLS (dialogue), 397
Risk, 269
Risk and utility, 452
Ritter, J., 417
Ritter, R., 364
Rivett, P., 21, 416

Sage, A., 364
SAM (dialogue), 335
Sampling (in simulation), 342
Sampson, D., 299, 464
Sanders, G., 542
Satisficing, 450
Sauceda, M., 299
Savage, L., 448

Savin E. Lavin (minicase), 349
Schaul, H., 364
Schlaifer, R., 299
Schmidt, C., 91
Schrage, L., 249
Schrage, M., 547
Schriber, T., 364
Scott, W., 367
Scott Morton, M., 329, 364
Scrap minimization model, 197
Security (minicase), 71
SEIZE (GPSS), 346
Self-interaction matrix, 520
Semi-Markov property, 147
Separability (in DP), 227
Sequential decision process, 257
Sequential Unconstrained Minimization Technique, 200
Service facility (in queueing), 302
Shadow prices, 44
Shaffer, L., 417
Shannon, R., 329, 364
Shetty, C., 223
Shier, D., 190
Shortest route algorithms, 150
Shortest route through a network, 147
Silver, E., 440
SIMPLEX algorithm, 11, 26, 36, 37, 52, 92, 109, 150, 168, 200, 204, 205, 467, 477, 480
Simplified Primal algorithm, 111
SIMSCRIPT II.5, 334, 346
SIMULATE (GPSS), 344
Simulation (discrete), 328
Simulation (continuous), 365
Sisson, R., 329, 364
Slack variables (in LP), 43
SLAM, 334, 347
Snell, J., 392
SofSneez (minicase), 483
Solberg, J., 364
Spacetrek (minicase), 490
Specified integer values (in ILP), 99
Spengler, O., 4, 21
Spira, P., 190
SPMS method, 6
Stagecoach problem, 225
Stallings, M., 91
Standardized normal distribution, 548
Starr, M., 90
START (GPSS), 344
State-dependent queueing system, 311
State transition diagram, 371
States of nature, 254
Stationarity, 372, 419

Statistical approximation method, 342
Steady state simulation, 331
Steady state system, 307, 331, 374
Stem, C., 546, 547
Stockout, 421
Strategic control, 526, 529
Sturms, E., 91
Stutz, J., 190
Subjective factor measure, 527
Subjective probability, 445
Successive linear programming, 199, 205
SUMT, 200
Surplus variables (in LP), 49
Surrogate variables, 93
System (definition), 8
System dynamics, 366
Systems analysis, 223, 410
Systems approach, 2, 8

Table function, 340
Taha, H., 91, 144
Taylor III, B., 495, 507
Technological forecasting, 364, 520, 543
Teletronix Industries (dialogue), 34, 47
Temporary entities (in simulation), 333
TERMINATE (GPSS), 346
TEST (GPSS), 345
Thesen, A., 5, 21, 364
Time of first passage (Markov chains), 377
Time-persistent variables, 342
Time-sequenced decisions (in DP), 226
T. N. Crumpets (minicase), 533
Toffler, A., 508, 542
Touring Europe (minicase), 241
Toynbee, A., 4, 21
Transformation (in ILP), 114
Transformation (in LP), 50, 52, 57
Transformation (in NLP), 197, 201, 203, 212, 221
Transient Markov process, 271, 375
Transient simulation, 331
Transient states, 375
Transitivity of preference, 271
Transportation model, 158
Transportation tableau, 183
Transshipment model, 164
Traveling salesman model, 115
Travis, L., 364
Trees, 514
Triangular distribution, 403

UFO (dialogue), 277
Ulgen, O., 363
Unbounded solution (in LP), 50

Uncertainty, 445
Uniformly distributed random variable, 324, 338, 342, 345
Unrestricted signs (in LP), 50
Upper-bounded variable (in LP), 53
Utility functions, 269
Utility theory, 268
Utility transformation for incommensurable objectives, 482

Validation, 9
Value of imperfect information (EVPI), 261
Value of perfect information, 260
Values, 7
Values in specified intervals (in ILP), 101
Variables unrestricted in sign, 50
Verbal models, 3
Vertex, 38
Villanueva, R., 364
Visual and Multiattribute choice models, 508
Visual interactive simulation, 348
Von Neuman, J., 299, 464

Wagner, H., 46, 91, 106, 144, 190, 224, 249, 326, 378, 392, 440
Waiting lines, 300
Wald, A., 446
Walton, R., 547
Waren, A., 223
Warfield, W., 542
Waterman, R., 21
Watson, H., 364
Weighted center of gravity model, 217
Weill, P., 547
"What if" analysis, 46
Whitin, T., 440
William Hill Distillery (minicase), 60
Williams, A., 91
Wilson EOQ model, 419
Winkler, R., 299
Winston, W., 91, 144, 190
Wiseacre (minicase), 55
Wolfe, P., 203, 223
Woolsey, R., 21, 440
Worth tree, 515

Young, R., 111, 144, 364

Zadeh, L., 483, 507
Zero-one variables, 103, 112, 114
Zionts, S., 144
Zuboff, S., 547